Lee Baxandall's WORLD GUIDE TO

NUDE BEACHES AND RESORTS

N Editions / P.O. Box 132 Oshkosh, WI 54902

Jerry Derbyshire. Bryce Canyon National Park, Utah.

Jerry Derbyshire. Royal Arch Creek, Grand Canyon, Arizona.

IMPORTANT NOTICE

MUCH CARE IS TAKEN to verify the information presented here. Reports from readers, however, are necessarily a basic resource, and the editorial team and publisher cannot and will not take responsibility for errors, let alone altered legal status of nude use.

Before you take off all of your clothing in a public place, be certain to check with persons knowledgeable about clothes-optionality in the specific circumstances. To deliberately give offense with your nakedness to those who are unwilling to share it, is indefensible and may lead to a charge of disorderly conduct.

The *Guide* should not be construed to justify private-property trespass if both owner acquiescence and a public, common-law, right-of-way are absent. We will correct any such inadvertent listing.

To describe and give access information to the world's most desirable, well-established, clothing-optional recreation sites, private and public, is our aim. Note that an established public nude site doesn't always receive governmental designation. The most popular, enjoyable, clothes-optional zones often lack official nude status: they thrive on community acceptance and permissive law enforcement policy. Official advisory signage is only one way that nudity as the norm is claimed. So again, ask knowledgeable locals before you remove all clothing.

SITES COMPILER: RUTH A. PERCEY
PHOTO & SITES EDITOR: LEE BAXANDALL
DESIGNER: LARRY BILOTTA
PRODUCTION ARTIST: GLORIA DALMAN

Copyright © 1998 by Lee Baxandall

Published by N Editions, a division of The Naturists, Inc.,
P.O. Box 132, Oshkosh, Wisconsin 54902, USA

N EDITIONS and colophon are trademarks of The Naturists, Inc.

The Naturist Society consists of The Naturists, Inc.,
The Naturist Action Committee, Inc., and
The Naturist Education Foundation, Inc.

Library of Congress Catalog Card Number 80-50931
ISBN: 0-934106-21-5

10 9 8 7 6 5 4 3 2

Printed by the Castle-Pierce Printing Co., Oshkosh, Wisconsin

Next Two Pages: Leif Heilberg.

THIS EDITION IS DEDICATED

to the past and ongoing efforts of these friends and comrades in the great adventure of recreating natural values and experiences within this market-driven culture —

JOHANNA MOORE BAXANDALL
Life partner & the NAC-NEF comptroller

FRANK & MARIANNE CERVASIO
and MARVIN & JAN FRANDSEN
Untiring heroes in Canaveral National Seashore action

MARIANNA HOPPE HANDLER
The 'Mom' of Moonstone (RI) & San Onofre (CA) nude beaches

RICHARD & SHIRLEY MASON
The architects of Miami-Dade's Haulover nude beach

MORLEY SCHLOSS
Naturist Rochester & NAC, both from the beginnings

JUDY WILLIAMS
Before TNS Judy created the Wreck Beach Preservation Society

BONNIE ZIEGENHAGEN CASE
The Naturist Society's first employee (1976-), still mailing your Ns

ACKNOWLEDGEMENTS

PHOTOGRAPHY

Front cover – Jerry Derbyshire. Back cover – Paulo Sergio Moscoso.

Within this Guide – Doug Ball, Richard Bangs/Sobek, Lee Baxandall, Jerre Blank, Marty Brittan, Eugene Brousseau, Vittorio Buono, David Bybee, D.G. Byrd, Sheryl Campbell, Canyon State Naturists, Sung-wei Chen, China Tourism, Tom Chittenden, Michael J. Cooney, Rob Coykendall, Chris A. Crumley, Rod Dailey, Yang Dan, Dave Davis, Jerry Derbyshire, Stanislaw Dziedowicz, Jack Falat, Giuseppe Feroldi, Kathleen A. Galley, Illiona Gencheva, Bob Gereke, Dennis Budd Gray, Leif Heilberg, Bill Heyne, Wolfgang Hiob, Bowen Kerrihard, John Kramer/Sobek, Merv Krull, Pedro Lacomba, Dana Levi, Jayson Loam, Leonard Lujan, Charles MacFarland, Ron Marsh, Glen Martin, Eduardo Masferre, Steve Mattis, Ewe Meyer, Brooks A. Mick, Angelos Mimikopoulos, Dovel Moore, Paulo Sergio Moscoso, Gons Nachman, Bill Pennington & Camilla Van Sickle/Nudisk, Tom Numake, Lloyd Olson, Randy O'Rourke, Mark Orpen, Rich Pasco, Dave Patrick, Politikens Presse, Jim Rand, Karl H. Reddies, Claude Richards, Terry Roscoe, J. Riera Rovira, "Saule" (Latvia), John Saffre, Frank R. Shepard, Fred Sidell, Peter Simon, Gerhard Skagestein, Dennis Craig Smith, David Southall, George Sporn, Durand Stieger, Ed Stimpson, Walter Sullivan, Tahanga, Edin Velez, Doug Wahl, Richard West, Otto Wiesner.

Captions & credits of photos appear on the same or adjoining page, running parallel to the page "gutter."

LISTINGS

Individuals contributing new or refreshed site listings to this edition (partial list): Loren Adams, David Basford, Peter Bentley, Jorge Biagosch, Dave Bitters, Ken Bohls, Geert Bovenhuis, S.T. Brown, Glenn Bruckno, Vittorio Buono, Lyle Burke, Anthony Cadiz, Camping Bares, Lici Carr, Pete Carstensen, Gene Caywood, Mecislav Chorzempa, William Cottrell, Forest duBruyne Jr., Toni Egbert, Howard Feldman, Carl Flick, Gary Hanauer, Leif Heilberg, Charles Holmes, Les Hotchkin, Erkki Husu, William Jones, Roeland A.M. Laudy, David Lay-Flurrie, Al Lister, Jayson Loam, David Martin, Angelos C. Mimikopoulos, P. Morgan, David Morrison, Peter Norwood, Pierre Naslin, Ohio Buckeye Naturists, Bob Ohlwiler, Joseph O'Keefe, Sergio de Oliviera, Phil Owensby, Bill Pacer, Rich Pasco, Dave Patrick, Chuck Pearson, Bill Pennington, Rick Perkins, James Peterman, Michael Prescott, Joe Priestley, Celso Rossi, Morley Schloss, Don Schrader, Jerry Schrotenboer, Camilla Van Sickle, Tahanga, Don Titmus, Cristian Vogt, Robert Walker, Brad Westervelt, Judy Williams, William Zacher. 1998: Richard Anderson, Allan Beatty, Bay Area Naturists, Christopher J. Berdos, David R. Branch, Marty Britton, Tom Caulley, Ron and Lorrie Curry, Oleg Dudkin, William Elbert, Jason Hernandez, Darin Jetton, Norman Lathrop, Bill Locey, Jere Lull, Juris Menke, Elizabeth Moynan, Naturist Rochester, Mark Nisbet, C. Olsen, Virg and Peg Peters, Chris Plumb, Shawn Presson, Jeff Reuteler, Jeff Riddlebaugh, Klijsen Schoenmode, Gary Schroeder, Raghu Nandan Singh, Bryan Simmons, Dale Smith, Steve Sorenson, Kevin Stewart, Mark Storey, North Swanson, Richard Trotter, Herb Wallower, Sheila and Ken Watkinson.

The First Gathering Of The Naturist Society.
At Elysium Fields, Los Angeles County, October 24–25, 1980.

Pedro Lacomba. Lake Champlain, Burlington, VT.

CONTENTS

Next Two Pages: Jerry Derbyshire. Beaches Are Everywhere: In The Grand Canyon Of The Colorado River.

THIS BOOK HONORS
THE INTEGRITY OF
THE VISION OF
JERRY DERBYSHIRE
(1948–1989) —
A PHOTOGRAPHER
WHOSE IMAGES
CAPTURE THE
PHILOSOPHY OF
NATURISM IN
AMERICA.

INTRODUCTION

Relaxation or active recreation without garments— what the British call "costumes"—and without a sense of shame is today, for much of the civilized world, an uncontroversial amenity.

Indeed, one mark of a civilized country is its nude and topfree beaches.

It seems almost inconceivable, given the present acceptance, that earlier in this century a beachgoer who exposed a bare knee or shoulder from a cumbersome bathing costume invited arrest.

It has been said that self-acceptance is largely an extension of body acceptance. Social nudity permits us to enhance our awareness of the reality, not merely the idea, of how much alike and similarly vulnerable we are. Discovering this, we may learn to control our fear of the gaze of another.

Alienating barriers of social role and economic class, sex role and gender preference are reduced as we dispose of the trappings of difference, privilege and fear. Individuality can be strengthened without arrogance; integrity can be recovered.

The presence of our bodies—of breast and genital vulnerability in a natural context, "Naturism"—contributes to perspective and health. When the culture into which we are born strays too far from nature's laws, we suffer. A "naturalization" is in order. This will, conversely, make it possible to more completely "humanize" our culture.

This book is a guide to opportunities for you and your family and friends to enjoy recreation in the nude. And why should you and they not try it? You cannot imagine the taste of an apple if you haven't tasted one. It is no different with a nude beach or resort.

TAKING THE PLUNGE

Have you spent all of your adult years without once getting naked in a sociable, outdoor, recreational setting? Going through life with a clothes-compulsive personality is hard on a person. More stressful than you will ever realize, if you do not try the clothes-optional alternative.

Trying it is easy. You won't think twice about it once you've broken through the anxiety barrier. Thinking it through in private is one way to get ready to go public.

There's an "etiquette" to clothes-optional beaches and resorts as to all public situations. Once you get the hang of how people make themselves comfortable while naked among others, you are "home free."

You'll find it easier to first visit a well-established nude recreation site in the company of friends who are versed in the etiquette.

You will be with men and women who also, after growing up in a clothes-compulsive society, had to "get the hang of it." They are not unlike yourself and they already have broken patriarchal society's most fierce taboo: Thou shalt not be vulnerable, even among those whom you might be able to trust.

For the fear of going naked among others reflects the climate of indiscriminate aggression that the English author Thomas Hobbes describes as "The war of All against All." Not all times have militated against trust and vulnerability. Surely this era of ruthless careerism, industrialization, exploitation of nature, and national expansion has.

Only now are we finding the ways to transcend the misbegotten ethos of personal armoring that is wedded to aggression. Before Western civilization, nakedness was a normal element of life acceptable in many circumstances. Freud, in his *Civilization and Its Discontents,* describes how psychological repression of the awareness of our natural being was a necessary step in building urban civilization. Only people motivated by abstractions, rather than spontaneous perception and need, could build the cities and staff the factories, serve in the armies, and otherwise discipline themselves into taking part in vast and self-abdicating social projects.

Armoring of the natural individual has devastating effects, although nothing less might have served to accomplish the purposes of Western civilization. The post-industrial, newly greening era offers fresh options, a chance to integrate the natural human being with post-industrial values, technology and knowledge.

FIRST VISIT

So, let's take the plunge. You need not immediately undress if you feel self-conscious, awkward, embarrassed. That will be understood. But in your nervous state do not put needless "armor" between yourself and those you encounter. Leave camera, sunglasses, radio at home. At least seem at ease. Practice will make perfect.

Sit quietly at the edge of activity. Look around. Groom, lay back. Be open to a smile, a word, a shared refreshment. Bring something to share. Don't force the situation. Be receptive. Your open demeanor will best say that you are "getting it," that you are happy to be free of unneeded defensiveness.

After 20 minutes you will find yourself no longer acutely aware of being naked. You will see that "almost"-nude beaches, where bikinis and thongs are paraded, are more sexually titillating than a clothes-optional resort or beach. What is natural is more fulfilling, though it might not fit the tantalize-and-deliver titillation of our consumer culture. A new age is slowly being born.

What about erections? Will you get one on the first visit? Possibly, but just put it in the sand, the towel, or the water until your steamy imagination adjusts to the reality that sex, as you know it, is not the reason these people are unclothed.

Will people aim cameras, come-ons, or comments at you? Possibly. But the repression of a healthy nudity, especially for females, has been one of the chief means of mind and destiny control by the patriarchy. The women who take down straps and lie on their tummies, then roll over, get up and walk about topfree or fully naked, are shattering the invisible bonds of an inherited sex role. It may feel somewhat heroic to put up with the lascivious attentions of a beach gawker in Bermuda shorts and camera, but it is qualitatively no worse than many street experiences a free woman must endure, and the payoff—outgrowing sexist stereotypes—is of far greater benefit.

You will adapt to this new experience. Just ease yourself into a clothes-optional setting without putting up more defenses than necessary. The scary questions and hovering doubts you first had—Will I be accepted? Will I find friends?—begin to answer themselves. You'll find that you are putting behind you the obstacles to personal growth, in many ways that you could not have imagined before you went clothes-optional.

THE LAW

The "law" is a possibly hostile element of your new environment. But it will not be a problem if you first visit a private beach, resort, or club. And remember that the law as administered at many public recreational areas is on your side.

There isn't any countrywide law to ban nudity on federal land. Please check for possible assimilation of a state or county law to a federal jurisdiction and for special federal regulations. However, in general, National Park Service, Bureau of Land

NORTH AMERICA

Management, Forest Service, etc. view nude recreation—conducted with discretion and sensitivity for the varying values of others—as "a legitimate activity."

In many if not most state, county, and city jurisdictions, the Victorian Age confusion of nude with lascivious is rejected in the courts. Accordingly, law-enforcement personnel generally try to avoid citation or arrest actions that could lead to court tests and waste of taxpayer funds. "Nude is not lewd" is the rule of thumb in these responsible jurisdictions.

Nonetheless, painful and ridiculous incidents still occur. Individuals are misjudged—by elected or appointed government employees—as social deviates for enjoying the victimless "crime" or, more recently, the "misdemeanor," of innocent nudity. Archaic social codes and repressive values die hard.

Since 1975 an administrative trend has appeared to ban nudity as such—much as pets, glass containers, or bare feet may be banished—as a nuisance or nonconforming use, with no further reason required. The effective answer to such "mere nudity" curbs will be to demonstrate the community tolerance and support of naturist values. Certainly, the trend is decriminalization and de facto recognition of clothes-optional zones.

An enlightened culture—one providing for individual and minority liberties—lets the clad and the unclad equally share in private and public resources. No good comes from forcing a clothes-compulsive dress code upon all so long as a dwindling majority possibly clings to it. That is not democracy. It is domestic tyranny.

Provision not only for the diversity of recreational choice but also for the security, access, convenience and site maintenance is the right of every citizen.

The law is not an inherent adversary.

Increasingly, law-enforcement personnel and recreation managers are overcoming their timidity before the small minority of zealots who still consider social nudity evil. They should actively promote the principle of diversity of dress codes in recreation—very much as social resources are extended to accommodate both sexes, all races, the handicapped and the well, where tax-obtained funds are involved.

THE SUN

Long vanished is a time when you could claim a health belief as "a sunbather" for a good excuse to go naked. Excessive, irregular sunning is not the best thing for healthy skin. Not only can it possibly lead to skin cancer, it can prematurely dry, wrinkle, and age the skin. The health hazard is an excessive exposure to the sun between the hours of 10 a.m. and 2 p.m.

Nude recreation doesn't require much or any sun exposure. Haven't you enjoyed running naked in the spring rain? Haven't you enjoyed late afternoon sports on a clothing-optional beach under stormy skies? And haven't you skinny-dipped by moonlight? Take to nude recreation and not necessarily the sun. Start out early or late. Go out in the midday sun in moderation. And then, be active, turn your body this way and that as you run, play ball, throw a Frisbee, leap the waves. And when you are not active or at midday, put an umbrella, a tree, a tent, a sunscreen between you and the sun.

A sunscreen that you squeeze from a tube can be as good as a shirt or robe, and it won't interfere with your freedom to move and be one with the environment. May you enjoy your full freedom of body and spirit without injury!

E-MAIL & WEBSITE DIRECTORY

THESE ADDRESSES ARE CURRENT AS OF SEPT. 15, 1997. If the address you try is no longer in service, we recommend that you use Web search engines or check the Network section of our current *Nude & Natural* magazine.

Abbreviations: E = e-mail W = website

GENERAL

Altogether Christians **E:** nli@together.net
    W: www.together.net/~nli/
American Association for Nude Recreation **W:** www.aanr.com
A.O.L.
    E: exchange then Interests-Hobbies/General Special Interests/Naturist
Bare Necessities Tour & Travel **W:** www.bare-necessities.com
Barefoot Adventures **W:** www.threerivers.com/3rivtvl
Being and Nakedness
    W: www.best.com/~cgd/home/naturism
Christian Naturists **E:** markm@sierra.net or
    Usenet: alt.christnet.nudism
Clothing Optional Digest **E:** codigest@onramp.net
CompuServe **E:** go nudist or go hsx100
Cybernude & Campus-nude listserver **W:** www.cybernude.com
Delphi - Online Naturist Club **E:** custom 13
Gay Naturists International **E:** wrightmgt@aol.com
    W: www.gaynaturists.org/gni.html
Go Classy Tours **W:** http://goclassy.com
International Men Enjoying Naturism **E:** imen1@aol.com
    W: www.imengonude.com
Intl. Naturist Fed. (INF) **E:** naturism@inf-fni.org
    W: www.inf.fni.org
Internet Usenet newsgroups **E:** rec.nude or alt.cult.nudism
Naturally Magazine **W:** www.tiac.net/users/nat
Naturist Action Committee **E:** scootchdc@aol.com
    W: www.naturist.com
Naturist Society **E:** naturist@naturist.com
    W: www.naturist.com
Nudist Notebook
    W: www.breath-of.com/nudenote/opening.htm
Nudist Webring
    W: www.webring.org/cgi-bin/webring?ring=nudism;list
Prodigy **E:** jump: hobbies bb
Singles SIG **E:** 73244.2610@compuserve.com
    W: www.tiac.net/users/aeon/singsig.html
Skinny-Dip Tours **W:** www.skinnydip.com
Virtually, CD-ROM magazine **E:** rewest@interlog.com
    W: www.interlog.com/~rbwest

UNITED STATES

ALASKA

Alaskan Naturists **W:** www.alaska.net/~johnm/soc/aknat.html

ARIZONA

Canyon State Naturists **E:** csn@syspac.com
    W: www.syspac.com/~csn
El Dorado Hot Spring **E:** hotspring@el-dorado.com
    W: www.el-dorado.com/hotwater/
Hidden Valley Retreat **E:** azhvr@syspac.com
    W: www.syspac.com/~azhvr
Shangri-La II **E:** s12@sprynet.com
    W: home.sprynet.com/sprynet/s12/s12.htm

CALIFORNIA

Bay Area Naturists **W:** www.best.com/~pasco/sbn.html
California Action Project **E:** 76164.1156@compuserve.com
Camping Bares **E:** bdymind@inetworld.net
Desert Shadows Inn & Villas **E:** 76142.2071@compuserve.com
    W: www.cybernude.com/dshadow
Elysium **E:** elysium@hollywood.cinenet.com
    W: www.elysium-sunwest.com
Glen Eden Sun Club **W:** www.gleneden.com
Laguna Del Sol **E:** laguna@ns.net **W:** www.lagunadelsol.co
Lupin Naturist Club **E:** office@lupin.com **W:** www.lupin.com
Morningside Inn **E:** morningsideinn@juno.com
    W: www.morningsideinn.com
Olive Dell Ranch **E:** kilborn@earthlink.net
    W: www.cdiguide.com/909/a_res/olivedel.html
Raffles Palm Springs Hotel **E:** rafflesh@aol.com
    W: www.cybernude.com/raffles
Red Rock Beach **E:** jrl73@community.net
    W: www.community.net/~jrl73/redrock
River Dippers **E:** riverdippers@rocketmail.com
San Onofre Beach **E:** fosobch@aol.com
Silver Valley **E:** 76417.2477@compuserve.com
    W: www.kaiwan.com/~wem/svsc/svsctoc.html
Swallows Sun Island Club **E:** jshafer@znet.com
    W: www.swallowssunisland.com
Terra Cotta Inn
    W: www.ernestallen.com/tr/ca/theterracottainn

COLORADO

Valley View Hot Springs **E:** neil@vvhs.com **W:** www.vvhs.com
Wild Wood's Resort **E:** JCUC@msn.com

CONNECTICUT

Solair **E:** solair@neca.com **W:** www.neca.com/~solair/

FLORIDA

Central Florida Naturists **E:** cervasio@inspace.net
    W: www.inspace.net/cfn
Club Paradise **E:** clparadise@aol.com
    W: www.paradiselakes.com
Cypress Cove **E:** cypcove@phoenixat.com
    W: www.suncove.com
Haulover Beach Miami **E:** spsm4nude@aol.com
Lake Como Club **E:** lakecomo@nudism.com
    W: www.nudism.com/lakecomo

Palm Beach Naturists **E:** synergy@emi.net
Riviera Naturist Resort **E:** bigfoot@adpservices.com
    W: http://adpservices.com/rnr/index.html
South Florida Free Beaches **E:** brujude@juno.com
    W: pages.prodigy.net/dimi
Sunny Sands **W:** www.greyhawkes.com/sunnysands
Sunsport Gardens **E:** sunsport@earthlink.net
    W: www.sunsportgardens.com
Tallahassee Bare-Devils **E:** tbaredev@freenet.tlf.fl.us
    W: www.freenet.tlh.fl.us/~tbaredev
Tampa Bay Free Beaches **E:** TBFB@nudism.com
    W: www.nudism.com/tbfb/index.html

GEORGIA
Bell Acres **E:** bellacre@stc.net
    W: www.cybernude.com/parks/bell
Hidden Valley Resort **W:** www.cybernude.com/hiddenvalley
Mountain Grove **E:** mtncreek@stc.net
    W: www.cybernude.com/resorts/mtncreek
Serendipity **E:** office@serendipity-park.com
    W: www.serendipity-park.com

HAWAII
Kehena Beach, Hale Makala **E:** hamakala@ilhawaii.net
Kona-Honokohau Beach **E:** konasun@gte.net
Kona Banana Patch B&B **W:** www.ilhawaii.net/~banana
Shangri-La, Maui **E:** shangrla@maui.net

ILLINOIS
Blue Lake Club **W:** wpr.pair.com/bluelake
Chicago Sun Club **W:** www.cybernide.com/csc

INDIANA
Tri-State Country Club **E:** ekern@venus.net

KANSAS
Heartland Naturists **W:** www.sky.net/~rjw/outdoor.htm
Lake Edun **E:** bornnude@aol.com

MARYLAND
Assateague Beach **W:** www.infosponge.com/naturist
Maryland Health Society **W:** www.cybernude.com/maheso
Pine Tree Assoc. **E:** pinetr@erols.com

MASSACHUSETTS
Berkshire Vista Resort
    W: www.tiac.net/users/aeon/bkv1.html
Cape Cod Naturists **E:** eairs@aol.com
Pilgrim Naturists **E:** aeon@tiac.net
    W: http://www.tiac.net/users/pilhome.html
Sandy Terraces **E:** ftnancy@aol.com
    W: www.cybernude.com/stanude

MICHIGAN
Forest Hills **E:** cebrower@novagate.com
    W: www.aanr.com/clubs/foresthl.html
Turtle Lake Resort **W:** www.cybernude.com/TLR

MINNESOTA
Minnesota Naturists **E:** mnnature@aol.com
    W: www.geocities.com/HotSprings/4058

MISSOURI
Show Me Naturists **W:** www.cybernude.com/clubs/showme

NEVADA
Tahoe Area Naturists **E:** north11@juno.com

NEW HAMPSHIRE
Cedar Waters Village **W:** wwl.usal.com/~ggjn/cwv.html
Naturist New Hampshire **E:** mwm@together.net
    W: www.tiac.net/users/aeon/nnh1.html

NEW JERSEY
Paddling Bares **E:** pbares@aol.com
    W: http://members.aol.com/pbares
Sandy Hook & Tri-State Metro Naturists **E:** JSXT@juno.com

NEW YORK
Empire Haven **E:** mrobin2459@aol.com
    W: www.aanr.com/clubs/ehnude.html

NORTH CAROLINA
Bar-S-Ranch **E:** bars@interpath.com
    W: www.cybernude.com/bar-s-ranch
North Carolina Naturists
    W: web.infoave.net/~pixman/ncn4.htm
Triangle Area Naturists **E:** wwenck@email.unc.edu

OHIO
Bare Valley Nudist Camp **W:** www.ohnuderec.org
Buckeye Naturists **E:** bobsanns@midohio.net
    W: www.ohnuderec.org
Ohio Nude Digest **E:** bobsann@midohio.net

OKLAHOMA
Oaklake Trails **E:** oltom@nworks.net
    W: www.telepath.com/rlp/olt.html
Sun Meadow **W:** www.sunmeadow.com

OREGON
Hidden Springs **E:** mikpar@delphi.com
Restful Haven **W:** www.cybernude.com/restful
Rogue Suncatchers
    W: id.mind.net/~mikeknox/suncatcher/index.html
Squaw Mountain Ranch **E:** squawmt@aol.com
    W: members.aol.com/squawmt
Willamettans **W:** www.multinet.com/willies

PENNSYLVANIA
Beechwood Lodge **W:** www.netaxs.com/~cheefdan/beechwd
Mid-Atlantic pages **W:** www.netaxs.com/~cheefdan
Potomac Rambling Bares **E:** gwill607@smart1.net
Student Naturist Association **E:** naturist@dolphin.upennedu.
Sunny Rest Lodge **E:** buddy@ptd.net **W:** www.sunnyrest.com
Sunspot Family Nudist Park **E:** sunspot@epix.net

RHODE ISLAND

Dyer Woods **W:** www.dwoods.com

SOUTH CAROLINA

Carolina Foothills **E:** cfr@bigfoot.com
    W: www.teleplex.net/geneg/cfr.htm
Cedar Creek **E:** cdrcreeksc@aol.com

TENNESSEE

East Tennessee Naturists: **E:** lynna4nude@aol.com
Timberline Resort: **W:** www.bhm.tis.net/~bottom/tmln.html

TEXAS

Bexar Recreation Society **E:** nudentx@aol.com
Bluebonnet **E:** bluebonnet@pobox.com
    W: www.cybernude.com/bluebonnet
Central Texas Naturists **E:** ctnudists@aol.com
Hill Country Nudists **E:** hcn@oal.com
    W: www.sss.org/texnude/hcn.html
Live Oak Ranch **W:** www.aanr.com/clubs/liveoak.html
Longhorn Nudists **E:** nudists@uts.cc.utexas.edu
    W: uts.cc.utexas.edu/~nudists
Natural Horisun **E:** paulm@intertex.net
Riverside Resort **E:** genieb@world-net.net
    W: www.worldnet.net/users/genieb
Sahnoans **E:** lyman@bga.com
    W: www.sss.org/texnude/sahnoans.html
Sunny Pines **W:** www.cybernude.com/sunnypines.

VIRGINIA

Commonwealth of Virginia Naturists **E:** cvnnude1@aol.com
Potomac Rambling Bares **E:** gwill607@smart1.net
White Tail Park **E:** broche@gc.net **W:** www.wtpnude.com

WASHINGTON

Fraternity Snoqualmie **E:** Barebuns@worldnet.att.net
Lake Associates Recreation Club **E:** larc@sos.net
    W: www.lmrr.com
Northwest Action Project **E:** storey@aa.net
SLUGS **E:** rperkins@breath-of.com
    W: www.breath-of.com/slugs

WEST VIRGINIA

Avalon **W:** www.avalon-nude.com

WISCONSIN

Badger Naturists **E:** claude@globaldialog.com
Friends of Mazo Beach **E:** fomb@globaldialog.com

CANADA

Federation of Canadian Naturists **E:** information@fcn.ca
    W: www.fcn.ca
Fédération Québéçoise de Naturisme
    E: legrand@generation.net
    W: www.generation.net/~legrand/fqnhome.htm

BRITISH COLUMBIA

Sol Santé **E:** bare@islandnet.com
Sunny Trails Club **W:** www.abbotsford.com/sunnytrails
Vancouver Sunbathing Assoc. **E:** gskillen@uniserve.com
Wreck Beach Preservation Society **E:** judyw@direct.ca

MANITOBA

Crocus Sun Club **E:** lprucy@mb.sympatico.ca

NOVA SCOTIA

SunnyVale Nature Park **W:** www.auracom.com/~srverge

ONTARIO

Four Seasons Nature Resort **E:** gobare@thefourseasons.com
    W: www.thefourseasons.com
Lakesun Club **E:** rmbehr@istar.ca
Ontario Roaming Bares **E:** btempest@interlog.com
Ponderosa Park **E:** wwpowell@hookup.net
Sunward Naturist Club **E:** tonymilne@compuserve.com
Tylara Hills Naturist Resort **E:** tlhill@sky.lakeheadu.ca

CARIBBEAN

BAHAMAS

Cutlass Bay **W:** www.cutlass-bay.com

BONAIRE

Sorobon Beach Club **W:** www.sorobon.com

JAMAICA

Catcha Falling Star
    W: www.breath-of.com/nudenote/See'chelle_CatchaFallingStar.htm
Firefly Negril **W:** www.jamaicalink.com/firefly
Braco Village Resort/Grand Lido
    W: www.super—clubs.com/braco.html

ST. MARTIN

Club Orient **E:** orient@gobeach.com
    W: www.best.com/~paradise/orient

CENTRAL/SOUTH AMERICA

BRAZIL

Rionat-Naturist Societies (Rio de Janeiro)
    E: rionat@imagelink.com.br
Federação Brasileira de Naturismo **E:** rincao@mt2net.com.br
    W: //www.tca.com.br/naturis/fbnet/fbno01htm

EUROPE

FRANCE

Cap d'Agde **W:** www.cap-d-agde.com
French Naturist Fed.
    W: www.maison-de-la-france.com:8000/at/naturism

GERMANY

German FKK Assoc.
W: htttp://ourworld.compuserve.com/dfk

GREECE

East-Central European Doc. C. E: eedcnapo@groovy.gr

HUNGARY

Napóra Club E: jhalasz@ozon.zpok.hu

ITALY

Unione Naturisti Italiani E: natur@arpnet.it
W: www.services.csi.it~natur

NETHERLANDS

Nederlandse Naturisten Home Page
W: www.worldaccess.nl/~jozefvl/provincie.htm

NORWAY

Norsk Naturisforbund E: nnfoslonett.no

RUSSIA

Nat. Fed. Naturism (Carpov) E: vvk@aan.astufps.cactus.msk.ru
St. Petersburg E: kotzov@okst.spb.su

SPAIN

Club Catalá de Naturisme E: ccn@mx2.redestb.es
W: www.redestb.es/ccn

Costa Natura E: costanatura@wcostasol.es
W: http://wcostasol.es/negocios/naturista/costanatura
Todo Naturismo E: focus100@ctv.es
W: www.ctv.es/USERS/focus100/todnat.html

SWEDEN

Sveriges Naturistförbund E: nnf@sn.no
Swedish Naturist pages W: www.algonet.se/~brummer

UNITED KINGDOM

British Naturism W: www.british-naturism.org.uk
Broadlands Sun Club
W: www.paston.co.uk/broadlands/cover.html
Internet Usenet E: uk.rec.naturist
Robert Tedder's pages
W: www.personal.u-net.com/~tedder/natshub.htm

FAR EAST & SOUTH PACIFIC

AUSTRALIA

Australian Nudist Federation W: httw://aus-nude.org.au
Australian Sun & Health
W: www.winshop.com.au/sun&health

NEW ZEALAND

Naturism pages W: www.dbphoto.co/nz

POINTERS FOR GRACIOUS NUDE BEACH RECREATION

☞ **Stay Out of the Dunes** and other environmentally sensitive areas.

☞ **Obey Parking Regulations** and other posted rules.

☞ **Help With Litter**—bring along a trash bag. Carry out more litter than you create.

☞ **Don't Go Out of Established Nude Areas.** To wander nude into a clothed beach or parking area will offend many.

☞ **No Overt Sexual Activity.** Leave exhibitionism to those attending clothed beaches.

☞ **Respect the Property of Others.**

☞ **Ask Prior Consent for Photography.**

☞ **Privacy Is Fundamental.** Many are at club or beach for quiet time. Body language should tell you they don't want to be disturbed. It's not wrong to look for new friends—but it is rude to intrude when you're not welcome.

☞ **Come Prepared.** Bring beach supplies: beverage, food, sunscreen, towel. Mooching is not a good way to make friends.

☞ **Speak Up for Standards.** Don't let some newcomer who doesn't understand the situation or our values cause trouble. Instead of doing a slow burn, go talk, politely but firmly, to the couple starting sexual activity, the can-tosser, the wanderer into the dunes.

A N ever expanding source of timely information about nude recreation is found on computer networks. Your home computer, a modem, and a telephone line to dial out on can be your virtual gateway to the world of Naturism.

Brisk traffic with such information appears on major commercial systems including CompuServe, Prodigy, America Online, Delphi and the Internet in general. Computer-enlightened Naturists find they can also share the word about their lifestyle via home-run BBSs operated as small businesses or hobbies which are sometimes linked to amateur but expansive systems such as Fidonet. Many are now connecting to the Internet.

The result is a worldwide network where news about changes affecting your use of public lands or private resorts is traded at a speed never known before. Ever more information, often illustrated with color photos, has become available as development of the Internet's World Wide Web continues.

DELPHI: THE ONLINE NATURIST CLUB

Naturism has been flourishing on the Delphi network for over a dozen years. The "Online Naturist Club" was founded as a custom forum by Veal Johnson in 1984, and since 1989 has been coordinated and managed by Michael Corbin (naturist@delphi.com).

The club currently has about 2,000 active members, with 50 to 100 logging in on any given day. There is a file database from which users can download information on Naturism; most of it is in text form, though there are some graphic images available. Anyone may upload files to the database, but they are reviewed by Corbin beforehand.

To join the Online Naturist Club and Delphi at the same time without paying an extra fee, call 800-365-4636 with your modem. After making the connection, hit the enter key twice. At the username prompt, enter "joindelphi" (as one word). Then at the password prompt enter "customl3" (again no space) and press enter again.

Current Delphi members can join the ONC by requesting access from Corbin, either through the Custom Forums menu or by Delphi e-mail. To view a description of the ONC, type GO CUS at any Delphi prompt. Once in the Custom Forums area choose Custom Forum 13 from the menu, look over the club's description and, if you like, send a note to Corbin requesting permission to join the club and gain access. Requests are usually processed within 24 hours. Rates on Delphi vary from $16.95 to $19.95 a month through Delphi itself and $35 annually if accessed from another Internet service. Both text and Web-based interfaces will work on this system making it attractive to those with older non-multimedia systems.

COMPUSERVE (CIS)

CompuServe carries three moderated Naturist forums that contain a wide range of postings by Naturists across the world. Participation is especially heavy from North America and the United Kingdom though there is global participation.

The newest areas are part of the Outdoors Network of forums which hosts the majority of outdoor activities on the system. A leading menu linking all forums is available at the command GO OUTDOORS. Direct access to the "Nudist & Naturist Forum" can be made at GO NUDE or GO NUDIST. Here messages, archive files on Naturism, and live keyboard chat capabilities can be found. A weekly structured group chat also takes place.

The second forum, called the "Nudist Frontiers Forum," is located at GO NUDEF. Here images of Naturism, nude art and stage performance can be found, along with more controversial discussion subjects such as massage, body adornments, intimacy, and gender preference issues. Due to a repositioning of controversial content on CompuServe, the Nudist Frontiers forum requires passage through an adult gateway. Both of the Naturist areas in the Outdoors Network are managed by Dennis Kirkpatrick (CompuServe 76710,1773).

The third area on CompuServe where Naturism is found is the "Personal Support Forum" at GO HSX100 in Section 12. Personal Support is a general lifestyles interactive area covering many subjects and is the oldest home of Naturism on the CompuServe system.

CompuServe is the only major online service with extensive file libraries on Naturism. To access CompuServe you will need one of their proprietary programs for the DOS, Windows, or Mac platforms. These can be obtained by calling CompuServe or downloading the programs from their Web site at www.compuserve.com.

Current rates are $9.95 a month for 5 hours plus a metered rate after that. As of October 1997 CompuServe offers an unlimited access rate starting at $24.95. Other access option packages remain available.

PRODIGY

Prodigy carries a very active Naturist area in its Hobbies section (JUMP: "hobbies bb"). It is easy to find although a bit cumbersome and time consuming to use. Hundreds of people regularly visit the Naturist section. For help contact Ray Ferarra at GRGG95A on that system. For access software contact Prodigy.

Prodigy recently expanded its offerings by opening up "Prodigy.Net" with improved access to the Internet over its "classic" service. Pricing plans range from $9.95 to $19.95 per month to start.

AMERICA ONLINE (AOL)

AOL is a completely different story. On this fast growing service, the Naturism topic area is hidden away like a bad relative. In early 1997 it was reported that management also was interdicting user defined chat rooms with the "nudist" topic heading. This remains under investigation by Naturist activists for resolution. It's hard to find the message board section and, when you get to the section, there is not much available.

As a general service provider, AOL is relatively inexpensive and quite user-friendly; we can only hope that the quality of its Naturist area will catch up to what is offered on other services.

To access the Naturist Folder use the "keyword" Exchange in the dialog box. When the menu for this area comes up click on the icon for INTERESTS AND HOBBIES. Once there, select the "General Special Interests" message board area and within that locate the Naturist/Nudist folder. You may wish to set a date limit when accessing this folder for the first time as messages date back as much as two years. While this can be interesting reading, it is cumbersome if

you want to look at recent messages.

AOL access software is available for the Windows and Mac platforms in wide distribution, often packaged with online topic magazines. It is also downloadable from their Web site at www.aol.com. Two main access plans exist at $19.95 per month for unlimited usage and $9.95 a month for the same plan when accessed through another service provider.

THE INTERNET

USENET NEWSGROUPS

All major services now have portals to the Internet and provide access to the World Wide Web. Naturist transmissions from all over the world have been sailing along on the Internet for years.

Within the general structure of the Internet are the "Usenet" newsgroups, which are topical message posting areas. Two Usenet groups stand out as viable options for Naturist message exchanges.

The first is "rec.nude" consisting mainly of posts from North America but also from the rest of the world. The second is "uk.rec.naturist" which is set aside for information on Naturist venues in the United Kingdom and also draws some European content.

Usenet can be described as an ungovered free-for-all. There are no rules and anything goes, as long as someone posting abusive or off-topic information can endure the often colorful rebukes, or "flames," from other users. "Net etiquette" prefers civility, however, and messages not related to Naturism or inappropriate items should not be posted in rec.nude.

Dismaying as it may be, rec.nude is an important part of the overall Naturist network. Newcomers to rec.nude should check out the various "FAQ" (frequently asked questions) files, which are regularly updated volumes of information about Naturism in general, public and private access, legal and political trends, and how to get involved in clothing-optional recreation.

To get to rec.nude a user must have access to the Internet and the ability to reach the vast array of Usenet newsgroups. Various programs exist for this as downloadable "freeware" news exclusive programs and most Web browser programs can also access Usenet.

WORLD WIDE WEB

Tremendous possibilities for Naturist communications and promotion are opening swiftly on the World Wide Web (WWW). Individuals, clubs, and vacation resorts are quickly establishing "home pages" on the Web, often with direct links to other pages with related subjects. They are colorful, interactive, and contain a great deal of information. Crisp color photos and other graphics and sound make Web pages even more attractive.

If you have access to the Web, visit The Naturist Society's page by going to the "universal resource locator" (URL): http://www.naturist.com. To locate other Naturist pages you can use a "search engine" such as Yahoo, Lycos, AltaVista, or Excite with a search word such as "Naturist" or "nudist" and the search engine will return a list of links to explore.

Access to the Web can best be enjoyed by using special graphical user interface (GUI) software called a "browser." These are available in computer software emporiums or as free downloads off the Internet itself. Leading programs for which most Web pages are designed include Netscape's browser and the Internet Explorer by Microsoft. Both are available for the PC and Mac platforms.

INTERNET RELAY CHAT & VIDEO CONFERENCING

IRC is one of several new options that allow point-to-point "chat" communications over the Internet. Various computer "servers" host user defined topic areas including those for Naturists. Your keyboard is your gateway. You must have a direct Internet connection through an independent service provider (ISP) to use IRC. IRC software is somewhat advanced compared to the larger services point-and-click icon driven programs.

Also available on the cutting edge of technology are new video and voice conferencing programs that are in a class of their own.

FIDONET

Fidonet is an amateur network that links more than 30,000 private BBSs around the world. It has a Naturist area among its regularly transmitted conferences. Like the large commercial services there is frequently an international flavor to the message base on the Fido Naturist "echo" area. An undetermined number of these privately operated BBSs carry Naturist information and file bases, bringing information into the home computers of a rising tide of newcomers.

UPDATING

The quarterly journal of Naturism, *NUDE & NATURAL* magazine from The Naturist Society, now lists many groups' Web page URLs and E-mail addresses. As the new medium grows so will these listings in the Network section of *N* magazine and on TNS' own Web site.

– Dennis Kirkpatrick

NATURISM DEFINED

"Naturism is a way of life in harmony with nature characterized by the practice of communal nudity, with the intention of encouraging self-respect, respect for others and for the environment."

– International Naturist Federation, 1974

"Naturism: A way of living in greater fidelity to nature, with a norm of full nudity in social life, the genitals included, when possible and appropriate. We aim to enhance acceptance and respect for one's self, other persons and the biosphere."

– The Naturist Society, 1997

UNITED STATES

CLOTHES-FREE RECRE-ATION ENTHUSIASTS, we find freedom and take delight in our body acceptance. *The Naturist experience of play* is at the origin of innocence and the core of our beings, however it is inhibited by custom or demeaned by taboo.

EARLY HISTORY

The American frontier saw plenty of it, as skinny-dipping. Rural Americans from Vermont to Arizona, from Georgia to Oregon, quietly believe in skinny-dipping as a great experience of growing up. It is our equivalent of the Greek civilization's passion for Olympic games in the nude as a means of character building in a natural state of being.

However well a stalwart heart has been nakedly nurtured at the quarry, lake or pond, the child has to acknowledge the teachers of shame and assume the fig leaf of body reticence. Only the boldest of earlier American writers and artists—one thinks of Thoreau, Whitman, Eakins—dared to espouse the beauty and necessity of the naked body in social intercourse.

Around 1900 the puritan heritage incited opponents who were convinced enough of the importance of overcoming body denial to make a social issue of it. Free spirits like Floyd Dell, John Reed, Eugene O'Neill, and Max Eastman talked of naked joy in New York City's Greenwich Village in the winters and lived it summers in the country.

The first secular community to treat nude recreation as a social right may have been Home at Joe's Bay, Puget Sound, Washington founded in 1896 by University of Toronto graduate George H. Allen. With his comrades he wrote in an article, "The Nudes and the Prudes": "Home is a community of free spirits who came out into the woods to escape the priest-ridden atmosphere of the conventional society. One of the liberties enjoyed by Homeites was the privilege to bathe in evening dress or with only the clothes nature gave them, just as they pleased."

By 1915, several intentional farm-based communities in New England quietly practiced nudity. The 1920s saw a wider rebellion against genteel society. Bathing suits (a garment not known before the mid-19th century) diminished, signalling a weakened regulation of the sexuality and sensibilities of industrial subjects and consumers. But as quickly as human nature revived, it would be channeled by new social controls, masked by the advertising industry as gratifications.

NUDISM

Labor Day Weekend 1929 marked what is now regarded as the founding event for organizationally supported clothes freedom in North America. Drawing on experience in his native Germany, Kurt Barthel, an immigrant with an import-export business to Latin America, took his wife and two other couples to Bear Mountain not far out of New York City for the public-land nude camping experience that led to private clubs for free body culture.

Early "nudists" were hounded by opponents, and retreated into enclaves by 1931. Some confusedly saw the tactical necessity as an unalloyed good. For several decades, nudist park proprietary interests subsumed the objectives of a free body culture as a whole.

Nudist magazines of the 1950s, notably *Sunshine and Health*, at last won the battle against airbrushing of genitals and pubic hair—only to see magazines titillating a sexually immature public put them out of business.

The youth culture of the 1960s left no form of social control unexamined. Nude-ins began to occur in California. A new breed of proprietor, south of San Francisco, began to lease ocean beach and allow visitors to undress as they chose. By 1967, San Gregorio was described by *Time* as the country's first nude beach. The clothes-optional use of public shorelines was also under way at Massachusetts' Cape Cod and Martha's Vineyard, Vermont quarries and Lake Michigan dunes, Georgia's rivers and the Florida coast.

NATURISM

From 1975, a network of the free beaches emerged. It was coordinated from Oshkosh, Wisconsin. By 1980 this had evolved into The Naturist Society and the first edition of this *World Guide*—the nude recreation best-seller—was published.

New American Sunbathing Association president James Hadley brought ASA leaders to the first Naturist Society gathering at Ed Lange's personal-growth-oriented Elysium near Los Angeles (photo, pp. 6–7). The Hadley leadership marked renewed interest by club nudists in seeking legal nude use of public lands.

The paradigm was shifting for nudism. No longer did the energy lie in a smallish club, recruiting families from a hundred-mile radius, with weekend camping, volunteer workers and member-driven nudist priorities. These still exist in the dozens, especially in the northern tier of states. However, the trend has shifted to entrepreneur-driven, clothes-optional resorts. They amortize costs from year-round income as vacation destinations. A Trade Association for Nude Recreation (TANR) was formed in 1987 to enhance marketing.

The fading paradigm is the small trailer park where mom and dad relax and play volleyball and the kids skinny-dip with a safe pack of little friends. The trend is to exciting, even glitzy getaways from the kids serviced by a restaurant, poolside bar and night life. Clothed society sets most expectations that people want to experience (see *Nude & Natural* magazine, N 14.4, pp. 49–56). In this *Guide* you will find both the down-home club-in-a-woods with its above-ground pool or dammed-up stream, and the sophisticated and international nudist resort.

During the 1980s, the free beaches changed too. Thinly organized to begin with, most didn't hold their leadership, as short-term crisis and euphoria yielded to long-term hard work of organizing, lobbying and fund-raising. Those that continued, coalesced around leading personalities. Interaction of nudists and naturists, clubgoers and beachgoers, continued sporadically to grow. Neither club and resort nudism nor public-beach nudity has burgeoned as expected.

THE 1990s

In the 1990s, body-alienated church fundamentalists took up positions of authority in politics and administration which grew increasingly aggressive. They didn't hesitate to act against nude beaches, even in defiance of community acceptance surveys, such as a 1983 Gallup Poll (commissioned by The Naturist Society), which found that 3 in every 20 Americans said they'd tried coed nude recreation— and nearly three-quarters said that nude recreation is acceptable in appropriate places recognized for nude use.

Nearly three-quarters approval should gain official acceptance; but not if a conspiracy of the righteous think otherwise. Naturists had to defend against church-seated intolerance, and The Naturist Action Committee was formed in 1990.

The nonprofit NAC, with leaders elected from the membership of The Naturist Society, shares with the publishing arm, The Naturists, Inc., in the public-lands focus and work of The Naturist Society. The maturing of durable free beach groups and leaders gave rise to this strengthening and democratization of the Naturist movement.

RESOURCES

The **Naturist Action Committee** and the **Naturist Education Foundation** address the political-governmental and educational concerns of The Naturist Society. Both can be contacted at The Naturist Society address and phone. NAC publishes a monthly newsletter ($20/yr).

Updates on this *World Guide*, with current addresses and phones of Naturist Network-affiliated clubs, groups, SIGs and businesses, appear in **N: Nude & Natural,** the magazine of The Naturist Society. A sample issue is $8.00. P.O. Box 132-WG, Oshkosh, WI 54902. Phone (920) 426-5009.

The **Library of Naturism** provides a current index to *Nude & Natural* magazine and *N*'s precursors, *Clothed With the Sun* and the *Free Beaches Sun.* It is available on Mac or PC disk as a text-only document that may be imported into most popular word processing programs. Search the index with your "find" command to locate names, places and other subjects.

Once the initial disk is purchased, *Library* updates are available free upon request; simply return your original disk and a stamped self-addressed envelope.

Many nudist resorts and clubs appear in the illustrated *North American Guide to Nude Recreation,* published 1997 by the **American Association for Nude Recreation,** a trade group which also publishes a monthly tabloid *Bulletin.* 1703-WG N. Main St., Kissimmee, FL 34744-9988. Phone (407) 933-2064.

Undeveloped natural hot springs in wilderness settings are much prized by Naturists who often find them through guides created by the late Jayson Loam. These are now updated and published by **Aqua Thermal Access,** 55 Azalea Lane, Santa Cruz, CA 95060.

Gay Naturists International is at P.O. Box 7150, Corte Madera, CA 94976. **International Men Enjoying Naturism** is at P.O. Box 77122, Atlanta, GA 30357.

ALABAMA

GYMNO-VITA PARK

A clothing-optional, rustic recreation park owned and managed on-site by the former director of the Birmingham Zoo. Fish-filled creek, pool, sports, theater/ballroom, game room and nature walks. RV and tent sites with hookups, rooms. Couples and families only. April 1 to October 31. P.O. Box 121-WG, Vandiver, AL 35176. Phone (205) 672-7105.

BON SECOUR NATIONAL WILDLIFE REFUGE

A fine refuge in a protected environment, Bon Secour is little visited or patrolled. Nudity is legal on most remote federal lands where it does not offend others. The compacted sand makes hiking easy as you put a mile between your party and possible beach prudes.

☞ Route 59 to Gulf Shores. Right on Highway 180 West (Fort Morgan Road) for 8.7 miles to past the 12-mile marker, and left on unmarked dirt road. (Turn is at real estate billboard, "Dune Lakes East Boundary," with a power sub-station on your right after you turn in.) Parking is very limited so arrive early. Walk down the beach to the west for perhaps a mile.

ALASKA

Alaska offers fine experiences both clothed and unclad. These tips, offered by natives, will lead you to tested sites. You will surely go nude in other places as you hike or boat or simply bask, and when no one who might object is about.

It's only natural in this great outdoors state. In private saunas and the rare hot tub, too, hosts seldom expect their guests to wear anything.

The National Park Service owns 96 percent of Alaska, which makes the largest state potentially one huge zone for nude recreation. Temperatures are commonly in the 70s and sometimes 80s from late May into early August in much of Alaska south of the Brooks Range and away from the ocean. However, always be sensitive, don't let your nudity become offensive.

The **Alaskan Naturists** organize hiking, canuding and camping, and electronically publish *"The Skinny-Dipping News."* Contact at P.O. Box 221503, Anchorage, AK 99522-1503.

LIARD RIVER HOT SPRINGS

Actually at the B.C.–Yukon boundary, well-marked on maps. Nobody would look it up except while floorboarding toward Alaska! Enjoy!

FAIRBANKS RIVERS & TANGLE LAKES

Several rivers offer one- to several-day canoe trips around Fairbanks. The Chena, Tanana, and Chatanika are relatively easy, accessible at both ends by road, and have nice gravel bars and often sunny banks. In the Alaska Range, the Tangle Lakes are a network of such waterways off the Denali Highway, about 150 miles south of Fairbanks.

SOUTHWEST: NANCY LAKE RECREATION AREA

A state tract of about 35 square miles with some 24 small lakes, campgrounds, hiking and a canoe trail which traverses 16 lakes with 11 campgrounds; no motors allowed. Be prepared to portage. Fair fishing. Canude during the week and you may have the trail all to yourselves.

☞ North on Route 1 from Anchorage to Parks Highway (#3). Past the town of Houston, at mile 67 on the left is the Nancy Lake Parkway. The canoe trailhead is clearly posted about 4.5 miles into the Recreation Area.

STORMY LAKE

Stormy Lake's 50 campsites in the Captain Cook State Recreation Area are little used. Many sandy beaches for stripping down near the camping area, or canude to the far beaches.

☞ From Anchorage, Route 1 south to Kenai and take the spur road north for 26 miles to the Recreation Area and Stormy Lake.

ALASKA PENINSULA

Katmai National Park is one of the most geologically active areas in North America and on a cold and windy day the steam vents of Novarupta Volcano can be rather pleasant. Volcanoes and associated steam vents and hot springs occur up and down the Alaska Peninsula and the Aleutians.

UNALASKA ISLAND

Remote Unalaska Island has a beautiful and popular skinny-dipping lake nestled in a hidden valley. Drive to the top of "General's Hill" and park. Hike 1/4 mile to the first lake and another 1/8 mile to the second lake. Warm in July and August, with a fine sandy bottom.

Richard Bangs/SOBEK: River Guide.

23

ARIZONA

PHOENIX AREA

CANYON STATE NATURISTS

Over 600 members, family oriented and singles friendly, with at least one state-wide campout each month, regional day hikes, backyard pool parties, 4WD trips, a houseboat trip on Lake Mead each Oct.

CSN is involved with public education in the benefits of body acceptance; street festivals, seminars, weekly broadcasts on Public Access Cable TV.

Send long SASE for info. P.O. Box 33431, Phoenix, AZ 85967. Phone (602) 834-0039; fax (602) 832-3869.

ARIZONA WILDFLOWERS

Member pool parties, potluck suppers, some campouts. Meets at least twice a month year-round; 200 members strong. Mail SASE to P.O. Box 26465, Phoenix, AZ 85068.

☆ SHANGRI LA II

Phoenix's oldest landed nudist park offers lodging and tent/RV sites. Modern facilities include heated pool, sauna, hot tub, tennis, shuffleboard, horseshoes, volleyball, nude hiking in surrounding hills and nearby clothed horseriding. 46834 North Shangri La Road-WG, New River, AZ 85027. Phone 800-465-8760 or fax (602) 465-5900.

☆ HIDDEN VALLEY RETREAT

Desert range land, 65 acres, with pool, two spas, shower/toilets, sand and water volleyball, horseshoes, playground, tent/RV sites with hookups, 2000-foot airstrip. Adjacent BLM land to explore. Contact John Covert, 55551 W. La Barranca, Maricopa, AZ 85239. Phone 1-800-310-0809; fax (520) 568-4962.

☆ EL DORADO HOT SPRING

Only 40 miles west of Phoenix, near I-10. Private soaking pools and rustic RV/tent camping on 6.7 acres of desert with mountain views. Near to Alice's Restaurant, biking, hiking, and petroglyph and wildlife viewing. P.O. Box 10,

Tonopah, AZ 85354. Phone (602) 393-0750.

CENTRAL

SYCAMORE CREEK

Only about an hour from the valley; water is cool and running abundantly except in summer, the sandy beach a pleasure to sun on. Not a long hike but good shoes are recommended. Great place for a family picnic or an aggressive hike on many surrounding trails and canyons.

☞ From Phoenix, take State Road 87 (Beeline Highway) about 23 miles north from Shea Blvd. Watch for mile-marker 212, slow down, continue 0.5 miles and turn right just before the bridge onto a dirt road that immediately crosses a cattle guard. Follow the road left about 0.3 miles to an old concrete creek crossing. Walk or 4WD north across the bridge, up the trail about 1/4 mile. Turn right at the junction, look for pink rock, go about 200 yards, turn left at large pink river rock. Follow side path to ledge. Climb down uneven, steep trail approximately 100 feet to swimming hole.

GORDON CREEK

In the Tonto National Forest, Gordon Creek is at the base of the Mogollon Rim among the tall pines. Clear water runs most of the year, stopping in early June. Best time to go is late spring or early fall. Be prudent. Portions of the road are rough and narrow. You do not need a 4WD but low clearance or large motorhomes would not be recommended.

☞ From Payson, go east on State Road 260 about 20 miles to Christopher Creek. Continue about 3 miles (watch for the highway maintenance yard on the left), turn right on Colcord Road (Forest Road 291). Take FR 291 about 4 miles to FR 200. Turn right on FR 200 and travel about 6.2 miles to a turnoff just after descending a long hill (look for Trail 178 on the right). Turn right and follow the dirt road about 0.5 miles to the camping area. There are several areas of the creek to explore from this base camp. About 1/2 mile either upstream or downstream are good pools, jumping rocks and beautiful sunning areas.

VERDE HOT SPRINGS

Clothing-optional is the tradition at this Verde River site where the Tonto and

Coconino National Forests meet. The hot springs in this high desert canyon are all that remain of a resort, one of many built in Arizona in the '20s and '30s. Regulars have made many improvements to the camping area and the bathhouse—including the excavation of caves—which render wintertime soaking the more enjoyable. The heavily-mineralized water is rated at 104°F and additional hot springs along the river provide a usually mellow, rarely crowded setting.

☞ Drive I-17 to about 80 miles north of Phoenix and Camp Verde turnoff. Forest Service station here can advise on road and river conditions. Last source of supplies. Follow turnoff east 3 or 4 miles to Camp Verde. From Camp Verde, take State Road 260 east 4.7 miles. Go right on gravel Forest Road 708 for 13.7 miles. Bear right on FR 502 and go 7 miles to the end. Park or camp here and hike one mile-plus upstream, crossing river to the old bathhouse.

FOSSIL CREEK

Fossil Creek provides nude sunning, hiking and swimming opportunities. A perfect place to go when high waters in the Verde River make it impossible to reach Verde Hot Springs. At Camp Verde, take Route 260 for 4.7 miles. Go right on gravel Forest Road 708 for 17 miles. Bear left on FR 502 and go 5 miles. Park at bridge. Walk downstream and pick a pool!

OAK CREEK CANYON

Take US 89A north from Sedona or south from Flagstaff. Park at Grasshopper Point (about 4 miles north of Sedona) and hike downstream about 1/4 mile. Or park 1/4 mile south of Grasshopper Point and descend the canyon to the creek.

The area 1/4 mile south of Grasshopper Point down to Midgley Bridge is used for skinny-dipping and sunning. Rarely crowded, the area has several nice pools and a great view. The drive through the canyon is beautiful.

WET BEAVER CREEK

Wet Beaver Creek offers a beautiful hike near the red rocks of Sedona. East #298 off I-17 at Sedona Exit. Travel towards Wet Creek Beaver Ranger Station. Trailhead is at station. Must hike past Wilderness sign to get to nude water pools. First two miles of trail are clothed. Use discretion.

KAISER WARM SPRINGS

In Mojave County, small thermal springs create a lovely soaking pool that is rarely visited. Litter-free, complete privacy, beautiful scenery. Two tubs are a few yards downstream from the warm spring and a sandy beach with large red sandstone boulders and refreshing creek water is located where Kaiser Canyon meets Burro Creek, about 200 yards from the spring.

☞ From Nothing, take Highway 93 for 8 miles to Burro Creek Campgrounds. Continue north on 93 for 5.5 miles to Kaiser Springs Bridge. Go left on dirt road just north of bridge; close the gate behind you. Go 0.1 miles to the end and walk right, down the wash and into the canyon for 1.5 miles. Enjoy!

Nearby BLM **Upper Burro Creek Wilderness Area,** east of Highway 93, offers 27,440 acres of free camping, sunning/swimming at deep pools connected by small waterfalls.

SOUTHEAST

☆ JARDIN DEL SOL

A family-oriented nudist park in the Sonora desert 35 miles northwest of Tucson. Pool, hot spa, tennis and volleyball, community kitchen, cacti garden, desert trees, water fountain, zoo. Tent and trailer sites. Area attractions include Kitt's Peak, Tombstone and Biosphere 2. P.O. Box 39-WG, Marana, AZ 85653-0039. Phone (520) 682-2537.

SABINO CANYON

Tucson's Sabino Canyon Recreation Area has been posted clothed. Our directions take you beyond, into the Coronado National Forest where folks still skinny-dip.

☞ Exit Route 256 off I-10. Go east on Grant Road and left on Tanque Verde Road. Turn left on Sabino Canyon Road to the end at Sabino Canyon Recreation.

From the Visitors Center at Sabino Canyon entrance, take tram to Stop 9 (tram runs every half hour, check schedule for last tram out). At the stone wall overlooking the creek, go right on the uphill trail. After the wall ends, go left downhill to the creek. At the creek, go upstream until out of sight of the road.

TANQUE VERDE FALLS

The Pima County Sheriff is not always tolerant of nude use; contact Canyon State Naturists for the current status!

Near Redington Pass between the Catalina and Rincon Mountains, Tanque Verde Falls is the popular and rugged skinny-dipping spot for Tucson. Great solitude among granite boulders and giant saguaro, barrel and fishhook cacti. Nudity begins around the Falls and continues beyond. Regulars hike in the nude for miles above the Falls, but take note— in 1981 eight people died when swept over the Falls during a flash flood under sunny skies. The rainstorm was hidden behind mountains; it's crucial to hear weather reports for entire watershed. Some rocky shade. Often bone dry; running river and falls, July–August; some pools, April–November.

☞ From I-10 in Tucson, go east on Speedway. Turn north at Wilmot, which becomes Tanque Verde, which becomes Redington Road. When pavement ends, follow rough gravel road for 2 miles. Park on left side of road, and trek down the Upper Tanque Verde Forest Trail on your right about 20 minutes to the stream. Clamber upstream to the Falls, about a mile away.

WATSON WASH HOT WELL

The pool is 97°F in winter and goes up to 104°F in the summer. It is a well, not a spring as shown on the new Pima U.S.G.S. topo map. On BLM land; there is no problem with camping or getting naked. Tub has drain plug and adjustable water force. Avoid weekend parties.

From Route 70 in Thatcher, go north on Reay Lane to the end. Turn left on Safford-Bryce Road. After Watson Lane on the left, turn right up Watson Wash, marked by a dip in the road and derelict cars on their sides, used to channel the water. No problem for autos unless there has just been a gully washer. The tub is 0.2 miles up on the left.

Michael Cooney. Arizona. Top & Center: Tucson's Upper Tanque Verde Falls. Bottom: A Canyon State Naturists Outing In Table Mesa Area Of Tonto National Forest.

Arizona. Canyon State Naturists Houseboating On Lake Mead. Climbing the Ladder To Arizona's Ringbolt Hot Springs At the Colorado River (See Nevada). Bev Price, The Arizona Wildflower, Decorates A Saguaro.

EASTERN

GREENLEE & GRAHAM COUNTIES

For the remote hot springs see careful directions in *N* magazine, 17.2 (1997). Stop at the store at Coolidge Dam or at the Exxon Station at the east end of Globe, to buy ($5) a recreation permit for the San Carlos Apache Indian Reservation. Camping is permitted on the reservation unless otherwise posted or restricted. Permit in hand, check out San Carlos Warm Springs. Lots of water (3398 gal./min.) in the middle of the desert, warmed enough (84°F) to take the chill off.

☞ From Globe, go east on Highway 70 beyond the crossing of the San Carlos River (turn off to Coolidge Dam) about 5.5 miles to the only paved road heading off to the north. Take to (reservation Highway 8 but the roads aren't necessarily signed) north, then east for 15 or 16 miles. Turn left on a gravel road (reservation Highway 5) and go northerly 3 or 4 miles to the San Carlos River. On the upstream side of the ford, the springs are all over, on both banks and coming up through the sandy bottom, forming a large (probably 1200 feet long by an average of 50 feet wide) shallow pool. A few areas deep enough to swim along the south bank. Naked is probably okay.

HOOKER'S HOT SPRINGS

Hooker's Hot Springs in Cochise County, part of the Muleshoe Ranch, it is now owned by the Nature Conservancy which intends to protect it from cattle ranching and motor vehicle destruction. Only the guests staying in the casitas are allowed to use the hot spring. Campers are not allowed to use it and no provision has been made for day use.

☞ Leave I-10 at Wilcox. Find Airport Road and take it west past the airport (where the pavement soon ends) about 17 miles. Turn right and go 14 more miles. Or from Benson, cross the San Pedro River and go north on Pomerene Road through the town of Pomerene (where the pavement ends) for 17 miles. Turn right for 15 miles, then left for 14 miles to Hooker's. Reservations: phone (602) 586-7072.

ARKANSAS

NORTHWEST

FAYETTEVILLE & ARKANSAS NATURISTS

Nude recreation in this Ozark frontier developed a special complexion from the late 1960s as University of Arkansas-Fayetteville students started coed skinny-dipping. Law professor Bill Clinton is said to have joined them. It spread to the Buffalo National River and Ozark National Forest. Couples and groups could be seen nude in remote places along the Mulberry, White, Buffalo, Savoy, Spavinaw, and Illinois Rivers. There are literally hundreds, if not thousands, of remote swimming holes in the Ozarks that one may enjoy nude. Here are a few.

For a list, send an envelope and donation to **Arkansas Naturists**, P.O. Box 852, Farmington, AR 72730-0852. Phone (501) 442-6817.

BUFFALO RIVER

The Upper Buffalo River is used for skinny-dipping during the off-season when canoe traffic is down. Diving from the Buffalo's bluffs is not recommended. From Harrison, follow Highway 43 to Newton County, passing the community of Ponca. At the junction of 43 and 74, turn left and follow the winding road to the top of the mountain. Turn left at the entrance to Steel Creek and follow the steep road down to the river. The bluff walls on the sides of the river create an intriguing echo chamber. Make sure you choose a remote area.

Other areas located along the Buffalo include Lost Valley and The Old Homestead Swimming Hole. The latter is south of Boxley on the Upper Buffalo. Before Highway 21 ascends the mountain, turn right on an old road located near an old homestead. Park by old buildings and hike through field to river.

WHITE RIVER (Greenland)

Fayetteville's favorite spot, primarily because it is close to the university yet isolated from traffic. The rocks are rugged and can get really hot in the summer sun, so bring a thick blanket to lie on or an air mattress float.

☞ From downtown Fayetteville, US 71 south past the airport and the small town of Greenland. After crossing the White River (West Fork) Bridge, go 1/4 mile to the first road to the left. Make sharp left back toward the river, following the paved then gravel road 1 mile, bearing to the left at all forks. Past the red barns and white house on the left, follow the road downhill a few feet to the tree-shaded area and park. Be sure not to block the wire-strand gate—offending cars have been towed. Walk through that gate to the river, cross it (it's shallow here), and follow the trail upstream 1/4 mile to the swimming and sunning area.

OZARK NATIONAL FOREST

The Russellville region of this large national forest affords numerous opportunities. Rock faces of limestone and granite create wonderful waterfalls, while artesian springs and creeks are common. Some sites of particular interest are Devil's Canyon, Richland Creek, and Mulberry Creek, which, from Cass to Ozark, has many sites for nude camping and swimming. From I-40 take Highway 23 north of Ozark; pass Turner's Bend. After passing the town of Cass, turn right at the sign for Camp Redding. From the Camp, find sites along the river but away from the main road for nude use.

Write to the Ozark National Forest, Russellville, AR 72801 for maps covering all sites. Forest Supervisor J. R. Crouch in 1981 told a USFS survey: "We do not attempt to control nudity outside of developed recreation sites. There are no reports of other forest visitors being offended by the activity."

DEVIL'S DEN STATE PARK

Lee Creek is a terrific secluded swimming hole surrounded by boulders for sunning and diving.

☞ Take Route 71 south from Fayetteville and at West Fork go west and then south onto Route 170 to Devil's Den State Park. Pass the saddle camp, following a gravel road (Route 220) 6 miles to Lee Creek, near where the road again becomes paved. Find the swimming area secluded from traffic, and enjoy.

SPAVINAW CREEK

Spavinaw Creek has tall shade trees, bracingly cold spring water, bluffs, fish-filled, crystal clear water. Clothed bathers use area by bridge on Route 43. People skinny-dip downstream from the parking area, then lay out on the bluff above. It's the norm, but be cautious.

☞ Take Route 68 west from Fayetteville to Siloam Springs, then Route 43 for 7.6 miles north to Route 10. Continue on Route 43, 5.9 miles past Cherokee City and two Spavinaw Creek bridges. Continue a half mile after the second bridge to the cut in the hill; turn right on the narrow gravel road, follow it 0.9 miles, bearing right, to the creek; park under the tall trees and follow the trail downstream. The "No Trespassing" sign is a ruse. The farmer attempted to exclude the public but lost in court—the creek is public property.

BIG HOLE

Big Hole has been a skinny-dipper's delight at least since "Free people" from far corners of America came to the Ozarks in the late 1960s to settle on farms and communes. These same folks started the Electric Moo Festival; clothes-optional was the music festival's dress code. Big Hole remains their favored swimming hole. A waterfall spills into the pool. It's hard to reach—4WD is advisable. Those who come usually camp for a weekend. Do check the water depth before diving, and take your trash out. Ozark National Forest posts against nudity; use discretion.

☞ It's 48 miles from Fayetteville on State Route 16, southeast through Brashears, St. Paul and Pettigrew. A mile beyond the community of Boston, look for the first gravel road to the right. You'll see a microwave tower ahead as you turn before reaching it. This rough road leads down the mountain after 3 or 4 miles to Big Hole.

ARKANSAS RIVER

East of Van Buren, in the Ft. Smith area, find naturist sand beaches on the north shore of the Arkansas River, above and below Lock and Dam 13 near Barling. A short walk, either east or west, will provide many secluded beach areas. All along the river are roads, lanes and paths that lead to the river's edge. The Arkansas River is not for swimming.

CENTRAL

BEAR CREEK

Visited often by the **Hot Springs Naturist Society,** P.O. Box 1683, Hot Springs National Park, AR 71901.

From Hot Springs, drive north on Highway 7. Pass Jessieville and take the unmarked dirt road on your right just before Bear Creek Bridge. The dirt road forks; go north to reach Bear Creek (a truck is needed), or straight to Bear Lake. The road curves before reaching the lake. Parking is available on the north side and nude possibilities are upstream.

LAKE OUACHITA

West of Hot Springs and accessed by Mountain Harbor Marina at Mt. Ira, this Corps of Engineers lake is great if you rent a houseboat. Find a private cove, probably at the western end.

COSSATOT RIVER

Skinny-dipping sites are located on Cossatot River 10 miles east of Wickes on Highway 4. Park near bridge and locate sites north and south of bridge.

☆ – *The star symbol before a resort name is your guarantee that The Naturist Society card is accepted and earns a discount at the resort. To obtain Naturist Society membership, see the inside front cover.*

Bowen Kerrihard. Arkansas Naturists Bask At Flat Rock, Southeast Of Fayetteville.

INTRODUCTION TO

California—the Nude Beach Mecca! That's what many thought in the '60s and '70s as youth culture established its attractive but vulnerable clothes-optional havens.

Unsurprisingly, greed culture captured the hegemony by the '80s; and even the California-created, redwood hot tub community micro-culture lost its dynamism.

Free beachers have struggled to retain the major coastal enclaves, such as Black's Beach in San Diego County, and remote inland clothes-optional zones, such as Deep Creek Hot Springs in San Bernardino County.

On pristine headlands above nude beaches, such as San Gregorio, Pirate's Cove at San Luis Obispo, and Santa Barbara's Summerland Beach, Yuppies built lavish homes with views then complained of nude persons on public beaches. (Mostly it's been a stand-off.)

Some beaches—such as More Mesa in Santa Barbara—remain pristine and nude only because developers were soundly defeated on environmental and water supply grounds.

The Chad Merrill Smith decision (1972) of the California Supreme Court clarified the emerging social climate, declaring that public nudity, if not intended to be lascivious, is not lewd.

But Southern California church authorities, by exhorting the faithful and calling in city/county political debts, put teeth into a novel legal theory that regards "mere nudity" as contrary to "community" values and lacking First Amendment protection.

The prohibition of nudity, even when lewd conduct is absent—first voted into law in 1974 by the Los Angeles City Council—became a nationwide goal of radical "religious" right-wing politics. In 1995, it emerged in the California Assembly as the nearly-successful

CALIFORNIA

"Morrissey AB 1200 initiative" to sweepingly demean all nudity.

Obviously the nude bodies do not go away. But bodies in "public" may be discouraged by bad law and the promotion of designer threads.

Unashamed body owners may be forced to go to the obscure ends of difficult trails. Even there, at the nude havens from Black's Beach to Pirate's Cove, there's a new factor: the immigrant who buys a six-pack and goes with buddies to a coastal cliff there to sip some cold ones and gawk at the non-Mexican women brazenly getting all-over tans below.

Understandably the body anxiety and denial which gives rise as well to a pornographic exploitation of the repressed may today inhibit shy women from visiting California beaches.

For a secure experience in conservative times, California does have nudist resorts—but not many. There's a threshold of acceptance, financing and professionalism that is still to be crossed, before clothes-optional enterprises become a major economic fact and cultural resource.

Heritage Videos has produced several titles on California nudism. Segments on California naturism appear in titles from Fast Forward Images and our own video, *Vacation Naturally* (1997 ed.). For additional information, check these established in-state resources: David Patrick, *California's Nude Beaches* (Bold Type, Berkeley), and the annual San Francisco *Bay Guardian* nude beaches update by Gary Hanauer (issued in late June).

Dave Patrick. Black's Beach At La Jolla, San Diego County, In the 1970s.

31

Southern California

SAN DIEGO COUNTY

BLACK'S BEACH

Urban and yet remote below a 300-foot cliff, north of the University of California–San Diego at La Jolla—the shifting legal status and demographics of Black's Beach and its off-again-on-again turmoil with the city, the county and state parks reflect the advances and setbacks of nude recreation in all California.

In 1995, an emergency call box was installed at the foot of an access road, reducing emergency response time by as much as 10 minutes.

Nude use was condoned by San Diego City Council in 1974. Attendance happily shot up, with small children brought and altogether a good people mix. Declared illegal after intense radical "religious" right pressure and a bitterly fought, narrowly lost citywide referendum in 1977, Black's Beach became mostly avoided except by bolder regulars and visitors, those adults who—unlike most Americans—will "act outside the law" when a controversial freedom is at stake.

A lively beach culture continues and, as before, breezes soothe, surf rolls, hang gliders soar. You will be rewarded by almost daily horseshoes, volleyball, Frisbee, sandcastling, kite flying and body-painting. Contact: **Black's Beach Bares,** P.O. Box 12255, La Jolla, CA 92039.

☞ Driving from San Diego, exit at La Jolla Village Drive. Go west a half mile and turn right on Torrey Pines Road North. Just past the Salk Institute turn left at the sign to the gliderport. Park in the lot and take stairs on the left to the beach.

Stay south of Muscle Rock to avoid problems.

Alternative: continue on North Torrey Pines Road past the gliderport turnoff, and at the next light turn right onto La Jolla Shores Road and immediately right again onto La Jolla Farms Road. Go 1/2 mile and you'll see Blackgold Road on the right. A paved trail can be identified by a large black gate with a UCSD sign inside. You may be lucky and park on the street nearby—observe posted regulations or be towed.

☆ SWALLOWS SUN ISLAND CLUB

Many residents, room rentals, campsites, snack bar, tennis, volleyball, pool, spa, clubhouse, sauna, sun deck. San Diego's family nudist park. 1631 Harbison Canyon Road-WG, El Cajon, CA 92019. Phone (619) 445-3754; fax (619) 445-2370.

CAMPING BARES

Camping Bares enjoy garden parties nude and operas clothed—but most of all, they hyperactively climb mountains and run white water, hike and camp au naturel where others do not go. SASE to P.O. Box 81589, San Diego, CA 92138-1589. Phone (619) 685-8175.

SAN ONOFRE BEACH

San Onofre State Beach has an entry fee, showers, lifeguards, toilets, trash cans. In the past, north district San Diego sheriff's deputies issued citations and Camp Pendleton M.P.s evicted sunbathers. That no longer happens, but beach users are now alert to prevent sex acts by selfish interlopers, which could cause a closure order.

To the north you will see the twin globes—"Les Boobs"—of the San Onofre nuclear energy plant. On a clear day to the south you may view the headland of Torrey Pines State Beach just beyond which lies Black's Beach. San Onofre's own sandstone cliffs are more sculptured (if not as high or dangerous) as those of Black's Beach, with lizards, swallows and squirrels, and the broad beach is a delight.

Local beach group organizes activities; send SASE to **Friends of San Onofre,** P.O. Box 2552, Capo Beach, CA 92624; phone/fax (714) 443-0891.

☞ On Route 5 north or south, take the San Onofre Park/Basilone exit. Go south several miles to the entrance to the state campground. Pay $6 day fee. Go 3.5 miles to the end of the campground and park near the last rest room (#16). Trail 6 starts here. Go down to the beach, turn left (south) for about 0.5 miles past the last lifeguard station but do not disrobe until you pass the wash after that station. Stay north of the Camp Pendleton fence.

IMPERIAL COUNTY

PALM OASIS WARM SPRINGS

Palm Oasis is neat, clean, and more convenient than the now-closed Oh My God! Hot Well for San Diegans. Surrounded by a wood platform, head-high bushes and bullrushes and five palm trees. Water is 90°F, plenty of camping room, nude is the norm. Good nuding is also on the Highline Canal, a five-minute walk west.

☞ From Brawley, take Route 78 east for 15 miles until you cross the Highline Canal, marking the end of farmland. Take second dirt road on right, go 1.5 miles. On your right will be an oasis with the only five palm trees in the area.

RIVERSIDE COUNTY

RAFFLES PALM SPRINGS HOTEL

An 11-room garden Bed and Australian Breakfast Inn. Nine rooms have kitchenettes; all have refrigerators. Large spa and heated pool with mountain view. Reservations required. 280 Mel Ave., Palm Springs, CA 92262. Phone (760) 320-3949; fax (760) 322-1236.

MORNINGSIDE INN

With refurbished rooms and courtyard and light lunch on weekends, owners Ken and Sallie Smelker say they give the best value of Palm Springs B&Bs. Seven full suites have VCRs, kitchens; some have private patios; 3 cabanas with microwave/fridge. Heated pool and spa, exercise area. 888 N. Indian Canyon, Palm Springs, CA 92262. Phone (619) 325-2668.

☆ DESERT SHADOWS INN AND VILLAS

The Naturist Society's first luxury resort has 34 air-conditioned rooms with cable TV, VCRs, refrigerators, and 38 luxury villas built around three waterfalls and a pond. Grounds offer an incomparable view of 9000-foot San Jacinto Mountains. Sculpture fountain, three large heated pools, two spas, tennis, volleyball, game and exercise rooms, cafe restaurant, putting green, and Skinny-Dipper gift shop. See *Nude & Natural* magazine, *N* 17.1, pp. 32-40. 1533 Chaparral Road, Palm Springs, CA 92262. Phone (760) 325-6410 or 800-292-9298; fax (760) 327-7500.

TERRA COTTA INN

Heated garden pool and jacuzzi spa, barbecue facilities, 17 guest rooms with private baths, cable TV, VCR and air conditioning. Kitchens and private patios available. No children. 2388 E. Racquet Club Road-WG, Palm Springs, CA 92262-2629. Phone 1-800-786-6938 or (760) 322-6059; fax (760) 322-4169.

N/N GROUP

Palm Springs area Nudists and Naturists Group meets for parties, hot spring excursions, camping trips and visits to landed clubs. Send SASE to P.O. Box 8038, Palm Springs, CA 92263. Phone (760) 323-7291.

TURTLE BACK MESA

A Naturist B&B in the desert with hiking trails, soaking pools, beautiful scenery. P.O. Box 8038, Palm Springs, CA 92263. Phone (760) 347-5358.

☆ OLIVE DELL RANCH

A small well-equipped nudist park with rentals, restaurant, guest passes, an hour's drive from Los Angeles. 26520 Keissel Road-WG, Colton, CA 92324. Phone (909) 825-6619.

☆ GLEN EDEN SUN CLUB

The largest family nudist resort of the West, with many scheduled sports and social events. Volleyball, tennis, indoor and outdoor pools, sauna, tent and trailer sites. Co-op governance, many residents. 25999 Glen Eden Road, Corona, CA 91719. Phone (909) 277-4650; fax (909) 277-8020.

ORANGE COUNTY

☆ CAMP McCONVILLE

The oldest nudist park in California (1933) is set snugly high above the smog in a wooded gulch by a seasonal creek in the Cleveland National Forest. Cabins, tent and RV sites. Volleyball, swimming pool, hot tub, tennis, horseshoes, hiking, children's play area. P.O. Box 477-WG, Lake Elsinore, CA 92531. Phone (909) 678-2333.

LOS ANGELES COUNTY

☆ ELYSIUM FIELDS

The oldest clothing-optional educational facility in the nation, holding a variety of classes and workshops year-round. Elysium Fields also offers sun lawn, jacuzzi, pool, sauna, tennis and volleyball courts, picnic areas, community kitchen. Families and children welcome; guest passes available at nominal charge. Ask for a copy of its *Journal of the Senses*. 814 Robinson Road-WG, Topanga, CA 90290. Phone (310) 455-1000; fax (310) 455-2007.

SAN BERNARDINO COUNTY

DEEP CREEK HOT SPRINGS

Nude is the only way to enjoy these marvelous springs, and that is how US Forest Service rangers supervise it, asking only that you take litter out and do not camp at the springs. The chilly creek flows past a selection of large and small, naturally hot pools. Many hike au naturel. People are evicted in time to make the climb out before nightfall.

If you do want to camp, you may do so at the nearby Bowen Ranch, where you'll park, but you'll have to bring everything, since the ranch supplies nothing—not even water. Friends of Deep Creek oversee the site; contact them c/o Bowen Ranch, 6221 Bowen Ranch Road, Apple Valley, CA 92308.

☞ Go north on I-15 through Cajon Pass into the Mojave Desert. About 6 miles beyond the Pass, take the Hesperia/Phelan Exit. Turn right at the off-ramp stop sign onto Main Street and go 7.4 miles through Hesperia. Turn left onto Rock Springs Road; this turn occurs just after the road bears to the right, past a Silverwood Lake sign on the left. Go 2.5 miles to a T-intersection; turn left onto Kiowa. Go 0.5 miles and turn right onto Roundup Way. There is a Mariana Rancho sign here. Follow Roundup Way to the end of the paved section and go exactly 1.4 miles on the dirt section of Roundup Way. Turn right onto Bowen Ranch (no road sign here). Go 5.8 miles on Bowen Ranch Road, bearing right at the only major intersection, to the ranch house where there is a chain across the road. Honk your horn to get someone to come to the door. Pay the fee and continue another 0.3 miles to a large flat camping area. Hike 0.5 miles to the end of the road, go down the trail between the large rock pile and the Joshua tree and bear left through the fence, where there is a large iron sign which says Area Closed To Vehicles. Continue about 50 yards and bear right into the first canyon. Follow the Forest Service Trail about 1.5 miles (800-foot elevation drop) to the creek. The last part is a steep hill with a surface of decomposed granite—good track shoes are recommended. Ford the creek to the hot springs.

☆ SILVER VALLEY SUN CLUB

In the smog-free, blooming Mojave Desert, halfway between Los Angeles and Las Vegas, an oasis with small lake, islets and boats, cottonwoods shading tent/RV sites, shuffleboard, volleyball, clubhouse restaurant noted for hospitality. Information and list of area attractions: 48382 Silver Valley Road-WG, Newberry Springs, CA 92365. Phone (760) 257-4239; fax (760) 257-4670.

BUFF CREEK NUDIST RESORT

Formerly Treehouse Nudist Resort. Many residents, large pool, indoor and outdoor spas, sauna, tennis, minimart, restaurant, volleyball, rec hall, hiking trails. No singles. 1924 Glen Helen Rd., Devore, CA 92407-1500. Phone (909) 887-0803 or 1-800-899-NUDE; fax (909) 887-2390.

BEACHFRONT USA

Politically active group, publishes informative newsletter; enclose SASE with inquiry. P.O. Box 328, Moreno Valley, CA 92556.

> NOTE: captions to photos run along the inside edge of pages.

Central California

SANTA BARBARA COUNTY

RINCON (BATES) BEACH

Rincon is Santa Barbara's southernmost nude beach. Amenities: paved parking, rest rooms, picnic area, paved footpath to beach. Marine life in tidal pools and seals frolic offshore. Around the point to the east (where you must be clothed) find radical surfers. Popular for nudity but raided too often by sheriff deputies to be used without checking the current status.

☞ Access is from Highway 101 at the Ventura County line, 15 miles west of Ventura and 10 miles east of Santa Barbara. Look for the Bates Road Exit in Carpinteria. Take the exit and turn left, going under the bridge and towards the ocean. Signs for the beach will appear on your right, as will the beach gate. Enter the gate and go up a rise to the day-use lot. If the parking lot is full, turn left, drive up the hill and park. Take either the staircase at the end of the lot or the ramp near the picnic area down to the nude zone—north of the drainage pipe and near the volleyball nets.

MORE MESA

Many Santa Barbarans swear by More Mesa's white sand, sheltered location, and broad prospects. Sheriff's plain-clothes deputies did "riot" against beach-goers one infamous day in 1978, but this has long been a very mellow spot where troubles are forgotten. Sheriff's office now says it would issue citations "on complaint" only. Complainers are nonexistent; horseback riders, surfers, volleyball zealots, Frisbee hurlers, elderly and infants share the beach.

On the mesa top the sandy soil supports one of few remaining natural ecologies in greater Santa Barbara. That, plus the view, inspired environmentalists to preserve the large tract.

☞ From Route 101, exit on Turnpike Road to the south, then left on Hollister, going 2 blocks and turning right on Puente Drive. Follow Puente about 3/4 mile (road turns into Vieja Drive) and park near the entrance to Mockingbird Lane. Mockingbird Lane is an access road no longer open to vehicles, so walk to the end and take the established descent at the terminus of the ruts in a stand of eucalyptus trees. Any other route is dangerous. Considering the parking problem, the best solution is to take the Hollister/State Street bus. It stops at the end of Puente Road—a 20-minute walk from the beach.

GUADALUPE: NIPOMO DUNES

Little known are the fabulous 19-mile coastal Guadalupe Dunes—preserved by many miles of federal land including Vandenberg Air Force Base. It's not a simple trip in. You won't find much of a social nude beach; rather, an environment for free-spirited gamboling in the sun and dozing in the dunes.

☞ From Route 101 in Santa Maria, take Route 166 west to the town of Guadalupe, then farther west on Oso Flaco Lake Road to a parking area 40 minutes walking distance from the ocean; 4WD vehicles proceed onto the trackless sands. Ocean at the northern end.

SUMMERLAND BEACH

Summerland's clothes-optional area is just east of Lookout County Park. Easy descent to the beach makes this a popular spot with kiddies and oldsters alike. Lots of bodysurfing, volleyball, and swimming, and many users have come for a decade. It is wise to check out current conditions before disrobing.

☞ From Route 101, exit at Evans and take the immediate left on Evans under the freeway. Take next left as if going south for 0.3 miles and turn right just before freeway (at the sign for recycling center). Continue to the parking lot and turn south. The clothing-optional beach starts approximately underneath the only house on the cliff. More parking in Lookout Park, west of the exits from 101. Do not park on Finney Road.

BIG & LITTLE CALIENTE SPRINGS

Caliente Hot Springs receive a lot of use, both nude and clothed. There is a specific rule against nudity here, so caution is a necessity. The two springs are about 5 miles apart.

☞ Take the Gibraltar Road, which climbs 7 miles up the Santa Ynez mountain range behind Santa Barbara. It mounts steeply to the crest, where one gains almost breathtaking views of Santa Barbara and the Channel Islands. At the crest, turn right on Camino Cielo. The asphalt road turns to dirt after 7 miles and at Romero Saddle it becomes narrow, winding and rough with jagged stones and rocks—beware tire damage. (There are four campgrounds along this road; all free but without facilities so take food and water.) At Juncal Campground, the road doubles back to the left just past the concrete creek ford and goes 3 miles to the Pendola Ranger Station.

To reach Big Caliente, take the right fork from Pendola. The road goes another 3 miles to end at the spring.

To reach Little Caliente, continue straight ahead on the road at Pendola Station for 5 miles to Mono Campground. There is no longer a locked gate on the road just past the campground, so drive the last mile to the spring, taking the right fork. Follow the road to a point where it starts to climb and makes a horseshoe bend back to the left to cross a low ridge. Take the trail from the parking area marked by wood-retained steps to the right of the spring. Smaller and colder

than Big Caliente, Little Caliente is more isolated and freer of hassles. Not accessible during fire or rainy seasons, so check with Los Padres National Forest Ranger Station before setting out.

SAN LUIS OBISPO COUNTY

PIRATE'S COVE

Pelicans dive and seals frolic at this long-established nude beach. More recently, farm workers with the day off vie for space on the clifftop with developers building homes with a view. Hang in there, and get organized, nudies!

☞ Take the Avila Beach exit from Route 101, six miles south of San Luis Obispo. Drive west 2 miles on Avila Road. Take the blacktop spur cutting up to the left marked "Not a Through Road—No Overnight Camping." Follow over the sea ridge, about 0.5 miles to the parking area. After a rather steep descent, you'll be on the beach.

SYCAMORE HOT SPRINGS

Clothing-optional secluded redwood hot tubs about the grounds and a private hot tub on the balcony of each motel room. Swimming pool, massage. Nearby Pirate's Cove on Avila Beach. 1215 Avila Beach Drive, San Luis Obispo, CA 93405. Phone (805) 595-7302.

HEARST STATE PARK

Hearst State Park at San Simeon has a parking lot (fee charged) from which you can walk to "the cove," a beach beyond a row of state park pilings that serve as boundary markers. Nude sunbathing in the cove has annoyed Hearst Corp. managers but it's public land to the high tide mark. Go past all buildings before disrobing.

KERN COUNTY

REMINGTON HOT SPRINGS

Two miles from a Forest Service campground; two small volunteer-built cement tubs; water temperature 104°F; the site is kept extremely clean. If spring is closed by high water, visit Delonegha Hot Springs.

☞ From Bakersfield take Route 178 a few miles past Delonegha Hot Springs and turn on Borel. While it quickly dead ends, turn right and drive over a mile, passing Hobo Campground, to a large turnout with a telephone in the middle. A trail leads to the springs. The

descent is steep so wear appropriate footgear.

DELONEGHA HOT SPRINGS

On Kern River between Bakersfield and Lake Isabella, Delonegha is a popular nude soak. Recently three new pools were built and there is a small 2-person pool on the downstream side of the cliff.

☞ Take Route 178 (old highway) up the river from Bakersfield. After miles of a winding 2-lane highway, it crosses the Kern River and becomes a 4-lane highway. The springs are located between mile-markers 32 and 32.5. Pull off at the first curve after the start of the 4-lane section, and park in the lot marked "Emergency Parking Only." The springs are down the river a hundred yards below the road, overlooking the creek. These springs are hot, with a clean rocky bottom and beautiful setting.

INYO COUNTY

SALINE VALLEY WARM SPRINGS

Well-maintained by regular users, who have created a unique drop-in (and even fly-in) community of free spirits and self-governance. Was BLM land; in 1994 assimilated to Death Valley National Park. Signage confirms clothing-optional status. Two springs flow into four cement-lined soaking pools; a fifth pool is used for baths and shampooing.

Terrain is rough, the road passable by 2-wheel-drive vehicles with good ground clearance unless directly after a heavy rain. The last 8–10 miles are the most difficult. Be sure to fill your tank before entering the region, and have a spare tire and tools along as it's 80 miles to the nearest tow service. Stay on the road at all times (no off-road vehicle activity allowed) and if possible travel in groups of two vehicles or more. Bring plenty of water; keep tents and food secured to avoid raids by wild donkeys.

☞ From Los Angeles, take Route 14 to 395 north. Exit at Olancha (south end of Owens Lake) onto Route 190 and follow signs to Death Valley. Continue for 17.2 miles, turn left onto blacktop road marked Saline Valley Road. About 8 miles beyond take the right fork keeping on the paved road. Follow the road winding up the canyon, after 5 miles there's a sudden drop-off into Panamint Valley to your right. Continue for 2.4 miles, turn left and descend into Grapevine Canyon. You emerge from the canyon after 5 miles with views of the Saline Valley salt lake far below. Drive past the salt lake (20 miles), then go 5 more miles past the sand dunes on the right-hand side. Turn right at a green painted post onto a narrower dirt road

heading east. The springs are 6 miles from here. Roads to avoid are "Eureka Corridor" and trails to "Racetrack." "Painted Bat Rock Road" is okay; take this until the road forks and go left. Watch for tall brush and other campers about 7 miles past the painted rock: this is Lower Warm Springs.

At the junction of routes 395 and 136 is an information center where you can pick up maps and other information.

OWENS RIVER

Located on the Eastern Sierra portion of Bishop, CA, the Owens River affords many private swimming and sunning areas. A good spot is 3 miles north of Bishop, between 5 Bridges Road and Laws, Highway 6. Fishing, swimming, and sunning are possible at this little used site.

TECOPA HOT SPRINGS

A nice respite on the way to Death Valley. "Nudity required," according to terms of Inyo County treaty with the local Indian tribe. Separate bathhouses make mixed-bathing impossible. Open 24 hours, no charge. Located between Baker and Death Valley; lodging can be found at the Tecopa Hot Springs Resort, off Highway 127. Phone (619) 852-4373.

From Shoshine, CA, take CA 127 south toward Tecopa. Approximately 5 miles down the road, there is a sign for Tecopa Hot Springs. Turn left and follow signs for 3 miles. The springs are directly across the street from an RV park. The parking lot is shared with the Inyo County Library.

KEHOUGH HOT DITCH

The Ditch consists of five rock pools below the hot springs. Clear, hot water, view of the snowcapped Sierra and the dry Owens Valley.

☞ One hundred miles south of Bridgeport and 9 miles south of Bishop, just off of Route 395.

MONTEREY COUNTY

ESALEN INSTITUTE

Esalen Institute is a world-renowned center offering workshops in a wide variety of human potential development areas. The naturally hot sulphurous baths and the swimming pool and lawn are clothing-optional to registered guests only. The hot baths are open to the general public 1–3 a.m. daily; reservations required: (408) 667-3047.

Ask for a catalog, you may want to go for a two- or five-day program. By itself on the coastal slope of Route 1, 45 miles

south of Monterey, 50 miles north of Hearst Castle.

PFEIFFER BEACH

The wild and rugged Big Sur coast offers many opportunities for solitary clothes-optional activities. Pfeiffer Beach provides, quite simply, a social occasion with a fine breeze and a view of offshore rock formations and huge floating kelp.

☞ Pfeiffer Beach is in Los Padres National Forest, 12 miles north of Esalen Institute on Highway 1, along Big Sur. Just over the Pfeiffer Canyon bridge, turn off toward the ocean on unmarked Sycamore Canyon Road (diamond-shaped signs show that there is a cross-road only on the ocean side of Route 1. The crossroad is like a "Y"; veer left coming from the south or cut back sharply coming from the north). At the end of the 3-mile-long road is the federal beach parking lot; park ($5 fee) and take the path to the beach. Walk north about 1/4 mile to the nude haven, well out of view of the casual beach tourists.

GARRAPATA BEACH

This half-mile of beautiful state park beach with many caves and coves for wind protection is treasured by the locals. Equally warm in winter and summer. High cliffs with a variety of wild flowers give privacy; swim with caution. Unimproved and unhassled, and the **Friends of Garrapata Beach** hope to keep it that way. Contact them at 1225 Military Ave., #A, Seaside, CA 93955.

☞ The Garrapata River runs beneath Garrapata Bridge into the south end of Garrapata Beach. It is the 6th bridge on Highway 1 going from Rio Rd. in Carmel (the main beach entrance is exactly 9.6 miles from the junction of Highway 1 and Rio Road). Driving north from Big Sur it's the second bridge on Highway 1 in Carmel after the Rocky Point Restaurant, about 1/2 mile beyond it. A landmark stone house is sited on the cliff near the bridge, where you park and descend the 20-foot cliff on wooden steps to the riverside. From there it's an easy walk to the beach. Nudity occurs on the north and south ends of the beach; the middle area is clothed.

ARROYO SECO CANYON

Arroyo Seco Canyon in Los Padres National Forest has a lovely river for sun-bathing.

From Salinas, take Route 101 south past Soledad to Arroyo Seco Road. Follow it west to the campground. Continue about 1.75 miles past campground entrance. Park before "Road Closed" sign indicating a 2.25-mile hike to

fairly easy descent to creek. (The gorge is a hike beyond that.) Other slippery, steep descent trails are available for skilled climbers.

At some areas the canyon becomes so narrow one can touch both sides at once and at other areas one must wade or swim. The experience is worth it!

FORT ORD'S CRATER

Clothed and the unclothed have begun hanging out at what used to be an Army artillary range. Users gather at the bottom and sides of the enormous hole that is surrounded by miles of dunes, part of the old Fort Ord military base.

☞ Take Highway 1 to Seaside's Fremont Boulevard overcrossing. Park in last block on north end of Fremont, facing south near old motel. Walk north past traffic light, and hike up the large sand dune to the top; the crater is on the other side.

SANTA CRUZ COUNTY

BAY AREA NATURISTS

House parties and beach and backcountry outings. Write for the West's best Naturist monthly newsletter. Send long SASE to P.O. Box 23781, San Jose, CA 95153.

BONNY DOON BEACH

A showplace of California naturism. The community spirit of the regular visitors added to the natural beauty should put Bonny Doon on any itinerary. Bonny Doon can be windy. The cliffs offer protection—but unstable rock makes it dangerous to stand or lie directly below the cliffs! Remove trash, even if it's not your own.

☞ Highway 1 to the intersection with Bonny Doon Rd., 11 miles north of Santa Cruz or 2 miles south of Davenport. At the intersection, park in the lot on the west side of Highway 1 (it is illegal to park on Bonny Doon Rd. or on the shoulder of Highway 1) and walk up behind the highway 27.6 mile-marker sign, over the railroad tracks, and down the steep trail to the beach. At the beach, walk north to the cove at the end of the beach.

SHARK'S TOOTH BEACH (DAVENPORT COVE)

Named after a massive rock formation 50 yards from shore, Shark's Tooth is a deep sandy beach in a cove with cliffs to the north. The cold water, small beach area and steep trail to the cove deter many. Don't go nude at Davenport Beach.

☞ Access from a pull-off (blocked by a long barred gate) a half-mile south of Davenport, or you can walk north a half-mile from Bonny Doon Beach.

RED, WHITE, AND BLUE BEACH

A benevolent proprietary utopia run by Ralph Edward & Son, this fine beach has the amenities of a state park plus clothes-optional everywhere. Edward keeps out gawkers, forbids photography, and encourages sociability and trust. The 600 yards of deep, sandy beach are bounded by beautiful cliffs—and those on the south can be passed at low tide, opening up another mile of unspoiled beach. Edward claims to be in it only for the money but don't believe him; he's one of the pioneers. Entrance fee ($7 for day use), overnight camping ($12–$16 fee). Day use 10 a.m.–6 p.m. in summer months. Phone (408) 423-6332 for weather information.

☞ Access is by Highway 1, seven miles north of Santa Cruz or four miles south of Davenport. Look for a large red, white, and blue mailbox with the number 5021 on the west side of the road. Turn onto Scaroni Road, a crescent—the first entrance, 100 feet past mile-marker 24.67, coming from Santa Cruz; the second, larger entrance, 30 feet before marker 25, go in through the gate.

PANTHER BEACH

Panther has a spectacular setting—high rock tower, natural bridges and caves. Not a well-known nude beach, it has on a good day no more than 100 visitors. Beach too crowded? Try Hole in the Wall Beach by going through a hole in the wall at the south end of Panther Beach.

☞ The beach is 10.6 miles north of Santa Cruz on Highway 1 between mile-markers 95 and 96. Park on the small dirt road on the west side off the highway and climb down to the beach from the north end of the lot. The path is steep and eroded; wear appropriate footwear.

FOUR MILE BEACH

A young crowd gathers here to surf, sun, and party—unfortunately leaving trash as a trophy of their festivities. Now part of Wilder Ranch Estates State Park; portable toilets have been added and rangers have, on occasion, admonished the 10 to 20 nude users on the south end of the beach.

☞ Starting from Santa Cruz, Four Mile Beach is 4 miles north of the junction of Mission Boulevard with Highway 1. It is at the Baldwin Creek crossing of Highway 1. Park on the unpaved turnout, walk 1/4 mile down the dirt road to cross the railroad and wind to the left of a marsh and standing water to the beach.

2222 BEACH

A 100-foot cliff is all that segregates this tranquil clothing-optional cove from the expensive homes of West Cliff Drive. Named for the facing house number, 2222 Beach establishes a model for urban nude beaches, with its durable acceptance in a residential neighborhood.

☞ In Santa Cruz turn off Highway 1 on Swift Street to the Pacific, then right (north) on West Cliff Drive for five blocks. 2222 Beach is between Auburn and Chico Avenues—do not park on West Cliff Drive, look for the nine-car lot on the sea side of West Cliff. If the lot is full, park on Chico Ave.

KIVA RETREAT HOUSE

Hot tubs (community and individual), cold plunge, showers, sauna, social room, sunning lawns, library/reading room with fireplace, at this entirely clothes-optional retreat located near downtown Santa Cruz. $8 per day; massage extra. 702 Water Street, Santa Cruz, CA 95060. Phone (408) 429-1142

HEARTWOOD SPA

Friendly establishment with clothes optional in community hot tub and sauna in beautiful garden area; private tub, massage, other bodywork available. Sunday nights are women only. Noon to 11 p.m. daily; $8 for the day. 3150-A Mission Drive, Santa Cruz, CA 95065. Phone (408) 462-2192.

HENRY COWELL REDWOODS PARK

Nearly a mile of secluded creek in a lushly wooded steep canyon; several small swimming holes, sand beaches. Garden of Eden, where the San Lorenzo River makes an "S" bend, if not deserted, is a friendly mix of textiled and nude. Main problem is summer fog, which usually but not always burns off by noon.

From the main parking lot, go south on the Redwood Loop Trail; from the south end of the loop follow the railroad tracks south over a bridge and another quarter-mile until you see well-used path to left and signs against diving in the river.

Cowell Park has a campground which fills rapidly in summer. For reservations or trail map, write Henry Cowell Redwoods State Park, 101 N. Big Trees Road, Felton, CA 95018. Phone (408) 335-4598.

Begin or finish a memorable day by riding through the big trees on the authentic, 1890s steam-driven, narrow-gauge Roaring Camp & Big Trees Narrow Gauge Railroad—phone (408) 335-4484, with a stop at Cowell Park headquarters on Graham Hill Road.

☞ From San Jose, Highway 17 south to Scotts Valley, take the Mt. Hermon Road turnoff, continue to Felton. Take Highway 9 south past the main entrance of Cowell Park, 1.3 miles to roadside parking at the park maintenance road gate (Ox Road Trail).

SANTA CLARA COUNTY

☆ LUPIN, A FAMILY NATURIST CLUB

Full-service restaurant with scenic terrace, lodgings, tent sites, two pools and hot spas, sauna, tennis, volleyball, massage, children's playground, hiking on 110 wooded acres in Santa Cruz mountains. Near San Francisco and Santa Cruz/Monterey nude beaches. Frequent site of Western Naturist Gatherings. P.O. Box 1274-WG, Los Gatos, CA 95031. Phone (408) 353-2250; fax (408) 353-2230.

ALAMEDA COUNTY

☆ SEQUOIAN FAMILY NUDIST PARK

Sequoians has a 40-plus years tradition, 80 acres and over 150 members. Volleyball, pool, hot tub, tent and trailer sites. P.O. Box 2095-WG, Castro Valley, CA 94546. Phone (510) 582-0194 or 1-800-404-NUDE.

SAN MATEO COUNTY

MONTARA STATE BEACH

Nude use is discreet, and only at the north end of the state beach; dunes, secluded coves—and possible problem with rangers. A nearby youth hostel can provide comfortable overnight accommodations for as little as $7 per person; phone (415) 728-7177 or write to Point

Montara Lighthouse-AYH Hostel, P.O. Box 737, Montara, CA 94037.

☞ On Highway 1 south of Pacifica, Montara Beach is located 1.1 miles south of Devil's Slide.

SAN GREGORIO NUDE BEACH

The historic "first" among recognized nude beaches in America. The 120 leased acres include caves, cliffs and 2 miles of beach with a relaxing atmosphere. Attendance is 800 maximum on a weekend. Jogging, volleyball, driftwood shelters in the sand, nature walk to lagoon behind the beach. Users include families, singles, and to the north, gays. No camping, fires, food or water but there are now chemical toilets near the parking area. There is a fee. In addition to beach sex, fog is a big problem here; call San Gregorio State Beach for weather info at (415) 726-6238.

☞ From San Francisco, go south on Highway 1. Pass Half Moon Bay and after about 11 miles, look for the intersection of Hwy 1 and Hwy 84. Just opposite and 100 yards north of this intersection, turn in and go through the large white gate bearing the sign "Toll Road;" pay the fee and park. A trail leads to the beach.

POMPONIO STATE BEACH

Clean, quiet, sandy beach extends for over a mile. State officials indicate there will be no problems unless complaints are made. Rest rooms located at main beach.

☞ Four miles south of San Gregorio Nude Beach on Highway 1. Enter the park and turn south. Park in the lot past the circular parking lot and do not leave valuables in your car. Walk to the circular lot, take the trail down to the beach; the southern end is the nude area. The last part of the trail is steep and narrow so wear appropriate shoes.

GRAY WHALE COVE

State-owned and privately-leased Gray Whale Cove features 300 yards of clean beach with rest room facilities, a hot dog stand and soda machine. The water is cold for swimming and the undertow is strong, but one can join in a game of Frisbee, volleyball or paddleball and there is plenty to do for those who like to explore tidal pools and the nearby rocks. Admission is $5; beach closes at 7 p.m. and is not open on rainy days. For road and weather conditions, phone (415) 728-5336. No fires, camping, cameras or binoculars allowed.

A Family Grows In Naturism

☞ Highway 1, five miles south of the San Francisco suburb of Pacifica, and 1 mile north of the town of Montara. Look for Devil's Slide—a cliff that drops dramatically to the sea—then spot the sign "Beach Parking" on the left. There is a huge asphalt parking lot; cars parked along the road are often towed. Transportation to the beach is provided for the handicapped, pregnant or elderly; all others must take the stairs that lead down to the beach.

SAN FRANCISCO COUNTY

GOLDEN GATE: BAKER BEACH

Seaward and south from the Golden Gate lies Baker Beach, its secluded sands offering a great view. From downtown, go west on Geary, turn north on 25th Ave., up to Camino del Mar. Turn right (a sign points right for the Presidio) and travel about 1/4 mile to the second appearance of Bowley St. (the first one is one-way out). The park-

ing lot is on Gibson Road; enter, take a small road to the east parking lot, and park as far east as possible. The clothing-optional section is about a five-minute walk along the beach. If one con-

tinues about a half mile farther along Camino del Mar (which has now become Lincoln Blvd.), a steep beach access directly to the clothing-optional section is available.

Northern California

MADERA COUNTY

ANGEL FALLS

Over two decades of nude use at this beautiful area north of Fresno, with easy access. Large, smooth rocks for sunning and numerous whirlpools perfect for swimming. Usually not crowded; a summer weekend brings about 30 people, half being nude.

☞ From Fresno, take Route 41 north, turn right on Highway 274, the Bass Lake turnoff. Go about 4 miles to two forks in the road. Keep to the left both times, staying on Highway 274. You will immediately see the Mountain Government Center on your left. Go about a half-mile, turn left onto a small driveway in which you can go left or down to the right, go to the right through a steel green gate and free parking is along the stream (if you cross over a bridge you have gone about 200 feet too far). Hike up along this stream to Angel Falls (about a 10-minute walk on trail left of the stream). If you cross the stream and hike another ten minutes along the right side of the stream you will reach Devil's Slide with more pools in the rocks. Clothing-optional use is from the parking area up to Devil's Slide (Angel Falls is halfway in between). This is the stream that replenishes nearby Bass Lake.

TUOLUMNE COUNTY

TUOLUMNE RIVER

From Groveland east of Stockton, near the west side of Yosemite National Park, drive about 15 miles east on Route 120 to the South Fork of the Tuolumne River. Just after crossing the bridge, turn left. Another immediate left leads to the Rainbow Pool (on the upstream side of the bridge). Skinny-dipping is common above and below the main swimming hole, and occasionally in the Rainbow Pool itself. The most attractive sites are to be found by parking near the blocked dirt road, descending from the road down to Rainbow Pool, and hiking down the steep dirt road about 3/4 mile to the confluence of the South and Middle Forks.

For **Preston Flats,** follow the above instructions as far as crossing the bridge and turning immediately left. But then, having turned left, immediately turn right instead of another left; this puts you onto the road towards Cherry Lake. Follow 8 miles to the Tuolumne River at Early Intake. Cross the bridge, turn right, and continue past residences and Kirkwood Powerhouse to the end of the road. Park and follow the trail 1/4 mile to 4 miles upstream. The trail is easy, with gentle slopes and good camping. Best spot, 3 miles up.

MONO COUNTY

BENTON HOT SPRINGS

Clothing is optional at Benton Hot Springs, the only business in the town of the same name. A naturally-vegetated setting and individually sited facilities for privacy. Groups/private parties can be arranged. Located on Highway 120, four miles west of Route 6. Phone (619) 933-2507.

MAMMOTH LAKES

East of Mammoth Lakes are several au naturel hot springs. Crab Cooker (112°F) has a cement pool with water/temperature valve, a nearby cold water spring and beautiful view. Shepard Hot Spring has adjustable temperature and room enough for two people. Dave's Warm Tub can hold one person in its porcelain tub. Red's Pond is within walking distance from Mammoth Lakes; up to fifty percent of the bathers may be nude and others are topfree. Pulky's Pool, off Benton Crossing Road north of a cattle guard, has a large cement-and-rock pool with hot and cold water valves. Other recommendations are Crowley Hot Spring, Hot Tub, and Wild Willy's. To locate, ask locals for directions and check Jayson Loam's *Hot Springs and Hot Pools of the Southwest.*

"BIG HOT" WARM SPRINGS

Geothermal pools; some quite deep. Water temperature 80–85°F. Located less than two miles east of Route 395, south of Bridgeport in Mono County. Walking or 4WD is recommended for the last part of the road. Close any gates you open.

TRAVERTINE HOT SPRINGS

View the Sierra from one of two pools where locals have built a concrete tub and a smaller shallow tub. Sunning area, camping space. Afterwards visit the ghost town, Bodie, or explore an abandoned mine.

Friends of Travertine oversee the sight. For information, write c/o Michael and Sharon Mooney, P.O. Box 282, Bridgeport, CA 93517.

☞ From Bridgeport, take US 395 south for 1/2 mile and turn left onto Jack Sawyer Road. At the second fork, take the dirt road straight and continue to the right on the road up the hill. Continue straight a half-mile and park in the lot near the hot spring. Walk down slope to reach the pools.

AMADOR COUNTY

RANCHO CICADA RETREAT

In the Sierra foothills 45 miles east of Sacramento. Fifty wooded private acres of prime river frontage for swimming and rafting, hiking, games. Accommodates groups up to 40 on modern tent platforms with mattresses, community kitchen, hot showers. Catering available for groups. Reservations necessary. P.O. Box 225, Plymouth, CA 95669. Phone (209) 245-4841.

COMANCHE RESERVOIR

A man-made lake near Lodi, filled by the Mokelumne River. About 52-mile shoreline has access gates at north and south. Sunbathing, fishing, boating, water-skiing, camping, horseback riding are popular year-round. Skinny-dippers mostly use small coves reached with the boats that may be rented from concessioners located at the access gates. For sunning without a boat, try the north shore camping area. Skinny-dippers have coexisted with the clad without hassle, and if you are considerate of others' rights, this situation should continue.

SACRAMENTO COUNTY

☆ LAGUNA DEL SOL

Twenty miles southeast of Sacramento. A 238-acre nudist resort with grassy camping areas, RV hookups and motel, restaurant, gleaming entertainment center, lake with fishing and boating, fitness center, two spas, tennis, volleyball, two outdoor pools and new indoor pool with spa. 8683 Rawhide Lane, Box 1-WG, Wilton, CA 95693. Phone (916) 687-6550; fax (916) 687-7860.

HOUSEBOAT HOTLINE

For Delta houseboating, give the Houseboat Hotline a call. Receive an hour of training before you shove off on a rented houseboat that can accommodate up to 10 people and comes equipped with everything except bedding and linen. 6333 Pacific Avenue, Suite 152, Stockton, CA 95207. Phone (209) 477-1840.

RIVER DIPPERS

An informative newsletter, family events. Send SASE to P.O. Box 188366, Sacramento, CA 95818-8366. Phone (916) 484-4127.

PLACER COUNTY

AMERICAN RIVER

The north fork of the American River has a sandbar in the undeveloped Auburn Ravine that is well-known to skinny-dippers. The area has some sand beaches and many sunning rocks.

☞ Drive I-80 northeast from Sacramento to the Elm Avenue Exit at Auburn. Follow Elm east to the first traffic light (High Street), turn left on High Street, which becomes Route 49. Continue on 49 for 2 miles, to a wider stretch of road with parking space on both sides. This is 1/2 mile before the Route 49 bridge over the North Fork American River. From the parked cars, take the path down to a wider dirt road, formerly a railroad grade; cross over this dirt road and, nearby, you'll find the footpath leading directly down to the nude beach. At the beach, gays usually go right, others go left.

FOLSOM LAKE

Folsom Lake offers many skinny-dipping coves and beaches, but perhaps the best, especially for those without a boat, is just upstream from Beeks Bight. The Folsom Lake State Recreation Area maintains toilets at the parking lot, among other amenities, and the town of Folsom is quaint and fun to visit.

☞ Enter the park at the Granite Bay access off Douglas Boulevard (admission is charged). Drive north from Granite Bay, past Dotons Point to the Beeks Bight parking. Take the footpaths near the shore for 15 minutes to the north shore of Beeks Bight and a number of beaches and coves that are separated by rocks (difference in water level makes a difference in how much beach is exposed). Proceed far enough north along the point so you are not in view of the clothed folk on the south shore of Beeks Bight.

LAKE TAHOE

EMERALD BAY

If much of Lake Tahoe's California side is private, naturists have hunkered on the southwest shore between Emerald Bay and Bliss State Park, and south from Eagle Point at the south side of the Emerald Bay inlet. Access involves some walking. Obtain a map of the Tahoe Basin from the US Forest Service Visitors Center several miles south of Emerald Bay.

NEVADA COUNTY

OREGON CREEK

Oregon Creek widens into a pleasant little pool with several waterfalls. Warm spring water. Flat granite ledges for sunning surround the pool. Mostly nude use by local families.

☞ From Sacramento area, take I-80 to Auburn, then Highway 49 north past Grass Valley and Nevada City. Continue on Highway 49 about 3 miles past North San Juan, where you will cross the Yuba River and the Oregon Creek Campground. Immediately after the second white guardrail (or 1/2 mile past campground), take the dirt road that leads to the large dirt parking lot, then hike the short and easy trail to the pool.

YUBA RIVER, SOUTH FORK

The South Fork of the Yuba River near Grass Valley is popular skinny-dipping for locals who keep the area free of litter; do likewise. Route 49 northwest out of

Auburn; at Grass Valley take Route 20 west for 8 miles to Pleasant Valley Road; turn right (north) on it, past Lake Wildwood, to South Yuba River. Cross the new bridge, and park in lot. Walk on the dirt road toward the river and then upstream until you notice a dip in the road, about a 3-minute walk from the parking area. From here, take a footpath on the left, go up a hill and walk for 7 minutes until you reach a nearly-level former flume grade. Follow the footpath upstream along the grade, walking by the downhill paths at the 11- and 14-minute points until you cross the dry French Corral Creek on the wooden bridge and pass the State Park boundary sign. Once past the sign, continue walking for about 2 minutes. Look for a trail on the right, going about 40 or 50 yards down to the river, where you will find a sandy, clear area that is used for skinny-dipping.

Another site for family skinny-dipping is at **Edwards Crossing Bridge.** Where Spring Creek enters the Yuba River and acts like a natural jacuzzi is the most popular (be sure to arrive early). From Nevada City follow North Bloomfield Road 8.5 miles. Park just before the bridge. Facing downstream, take the trail on the right bank for 10 minutes until you come to Spring Creek. Cross it and look for a trail roughly parallel to the creek leading down to the river. BLM's South Yuba Campground is near the bridge with other campgrounds at Malakoff State Park and Grizzly Creek.

Purdens Crossing, upstream from Edwards, is also a great place to take children.

NOTE: captions to photos run along the inside edge of pages.

Facing Page Top: Leif Heilberg, A Game For Adults At Elysium Fields, Near Los Angeles.
Facing Page Bottom: Michael Cooney, Bonny Doon Beach In Santa Cruz County. This Page: See Overleaf.

SIERRA COUNTY

SIERRA HOT SPRINGS

Rustic spiritual retreat renovating century-old hotel offers hot tubs, soaking pools, campsites, private lodge rooms, on wooded 700 acres. Massage available. Twenty-five miles north of Truckee on Route 89; right on Route 49 in Sierraville at T-intersection; go 3/4 mile and turn right on Lemon Canyon Road; go 1/2 mile and turn right on Campbell Hot Springs Road; 1/2 mile to parking lot at second trailer; 5-minute walk. P.O. Box 366, Sierraville, CA 96126. Phone (916) 994-3773.

PLUMAS COUNTY

WOODY'S FEATHER RIVER HOT SPRINGS

Offers hunting, fishing and swimming on the Feather River; two soaking pools, restaurant, motel; RV sites with hookups. P.O. Box 7, Twain, CA 95984. Phone (916) 283-4115.

MARIN COUNTY

EAST BONITA COVE

In the Marin County headlands, this cove offers two separate beaches. One is about

1/4 mile in length, with dark sand. The other (Central Bonita) lies to the west of this and is separated from it by a large pyramid-shaped rock. The water is cold and a strong ocean current makes it dangerous for swimming. But the cove is indeed a paradise, with an excellent view of the San Francisco skyline, the bridge, some interesting rock formations, a cave in the distance, and an abundance of wildlife.

Central Bonita Beach can be accessed by hiking to the right of the parking lot for East Bonita. The downhill trek is difficult and not for small children.

☞ The access is somewhat tricky. After crossing the Golden Gate Bridge from San Francisco, take Alexander Avenue (the first major turnoff to the right) toward Sausalito. Cross the highway to the left after a couple hundred yards and turn left on Conzelman Road. Follow Conzelman and traverse McCullough until it becomes a one-way road. When you come to the YMCA and the turnoff to the lighthouse, turn right. The next turnoff to your left will be Battery Alexander parking lot. Park here.

Take the broad path on the ocean side of the lot and look for the second intersecting path; follow this to the beach. If you get lost, go to the Rodeo Beach Ranger Station and ask for a copy of a map outlining the trails through the entire Golden Gate National Recreation Area. The mile hike down to these spots is well worth it, but contracting poison oak is not. Be sure to wear long pants, socks and shoes.

MUIR BEACH

The beach is very popular and relatively hassle-free. The unclad part is, in fact, located in front of private property. To reach it, you must either climb over the rocks that divide it from the public Muir Beach, or wade around at low tide. An excellent site for swimming, since the waves are small and it has a sandy bottom. Arrive before 11:30 a.m. on weekends to get a parking spot.

☞ North from San Francisco on Highway 1. Muir is just south of Stinson Beach; turn left from Highway 1 onto Pacific Way, and park in the public lot for Muir Beach (cars parked on Pacific Way will be ticketed). From the lot, go right and head north along the sand that starts at the bottom of the hill behind the phone booth. Carefully cross the rocks to reach the beach.

RED ROCK BEACH

With merely a hundred yards of sand between two points, Red Rock has a lot going for it—Frisbee, hot pool and ocean swim, sun and conversation.

At low tide visit the hot spring. About 50 yards up the trail to the parking lot is a saddle. Go down to the beach from this saddle and along the shore to the hot spring; you'll have to wade even at low tide.

Recommended lodging: Steep Ravine Environmental Cabins. A bargain at $30/night. Located within walking distance of Red Rock, Steep Ravine has 10 cabins with ocean views, wood-burning stoves; no showers, electricity or indoor plumbing. Reservations required. Phone Mistix (800) 444-7275.

☞ A half-mile south of Stinson Beach on Highway 1 find a large red rock and join the cars parked in a turnout on west side. The long trail begins near the trash bin; keep an eye out for poison oak. From Steep Ravine Environmental Cabins, take the trail from the cabins to the beach and walk 400 yards to the hot spring.

POINT REYES NATIONAL SEASHORE

San Franciscans seem scarcely aware of the natural resource they might enjoy in less than an hour's drive up coast on Route 1. Point Reyes National Seashore

stretches from Bolinas at the south to Tomales Bay State Park at the north. Together they comprise a refuge peninsula 30 miles long, and 12 miles from Tomales Bay inlet on the east to the outermost point of Point Reyes Lighthouse on the wild Pacific.

Clothing-optional use: little-used **Limantour Beach** has 7 miles of rolling sand dunes. The sole tree in sight marks a campground 2 miles distant. Then, **Sculptured Beach** adds high cliffs to sand dunes, tidal pools, sea lions and no civilization for miles. From Limantour Beach, hike south 3 miles, passing Coast Camp, for Sculptured Beach and time your visit to low tide.

Bass Lake lies on the Palomarin Trail about 2.8 miles from the Palomarin trailhead at the end of Mesa Road. Take Route 2 from Stinson Beach and just north of Bolinas Lagoon, turn right on the exit to Bolinas. Follow the road back on the west side of the Lagoon. The road will dead-end at Olema-Bolinas Road. Take a left and continue 0.5 miles to a stop sign at Mesa Road. Turn right and follow road to the end (it becomes a dirt road) to a parking lot and trailhead.

Never more than a dozen people hang out at the 150-foot **Mount Vision Pond,** and about half are nude. Grassy area surrounding the cold water pond is perfect for picnics. Find the pond on map available from park headquarters in Olema.

All food must be brought and don't forget binoculars for bird, whale and seal watching. Warm days of spring and autumn are the best and most fog free. Phone (415) 663-1092 for weather and tide.

☞ Point Reyes National Seashore is 40 miles north of San Francisco. Exit Highway 1 at Olema, parking at Seashore headquarters to pick up trail map and follow Limantour Road to the end.

SHIBUI GARDENS

Shibui Gardens has a unique Japanese style and rents private outdoor hot tubs, sauna by the hour. 19 Tamalpais Avenue, San Anselmo, CA 94960. Phone (415) 457-0283.

SONOMA COUNTY

MEEKER FALLS

A clothing-optional waterfall in the middle of a forest. Pools are located at the top and bottom of the falls.

☞ Take Highway 101 north past Petaluma to Highway 16. Take it west to Sebastopol. Turn left (west) into the Bodega Highway. At the town of Freestone, get on the Bohemian Highway, toward Monte and Russian rivers. Several miles north of the town of

Occidental, look for the "Camp Meeker" sign. From the sign, continue driving 1.8 miles to the "Slippery When Wet" sign. Park about 50 yards north of the sign in the turnout on the right side of the highway. Follow the path on the right side of the cliffs for less than a half-mile to the waterfall.

HIGHLANDS RESORT

On the Russian River. Swimsuit optional policy at pool and outdoor hot tub. Activities include billiards, barbecue, nearby water sports and hiking trails. Day use $10. Phone (707) 869-0333.

MENDOCINO COUNTY

ORR HOT SPRINGS

Splendid individual and group hot tubs, warm creek-flow pool, sauna, flower and vegetable gardens, lodge and community kitchen; massage available. No visit is complete without a half day, perhaps picnicking, two miles west by a stream in primeval Montgomery Redwoods—many trees 300 feet tall and 1,000 years old. 13201 Orr Springs Road, Ukiah, CA 95482. Phone (707) 462-6277.

SWEETWATER GARDENS

Clothing-optional hot tubs of various sizes in Mendocino. Massage available, private room for overnight rental. Group tub and sauna available with no time limit. Free hot tub with a massage on Mondays, Wednesdays and Fridays (excl. holidays). Phone (707) 937-4140 or (800) 300-4140.

LAKE COUNTY

HARBIN HOT SPRING

Formerly a major society spa, now Harbin's unceasing waters, clear air and skein of hillside trails lead to a new age. Cold, hot and hotter pools, sun deck, massage, vegetarian restaurant. Clothes-optional at the pools. Day visits, camping, cabin rental, conferences. 18424 Harbin Springs, Middletown, CA 95461. Phone (707) 987-2477 for reservation and directions.

COLUSA COUNTY

WILBUR HOT SPRINGS

A spacious former stagecoach hotel in the boonies with a San Francisco clien-

Previous Page Bottom: Martin Brittan. South Fork, Yuba River, Nevada County. Top: Michael Cooney. Sierra Hot Springs, Sierra County.

tele who return for the relaxation, yoga, massage, Japanese-quality soaking pools, swim pool, sun deck, community kitchen. 240 acres in open hilly terrain great for hiking, biking. Wilbur Hot Springs, Star Route, Williams, CA 95987. Phone (916) 473-2306.

BUTTE COUNTY

BIDWELL PARK

Families as well as Chico College students play here. Lower Bidwell Park goes right into downtown Chico; use only Upper Bidwell Park for skinny-dipping.

☞ From Highway 99 exit, go east on East Avenue. After a mile or two, turn left into park on Wildwood Avenue. Continue on Upper Park Road, which becomes gravel, to Parking Lot M. A trail leads to a small canyon between 100-foot basalt sides to the creek, a 5-minute walk. You'll find two small beaches of fine gravel, small rapids for sliding in, lots of fish for chasing.

BUTTE CREEK

A popular area with Chico College students. Spring and summer offer ample water.

☞ From Chico, take Skyway Road east a half mile to Honey Run and turn left. It follows Butte Creek going east and northeast. At the point where there is a parking area and pedestrian covered bridge on the right, veer left. Several miles later you come to Helltown Road and then Humbug Road. Park, walk down the road and across the bridge, and follow trail to the right upstream along Butte Creek about 1/4 mile.

HUMBOLDT COUNTY

EEL RIVER BEACH

Diving from rocks not recommended. Water is cold; shoes are suggested. Not entirely hidden from view of nearby houses.

On Highway 101 heading north, take the first exit to Garberville. Turn left at the sign to San Francisco but instead of getting on on-ramp, go straight. Turn right on first paved road as you're going downhill. Park at the pile of gravel and take path to river.

TRINITY RIVER

Both Trinity River and Willow Creek (west of the town with the same name) offer a number of skinny-dipping areas. The Elbow, a favorite, lies about 7 miles southeast of Willow Creek and 1.7 miles northwest of Hawkins Bar/Trinity Village, at a small horseshoe bend in the Trinity River. A narrow dirt road (Dead Road 6N51) runs inconspicuously off Route 299 to the northeast for a 1/4 mile along a narrowing ridge. Park away from the bushes (poison oak) and hike 200 yards down a steep trail to the river, where it makes a sharp bend. This Forest Service land includes cliffs and wooded hillsides, and at the river beach you can tan, raft, fish and swim.

Or try **Boogie Bar,** 3 miles east of Willow Creek on Route 299. Cross the Trinity River Bridge, immediately turn right onto South Fork Road and look for the parked cars 5 minutes farther. Path to the beach is after the meadow and junkyard.

COLLEGE COVE

Part of Trinidad State Beach, College Cove is popular on the relatively few sunny days that the region enjoys. Nude use is south of the big rock; water is icy.

☞ From Eureka, drive north on Highway 101 about 25 miles to Trinidad. Follow signs to Trinidad State Beach parking area, but continue on the old highway about 3/4 mile more (crossing a lovely fern-shrouded ravine) and look for the dirt parking lot on the left (if you reach Abalone Beach, you've gone too far). Park and follow trails that begin on the left side of the parking lot. A trail on the north side of the lot leads to **College Cove North,** where about 25% of the users are nude. Expect more nudes at **College Cove South** in part due to the more difficult trail.

If College Cove is too crowded, turn around and head for **Baker's Beach,** which is 12 miles north of Arcata on Highway 101. Take Westhaven Exit to Scenic Drive north. Stop at parked cars and large, vine-covered residence sign and its rusted metal "Private Property" sign on right. Parking on Scenic Drive has caused some problems for residents; be sure to leave enough road clearance for passing traffic.

MAD RIVER FISH HATCHERY

Upstream from the Mad River Fish Hatchery is the clothes-optional Mad River fun spot; used mid-April to late September.

☞ From Coastal Route 101 just north of Arcata take Route 299 east, through Blue Lake by the off-ramp, and then following Fish Hatchery Road. At the hatchery, cross the Mad River and hike upstream about 3/4 mile to the sandbars and swimming holes. You could also check out the Mad River at Maple Creek and at Swinging Bridge (ask locals for directions).

TRINITY COUNTY

BIG BEND HOT SPRINGS

A commercial spa with three clothing-optional concrete soaking pools over the river and several pools in the riverbank. Rental cabins available. No smoking, alcohol or drugs. 196 Hot Springs Row, Big Bend, CA 96001. Phone (916) 337-6680.

HELLS GATE CAMPGROUND

The South Fork of the Trinity River and its hiking trails are a skinny-dipper's delight. Recommended is the Hells Gate Forest Service Campground 2 miles from Forest Glen. Good camping facilities and a mellow crowd of young people from May to October, with nudity the norm along the riverbank. This remote and little used area is about 50 yards long and 25 yards wide. Backed by thick woods with sheer cliffs in the front, the beach is hassle-free.

☞ From I-5 at Red Bluff, drive Highway 36 west for 70 miles. Upon reaching Hells Gate Campground, follow the campground road for about a mile to its end. Park here or at any campground area. Walk upriver for 500 yards; the small beach is to the right.

SHASTA COUNTY

BRANDY CREEK

Located in the Whiskeytown-Shasta-Trinity National Recreation Area, the site is traditionally clothing-optional with a good flow all summer. Access to some of the best spots requires rock hopping and shallow wading or scrambling up and down fairly steep wooded trails.

☞ Drive west on Highway 299 toward Eureka, 7.75 miles from downtown Redding. Turn left into Whiskeytown Recreation Area passing the visitor center. Continue about 4.5 miles, going across the dam, to about 100 yards beyond the

John Kramer/SOBEK, Angels Camp, California.

Northern California

entrance to Brandy Creek Beach on the right. Then, just before crossing the little bridge over Brandy Creek, turn left up the hill. Continue 2.9 miles on the road which quickly turns to gravel and dirt. About a third of the way up this road there is a left fork to Peltier Valley, followed a few feet later by a right fork to a parking area and Brandy Creek Camp 1 (unmarked). Go straight between these turnoffs. At about two thirds of the way there is a right fork

to Sheep Camp, but stay left and continue, going through the little brook, all the way to Brandy Creek Camp 2 at the end. Stop at either of two parking areas just before the road crosses Brandy Creek itself, and becomes impassible. Although nude use does occur along the entire creek, most people enjoy their naked play within a few hundred yards of these parking areas. You may obtain a wilderness permit at the visitors center and camp in the area.

LAKE SHASTA

Just north of Redding on I-5, you'll find dozens of houseboats for rent. One can stay nude for days on the man-made lake with 360 miles of shoreline. Sheriff might check for fishing license but enforcement of anti-nudity ordinance is situational; typically on drunk college students.

Jerry Derbyshire. Conundrum Hot Springs, Aspen.

COLORADO

ASPEN AREA

CONUNDRUM HOT SPRINGS

Conundrum: How do Aspen visitors get closer to nature, and maybe 25 other tired hikers at 11,200 feet? *Answer:* Hike, from June to September, up a spectacular 8-mile trail.

Conundrum Creek trailhead is reached by driving about 5 miles southwest from

Aspen on Castle Creek Road. You'll find a dirt track on the right (Forest Service Road 128) that descends and crosses Castle Creek. Take this road 1.5 miles to the trailhead; it is narrow, rocky and steep, unfit for large or ailing vehicles. Park and follow the well-marked trail along Conundrum Creek for 8 miles. The US Forest Service supplies maps and advises that you stay overnight, but don't camp closer than a mile to the thermal pool, and do bring a primus stove—firewood is nearly nonexistent. Don't forget your sunblock.

ROARING FORK RIVER GROTTOES

On hot summer days Aspen folk head for the "grottoes"—potholes carved in rock by the icy runoff waters of the legendary Roaring Fork River. The area becomes a sort of "cold springs" retreat, the contrary of Conundrum's function. Take Route 82 east from Aspen. After several miles, find the wooden sign with inlaid white lettering, "Grottoes," and an arrow pointing to the right (visible from eastbound lane only). Park and hike in.

Colorado

DENVER AREA

☆ MOUNTAIN AIR RANCH

A 150-acre resort with cabins, tent and RV sites, pool and spa, rec and dance hall, restaurant, playground, and mountain view. P.O. Box 855, Indian Hills, CO 80455-0855. Phone (303) 697-4083; fax (303) 697-4563.

THE ROCKY MOUNTAIN BARES

This large Denver area group offers frequent health club nights including swims and backcountry excursions. Send SASE to P.O. Box 740159, Arvada, CO 80006. Phone (303) 420-4565. Providing information for much of Colorado is Colorado Naturists, P.O. Box 652, Elizabeth, CO 80207.

NORTH CENTRAL

STRAWBERRY PARK HOT SPRINGS

"Woodstock never ended at this outdoor recreation area seven miles north of town on Park Road," writes the Colorado Springs *Gazette Telegraph* of this delightfully primitive and increasingly popular Steamboat Springs retreat. Geothermal fissure flow collects in several pools. Sauna, massage, cross-country skiing, and saddle-horse trips by appointment. Rental cabins and campsites. Nudity after dark. From US 40 in Steamboat Springs, turn north on 7th Street. Follow signs 7 miles to area. P.O. Box 773332, Steamboat Springs, CO 80477. Phone (970) 879-0342.

SOUTH CENTRAL

COTTONWOOD INN

Several small thermal pools, cabins, restaurant and meeting rooms available at this rustic lodge near the San Isabel National Forest that permits nudity in private jacuzzis only. Swedish massage, deep tissue work, sports massage, polarity, Reiki, body scrubs and facials available. 18999 Highway 306, Buena Vista, CO 81211. Phone (719) 395-6434.

DESERT REEF BEACH CLUB

Artesian well water cools from 130°F, flowing into new pool with waterfall and a spa to create a nude recreation oasis. Volleyball, horseshoe pit, picnic lawn. Close to Colorado Springs. Entirely clothing-optional; about half the visitors choose nudity. Nonmembers admitted with reservation. Open 10 a.m. to 10 p.m. Wednesday, Thursday, Saturday and Sunday year-round. P.O. Box 503, Penrose, CO 81240. Phone (719) 784-6134.

THE WELL

A copious thermal well and pool with food and drink services, located in a desert valley surrounded by majestic mountains. RV and tent sites (no hookups). Open year round from 10 a.m., closed Tuesdays. 0001 Malibu Blvd., Highway 50 at Penrose, CO 81250. Phone 1-800-898-WELL or (719) 372-9250.

VALLEY VIEW HOT SPRINGS

Located on the west slope of the Sangre de Cristo Mountains at 8,700 feet, an hour from the Monarch and Wolf Creek ski areas, Valley View Hot Springs overlooks the San Luis Valley. Entirely clothes-optional. Hiking and music-making, four natural pools for soaking and an 80-foot swimming pool. Rustic cabins and rooms available (reservations recommended!) or camp out. Nearest food service and purchase is 13 miles away. Kitchen facilities and sauna, firewood provided. Children free. Weekdays open to the public. Weekend and holiday use reserved for members and their guests. P.O. Box 65, Villa Grove, CO 81155-0065.

WILD WOOD'S RESORT

An emerging campground on 80 acres within view of Pike's Peak and the Sangre de Cristo mountain ranges. Volleyball, horseshoes, organized activities. Tent/RV camping. P.O. Box 408, Calhan, CO 80808. Phone (303) 210-1715.

SOUTHWEST

RAINBOW HOT SPRINGS

Also called Wolf Creek Pass Hot Springs; north of Pagosa Springs on Route 160. Sign in at San Juan National Forest ranger station and hike 5 miles on a well-maintained trail to the camping area where you will find volunteer-built 100°F pristine pools at the bottom of the San Juan River. Arrive early to set the clothes-free usage trend.

ORVIS HOT SPRINGS

Less than an hour from Telluride, 1.3 miles south of Ridgeway from Route 550 in the direction of Ouray, this rustic lodge with a scenic view of the Mt. Sneffels Range rents tent sites and six guest rooms, bicycles, cross-country skiis, and access to four indoor tiled soaking pools and several outdoor clothing-optional hot ponds. Day or overnight rates. 1585 County Road 3, Ridgeway, CO 81432. Phone (970) 626-5324.

☆ – The star symbol before a resort name is your guarantee that The Naturist Society card is accepted and earns a discount at the resort. To obtain Naturist Society membership, see the inside front cover.

CONNECTICUT

SUN RIDGE RESORT

Convenient to Rhode Island, Connecticut and Massachusetts, Sun Ridge Resort offers swimming and heated conversation pools, rec area, outdoor pavilion, playground, tennis and volleyball courts. Tent sites, electric and water hookups; rest rooms with hot showers, on-site laundry facilities and camp store. Open May 15 to October 15; reservations recommended. 131 Calvin French Road, Sterling, CT 06377; phone (860) 779-1512.

HIGGANUM RESERVOIR PARK: MILLER'S POND

Higganum Reservoir State Park offers this small and quiet retreat with clean water, an adequate beach, good hiking trails, and a skinny-dipping tradition.

☞ At Exit 15 on I-91, take Route 68 East to Route 17 in Durham. Turn left (north) and take the first right (Maiden Lane). Go 1.8 miles to the end. Go right on Haddon Quarter Road, pass-

ing Arbutus Road, for 1.7 miles to a stop sign. Turn right on Foot Hill Road, go 0.5 miles. At Wiese Albert Road, park in the well-defined dirt area, right. Follow the trail on the right to the pond, then turn left. Go on the second trail leading right, marked by a huge fallen oak on the left, and follow it to the rock outcropping that marks the nude area.

LYME: NEHANTIC STATE FOREST

Nehantic State Forest has long had both clothed and nude users. Some recent policing for nudity; avoid weekends.

☞ Twenty-five miles west of New London. From Lyme, go 4.5 miles north of Route 95 on Route 156. Look for the well-marked entrance of Nehantic State Forest on your right. Proceed for 2 miles on the narrow paved road, and pass the boat launch to the right (stay left). The first skinny-dipping spot is 0.5 miles after the boat launch and is reached by taking the turnoff to the right. Continue

up the hill and park near the path to the right that leads to the lake. The second spot is 500 yards (0.3 miles) beyond. Take the right-hand turn, turn right again almost immediately and park in the "developed" and therefore non-nude area. Approach the water bearing left after you park. You'll pass the outhouses. Follow the path as it descends the hill to the lake. Though not the best place to sun, the water is clean and clear.

OUTSOURCING

Connecticut residents deserve better than to have to cross state lines for skinny-dipping. Still, here goes. You may take the Bridgeport ferry to Port Jefferson on New York's Long Island. This summertime special departs from Bridgeport Harbor Terminal at the Union Square Dock (Exit 27 on the Connecticut Turnpike). A charter bus transfers passengers from Port Jefferson to Smith Point Park on Fire Island. Not costly. Phone (888) 443-3779 for schedules.

DISTRICT OF COLUMBIA

They call it life inside the beltline. Members of that exclusive club the U.S. Senate may frolic in the Russell Senate Office Building Pool without a belt or a stitch; your public servant has a clothing-optional health club key. The few female Senators make appointments to assure there won't be nude males on hand. Men in the House of Representatives, less privileged, get only a clothing-optional steam room.

Apart from Congress, there are no known nude recreation facilities in DC.

FLORIDA

Florida is suffering through a "cultural war" that is organized by an intensely "religious" radical right-wing in order to suppress any value or activity that is not its own.

For these extremists, skinny-dipping is *not* a traditional value—even if slipping off to a pond for a dunk has been a rural pleasure for centuries!

Families—parents and children—have no right to be nude, together at home or at a beach with other families, claims a so-called Florida Family Association. Never mind that family naturism is a cherished right of childhood in Europe. Never mind that America needs more, and not less,

body acceptance.

The radical cult is using the political process to get laws passed to block the preference for body acceptance of naturists. A dozen Florida counties have already passed anti-nudity laws. The "family association" is trying to get a state law passed.

Public opinion polls, the media, civil rights organizations, business and tourism groups, all reject the anti-nudity cultists and ridicule their unprecedented demands.

Nonetheless, the zealots are powerful because they do work the politicians, and they are curtailing our rights.

Naturists are learning to be politically effective. Please find the appropriate naturist organization for you,

and contact them for information, for your security, and to protect your rights.

FLORIDA KEYS

KEYS NATURISTS

Florida Keys Naturists, 22386 Lafitte Drive, Cudjoe, FL 33042-4218; (305) 744-9986 voice and fax.

KEY WEST GUEST HOUSES

Key West—behavioral outpost. Unisex thongs throng carnival-like streets (see *N* 17.2).

Topfree is the dress code, for both sexes, at the posh downtown **Pier House** pool and beach. And topfree and g-strings are common on the **Higg's Beach** wooden pier and around the West Martello Tower on the south side of Key West and west of the large county beach and White Street fishing pier. Take US 1 to White St., turn left and follow it until it meets Atlantic Blvd., and you're there!

Gay-owned guest houses feature sophistication, patios with pools, nude sunning decks. **The Blue Parrott, The Chelsea, Lime House, La Di Da, Sea Isle, Island House, Garden House,**

Florida

Southwind, Colours, Newton Street Station and Normandy South Miami Beach are dress-optional in part. Most accept guests without concern for gender or gender preference. Atlantic Shores Motel, a perfect choice for first-timers, offers a clothing-optional pool and pier area, and Deja Vu Resort is totally clothing-optional.

A water taxi ($4 one way) takes you to Tank Island where nudity is possible on the southwest shore. Take food, beach shoes and snorkel gear for exploring the cove near the only grove of palm trees on the island.

While many captains are accepting of nude cruising, a favorite is Witt's End Charters of Key West, run by Naturists Greg and B.J. Witt. P.O. Box 4594, Key West, FL 33041-4594; phone (305) 296-9916. Or try Reef Raiders, where the chartering party sets the dress code. Half or full day voyages; 12-person capacity. Phone (305) 294-3635.

SOUTHEAST

SOUTH FLORIDA FREE BEACHES

The information and activities resource for Miami and southeast Florida. Info pack is $3. Plug in to a fast-changing situation. P.O. Box 330902, Coconut Grove, FL 33133. Phone (305) 893-8838; fax (305) 782-7400.

HAULOVER BEACH

South Florida Free Beaches has encouraged and cooperated with Dade County Parks and Recreation to establish this model urban clothes-optional beach, attractive to tourists and residents alike. (See *N* 16.2 pp. 19–22; *N* 16.4 pp. 76–77.) A half-mile of perfect sand and sea with a parking field, trash cans, food concessions, signage for nudity, rest rooms, lifeguards, on State Road A1A between Bal Harbour and Sunny Isles. Ocean Palm Resort Hotel is nearest to the beach (phone 1-800-231-6932); or for a list of other nearby accommodations, phone Sunny Isles Resort Association (305) 947-5826.

☞ From I-95, exit at Golden Glades Interchange on to State Rd. 826 east (167th/163rd St.). Or go east on 125th St. Find Haulover County Park at about 150th St. on Collins Ave. (Route A1A) and park in the northernmost lot ($3). Walk to the beach through the tunnel underpass. Handicap accessible.

MIAMI BEACH

In the Miami Beach downtown art deco revival zone, the 20th Street Beach offers a wide sunning arena backed by metered public parking, with lifeguard station, refreshment truck, lounge chair rentals. This "European-style" zone is from 20th to 23rd Streets. Lummus Park, between 5th and 15th Streets, also sees topfree.

Topfree sunning has been accepted since 1986. Progressive Miami Beach hotels include the Shawnee, Sasson, Shellbourn Condominium, Sea Breeze, Deauville, and the Rodney.

SEMINOLE CLUB

Nudist facility west of Miami. Restaurant, game room, swimming pool, whirlpool, volleyball. Cabins, tent and RV sites. Seminole Health Club, 3800 S.W. 142nd Ave., Davie, FL 33330. Phone (954) 473-0231.

PALM BEACH NATURISTS

For information send a long self-addressed stamped envelope (SASE) to P.O. Box 432, West Palm Beach, FL 33402. Phone (407) 844-5434.

☆ SUNSPORT GARDENS

Semi-tropical nudist park, site of annual February Naturist Gatherings. Social club, restaurant, volleyball, pool, spa, sauna, fishing, nature trails, tennis; tent and RV spaces available; 20 miles to North Palm Beach. 14125 North Road, Loxahatchee, FL 33470. Phone (561) 793-0423 or 800-551-7217.

☆ SUNNIER PALMS

Naturist cooperative with 50 full RV hookup sites, tent areas, heated pool, hot tub, clubhouse, rental rooms, 12-acre wildlife preserve; see *N* 16.3 pp. 57–62 for more information. Open year round. Public welcome. 8800 Okeechobee Rd., Ft. Pierce, FL 34945. Phone (561) 468-8512; fax (561) 468-9786.

EAST CENTRAL

CANAVERAL NATIONAL SEASHORE: PLAYALINDA

For many years, a terrific beach. Playalinda Beach Naturists currently face bias and misrepresentation from the county Radical Right and citations by Brevard County deputies. Before you visit, contact Central Florida Naturists for an update of the legal status (P.O. Box 2004, Merritt Island, FL 32954-2004; phone (407) 381-0637).

We and CFN urge a boycott of Brevard County stores and motels until county law is corrected.

Playalinda federal beach offers refuge for such endangered creatures as sea turtles, skinny-dippers, and ibises.

Skinny-dippers are restricted in practice to upper (north) Playalinda Beach. Playalinda closes for NASA space launches—phone (407) 867-2805 before going, to avoid disappointment. If closed, try the beach at South Apollo. Camping is permitted at Playalinda from October to May 15, and campgrounds may also be found nearby. A stiff ocean breeze will hold down insects but bring insect repellent just in case. Consider touring the NASA facility, reached by another road from Titusville. Exit the Seashore by way of the Merritt Island N.W. Refuge dirt road for a direct encounter of other endangered species.

☞ From Highway 1 or 95, Route 406 east through Titusville. Cut onto Route 402, pass the Seashore headquarters, and continue on to the beach. Turn left (north) through the gates and for 5 miles follow the paved road behind Playalinda Beach. Get as close to the dead-end as possible and park. Parking is limited; arrive early! Continue north on foot to where you find others are clothes-free before getting natural. Even then, be tactful, as prudes are occasionally great walkers. Stay out of the dunes no matter what.

SOUTH APOLLO BEACH

The northern access to Canaveral National Seashore is by way of South Apollo Beach. Klondike Beach is the name of the wild shore colonized by naturists which, 10 miles south, becomes Playalinda Beach. It is not affected by space shot closings, but arrive by 8:30 a.m. due to very curtailed parking.

☞ Route I-95 or Highway 1 to exit at New Smyrna Beach. East on Route 44 to the Cape and A1A south to Apollo Beach, about 8 miles from town. Park at the southernmost available area and walk farther south to marker #29 or so. Leave nothing but footprints. Camping is permitted but you must apply on arrival for a wilderness permit. No glass allowed. Seashore phone (407) 267-1110.

CENTRAL

☆ SUNNY SANDS

Tent and RV sites, fully-furnished rental units. Take-out restaurant and snack bar, playground, pool, rec room, hot tub, 50 acres with hiking trails. Less than an hour from Daytona Speedway, Universal Studios and Cape Canaveral. 502 Central

Boulevard, Pierson, FL 32180. Phone (904) 749-2233; fax (904) 749-0240.

☆ CYPRESS COVE

Convenient to Disney World, Cypress Cove is a showplace among clothes-free resorts—with manicured lawns, paved streets for the many residents, pool, 50-acre lake, water-skiing, tennis, volleyball, basketball, whirlpool spa, a social activities director, nudism's library, and a bar and restaurant. Villa apartments, motel rooms, tent and trailer sites available. 4425 Pleasant Hill Road, Kissimmee, FL 34746. Phone (407) 933-5870.

SOUTHWEST

SANIBEL NATURISTS

Established with Naturist Society help to protect Bowman's Beach (now named Silver Key Beach) in 1981, this dynamic group continues to keep beaches in use. Newsletter, social and beach activities. SASE to P.O. Box 6789, Ft. Myers, FL 33911. Phone (941) 939-1784.

SILVER KEY BEACH

Located on renowned Sanibel Island, a delightful spot once called Bowman's Beach. Since 1982, the beach has been patrolled from time to time, with citations for nudity possible. You do need to contact Sanibel Naturists for current status. If time permits, visit the astonishing Ding Darling National Wildlife Refuge on Sanibel.

☞ From the end of the Sanibel Causeway ($3 toll), turn right at the first intersection onto Periwinkle Way. Continue 2.5 miles, then turn right onto Palm Ridge Road, which becomes Sanibel-Captiva Road at the Tarpon Bay stop sign. Continue straight for 5.1 miles. Turn left just past the firehouse onto Bowman's Beach Road and then right at the park gatehouse. Park in the lot and walk north. Pick a spot just before the last blue trash can and up to the renourished area. There's plenty of wee beaches among the dead trees but swimmers should use caution and beware of limbs sticking out of and under the water. The beach on the south end of Silver Key is the recommended area until after 4:30 p.m.

Parking on Sanibel Island is metered. Estimate length of stay and feed meter accordingly. Meter will spit out receipt; place it on car window.

CAYO COSTA ISLAND

A delightful offshore paradise near Ft. Myers, the north end of Cayo Costa is a great place to sun in the buff, swim in the warm Gulf or explore trails. One of three islands comprising the Cayo Costa State

Park system, it is accessible only by boat. Ferries leave from Pine Island near Ft. Myers for the 1-hour trip. The Tropic Star operates daily, phone (813) 283-0015. Rental bikes, cabins and tent sites available on the island.

SOUTHERN EXPOSURE

Started with Sanibel Naturists, Southern Exposure has acquired land. Serving the Naples area. P.O. Box 990192, Naples, FL 33999. Phone (941) 649-4380.

WEST CENTRAL

TAMPA BAY ISLANDS

Boaters may escape the clothing code by cruising out on Tampa Bay to one of several popular islands. For local activities, contact Tampa Bay Free Beaches, P.O. Box 274121, Tampa, FL 33688.

About 85 percent of visitors to **Beer Can Island** go nude (actually it's not trashy). On **Egmont Key,** you'll find only a lighthouse and other sunbathers; 3 miles long and recently taken over by the State Parks Department, Egmont Key's continued nude use is uncertain at this point and visitors should assess the situation before disrobing on the island. The island is a good spot for shell hunting and its north point has forts from the Spanish-American War.

☞ Beer Can Island is sighted from Davis Island boat ramp as the third one out in Tampa Bay; 6 miles out, it is still protected from the gulf storms.

Egmont Key is at the entrance to Tampa harbor; the DeSoto National Monument offers a convenient boat launch, parking and refreshments.

Cape Freedom is a sandbar off the north end of Fort DeSoto County Park. A storm separated this sandbar from the previously adjoining sandspit that allowed rangers to drive its length. Cape Freedom has been freed from the mainland by a channel too deep to drive through.

☞ To reach Cape Freedom, take I-275 into South Petersburg and exit at 54th Ave. South. Go west on Route 682 where there is a $.50 toll for about 2.5 miles. Then turn south on Route 679 for about 4 miles where there is a $.35 toll. Continue along the road until the road tees and turn right, toward North Beach. Cape Freedom can be easily reached by parking at the north parking lot and wading across at the northeast end of the sandbar. Patrol boats pass on occasion. Set up your "Attention Nudity" signs and enjoy!

CLEARWATER COAST

Anclote Key is a wildlife preserve in Pasco County. Three miles of unspoiled

beach on its western side, virtually deserted weekdays. Weekends, first to arrive set dress code. North from Honeymoon Island; about 3 nautical miles west from the mouth of the Anclote River at Tarpon Springs where there is a boat ramp.

Three Rooker Island, south of Anclote Key and north of Third Island, has nude use. Access is by boat only.

Third Island, a.k.a. Dog Island, is a sandbar evolving into an island about 2 miles north of Honeymoon Island. Hard to see with naked eye. Access by boat only. Caution, shallows on east side! A Pinellas County sheriff's boat comes by occasionally.

Little Honeymoon is the sandspit on the north end of Honeymoon Island, an attraction of the Clearwater coast. It's a popular if not hassle-free nude beach; vehicles can be heard approaching. Road access is lacking to the narrow beach on the east side of the lagoon. Causeway from Alternate 19 between Dunedin and Tarpon Springs.

Caladesi Island, directly south of Honeymoon Island, has nude use at the south end. It's just opposite the north end of Clearwater Beach, also so used. Ferry service is from Honeymoon.

☆ CLUB CALIENTE

Opening in Spring 1998. Residential community and resort on 95 acres. Planned amenities include several beaches and pools, hot tub, boutique shops, restaurant and sports courts. Under construction at press time; please call for latest information toll-free 800-326-7731 or fax (813) 949-3616. P.O. Box 1255, Land O' Lakes, FL 34639.

☆ CLUB PARADISE

North by 17 miles from Tampa Airport via Dale Mabry Boulevard; Paradise Lakes has 80,000 annual visitors and 5,700 members. Club Paradise at Paradise Lakes is an upscale, partying, vacation resort with over 100 rental condos and hotel rooms, 70 RV spaces, retail stores, restaurant, nightclub, poolside bar and grill, spas, sports courts and, oh yes, a cypress-bordered lake where ospreys fish; all on 73 acres. Nightly entertainment, supervised children's activities. P.O. Box 750-WG, Land O'Lakes, FL 34639. Phone (813) 949-9327 or 800-237-2226.

☆ GULF COAST RESORT

Formerly City Retreat. This laid-back alternative to urban crowding offers pool, restaurant, hot tub, outdoor showers, store, laundry, rec room, volleyball, tent and trailer (incl. rental) sites in spacious wooded park. 13220 Houston Avenue-WG, Hudson, FL 34667. Phone (813) 868-1061.

LAKE COMO CLUB

This pioneer nudist park has 250 acres, much of it in orchards, on its own lake, 20 miles north of Tampa Airport. Pool, whirlpool, sauna, tennis, volleyball, nature trail, fishing, rec hall, shuffleboard. Trailer hookups, tent sites and rental rooms, restaurant. Clean, reasonable; many snowbirds and retirees. 20500 Cot Road, Lutz, FL 33549. Phone (813) 949-1810. Continuous improvements are taking place since the property became a membership cooperative in the mid-1990s (see *N* 16.4 p. 6).

PANHANDLE

TALLAHASSEE BARE-DEVILS

The Tallahassee Bare-Devils offer weekend swimming, sunbathing, and camping at their secluded 40-acre naturist retreat. The club sponsors full-moon skinny-dips, nude hiking, canoeing and trips to remote springs. Send SASE to the Bare-Devils, P.O. Box 6866, Tallahassee, FL 32314. Phone (850) 847-8537.

☆ SUNBURST RESORT

Heated and unheated pools, hot tub, 20 wooded acres, jogging track, snack bar, clubhouse with wide-screen TV and sofas. Rooms, tent and RV sites. 2375 Horn Road, Milton, FL 32570. Phone (850) 675-6807.

PANHANDLE FREE BEACHES

Formed from the core users of Navarre Beach. Panhandle Free Beaches, Inc., P.O. Box 5488, Navarre, FL 32566.

GULF ISLANDS NATIONAL SEASHORE

This federal recreation area extends across the state lines of Mississippi and Florida. Here, clear blue water, mild surf and gently sloping beaches abound. Add to that a history dating back to the 16th-century Spanish explorations and you can see why this is a popular spot for tourists. The Florida portion consists of the islands and peninsulas surrounding Pensacola Bay.

Perdido Key. A fairly secluded place used by local sunlovers. Federal rangers issue warnings for reckless nudity, be discreet! Drive onto Perdido Key (reached by Route 292 from Pensacola), by taking Perdido Key Drive to the Gulf. Cross the bridge and 1 mile farther, turn left onto Johnson Beach Drive. When road ends, you may park on sides of the road, then walk 15 minutes east to a beautiful beach. Lodgings at Perdido Key or at Gulf Shores, Alabama, only 10 minutes away.

Florida

Navarre Beach. On Santa Rosa Island, 13 miles of superb white sand and lightly visited; the sunsets are terrific! County officials from time to time "crack down," even making a hot pursuit of nude bathers who go onto adjacent Eglin Air Force Base beach. Concession stand, toilets, where tollroad makes right turn.

☞ Take I-10 or US 98 for 12 miles west from Fort Walton Beach, or 25 miles east from Pensacola. In the town of Navarre, take the very large bridge leading over to Santa Rosa Island on Route 87 and continue to a caution light near a convenience store on your right.

Notice the large domed building on left, part of the Eglin Air Force Base where you're headed. Turn left here where main road angles right onto Santa Rosa Island. Drive through picnic site, down a shell road about 1/4 mile and park. Walk east to Gulf beach and along it to military area. Do not go on the Eglin side of the fence; you risk a ticket from federal marshals.

☆ RIVIERA NATURIST RESORT, INC.

Formerly Ethos Trace. Nudist park with pool, hot tub, volleyball, sun deck, horseshoes. RV, tent and trailer sites. Close to the Gulf of Mexico and 5 minutes from Pensacola. P.O. Box 2233-WG, Pace, FL 32571. Phone (850) 994-3665.

> ☆ – The star symbol before a resort name is your guarantee that The Naturist Society card is accepted and earns a discount at the resort. To obtain Naturist Society membership, see the inside front cover.

GEORGIA

ATLANTA NORTH

☆ BELL ACRES

Bell Acres Recreation Enterprise (BARE) approached its 10th anniversary with a steady growth in membership, facilities and community acceptance. Large pool, clubhouse, hiking trails, hot tub on 70 acres of hilly woods; 70 miles northeast of Atlanta. P.O. Box 302, Maysville, GA 30558. Phone (706) 677-2931 or (800) 432-1436.

☆ MOUNTAIN CREEK GROVE

North Georgia's Mountain Creek Grove has 75 acres bisected by the swift-flowing Blue Creek. In-ground pool, hot tub, indoor and outdoor showers, toilets, clubhouse, and snack bar. RV and tent sites and motel available. Mountain Creek Grove, 258 Grove Lane, Cleveland, GA 30528. Phone (706) 865-6930 or (800) 863-NUDE.

☆ SERENDIPITY PARK

Forty-two wooded acres, Serendipity is 80 minutes from Atlanta. Families and singles-friendly. Tent and RV sites, cabins with kitchens. Heated pool and spa, sauna, clubhouse with exercise and tanning rooms, TV and dance floor. A motel planned. 95 Cedar Hollow Road, Cleveland, GA 30528. Phone 1-888-NUDEONE.

☆ HIDDEN VALLEY

Family-oriented, 110-acre resort in the northern Georgia foothills near Lake Lanier. Pool, spa, volleyball and tennis courts, horseshoes, nature trails, restaurant/snack bar, clubhouse. Sports tournaments, dances, Octoberfest. Tent and RV sites, motel rooms. (See *N* 16.4 p. 6.) 49 Valley Drive, Dawsonville, GA 30534. Phone (706) 265-6110; fax (706) 265-1533.

LAKE LANIER

A lovely lake 40 miles northeast of Atlanta, with many coves for sunbathers with a boat. Those landlocked can drive I-85 from Atlanta to the Buford exit, follow Buford Dam Road to the Buford end of the dam, explore for small roads that lead to the coves on federal land. Weekdays best; discretion called for on weekends.

AUGUSTA AREA

CLARKS HILL LAKE

Secluded coves and small islands, 1,000 miles of shoreline, mostly within the Sumter National Forest, guaranteeing little development. Located near intersection of routes 150 and 221 northwest of Augusta.

SOUTHEAST

WASSAW REFUGE

The two islands of the Wassaw State Wildlife Refuge near Savannah are reached only by boat. Avoid weekends and anchorages, try beaches with south/eastern exposure. Consult Ocean Survey chart 11509 (large scale) or charts 11511 and 11512 (detail). Day charters available. Remember bug repellent.

☆ HOLLY ACRES

South on I-95, 55 miles from Savannah, emergent Holly Acres offers limited facilities and plenty of forest and wildlife. Tent and RV camping w/water and electricity, picnic area, outside showers, children's playground, nature trails. Reservations required. P.O. Box 409, Darien, GA 31305. Phone (912) 437-6415.

CUMBERLAND ISLAND NATIONAL SEASHORE

Eighteen miles of white sand ocean beach with gentle dunes, marshes, freshwater ponds and the appropriate birds. Limit 300 persons per day. The NPS-run ferry is the only general access with no cars, bicycles or pets admitted; bring everything you will need as the island has no shops. Or reserve at the posh Greyfield Inn (904-261-6408) which runs a guest ferry from Fernandina Beach, FL.

☞ Take Georgia Route 40 east from I-95 near Kingsland to coastal St. Marys. Round-trip NPS ferry $7.95. Four primitive campsites. Reservations at 16-place developed campsite (seven-day limit) and on ferry is mandatory: P.O. Box 806, St. Marys, GA 31558. Phone (912) 882-4335. Daily ferry in June, July and August—Thursday through Monday off-season.

HAWAII

A world-class if obscured Eden, where clothes are not important, lies just beyond the customary tourist stops. Sadly, the return of body acceptance from the mainland causes some native Hawaiians to call for enforcement of recent state bans on nudity. Other Hawaiians are happy for the Naturist havens at secluded beaches.

The Polynesians wore little clothing, and then not in or at the sea, until Christian missionaries arrived with Captain Cook in 1776. See *Clothed with the Sun*, 8.1, pp. 48–65; 8.2, pp. 46–50; *Nude & Natural* magazine, N 10.4, pp. 54–55; "Nudity On Beaches Not Anything New" by NPS Hawaii historian Russ Apple, N 11.2, pp. 86–87; and N 16.1, pp. 40-42.

OAHU

Photographer Leif Heilberg has done much to disclose the marvelous beaches of the Hawaiian Islands for

Naturist visitors. Of Oahu, the first island to become a tourist mecca, as well as seat of military and government, he says: "Over 80% of Hawaii's inhabitants now live there. Overpopulation has effectively crowded all beach areas with private houses or state park beaches, virtually exiling nude beach activities to the other islands." Here's what remains on Oahu—

MALAEKAHANA STATE PARK

This bird sanctuary includes offshore Goat Island—Mokuauia in Hawaiian—which may be visited midweek for sunbathing. Malaekahana proper is a narrow coastal strip with a wide sandy beach and facilities. Avoid in the rainy season.

You wade up to your waist to reach the island and you need to wear tennis shoes to avoid cutting your feet. Because of these deterrents, you'll probably be in secluded skinny-dipping heaven when you do reach the island. It has two fine beaches facing the mainland, and its 18 acres are covered with ironwood, sea grape and grassy cover for the sea birds that nest. Its better beach is 300 yards long and 25 yards deep with a gentle lagoon of good sand. Note: Goat Island is sometimes closed due to hatching—phone ahead. Camping in the park requires a permit. Nearby lodging is in Laie, a Mormon community, at the Lanikoa Lodge, or in the Kuilima Hotel at Kahuku a few miles north.

☞ Malaekahana State Recreation Area is in the northeast of Oahu. From Honolulu, take H1 to the Likelike Highway. Go west on Likelike through the tunnel. Take the next exit, Highway 83, and follow all the way to Laie. Just past a refuse dump, watch for the first road on your right. This is the park entrance. Park in the picnic area and walk toward the ocean. Keep between the shower house (on the right) and the pavilion (on the left). Once at the beach head, walk from point to point, straight out across to the island. Keep to the right of the big blue sign, and once on the island, go left. The beach is a long, shallow half-moon. Watch for jelly fish when the surf is high.

Or, the #52 bus, Kaneohe-Wahiawa, runs from the Ala Moana shopping center near Waikiki to Malaekahana. From the parking lot, walk south on the beach 1/4 mile to Kalanai Point. It's only 250 yards to ford here. Be sure to walk straight out!

TURTLE BAY HILTON & KAHUKU POINT

Near-deserted wide coral and sand beach about 2 miles long, just up the coast on Route 83 from Laie and the now-defunct North Shore Naturist Park. Most tourists don't travel full length of beach; there is a good sandy stretch about a mile east of Turtle Bay. Everywhere else is rough lava rock at water's edge, but good sandy areas above the water.

Follow directions to Malaekahana State Park, but continue on Route 83 five more miles until you see the resort on your right.

MOKULEIA: POLO BEACH

A half-mile of gorgeous beach backed in part by a polo field and, to the east, by trees, 4.5 miles west of the town of Waialua on Route 930, before the Dillingham Airforce Base. Best access from Honolulu is H1 west to H2 north. H2 will turn into 99. From 99 take the 930 exit and follow to just before Dillingham Field. Parking is along the road. Walk across the east end of the polo field. It can also be reached by way of condominiums directly west of the field. Relatively deserted weekdays. Keep a low profile.

KANEANE BEACH

Kaneane Beach, at Makaha, has become the unofficial clothes-optional beach on the western coast. With few users on weekdays, even Makaha Beach itself gets some nude use. Kaneane Beach is not too good for swimming but it is great for sunbathing and shelling. It's often sunny when Waikiki is rainy.

☞ Take H1 to Highway 93. Follow 93 (Farrington Highway) north to the Cave on your right. Continue past the Cave parking area 1/4 mile north, and pull off to the shore side and park. (Car theft is a problem in the regular parking lot.)

An alternative west coast site for isolated nudity is Kaena Point. From Yokahama Bay, take the rugged 2-mile road leading up to a satellite station above the point; 4WD is suggested. Park at the "Y" and walk 50 minutes to sand dunes and wading pools. The dune area around the Point is a bird sanctuary; stay on the trail. The nonexistent beach has a lava rock coastline and rough water; few visitors.

MANOA FALLS

The Falls have been published in several tour guides, so there is now a steady stream of tourists on the main trail. However, there is an entire network of trails that provide nude possibilities. The area is along the boundary of a tropical rain forest and weather changes rapidly; the trails get very dark if the sun is blocked.

Take H1 to the University exit. Take University north to Oahu, then to Manoa Road. Follow to the bitter end to Paradise Park and follow the trailhead to the falls.

KAUAI

The most scenic and "natural" island with the most clothing-optional beaches—from Haena State Park and the NaPali Coast in the north, girdling Kauai to Polihale State Park in the west. Lihu'e has the airport and is a good center for your visit.

LIHU'E EAST: NININI BEACH

In Lihu'e drive eastward on Rice Street, towards Nawiliwili Harbor. Turn north on Kapule Road then, 0.3 miles north of Rice St., go right on a private road, past a guard station, where you simply tell the guard you are driving to the Ninini Beach Lighthouse. You'll find a spectacular view with a picnic table provided. Hike down a small cliff to either of the two coves with small sand beaches, adjoining the golf course, to get naked.

DONKEY BEACH

On the eastern shore, minutes north of central Kapa'a, enjoy a well-accepted, crescent nude beach with a lovely meadow and ironwood trees.

☞ Take Route 56 north from Kapa'a through Kealia toward Anahola. At the 11 mile-marker the road begins to climb slowly, then descend. Watch for a cane plantation road on the right. Take this road to another cane road (not a through road) fronting the ocean, then left 100 yards to the south end of Donkey Beach. If the cane road is barred you may park on the highway and walk in.

For a shorter walk to the beach, continue on the highway north about 1/4 mile as it descends before crossing a small valley. Park in front of the metal guardrail on the right ("nude beach" is spray-painted on it). Climb a short hill behind it and take the trail to the beach.

As car break-ins at the beach are frequent, most nudists prefer to park on the highway and walk in. Gays generally congregate at the north end. Vicious tides can make the surf dangerous for swimming.

CRACK BEACH

This is the bay north of Donkey Beach, between Ahihi and Anapalau points. Look for a closed tubular steel gate along Route 56, just 200 feet beyond where you'd park for Donkey Beach. The gate is to stop vehicles; you may easily pass through and follow the path, keeping to the left, a 7-minute walk to the bay, which also has a milder surf than Donkey Beach.

ROCK QUARRY BEACH

Larger, nicer and more scenic than the Donkeys. The beach is beside the parking—75 feet wide, 500 feet long, with a freshwater estuary at western end. A short climb over the rocks at the right end will take you to a small sand beach which is almost always nude. Some camping, busy weekends, mostly nude. A good alternative to Secret Beach when its descent is slick and surf dangerous in winter.

Drive north from Kapa'a on Route 56. Pass Anahola and after 15 minutes note mile-marker 21, go another 0.6 miles, and turn right on Wailapa Road. Go 0.15 miles and find fenced open field on left with two small shacks in it. Veer left on rocky dirt road, drive 0.6 miles to space for a dozen cars.

SECRET BEACH

Secret, also known as Kauapea Beach: its 300-foot protective cliff lurches upright from the sand. A stream cascades down its slope. Elsewhere, freshwater flows from the lava rocks, slaking thirst. High, even excessive surf. Most visitors are nude and you can walk a good half-mile. Interesting tidal pools at the western end. There's an excellent view across the waters to the NaPali cliffs. It's said the wimps who won't risk the Kalalau Trail do come here to admire it! In winter months, the east end of the beach disappears but nude use continues on the west end, where there is plenty of beach for everyone.

☞ From Kapa'a take Route 56 northwest to Kilauea. Beyond the 23 mile-marker, turn right onto paved Kahiliwai Road. Immediately after telephone pole 19, turn right onto a dirt lane about 150 yards from Route 56. Go 0.4 miles over a steep rise to parking. Walk left beside a wire fence for 50 yards to a trailhead that descends a ravine on your right to the beach.

A bit closer to Anahola (southwards), take Koolau Road and watch for telephone pole 29, where you will see a metal pole with the designation "Beach Access." Drive 0.95 miles to the road's end and park. Walk between two posts about 150 yards to the edge of bluff where the trail splits. The left path is the easiest to pleasant **Larsen Beach,** a beautiful, secluded beach area with shade trees, perfect for skinny-dipping.

TUNNEL POINT BEACH

A gorgeous panorama view, near Haena. Surfers delight in "tunnel" waves here. Backed by vacational rental houses, but nudity is a tradition near to the point.

Take Route 56 north. Route 56 ends at mile-marker 28, then is renamed Route 560. Continue on Route 560 along the north coast to end, through Hanalei Bay

Leif Heilberg. Picnic At Rock Quarry Beach, Kauai.

Hawaii

Village. About 0.9 miles past Charo's Restaurant is a tree with a red stripe (near mile-marker 8). Turn right, then left, and park on the edge of the road if the lot is full. Follow the fence about 100 feet to the beach and turn right. Walk past the main Tunnels Beach and an additional 200 yards to Tunnel Point Beach where prudent nudity is accepted.

HANALEI BEACH

A small beach just beyond the Hanalei Colony Surf Resort and the better-known Charo's Restaurant. Swimming and snorkeling are probably the best on Kauai—unique in the area.

☞ Continue north from Hanalei on Route 560 to mile-marker 8. About 0.4 miles farther, turn right onto a narrow dirt road through the jungle to the beach. A white pipe states "Beach Access." Take a short walk through private properties to the beach. The nude area starts to the north (left) and continues about 150 yards.

KE'E BEACH

Located at the very end of Route 560, Ke'e Beach is the trailhead to the NaPali Coast. Nudity at this lagoon is sharply curtailed at present due to tourist presence.

About a quarter-mile along the shore east of the Ke'e lagoon, at the outlet of Limahuli Stream (you can spot the stream from Route 560), nudity is still okay on weekdays only, avoid when local families appear on weekends and holidays.

NAPALI COAST: KALALAU BEACH

On the NaPali Coast, this is the Paradise of paradise. Shielded from conventional tourists by 12 very difficult miles of trekking—often along a 1,000-foot cliff face, slippery with mud when it rains, as it frequently does—the NaPali Coast is not forgiving of the idle mind. It's located on the northwest edge of the 553 square miles of Kauai. You need a state parks permit, good shoes, water, a complete food provision and other supplies.

The reward: unbelievable green sculptured cliffs, wild goats scampering amid a rainbow of blues, violets and orange blossoms.

Camping is permitted at Hanakoa, Hanakapiai and Kalalau Beaches; permit required. Nudity occurs along the trail but is mainly confined to the camping area at Kalakau and the far end of the beach. *Hiking Kauai* by Robert Smith is recommended.

Hawaii

☞ Begin hiking at Ke'e Beach, at the end of Route 560. But let's get serious: begin by writing for a map, regulations and permit for "Kalalau Trail." Dept. of Land & Natural Resources, Division of State Parks, Box 1671, Lihu'e, HI 96766. Phone (808) 245-4444.

KAHILI MOUNTAIN ROAD POND

Take Route 50 west from Lihu'e. Half a mile past Route 520—Tree-Tunnel Road that leads south to Koloa—find a sign on right for Kahili Mountain Park. Turn here, go 0.8 miles and where most traffic veers left, continue straight on a rougher plantation road 0.4 miles to a "T." Go right, then immediately right again, and park. The wadeable pond has low waterfalls, swimming, and copious flow; nudity okay.

WAHIAWA BAY

Continue westward on Route 50 past Kalaheo, then angle left on Route 540 (McBride Hill Road) southwesterly to Numila. Go a total of 3 miles, and on left, just before a bridge, find sign for Kauai Aggregates. Turn left on this red dirt road, go 0.4 miles, keeping to right, the sea ahead, descending. Where a brick wall on right ends, turn left. At a stone wall 0.4 miles farther, make a sharp right. At 0.2 miles down this steep road you reach a yellow gate. Turn left onto a deserted, wide, 1/4-mile beach; almost certainly, Wahiawa Bay.

MAHA'ULEPU BEACH

Two miles east of Poipu beyond the coast guard station. Follow Route 50 south from Lihu'e and take the turnoff (Route 520) to Koloa. Take the main street (Route 530) in Koloa Town west from the intersection with Route 520 for a very short block. Turn south at the first street going to the left. This is Poipu Road. Follow until the paved road ends and continue straight on a cane road, past the Hyatt and the Shipwreck Beach entrance; turn right at the "T" to pass through the control booth to the beach with parking in front of the sand dunes. Walk right to the beach, then northeast 200 yards to the nude area.

KEKAHA BEACH PARK

On Kauai's southwest coast, west from Kekaha and extending miles and miles, is a beautiful, open and unshaded beach beside the highway, largely invisible to automobiles. Many turnoffs will take you in; best access is just west of Kekaha on the last stretch of beach before the canal. It gets low use in midweek.

PRINCEVILLE BEACH

Take the road to Princeville at the traffic light on Route 56, and follow road to the Princeville Hotel at the end. Park in the hotel parking lot at the far right corner next to the Puu Poa condominium. Make your way around the fence post close to the cliff and descend steep steps to a small white sand beach. Outstanding snorkeling.

POLIHALE STATE PARK

A beautiful beach on the southwest tip of Kauai—with moderate clothed use close to the parking lot, and beach buggies to intrude on privacy. Unbelievably hot; bring water, and perhaps a beach umbrella as there is no shade. The sea is splendid. Many dunes provide secluded off-beach hideaways. The sign warning against nudity is still up, unmolested and often disregarded. The southward expanse of this beach is not established as nude—it's just so huge you won't meet anybody. Both ends have considerable use by people cruising in pickups; don't leave valuables in your car. Camping at the north end. Strong currents in winter make swimming unsafe.

☞ At the western end of Route 50 you'll find the state park. Leave the highway at the sign pointing left to Polihale. Take the 15-minute drive down the unimproved road (muddy when wet) to the huge tree with an attached sign pointing right to the state park. (This road is longer, bumpier and will lead to a clothed beach with facilities.) Instead, turn left. After a short drive you'll come to a turnoff to the right, leading to a parking area. The area is much more private, with people spaced several thousand feet apart.

HAWAII (THE BIG ISLAND)

KONA: CONTACT & LODGE

Kona Sun Klub. Organized in 1995 to conserve nude use of Honokohau Beach, provide tourist information and conduct government relations. Contact John Kinman, P.O. Box 390304, Kailua-Kona, HI 96740. Phone (808) 326-2752.

Hale Makala. Sue & Len Welter's

House In the Sun. Private garden with pool and waterfall, barbecue, kitchen, indoor rec area. Sleeps 6, 2 bedrooms, 5 minutes from downtown. P.O. Box 1836, Kailua-Kona, HI 96745. Phone/fax (808) 329-9576.

The Kona Escape. Attractive private garden B&B, 15 minutes south of Kailua-Kona. Hot tub, ocean view, 3 bedrooms, private verandas, baths, and entrances. P.O. Box 197, Holualoa, HI 96725. Phone (808) 322-3295.

The Banana Patch. Authentic banana farm offers clothing-optional cottage and bungalow, each with fully-equipped kitchen, shared hot tub, private sunning area. Within minutes of beaches, restaurants, golf and tennis facilities. Information or reservations 800-988-2246 or 800-322-8888; fax (808) 323-2348.

Hale Luana rents lower level of home, complete with two bedrooms, bath and shower, kitchen, screened lanai with exercise equipment. Only 15 minutes to the beach. Information/reservations; John and B.J. Kinman, 77-409 Puuwai Alii Place, Kailua-Kona, HI 96740; call/fax (808) 326-2752.

KALOKO-HONOKOHAU BEACH

The NPS superintendent of Honokohau Beach enacted a ban on nudity in January 1997. However, he violated just about every procedure of rule making in doing so, and the ruling may well be reversed. For current information, contact Kona Sun Klub.

Three miles north of Kailua-Kona is the emergent Kaloko-Honokohau National Historical Park. Beach nudity was the practice and custom of the ancient Hawaiians and Honokohau Beach remains the Kona Coast's most popular unclad area. Toilets, trash cans and security are now provided by NPS. With its pond and lush grasses behind the beach, the sloping sands to the water along a half-mile crescent, and historic Queen's Baths, Honokohau Beach is a pleaser. Easy access and nude users outnumber clothed. Worth a swim and snorkel too.

☞ North from Kailua on the "airport" road. Or south from Keahole Kailua-Kona Airport. Turn to the sea on the Honokohau Harbor Road. Now keep bearing right until you dead end, more or less, on a bumpy dirt road just past Kona Marina. Follow the main road circumventing the marina. A sign points to the beach as well as "NB" painted on rocks along the road. Park, lock, and take the grassy trail that leads north to the beach.

MAKALAWENA BEACH

North 2.5 miles from the Keahole Airport turnoff, find sign for Kona Coast State Park. Turn west onto this rough road and go 1.5 miles. At 200 feet from the clothed-beach parking, pull off on your left and park, scramble through the fence across the road, and walk 15 minutes northward on a rough jeep trail through lava rock to the north end of Kona Coast State Park. Here you'll see an abandoned house with palm trees, marking the now mostly-clothed Mahai'ula Beach. Toilet facility here.

Behind a water tower at the north end of Mahai'ula Bay you'll find and follow the narrow, tortuous King's Trail path for 20 minutes, northerly through trees and across dunes, to Makalawena Beach. Difficulty of access makes this long crescent of white sand an almost entirely nude beach.

KUA BAY BEACH

Kua Bay has soft and silky white sand—scenically and tactilely, the best beach on Kona Coast to be nude. But you must come very early and on a weekday.

At 12.1 miles north of Kailua-Kona, the road cuts through a knoll. Just as you come out of this cut find a dirt road entering from the left, it has a stop sign. Turn down this road. Near the beach a steel gate stands at an angle on the right. Park, go through the gate and walk 10 minutes to the beach. In 1994, the gate was unlock-ed and increasing numbers of cars were overnighting—bad for nudity. Do check the current usage before getting naked.

KOHALA: POLE 67 BEACH

In Kohala, north of the Kona district, a 45-minute drive north of Kailua, turn left at Puako Beach Drive. Take the first right on Puako Road and continue to telephone pole No. 67.

Hike or 4WD on the beautiful white sand beach; the north end is traditionally nude. There's also shade here, and an opening through the sea rocks for swimming.

Beach squatters may still be a problem. Most users are employees of the resort hotels, with a day off.

MAU'UMAE BEACH

Early in the day before a daily quota is filled, arrive at the guard station of the Mauna Kea Beach Hotel—35 miles north of Kailua-Kona on Route 19—and ask for a beach pass. Drive towards the sea 0.45 miles, and where a sign on left says Villas of Mauna Kea, turn right. Go 0.1 miles and turn left onto a gravel road, go 0.45 miles and park at telephone pole 22 on left. Take path towards sea; a minute's

walk brings you to a "T" and a pole saying Ala Kahakai. Turn left and walk 2 minutes to this smooth gray sand beach backed by shade trees. An easy walk, mild surf, and never a problem to get nude, even if you're the first. On leaving, you may want a drink or lunch at this luxurious Rockefeller resort!

SOUTH POINT: GREEN SAND BEACH

Take a day to drive and explore—or skip this 100 yards of olive-green sand below towering volcanic cliffs near the southernmost point of the U.S. The undertow is rough, with strong waves.

☞ It's 61 miles south from the Kona airport to the South Point sign where you turn and go to Land's End. At 300 yards before that point, take the left fork to a boat ramp. Park, and prepare to hike an hour to the east. Only 4WDs can drive this track to the high volcanic cliff overlooking the ocean.

HILO COAST: CONTACT & LODGE

Kalani Honua Retreat & Conference Center. Nearby Kehena Beach natural steam baths are clothing-optional. So too the Kalani Honua pool-spa after 7 p.m. Community kitchen, bath in each lodge, 20 lush acres, sauna, 24-meter pool, jacuzzi, arts and crafts, yoga, dance, bicycling. Brochure from P.O. Box 4500, Kalapana, HI 96778. Phone (808) 965-7828.

KEHENA BEACH

Pronounced *keh-HEH-nuh* (if you get lost and need to ask), Kehena Beach has a good mix of amiable folks, sunning, swimming, bodysurfing, snorkeling, fishing, beach surfing, some windsurfing, and scuba activity. Frequent sightings of whales, dolphins, sea turtles. Good anytime. A lava flow from Kilauea in 1955 created its black sand, shaped by the waves and weather. Food and showers available at Harry K. Brown Park at Kalapana, just down the road on Route 130 from the Route 137 turnoff. Complete the day at the Steam Vents.

☞ Take Route 130 south for 30 miles from Hilo; you must do almost a U-turn into Route 137 on your left as you reach the coast. If you get to Kalapana you've gone too far, turn around and go back to Route 137. At 4 miles from Route 130, mile-marker 19, park, descend the easily negotiable footpath about 125 yards northeast of the "Scenic View" parking atop the sea cliff. At the beach go left (northeast).

PAHOA STEAM VENTS

South of Hilo, in the Puna District. The

rising steam from several small cones or hills in the woods is visible from the highway. Remember to bring some wash-off water in gallon jugs. Best time to go is dawn or evenings; daytime is much too hot.

☞ Going south from Hilo for 22 miles on Route 130, about 3 miles south of Pahoa is a "scenic point" turnoff. Three short trails lead from the roadside to the last cinder cone. Climbing it, you'll discover a bi-level natural sauna!

The Natural Food Store in the center of Pahoa may provide updates on naturist sites.

Looking for a place to stay? Only 30 miles from Pahoa is the **Na'Alii Plantation** which offers a rental home on a working anthurium farm. Reservations required. 2939A Pulima Drive, Hilo, HI 96720; (808) 935-2109.

MAUI

CONTACT & LODGE

Shangri-La, also known as Hale Akua. Secluded naturist resort near Kahului airport, operated by a clothing-optional community on an elegant garden estate. Hot tubs and 60-foot pool overlook a canyon with panoramic ocean view. Yoga, massage available. Star Route 1, Box 161, Haiku, Maui, HI 96708. Phone (808) 572-9300; fax 572-6666.

Little Beach. Contacts for lodging include the luxurious Makena resort **Maui Prince,** 800-321-MAUI; and **Maui Intercontinental,** 800-367-2960.

Hana Plantation Houses cater to naturists, phone (808) 248-7049. The Sea Cottages of the **Hana Ranch** are close to the trailhead for Red Sand Beach, phone (808) 248-7238.

☆**Honokalani Ranch,** a private naturist resort with camping and cabins in a secluded setting by a black sand beach, secret coves and a picturesque coastline. P.O. Box 349, Hana, Maui, HI 96713. Phone (808) 248-7220.

MAKENA: LITTLE BEACH

Relax, swim, snorkel, bodysurf or boogieboard surf, and sunbathe in paradise at Maui's nude beach, listed in local guides and known worldwide. Saved for nudity by Friends of Little Beach organized by Peter Rowley in the 1980s, hundreds of visitors frequent the sheltered cove every day, unaware of the sacrifice and effort put forth to preserve their freedom. Friends of Little Beach/Maui SunSeekers, P.O. Box 841, Puunene, 96784, Maui. See *N* 11.3, pp. 95–96.

☞ Little Makena Beach is the reward at the end of Route 31 (Pilani Highway). Take it south past the expansive Wailea golf resort complex. When

Maui Christmas!

the road ends, take a right turn on Waikea Iki Drive. Take a left on Wailea Alanui Drive, which becomes Makena Drive. Drive exactly one mile beyond the Maui Prince Hotel, watch for the cone hill (lava formation) on the right, and turn on a neatly graveled road marked "Makena La Perouse State Park" to the first of Makena's two parking areas. Little Makena is reached by walking north on Big Beach (to the right as you face the water), clambering over the lava-flow barrier berm to Little Beach.

HANA: RED SAND BEACH

Located on Maui's east coast on Kaihalulu Bay south of Kauiki Head, Red Sand Beach is a well-known site accepted by locals for skinny-dipping. Take a day to drive the Hana Road, then stay overnight and go to the beach early, before 11 a.m. as later sun is blocked by towering cliffs. A mini-reef creates a fish basin—bring snorkel gear, as well as shoes and a towel against the sharp sand.

☞ Entering Hana from the north on Route 36, take the left fork and follow signs to Hana Bay Park. At the park entrance, take Ua'Kea Road two blocks south to the Old Hana School, now labeled "Hana Community Center," on your left. Park. Walk down the dirt road behind the school to a Japanese cemetery. Just before you reach it, find a path descending to the shore. Then walk about 200 yards left and around a point to the coarse volcanic sands of Red Sand Beach.

SEVEN POOLS

Seven Sacred Pools are a large number of natural stone basins on the southeastern slope of a 10,023-foot volcano, in the Halea Kala National Park. Rains cascade from one pool to the next from Oheo Gulch to the sea. The ascent takes 45 minutes at 25 mph on a narrow, winding, bumpy road ($3 entrance fee). Or park at bottom, hike the 1-mile ascent trail that begins across the road from the parking. Arrive early in the morning for the best opportunity to skinny-dip. Be sure to leave while there's still light if your return trip on the Hana Highway is long—it's not wise to drive the highway after dark.

☞ Drive to Kipahula,15 miles beyond Hana. Skinny-dippers seclude themselves in the upper pools, and rangers observe the same policy as in all national parks: if the nudity is discreet, it's legitimate.

WATERFALLS

You'll be greatly assisted in finding waterfalls and other elusive *wailele* if you'll write the University of Hawaii Press for its "Reference Maps of the Islands of Hawaii" as also its Atlas of Hawaii where dozens of waterfalls are listed by height, volume, and directions. The alternative way to find waterfalls: look for the parked cars!

Nudity is at your risk at waterfalls—with luck you can have a marvelous natural experience. Maui is the island for waterfall delights. The 52-mile, extremely curvey road to Hana is the access. Twin Falls, at Hoolawa Bridge along the notorious Route 36, is the first of a dozen Hana coast waterfalls. Follow the marked paths.

> NOTE: captions to photos run along the inside edge of pages.

IDAHO

Idaho shelters more "unimproved" (translation: natural, noncommercial, and clothes-optional) hot springs on public lands than do the other northwest states taken together. Rafting the wild and scenic rivers remains the readiest way to reach many of the hot springs, as they're often distant from roads. Rafting is also a tremendous rush—and the Forest Service has confessed that there is hardly a Salmon River raft trip that's not naked.

The following entries are a sample of what Idaho offers. An additional source: *Sun 'n' Soak Naturally: Clothing-Optional* by Phil Owensby, 1089 Medford Center #170, Medford, OR 97504. $21.95.

MISSOULA AREA

JERRY JOHNSON HOT SPRINGS

Missoula is across the Idaho border in Montana. Legendary Jerry Johnson Hot Springs flows out of a mound of minerals of its own making at the fabulous rate of 450 gallons per minute. The 115°F water runs into crudely formed boulder tubs, where it mingles with icy waters from Warm Springs Creek. Hence, part of you can be parboiled while the rest is chilled—a stimulating experience. Most seem to choose to soak seated, moving from cooler to warmer mixes, though some like to take an icy plunge for variation. You can camp nearby; evening soaking is popular; year-round use.

☞ Jerry Johnson is located off US 12, 20 miles into Idaho from the Montana border. Find the Warm Springs Park bridge trailhead a half-mile west of mile-marker 152. Hike 1 mile southeast on Forest Service Road 49 to the first set of pools, which will be down an embankment to your right; shallower pools are 100 feet farther up.

BOISE NATIONAL FOREST

MIDDLE FORK OF THE PAYETTE RIVER

An adventure bouncing along the back roads, then hiking and fording a river several times, will bring you to hot springs—Moon Dipper, Pine Burl, Bull Creek—which await the deliciously weary traveler on the south bank of Dash Creek before they spill into the Middle Fork of the Payette River. Each has primitive rock and log pools which allow you to mix cold river water with the hot mineral water.

☞ Purchase a Boise National Forest map at any ranger station and follow Forest Service Road 698 north from Crouch to Trail Creek Campground and the Boiling Springs USFS guard station (20 miles of unpaved road). From here hike north for 2 miles on a clear but unmarked path along the river to where the springs appear on the map. Wear shoes that can get wet.

VULCAN HOT SPRINGS

The boiling hot creek is tamed to a mere 105°F in a soak reservoir behind a log dam on the South Fork of the Salmon River. From Cascade, take Forest Service Road 22 to FSR 474 and travel south 7 miles (a mile past Stolle Meadows) to Vulcan Hot Springs camping. Park, hike 1 mile west to the springs.

MOLLY'S TUBS & HOT SPRINGS

Same as road to Vulcan Hot Springs. From Forest Service Road 22, along South Fork of the Salmon River, turn south on gravel FSR 474 for 1.3 miles to a pullout on the right. Hike down to several tubs. For Molly's Hot Springs, go south another half-mile to intersection with road heading east to Warm Lake. Park here and hike west on blocked road for 300 yards, cross bridge, take a right on unmarked path for 100 yards.

CHATTANOOGA HOT SPRINGS

A large, sand-bottomed pool at the base of a thermal cascade amid spectacular scenery enjoyed by a well-established group of nude users. From Boise take Route 21 north 15 miles. Turn right onto Forest Service Road 268 and continue to Atlanta, about 35 miles (estimate an hour driving time). Hot springs are located 1/2 mile past Riverside Camp-ground. Park in the area at the top of the cliff.

TWIN SPRINGS RESORT

Three modern rental cabins, each equipped with kitchen, private deck and hot tub overlooking the river. Clothing is optional on the private decks and in a big communal pool fed by a hot spring. Located a half hour from Boise on the road to the historic mining town of Atlanta. Reservations mandatory, phone (208) 338-8529.

ILLINOIS

NORTHERN

Our midwestern Second City gave rise to Hugh Hefner, Ed Lange and Dick Drost—each man a repackager of flatfooted nakedness into spiritedly bankable fantasies on nudity (and each, significantly, moved on to Southern California).

What Illinois has not given rise to is viable nude recreation sites at home either public or private. Prurient or repressed ideas of nudity pervade Illinois: it has been impossible to serve body acceptance and commerce too. Where Eastern poet Walt Whitman "sang the body electric," Illinois' poet Carl Sandburg apotheosized the working person not the sunbather. Illini who don't migrate seek nude community in Wisconsin, Indiana and Michigan.

CHICAGO SUN CLUB

Health club, social, and lakeside activities. SASE to P.O. Box 508135, Cicero, IL 60804; (630) 243-9614.

ELGIN QUARRY

Nude sunbathing and swimming occur at some of the 12 quarries. If clothed folks are there first, ask before undressing.

☞ From the village of West Chicago, take IL 59 north for 7 miles to West Bartlett Road and turn left (west). Drive 2 miles. At Gifford turn right and proceed north 1.9 miles to the dead end at Bluff City Blvd. and park. Walk south on Gifford Road; the larger, more scenic quarries are on the east. At the bottom of the first hill by a 45 MPH sign is a low spot in the barbed wire. At the top of the next hill is easy access to west side. Clothed visitors predominate and fish and swim on both sides. South end of both sides is company patrolled.

☆ BLUE LAKE CLUB

Wooded 20 acres in Moline area's Rock River Valley. Motel and tent/trailer sites, lake, chlorinated swimming pond, volleyball, rec hall, snack bar, whirlpool. May–October. P.O. Box 13-WG, Erie, IL 61250. Phone (309) 659-9297.

LAKE CARLYLE

Near St. Louis in southwestern Illinois and created by Corps. of Engineers, the fairly large Lake Carlyle is popular for boating, sailing—and skinny-dipping. Singles and families enjoy the 250 yards of beach au naturel on weekdays with little or no hassle from the rangers.

☞ From St. Louis, take Route 64 to Route 50; go east on Route 50 to Carlyle. Continue east 5 miles past Carlyle to Route 2300E and turn left. Take to the end of the road, park and walk 100 yards to the path on your left. Follow the path to the beach.

☆ – The star symbol before a resort name is your guarantee that The Naturist Society card is accepted and earns a discount at the resort. To obtain Naturist Society membership, see the inside front cover.

INDIANA

NORTHERN

LAKE MICHIGAN: THE INDIANA DUNES

Sixty miles east of Chicago are 12,000 acres of sometimes huge sand dunes among wetlands, administered by the Indiana and national parks systems. US 12, I-94, Route 49 and the Indiana Toll Road bring you into the area.

From US 12, go to **Central St. Beach.** Park at Central St. Beach and walk to the lake. Go right (east) past a large sand dune to where a small creek enters Lake Michigan. Visited by area family naturists; kids love to play in the shallow creek.

Kemil Road Beach is in a wildlife refuge with few patrols or sunbathers, north of the federal Visitor Center. Follow US 12 to Kemil Road. Take the road to the Kemil Beach parking lot. Little parking, so you may want to bike. DO NOT turn left into the state park when you reach the beach. Kemil Beach is guarded in the summer from 10 a.m. to 6 p.m. Head east, away from the guarded section, where you will find a long stretch of quiet beach between Kemil and Lakeview Beach (clothed) that can be used nude. The beach is not heavily used evenings.

Bailly Beach. Pristine dunes backed by woods; no hassle, few visit. Bordered by Cowles Bog on the south, Bailly Generating Station on the west, and the Town of Dune Acres on the east. Access is by boat—or a long trek on the Cowles Bog Trail, starting from guard station at entrance to Dune Acres. The Cowles Bog parking area is on the east side of Mineral Springs Road north of US 12 and south of the entrance to Dune Acres. Park, and walk across the street to Cowles Bog Trailhead. It is at least an hour walk from here to the beach so bring plenty of water.

You can also get there by taking the South Shore Line, from Chicago or South Bend, and ask to get off at the intersection of Mineral Springs Road and US 12. The Line will pick you up. Trains run every two hours on the weekend and less often during the week. There is a guard at the entrance station of Dunes Acres; stay well west of the Dunes Acres homes. Remove your litter, bring your own water.

☆ LAKE O' THE WOODS

An hour from Chicago, a cooperative gated weekend community of 130 wooded acres with 26-acre lake, water sports, winter sports, volleyball, hiking, camping and RV w/hookups, sauna, hot tub, heated pool, rec room. Open year-round. P.O. Box 53-WG, Valparaiso, IN 46384. Phone (219) 477-6643.

☆ SUNNY HAVEN

A relaxing, family-oriented spot in the South Bend area. Heated pool, sauna, hot tub, volleyball, weekly social activities, miniten, natural trails, general store, shuffleboard and restaurant. RV, tent and trailer sites. 11425 Anderson Road, P.O. Box 100, Granger, IN 46530. Phone (219) 277-5356.

CENTRAL

☆ SUNSHOWER CLUB

Near Indianapolis, Sunshower Club is a full-service resort on 20 acres surrounded by a 65-acre woodland. Beautiful pool, volleyball, playground, rec room, shuffleboard, nature trails. Tent and RV sites, rental cabin. Open May 15 to October 15. P.O. Box 33487, Cleveland, OH 44133. Phone (765) 855-2785.

PURDUE UNIVERSITY

The Purdue Nude Olympics occur on the coldest night of the year in Lafayette. Undergrads—male and female—burst from their dorm rooms at Cary Quadrangle to race nude around the sidewalk of Spitzer Court. The winners of the Nude Olympics stay the course the longest.

The Nude Olympics streak goes back to 1957. Purdue officials took harsh countermeasures in the late '80s, yet failed to stop the Olympics. Other universities also maintain proud traditions of ritual mass nuding. Princeton, NJ, at first snowfall; Ann Arbor, MI, at the last spring class; Stevens Point, WI, when it feels right. But Hoosier engineers have the best, and are relentless. They have thick skins.

SOUTHERN

HOOSIER NATIONAL FOREST

Blackwell Lake. From Bloomington take Route 446 southeast 12.5 miles to Tower Ridge Road. (Sign: Maumee Reservation Boy Scout Camp.) Turn left (east), drive 0.3 miles to information sign; turn right at sign, park. Nude use not recommended during weekends when the nearby information cabin is staffed.

Terril Ridge Pond. Continue past Blackwell Lake another 6.3 miles and park at Hickory Ridge Lookout Tower on the left. From the end of the parking lot begin on the wide trail that is roped off to prevent cars from entering. A short distance later take the first marked hiking trail on the right, Sycamore Loop. Watch for unmarked trail to pond at roughly 1.5 miles.

Grouse Hollow Lake, a camper's paradise. The most promising skinny-dipper site in the Hoosier National Forest. From Bloomington, take Route 446 southeast 15.3 miles, turn left on Hunter Creek Road (just over county line, unmarked but look for a Hunter Creek church sign), immediately turn right and travel 1.2 miles to road L4E7N and turn left. Drive 3.2 miles to parking on left; hike 0.5 miles to lake.

SAUNDERS QUARRY

A classic stone quarry with sunning rocks. In Bloomington, south of the old business district when one-way streets allow, go south on S. Walnut. Continue south to Fairfax. Go left (east) 2.2 miles past old school building converted to a business with signs "No quarry parking – will be towed." As you go downhill, the path on the right is next to a few posts before Norton Street. Parking is scarce. No parking signs abound even on side streets.

Follow the path until you see a few deep quarries on the right. The path will "Y." To the right is the famous quarry in the movie "Breaking Away," which is textiled. Follow the left branch of the "Y" and you will come to another quarry, called Ray Hole. There is a road to the left which will take you to the water. The second left is where the best sunning area is.

LOTHLORIEN NATURE SOCIETY

Ninety-two acres of forest preserve, miles of winding pathways, camping, ceremonial grounds, fire circles, solar showers and no electricity, a culture refuge for nature religions—and "not for an exclusive few. We share the sanctuary with all who live the peaceful path of harmony…One may skinny-dip or sunbathe without hassle. If you wish to hold a play, play a tune, celebrate a season, or howl at the moon, it's okay with us. We're especially interested in experimenting with alternative and ecologically sound life-styles."

Best time to get acquainted is at one of several festivals at Lothlorien. Membership otherwise required. P.O. Box 1082, Bloomington, IN 47402.

FERN HILLS CLUB

About 7 miles from Bloomington with 70 acres, tent and RV sites, pool, sauna, volleyball, rec hall. May–October. 7330 S. Rockport Road, Bloomington, IN 47401. Phone (812) 824-4489.

☆ TRI-STATE COUNTRY CLUB

A natural getaway for the Indiana, Ohio or Kentucky nudist happy with a tent or small RV and the great outdoors, aboveground pool, rec hall, community kitchen, snacks. Tent and trailer sites, cabins. Memorial Day to Labor Day. 79 Drakes Ridge-WG, Bennington, IN 47011. Phone (812) 427-3914.

> NOTE: captions to photos run along the inside edge of pages.

KANSAS

NORTHEAST

HEARTLAND NATURISTS

Heartland Naturists, formerly Kansans for a Natural Society, do their best to keep at least one clothes-optional spot going. Write c/o Stan Severance, P.O. Box 9103, Shawnee Misson, KS 66201.

☆ LAKE EDUN

Southwest of Topeka, Lake Edun is a 10-acre skinny-dipping pond set in 65 wooded acres with hiking trails and sauna. Occasional parties. Day use fee or annual membership. Fishing (license needed) is permitted. No hunting. Box 1982, Topeka, KS 66601.

From Topeka, exit I-70 at Auburn Road. Go about 5.5 miles south to SW 53rd St., then 1 mile east to Indian Hills Road. Go about 1/4 mile south on Indian Hills Road until you see a bluish-gray barn on the west side of the road. Park on either shoulder or in the lot if the gate is open. Follow trails to the barn, sign in and pay visitor fee.

SOUTHEAST

SANDY LANE CLUB

Weekends only, seven miles from Hutchinson. Forty acres, pool, tent and RV sites, cabin. Guests welcomed to groomed grounds in a catalpa grove. P.O. Box 1866-WG, Hutchinson, KS 67504. Phone (316) 543-2645.

☆ – The star symbol before a resort name is your guarantee that The Naturist Society card is accepted and earns a discount at the resort. To obtain Naturist Society membership, see the inside front cover.

KENTUCKY

EASTERN

RED RIVER GORGE

Eastern Kentucky is graced by the large wilderness tracts of Daniel Boone National Forest. The many trails, seclusion and scenery of Red River Gorge, near Lombard, offer naturist delights to the discreet woodsperson following in the tracks of Boone, who himself never wore a stitch when enjoying a dip. Do use with caution and pick up before leaving.

☞ Entering the Gorge from the Nada Tunnel, follow the paved road to the bridge at the Powell-Menifee county line. Immediately after the bridge a gravel road turns off to the left (County Road 1067, if you have a map). Take it. Likely spots begin almost immediately, for a fallen tree 0.4 miles up the road prevents canoes from reaching the points beyond, guaranteeing you a relaxing cove.

CENTRAL

GREEN RIVER LAKE STATE PARK

Many coves where you may tie up a boat and be au naturel. Campsites on upper west shore. Southeast of Campbellsville; several roads off Highway 55 lead to lake.

WESTERN

LAND BETWEEN THE LAKES

Kentucky has many backcountry sites where a girl and her fellow can skinny-dip, but the best-established nude water recreation area in the state lies along the many miles of shoreline of the Land Between the Lakes, extending nearly 50 miles along either side of Route 49 between Padacah and Fort Donelson, Tennessee. Murray State University students are the Daniel Boones of this area.

For more info, send an SASE to **Ken-Ten Naturists,** c/o Charles Holmes, P.O. Box 822, McKenzie, TN 38201.

JOE FORD NATURE CENTER

Discreet nude use occurs at the Joe Ford Nature Center of Owensboro. This is not a naturist park; however, the wooded grounds include two ponds and nature trails perfect for solitary strolls or bird-watching.

NOTE: captions to photos run along the inside edge of pages.

MAINE

SOLAR BARES

Maine delights the sailor, canuder or hiker with the feeling of breeze and sun on naked skin. The rocky shoreline is great for basking. We've provided a few social settings and backcountry destinations; the explorer will not be limited by these suggestions.

Information on the ever-changing possibilities of Maine: Maine Coast Solar Bares, c/o Stanley W. Wright, P.O. Box 104, Norway, ME 04268. Phone (207) 583-4637.

PORTLAND AREA

CASCO BAY

Casco Bay is enjoyed for nude sailing and so are other waters away from Portland Harbor and the islands immediately outside the harbor.

MT. DESERT ISLAND

LAKE WOOD

In Acadia National Park, a sun-warmed, naked-granite beach, sloping to the warmest freshwater lake on the island. Look for blueberries in August.

From Main Street and Route 3 in Bar Harbor, follow Route 3 for 3 miles to Hulls Cove. Turn west on Crooked Road. Drive 0.7 miles, past the gravel pit/quarry to 2 lefts just after the gravel pit, and take the second left. There's a semiconcealed park sign up the road indicating day use only. This road starts rough, gets better. Drive 0.3 miles to developed parking, or park on grass.

Leave no valuables in car. A maintained trail leads from the parking area to clothed swim area. For nude area, walk clockwise to left around lake, either at shore or on grassy ridge above (trail starts at grassy parking). Ledges for nude sunning and leaping are 1/2 mile easy hike halfway down east side of lake. On private property but no one complains.

Or try **Long Pond,** also called Great Pond. Rowboat and canoe rental to access the coves, or skinny-dip as you hike around the pond. Easily found on maps.

MARYLAND

OCEAN SHORE

ASSATEAGUE NATIONAL SEASHORE (NORTH SEGMENT)

Assateague Island is at risk from rowdy recreational sprawl at Ocean City. A more apt breed of shore visitors are the Naturists. Ecologically aware of impact and alert to stop misbehavior, naturists have been a boon to coastal administrators.

☞ From Baltimore and Salisbury take Route 50 east. At Ocean City West turn right on Route 611 and cross bridge to Assateague Island and continue straight east to State Beach paved parking (entry fee) with showers and concession stand. Walk to main beach, then to the left at least 1 mile north before taking it all off, which brings you within the northern segment of Assateague Island National Seashore. The area north of the pole numbered 70 is naturist (about a 45-minute walk). Stay out of the dunes.

ANNAPOLIS AREA

PINE TREE ASSOC.

Among largest, oldest East Coast nudist parks. Ninety rolling secluded acres, an hour from Washington and Baltimore. Mostly wooded with private cabins. Tent and RV sites, rental rooms, trailers available. Twenty grassy acres for sunning and sports. Heated indoor pool, outdoor pool, tennis, volleyball, shuffleboard, sauna, hot tub, rec hall. Snack bar in summer. Open year-round; nudity required. P.O. Box 195-WG, Crownsville, MD 21032. Phone (410) 841-6033 or (301) 261-8787.

MARYLAND HEALTH SOCIETY (MAHESO)

An independent, rustic nudist cooperative, MAHESO has 100 acres of woods, a large pool, clubhouse with full kitchen, tent and RV sites, 12 cabins. Volleyball, shuffleboard, hiking trails. P.O. Box 126, Davidsonville, MD 21035; phone (410) 798-0269. Fax (410) 798-4705.

CHESAPEAKE BAY

Citizens of several states congregate to skinny-skipper their craft on the relatively calm waters of this giant bathtub. Taking your values to sea may be the best solution in officially unliberated Middle Atlantic states. Bring along your friends, they'll thank you. But be aware that the saline solution grows more toxic with each year—think before you open your mouth while skinny-dipping from your boat, and join the Naturists concerned to clean up the mess. Save the clams!

BALTIMORE AREA

PATUXENT RIVER

Excellent area for tubing and good sunning spots. Some clothed fishing and canoeing. From Capital Beltway I-495 in MD, take New Hampshire Avenue north (Route 650) to small town of Ashton. Turn right on Sandy Spring Road (Route 108) and go about 2 miles to paved Mink Hollow Road. Turn left and continue to the bridge that crosses the Patuxent River. Park before the bridge (space enough for 2 cars), follow path right (downstream).

ELK NECK STATE PARK

Crowded with boaters on weekends. Weekdays a few skinny-dippers appear at this coastal park. Low tide is best for walking to privacy down shoreline, past fallen trees.

☞ Reached by I-95 north out of Baltimore for about 50 miles to North East-Rising Sun Exit (Route 272), taking 272 south through town of North East about 13 miles to the park entrance (sign on left). Drive Route 272 to 1 mile past swimming/picnic area, and choose one of the unpaved parking spots along road. The last of these is across the road from boat launch. Park, follow footpaths down hill through woods 100 yards to beach. Locate a secluded spot—be discreet!

GUNPOWDER FALLS STATE PARK

All but 300 of the 10,000 acres of Gunpowder Falls State Park remain undeveloped. Nude use is sparse but the potential for frustrated skinny-dippers is excellent. Of note is the area on the **Big Gunpowder River** just above Prettyboy Reservoir—great swimming and tubing, with waterfalls and rocks for sunning. Local teens stake out the most accessible sites for boozing and whatnot—you should be able to locate some less-accessible seclusion with no problem.

☞ Take I-83 north 15 miles from Baltimore to MD 137 (Hereford Exit), then north 2 miles on MD 45 to the river. Or take MD 137 west 1 mile to Masemore Road (on right) and to parking area. Also of interest is Little Gunpowder Falls. Follow MD 147 10 miles northeast from Baltimore, left on Fork Road 2 miles, right on Bottom Road 2 miles to the picnic area. From this access point, scout along the trails. Little Gunpowder is too shallow for tubing or canoeing.

NORTHWEST

PEN MAR CLUB

Sixty-eight country acres with pool, volleyball, playground. Tent and RV sites, showers, community kitchen. Weekends, May–Sept. P.O. Box 276-WG, Hancock, MD 21750. Phone (717) 294-3262.

MASSACHUSETTS

Lee Baxandall. Bottom: Cape Cod Surf's Up! Top: Beach Camaraderie in the 1970s.

CAPE COD & THE ISLANDS

SOUTH CAPE BEACH & WASHBURN ISLAND STATE PARK

Two excellent getaways on the Inner Cape near Falmouth. From Boston, take Route 3 across the Ship Canal to Route 6 and turn onto Route 130 (second exit) south to Mashpee Center. Turn right and follow Route 28 to Mashpee rotary. Take second right, 28 N toward Falmouth.

For South Cape Beach in New Seabury: at intersection of Routes 28 and 151 take Great Neck Road south to the end. Left goes to the state beach. Instead, turn right to find 2 miles of beach where couples and singles enjoy the sun naturally.

Not far west of South Cape Beach, Washburn Island is located between Waquoit Bay and the Childs River. Over 2 miles of hiking trails in woods of pitch pines and summer wildflowers. Do not disrobe until you are off the beach area and into the woods. Campsites available on the Mashpee side; reserve through the Massachusetts DEM.

For Washburn Island: go as to South Cape Beach but drive farther west on Route 28, cross Childs River, take next left to Seacoast Blvd. and follow to Bayside Drive. Turn left and continue to the shoreline. Park on any street except at the community beach. From the boat launch at the community beach, launch your canoe or rubber raft and navigate the 100 feet or so to the island. Water is in the 70s throughout the summer.

☆ SANDY TERRACES

Sandy Terraces Associates owns 10 wooded acres on a spring-fed lake 15 minutes from Hyannis, an hour from the beaches of Truro and Provincetown. Volleyball, tennis, shuffleboard, lake

swimming, sauna. Tent and trailer sites; families, couples welcome. P.O. Box 98-WG, Marstons Mills, MA 02648. Phone (508) 428-9209.

CAPE COD NATIONAL SEASHORE

The National Park Service's only special regulation anywhere to ban nudity, not an offense as such under federal law, was enacted here in 1975. It doesn't deter thousands of nude bathers annually from seeking their own liberated patch of sand on the Cape. See *Clothed with the Sun* magazine, 8.1, pp. 88–91; *Nude & Natural* magazine, *N* 11.4, pp. 85–87; and *N* 13.3, pp. 89–91.

Many go to the ocean beach of **Truro,** nearly at Cape tip out Route 6, between Ballston Beach and Long Nook Beach; or for solitude, they walk north from Long Nook Beach. Parking permit available at Truro town hall. Some motels in Truro give free parking passes. **Herring Cove Beach** just outside Provincetown also has nude use, much of it gay, and can be reached by foot, bike, or paying NPS daily parking fee.

Check out Seascape Motor Inn, a fine non-naturist facility run by an avid, knowl-edgeable naturist; phone (508) 487-1225.

Cape Cod Naturists, c/o Ed and Ann Ayres, P.O. Box 216, S. Wellfleet, MA 02666; off-season: 55 Essex St., Cambridge, MA 02139; phone (617) 576-3855.

MARTHA'S VINEYARD

Gay Head Lighthouse Beach. See *Nude & Natural* magazine, *N* 11.4, pp. 87–90. Park in the lot before the lighthouse. Walk back along Moshup Trail and take the first path to right, leading down to the beach. On beach walk right 0.3 miles to secluded nude area beneath the cliffs—or walk left, about a mile, to historically nude Zack's Beach.

Chilmark: Lucy Vincent Beach. This town beach, in part zoned nude, is strictly for use of locals and guests of local lodgings. Consider reserving at the Chilmark Inn.

NANTUCKET: MIACOMET BEACH

Miacomet Beach is the "social nude beach," between Surfside (to the east) and Cisco (to west). Reach it from Surfside Beach by walking to the right (west) past the fences for the bird sanctuary and a bit farther. Coming directly from town, bicycle along Atlantic Avenue, noting signs for Surfside Beach, but soon after the high school, find bike path on the right. If you've a car, go on, look for road on right, Miacomet Avenue—do not take it, but a bit farther turn right onto a paved road. Go southerly about 1.5 miles. Miacomet Pond will appear on your right, and the road ends at the ocean. You turn left into a small dirt road along the backside of the beach dunes. There are several parking turnouts. Hike through dunes to beach. For more privacy—

Pebble Beach. On the south coast stretching from the old Navy Station to the village of Sconset. Reach it with a right off Milestone Road to Sconset, taking Tom Nevers Road to the Navy Station.

Snapshots From The Truro Nude Beach

Lee Baxandall. Golden Memories Of Cape Cod…Not Forgetting the Free Beach Celebration Of 1975 With Seashore Rangers As Hosts (Photo, Tom Chittenden).

Eel Point. On the west side, take Eel Point Road to beyond Dionis Beach, keep walking at end of road, past last beach house, to Eel Point tip.

Nantucket Harbor offers a wonderful destination for skinny-dipping, the Coatue Wildlife Refuge of low dunes on the Sound that protects Nantucket harbor. Go by sailboat or 4WD (getting a sand permit) by way of Wauwinet, or from Wauwinet by hiking.

Madequecham is a secluded coastal valley near Nantucket Airport. Get an island map (Nantucket Information Bureau, 25 Federal St.) and bike out to the end of Old South Road, and the old rutted track that continues on to shore will take you into Madequecham Valley. No beach stickers needed—but respect every "Private Beach" sign and stay out.

Phone (508) 228-0925 for room rentals and (508) 477-8600 for ferry information. Rent bicycles near the ferry wharf. (Young's at the steamship wharf is good; no need to reserve.)

EASTERN

CONTACTS

The Pilgrim Naturists and **NENA** merged in 1996. Cold-weather monthly events at a large health club, and leadership in summer activities, including whale-watch cruises.

Contact Dennis Kirkpatrick, P.O. Box 273, Boston, MA 02132. Phone (617) 624-6775; fax (617) 325-1883.

Young Urban Nude Beach Enthusiasts (YUNBE), unofficially based at Boston University, accepts members from colleges and universities in the Boston area. Activities geared to the 18- to 30-year-old crowd. Send SASE for information. P.O. Box 410411, Cambridge, MA 02141.

CENTRAL

☆ SOLAIR

Founded 1934, 350-acre member-owned Solair is 10 miles south of Sturbridge Village in Woodstock, CT. Features a private lake and wooded hiking trails, pool, snack bar, tennis, volleyball, boating and fishing, hot tub, sauna, whirlpool, dances, playground. Rental units, tent and RV sites. April to November. P.O. Box 187-WG, Southbridge, MA 01550. Phone (860) 928-9174.

WESTERN

☆ BERKSHIRE VISTA

Just over the line from New York State in Hancock, MA. Berkshire Vista Resort (formerly Renaissance Resort) is the only nudist park in the Berkshires; convenient to Pittsfield, Tanglewood, Williamstown. Grassy mountainous setting; mellow, friendly crowd. Volleyball, heated pool with bar, hot tub, sauna, tennis, DJ dances and weekend activities, restaurant and bar. Tent and 135 trailer sites w/hookups. For information: P.O. Box 1177, Hancock, MA 01237. Phone (413) 738-5154.

LITTLEVILLE LAKE

North from Granville, Littleville Lake is at the Middle Branch of the Westfield River.

Controlled by the Army Corps of Engineers, Dayville Dam created Littleville Lake. Great fishing! On the other side of the lake from this site one can launch water craft. Great sun alignment with late sunsets on the east side. Officially, there's no camping but some people have been doing it for years.

☞ At Routes 20 and 112 in Huntington, go north on 112, take the first left: "Middlefield–Skyline Trail." Go left at the fork, follow the West Branch upriver. Take the first right: Skyline Trail, to the top, taking the first right, "Littleville Fair–Little Lake." Go down hill to the valley floor of the Middle Branch. Bear right at the bottom, park, and walk straight ahead to Littleville Lake. The farther one walks, the more privacy one finds.

WEST BRANCH OF WESTFIELD RIVER

A short distance west from the Littleville Lake site is the West Branch of the Westfield River, near Chester, which has been cleaned up from 30 years of trash and neglect by partiers and now looks great! Great white water canoeing and rafting in spring when it's too cold to be nude, of course. Good fishing in summer. Large, shallow pool and good sun alignment. People often camp overnight.

☞ From Routes 20 and 112 in Huntington, go north on 112. Take the first left toward Middlefield, then left on Basket St. and follow the West Branch for 4 miles until the road bears left across a bridge. Go straight 0.6 miles, following the right side of the river. Bear left to camping and pool.

FORTY FOOT POOL & FLUME

Forty Foot Pool and Flume, Huntington, on the East Branch of the Westfield River, is located in small, well-kept C.M. Gardner State Park with a sandy beach, large sunning rocks, fireplaces, picnic tables, outhouses, even a small pavilion. Prior to Memorial Day and after Labor Day, the park is sparsely visited and the unclad as well as the clad appear—the former downriver, the clad gravitating upriver. In the spring and after heavy rains the East and West Branches of the Westfield River offer Class II and III white water rafting and canoeing—a good time to visit.

☞ From Westfield, exit 3 on I-90, the Massachusetts Turnpike, turn south on Routes 10 and 202, to US Route 20 west, which is a right turn. Go for 12 miles to Huntington. From the center of Hunting-ton, at the intersection of Routes 20 and 112, go north (right) on Route 112 for 2.4 miles. C.M. Gardner State Park is on the left.

Also nearby is a brook with several spots for cool dips above the upper Knightville Road. From the intersection with Ireland St. (with delicious Bradford Restaurant and The Academy for summer concerts), drive south on Route 112 for one mile. Two turnoffs are on the left beside the small, clear brook.

KNIGHTVILLE DAM PONDS

Knightville Dam Flood Control and Wildlife Area is a 12-mile wilderness area along the East Branch of the Westfield River. No camping is allowed but overnight parking is. Pools and sunning areas are just about anywhere one chooses to go, and wildlife abounds, including bald eagles. Nude use has been established here for over 40 years—appropriate behavior is expected, including removing your trash. Knightville lies directly below privately-owned Chesterfield Gorge; neat to look at but swimming (clothed or otherwise) is prohibited.

☞ To the main pool—from Westfield, take exit 3 on I-90, the Massachusetts Turnpike; turn right (south) on Routes 10 and 202. Go to US Route 20 west, which is a right turn. Go for 12 miles to the center of Huntington, and turn right on Route 112, north. Go for 4 miles, past the main entrance which is on the right, and continue north on 112. Cross a long, narrow bridge which is very high above the river, and go up the long hill and across a cement bridge which spans a small brook. Immediately after the bridge, take a right turn on the old access road which is marked. Go down the hill to the valley floor and turn left, which is upstream. Go about 0.8 miles upstream and park near the barricade (there is room for 50 or more cars). Cross a narrow cement bridge and walk 0.5 miles farther upstream from the main pool on the right, with prominent paths leading to it, just before the first gate.

POND BROOK FALLS

Pond Brook Falls has a goodly flow of water over tiny cataracts and into glacial potholes, even in time of drought. The water is regulated by beaver dams located upstream. Pools range from the size of a trash can up to a good-sized jacuzzi. Downstream 100 yards you'll find a spot deep enough to swim in. There are twin tubs just before the last cataract. Located near the road, but still very private; anyone walking in can be seen from most parts of the falls. Good for couples and small groups. Totally litter-free.

☞ From Westfield—exit 3 on I-90, Massachusetts Turnpike—take US Route 20 west and go 4.5 miles crossing the Russell/Westfield town line. Go another mile and take a left on Route 23 west. Go 6 miles to Blandford. From the center of town at the only flashing yellow light, go 2.4 miles on Route 23 west, to Blair Road, a marked dirt road just over the brow of a steep hill on the right. (If Blair Road is closed, park safely off Route 23 and continue on foot.) Slow down, and go 0.1 miles farther, then turn left on Hiram Blair Road. Go 3/4 mile, cross a culvert and park immediately afterward on the left. Follow the trail downstream a short distance to Pond Brook Falls.

HEAVENLY HIDEAWAY

The Heavenly Hideaway, a half-mile of tiny cataracts and pools of clear spring water, is on Goldmine Brook in the Chester-Blandford State Forest. Because the stream is diminutive it accommodates couples or at most small groups. Chester-Blandford State Forest Campground is 1/2 mile west on Route 20. Camping with permit; go to headquarters located at Boulder Park, the main entrance.

A mile beyond that is Sanderson Brook Falls, a 100-foot-high cataract thrilling to see in the spring or after a heavy rain. Intermittently, a bridge on the access road is closed. Park and walk; it's worth it, or go back on Route 20 to Route 23. Follow 23 to the center of Blandford; go right at the flashing light on North St., cross the Massachusetts Turnpike, I-90, and take the 2nd right on a sweeping left-hand bend. Follow the dirt road down to the falls. Or proceed to the next right, also dirt, and follow to the falls.

The falls are viewed by the public from a great distance; on its various levels are glacial potholes, up to 5 feet deep, that can accommodate 2 or 3 folk. Tubbing au naturel is OK; covering immediately after leaving the water is advisable. Use caution when climbing here; several have died as a result of falling down the steep faces. Above the falls, which can be reached by skilled rock climbers only by going directly up the falls or up the sides, or by going around on any of several

trails, is a 1/4-mile-long gorge with many small pools and plenty of privacy for natural swimming/sunning.

☞ From Westfield, Exit 3 on I-90, the Massachusetts Turnpike, take US Route 20 west to Huntington, a distance of approximately 12 miles. From the center of Huntington, go west 1.4 miles and pass the Chester/Huntington town line. Go 1.9 miles, past the main entrance to the Chester-Blandford State Forest on the left, and park in a small gravel turnoff on the right, immediately before Route 20 crosses a small cement bridge at milemarker 39.160. Cross the highway towards the Goldmine Brook, and follow a trail uphill that starts about 20 feet east of the bridge. At the brook, head upstream. The largest pool is the uppermost one, and the best sunning area is 100 yards farther up, where a power line crosses the brook and where the brook becomes completely subterranean for several hundred feet. This in itself is an interesting sight.

THE WHIRLIES

A short, smooth rock natural water slide with potholes and good sun on the Cold River, with long nude use. Half-mile from Mohawk Trail State Forest which has RV and tent sites.

☞ I-91 north to Greenfield, then Route 2 west. From post office in center of Charlemont, take Rt. 2 west for 4 miles. Park in turnoff on right just before cement bridge. If area is full, drive 0.2 miles farther west on Rt. 2 to either of two large dirt parking lots on the right just before the Mohawk Trail State Forest entrance. From either parking area, follow trails to the right to Cold River. The water slide is 100 yards upstream of a small brook flowing in from the west.

CUMMINGTON: WESTFIELD RIVER

Take Route 9 northwest from Northampton to the Cummington, MA town sign. Continue a little more than 1 mile. Park on the left in the large parking area. Walk to the west end of parking area and follow path down to the East Branch of the Westfield River. Cross the river and go up path through the woods until you reach the river again. All use here is nude. Mostly gays but some couples during weekend.

ELWELL STATE PARK

A small park—just 2 or 3 acres—close to the center of Northampton, MA. Trails

lead down to the Connecticut River.

☞ From the intersections of Route 9 and I-91, go 0.7 miles west of the center of Northampton, turn left (north) on Damon Road. Elwell State Park is on the right.

Naturist areas are best reached by boat. At the north (upriver) end of the parking lot is an old railroad trestle turned into a bicycle path. Put in here and paddle upriver 0.1 miles and you'll see a series of islands on the left (west) bank of the river. There are more islands upriver, all uninhabited, for naturist exploration.

GREENFIELD: GREEN RIVER

From I-91 at Greenfield, take Exit 26. On Route 2 West heading out of town, take the first right marked Colrain Road. Follow to a fork, bearing right on Plain Road. Go until Green River Road comes in on the left; proceed until the road becomes dirt, about 1.3 miles after Plain and Green River Roads merge. The road is wide and then becomes narrow, parking spots are on the right. Park and take the steep path to the pools.

This is a privately-owned site and the owner requires that you help keep it clean. Upriver are more pools.

QUABBIN RESERVOIR

Quabbin Reservoir, with easily more than 100 miles of shoreline, is 150 square miles of nothing but water, woods and rocks, including the Federated Women's Club State Forest and Petersham State Forest. There are many dozen parking spots on state highways and several MDC access roads lead to the water.

No swimming is allowed at Quabbin—if caught by MDC staff, one invites a stiff penalty. The plus side is Quabbin is virtually heaven for those enjoying nude hiking and sunning. And even if one isn't an animal lover, it's a thrill to see the ever-growing population of wild turkeys, deer, and the American Bald Eagle, for which special habitat has been created. Boats with limited-size motors are allowed on Quabbin at several launching sites, giving one access to more than a dozen islands, the largest of which is almost five miles long.

☞ Quabbin can be accessed from State Roads 202, 9, 32 or 122. Pick a road and find a spot.

Reports persist of skinny-dipping spots below the Windsor Dam on the Swift River—Quabbin's overflow and also the Belchertown/Ware line.

MICHIGAN

Jerry Derbyshire. Offshore Freedom In Michigan: Lake Huron, Eastward Of the Soo Locks.

DETROIT AREA

WHISPERING OAKS

Thirty-five miles north of Detroit; 52-acre landscaped grounds with small lake, pool, spa, sauna, game room, volleyball, shuffleboard, tennis, playground, exercise equipment, softball diamond, dance lounge. A hundred tent and RV sites w/hookups. April–October. 5864 Baldwin, Oxford, MI 48371-1014. Phone (248) 628-2676; fax (248) 628-7200.

SOUTHEAST MICHIGAN NATURISTS

House parties, trips to Turtle Lake and Mazo Beach (WI), and volleyball picnics are some activities of this fun group. Send SASE to P.O. Box 8127, Ann Arbor, MI 48107; or phone Tim Downing (313) 434-7859.

SOUTHWEST

☆ TURTLE LAKE

This year-round facility is halfway between Detroit and Chicago. Winter events are held almost weekly in the 10,000 sq. ft. clubhouse with heated pool and hot tub. Miniature golf, fishing, boating and canoeing, horseshoes, shuffleboard, volleyball (sand and mud), water slide and five playgrounds. Rental units, 200+ full hookup RV sites on 160 well-manicured acres. See *Nude & Natural* magazine, *N* 13.4 pp. 49–51; *N* 14.4 pp. 46–48; and *N* 16.4 pp. 42–44. P.O. Box 55, 2101 Nine Mile Road, Union City, MI 49094. Phone (517) 741-7004; fax (517) 741-7919.

☆ SUNSHINE GARDENS

Eight miles from Battle Creek. Welcomes couples, families and singles to its 140 rolling wooded acres. Spring-fed pond, fishing, boating, tennis, volleyball, large indoor heated pool, spa, sauna, nature trail, snack bar, game room and TV lounge. Cabins, rooms, tent and RV sites with hookups, barbecues. Handicap accessible. May to October. 21901 Collier Avenue, Battle Creek, MI 49017. Phone (616) 962-1600.

☆ FOREST HILLS

A co-op nudist camp with 45 wooded acres. Heated pool, sauna, hot tub, hiking trails, volleyball, badminton, restaurant. P.O. Box 105-WG, Saranac, MI 48881. Phone (616) 642-9526.

LAKE MICHIGAN

Michigan has 255 miles of dunes along the Lake Michigan shoreline. Despite efforts to protect the largest

system of freshwater dunes in the world, they're threatened by development. Private construction is stripping the vegetation, causing instability and erosion, disrupting century-old scenic wonders for the sake of condominiums and resorts.

SAUGATUCK DUNES

Located south of Holland—the showplace of Dutch ethnic pride in America. While in Saugatuck, Newnham Bed & Breakfast is recommended lodging.

Saugatuck Dunes State Park—an easy drive from Kalamazoo and Grand Rapids. No state park in Michigan is truly secure for nude use and this one is no exception: use discretion. Drive north from Saugatuck on the Blue Star Highway. On the north side of Blue Star, the road meets US Highway 31; just south of this, go west on 64th St., then turn left onto 138th St. to the parking area. Or just follow Saugatuck Dunes State Park signs to the parking lot. Park, take the trail to the beach, and walk 1 mile north before you get naked.

Oval Beach County Park—check on current enforcement, where both gays and heteros walk north from the public area before disrobing. Then there's private Oval Beach...

HARDY LAKE

Near Muskegon. Only a boat can bring you to the lovely west shore of Hardy Lake, the reservoir created behind the Hardy Dam on the Muskegon River. Owned by Consumers Power Co. and no development has occurred at all. Any quiet cove will serve.

LUDINGTON STATE PARK

Located on Big Sable Point, north of Ludington, this state park is halfway up the Lake Michigan coast. Much of the beach stretches along the highway. The north end is relatively quiet and is the best bet for enjoying the great outdoors in your birthday suit. Care should be taken not to offend the casual stroller, so get as far away from the main beach as possible. One drawback to the northern end is the easy access from the campground, so use caution.

If you go, ask to camp in The Pines. Then, for skinny-dipping, hike or bike out the dirt service road to the lighthouse (this 1.5-mile trek starts at The Pines). Swim and sun on the beach beyond the lighthouse; this gets you away from the casual walkers. The dunes east of the lakeside road are generally deserted and you'll find rain-filled pools among them, sometimes 200 feet long—waist-deep, and warmer than Lake Michigan.

Middle: Leonard Lujan, The Chocolate Pudding Battle. Bottom: Mark Orpen, Turtle Lake's Water Slide.

NORDHOUSE DUNES

This is a 5,000-acre area, north of Ludington State Park and south of the Lake Michigan Recreation Area. About 700 acres of open sand, 1200 acres of wooded sand dunes, 4 miles of beach on Lake Michigan—and no vehicle access. Real wilderness camping is permitted in the dunes; fancier but still primitive camping is at Lake Michigan Recreation Area. Seven miles south of Manistee on US 31. A little north of Ludington go west on Forest Trail (marked by a street sign) a few miles to the beach. Most sunbathers go at least another 1/4 mile along beach, then cut into the dunes for a private site. It's possible to walk over 2 miles without encountering other visitors. Take something to drink, it gets hot!

SLEEPING BEAR DUNES SEASHORE: OTTER CREEK

Otter Creek is sand beach with clean water and a great lake view just 22 miles west of Traverse City, the northern Michigan convention mecca. Naturists aren't bothered when no one complains. They're discreet and assist to keep the Seashore clean.

Sleeping Bear National Lakeshore is at Box 277, Empire, MI 49630. Camping is available several miles south at Platte River Campground.

☞ Empire is a village 22 miles west of Traverse City by Route 72. From Empire drive south 4 miles on Route 22 to Esch Road. Turn right, drive to beach and park; walk north (right) on beach for at least 1 mile. The walk does involve some climbing through, over, under and around a jumble of tree trunks and limbs but the high dunes of Otter Creek are well worth the work to get there.

TRAVERSE AREA NATURISTS

A nudist group in northern Michigan that enjoys beach outings and home parties. Send SASE for info. c/o Patrick Bell, 8700 W. 6 1/2 Road, Mesick, MI 49668-9347. Phone (616) 275-7979.

NORTHPORT: CAT HEAD BAY

Cat Head Bay in Leelanau County north of Traverse City has a beautiful beach and great swimming. Find the road from Northport past the airport, take the first left and park in the lot (day permit required) for the new 1200-acre state park. Walk the shortest trail to the beach (20 minutes) and then go north for privacy. Camping available at nearby Grand Traverse Lighthouse.

MICHILIMACKINAC WILDERNESS PARK

West of Mackinaw City, the breathtakingly lovely, secluded Wilderness State Park on Sturgeon Bay is worth any naturist's visit. The little-visited beach is about 10 miles long, on the southside of the Wilderness. The home-cooked Polish specialties at Leggs Inn, Cross Village, will send you to your tent tired but satisfied—or you may lodge at the inn.

☞ Exit from I-75 at Mackinaw City (Exit 338). Go north one long block to Central Avenue. Turn left (west) and follow Scenic Route 1 approximately 15 miles to the Lake Michigan shore. Or, from Carp Lake on US 31, take Gill Road (which becomes Lake Shore Drive) for 9 miles west to Lake Michigan. Park and walk to the Wilderness Park area, about 1/2 mile. The 2-mile, wide sandy beach with low dunes appears when you've walked north 1/2 mile and rounded a large point.

BEAVER ISLAND

Due west from Mackinac Island, Beaver Island is 25 miles at sea, linked by ferry service to Charlevoix on the Lower Peninsula. Airstrips available too. The southwestern third of Beaver Island, undeveloped and uninhabited, is reached by a road from St. James, the ferryport. Car and bike rentals, motels and restaurants in St. James. Bare backpackers will love the pristine isolation and wildlife.

Winter visitors might want to drive to Boyne City at the southeast end of Lake Charlevoix. Starting in 1937, Boyne City fishermen began inventing new ways to have fun while hanging their lines in the frigid waters beneath the shanty-city-on-the-ice, dubbed Smeltania. Soon *Life* magazine came around and took pictures. That cinched it: there had to be a more outrageous Smeltania each year. Nudity got mixed in centrally by the Charlevoix Buffs when the lake refused to freeze in time for the smelt festival one year. A William Underhill allegedly "danced naked in downtown Boyne City to get ice for the ice fishing festival...It is an old custom and it worked, the lake was frozen the next day." Anyway, these Michigan backcountry sportsmen have unsuspected tricks up their sleeves.

UPPER PENINSULA

In addition to the sites listed here, northern Route 28 east of Marquette (between Harvey and Shot Point on Lake Superior) and farther east along Au Train Bay offers numerous opportunities to park and walk a short distance to the water in relative privacy. There are similar sections of beach along Route 2 east of Naubinway and well west of St. Ignace. There's a small gray road (on the Michigan official state highway map) that runs east from Route 123 toward Bay Mills; here you'll find pleasant sandy beaches, protected from road view, on both sides of Naomikong Point.

HIAWATHA NATIONAL FOREST

A popular spot for the locals is along the Au Train River which flows through the Hiawatha National Forest for 4 miles between two bridges on Route H03 that are 3/4 of a mile apart by road. The river is warm, crystal clear and has a beautiful white sand bottom. Many of the banks are high enough that you are out of sight at water level. One swimming hole has a rope tied 100 feet up in a cedar tree, so you can swing and drop into the center of the river.

The bridges are on H03 just south of Au Train. Access is by canoe from the upstream bridge; and when you reach the downstream bridge, it's only a 10-minute walk back to your car. Canoes can be rented at a resort located at the first bridge. Another way to get there is by hiking an old logging trail that bisects H03 between the two bridges.

The rangers do not patrol this part of the forest and the Scandinavian miners who settled the area are tolerant of nudity—hence, no complaints, no rangers. In fact, almost all of the local resorts have large wood-fired saunas in the yards.

BIG KNOB STATE FOREST

From the Mackinac Bridge take US 2 for 50 miles west of St. Ignace. Then measure 1.5 miles west of junction of US 2 with Route 117, to Big Knob Road on left (south) side. Take it 4.5 miles to campground with 23 sites, pit toilets, sandy beach, dunes, nature trails.

PICTURED ROCKS NATIONAL LAKESHORE

Backpackers enjoy sunning nude on the rocks, and there is a sandy beach area. Multicolored sandstone cliffs, waterfalls, forest and a variety of wildlife. From 12 Mile Beach Campground walk east or west, at least a mile in either direction.

MINNESOTA

MINNEAPOLIS AREA

MINNESOTA NATURISTS

For clothing-optional information, contact Minnesota Naturists—a friendly group that enjoys regular activities. Enclose SASE with inquiries. P.O. Box 580811, Minneapolis, MN 55458.

TWIN LAKE

Also known as Sweeny Lake, Twin Lake is in suburban Golden Valley west of Minneapolis city limits. Nudity and topfreedom are common but illegal; plainclothes police do conduct heavy-handed surprise raids. All things considered, it is a lovely and appropriate site—ducks and geese, reeds, cool and spring-fed, little algae even in late summer—and if you paddle out on a raft to strip and sun, there's little the boys in blue can do.

☞ Take Highway 55 west from Minneapolis past the traffic light at Wirth Parkway. Continue on 55 another 1/2 mile to the service road exit near the motel on the right. Double back on the service road to Ottawa Avenue and park in the rear of the parking lot behind the motel. Walk north on Ottawa 1/4 block to the railroad tracks. Follow the tracks to the right for about 1 block. At this point there will be a well-used path on your left. Follow it to the lake. Or, on the service road, go past Ottawa to the first business on the next block. Park behind the building. Follow the path up the hill, past the radio tower. Across the tracks, the path will lead to the lake.

Or take Highway 55 to Indiana Avenue (off the frontage road). There is parking here. Then cross over the railroad cars that are always parked in the yard. Continue on the other side of the cars to the main railroad tracks. At the tracks, head left (west) for 1/4 mile. It's a nice amble down the train tracks, then through a woods, to the small lake. If you reach Ottawa Avenue, go back 50 yards. There is a forked path, take the left fork and walk 5 minutes to the lake. A lakeside trail leads to several coves.

AVATAN

A small rustic park of 40 acres of woods and grassy areas offering a respite to stressed Twin Cities folk. Pool, volleyball, sauna, tent and trailer sites. Box 580950, Minneapolis, MN 55458-0950.

DULUTH AREA

PARK POINT BEACH

Opposite Wisconsin Point, on a Lake Superior breakwater jutting northwest from Superior (WI), is Minnesota Point which reaches southeast into the lake from Duluth (MN).

A sandy beach is at the tip of Minnesota Point. It is isolated by a forest and reached only by an hour's walk that keeps the shore hassle-free for the dedicated hiker and sunbather. The water is never warm—try 42°F—but some days when the wind is right it's just great.

☞ Drive southeast on Duluth's Lake Avenue over the Lift Bridge and another 3.5 miles, as far as you can go, leaving your auto in the Park Point Recreation Area on Minnesota Point near the Sky Harbor Airport.

Walk across the dunes to Lake Superior and then turn right (southeast) traversing a bird sanctuary and two miles of uninterrupted sand beach. The last mile is deserted and many driftwood windbreaks are found for nude sunbathing.

On reaching the end of this beach, you can continue through the forest on a path near the lake to a concrete breakwater. By wading over rocks a brief distance you will reach a final sandy beach inside the breakwater which offers a quarter mile of weekday privacy.

LESTER RIVER WATERFALLS

The locals have made some nice soaking pools at these waterfalls. The area is flat granite, ideal for sunning, but the water is cold.

☞ The Lester River is at Duluth's eastern end. Take Superior St. east from downtown to the stop sign at 60th Avenue East. Go straight another two blocks, crossing over the Lester Avenue Bridge, looking for the Lester Park Golf Course sign on your left.

Turn left from Superior Street onto Lester River Road. Check your odometer: go exactly 1.2 miles. Look for a small car park on the left-hand side of the road. If it is full, park alongside the road but well onto the shoulder.

Walk down the gravel road from the car park until the gravel stops. Take the path to the right down to the waterfalls of the Lester River.

MISSISSIPPI

RUNNING BARE BED & BREAKFAST

Mike and Linda Piety have opened their large home on the Mississippi Gulf Coast to lodge naturists. The modern home is on one acre of land with a 16 x 32-foot in-ground pool, hot tub, and large backyard with surrounding fence. Several rooms to choose from. The Pietys offer nude boat excursions on the Sound and Gulf to the barrier islands. Nearby attractions include restaurants, shops and casinos; less than an hour from Mobile, AL, and New Orleans, LA. Contact the Pietys at 5118 Mitchell Road, Long Beach, MS 39560. Phone (601) 868-8631.

GULF COAST

GULF ISLANDS NATIONAL SEASHORE

Also see Gulf Islands listing under Florida. Ship Island is the most often visited as ferries go twice daily, June through August, from Biloxi Small Craft Harbor and from Gulfport. The National Park Service rangers throw up no obstacles to nude bathers as long as they keep away from conventional bathers, so once on Ship Island you'll head for the southeast shore—the first one there establishes the dress code. The south coast has the best surf but also a dangerous undertow. Camping is permitted, with mosquito netting suggested. If you own a boat or rent one, you can organize outings to such unvisited sites as Cat Island.

Better yet, try **Horn Island,** accessible only by boat. The island, about 20 miles south of Ocean Springs, MS, is about 12 miles wide and rangers seem more concerned with glass bottles than nudity. The northwest end of the island and very west end of the south side attract a lot of swimsuits; naturists go to the western point on the south side of the island, then travel east 1/4 to 1/2 mile down the beach. No facilities on the island; bring everything you'll need.

MISSOURI

SHOW-ME NATURISTS

Members organize trips to public land sites. Send SASE to Show-Me Naturists, 7201 N. Route E, Columbia, MO 65202.

ST. LOUIS AREA

JOHNSON'S SHUT-INS STATE PARK

Lustrously smooth rocks shaped by flowing water attract 100-plus clothed people on weekends. Be discreet; avoid weekends. On weekdays, go 1/2 mile past the clothed area to where there are sunning rocks and pools of water about 5 feet deep. The park has 52 campsites and 46 picnic sites. Ticks are prevalent in the woods, nude hiking is not recommended.

☞ From St. Louis, take Route 21 south to Glover, Lesterville, and turn right on N to entrance of park. Or take I-55 south to Route 67 south to rendezvous with Route 21, continue west past Lesterville and look for signs to the park. Park in any of several large lots. On a nice day the lots fill up by 1 p.m. so arrive early.

The trail to the Shut-Ins begins near the entrance of the main lot. Follow trail past main swimming areas to the top of the bluff; trail gets rocky as you go up. Go down bluff to river and continue until you reach the 90-degree bend in the river. Take one of the several trails on your left for about 50 yards to reach the bend of the river. Strip here or move farther down the bend for more privacy. The total hiking distance from the parking lot is 3/4 mile.

HAWN STATE PARK

In the peaceful Ozark Mountains this scenic, moderately-rugged 10-mile trail offers small creek pools to dip in. The park receives little use during the week. Most people stay in the picnic area and very few reach the last 5 miles of the trail. From St. Louis, take I-55 south to Route 32. Go west on Route 32 to Route 144 to the clearly-marked park entrance for Hawn State Park. Park in the main picnic area, where you'll find the trailhead. Once on the trail, bear right after the small wooden footbridge where you will find the river on your right. If clothed folks are here, continue hiking another 5 minutes to where the trail crosses the river and hike upstream to large pools with flat sunning rocks. If you fill out the day hike card, make sure you get back by dark;

the ranger is very picky about that.

BLACK RIVER CANUDING

Black River originates out of the Clearwater Lake reservoir, and after a few miles flows through Mark Twain National Forest to the city of Poplar Bluff and beyond. The stretch below the Clearwater Dam is little used due to a shortage of commercial canoes and poor vehicle access. You can put in just opposite the Clearwater store below the dam and enjoy canuding.

SOUTH CENTRAL

PULASKI COUNTY: GASCONADE RIVER

From I-44 at Ft. Leonard Wood, drive 6.5 miles north on Highway Y to the "State Maintenance Ends" sign and then continue another 0.5 miles to Riddle Bridge. The Gasconade is a clean, shallow river with many gravel bars. Bring lounge chairs for sunbathing, or use tubes or rented canoes to head downstream. Apparently the locals don't mind, as the beach can be easily seen from the road. Use discretion, take litter upon leaving.

Alternate access site: Take exit 150 off Highway 44 and follow signs for Highway 17. On Highway 17, go south 6 miles until you reach the town of Fairplay. A little farther south on 17 is a gravel road, Sanora Lane, which descends to the Gasconade River. Good fishing and nice, deep pools for soaking. Do not go nude until away from parking area and cover up on site of canoers that occasionally float by.

MARK TWAIN NATIONAL FOREST

Hercules Glades Wilderness, a large wilderness area near Branson, has trails several miles long. Don't expect to see others; if you do, cover up until they pass. Hiking, camping, horseback riding. Access roads into Mark Twain National Forest are off Routes 125 and 160. Three miles from the Hercules Lookout Tower is Hercules Falls, located on Long Creek. Upper Pilot Knob and the Blair Trail are two more nude use possibilities.

PARTY COVE

Party Cove at the west end of 98-mile Lake of the Ozarks attracts boat enthusiasts from Nebraska, Illinois, Indiana,

Iowa and Texas who enjoy water-skiing, parasailing, fishing and nuding. Thongs are well-accepted among the large, friendly crowd and full nudity is not uncommon. About the only restrictions are that boats cannot run louder than 85 decibels and the captain can't be drunk.

NORTHWEST

HEARTLAND COVE

Heartland Cove is about 8 miles north of Smithville, on Lake Smithville. Weekday use is best. Underwater branches and tree trunks in the cove can make swimming dangerous; use the buddy system.

Follow 169 north, turn right (east) on Route W. Continue to Route F. Turn left on Route F and then right (south) on SW King Road. Follow the gravel road to the end. Park and walk back 0.25 miles to the entrance that is marked with a stake and the letters HC alongside the leftmost gate. Cross the field to the cove.

ST. JOSEPH: WILLOW RIDGE

Sixty miles north of Kansas City, a clothing-optional picnic ground is emerging on a farm. Facilities currently include pond, picnic area, outdoor toilets, horseshoes, badminton, volleyball, 2 cabins on 50 acres. Daily fee, $6.

Write George Tunks, 2274 N.W. Mill Road, Maysville, MO 64469. Phone (816) 449-5303.

GRAND RIVER

The Grand River offers lots of secluded sandbars for camping and skinny-dipping. The river runs shallow-to-deep-to-shallow again. Canoes are necessary when traversing the waters where the Grand River and the Thompson River join. The canuding is excellent and several campgrounds exist in the Chillicothe area.

Go 3 miles west of Chillicothe on US 36 to the bridge crossing the Grand River. Park on the northwest side of the bridge, between the highway and the old abandoned railroad. Wade across river and proceed west upstream about 1,000 yards to where the rivers meet and to the sandbars.

NOTE: captions to photos run along the inside edge of pages.

MONTANA

MISSOURI RIVER CANUDING

Montana offers few amenities to a sedentary nudism, but the wild and scenic Missouri River is terrific for canuding—with towering snow-white sandstone cliffs, badlands and forests.

A good put-in spot is Coal Banks Landing, near Fort Benton, with take-out 130 miles below at Fred Robinson Bridge. A road crosses the river only once and discretion might be advised there, and at several permanent settlements. However, it's possible to canude for days and not see another party, and camping is at your whim. From mid-July through August the river is lower, slower, lukewarm and nice for swimming.

Outfitters offer canoe rentals and shuttle service. Write: Bureau of Land Management, District Office, Airport Road, Lewistown, MT 59457. Phone (406) 538-7461. BLM sells waterproof maps that explain the trip well.

NEBRASKA

OMAHA: PLATTE RIVER

Almost any portion of the slow-moving Platte River can be used for skinny-dipping. The most popular area is just outside Two Rivers State Recreation Area. The spot is accessible from June to the end of September. For at least 25 years, it has afforded hassle-free sunbathing on white sand; and in the hot Midwestern weather a cool dip in the admittedly brown Platte feels awfully good! Watch for the deep holes in the river bottom; go with friends.

☞ West from Omaha on Route 92 (Center Street and West Dodge Road) about 20 minutes. Then south at the Venice Inn, where double yellow overhead lights flash and a sign announces the Two Rivers State Recreation Area. Follow the signs, pay the fee, turn left (south) just past the entrance, and go through TRSRA to a camping area where parking is available under the shade trees. Then walk farther down a dirt road at least 1 mile southwest and onto the sandbars, outside the TRSRA, where you feel comfortable. On this private property you needn't look for the game wardens.

NEVADA

LAS VEGAS

LAKE MEAD RECREATION AREA

Sprawled out behind Hoover Dam, Lake Mead supports a wealth of recreational boating and with it much skinny-dipping and sunning. Rent a boat, pick a secluded cove, and enjoy. Road-accessed coves are limited. Also check out the Colorado River hot springs below the dam.

☞ Take I-93 for 2.3 miles past the Hoover Dam toward Kingman (AZ), look for a road leading to the left, take that 3.6 miles to a small parking area. The nude beach coves are there.

Or take I-95 north toward Utah, after passing downtown Las Vegas look for the Lake Mead Blvd. exit and turn right. (Don't confuse this with Lake Mead Drive which is south of Las Vegas.) Follow Lake Mead Blvd. across Sunrise Mountain. The road will end at a "T" intersection. Go left. After exactly 4.8 miles look for a sign "Mile 8.0 Road." Vibrate your way down this gravel road, and veer left at every fork in the road. Park in the lot overlooking the lake and head north into a little ravine and over a hill along a narrow trail, for five minutes. You will see the beach sort of segregated between males and couples. Camping permitted.

RINGBOLT (ARIZONA) HOT SPRINGS

Among the hot springs along the Colorado River, Ringbolt is one of the easiest to reach. Located above a waterfall, a ladder has been provided by the Lake Mead administration for convenient access.

☞ From Las Vegas take Route I-93 south to Boulder City and Hoover Dam. Continue to the 4-mile marker. Just past the guardrail is a parking area on the right, down a steep hill. Park and take the signed trail about 2 miles. When you reach the river, go left across a sandy area and over two ridges. A trail marker will be on top of the second ridge. Follow the water upstream a short distance to a small pool. Go through the pool until you see a steel ladder about 13 feet high. Climb the ladder and walk a few yards to the pool. The trip out takes longer than the trip in; plan your leave accordingly.

You can more easily reach Ringbolt by water. Rent an outboard-powered boat at Willow Beach Resort, off I-93 13 miles south of Hoover Dam, and go upriver. If you've already been here once on foot, you'll recognize the approach from the water. If you haven't and you miss it, continue on until you see a sign on the left bank of the river, "Caution–Rocks and Reefs Beyond This Point;" or beach your boat about 200 feet beyond the sign for another good soaking point. Yet another good site is 1/2 mile past the 1-mile river marker where three springs of interest feed into the water. One comes out of a tunnel like a steam bath, another is too hot to get into and the third is a series of springs and pools descending a canyon that includes a three-foot-deep pool inside a cave formed by massive boulders.

COLORADO RIVER: LAKE MOHAVE

Cottonwood Cove, where outboards to visit the Colorado River hot springs may be rented, has a sandy beach among small hills and trees. From Las Vegas, the turnoff eastward from US 95 is at Searchlight. Between mile posts six and seven, turn right onto Power Line Road. Just after the cemetery on the right, there is a diagonal road off to the left with a small sign for Six Mile Creek. Take this turn to the coves. Use the furthermost coves; avoid weekends.

PAHRANAGAT REFUGE

Isolated Crystal Springs make an oasis of vegetation and birds in Pahranagat Valley to delight any naturist. Tremendous flow of warm water forms a stream, flume and soaking pools, completely undeveloped. Off Highway 93 in Lincoln County, just west of the turnoff for Route 375, about 100 miles north of Las Vegas.

LAKE TAHOE

LAKE TAHOE

The California side of Lake Tahoe did have nude bathing sites; these dwindled as the Nevada side became accepted and popular.

The US Forest Service has jurisdiction from Incline Village to Cave Rock. Its rangers are unconcerned about discreet sunbathing, and they post advisory signs for an unwitting public where it occurs. But there are problems being created by officials who are eliminating parking, roadside or other, so they'll have fewer visitors to manage for. Update yourself! Contact: **Tahoe Area Naturists,** c/o North Swanson, P.O. Box 10036, Zephyr Cove, NV 89448.

SECRET HARBOR CREEK BEACH

Secret Harbor Creek Beach has been under the protection of Tahoe Area Naturists, who take great care to set standards and conserve the area. Hiking, volleyball, paddleball, frequent cookouts. The water is not as warm as Paradise Cove or Whale Beach but the friendly atmosphere and family-oriented activities make this the most popular of the beaches. See *Nude & Natural* magazine, *N* 14.1, pp. 42–44.

☞ Located on the southeast shore, access can be gained by docking at Boat Beach and hiking a few minutes south. From Spooner Summit (US 50), drive north 5 miles on Nevada 28 toward Incline Village. From this point to the junction of the dirt Forest Service Road (about 1/2 mile) you may park off the pavement on the narrow road shoulder. Caution: be sure to have all tires off the pavement or you risk a ticket and the possibility of getting towed. Also be sure to remove all valuables and lock your car before leaving.

Walk over the side and down any of the footpaths you will see. Stay on the paths to avoid erosion! The two large dead pines on Nevada 28 can be a good marker. All trails from there intersect the dirt Forest Service Road, which has a more gradual descent and is open to foot traffic only. The trails that stem off of it will lead you to a lakeside path that accesses all the beaches. Remember to take all you need as it's a long walk back; and clean up after yourself before leaving.

WHALE BEACH

Named after boulders that resemble whales nosing in to have a look. Whale Beach offers warm, shallow water for sunning on rafts or rocks. South around the bend from Secret Harbor Creek Beach, and two miles from the beginning of the Forest Service Road.

PARADISE COVE

Known also as either Secret Cove or Frankie Loves Dougie Beach (for the graffiti on a large gray boulder that used to be on the east side of the road), Paradise Cove is well hidden with shallow warm water and large rocks for sunning. It is also the closest beach to the dirt Forest Service Road (see above) and requires the least amount of walking to get there. Find the two trails on the dirt Forest Service Road that are on either side of the trash cans. Take either trail (they intersect farther on) and a short walk of 10 or 15 minutes will lead you to the stairs that descend to the beach.

CHIMNEY BEACH

Part of the same Toiyabe National Forest, Chimney Beach is undeveloped shoreline left to the state by millionaire George Whittell; it is named and marked by a remnant of Whittell's estate. The northernmost free beach on the shoreline,

Chimney Beach has been quite popular—up to 1,000 visitors on a good day—and clothing is optional. The nude area was formerly in the north end by the old chimney, but lately it has shifted to the south. Find it 2.3 miles south of the car entrance to Sand Harbor. Park along the road and follow the trail down to the beach (20-minute walk).

Another popular spot within walking distance of Chimney is the small **Black Sand Beach,** 15 minutes to the south. Large boulders for sunning; can be crowded.

SPENCER HOT SPRINGS

Near Austin, east of Lake Tahoe. A natural hot spring at an elevation of 5,700 feet, with ambient camping. Pools include natural ones as well as a metal stock tub with bench.

☞ From the intersection of US 50 and NV 376, go 100 yards on 376, then go about 6 miles southeast on a gravel road. Bear left on a dirt road which leads to the hot springs.

NEW HAMPSHIRE

SOUTHERN

CEDAR WATERS VILLAGE

Near the New Hampshire coast, with almost 400 acres of woodland and a private 20-acre lake with small beaches, Cedar Waters Village, perhaps the largest Christian nudist park, was founded 45 years ago. Miles of nature trails, sauna, hot tub, swimming, boating, windsurfing, volleyball. Sunday services, new rec hall. Tent and trailer sites with hookups, 6 rental cabins (5 on the lake). Couples and families only. 24 Smoke St., Nottingham, NH 03290; phone (603) 679-2036.

COLD RIVER POOLS

Too many heedless partiers from Keene here—please, set an example, remove trash. You may have to tolerate or convert the many clothed visitors.

☞ From I-91, north of Brattleboro (VT), take exit 5 onto US 5, and go south following signs for Walpole (NH). Cross the Connecticut River bridge and turn left (north) on Routes 12/123. When Route 123 leaves Route 12 and turns northeast at Whitcomb Construction, turn right on Route 123. Go 0.2 miles, taking the first left turn on Cold River Road, clearly marked with a steel sign. The Cold River will be parallel on your right.

Just short of 2 miles along this road is a small parking lot on the right where the clothed gather. For the next 3/4 mile find turnoffs on the right. Take path along the field to the river. Upriver in the deeper part of the gorge, are private opportunities for natural recreation.

FIELDS BROOK WATERFALLS

On the east side of Lake Winnipesaukee near the Ossipee Ski Area, Fields Brook Waterfalls has cold, clear and drinkable water, and several very nice campsites. No one knows who owns the property but there are no signs barring its use.

Take Route 109A north from Wolfeboro, to Tuftonboro. Turn left on 171 and follow it 3.5 miles to the brook crossing. Go over the brook and park. The trail begins here. (If you reach a junction on the left, you've passed the turnoff.) Walk about 1/4 mile to the first and deepest pool. More falls and pools are located upstream.

WHITE MOUNTAIN NATIONAL FOREST

Fully 12 percent of the "Live Free or Die" state is federal land. Splendid sites are available for discreet skinny-dipping—with emphasis increasingly put on caution.

Federal law includes no general prohibition of nudity, and a temporary USFS order banning nudity in the Northeastern region federal forests, from Wisconsin to New England, was lifted in 1994. Cooperation of naturists with the rangers to avoid offending clothes-compulsive visitors can preserve the more secluded sites, and forestall another closure.

The Kankamagus Highway is fine for access to the White Mountains; and the Pemigewasset River, north of it, for discreet nude adventure.

Pemigewasset River. Hike the Wilderness Trail, an old lumber route, to where it follows the river. Skinny-dipping is perhaps 10 minutes from the highway,

and a great site is only a mile's walk (20 minutes), at a bend of the river which has large flat rocks and a sandbar for sunning amid the chilly waters. A bit beyond, there's a natural flume, or slide.

Sawyer Pond. Route 302 brings you to the Sawyer River, which puddles into a number of pools that are preferred for skinny-dipping and sunning. Park at the first wide parking area you reach at the river, and walk a mile up the dirt road to where the river forms a deep pool. If swimsuits prevail here for the day, just go upstream. A half mile up is a former logging settlement. You'll reach a waterfall, and at the road's end a trail leading to Sawyer Pond. It's 1 1/2 hours in all to the six-site campground.

Naturists interested in joining an in-state group can send a self-addressed stamped envelope to **Naturists New Hampshire,** 20 Canal Street, Franklin, NH 03235.

NORTHERN

GEORGIANA FALLS

Hardly known even to local people, and yet in the White Mountain National Forest and Lincoln township. Not on the Wilderness Trail or the usual hiking maps, so skinny-dipping may have a long existence here. The access is unmarked, so if you like company bring your own. Georgiana Falls is a 1 1/4 mile walk off Route 16 at the southern end of the Franconia Notch: A series of cascades dropping into pools and falling over ledges a vertical distance of about 350 feet. Water supply is steady, coming from a pond, and quite cold. The best pools are near the top of the falls, as are the best sunning rocks.

☞ Drive north on I-93 and exit at the (temporary) end of the highway, joining US 3 northbound. In less than a mile Hanson Farm Road (hard to spot) turns off to the left opposite the Longhorn Restaurant. (Just beyond the restaurant is a Chamber of Commerce information booth—if you reach it, you've gone 75 yards too far. Fantasy Farm on the left is also beyond the turn.) Go 50 yards down Hanson Farm Road and park at its end; don't block driveways. Ford the stream (or cross the bridge, if the owner looks benign) and head across the field on a

logging road. At far end of the clearing, before reaching another stream, take a sharp right onto another logging road that enters the woods. This road follows the second stream, Harvard Brook, for a half mile, ending in a clearing. A footpath continues upstream to the falls. The walk along this rushing mountain stream is attractive and litter-free.

GORDON POND

Choose this for a premiere, all-day experience. The Gordon Pond Trail is 4.5 miles, requires 3 hours and is Class 1. Find it off

Route 112, 1/7 mile west of North Woodstock. It shortly bears right on an abandoned railroad track, crossing and then recrossing a power line swath. Soon the trail switches to the north bank of Gordon Pond Brook and parallels the brook at a gentle grade. At the head of the valley the trail crosses the brook again, just above the beautiful Gordon Falls, and in a short time reaches Gordon Pond.

NEW JERSEY

NORTH JERSEY COAST

GATEWAY NATIONAL RECREATION AREA: SANDY HOOK

Gunnison Beach on Sandy Hook is now the principal nude beach for the Middle Atlantic states. The National Park Service provides lifeguards, security, maintenance, advisory signs. See *Nude & Natural* magazine, *N* 10.3, pp. 43–45; *N* 11.4, front and p. 5; *N* 13.1, pp. 6–7.

Thousands attend Sandy Hook on a warm, sunny weekend. Often one can't get on any beach after 11 a.m. on nice summer weekends, so plan to arrive early.

☞ Take the Garden State Parkway to exit 117, which is plainly marked, then Route 36 east following signs to Sandy Hook (about 12 miles). At Sandy Hook follow signs to North Beach until you come to the Old Gun Battery on the right (about 5 miles past the park entrance). Follow the main road to just beyond parking lot L where the road forks; take the right-hand fork to Gunnison Beach, past the pedestrian crosswalk and park in lot G on your left. Follow the boardwalk past the gun battery to the beach. Head south (turn right as you face the ocean) along the beach for about 1/4 mile to the nude area.

From the south: take I-95 east from Washington, DC and Baltimore into the state of Delaware. Approaching Wilmington, DE, follow signs for NY, via the NJ Turnpike. Go north on the Turnpike to Exit 7A. From Exit 7A, go east on I-95 until it becomes Route 38 (at the Garden State Parkway Interchange). Do not enter the G.S. Parkway, but continue east on Route 38 for another 3 miles, until you see the entrance to

Route 18 North. Follow Route 18 about 8 miles north to the Route 36 East exit. Do not go north to Exit 117, which is past the exits for Sandy Hook, at the northern end of Route 36. Go east on Route 36 to Long Branch, NJ. Entering the town of Long Branch, you will pass a sign to the Little Silver railroad station, then you will pass the Long Branch McIntosh Inn. Route 36 continues all the way to the seafront, where it makes a sharp left turn and follows the coast due north to the clearly-marked entrance to Sandy Hook.

NORTHERN

SKY FARM

Operated continuously since 1932, Sky Farm is North America's first nudist park. Co-operatively owned. See its history in *Nude & Natural* magazine, *N* 12.4, pp. 75–88; *N* 13.1, pp. 19–23. Heated pool, jacuzzi, spa, sauna, sun lawn on a brook amid wooded hills with members' cabins; volleyball, shuffleboard, clubhouse. Prospective members allowed three trial visits. West of Newark. P.O. Box 17, Basking Ridge, NJ 07920. Phone (908) 647-2310.

☆ ROCK LODGE CLUB

An hour from New York City, with 100 wooded acres and a 5-acre private lake, a sandy beach, hiking trails, sunning and picnic lawns. Tennis, volleyball, fishing and boating, sauna, hot tub. Rental cabins and rooms. Day visitors welcome. P.O. Box 86-LB, Stockholm, NJ 07460; phone (973) 697-9721.

☆ GOODLAND COUNTRY CLUB

Sunning lawn, woods and creek, large pool, 2 whirlpools, 2 saunas. Volleyball,

badminton, shuffleboard, tennis. Cabins, tent and RV sites available. Families, couples and singles welcome. Delaware Water Gap, Waterloo Village, state parks nearby. P.O. Box 575-WG, Hackettstown, NJ 07840. Phone (908) 850-1300.

DELAWARE RIVER GAP NATIONAL RECREATION AREA

Delaware River Islands. A 300-acre haven in the Delaware River is Minisink Island,

a canuder's delight you can moreover hike to on the Jersey side. Take NJ 206 to the Delaware Toll Bridge, joining Milford, PA and Montague, NJ. From where NJ 206 intersects with NJ 521, take NJ 521 south 1.95 miles, find mile-marker 39, park and hike over to the river. Or contact the **Paddling Bares,** a naturist canoe club familiar with water routes as well as the rangers: P.O. Box 22, Milltown, NJ 08850; phone (908) 432-9109.

Kittatinny Campground is north of Milford and many state parks and other attractions are in the area.

Crater Lake. Although it's reverting to wilderness status, an inhibited home owner remains in this lightly-visited park, and other, easily-startled types might appear at any time. Do use a secluded area. From NJ 94 at the Fredon Township School, about 3.5 miles south of Newton, take the county road west and follow signs to "Fairview Lake–YMCA." At Fairview Lake continue another mile, and turn right onto a dirt road near the top of the mountain. Go 2.2 miles to the end of the road, park, and walk right to privacy.

SOUTH JERSEY

HIGBEE BEACH

This established if unofficial nude beach has had parking problems imposed, and use is problematic. Parking is only at Sunset Beach, at the Cape May point where the sunken concrete ship is found. Park, walk straight out to the beach; go right and down the beach, to past the stakes in the water, for the nude area. Do not go into the dunes for any reason. Before going, phone (609) 794-3423.

☞ These are the directions to the parking closest to Higbee Beach— which currently is closed from Memorial Day to Labor Day! At the end of the Garden State Parkway, follow signs to the ferry. At the second light, make a left, go over the Inland Waterway bridge. Make a right at the end of the bridge, follow this road out to the end and park.

Alternate parking is 0.8 miles down the road at Hidden Valley. The lot holds 30 cars; many will drop their buddies off at the closed lots, park at Hidden Valley and

walk back to the beach.

Or park at Sunset Beach at the end of Sunset Blvd. Walk 0.5 miles through the hot and wet sand from Sunset to Higbee's.

NORTHERN

TRI-STATE INFORMATION

Tri-State Metro Naturists—New Jersey, New York, Pennsylvania—is your best regional source of information and activities. P.O. Box 1317-WG, FDR Station, New York, NY 10150-1317. Phone (215) 741-0270.

Mike Gesner's similarly-named **Tri-State Sun Club** sends information on its regionwide events. P.O. Box 532-WG, Broadway, NJ 08808. Phone (908) 689-4911.

NOTE: captions to photos run along the inside edge of pages.

NEW MEXICO

HOT SPRINGS

Ask for free *New Mexico Vacation Guide* (1997), Dept. of Tourism, P.O. Box 2003, Santa Fe, NM 87503; phone 1-800-545-2040.

Most New Mexico hot springs "have no clothing requirements, though some require bathing suits," confirms the official *Vacation Guide.*

Singled out for "clothes-optional" status are the Battleship Rock and McCauley Hot Springs, Spence Hot Springs and the Jémez Springs Bath House, p. 33. The Faywood Hot Spring, Lightfeather Hot Spring and San Francisco Hot Spring, p. 108. Black Rock and Stagecoach Hot Springs, p. 122.

Please be courteous with first-time soakers who may not know that nudity is traditional at natural springs. You may inform them of the state's advice.

CENTRAL

NUDE & NATURAL

Newest state group, Nude & Natural of New Mexico. Activities include camping trips to hot springs and a health spa, backyard parties. 1327 Barelas Road, S.W., Albuquerque, NM 87102.

ALBUQUERQUE: RIO GRANDE RIVER

Nudity is often found at the Rio Grande River, for instance at North Beach, great for sunning and wading (the water depth ranges from 6 feet in spring to 6 inches in the late summer). Located 2.5 miles north of the Corrales Bridge.

☞ Take Alameda Exit on I-25 North and go west until you get to the river. Just before you go over the Barralas Bridge, there is a gate to the right for Rio Grande Recreational Area. Make a loose right through the gate, go down the hill, and follow the dirt road for about 100 yards to the parking area. Walk at least 1/4 mile north before stripping down.

JÉMEZ SPRINGS

Jémez Springs Bath House has clothing-optional segregated bathhouses and outdoor clothing-optional hot tub. P.O. Box 112-062, State Highway 4, Jémez Springs, NM 87025; phone (505) 829-3303.

SANTA FE NATIONAL FOREST

Spence Hot Springs—on the southwest slope of Valle Grande, one of the world's largest volcanic craters. The 106°F pools accommodate 15 people maximum.

USFS here first set precedent of a clothes-optional policy in the early 1970s. See history in *Nude & Natural* magazine, *N* 14.1, pp. 38–39.

☞ From Route 44 in San Ysidro, take Route 4 north 17.5 miles to Jémez Springs. Go 6.8 miles to large turnoff on right, 2 miles after Battleship Rock. Follow trail to river, then up opposite bank to several pools and two hot showers. Another much more private spring is located 50 yards uphill and slightly left.

McCauley Hot Spring—close by Spence Springs, more isolated and larger (30- to 40-foot diameter), with an average temperature of 88°F that is more apt for summer soaking.

☞ Either (a) find Battleship Rock Picnic Grounds on Route 4, a couple of miles below Spence Hot Springs; hike a trail along the stream for five minutes or so, then take trail 137 up the hillside for 1/2 hour to the springs. Or (b) take a much more clearly-defined access: drive over a rough 2-mile road from Route 4 to Jémez Falls Picnic Area. From there, a 2.5-mile trail will get you to the hot spring in about 40 minutes.

SAN ANTONIO HOT SPRINGS

Among the state's nicest. Take Route 126 toward Cuba from La Cueva. Go about

1/4 mile past San Antonio Campground to Forest Service Road 132 on the right. A beautiful 3-mile clothing-optional walk through the woods begins where the forest road leaves the pavement and leads to the hot springs. Unable to walk far? Park about 300 yards from the springs on Forest Service Road 376 (dirt). No Trespassing signs posted; possible $50 fine if enforced.

NORTH CENTRAL

TEN THOUSAND WAVES

Don't miss it! Much like the great hot spring resorts of Japan, Ten Thousand Waves offers hot tubs, saunas, massage, acupuncture, yoga and facials; just 3.5 miles from downtown Santa Fe. Kimonos, towels and sandals are provided but the facility is largely clothing-optional. Light food, pastries, mineral water, juices available in lobby. P.O. Box 10103, Santa Fe, NM 87504; phone (505) 982-9304.

ROADRUNNER NATURISTS

Monthly activities include home parties and traveling to hot springs. P.O. Box 956, Los Alamos, NM 87544.

TAOS: BLACK ROCK WARM SPRING

Black Rock Warm Spring—a.k.a. Arroyo Hondo Warm Spring. The 10-foot diameter unimproved pool has a sandy bottom and 97°F waters. Since the spring is adjacent to the Rio Grande it doesn't maintain its temperature when the river is high. You can watch the river rafters go by. Rio Grande National State Park, phone (505) 344-7240.

☞ Drive north on Route 3 from Taos for about 15 miles. After passing a sign for the village of Arroyo Hondo, take the second dirt turnoff to the left (west) over a small bridge and follow it for a little over a mile, take a right at a crossroad and go another mile. Its terminus is a gravel road going both right and left. To the left is the fishing and camping area, but soakers take a right and follow this for 1.1 miles to the Rio Grande Gorge. Coming up the far (west) side of Rio Grande Gorge, find the small parking area at the end of the first switchback mounting the west face. The trail starts in the parking area and leads to the south-

west for 1/4 mile.

Stagecoach Hot Springs—named for the old ruts that lead to it, this spring has two unimproved pools which hold 5 to 6 people each; 90°F water. Same route as for Black Rock Hot Spring, but instead of turning right at the gravel road, take the left to southwest for 2.3 miles to pools on the east side of the Colorado River Gorge in the ruins of the old Sante Fe stagecoach buildings.

SOUTHWEST

GILA NATIONAL FOREST

Lightfeather Hot Springs is a half-mile hike north from the Gila Visitors Center on the Middle Fork of the Gila River—north in turn on Route 15 from Silver City. The spring flows into Lightfeather at 150°F and cools moving to the outflow, so pick your ideal spot by its poaching temperature. A nice treat after visiting the Gila Cliff Dwellings National Monument!

Meadows Hot Spring—another 9 miles hiking up the Middle Fork. First get a wilderness permit at the Visitors Center. The trail fords the river, so neither hot spring is accessible in the rainy season.

Turkey Creek Hot Springs. After the trail leaves Turkey Creek at Skeleton Canyon to climb the ridge, follow the creek upstream. Expect thirst and exhaustion as you rock hop and wade for a half mile, where the water becomes noticeably warm. Continue upstream around several bends and minor obstacles until you reach a huge rock overhang with a dry sand floor where overnight camping is possible. Nearby hot pool (90°F to 97°F) is perfect for soaking or go below the hot pool where the creek turns into a water slide.

Bubbles Hot Springs (120°F), has a large sand-bottom pool. Additional hot springs are located downstream. Drive northwest for 50 miles from Silver City on Route 180, about 3 miles before Pleasanton and cross a bridge over S. Dugway Canyon. Go 1.4 miles farther and, just before a curve in the highway to the right, turn left onto a gravel road marked #519. Go 3 miles to San Francisco Hot Springs (privately owned). From there, continue one mile to Bubbles. A local realtor is waging a media campaign of lies to rid this federal site of "low-rent hippies" but she's way out of line! The state tourism bureau validates nude use.

FAYWOOD HOT SPRING

This 110°F privately-owned hot spring has a long history of providing clothing-optional areas. Three separate soaking pools, each a different temperature. Water and electric RV hookups, tent sites. Interesting features are the many mortar holes for grinding grain, made by nomadic hunter-gatherers. Artifacts found around the spring indicate this was an important center of activity.

Located between Deming and Silver City, just off US 180 on Route 61; City of Rocks State Park is next down the road. Faywood Hot Spring, HC 71, Box 1240, Faywood, NM 88034; phone (505) 536-9663.

TRUTH OR CONSEQUENCES

T-or-C (the local name)—created long ago for tourists and snowbirds—perches on an artesian hot well field alongside the Rio Grande, with lots of Mexican restaurants.

Riverbend Hot Springs Resort Hostel is the first new establishment in 50 years, and the first with artesian out-of-doors thermal tubs. Three are stepped in a deck with a capacity of 18; mountain/ river view; more are planned. Phone ahead to Silvia to reserve for group nude use: 10 a.m.–5 p.m. or late evenings only, $5/hour/person.

Riverbend Hostel overnight guests, if clad, soak free 8–10 a.m. or 6–9 p.m. Choose shared bunk houses, private rooms, or the tethered houseboat. A block off main street at 100 Austin Ave., Truth or Consequences, NM 87901; phone (505) 894-6183.

The older bathhouses have small indoor tubs only. The **Marshall Bathhouse** has hottest thermal flow.

Artesian Bathhouse and RV Park has six small tubs and six 2-to-6-person tubs, powerful 107°F flow, low rates, massage available, warmhearted manager. 312 Marr St.; phone (505) 894-2684.

Indian Springs, offers 10 x 10 sunken pool, high rate of flow, 105°F water in a small room; $5/person/hour but use may be limited as it is very popular with locals. 218 Austin Ave.; phone (505) 894-2018.

Charles Motel & Bathhouse with sauna and massage; 601 Broadway; phone (505) 894-7154.

NEW YORK

Jack Falat. Dune Crossing To a Nude Beach, Fire Island National Seashore.

The history and status of New York State nudity law is told in *Nude & Natural* magazine, N 11.3, pp. 43–66; N 11.4, pp. 53–55; N 12.2, pp. 32–44.

New York's Exposure of a Person law prohibits genital nudity in public places; yet there are such places, described here, where toler-ance is the rule. The state Court of Appeals moreover, in response to a carefully prepared and pursued test case, declared women's pari-ty with males in the right to be topfree, in 1992.

NEW YORK CITY

TRI-STATE CONTACT
Tri-State Metro Naturists—New Jersey, New York, Pennsylvania—is your best regional source of information and activi-ties. P.O. Box 1317-WG, FDR Station, New York, NY 10150-1317. Phone (215) 741-0270.

Mike Gesner's similarly-named **Tri-State Sun Club** sends information on its regionwide events. P.O. Box 532-WG, Broadway, NJ 08808. Phone (908) 689-4911.

SKINNYDIPPERS
The Skinnydippers is Peter Kacalanos. 51-04 39th Ave., Woodside, NY 11377-3145. Phone (718) 651-4689; fax 424-1883.

STATEN ISLAND
This 1840s farmhouse B&B on Staten

Island offers the quiet seclusion of tall trees, evergreen hedges and lilac bushes for local and visiting naturists. The yard is perfect for sunning. Coming by air, train, bus? Your transportation may be met. Venturing into the Big Apple? Your hosts can provide information on what to do, where to go and how to get there. White Pickets, 67 Brewster St., Stapleton, NY 10304; phone (718) 727-9398.

LONG ISLAND

JONES BEACH

A very popular beach for those with autos. In the dunes of the Tobay Beach area a mile to the east of Lot 9, sun worshipers have long congregated. It's a very sociable group, with the clothed and the nude, the gays and straights, mixing easily.

☞ Take any freeway from New York City out to Long Island. Turn off going south on Meadowbrook Parkway and follow it to Jones Beach. Park in Field 6 near the east bathhouse. Walk east along the beach about 30 minutes. Since Field 6 may be filled by 8 a.m. on weekends, consider using Field 5. In this case, drop passengers and equipment along the beach road between the light poles marked 248 and 260, drive to Field 5, and walk the 3 miles back.

The beach is also accessible by public transportation; Long Island Railroad to Freeport, then bus to the beach from the station. From the beach, walk east, past the obelisk and Field 6 (last stop for refreshments) for about 20 minutes, passing the old Field 9 and a bird sanctuary, until you see other naturists.

FIRE ISLAND

A low-slung barrier reef 32 miles long and 900 yards to less than 200 yards wide. Fire Island is reached from the southern coast of Long Island. For those who choose to visit the several sections where nudity is not uncommon, it offers an exciting experience of wind, surf, sky and one's own natural being. The Fire Island National Seashore rangers are responsible for preserving the dunes and vegetation, and they are generally of assistance to the nude as well as the garmented visitor.

You may drive to Smith Point and to Lighthouse Beach only. To reach the other destinations, you must take a ferry or perhaps a private boat or seaplane; no roads serve most of Fire Island. Most people go by the Long Island Railroad, phone (718) 217-5477, from New York City, connecting by taxi to the correct ferry. Taxis meet the train.

FIRE ISLAND LIGHTHOUSE BEACH

An attractive nude sunbathing site, which former U.S. Interior Secretary Manuel Lujan viewed and pronounced a "no problem nude beach." Still, there were some problems, resolved in 1995 by NAC and Friends of Lighthouse Beach, P.O. Box 571, Babylon, NY 11702.

No facilities or lifeguards. Please respect the efforts of naturists to avoid life-style conflicts.

☞ Drive east on Long Island by Southern State Parkway, Sunrise Highway, or Montauk Highway. At West Islip turn right (south) on Sagtikos State Highway and Robert Moses Causeway to Robert Moses State Park. Drive left (east) and park in Field 5. Hike east 1/2 hour to Lighthouse Beach and 200 yards beyond, to be out of sight of casual tourists at the restored landmark. Avoid Kismet residences to the east. Memorial Day to Labor Day.

You can also take the Long Island Railroad to Bay Shore, then taxi to the Kismet ferry, and on Fire Island walk a short distance west. Or take the LIRR to the Babylon Station and then take a bus straight to the beach. The bus will stop at Field 3. It's a long walk east—pass Fields 4 and 5 and begin the hike as stated above.

New York

WATCH HILL

For access, see Davis Park. The Watch Hill attraction is the beach—and a visitor center and campground where you must reserve. Four-night limit. Phone (516) 597-6633 for family camping or (516) 289-4810 for group camping. Showers, picnic tables, snack bar, groceries and ice. From Watch Hill it's a seven-mile wild beach east to Smith Point Park, much of it hikable *au naturel*.

DAVIS PARK

Couples, singles, and families enjoy the clothes-optional beach to the west of Davis Park. The curious clothed may wander over to check the scene, but they're harmless and some stay to join. Food and drink pavilion at the ferry arrival point.

☞ Ferries from Patchogue run to both Davis Park and Watch Hill. Take the Southern State Parkway to exit 44 east; follow the Sunrise Highway east for 9 1/2 miles to South Ocean Avenue in Patchogue. Take a right onto South Ocean for 2 miles to Maiden Lane. A right again onto Maiden Lane (it jogs into Brightwood Street) will bring you to the ferries. Davis Park and Watch Hill schedule: phone (516) 475-1665.

POINT O'WOODS

East of Point O'Woods, clothed and unclad bathers generally coexist amiably. If you experience difficulties, hike farther east past Sunken Forest and Sailors Haven to Cherry Grove. Road connection and ferry schedule from Bay Shore to Ocean Bay Park.

CHERRY GROVE & FIRE ISLAND PINES

These twin communities—favorite celebrity havens—are known for the most extravagant personalities on Fire Island. Clothes-optionality was pioneered here. Many summer visitors rent cottages together, forming a stable and strong-minded community that sets, for National Park Service purposes, "the community standard" of dress (or undress) code. Gay is prevalent with heterosexual concentration on the beach west of Cherry Grove or east of the Pines.

☞ Ferry service is from Sayville. Schedule: for Fire Island Pines (516) 589-0810; Cherry Grove (516) 589-3622.

To get to ferries: from the Grand Central Parkway, take Meadow Parkway South, exit the Meadowbrook at M6 (Southern State Parkway East) Eastern

LI. Pass through exits 48, 41 bear right to Eastern LI. Take Exit 44E-Route 27 East, Eastern LI. Follow Route 27 about 5–6 miles to Lakeland Ave.-Sayville (you'll see traffic lights & sign). Make right and take this into the town of Sayville. At traffic light past the railroad tracks, continue 3 blocks until road ends. Go left to Foster Ave. and turn right. Go 2 or 3 more blocks until you see sign for Fire Island Ferries. Make left, then next right and enter parking lot of your choice.

SMITH POINT COUNTY PARK

This remains a delightful haven because nude recreation—accepted alike by federal rangers and Suffolk County deputies—begins 1 mile west by foot from the parking and concession stand. A red post at the dune line is the apparent demarcation. The beach is then wild for 6 miles west to Watch Hill, and with some tact may be hiked nude. Gawkers usually lack fortitude to hike in.

☞ Take the Southern State Parkway to exit 44 east; follow the Sunrise Highway east for over 17 miles to the William Floyd Parkway (Route 46) in Shirley. Go right on William Floyd Parkway 5 miles across the bridge over Narrow Bay to the Smith Point parking lot. Park in the west end and follow the boardwalk west. Distance from Manhattan: 74 miles and worth it, with no ferries to hassle. Information: phone (516) 597-6455.

SOUTHERN

WEST POINT: BLACK ROCK FOREST

Black Rock Forest is a 3,600-acre, Harvard-owned, experimental area just west of the West Point Military Reservation, with a maze of lightly-used hiking trails and 8 wilderness lakes. Swimming is allowed only at Sutherland Pond. Skinny-dipping should be done from the rocks to the right of the main swimming area, separated from it by trees and bushes. The other lakes are reservoirs and are attractive and more private locations for picnicking and sunbathing. Hiking should not be done without a trail map, which can be obtained from Walking News, Box 352, New York, NY 10013.

☞ Sutherland Pond is about a mile from the nearest trailhead, but this mile includes an initial steep climb. This trailhead is reached by going east from Route 32 in Mountainville on Angola

Road and then south on Mine Hill Road to a parking area at the trailhead. Another access is from Route 9W several miles south of Cornwall-On-Hudson. Here you can turn onto a dirt road at the sign for Black Rock Forest and drive to a small parking area by the gate at the Upper Reservoir. From here you can take longer and more interesting hikes to Sutherland Pond.

MINNEWASKA: MOHONK PRESERVE

The privately-operated 5,400-acre land stewardship in 1995 posted the entry to Coxing Kill stream and the Split Rock upper area as "no nudity" while permitting it 10 minutes downstream. Any sexual activity will be prosecuted.

☞ Drive west from New Paltz on Route 299, then turn right on Route 44/55 for about three miles in the direction of Kerhonkson. Exit right on Trapps Road from 44/55 (if you reach Minnewaska State Park, you've gone too far). At the "Y" bear left, this is Clove Road; continue 3 miles to a parking lot on the right, visible about 75 yards from the road. Parking has a fee and the lot fills up fast so arrive early. Hike downstream on the right bank for several hundred yards until you reach a wide area of the flat rock streambed, below Split Rock, which is now posted with signs permitting nudity.

MINNEWASKA STATE PARK

Acquired by the State of New York in 1987 were 1200 acres of woodland surrounding Lake Minnewaska, combining for a 17,000-plus acreage now forming Minnewaska State Park. The NYS Office of Parks, Recreation, and Historic Preservation (OPRHP), administrators of the Minnewaska park through their staff at Bear Mountain Park, have never appeared permissive. Fitfully the rangers have interfered with nude bathing along the Peterskill stream running through state property. Generally the ranger will move on if presented with a show of compliance, followed by absence. Money is very short, so enforcement is generally an early-season show of authority, followed by absence.

Nude swimming is a tradition in the runoff falls and streams of Lake Minnewaska—a lovely spot on top of the mountain—and skinny-dipping and sunning in this beautiful woodland continue to flourish.

☞ The prime dipping spot is reached by driving west from New Paltz on Route 299, then turning right onto Route 44/55 and up into the mountains in the direction of Kerhonkson. Route 44/55 essentially splits the mountain in two, creating an uphill section and a downhill section. Downhill are Lower Falls; uphill lie Minnewaska and Peterskill parks.

Minnewaska and Peterskill parks are the sites upstream. Plenty of nice pools with sunning rocks. Reached by staying on 44/55 to 0.2 miles past the main entrance to Minnewaska State Park, to a smaller state park sign and entry gate to a larger parking lot (fee may be charged). Walk south past the gate for 15 minutes on a shale road. Find a footpath down to the Peterskill Stream on the east side of the road and stake your claim to the site you like best.

For more information on Mohonk Preserve and Minnewaska State Park, see *N* 15.4 pp. 58–60.

CENTRAL

☆ FULL-TAN SUN CLUB

Campground located 16 miles from Amsterdam and 3 miles from Canajoharie, in the heart of the beautiful Mohawk Valley. Fishing pond, small inground pool, sauna, large clubhouse. Volleyball, sunning lawn, hiking. Tent and trailer sites; reservations required. Route 1, Box 34, Sprakers, NY 12166; phone (518) 673-2886.

☆ HUDSON VALLEY

Clothing-optional campground 25 miles south of Albany. Two ponds, pavilion, bathhouse; additional facilities are planned. Tent/RV sites. P.O. Box 1, Athens, NY 12015; phone (518) 945-1399 or (908) 689-4911.

WHITE CREEK

Northwest of Bennington, VT, White Creek has a long history of nude use, according to locals. The site accommodates up to 10 cars. The creek is cool, litter-free and quiet.

From the intersection of Routes 22 and 372 in Cambridge, NY, go south on 22 for 0.6 miles, passing the grammar school on the right, then Richardson's used car dealer/repair shop. Take the second right, White Creek Road, a near 180-degree turn. Drive 0.3 miles to just before or just after the tracks and park so as not to block the dead-end road (which shows as a through road even on good maps), since the farmer who plants crops IN the road a short distance past the tracks occasionally needs access. The last house on the left before the tracks is occupied by friendly folks who'll let you park near them if you stop, ask, and tell them you'd like to go "hiking along the creek." Follow the old Delaware and Hudson R.R. tracks to the right, north, for a 7- to 10-minute walk to where White Creek passes under the tracks. Climb down the abutment on the left side before crossing the creek.

WESTERN

☆ EMPIRE HAVEN

Heated pool, spa, sauna, restaurant, volleyball, tennis, congenial atmosphere, mountain air and scenic setting. Empire Haven's 97 acres in the Finger Lakes near Cortland make a base for area day trips. Rooms, tent/RV sites. May–Sept. RD 3, Box 297, Sun Lane, Moravia, NY 13118; phone (315) 497-0135.

BUCKRIDGE

Located in the Finger Lakes Region, Buckridge offers a snack bar, wooded campground, lake swimming and fishing, hiking trails. RV and tent sites. 215 Tuttle Hill Road, Candor, NY 13743.

ITHACA: POTTER'S FALLS

Ithaca is a liberal college town and there are many creeks, waterfalls, gorges, and small ponds near Ithaca that can be used nude. Potter's Falls is a high waterfall and pond at the bottom of Six Mile Creek near Ithaca, regularly used by naturists. Strong swimmers can swim underneath the falls and there are large flat rocks for sunning. The gorge at the top of the falls is fun to explore.

☞ From Ithaca take Route 79 out State Street southeast. Shortly beyond the intersection of Pine Tree Road, watch for a gate with a sign stating "Watershed, City of Ithaca, No Visitors." Park on the edge of the road and walk past the gate down the service road until you reach the dam at the end of the reservoir. Turn right just before the dam and walk on the path about 7 minutes to reach Potter's Falls.

WESTFIELD: CHAUTAUQUA GORGE

Local residents posted a 2-mile stretch of the gorge for clothes-optional use. Skinny Dip Falls is especially popular with young hikers and campers. Weekends are best. The local Chautauqua Institute has many cultural events and there is a spiritualist center at Lily Dale Assembly in Cassadaga.

☞ From Buffalo, follow I-90 south to Westfield (Exit 60). Follow Route 394 a short distance south to the center of Westfield and turn right onto Route 20. After crossing a bridge, turn left on Chestnut Street (after Welches Street) and follow it uphill (away from Lake Erie) for 3.4 miles to Ogden Road. Turn left on Ogden and go 1.5 miles to a dirt road marked only by a snowmobile trail sign. Turn left on it, go 0.6 miles to the end and park off-road or in the parking area at the top of the trail. Although the trail is rough in places, with a 4WD one can drive down to the stream. For those on foot, take the trail that leads down to the streambed, then follow the gorge downstream 1 mile for the best spot, Skinny Dip Falls.

ZOAR VALLEY BEACH

In the mid-60s the "hippie" movement brought hundreds of people to gather in this Buffalo-area river site. It has remained liberated, notwithstanding several citations on one day in 1997 due to a specific complaint. No facilities, no camping, and the park closes at sunset. It is a good hiking area, with both forest and plains.

You can camp at Evangola State Park, along Lake Erie near Angola, 25 miles south of Buffalo, beautiful in its own right and with skinny-dipping possibilities.

☞ From Buffalo, take Route 62 for 25 miles south to Gowanda. At the traffic lights in the center of town (junction of Routes 39 and 62), turn left onto S. Water St. Soon you will see Cattaraugus Creek on your left. Follow S. Water St. (it becomes Commercial St. and then Palmer St.) for 0.5 miles. Turn right on Broadway Road, go 0.9 miles, turn left on Point Peter Road. Go 1.8 miles to a prominent Y in the road. This is Forty Road. Go left, follow it to the parking area at the end.

Follow the creek downstream (clothed go upstream) about 2 miles. The clothing-optional area is where the two branches of the creek come together. This is a pretty wilderness area; please remove your trash.

☆ STEPH'S POND

Beautiful pond on 65 acres of near wilderness. Swim, canoe, raft, camp, go for a hike or join a game of volleyball. Campsites have water; no hookups. Sauna, showers. Family-oriented but most singles accepted. Reasonable fees; daily or seasonal. P.O. Box 195, Ontario, NY 14519; phone (315) 589-9646.

☞ From Rochester, take Route 104 through Webster and Ontario. Turn left onto Salmon Creek Road (after Spencer Speedway). Take the second left onto Eaton Road. Turn left into the only unmarked driveway disappearing into the woods. Drive slowly as roadway is bumpy. A half-hour drive from downtown Rochester.

Top: Randy O'Rourke, Potter's Falls Near Ithaca. Bottom: Frank R. Shepard, Zoar Valley Near Gawanda.

GENESEO

S.U.N.Y. Geneseo students have discovered a new skinny-dipping streambed and waterfall to replace Triphammer Pond, destroyed several years ago when a dam broke. Tan in the many nooks near the stream, which does dry up on occasion.

☞ Take I-390 to Geneseo exit, drive through the town past the college and bear right at the fork onto Routes 20A and 39. Continue downhill on 20A to the valley below. A guardrail on the left starts with a white marker. If you pass an alfalfa mill on the left, you've gone too far. Behind the marker is a metal gate to a cow pasture. Follow the path around the base of the hill to a small stream. Cross the stream and follow a path upstream to the falls (about a quarter mile).

SENECA POINT GORGE

Four waterfalls comprise the gorge; the first, about 25 feet high with a 6-foot-deep clear water pool, is the most popular for swimming and sunning.

☞ From Rochester, travel east on the NY State Thruway (I-90) to Canandaigua Exit 44. Go straight on 332 to Canandaigua through downtown to Routes 5 and 20. Turn right onto 5 and 20. After about a mile, turn left on Route 21 south. About 2 miles past the village of Cheshire, turn left onto Seneca Point Road. Follow signs to Bristol Harbor Golf Course. Go down the hill past Bristol Harbor to the first bridge by a large house on the right side of the road. Park just past the stream at the sand quarry and walk up the path on the left side of the stream. The first fall is about 0.5 miles up the road. Wear something on your feet as there are sharp rocks in the stream.

NORTHERN

DEER CREEK MARSH

Deer Creek Marsh Wildlife Management Area has about a mile of undeveloped sand dunes nestled between the pristine waters of Deer Creek and Lake Ontario. Put your towel somewhere in the middle and it's a short, naked walk to either side for swimming.

From Syracuse go north on Route 81 to the Pulaski (Route 13) exit. Go west to Route 3, turn right (north) and go about 3 miles to Rainbow Shores Drive. Turn left and follow to the lake. Go left on the dirt road for 1 mile until you see another dirt road veer off to the left. Take it. Follow to parking area and walk on the path to the beach or dunes. The farther south you walk the better it gets.

For those with canoes, takeout is at the

NATURIST ROCHESTER

A dynamic naturist club which reflects the interests of founder Morley Schloss—in whose basement, members enjoy a clothes-free pool, sauna and hot spa. 237 Vassar St., Rochester, NY 14607; phone (716) 244-1219.

DURAND EASTMAN BEACH

From Rochester, take Route 590 north until you can see the Sea Breeze roller coaster. Turn left at the Durand Park sign onto a road (in places called Sweet Fern Drive) which crosses Culver and winds through the park becoming Lakeshore Blvd. Park in the first parking area on the right side of Lakeshore Blvd. Walk right (east) along the beach just past the last set of steps to houses on the hillside. The ideal spot is below a large white house with lavender shutters which can be seen from the water. Avoid areas near clothed people and don't walk too far beyond the steps as there have been arrests on the Irondequoit section of the beach.

BARE ASS BEACH

Bare Ass Beach, a.k.a. Dutch Street Beach, is mostly pebbles with some sandy places. From Rochester take Route 104 east to Huron. In Huron, bear left onto Old Ridge Road. Continue east past Alton and Resort. Turn left at Dutch Street and take the street to the end at the beach.

CHIMNEY BLUFFS BEACH

On the south shore of Lake Ontario, Chimney Bluffs with its sandstone formations is seeing increased use.

☞ From Rochester, take Route 104 east to Sodus. Turn left on Lake Bluff Road. Continue left (north) on Lake Bluff Road past Lummisville Road. About 1 mile past Lummisville Road, Lake Bluff Road turns into Gardner Road. Continue north until the road curves (east). Just past the curve is a small dirt road on the left which leads to the west end of Chimney Bluffs and the secluded part of the beach.

launch point about a mile south of Rainbow Shores Drive for a nice 45-minute paddle to the lake.

ADIRONDACK HIGH PEAK

New York's vast Adirondack Park offers possibilities for nude recreation. The High Peak Area is of particular interest—well-marked trails crisscross a number of creeks with crystal clear water and warm sunning rocks. Owners support skinny-dipping and despise litterers.

Twelve minutes east of Lake Placid on Route 73, about 1 mile west of Keene, look for turnoff to north, Alstead Hill Road. Follow it 1.5 miles to end of pavement. Turn right on unmarked dirt road. After less than a mile it branches three ways. Take sharp left onto Lacey Road, drive half mile to iron bridge. Park off road and don't block driveway at end of road! Follow short trails south to a series of small falls and pools.

Adirondack Park also boasts the St. Regis Canoe Area; 58 bodies of water for canoeing, fishing, hiking and camping. Campsites available at Fish Creek Ponds off Route 30. Adirondack Park phone (518) 457-2500; camping reservations call 1-800-456-2267.

Alternative site: West Fork of Ausable River in the NY State Wilderness Area. Take Route 73 4 miles east of Lake Placid Village to Adirondack "Log" Road. Go south to High Peaks lot and park where the river crosses the road. The trail off parking area meets the riverbank 500 yards from the road and continues along the shore. Rocks and pool offer many opportunities to sun or soak in a wilderness setting. Only 1 mile from High Parks Trail. Use with discretion.

INDIAN LAKE

In Adirondack Park (phone 518-457-2500) Indian Lake island campsites—accessible by boat only—are a natural retreat and a treat. Access is by reservation from Ticketron. Take I-87 to the junction with I-90, continue north on 90 beyond Albany to Amsterdam. Then Route 30 north through Speculator to Indian Lake. Park at the main gate, present your permit, and paddle away to your naked hide-out.

BEAR SLIDE

Bear Slide, located in Warrensburg State Forest, is a large rock slide stretching some 150 yards down Buttermilk Brook. Riding the slide can be a real rush, however, take a square piece of burlap or carpet to protect your skin from being scratched by sand in the pool or from hitting the small crevices that the slide goes through. DO NOT try the full length of the slide in your birthday suit! Good

alignment to the sun makes Bear Slide a good tanning area all day.

☞ From Route 9N in Lake Luzerne, NY, turn onto Mill St., in the center of town, then turn onto River Road. Go for 5.3 miles, through the Lake Luzerne Rod and Gun Club grounds, staying on the public road and cross a narrow bridge. After the bridge, park and follow the side trail up the hill to the right. Walk for 12 minutes, and you will walk right onto Bear Slide. Bonus Time! The Rod and Gun Club is looking for new members. Cost? A mere $8 per year, which entitles one to unlimited use of the extensive park, including camping, fishing and a half mile of private frontage on the Hudson River, which offers more opportunities for nude use. Apply for membership at the Potash Inn, north of town on the west side of Route 9N.

SACANDAGA RIVER/LAKE

Sacandaga River and Sacandaga Lake is a naturist's paradise! The river is only little more that two miles in length, but all along the way, on both sides, are dozens of secluded spots that are perfect for nude recreation. The lake itself offers miles of good spots, because much of the shoreline drops off so quickly that one is invisible from the road when at the edge of the water.

☞ From the center of Lake Luzerne, take Conklingville Road, County Route 4, west for just over 5 miles. Take a left on CR 8, which goes over the dam when the north end of the lake becomes visible. After crossing the dam, for lake sunning/swimming, take a right and pick your spot. There are a few houses on

Sacandaga Lake, since it is used primarily for hydropower by Niagara Mohawk Power Co., so there are many private spots along its shores. People here in boats pay little or no attention to naturists. After crossing the dam, if one is looking for nude river recreation, turn left, go down river, and select an area. There is a public campground on the left side. Heading back east on CR 4 for 0.5 miles, one will find a public picnic area, owned by Ni-Mo. It offers many secluded spots right on the river.

NORTHWEST BAY BROOK FALLS

A string of falls, flumes and pools, stretching for over a quarter mile, with good alignment to the sun until very late in the day. Feast on blueberries in June/July. Litter is virtually nonexistent; help keep it that way.

Upper Lake George, surrounded by popular tourist attractions, is replete with opportunities for nude recreation, including on the lake proper in the Tongue Mountain Area. Watch for rattlesnakes.

☞ From Exit 25 on I-87, The Northway, take Exit 24 east towards Bolton Landing. Turn left, north on Route 9N. Go for 4.7 miles and keep your eyes open, because many signs are partially obscured by the foliage. Along the way, on the right, you will see a sign which reads "No Parking. Parking One Mile," with arrow pointing north. Then, cross a brook, and climb a steep, windy hill. At the top of the hill, on the right is an old quarry and a small parking lot. Park at the old quarry and look directly across the road where you will see two unmarked but distinct foot trails leading

into the woods. Follow either one of them and, as soon as the traffic noise ceases behind you, waterfall sounds will become evident in front of you. Follow them, angling off to the left, and enter a naturist's paradise.

SCHROON RIVER

The Schroon River is a cool, fast-flowing river which empties out of Schroon Lake, flowing south to join the Hudson River in Warrensburg, paralleling I-87 most of the way. Much of the country that it flows through is very rural, yet the river is never more than a few minutes away from the interstate. There are many, many spots along the Schroon, and below are two of them that are easy to find.

☞ Upper Schroon: In Chester, NY, take exit 25 off I-87 and go east toward Hague on Route 8. Pass signs for a campground on the left, cross the bridge over the Schroon, and take the first right after the bridge. Take the next right and go for 0.4 miles to a distinct

turnoff on the right. Follow the path down to the river to a small sand beach, large sunning rocks, and a nice pool.

Lower Schroon: Take exit 24 off The Northway, turn right at the sign which reads "Bolton Landing 6 miles." Cross the Schroon over one of those neat steel deck bridges, take first right turn, which goes back under the interstate and follows the river south for over 4 miles. Along the way, there are over six turnoffs on the right where there are no houses on either side of river. Pick one, take the 30-second walk to the river, and enjoy!

JABE & LITTLE JABE POND

Jabe and Little Jabe Pond, Hague, NY, are two ponds, high up on the mountain on the western side of Lake George, that feature clear water and miles of private shoreline. Owned by the State of New York, both ponds are little used, offering absolutely one of the best opportunities for naturist recreation in the Lake

George/Plattsburgh area.

Jabe Pond has several islands which are totally private, so bring along your boat. Little Jabe Pond is a 15-minute walk from Jabe Pond over gentle terrain.

☞ From Route 9N in Hague, NY, take Splint Rock Road west for 1.8 miles. It changes to dirt at 0.8 mile point. Turn left into a well-marked parking lot. If you have a car with low clearance, such as a large sedan, park here. If you have a car with reasonable clearance or a 4WD, continue on until you meet the ledge in the road—this will save you 9 minutes of walking. Park at the ledge, walk for 9 minutes and you will find yourself at Jabe Pond. To go to Little Jabe Pond, go back from the trashy beach at Jabe Pond for a distance of about 50 yards toward where you came in, and look off to the left. There you will see a distinct woods road which quickly changes to a foot trail. Follow this for a 15-minute leisurely walk, and you will arrive at Little Jabe Pond, which is good for swimming anytime, and is best for sunning after noon.

NORTH CAROLINA

OUTER BANKS

There's a stark, seemingly desolate, light-drenched and humidified beauty to the Outer Bank Islands—a timeless quality that draws many to experience the sand and sea. The Cape Hatteras and Cape Lookout National Seashores between them preserve 120 miles of magnificent beach. Ferries service most islands. Unfortunately, the state passed a vague and overbroad law in 1985 criminalizing consensual nudity. While it is aimed at the commercialized sleaze trade in women's nudity, some religionists and park officials believe it is their duty to enforce it against skinny-dippers.

CAPE HATTERAS NATIONAL SEASHORE

Cape Hatteras has long stretches of lovely uncrowded barrier island—for many the best in the Middle Atlantic states, ideal for enjoyment au naturel. Sadly the two most popular areas, Pea and Ocracoke Islands, are subjected to zealous Seashore enforcement which assimilates revised NC nudity regulations that require covering the genitals in public in the presence of the opposite sex without exception.

However, being topfree or in a g-string is legal! Indicative of the mood on Ocracoke: a woman was reprimanded by

a ranger for walking her dog without a leash. When she told him she didn't have a leash, he told her to use her bikini top.

Until 1985, nudity on Ocracoke was tolerated from a mile or so northeast of the campground north to Hatteras Inlet. It cannot now be recommended. Until 1990, Pea Island was still enjoyed by the initiated. Its USF&WS management is now replaced by CHNS policy and must be avoided until political changes are achieved.

Many dedicated naturists now own boats and, sailing the sounds inside the barrier islands with their friends, set their own undress codes.

CAPE LOOKOUT NATIONAL SEASHORE

Cape Lookout National Seashore is a 58-mile, mostly day-use barrier island, sparsely visited on weekdays. Most visitors head for the southern tip to go shelling, conceding the wild area north of the lighthouse, and Shackleford Banks too, to the occasional stroller and the naturists. Shackleford Banks currently has no rangers and no ferry access—bring-or-rent-or-hitchhike with a private boat.

The ride to Core Banks from Harkers Island takes about 45 minutes. For another fee, the Park Service will carry you and your gear in a tractor-drawn wagon 1/4 mile to the lighthouse point or a few miles down the beach. Go at least 1/2 mile north of the lighthouse to avoid the clothed. Take everything you will need

including water. The last ferry returns to the mainland at 4 p.m., keep an eye on the time as well as the horizon.

Consider launching a boat from the mainland—or ferry over a johnboat and light trailer with your vehicle from Atlantic (this will pull best in the damp sand of low tide without 4WD)—then, you can drive to the Cape's far north end, where Portsmouth Island has its own ghost town, Fort Portsmouth, and Ocracoke Inlet offers many fascinating creeks and channels; the price of this adventure is that strong insect repellent is absolutely essential.

☞ Cape Lookout National Seashore is accessible by a passengers-only ferry from Harkers Island Marina, south on US 70 from New Bern and east of Beaufort; the turnoff at Otway is well-marked, reservations are a good idea: (919) 728-3907; the ferries cost $12 per person round trip. Another ferry, this to central Cape Lookout—$55 round trip for a vehicle—runs from Atlantic at the very end of I-70.

AUDUBON WILDLIFE REFUGE

Access the Outer Banks by Route 158. The Audubon Wildlife Refuge in North Duck, on the way to Corolla, has a pleasant, 3-mile secluded beach with few users.

☞ Going north on Route 12 as you leave Duck, park in the lot of the Sanderling Inn (a resort with restaurant, health club, rental horses). Walk around the building to the beach. Turn left and head north for 10 to 15 minutes, out of sight of the resort. The beach abutting the refuge continues for about 3 miles, backed by a fence warning you not to enter the refuge.

The refuge may be reached from the road via an observation tower about 2 miles north of the Inn and across the road from the indoor tennis court complex. No parking is allowed but one can bicycle to the entrance.

HAMMOCKS BEACH STATE PARK

The park on Bear Island is reached by a 20-minute ferry ride from Swansboro. Take Route 17 or 258 south to Jacksonville and then Route 24 east. Ferry runs from June through August, usually 9:30 a.m. to 5:30 p.m. Vehicles not permitted.

Rangers have acted against nudity only on complaints as long as it is well away from the clothed beach. From the ferry follow the path to the right 1/2 mile over the dunes to the ocean. Then go left up the beach another 1/4 mile or so to be out of view of the textiled. Beach facilities include bathhouse and refreshment stand.

WILMINGTON: WRIGHTSVILLE BEACH

A shallow-draft boat, rented at one of the Wrightsville marinas, plus a high tide and some skill at negotiating muddy channels, entitles you to the widest selection of fine beaches across the Masonboro Inlet. Any boat at all, and no skill at all, will still get you to Masonboro Island with its 8 miles of wonderful beach (choose north or south end), or to Hutaff or Lea Islands (reached best by launching at Scotts Hill, Hampstead or Topsail Beach). Get skilled quickly—get the *North Carolina Chart Book* for $14.95; phone (703) 750-0510.

Of course, going is the fun—channel navigation makes you feel like a skipper, spartina grass varies with the seasons, the egrets, herons and ibises abound, ghost crabs are amusing, ospreys are breathtaking, and you may see dolphins from the outer beaches. Camping is permitted.

☞ From Wilmington follow Routes 17/74 east, then Route 74 leading to Wrightsville Beach. Continue south to the Wrightsville marinas, rent a boat. Go out Banks Channel behind the north end of Masonboro to find your private cove, or at least a harbor to begin your walk to a trackless hideaway.

From Carolina Beach you can take the Intracoastal Waterway north to green marker #155A. Turn right into the Carolina Beach Inlet channel. Moor the boat in the sheltered water of south

Masonboro Island and again walk off 10 minutes to your private paradise.

A shallow-draft boat will open up much of the leeward side of marshy Masonboro Island. Try at high tide to navigate into Dick Bay, opposite red marker #152, or John Creek, near red marker #150.

SOUTH COAST

WHISPERING PINES

A 50-acre Christian campground and nature preserve close to N. Myrtle Beach. Two hot tubs, Swedish sauna, heated pool, pool table, clubhouse/snack bar, dance floor, arcade, big screen TV. The one-acre lake is perfect for swimming. Fully-equipped rental units, tent and RV sites with hookups. P.O. Box 148-WG, Longwood, NC 28452. Phone (910) 287-6404; fax 287-4967.

BIRD ISLAND

Bird Island is a large island off the southwestern tip of Sunset Beach. You may walk to it at low tide but a short swim or boat is necessary at high tide when the waters are quite rough. The beach is wide with fine white sand. There are no rocks in the water, which is warm and ideal for bodysurfing. The land is privately owned but the owner has never objected to nude use. Conveniently located near Whispering Pines—the management has tide charts for the island.

☞ From Whispering Pines or US 17, take Route 904. Turn right onto Route 179 and follow signs for Sunset Beach. At the road nearest to the beach, turn right and park as far south as possible. Take a public access walkway over the dunes to the beach. Walk right on the beach to Bird Island.

INLAND

☆ BAR-S-RANCH

Nice 180-acre club in the Piedmont, north of Greensboro, with a 7-acre pond, sun lawn, pool, snack bar, twin gazebos, large hot tub, tent sites. 313 Bar-S-Trail, Reidsville, NC 27320. Phone (910) 349-2456.

TRIANGLE AREA NATURISTS

Triangle Area Naturist concerns range as widely as the Outer Banks. SASE brings newsletter. P.O. Box 527, Carrboro, NC 27510. Phone (919) 942-7810.

RALEIGH: FALLS LAKE

Recommended where the sunbathing is not visible to casual Falls Lake boaters. In

Wake County on Highway 98, go 0.8 miles west of US 1 and turn left onto SR 1967. You will pass Keith's Country Store on your left at the intersection with SR 2000. Continue on SR 1967 until you come to a red and white barricade; go around it and proceed to the barricade at the end of the paved road. Park and walk down the trail over two dirt banks toward Falls Lake. Turn left onto one-lane road and walk over two more dirt banks. At the top of the hill (in woods) there is a cable between two trees blocking an old road. Go right on brown dirt trail to small field. Go left on trail in field, about 3/4 mile from parking area. An alternative site is to continue past the cable and past one dirt bank to a cove, about 1 1/2 miles from the parking area.

PISGAH RANGER DISTRICT: CANTRELL CREEK

Serving Asheville with secluded skinny-dipper pools and easy access. Take Highway 280 for 18 miles south from I-40, to Henderson-Transylvania county line. Turn right onto Forest Road 297 (Turkey Pen Road) and follow it about 1.5 miles until you reach South Fork Mills River. Walk down Trail 133 to Swinging Bridge and follow river until you reach the former site of the historic lodge. Just after the lodge site, turn right (NNW) onto Trail 148 which parallels Cantrell Creek.

EAST FORK PIGEON RIVER

The East Fork of the Pigeon River has waterfalls, hiking, vistas, and free parking, all within an easy walk of the Blue Ridge Parkway. Originally mapped and used nude by North Carolina Naturists.

From Blue Ridge Parkway MM 417, Looking Glass Rock Overlook, walk north 0.1 miles to the grass on the left side of the road. Follow the trail paralleling the parkway to the stream; fork left, cross it and go right to the first campsite area, complete with small beach. More trails both farther up and downstream lead to waterfalls, nude swim areas, and campsites. Best bet is to obtain a map at the ranger station and plot your course to relaxation.

NORTH CAROLINA NATURISTS

North Carolina Naturists will provide detailed, accurate maps to over 50 sites across the entire state. $14 complete. P.O. Box 33845, Charlotte, NC 28233; voice mail (704) 565-5023.

OHIO

BUCKEYE NATURISTS

With info on clothing-optional sites in Ohio, the Buckeye Naturists also publish an excellent bimonthly newsletter for 250+ members. Send SASE for information: P.O. Box 182, Dublin, OH 43017. Phone (614) 341-7297.

SUNN JAMMERS

Sixty-two acres of woods and open areas. Clubhouse w/fireplace, community kitchen, hot tub, rest rooms and hot showers, wraparound deck, playground, stocked lake with beach, concrete court for basketball, volleyball and badminton. 3207 Brownsville Road, S.E., Newark, OH 43056. Phone (614) 763-4217.

BARE VALLEY FAMILY NUDIST CAMP

Fifty acres nestled in the heart of the Hocking Hills, nine miles northeast of Logan. Pond swimming, wooded hiking trails, volleyball. Tent and RV sites; rental units available. Singles and families welcome. P.O. Box 57, Unionville Center, OH 43077. Phone (614) 873-4601.

GREEN VALLEY OUTING CLUB

Akron-Cleveland area, 30 wooded acres. Heated pool, pond, Frisbee golf, volleyball, basketball, miniten, horseshoes, hiking trails, rec hall. Tent sites and RV hookups, rental trailers. P.O. Box 740, Bath, OH 44210. Phone (216) 659-3812.

PARADISE GARDENS

Thirty-five acres include Olympic-sized pool, volleyball courts, one-acre pond, large sunning area, playground, party rooms, sauna and whirlpool, snack bar. Year-round activities. RV hookups, tent sites. 6100 Blue Rock Road, Cincinnati, OH 45247. Phone (513) 385-4189.

CAESAR CREEK

Topfree, thongs and g-strings are the norm at Caesar Creek in Warren County. House Bill 188 can change that though, so regular users have organized **Caesar Creek Sun-T,** a group dedicated to defeating pending antinudity legislation. C/O Dr. G. Roger Davis, 612 S. Poplar St., Oxford, OH 45056; phone (513) 523-8339.

From Cincinnati, take I-71 north to State Route 73. Exit on 73, then travel west about 5 miles to the park entrance.

Or, from the Dayton area, take I-75 south to State Route 73. Exit on 73 and go east 18 miles. Follow signs to the beach.

OKLAHOMA

TULSA AREA

☆ SUN MEADOW

Oklahoma's first naturist park, 20 minutes from downtown Tulsa. Heated pool, spa, sauna, volleyball, table tennis, shuffleboard, children's play area, fitness center, party pavilion with jukebox, jogging track and a community kitchen. Clubhouse has fireplace, TV, VCR, library and indoor games. Tent and RV sites. Must reserve in advance. P.O. Box 521068-WG, Tulsa, OK 74152. Phone (918) 266-7651.

☆ OAKLAKE TRAILS

Oaklake Trails Naturist Park has the largest land area in the U.S. Over 400 acres of rolling hills with eight lakes and ponds. Facilities include tent and RV sites with hookups, hiking trails, clubhouse, swim pool, volleyball. P.O. Box 470564-WG, Tulsa, OK 74147-0564. Phone (918) 455-8120 or (405) 390-1148.

KEYSTONE LAKE

On Lake Keystone, try Washington Erving North, which was closed in 1984 but is used by naturists during midweek.

Take Route 64 west from downtown Tulsa for 13 miles to 209th W. Ave. (Prue Exit). Turn north, go 8 miles, find semi-paved road on left. Turn onto this road (makes two small curves). Go 2 miles, past houses and a cattle guard, to end. Park just beyond "Dead End" sign, take trail 200 yards to a broad sandy beach on the lake.

LAKE TENKILLER

There are places on the west side of Tenkiller Lake, east of Muskogee, that can be used nude. The lake is closely monitored by Corps of Engineers.

OREGON

PORTLAND AREA

☆ RESTFUL HAVEN HEALTH CLUB

A pleasant base while visiting Portland, 26 miles northwest. The 104 wooded acres offer tent and RV sites/hookups, heated pool, sauna, hot tub, snack bar, community kitchen, rec hall. Open year-round. P.O. Box 248, North Plains, OR 97133. Phone (503) 647-2449.

SAUVIE ISLAND

Sauvie Island's north end on the Columbia River is a large, popular family recreation site managed by the state Dept. of Fish and Wildlife. People fish, wade, swim, hike, chat and sunbathe on Collins Beach—nearly all, au naturel.

West of Portland, Sauvie Island is free of the Columbia Gorge chilly breeze that bothers some at Rooster Rock Beach. Some regulars put boats in the water at Ridgefield, WA to come over. Security and portapotties provided; 10 p.m. curfew. For water level, check the *Oregonian* newspaper weather page for Columbia River measured at Vancouver.

The Sauvie Island naturist group, Friends Of Sauvie Island Clothing Optional Beach, is at P.O. Box 7459, Beaverton, OR 97007, phone (503) 645-2306. Report on its success in *Nude & Natural* magazine, *N* 13.1, pp. 63–70; *N* 14.1, pp. 39–41. Two nudist clubs that visit Sauvie Island and other public sites:

Sun Rovers, P.O. Box 3183, Portland, OR 97208, and Hidden Springs, P.O. Box 17600, Portland, OR 97217.

☞ From Portland, go 10 miles northwest on US 30. Turn right over Sauvie Island bridge. Buy a parking pass ($3) at the store at the bottom of the bridge, then continue beyond the store for 1.8 miles. Turn right on Reeder Road and go 10.7 miles until it becomes gravel (passing Reeder Beach and Walton Beach, both clothing-required). About 0.3 miles on the gravel road, watch for signs on the right, "Collins Beach, Clothing Optional Area, Nudity on Beach Only." Show your pass, park on the left (west) side of the road, lock the car, and take a trail to the beach.

INNER CITY HOT SPRINGS

This holistic health center 10 minutes from downtown Portland has a sauna and hot tubs on a secluded deck open to the elements. Nudity is the norm. Massage therapy, nutritional counseling, wellness workshops and classes, flotation tank. Open daily. 2927 N.E. Everett, Portland, OR 97232. Phone (503) 238-1065.

ROOSTER ROCK STATE PARK

Rooster Rock State Park on the majestic Columbia River has the clothing-optional area with the longest record of large-scale, legal use anywhere in the USA. Clothes-mandatory and nude beaches are side-by-side. Boaters gather and party on weekends. Sand Island, opposite the nude shore, is the place to wade to and socialize in times of low water. Toilets, snacks at central building.

☞ Drive 25 miles east from Portland on I-84, turn off at Rooster Rock State Park (exit 25), proceed to the far east end of the parking lot (fee charged in summer/on holidays) and walk eastward down to the river.

BAGBY HOT SPRINGS

A "world-class soaking opportunity"— said Jayson Loam, our geothermal guru. Two hours east of Portland in Mt. Hood National Forest. An exceptionally beautiful, volunteer-tended public resource reached by a 1.5-mile hike through a rain forest. The Friends of Bagby Hot Springs rebuilt and maintain the three bathhouses and expect visitors will help to do the same.

☞ Trailhead is reached by driving Route 224 to 40 miles southeast of Estacada, then follow Forest Roads S-46, S-63, and S-70 to the southwest end of the parking lot of Pegleg Falls Campground. Weekends and holidays are always crowded. The Friends welcome donations: P.O. Box 15116, Portland, OR 97215.

☆ SQUAW MOUNTAIN RANCH

Squaw Mountain Ranch is on the way to Mt. Hood. The West's oldest (1933) nudist club has 19 rustic acres, 2 hot tubs, sauna, lake, volleyball, tent and RV sites with hookups, community kitchen in lodge with rooms to rent. Music festival each August. P.O. Box 4452, Portland, OR 97208; phone (503) 630-6136.

HIDDEN SPRINGS NUDIST CLUB

Newsletter, family nude swims; reduced prices for TNS members. P.O. Box 17600, Portland, OR 97217-0600.

BREITENBUSH HOT SPRINGS RETREAT

Clothing is optional at the Meadow Hot Springs of the Breitenbush Community, which hosts workshops and retreats for up to 200 in the Cascade Range east of Salem. Steam sauna, tubs, cabins, vegetarian restaurant, hiking and cross-country skiing in an ancient forest. Massage, yoga, aerobics, aromatherapy and hydrotherapy, herbal wraps. Fee for use of the hot springs. P.O. Box 578, Detroit, OR 97342. Phone (503) 854-3314.

☞ From Salem, Route 22 to Detroit. Left on Route 46 at gas station. Ten miles to Cleator Campground. Just 100 feet past it, take a right over bridge across the Breitenbush River. Follow signs, taking every left turn after the bridge, to Breitenbush parking. Please phone to reserve.

EUGENE AREA

☆ WILLAMETTANS

Amid Douglas firs, in the Cascade Mountain foothills 15 miles northeast of Eugene, this friendly 40-acre co-op naturist park has pool, whirlpool, playground, seasonal snack bar, rec hall, volleyball and tennis. Rental units, ample camping with hookups, open May–Sept. P.O. Box 969, Marcola, OR 97454. Phone (503) 933-2809.

McCREDIE HOT SPRINGS

A cluster of natural thermal pools along both sides of I-58 in the Willamette National Forest, 9 miles southeast of Oakridge at Salt Creek. Traditionally

nude, and much appreciated by long-distance drivers, one mile from a campground.

☞ To the north bank of Salt Creek, drive from Oakridge on Route 58 past Blue Pool Campground. Just after mile-marker 45, turn south (right) into a large oval truck park near the creek and walk upstream. Water cools from 120°F.

To the south bank—go 0.5 miles farther east on Route 58, turn right across the bridge and stay right on Forest Service road 5875. Park at the first curve, walk to the creek and head downstream. Spring temperature here is a scalding 140°F before mixing with Salt Creek water. Warning: do not try to wade across Salt Creek—it's deep, with a strong current.

TERWILLIGER (COUGAR) HOT SPRINGS

Five creek pools surrounded by big boulders, wildflowers and forest, accessible year-round. Nearby lake fishing, swimming, water-skiing. Please leave a donation for the caretakers. Camping nearby but not at the springs.

☞ East from Eugene on Route 126 to about mile-marker 45. Turn right on FS #19 at the sign "Cougar Reservoir" (not dam), pass the bridge, turn right and go three miles to the dam, bear right and drive about four miles until you a see a small lake on your right. It has a waterfall on the right shore. Park on the left side and walk back to where a trail begins on the north side of the lake. The 1/4 mile trail is somewhat steep. Look for the pools in a small creek ravine.

MEDFORD AREA

KENO ROAD ROCK QUARRY

Exit I-15 at south end of Ashland. Take Highway 66 south a little way to Dead Indian Road. Go left (east) about 15–20 miles. After Howard Prairie Reservoir turnoff, watch for turn to right. Keno Road name appears after the turn. Go 3/4 mile to the top of the hill. Turn right at the gravel piles. Follow the gravel road around to Bare Lake; the beach is at the northeast end. Bring an air mattress.

The user group is Rogue Suncatchers, P.O. Box 3203, Ashland, OR 97520; phone (503) 488-1287.

☆ – *The star symbol before a resort name is your guarantee that The Naturist Society card is accepted and earns a discount at the resort. To obtain Naturist Society membership, see the inside front cover.*

PENNSYLVANIA

EASTERN

☆ BEECHWOOD LODGE

Rustic 35 acres 2 miles from Lehighton near Appalachian Trail. Pool, sauna, whirlpool, playground, restaurant, volleyball, large indoor and outdoor hot tubs, tennis court, bathhouse, snowmobile and cross-country ski trails, rec hall, exercise equipment. Rental rooms, restaurant/snack bar, tent sites with shower/rest room center, RV hookups. Dances and other events scheduled; open all year. P.O. Box 145-WG, Ashfield, PA 18212. Phone (717) 386-4449.

SUNSPOT

Secluded 135 acres north of Scranton. Heated in-ground pool, hot tub, sauna and pond. Volleyball, horseshoes, badminton, Ping-Pong, nature hikes. Tent/RV sites with hookups. Rental rooms, playground, snack bar. May–Sept. RR2, Box 57D, Susquehanna, PA 18847. Phone (717) 853-3060.

PENN SYLVAN HEALTH SOCIETY

Fourteen miles from Reading. Camping with hookups, pool, sauna, whirlpool, volleyball, tennis, rec hall. Eighty acres. R.D. 3, Box 3770-WG, Mohnton PA 19540. Phone (717) 445-6330.

☆ SUNNY REST LODGE

A 190-acre site in the Pocono Mountains. Heated pool, tennis, volleyball, whirlpool, sauna, exercise room, restaurant, game room, nightclub, restaurant, laundromat. Air-conditioned motel, campgrounds with hookups. May–Sept. 425 Sunny Rest Drive-WG, Palmerton, PA 18071. Phone (610) 377-2911.

METRO NATURISTS

Small naturist social club. Box 165-WG, Bensalem, PA 19020-0165. Phone 215-GET-NUDE.

CANUDING THE DELAWARE RIVER

Paddling Bares are the expert canuders. P.O. Box 22, Milltown, NJ 08850. Phone (908) 432-9109. The Tri-State Sun Club regularly organizes canuding trips on an 8-mile stretch of the Delaware. P.O. Box 532, Broadway, NJ 08808.

LANESBORO: DEVIL'S PUNCHBOWL

A roughly triangular pond with nearly vertical sides. The two creeks that cascade down the cliffs make it a delightful spot in spring. Best swimming is in early summer; late summer brings murky waters.

☞ From Binghamton, NY (the nearest city) take NY 17 to exit 80 and follow the signs towards Lanesboro (you will be parallel with the Susquehanna River). Look at your odometer as you pass into Pennsylvania, and take the dirt road on the left 0.6 miles from the state line. Follow the road over the railroad tracks and park just beyond. Trails lead from here to Devil's Punchbowl. Be careful descending the cliffs to the water's edge, and know that some locals tend not to be too tolerant of nudity.

HAMBURG: LITTLE SCHUYLKILL PARADISE

A splendid natural site with only moderate use. From PA 61 Exit of I-78, take 61 north to PA 895 east. Follow 895 east into Drehersville. Turn right at sign for Albany and Hawk Mountain Sanctuary. Cross the tracks, go 100 yards, turn right, go about 0.5 miles, park on the right at the last "State Game Lands" access. Walk to the river, turn left, go downhill over a small stream to the pine grove. The site sees some fishermen a little distance away. Paradise begins here, find an enjoyable spot.

An alternative, after crossing the tracks, is to park almost at once on the left, then walk 0.5 miles to the Little Schuylkill bridge.

BERWICK: POWDER HOLE

A small, wild gorge for skinny-dipping, sunning and hiking. From I-80 go northeast on Route 11 along the Susquehanna to Berwick. Downtown, turn right on Route 93, cross the bridge and go 1.3 miles, turning left onto Wapwallopen Road at the bottom of the hill. Go 3.9 miles and turn right (gas station is on your far right-hand side). From this point you'll be going up into the gorge area. All along are access points, however, to get to the uppermost falls continue 1.1 miles on curvy road and take a sharp right. Go 0.1 miles past a farm with a house on left and a barn on the right. Park on the road where the woods begin, and take the path to the falls. Most nude use is here.

WESTERN

WHITE THORN LODGE

Volleyball Superbowl tourney is the weekend after Labor Day. Co-op club is 1 hour NW of Pittsburgh. Pool, shuffleboard, hot tub, tennis courts, snack bar, sauna. Tent/RV sites with hookups; rental rooms. 383 State Line Rd.-WG, Darlington, PA 16115. Phone (412) 846-5984; fax (412) 847-4136.

BARE ASS BEACH

Take Route 448 south from downtown Ellwood City. Turn left over the Ewing Park Bridge (steel plant on your right). Make the first right after you go over the bridge, continue a short distance and make the next right. You are now in a park setting and make a right turn on this alley. Go a short distance and park in the church parking lot that is almost under the bridge. A path can be found heading down to the river near the bridge. Another wide jogging path will be found running parallel to the the very next path leading off to the right (toward river). Watch the briar bushes and the steep jump down to the sandy beach among the large rocks. Enjoy, but some local boys leave broken bottles, so be careful.

STEELTON: HEMPT BROTHERS QUARRY

Several ponds near Hempt Brothers Quarry are used to swim nude and enjoy the sun. Weekends are a good time to visit, as well as after 4 p.m. weekdays when the quarry closes for the day.

☞ From exit 18 of the PA Turnpike (I-76), go to the traffic light. Turn left onto Eisenhower Boulevard, go to the next light, and turn right onto South Front St. (Route 230). Drive about a mile and you will see the sign for Hempt Brothers. Make a right and drive back into the quarry where you will find several places to enjoy.

BELLEFONTE QUARRY

Serving Penn State University students, the quarry is not always nude; exercise tact if others already there are clothed.

Exit 23 from I-80. Follow 220/150 S. Take Milesburg exit 144/150 S. From the exit, it is 2.2 miles. Cerro Plant and the quarry are on the left, Penn State Sub Shop #6 is on the right. Park by Uni-Mart on the left. Follow the fence up the road with the sign, Private Road, Cerro Plant #5. The quarry is a 10-minute walk from there. Follow the paths to the left, away from the plant when the road ends.

From State College: take 26 North to 150 North through Bellefonte to Route 144 North. At the stop sign past Tussey Mountain Outfitters turn left. You will be on Route 144 North. The Cerro plant is 0.7 miles up the road on your right.

UNIVERSITY OF PENNSYLVANIA

An on-campus, officially recognized organization, the **Naturist Student Association** holds clothing-optional study hours, social events. C/O Philip Tromovich, 4619 Spruce St., #1F, Philadelphia, PA 19139; phone (215) 476-2307.

SPROUL STATE FOREST: YOST RUN

A large waterfall with lots of rocks, ledges, pools and hemlocks; the area is largely deserted in summer—but is popular with hunters during deer season.

☞ From State College follow Highway 26 north 14 miles to I-80. On I-80 go west 12 miles, exit at Highway 144 north. Follow Highway 144 through Moshannon and 13.5 miles past the intersection of highways 144 and 879, through Sproul State Forest. Park at a large turnout on the left side of the road. Walk back (south) on Highway 144 about 0.3 miles to a dirt road on your right. Follow this road 1 mile downhill past Camp Bloom (usually closed until fall) to Yost Run. The trail follows Yost Run down the narrow, wooded canyon to the waterfall.

RHODE ISLAND

SOUTH COAST

☆ DYER WOODS

A quiet, family-oriented campground on an old farm with 200 beautiful acres of meadows, woodland and a beaver pond. Sauna, hot tub, pond, volleyball, playground, clubhouse. Tent and RV sites. Visitors must prearrange. 114 Johnson Road, Foster, RI 02825. Phone (401) 397-3007.

NEW ENGLAND NATURIST ASSOCIATION

In 1996, New England Naturist Association (NENA) merged with the Pilgrim Naturists; see Massachusetts listings.

BLOCK ISLAND

A low-cost, less-developed alternative to Martha's Vineyard and Nantucket. "Sun Your Buns on Block Island," some local t-shirts promise. Accessible by ferry from Montauk Point, New London, Providence and Galilee. Ferry tickets are reasonable and bicycles are allowed. Mopeds may be rented on the island.

Go where Mehegan Trail meets Lakeside Drive (at what islanders call the Painted Rock), then go down the dirt road (Snake Hole Road) until it ends at the bluff above Black Rock Beach. After going down to the beach level, turn right or left—or, if you have the place to yourself, stay where you are. Also, the deserted beach south of the North Lighthouse on the west side is used for nude sunbathing and swimming, as is the beach at "Pots and Kettles" and many other remote beaches on the island.

SOUTH CAROLINA

NORTHWEST

CAROLINA FOOTHILLS RESORT

Located in the beautiful border foothills of upstate South Carolina. Situated on 50 acres of forest, the resort offers lovely trails, a creek, rest rooms and hot showers. Pool, volleyball, enclosed hot tub and deck. Tent and RV sites, rental cabin. Convenient to several airports and many interstates, the Blue Ridge Mountain Parkway, Smoky Mountains, Chimney Rock and Biltmore Estate are a few area attractions. Open year-round. P.O. Box 657-WG, Chesnee, SC 29323. Phone (803) 461-2731.

BAYNES CREEK

Baynes Creek waterfall and swimming hole can be used nude on weekdays. Picnic area along the deep creek with a 10-foot water slide and 4-foot-deep swimming hole. Signs indicate no trespassing but the owner doesn't mind nude use. May through September.

From Greenville, SC, take I-385 toward Columbia to Exit 23 and turn right. Go to the 4-way stop sign, turn left. Turn left at the next stop sign and continue 4.1 miles to Route 101. Keep going straight for 2.4 miles and turn left on Baynes Creek Road. Go to the bottom of hill and cross the wooden bridge. Walk up paved road

for 100 feet and then turn right and go down dirt road that leads to creek.

AUGUSTA AREA

☆ CEDAR CREEK

Beautiful 60-acre woodland park convenient to Augusta. Spring-fed creek, nature trails, in-ground pool, hot tub. Volleyball, horseshoes, miniature golf, annual music festival. Tent/RV sites, rental accommodations. Easy access from I-95, I-20 and I-26. Cedar Creek, P.O. Box 336-WG, Pelion, SC 29123. Phone (803) 894-5159.

SUNAIR HEALTH CLUB

Established in 1950, this 280-acre park near the South Carolina/Georgia border is located among tall pines with pure spring water. Tennis and volleyball courts, shuffleboard, jogging and hiking trails, swimming pond. Married couples only. Call for directions. Route 1, Box 126-WG, Graniteville, SC 29829. Phone (803) 663-6377.

COASTAL

FRANCIS MARION NATIONAL FOREST

Ten miles north of Charleston, opposite coastal Bull Island, lies this 250,000-acre federal refuge from dress codes. Many unimproved roads, trails throughout. Permit is needed for overnight camping. Along the northern boundary meanders the Santee River, the flowage from Lake Marion; it has many sandbars, a fully wild river.

OFFSHORE NUDING

Charleston's barrier reef islands give a boat skipper and a friend the option to find a "deserted" island and strip down...sort of a Robinson Crusoe with a witness!

Truth to tell, nothing's deserted any more. But try **Capers Island,** a fish and wildlife refuge. It permits overnight camping. The south end draws a number of boaters and campers, but farther up, oceanside, is generally hassle-free.

Dewees Island, privately-owned, has only a few homes on the southwest side. Come ashore at the southeast or north and you should trouble no one. Better, land on the small uninhabited island at

Dewees' north end; its dunes prevent a view from the inland waterway if you choose the ocean side.

Bull Island also has a nice beach for collecting shells and sun's rays. Moores Landing is the point of departure for the island at 8 a.m. with a return pick up at 4 p.m. Friday–Sunday; $12 per person. Call boat operator for reservations, phone (803) 928-3368; bring a lunch. To reach Moores Landing, turn east off US 17 onto Doar Road (20.8 miles north of the Cooper River Bridge that connects Charleston and Mt. Pleasant) and follow signs. Tent and RV camping 6.8 miles north of Doar Road at the Buck Hall Recreation Area.

DAUFUSKIE ISLAND

Daufuskie Island is a natural paradise, located one nautical mile from Hilton Head Island at the southeastern tip of South Carolina. Take the local ferry service, phone 803-681-7925, running from Hilton Head to Savannah, GA. The ferry will drop you off at Daufuskie Island's Freeport Marina. Rent a golf cart and explore the secluded beach at the opposite end of the island. The wind-eroded shoreline has exposed palm and pine roots, warm water and fine brown sand. En route to the beach, visit the Silver Dew Winery or the African Baptist church built in 1880 and still in use.

TENNESSEE

Creeks, cricks, fast rivers, ponds, falls and TVA reservoirs beckon skinny-dippers to the wilds of Tennessee. A 1994 state law bans public nudity but the rangers who patrol the backcountry are holding that the law is inapplicable to discreet skinny-dippers.

EASTERN

CLEVELAND: UPPER OCOEE RIVER

Take Route 64 east about 28 miles from Cleveland in the extreme southeast. The first half mile of the Upper Ocoee is a very popular area for the locals and the first few large pools are generally filled with clothed visitors. As you go farther up the river you should see only an occasional hiker. Take a maintenance road that is 1 mile east of the first parking area; the road is steep in some parts, and should only be attempted with 4WD and high-clearance vehicles. Parking areas at top and bottom of this road, which is less than a 1/2 mile long. Several camping areas nearby. Ocoee No. 2 Dam is a popular launch point for white water rafting.

BIG SOUTH FORK NATIONAL RIVER AND RECREATION AREA

Big South Fork offers over 120 miles of streams which feature waterfalls, gorges and rock arches. A true delight for those who enjoy outdoor recreation, Tennessee's newest national park has something for everyone. For invaluable maps contact park headquarters at Oneida, TN 37841.

PINEY RIVER SWIMHOLES

Several swimholes can be found in the first 3 miles of the Piney River Trail in Rhea County. Go west on Route 68 about 1 mile from US 27 near Spring City. Turn left on Shut-In Gap Road (the last street to the left before the bridge over Piney River), and proceed 1 mile to a picnic and parking area on the right side of the river. Piney River Trail begins across from the picnic area.

FALL CREEK FALLS STATE PARK

North of Savage Gulf on the Cumberland Plateau, this state park straddles Van Buren and Bledsoe counties. Cane Creek has a rarely-visited, delightful pool. From the foot of Fall Creek Falls, go 1/4 mile down Fall Creek and Cane Creek, occasionally scrambling through or under a rhododendron thicket, to a deep pool where Cane Creek falls 4 feet over a shelf of bedrock cutting diagonally across the stream bed. Approaching visitors can be spotted some distance away.

For even greater privacy, a second swimming hole can be found 2 miles farther downstream at the junction of Cane Creek and Piney Creek, with an excellent campsite nearby. Easier access to this spot is from a park trail which crosses the canyon a 1/2 mile downstream from the pool.

EAST TENNESSEE NATURISTS

Taking advantage of nude opportunities on and off public lands are the East Tennessee Naturists, 2118 Belle Terra, Knoxville, TN 37923; phone (423) 689-3043.

CENTRAL

DALE HOLLOW LAKE

Directly south of Louisville, KY, straddling Kentucky's southern border, but 90% inside Tennessee, is Dale Hollow Lake with 600 miles of shoreline and hundreds of isolated coves ideal for naturist use. Deer, osprey, eagles, fishing and swimming.

Hendricks Creek Resort offers an 18-passenger houseboat for 3-day, 4-day and week-long live-aboard rentals. Management says skinny-dipping is "very common." Summer week $3,495 for bare boat. Renter buys food, drinks, gas, brings own captain and crew. Hendricks Creek Resort, Burkesville, KY 42717; phone 1-800-321-4000.

☆ TIMBERLINE

Equidistant from Nashville and Knoxville, with 200 acres of woods, lake, pool, indoor hot tubs, poolside bar, elegant restaurant, lounge, guest lodge, entertainment. Fishing, hiking, sailing, canuding, volleyball. Tent and RV sites. P.O. Box 1173, Crossville, TN 38557. Phone (615) 277-3522 or (800) TAN-NUDE; fax (615) 277-3222.

CROSSVILLE: CANEY FORK RIVER

From Crossville, go west on US 70 to the second Pleasant Hill exit, a paved road 4385 (known locally as Browntown Road) and go 4 miles south. Here 4385 makes an unmarked T-intersection to the left and a turn to the right 0.4 miles later to resume its southward course. One mile farther, turn left on a gravel road that will take you on top of Pilot Knob Ridge and down to Blue Hole Falls Bridge. Across the bridge, a rough road on the right follows the Caney Fork River downstream 1 3/4 miles. This is the Blue Hole Recreation Area and nudity is not recommended here. Instead, swim or wade upstream for 1/2 mile to find private areas for discreet nude recreation.

There is a pristine, deserted area adjacent to the rest area at mile marker 267 with toilets, snack machines and free parking.

VIRGIN FALLS

Among the best hiking, camping and swimming areas is Scott's Gulf State Natural Area, White County, and it gets little use. From Crossville, take US 70S west to De Rossett. Turn south at 1000 Oaks Grocery on the De Rossett-Eastland-Pleasant Hill Road (a.k.a. 4385 or Mulberry Road). After 5.9 miles turn right on a gravel road marked Virgin Falls, and follow it 2.2 miles to the Virgin Falls Trailhead. Go 3.5 miles down this trail where a stream pours out of a cave over a cliff and vanishes into a sinkhole.

Below the falls the trail descends into the canyon of the Caney Fork where numerous campsites and secluded pools are suitable for swimming; or hike 10 miles up or downstream to find flumes, soaking pools, sunning rocks and waterfalls.

Maps are available near the parking area; many sites are well-marked, including Martha's Pretty Point, Big Laurel Falls, Little Branch Brook Falls and Sheeps Cave. They all offer some of nature's best hiking scenery, as well as nude opportunities and free camping.

SAVAGE GULF STATE NATURAL AREA

At the southern end of the Cumberland Plateau, the Savage Gulf preserve in Grundy County is reached by taking Route 127 south of I-40 to park headquarters. Walk 3/4 mile to Stone Door. There take the Big Creek Gulf Loop Trail west along the canyon rim, descending into the canyon after about 4 miles of easy walking. Leave the trail to descend to the creek bend at the first opportunity. Rock hop about 100 yards downstream to a large secluded swimming hole.

Additional site: Drive east from Grundy County Courthouse in Altamont to the end of the dirt road (if impassable because of mudholes, park beside the road and walk to the end). Take a trail down to an old mill hole on Firescald Creek. This pool is frequented by Altamont residents, as is the downstream Greeter Falls, and it is not advisable to skinny-dip if locals are in the area. However, with reasonable discretion nude hiking should be safe on weekdays.

RATTLESNAKE FALLS

For a gorgeous primitive high waterfall pool, visit Rattlesnake Falls. However, discretion counsels that you and your friends should be alone at this pool to use it nude, so try to come during the week. If others are present, continue downstream about 1/4 mile, past the shallow rock-bottomed stretch, to a smaller fall with dipping pool and sunning rocks.

☞ Take Route 31 south from Nashville to Route 43. Continue on 43 south through Mt. Pleasant; just beyond the town of Rockdale; at the top of the long hill you'll find a small dirt road leading off to the left at the end of the guardrail. Park here, or if you think your car can make it, drive in. Be sure to bear right at the fork; pass the makeshift dump. Park here and walk down the small path leading to the right, cross the creek and pick your spot. Be careful in the steep section.

ROCK HAVEN

A 25-acre park 40 miles south of Nashville. Pool, spa, rec hall, snack bar, country store, nature walk. Volleyball, tennis. Cabins, tent sites, trailer hookups. April–October. P.O. Box 1291-WG, Murfreesboro, TN 37133. Phone (615) 896-3553; fax (615) 848-1812.

WESTERN

KEN-TEN NATURISTS

A peripatetic group visiting the TVA lakes and state parks. Write c/o Charles Holmes, P.O. Box 822-WG, McKenzie, TN 38201.

MISSISSIPPI RIVER

Whenever the Mississippi is running low, sandbars emerge that extend for miles and miles—putting the beaches of California or Florida to shame for sheer length, natives like to say. And they're clean. The water may be muddy but it's not polluted. The river is under federal

jurisdiction and you should have no problems with the law for that reason, as long as you're discreet. You do need a boat to get to your sandbar; try the boat launch

ramps north of Memphis at McKeller Park or Martin Luther Park and tool upstream. You'll enjoy solitude if you don't bring your own company.

Jerry Derbyshire: Rock Climbing In Pedernales Falls State Park, Texas.

TEXAS

Texas' state park system is a resource of future and current Naturist areas, most with camping. Perfect directions and a map to most of them are free at the state's Welcome Centers or write to: Travel & Information, P.O. Box 5064, Austin, TX 78763. Request "Texas Public Campgrounds" and the official State Map; the booklet is keyed to the map.

EASTERN

☆ DALLAS: RIVER HILLS RESORT

Among sandstone hills and oaks overlooking Lake Ray Roberts Dam near Dallas-Fort Worth. Pool, spa, nature trails, volleyball, dances and cookouts. Non-member singles, day visitors welcome weekdays April–Oct. Tent and RV sites w/hookups. R.R. 2, Box 242-B, Aubrey, TX 76227. Phone (940) 365-9571.

☆ BLUEBONNET

Dallas, Fort Worth and Denton are within an hour's drive. Has 67 acres of rolling hills, oaks and meadows with nature walks. LBJ National Grasslands adjacent. Tent camping, RV hookups, rental trailers, hot showers, laundromat and snack bar. Playground, pool, sauna, jacuzzi, volleyball, tennis, shuffleboard, horseshoes. C.R. 1180 Box 146-WG, Alvord, TX 76225; phone (940) 627-2313.

SUNNY PINES

Sixty acres near Dallas in pine country. Horseshoes, pool tables, dance floor, volleyball, shuffleboard, large pool, sauna and spa. Tent and trailer sites, rental trailers. P.O. Box 133-WG, Wills Point, TX 75169. Phone (903) 873-3311.

AUSTIN CONTACTS

This large, diverse, creative south-central Texas group conducts many activities on public lands and at members' homes. Its newsletter is outstanding. **Central Texas Nudists,** P.O. Box 150053, Austin, TX 78715-0053. Phone (512) 873-9602; fax 396-4337.

Hill Country Nudists also serve the Austin area. P.O. Box 91802, Austin, TX 78709. Phone (512) 244-2543.

AUSTIN: BARTON CREEK & POOL

Barton Springs Pool is a spring-fed recreation facility with bathhouse within city limits. It offers a haven for women who prefer topfree sunning (legal throughout Austin, by the way). While not prevalent as in the '70s, it remains an option. Full nudity occurs discreetly in wooded areas upcreek from the pool.

☞ Cross the Colorado River from downtown Austin on Lamar or Congress. Find Barton Springs Road and proceed west to Zilker Park, where you angle left to Barton Springs Pool Parking Area (pool fee charged). Alternately, take I-35 across the river and Riverside Drive, then right on Barton Springs Road.

TRAVIS COUNTY: McGREGOR PARK (HIPPIE HOLLOW)

When the Lower Colorado River Authority transferred the regulation of Hippie Hollow to Travis County in the '80s, this new entity, McGregor County Park, was at last extended the support services that citizens have a right to expect.

The basics—sparkling Lake Travis, a rocky shore and dirt parking, nothing more—were improved. The County asphalted a perimeter trail, providing handicapped access. A large new supervised parking lot, deputies on horse patrols, trash receptacles and toilets: these were unheard-of amenities in a skinny-dipping haven. Open 9 a.m. to 8 p.m. No overnighting. Phone (512) 266-1644.

The Travis County attorney had first done his homework and issued an opinion. The County would not enforce the state lewd and lascivious statute at the park, he said, reasoning that a public facility where signs prepare the public for the fact that nudity may be encountered, cannot be "reckless and offensive."

The signage announcing the nude custom is at the entrance of all major trails. The shore is patrolled to ensure law and order. Gays gather at the far end.

Currently, children are excluded from Hippie Hollow by order of the county attorney. See *N* 16.4, pp. 121–123.

In the spring and early summer, the lake is high but cold, and many visitors bring raft floats. In the late summer and fall, the water is low but warmer. Do not dive recklessly from the limestone ledges, people have died doing it.

New rest rooms and a concession stand were built in 1997.

☞ From routes 2222 and 620 northwest of Austin, go west (left) on 620. Turn right at the Comanche Trail/McGregor Park Hippie Hollow signs. Go 2.2 miles to parking lot, pay fee, park and lock car. Walk down the paved trail in the southwest corner of the parking lot to any of the several cliffside paths that lead to the beach. When leaving, dress before reaching the parking lot; remove litter.

PALEFACE PARK

Travis County administers Paleface Park (Pace Bend), a fantasy come true for a travelling Naturist! Spend the day at Hippie Hollow, then drive (nude) a few minutes around pristine Lake Travis, pay $15 for hookups on a lakeside level cement pad, and watch (still nude) dozens of deer graze and frolic at sunset.

Or drive, dressed only in towels, three minutes within Paleface Park to Gracy Cove (#6 on the park map): use the #5 Thurman Cove entrance, bear right for lakeside parking, and you may spend the day nude. It's far less crowded than Hippie Hollow and few or no gawkers. Drive right up to azure water, with picnic tables, nice diving cliffs, nearby boat ramps, and gorgeous sunsets. Not formally posted nude, but the caretakers say there's never a problem and nude use is not threatened. Travis County provides areas for responsible Naturists.

☞ The distance on FM 2322 north from Route 71 is 4.6 miles. Use map at Ranger Station to find Gracy Cove. Cars $5. Camping $10; w/hookup $15.

☆ RIVERSIDE RESORT

Twenty-five minutes south of the Alamo on the banks of the San Antonio River, Riverside Resort has 17 wooded acres. Hot tub, rec room, restaurant, playground, volleyball and schuffleboard. Campsites and two-room motel. P.O. Box 14413-WG, San Antonio, TX 78214. Phone (830) 393-2387; fax (830) 393-2589.

☆ SAHNOANS

Forty miles east of Austin, Sahnoans Star Ranch provides nude living for families. Outdoor pool, heated indoor pool next to hot tub. Tent and trailer sites, rental cabins. Volleyball, tennis, playground, clubhouse, restaurant. P.O. Box 142233-WG, Austin, TX 78714. Phone (512) 273-2257; fax (512) 273-2822.

☆ LIVE OAK RANCH

Largest club in Texas, with live oak trees and rolling green grass. Pool with waterslide, whirlpool, volleyball, rec hall, rental cabins, tent/RV sites with hookups, restaurant, playground, entertainment. Lounge in a shady hammock, stroll the spacious grounds or hang out in the hot tub. North of Route 290 by Route 6 from Houston or Austin. R.R. 1, Box 916-WG, Washington, TX 77880. Phone (409) 878-2216; fax 878-2788.

BOLIVAR PENINSULA

Bolivar Peninsula juts from the mainland toward Galveston Island, all but sealing Galveston Bay from the Gulf of Mexico. The Intercoastal Canal runs the length of the peninsula, paralleling the Gulf Coast, and the small beaches dotting the shoreline can be "liberated" on a first-one-here-sets-the-rules basis.

Bolivar Beach has been used over the years by a number of naturists who finally decided to join each other. In 1992 the Bolivar Beach Society formed to stake out this 3-mile section for nude use. Bolivar Beach Society, c/o William H. Hoover, Jr., P.O. Box 667002, Houston, TX 77266-7002. Phone (713) 521-9494.

☞ From Houston, drive east on I-10 to the town of Winnie. Turn south on State Highway 124 and go through the town of High Island. The intersection with Highway 87 is about 19 miles south of I-10. Look for the barricades. The nude beach is approximately 4.5 miles east past the barricades on Highway 87. Watch for drifting sand and missing roadway. Follow the path taken by other vehicles. The clothing-optional area is marked with numerous signs posted by beach regulars.

Other semi-private beach sections are accessible only by boat; the passing barges can do little but wave. Park at the Galveston Yacht Club to launch. Travel parallel to the ferry route, turn left upon reaching Bolivar Peninsula and enter the canal. Weekdays best bet, weekends are getting crowded.

☆ NATURAL HORISUN

On a 33-acre pecan and oak orchard, this family nudist park is 34 miles southwest of Houston. Open year-round offering RV sites, tenting space, clubhouse, swimming pool and whirlpool, volleyball and horseshoes. P.O. Box 809-WG, Needville, TX 77461. Phone (409) 657-3061 or 1-800-NHI-NUDE.

MATAGORDA ISLAND

A barrier island just off the Texas coast from Port O'Connor, about 34 miles long by about 2 miles wide, with the southernmost 10 miles owned and managed by the federal government. The rest is under management by the Texas State Parks and Wildlife Department; a primitive area where whooping cranes and alligators share the land with humans.

A two-mile beach and 7,325 acres of grass and ponds comprise Matagorda State Park. A ferry transports visitors once a day on Saturday and Sunday only from Port O'Connor. Saturday ferry leaves Port O'Connor at 8:30 a.m. and returns to the mainland at 2 p.m. The Sunday edition leaves the mainland at 10 a.m. and returns from the island at 4 p.m. The ferry holds 52 people; reservations are advised. Bring everything you will need, there is no food or drinking water on the island. Port O'Connor has three motels.

Once on the island, board a bus for the Gulf side where 4WD trucks will then take you to the beach. Go south one mile before disrobing. Beachcombing is excellent. Camping is allowed on the beach.

PADRE ISLAND NATIONAL SEASHORE: NORTH BEACH

Access PINS from Corpus Christi. Pick up your food and drink needs at Bob Hall pier area, drive 20 miles south, park car at the barricade and walk 2 miles south into "wilderness" area to North Beach on the Gulf shore. Take care to remove litter and preserve the dunes.

Driving with 4WD down the beach is the best bet. It goes for 60 miles and a complainer would have to go a long way to find a ranger. A ranger impelled by church imperatives has spearheaded nudie citations—so check with other users on current enforcement.

In truth, PINS has no legal basis to cite discreet sunbathers; certainly not under the Texas law which condones Hippie Hollow.

At milepost 15 there is a campground and beginning at marker 32, there are more than a dozen washover channels making crossing to Laguna Madre easy.

YUCANTAN CLUB

Larry Gooden, owner, Yucantan Nudist Club, will transport sunbathers on his boat to the dredge "spoil islands" of Laguna Madre. Tent and camping equipment for rent. 1005 Green Bay, Corpus Christi, TX 78418. Phone (512) 937-4001; fax 937-6488.

SOUTH PADRE ISLAND

The south Gulf Coast of Texas is known to students on spring break and to snowbirds for gentle breezes, sunny skies, abundant shells and fishing. Contact South Padre Island Naturists, Box 9230-WG, Port Isabel, TX 78578.

About 8.5 miles up the hard sand beach from South Padre Island town, far from the last sign of pavement, begins the informally naturist section, as marked by a large plastic tank buried in the sand and a big log with "Nude Beach" painted on it.

Low tide access is best for conventional vehicles and RVs. Vehicles with flotation tires or 4WD come and go any time. If the sand is dry, don't drive on it; you'll become hopelessly stuck. If stuck, don't spin your wheels—you'll only dig in deeper. Instead, deflate all the tires so they look 70% flat; in most cases you can drive out with ease.

☞ From Port Isabel, take Highway 100 to the Island. On South Padre Island, go 12 miles north on Route 100, turn right at Beach Access #3, then left (north) for 8.5 miles.

SANDPIPERS HOLIDAY PARK

Near Mexico and South Padre Island. Rental mobile home suites and RV lots. Weekend restaurant. Large heated pool with diving board, water slide, toddlers pool, jacuzzi, hot tub. Lighted tennis, volleyball, shuffleboard and horseshoe courts. Golf, fishing nearby. R.R. 7, Box 309-WG, Edinburg, TX 78539. Phone (210) 383-7589.

TEXAS CONTACTS

Bexar Recreation Society: A "backyard nudist group" established in 1995 that meets at Riverside Resort and members' homes. C/O Jim Morris, P.O. Box 13126, San Antonio, TX 78213.

Based at the University of Texas-Austin, **Longhorn Nudists** organize naturist trips, fund raisers and weekly activities. Send SASE to Texas Union #135, P.O. Box 7338, Austin, TX 78713.

The Natural Travelers. Events include visits to area clubs, camping trips and house parties. 3230 S. Gessner #613, Houston TX 77063; phone (713) 784-0621.

Sunbirds Sun Club serves the Fort Worth, Dallas and Denton areas. P.O. Box 111524, Carrollton, Texas 75011; phone (214) 373-2036.

WESTERN

AMARILLO: PALO DURO CANYON STATE PARK

This lovely part of the Panhandle has so many canyons and other isolated areas that a complainant, or ranger, is unlikely to stumble upon you. A wonderful place for nude swimming and hiking. South from Amarillo on Route 27, east on Route 217 from Canyon, to the park headquarters for directions/trail maps.

BIG BEND NATIONAL PARK

Primitive campsites along the Rio Grande at the Mexican border are spaced miles apart, permitting nude and natural highs for the friends you assemble to bring in.

The park's higher desert also has many camping areas with beautiful vistas. Primitive areas can be reached only with high-clearance vehicles. Bring plenty of

UTAH

NATURIST CONTACTS

Utah Naturists—organizer of river rafting and houseboating trips and Salt Lake City activities. P.O. Box 9058-WG, Salt Lake City, UT 84109. Phone (801) 278-9740.

SOUTHERN

LAKE POWELL HOUSEBOATING

Next in Utah to private homes, Lake Powell is the sociably naked place to be. Folks who don't normally recreate au naturel may camp or float nakedly in one of the many secluded coves.

Fantastic scenery including Indian ruins, dramatic canyon walls and the famous Rainbow Bridge. See *Nude & Natural* magazine, *N* 13.3, pp. 45–48, for detailed report.

MOAB AREA

MILL CREEK CANYON

From downtown Moab go east on Center Street four blocks to 400 East Street, then go south a similar distance, and turn left (east) onto Mill Creek Road. In about one mile, turn left onto Powerhouse Lane and go to the end. Park and continue on foot up Mill Creek Canyon past the dam. About a mile upstream the canyon forks; the north fork leads to beautiful waterfalls and pools well worth a dip. It is unlikely you will run into anyone easily bothered by nudity, but when in doubt, ask first.

The south fork of the canyon also has some nice pools and since the hike is a little longer, it is less populated.

NEGRO BILL CANYON

A beautiful box canyon spanned by Morning Glory Arch. Remember to bring drinking water; at least 1/2 gallon per person. From Moab take Main Street (Route 191) north 2 miles, turn right (east) onto Route 128 and follow it upstream along the Colorado River for 3

water and food as it is a long, slow and rough drive back to the ranger station. Maps and information from Big Bend National Park, TX 79834.

miles. Park in the lot 100 yards past mile-marker 3. Hike up the canyon about 2 miles; follow the right (south) fork of the canyon another mile. Along the hike you'll find many pools to cool off.

ARCHES NATIONAL PARK

Most areas of Arches National Park are approachable by car—easy hikes to relatively secluded and beautiful red rock landscapes that defy description. A short scramble off any established trail can provide privacy. Cross-country hiking off the trails is readily available. This always sunny area is great except mid-June through August, when it's too hot for the comfort of most. Water is scarce away from the campground, and the few swimholes are difficult to find.

About 28 miles south of I-70 and four miles north of Moab on US 163 is the entrance. Arches National Park personnel can provide directions to the trails.

CANYONLANDS NATIONAL PARK: NEEDLES DISTRICT

This has to be the greatest sandbox for adults anywhere on earth. Replete with beautiful red rimrock and alternate red and white layers of sandstone, a very warm beauty, and a myriad of trails and paths through an infinite variety of scenery.

The area south of the campground is limited to foot traffic and includes dozens of miles of easy-to-hike trails, marked simply by rock cairns. Skinny-hiking on the established trails poses no objection unless it's done in sight of the campground.

☞ Needles District of Canyonlands National Park lies southeast of the Colorado River. Drive 40 miles south of Moab on US 191 or 15 miles north of Monticello to the park entry. Drive west 37 miles on Route 211 to the Ranger Station and 3 miles farther to the Squaw Flat Campground. A handout schematic map is available. It's all one needs to guide oneself to several days' adventure.

Ed Stimpson: 1500' Bluff Above Rainbow Bridge Region Of Lake Powell, Utah; The Houseboats Look Like Toys.

VERMONT

ermont's attorney general in 1973 issued a memorandum of enforcement policy on nudity that seems to sum up the live-and-let-live tolerant attitude of Vermonters:

The state has no legitimate interest in nudity on private land out of public view. Nor has it a nudity interest in public if secluded areas—unless a citizen should complain, in which case the person shall be asked to dress.

The then attorney general is now U.S. Senator Patrick Leahy. If only all North America were to be "Vermonticized!"

The standard guide is *Vermont Unveiled* (1996) by Jim C. Cunningham, from P.O. Box 300, Troy, VT 05868; phone (802) 744-6565.

QUARRIES

Any lake, pond, or stream that is away from thoroughfares is likely to have its share of skinny-dipping. To locate sites not mentioned here, simply watch for the telltale parked cars on roadsides near water. If you're a boater or hiker, you will find many more suitable sites.

One word about quarries. They offer sunning rocks and cold refreshing waters; if you find a "No Trespassing" notice sign be aware that owners often post them to shed liability if anyone is injured on the property. An owner determined to get rid of swimmers has more than mere signs available. Swimmers emerging from a quarry covered with drain oil might surmise it was poured there on purpose. If you find manure laid out along the quarry perimeter, that could be because it draws vicious horseflies.

When you do find a quarry whose owner is tolerant of visitors, be a respon-

sible guest, closing access gates behind you, etc., and you will seldom be turned away. Just know that your safety is your concern. Look before you leap.

SOUTHERN

NEPCO'S HARRIMAN RESERVOIR: THE LEDGES

Close to Massachusetts and cherished by many skinny-dippers as the premier site of Vermont as well as exemplary of what a more body-tolerant corporate America should support and enjoy in its natural preserves.

Located on private property of the New England Power Company (NEPCO) a short distance from company's clothed picnic grounds, and a portion of the Green Mountain National Forest, large flat rocks offer sunbathing and diving platforms. The water level of Harriman Reservoir is higher early in the season. Some folks paddle a raft in, rather than hike the shore trail. Stay dressed until you reach the nude area.

☞ From Brattleboro: take Route 9 west towards Wilmington, and bear left onto Route 100 south. Watch for the NEPCO sign on right and bear right up the dirt access road, passing a few homes and continuing almost a mile to the picnic grounds. Once there, park as close to the lower right parking and picnic area as possible. Continue to the right along the shore until a well-trod path becomes evident, and follow it 5 minutes to The Ledges. It's close enough to carry lounge chairs and coolers. Portatoilets at the picnic grounds. The Ledges can also be accessed by boat from a launch site in Wilmington at the north end of the reservoir.

GREEN MOUNTAIN NATIONAL FOREST

Over 100 miles of hiking trails, plus windsurfing, powerboating, water-skiing, canuding, camping—all potentially clothes-optional on 250 sq. mi. of wilderness controlled by NEPCO and the Green Mountain National Forest. Rangers don't hassle discreet nudity. Avoid the developed areas; recommended sites are below.

Somerset Reservoir has a powerboat ramp on a six-mile lake where nude boating, water-skiing and windsurfing are possible. **Grout Pond,** Somerset's northern sister, has crystal clear water and over 30

private camping areas (14 night max.).

Branch Pond is almost a mile long. Free camping. Total wilderness: bring what you need. Obtaining a map before venturing in is a good idea.

Stratton and **Bourn** ponds are more remote than Branch Pond, accessible only by hiking. There are good-sized islands and the sunsets/sunrises are particularly inspiring. Long Trail and Appalachian Trail cross the area; many mountaintop vistas provide four-state views.

Downer Glen is a most unusual geological formation. Natural use in this area has occurred as far back as any local can remember. It's well worth the hike to pick your pool and enjoy.

Kelley Stand is a 12-mile good dirt road leading from Arlington to Grout. Along the way, it closely parallels Roaring Branch Brook and after the first 3 miles, the homes end, providing dozens of neat little spots for nude sunning on huge boulders below the many small falls or swimming in the chilly waters of the brook.

☞ After turning right on Somerset Road in Searsburg, go 6.2 miles where you come to the junction with FH-71 (Snowmobile Trail No. 7) on the left. To Somerset Reservoir, continue on Somerset Road for 3.25 miles to the reservoir. Campsites are available at the junction of FH-71 and Somerset Road. There is an information board on the left side of the road as you turn onto FH-71.

To Grout Pond, turn left on FH-71, bear right at the split (2.5 miles) with

Vermont

Snowmobile Trail No. 7AS and follow to its end, about 10 miles, at FH-6. Turn right on FH-6 and go about 1 mile. Look for the entrance to Grout Pond on the right.

Note: FH-71 and FH-6 (up to Grout Pond Entrance) are not maintained in the winter. Alternate route: From the center of Wilmington, go north on Route 100 to West Wardsboro. Turn left on FH-6 toward Stratton. Go through Stratton and proceed to the entrance of Grout Pond, on the left.

For information, write the Green Mountain National Forest, 151 West St., P.O. Box 519, Rutland, VT 05701.

BIG BRANCH BROOK

Big Branch Brook offers free parking for RVs (14-day limit), clean water and nude hiking/swimming opportunities.

☞ From Manchester, VT, go north on Route 7 or 7A to Danby. Turn right (east) on National Forest Highway 10, crossing Otter Creek. Enter the White Rocks National Recreational Area and just before the road crosses Big Branch Brook, park in the turnoff. Hike upstream as far as you choose.

MANCHESTER: PIKES FALLS

A beautiful area of cascades and small waterfalls with many potholes to dunk in, and one very large pool at the bottom of the main falls. Usually clothed and nude

mix fine. If crowded you can always retreat upstream.

☞ From the intersections of Routes 100 and 107 in Stockbridge, go 0.2 miles north on Route 100, around a sharp curve, and park in the dirt turnoff. Follow trails upstream.

OLD JELLY MILL FALLS

A 1/8-mile-long sheet of solid granite over which flows the crystal clear water of Stickney Brook. A short rock slide and small pool complete the geological phenomena. Few go here, even on summer weekends, so expect to be by yourself.

☞ From the center of Brattleboro, go north on Route 30 for 4.9 miles, passing Stickney Road on the left and crossing a small bridge spanning Stickney Brook. Park in the turnoff on the immediate left and follow the roaring sound of the falls to the pool.

Before leaving the area, check out the lattice-covered bridge 2 miles up Route 30 from the falls. Built in 1972, it is the longest covered bridge in Vermont and possibly the second longest covered bridge in the world.

INDIAN LOVE CALL

From the center of Brattleboro, follow Route 30 north for 6.9 miles to the Maple Valley Ski Area. Park at Maple Valley and walk north on Route 30 for 0.4 miles to Indian Love Call, marked on some

maps as a picnic area near the store Vermont Natural Castings (worth visiting). Walk through the closed parking lot. Day use only.

NEWFANE: ROCK RIVER

Low cliffs are suitable for diving and a sandy beach for picnicking. The first pool is used mainly by clothed swimmers; the three pools upstream by skinny-dippers. Drive Route 30 northwest from Brattleboro; 1.4 miles beyond Maple Valley Ski Area turnoff, take a left towards South Newfane and Williamsville. Parking is along Route 30. (The Rock River bridge is just beyond.) Go up the steep hill about 1/2 mile, cross over guardrail and follow path to the river. Gay areas farther left.

MANCHESTER CENTER: TOLLGATE ROAD FALLS

The flumes, slate slabs for sunning, tumbling white water, natural tubs and pools amid birches and pines—it's a classical Vermont skinny-dipping experience, 8 minutes from Manchester, 20 seconds from Route 30. Just east lies Green Mountain National Forest.

☞ From the overpass of Route 7 on the east side of Manchester Center, drive east 2.4 miles on Routes 11-30. Turn left sharply on Tollgate Road at the sign for Mistral's Restaurant. After just 50 feet turn sharply right onto a short gravel road; if you reach the restaurant you've gone too far. Drive 100 feet and park. If the few spaces for autos on this cul-de-sac are occupied, please return to the highway and go on—the Falls won't comfortably accept more bathers than can be parked.

LYE BROOK FALLS

Lye Brook National Wilderness Area has a winding brook that cascades for 2 miles. You'll catch the sun at one pool or another at any time. The water is crystal clear and potable. Walking the rocks in the gorge is fun. Litter here is nonexistent so take your trash out. Overnight parking of RVs for up to 14 days is allowed.

☞ Richville Road south from Route 30 in the center of Manchester, and turn left on East Manchester Road. Go to the first underpass and cross underneath US 7. Immediately take a right on Lye Brook Falls Access Road, and follow it 0.7 miles to the end, which is a large cul-de-sac. Park and follow the well-defined trail to Lye Brook. Walk in

the direction of water noise and you'll find it on the right. Follow the brook upstream for as far as you like.

DORSET: UPPER QUARRY

The magnificent Dorset back or upper quarry is a super-Olympic-sized marble pool with clean water in a birch and pine woods. Nudity is intermittent—troubled by rowdies and sexual show-offs—but often happens. The lower or front quarry is behind bushes next to the highway.

☞ Turn off Route 7 at Manchester Center, find Route 30 and drive it north for 5 miles. Or drive it for 3 miles south from Dorset Center. The long, one-story Mountain Weavers building is on the west side. On east, find gravel Kelly Road. Go up it 100 yards to trailhead in the woods to the upper quarry, follow it a quarter mile.

LUDLOW: BUTTERMILK FALLS

Icy water and far too many visitors not used to nudity have still not stopped Vermonters from enjoying these cascades, pools deep enough for diving, small sand beaches and large rocks for sunning au naturel.

Drive northwest on Route 103 from Ludlow towards Rutland. Watch for the turnoff on the right for Route 100. Drive just past it, to "old Route 103" on the right, marked by a large white VFW building. Turn onto it and go 1.3 miles to the several paths down to the water on the right side of the road. The road ends at a barricaded bridge. Cross the bridge, following paths on the left to the pools affording the best possibilities for nude recreation.

WALLINGFORD: LITTLE ROCK POND

North on Route 7 from Manchester Center towards Rutland, this Green Mountain forest pool beneath a 50-foot rock accepts 25 or so skinny-dipping hikers. Access by the Long Trail where it crosses Forest Route 10, east of Mount Tabor. Hike the trail north for 2.5 miles. Or turn east off Route 7 just south of the South Wallingford Congregational Church, cross a bridge and follow a curve to the right. On the left is South Wallingford Community Center. Park there, find Homer Stone Brook Trail at the driveway to the right of the next house (don't park near this house), and hike this route 2.5 miles—a bit steeper than the Long Trail. There are some gorgeous vistas on the Appalachian and Long Trails; camping nearby.

RUTLAND: MILL RIVER

South from Rutland on Route 7 past junction with Route 103 and a rest area on the right, take the next left. Immediately take the next right, and drive on this dirt road, (old Route 7, which changes to paved road) to the dead end and park. Most bathers at the bridge wear suits; nudity is more common beginning a half mile upstream along Mill River. Trails extend upstream for several miles where there are beautiful rock formations, pristine pools and very secluded areas.

In Shrewsbury, farther up from the Mill River, is the **Clarendon Gorge,** a mile-long canyon with 100-foot high walls.

☞ From the intersection of Routes 7 and 103 south of Rutland, go south on 103 for 2.1 miles. Park in the lot on the right, where the Long/ Appalachian

trails and the railroad crosses 103. Several trails to choose from; the easiest is farthest from the right of the railroad track, beginning at the middle back edge of the parking lot. The best nude areas begin downriver just out of sight of the suspension bridge.

Long-term mixed nude/clothed use is at the **Clarendon Quarry;** clear, warm water, nice diving ledges; good sun window. From Route 4, a divided expressway at West Rutland, go into town to Route 4A, then south on Route 133 for 2.3 miles. Go left at Clarendon Springs fork for 0.3 miles; park on right, before a small bridge crossing the Clarendon River. Follow trail to right.

BRANDON: SILVER LAKE

Route 7 to Route 53 east exit between

Michael Cooney: Harriman Reservoir, The Ledges

Brandon and Middlebury. South on Route 53 to Branbury State Park. Park and follow signage on east side, hike 10 minutes up to Falls of Lana picnic area and pools. A farther 30-minute steep hike brings you to the clean sandy beach, primitive camping and toilet, freshwater well with hand pump, and large swimming area of Silver Lake.

FELCHVILLE: READING SWIMMING HOLE

Between Springfield and Woodstock on Route 106, find Felchville. You'll know it by the Reading Country Store with a big Shell sign on the west side. Turn west here, towards South Reading and Tyson. Go exactly a mile and park on the crest of a small hill—along the road, not blocking any driveway. Paths lead down to the left: first a 50-foot scramble, then 20-foot-high cliffs, and at the base, a blue-green pool in the North Branch of the Black River, known as Twenty-Foot Pool. This site is usually clothed; but a hundred yards downstream is Ten-Foot Pool where clothing is optional. So too farther on at Fifteen-Foot Pool.

NORTHERN

WATERBURY: MAD RIVER PUNCH BOWL

Privately-owned and supervised, the Punch Bowl is open to the public and offers a litter-free beach, sunning rocks, no gawkers, good diving, a small waterfall and an island. Take I-89 to Waterbury. South on Route 100 to Irasville. From Routes 100 and 17 in Irasville, take 100

south for 2.7 miles. On the right is a private driveway, then an open field. At the south end of the field, 0.3 miles north of the steel bridge over Mad River, follow the tracks through the field to the end. Turn right onto a dirt driveway (a quarter mile before Texaco Station) that leads along the Mad River to the end of a field. Park and walk left down to the river. Take home your trash when leaving.

HUNTINGTON RIVER & GORGE

This rushing river and falls pass through a gorge populated by nude daredevil divers from the cliffs in summertime. The gorge is over a mile long, with shallow areas for children and an easy access. Downriver, below the farmhouse, pools and ledges call for sunbathing; steep trails lead to some. Please take out your trash.

☞ Exit 10 (Waterbury) or 11 (Richmond) off Route 2 will bring you to Jonesville. Then south across the Winooski River Bridge, and west (right) to a narrow, unmarked road that follows the Huntington River upstream on its right (northwest) side. Both down and upriver from a horse farm, parked cars will indicate trailheads leading to favorite sites.

To reach the Huntington Gorge: from the general store on Route 2 in Jonesville, head east 0.2 miles, turn right over the tracks and cross a steel bridge, then a smaller bridge. Go left at the next fork on Dugway Road. At the 0.5 mile mark, turnoffs can be seen at intervals along the road. The first ones offer the easiest descent to the river; the ones farther up offer better scenery. Caution: the upper gorge is extremely dangerous during

high water; avoid.

WOODBURY QUARRY

Midday sun challenges the quarry's icy water with its sunning rocks. Horseflies can be thick in early summer. Take Route 14 from Barre or Hardwick and in the village of Woodbury, with a white United Methodist Church on west side, take the facing road to Cabot eastward. After road climbs for 3/4 mile turn left on a dirt road. At the fork stay right. At 3/4 mile from the road to Cabot is the entrance to a working quarry on right. Go past, for another 1/2 mile on the worsening road, to the swimming quarry with spectacular cliffs and shelving ledges.

STOWE: BINGHAM FALLS

The West Branch of the Waterbury River offers easy access to lovely falls and pools where the unclad and clad frequently mingle. No one questions their nude use. No sandy beaches, only rocks.

From Waterbury on I-89, north on Route 100 to Stowe. North on Route 108 towards Mt. Mansfield. Just past "The Lodge" hotel on your left, park in the turnout on the same side of the road. The trail down to the falls is opposite the turnout, on the right (east) side of the road.

SHELBURNE POINT

Lake Champlain has many boaters who sail au naturel or look for a quiet cove to enjoy as nature intended. Shelburne Point has some of the more popular coves where you might find like-minded naturists. Possible to hike nude for miles.

☞ To reach Shelburne Point, travel north on Route 7 to Shelburne Village south of Burlington. At Village stop light (a Texaco Station will be on the corner), turn left. Cross railroad tracks 200 yards from stoplight and continue 2.5 miles through the 4-way stop signs. Turn right on Ticonderoga Drive, about 1.4 miles past the 4-way stop signs, and go about 100 yards. Turn left on General Greene Drive. Continue 100 yards past the driveway on the right on Gen. Greene Dr. and park on either side, keeping all wheels off the road. Walk 50 yards and turn left on Chatuguay Drive. Walk 100 yards and turn right at the T-intersection. Continue on road past the beach on the left for 100 yards, where you will turn right and go on dirt road with a "No Trespassing" sign. (There have been no reports of hassles; this is a well-known nudist area.) About 200 yards from the gate, the path bears left through the woods and another 200 feet, the path opens into a large meadow and woods. Just before entering the woods, the path

Vermont

forks. Either direction will take you to one of three beaches where you can find up to 40 naturists on a good day.

BURLINGTON: RED ROCKS PARK

The startling bluffs at the north end of Red Rock Park are established for social sunbathing. One may enjoy inspiring vistas of Mt. Mansfield and Mt. Marcy.

☞ To Red Rock Park, take Route 7 south (Shelburne Road) from Burlington. After I-89 intersection take right turn before Gulf station (Queen City Park Road) for one-third mile, across a narrow one-lane bridge, and the next left (Central Avenue) to the park entrance. Pay to park. At shore, clothed sandy beach is at left. You go right (north) about a mile on a broad bicycle path to the accepted nude use area just before the cliffs.

GRAND ISLE STATE PARK

Grand Isle State Park's south beach on Lake Champlain is developing a clothes-optional area. Skinny-dippers remain discreet especially in heavily-used areas. To get from Burlington to Grand Isle, take Route 89 north to Route 2 west and follow the well-marked route.

MAPLE GLEN

Close to Lake Champlain near Canada east of Swanton. Begun for the French-Canadians to avoid a Catholic orthodoxy which governed Québec into the '60s. While Québec now has nudist parks, Maple Glen keeps a French-speaking membership. Tent and RV sites with hookups, volleyball, tennis, pool, rec hall. P.O. Box 445, Sheldon Springs, VT 05485.

JEFFERSONVILLE: BREWSTER RIVER

Route 15 northeast from Burlington to Jeffersonville. Turn south on Route 108 as if to Smuggler's Notch—just out of town on your left, you'll see Brewster River Mill Gift Shop. Take the next left towards a covered bridge but instead of crossing it, turn right onto a narrow dirt road upriver. Go past the first pools on the left to park at turnabout and stroll the broad trail farther upstream, wading the stream once. Away from the suited, and to the better bargain, a nude pool and waterfall. Early afternoon has best sun. The bold may clamber farther up the gorge.

WESTMORE: LAKE WILLOUGHBY STATE PARK

Hassle-free, sandy wading beach for children and water sports; clean but chilly water with fine trout fishing and water-skiing, and spectacular view of Mt. Pisgah. North on I-93 or I-91 and exit from I-91 at Lyndon. Route 5 north to West Burke, then bear right onto Route 5A to south end of Lake Willoughby. Park either at clothed beach by the road, or about 200 feet south of this on the left. A trail from the latter leads down to the lake at Cunningham Cove around a small point from the clothed beach. Named for Jim Cunningham whose family pioneered nude use.

White Caps campground and store is a few minutes on foot. Motels, restaurants nearby.

BOLTON SKI AREA: JOINER BROOK

I-89 to Waterbury. West on Route 2 towards Richmond. A paved road on right leads up to Bolton Valley Ski Area; take it, and look for "Bolton Valley Resort" sign on right. Just 1.5 miles beyond, another sign urges: "Steep Hill Use Low Gear." Park in the next turnout on right. Cross the road, cross Joiner Brook, and follow trail upstream to the mother of skinny-dipper pools on this stream. You might also check other turnouts with parked cars descending to Route 2, as many will beat trails leading to nice parts of Joiner Brook.

VIRGINIA

☆ WHITE TAIL PARK

Family-oriented resort with 600 members. Trails, heated pools, hot tub, snack bar, rec halls, playground, volleyball with 160 campsites; rental units. Near Williamsburg, Jamestown, Virginia Beach. Families, couples and singles welcome. 39033 White Tail Drive, Ivor, VA 23866. Phone (757) 859-6123; fax (757) 859-6724.

SHENANDOAH NATIONAL PARK

A number of large streams suitable for impromptu dipping: pick up *Circuit Hikes in Shenandoah National Park* from the Potomac Appalachian Trail Club, 1718 N St., N.W., Washington, DC 20036 or any outdoors store.

Overall Run has been popular, with its rock bathtubs and slides, especially weekdays. Big Blue Trail will also delight the naturist backpacker, with its frequent remote streams, ponds, and lakes, as it follows a 144-mile route from Hancock, MD, south through West Virginia, then east across Shenandoah Valley into the north part of Shenandoah National Park.

Go 10 miles south of Front Royal to Bentonville. Turn left on Bentonville-Browntown Road. After a mile or so turn right on Thompson Hollow Road. Follow road several miles until you see a "No Parking After This Point" sign. Walk along road until road goes uphill toward a house. Veer right on the trail (you will see trees blazed blue). The trail, Thompson Hollow Trail, merges with Big Blue Trail, and later intersects with Overall Run. Big Blue Trail, several miles long, offers nude hiking opportunities. At the end of Overall Run (the last half mile is very steep), are several beautiful falls and nice pools. Trails are marked and trail junctions have concrete pillars. Bring water and bug spray, pack out what you pack in.

TOTALLY BUFF BLUFF

A superb, sandy beach location on the lower James River's tidewater adjacent to historic Williamsburg and the Busch Gardens theme park. Virtually exclusively naturist, this lightly-used sandspit is formed by the meeting of an unspoiled salt marsh, the James and a sandstone bluff containing fossil deposits laid down five million years ago on the bottom of a warm, shallow sea.

The southeasterly orientation of the site and the protection of the bluff allow for unsurpassed enjoyment in the spring, when Chesapeake rockfish make a salmon-like spawning run past the beach and into the marsh as bald eagles wheel overhead. Like many hassle-free nude beaches in the Old Dominion, this area is all but inaccessible.

☞ From Interstate 64 East out of Richmond, take the Route 199E exit to Williamsburg/Busch Gardens and then Route 60E exit, still following the Busch Gardens signs. Turn right onto Kingsmill Drive. Stop at the security gates (note: these are real police) and request a guest pass to marina. Continue on Kingsmill Drive to convention center, follow signs to parking at marina. Walk west one mile to the bluff. Low tides are best. Consult Jamestown Island tide table.

Alternatively, bike up Country Road from Carter's Grove Plantation off Route 60 to the top of the hill past the first salt marsh bridge. Turn left off road and hike through the forest 10 minutes to the beach.

SMITH MOUNTAIN LAKE

Although heavily populated, anyone with access to a boat will find secluded coves to skinny-dip in along the lake's 500-mile shoreline. The best area is the side toward the dam. The lake is patrolled by rangers on the lookout for drunks and reckless boaters. Weekdays are best due to low use; weekends are crowded but one can still find a nice cove if you get there early and claim your spot. Several campgrounds and restaurants are nearby.

☞ Between Roanoke and Lynchburg, take Route 122 from Bedford.

VIRGINIA CONTACTS

Potomac Rambling Bares. Hosts year-round clothing-optional activities at member's homes, on public lands, and at Avalon in WV. P.O. Box 515, Oakton, VA 22124-0515. Phone (703) 742-7987.

Commonwealth of Virginia Naturists, formerly Central Virginia Naturists. P.O. Box 2241, Virginia Beach, VA 23450-2241; Lynchburg phone (804) 332-1366; Charlottesville (804) 985-2025.

Fred Sidell: Assateague Island, Pony Round-Up.

WASHINGTON

EASTERN

SPOKANE: LATAH CREEK BEACH

The bus from downtown Spokane stops a mile west on the corner of Riverside and Clark, and some who get off hike through a reforested area to former Peoples Park. One of the nation's best-established nude beaches, its origin was the Spokane Expo '74. Homes in the area were condemned to enlarge High Bridge Park. Workers at the Expo set up rough camping. Skinny-dipping was part of it, and never has gone away. In 1982, prudes invoked the Spokane lewdness ordinance and several citations were issued before an ACLU lawyer (with aid from the Naturist Society) stopped the nonsense that nude was lewd. After nearby residents pushed for a traffic closure, the park board installed a concrete barrier and the complaints regarding parties and traffic decreased considerably.

☞ Go west from downtown on Riverside Avenue for 1/2 to 3/4 mile. At the bottom of a long hill, where Riverside intersects Clark (the concrete road barrier was installed here), you will see the Spokane River curving around to the right. Park in the lot where Clark Street dead-ends and walk 0.25 miles along the river trail to the nude beach that runs along Latah Creek at its intersection with the Spokane River. Or take bus #10 to the park entrance.

✰ KANIKSU RANCH

On 240 forested acres adjacent to Kaniksu National Forest, Kaniksu Ranch is 50 miles north of Spokane. The reasonably-priced nudist park has heated pool, large hot tub, sunning area, hiking trails, volleyball courts, large clubhouse and snack bar/dining room. Tent and trailer sites, rental rooms. May–October. 4295 N. Deer Lake Road, Box 5-WG, Loon Lake, WA 99148-9650. Phone (509) 233-8202.

FRANKLIN ROOSEVELT LAKE

This 200-mile-long reservoir has many places along the shore where one can enjoy a secluded swim and picnic. Pick a spot away from established camping areas and marinas and dress down; late arrivals who complain about nudity will probably be asked to find another spot on the lake.

From Coulee City on Highway 2, drive east about 25 miles to Highway 174. Head north 1 mile, turn right onto Highway 21 and go 14 miles to the lake.

Boat rentals are availalbe or ask for a map and explore the area in your vehicle.

CENTRAL

COLUMBIA RIVER: WANAPUM DAM RESERVOIR

Located upriver from the Vantage Bridge at I-90 on the Columbia River. Families and singles sun nude without hassles weekdays. Weekends, it may be wise to use the farthest beaches. Volcanic basalt rocks, good sailing, swimming, Frisbee.

☞ Five miles east of Vantage on I-90, take exit 143 and turn left onto the Champs de Brionne Winery Road. After 0.8 miles (mostly north) you will reach a T-intersection. Turn left onto Silicia Road for 5 miles, following the signs to the Wanapum Dam Reservoir on the old highway (no road name) for 5 miles, passing a "dead-end" road sign. The road ends at a boat landing and parking lot with an outhouse. A sand road on the left continues downstream past two trees with nice beaches and on to the bluff. People with trail bikes ride the sand roads and trails.

MOSES LAKE: POTHOLES RESERVOIR

Potholes Reservoir is ideal for amphibious naturists, for hundreds of sand islets are closely spaced over 10 square miles in the northwest half of the reservoir. The shallows keep the motorboats at bay, providing the desired privacy. A shallow-draft kayak or canoe is recommended but not mandatory: you can easily reach the island of your preference by wading. Indeed, nobody congregates here. Nude use is growing but it is dispersed. Free overnight camping with no facilities.

☞ West of Moses Lake on I-90, take exit 174, follow Mae Valley Rd. over the freeway to the T-intersection and turn right on south frontage road. Go west 2.4 miles to gravel road just beyond the power-lines crossing, marked D5-N.E. Take it for 3 miles and a series of forks going down to the lake appear. Explore; find your spot.

YAKIMA RIVER SITES

Between Ellensburg and Yakima snakes Canyon Road alongside the Yakima River. Numerous turnouts permit the skinny-dipper to refresh almost at whim.

WENATCHEE: DOUGLAS CREEK

Spring-fed creek offers many slides and pools as it flows through a lovely limestone and basalt canyon on BLM land. Most nude use is weekdays as non-nude picnickers emerge on weekends. No harassment.

☞ From Wenatchee take Route 28 east past Rock Island State Park to Palisades Road just past Nelson's Produce Store; turn left and follow it to town of Palisades. Where Palisades Road cuts east away from Douglas Creek you soon turn left, then the next right, and follow over and down a steep hill, taking a sharp right at the bottom; follow creek (6 or 7 miles beyond Palisades town) to picnic and parking areas alongside County Road I (rough road).

WESTERN

SCENIC HOT SPRINGS

Spectacularly situated as if to reward a steep 2-mile hike, these popular pools benefit from a 122°F thermal flow.

☞ From Seattle take I-5 north, then Route 2 east to Old Fairhaven Parkway and for 10 miles beyond. Cross a bridge over railroad tracks, and just after milepost 59 turn right onto a dirt road. It leads you on a very rough right-of-way for 2 miles beneath a power line (4WD helps; you may want to park along the road shortly after you get off Route 2). At the crest of the hill your trail doubles back to the right, up to the springs.

COOPER POINT

Evergreen State College students use Cooper Point clothing-optional beach 3/4 of a mile from campus parking. Located on state property outside the city limits of Olympia. From I-5 take Route 101 to the campus, then Cooper Point Drive to Driftwood, and left to parking lot F. Nature trail starts at rear of lot. Go right at each fork of the trail to the pebble beach.

OLYMPIC HOT SPRINGS

Olympic National Park removed the hot

springs from its introductory map. No doubt, this action reduces the visits by shockable, casual tourists, and a good thing. The dedicated hot spring user will not be daunted—not even by roadblocking boulders which ONP dumped across the access road to discourage vandalizing teenagers. Of the six pools, they get cleaner and hotter as you go to the top.

☞ Cross from Seattle to the Olympic Peninsula by the ferry or by driving through Tacoma and north along the Hood Canal. Take Route 101 along the north shore to Port Angeles and 8 miles farther west to the Elwha general store. Here turn south following the Elwha River Valley into the mountains. At the ranger station take the right fork up Boulder Creek to the head of the road. Park here and hike an easy 2.5 miles to the springs.

SNAKE RIVER DUNES

In southeastern Washington the Snake River dunes are a game preserve which has nude use. The size of the beach varies according to the amount of water held back by the dams downstream, but there is almost always some beachfront available. Boaters and water-skiers pass by frequently on weekends; weekdays are quieter.

☞ From Colfax or Pullman, follow Almota Rd. to Boyer Park. When you reach the river go past Boyer Park and Marina and cross over the Lower Granite Dam to the south shore of Lake Bryan. Follow the road 2–3 miles downstream. About 1/2 mile past the Illia boat landing and trailer park, you'll see a small parking area on the right. Park there and pick a trail to the beach. Please don't contribute to the litter problem.

SKYLINE LAKE

An hour and a half east of Seattle is Steven's Pass and Steven's Pass Ski Area. Across the highway from the ski area is a parking area with a closed minimart. Park here and walk up the gravel road leading to the A-frame cabins above. Past the first two cabins the road winds to the right but it is the only road so stay on it a mile or less. Pass the lookout tower and go left at the only fork in the road a bit farther up. This road leads to Skyline Lake a quarter mile farther. Here you can sun or fish nude and it's a scenic area for taking pictures. Nude hiking is possible on the west side of the lake where there is a slight trail heading a quarter mile up to the ridgetop. The views are tremendous and the ridge stretches for miles in either direction.

SNOQUALMIE FOREST: GOLDMYER HOT SPRINGS

Fabled Goldmyer Hot Springs is a

rugged 7-mile hike north of Snoqualmie Pass on the Cascade Crest Trail. The 120°F water provides an oasis of relief for the trail weary. A quota of 20 visitors per day is established. Nude use is permitted as long as others in tub do not object. Reserve before coming to be assured entrance. Midweek is best, Summer–Fall; do carry out your trash. P.O. Box 1292, North Bend, WA 98045. Phone (206) 789-5631.

THE SLUGS

Dynamic Seattle-area Naturist group headed by personable Rick Perkins, author of *The Nudist Notebook* which includes the states of Washington, Oregon, Idaho, Montana and Wyoming. P.O. Box 2335, Lynnwood, WA 98036.

FRATERNITY SNOQUALMIE

Forestia, owned and operated by Fraternity Snoqualmie, is the result of years of hard work and dedication by its members. Forty acres, convenient to Seattle; modern camping facilities, heated pool, whirlpool, sauna and outdoor games. Open weekends only. P.O. Box 748-WG, Issaquah, WA 98027. Phone (425) 392-NUDE.

☆ LAKE BRONSON

Lushly-forested nudist park on 320 acres northeast of Seattle with a 7.5-acre spring-fed lake, grassy beach, trout stream, high waterfall and hiking trails. Fishing, swimming, canoes, paddleboats, tennis, volleyball, shuffleboard, rec center. Snack bar, whirlpool, sauna, laundromat. Rental accommodations, tent and RV hookups. East of Everett. P.O. Box 1135-WG, Sultan, WA 98294. Phone (360) 793-0286; fax (360) 793-0841.

☆ LAKE ASSOCIATES

Halfway from Seattle to Vancouver, BC, LARC is a family-oriented park on 42 wooded acres at the edge of the Cascade Mountains. Tent and RV sites, volleyball courts, hot tub. Hike along a sparkling stream to the waterfall. P.O. Box 654-WG, Conway, WA 98238. Phone (360) 376-NUDE; fax (360) 445-5050.

GLACIER PEAK WILDERNESS: KENNEDY HOT SPRINGS

Located at 3,300 feet in the Glacier Peak Wilderness, a 5-mile hike from Owl Creek campground. The 96°F hot springs fill a 4 x 5 foot soaking pool that is traditionally clothing-optional and extremely popular. Open all year. In summer a park ranger lives on-site. Overnight permits from the

Mt. Baker-Snoqualmie National Forest ranger station.

☞ I-5 north from Seattle. North of Everett, take Route 520 east to Darrington. There drive on Forest Service Road 20 southeast for 8 miles to FSR 23. Turn on FSR 23 and go to its end—trailhead for 643 up White Chuck Canyon, to spring. Seek map and conditions at the ranger station in Darrington.

LARRABEE STATE PARK: CLAYTON BEACH

Although Whatcom County has closed the traditional skinny-dipping beach at Teddy Bear Cove south of Bellingham, another nearby well-loved clothing-optional beach has recently been added to Larrabee State Park. It is Clayton Beach.

While rumors abound that the Parks Department may close Clayton Bay, or ruin its natural beauty by building a parking lot adjacent to it, visitors currently still may enjoy its rugged beauty. The Pacific Northwest NAC group is presently engaged in negotiations with State Parks about potential clothing-optional designation for this and other Washington sites.

☞ On I-5 going north from Seattle, watch for the Old Samish Parkway (exit 250), and exit west for about a mile to the first light. Turn south onto famed scenic Chuckanut Drive. You'll know you're headed in the right direction when you pass Fairhaven Park on your left. Continue about five miles south. Just south of the southern park entrance is a new paved parking lot. People must park in the lot, not on the road. To get to the beach, cross Chuckanut Drive to the signed path leading to a set of stairs. Follow the stairs and trail to the beach. Expect to scramble down a steep rock face at one point on the trail. Traditional nudity is practiced at the most-northerly cove. Discretion is advised. Overnight camping (clothed) at Larrabee State Park main campground to the north.

SAN JUAN ISLAND

A number of fine beaches from South Beach to Eagle Cove get very little use, and yet they are within the San Juan Island National Historical American Camp Park, making them virtual havens for skinny-dippers. Driftwood from stray log booms may obscure the view of these beaches at high tide.

☞ From the ferry landing in Friday Harbor drive up hill on the main street a couple of blocks, to where the street branches into a Y. Take the left branch, Cattle Point Road, south past the county fairgrounds. Cattle Point Road makes several right-angle turns but eventually arrives at the southern tip of the island, rightly named Cattle Point. Just beyond the American Camp (6.7 miles

from the ferry) make a right turn off the main road, and take this new road over the low ridge and down to South Beach. Park in the lot and walk west, either on the beach or in the meadow above the bluffs, to your pick of coves (they keep getting nicer). Rangers don't see any problem with the nude use.

ORCAS ISLAND: DOE BAY RESORT

Often called the "best" of the San Juans, 56-square-mile heavily-wooded Orcas Island is a naturist's delight. Animal life and wildflowers abundant, isolated pebbly beaches all along the 125-mile coast, and Mount Constitution offers a spectacular view.

Secluded beach areas on the southeast side of the island hold nude possibilities—and 106°F clothing-optional group hot pools and sauna are found in Doe Bay Village, where campsites go for $12 and up, and indoor overnight lodging ranges from $30–$65. Doe Bay Resort (360) 376-2291. Nearby Moran State Park has over 150 campsites and the arts and crafts town of Deer Harbor has a luxury hotel.

☞ From Seattle, drive north for an hour to the ferry terminal in Anacortes. The ferry goes daily from Anacortes to Deer Harbor town on the southwest side of Orcas. Drive north on Horseshoe Highway through Eastsound to Doe Bay. Bicycles available for rent at the resort and cars/RVs are allowed on the ferry.

Michael Cooney. Phyllis Gaffney, Avalon; Now At Paw Paw, West Virginia.

WEST VIRGINIA

EASTERN

☆ AVALON CONSERVATION CLUB

Two hours from Washington, DC, and a half hour from Winchester, VA, with over 200 acres, Avalon is the only nudist facility in West Virginia. Restaurant and lounge, pond, heated pool, hiking trails, volleyball and other sports. Clean, comfortable motel rooms with private baths and air conditioning; campground with hot showers/flush toilets and RV hookups. Estab. 1995. P.O. Box 369, Paw Paw, WV 25434. Phone (304) 947-5600.

CENTRAL

TYGART LAKE STATE PARK

Discreet skinny-dipping from the shores of this large lake. From Clarksburg, take Route 50 east, pass under I-79, and continue to Grafton. Here follow US 250 south toward Philippi until you come to the Arden turnoff, marked "Arden 6." Follow this road about 4 miles to Arden. Cross the bridge here and turn left downstream. This section of road is not paved. Cross a small bridge and continue another 1/4 mile or less. Park along the road anywhere for the next couple of miles, and choose among the several spots which are secluded from the road. You might also drive to the next bridge across the Tygart, park, and hike downstream for more privacy.

Local police are said to act only on complaints; they'll ask that you cover up. From a tavern near the falls (about halfway between the first two bridges), liquid refreshments may be purchased. Camping is available near the falls or in the national forest area 25 miles east.

SENECA ROCKS

Climbing is exhilarating at Seneca Rocks with Spruce Knob the highest point in the state. Seneca Falls are cold—go down to the deep swimming holes, rapids, lots of sunning rocks. For map, brochure: Monongahela National Forest, Elkins, WV 26241.

☞ From Washington, DC: take I-66 west to I-81, north on I-81 and exit on US 50 at Winchester, VA. Take US 50 west 50 miles, then left (south) on US 220 to Petersburg, WV. Turn right on WV 28 (west and south) 20 miles to US 33 at Mouth of Seneca. Then US 33 west 5 miles to secondary Route 7 on left, follow it 2 miles past campground to trailhead on left. Park either at trailhead or campground. Falls and rapids are 3–4 miles up trail following Seneca Creek.

SOUTHERN

GREENBRIER RIVER TRAIL

A serpentine trail along the river of the same name; both twist their way among the Allegheny Mountains, offering many spots for nude recreation. The steepest grade is less than 3 percent with natural clearings for picnics or resting. Bring everything you need, there are virtually no services for the entire 80 miles of trails.

Check out the Marlinton to Clover Lick section, 15 miles long and very remote with about 6 good tenting areas and several points of interest, including Sharp's Tunnel and limestone caves.

☞ From Route 39 on Main Street in the center of Marlinton, go west from the restored Marlinton Rail Station (free maps are available here).

GLADE CREEK GORGE

An isolated, rugged area for experienced hikers and campers, Glade Creek Gorge is some 700 feet deep with beautiful waterfalls and pools along the creek. Avoid in rainy weather.

☞ Take Route 19 out of Beckley to Route 307. Follow 307 to Route 9. Take Route 9 a short distance to the old Route 22 and hike or 4WD down the road to the bottom of the gorge. Away from the construction site where an interstate bridge is being built, you can hike along Glade Creek all the way to New River.

☆ – *The star symbol before a resort name is your guarantee that The Naturist Society card is accepted and earns a discount at the resort. To obtain Naturist Society membership, see the inside front cover.*

Michael Cooney. Top: Hiking In the Baraboo Woods of Wisconsin.
Bottom: Two Moods of "Mazo" Beach Near Madison, WI.

Michael Cooney: Scenes From the Mazomanie Beach.

WISCONSIN

Wrote Roman Catholic priest/explorer Louis Hennepin in his *New Discovery of a Vast Country In America* (1698): "**They go stark naked in summertime**, wearing only a kind of Shoes made of the Skins of (Buffalo) Bulls."

Hennepin was describing Native Americans on the west shore of Lake Michigan. Sweltering in ecclesiastical garb, Hennepin must have appeared as strange to these "Indians" as they to him.

In the late 20th century, controversy continued at Milwaukee. The Wisconsin Court of Appeals ruled in 1994: "This County would have this court hold that any public nudity is per se indecent. We reject this argument." See *Nude and Natural* magazine, N 13.4, pp. 94-101. The County attorney shut down Paradise Beach anyway—N 14.1, pp. 45-47; 14.2, pp. 58-60.

DANE COUNTY

☆ VALLEY VIEW RECREATION CLUB

Rustic cooperative club, 25 miles east of Madison, 40 wooded acres. Day visitors welcome. Cottage, RV hookup, tent site rentals. Sun meadow, heated pool, rec hall, volleyball, community kitchen, playground. May–October. P.O. Box 605, Cambridge, WI 53523. Phone (608) 423-3060.

WISCONSIN RIVER: MAZO BEACH

Popular, wild and scenic, this clothing-optional site in the Mazomanie State Wildlife Refuge seems immune to lifestyle complainers—the core users have high moral, etiquette and conservation standards. Cooperation with authorities is constant. See *Nude & Natural* magazine, N 12.1, pp. 29–35. National Nude Weekend is a big event.

Friends of Mazo, P.O. Box 42, Sauk City, WI 53583, phone (608) 798-1954; fax (608) 798-FAXX, sponsor weekend activities such as clothing drives, corn roasts, Christmas on the Beach and volleyball tournaments.

Canuding the Wisconsin River is quite popular. Rent your canoe early, as outfitters often run out of canoes on hot summer weekends. Sauk City to Arena is a nice 1/2 day trip; picnic on a grassy sandbar or explore a wooded bluff. If camping on the river, take long tent stakes (the soft ground doesn't hold short stakes well), lots of bug spray and protective clothing from poison ivy. Remove your trash.

No glass. No roadside camping. Nearby on Route 12, Cedar Hills Campground is favored by the Mazo Beachers. Ganzer's Motel in Sauk City is naturist-friendly.

☞ From the Northeast: off Highway 41 to right on Route 26. Right on Route 151, and continue south to Sun Prairie. Here turn on Route 19 west to Route 12. Turn right (north) for 9.1 miles to County Y. (It's really Y only if you get to the top of the hill before turning left.) On County Y drive west and north exactly 5.2 miles, and turn right on blacktop Laws Road, which leads left in 1/2 mile onto gravel Conservation Road along the

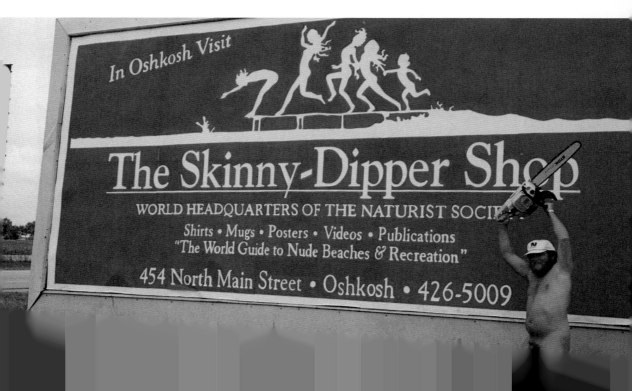

BADGER NATURISTS

Founded by Jim Urban in 1982 with direct assistance of The Naturist Society. Summer activities at Wisconsin River's Mazo Beach. Winter parties. Send SASE. P.O. Box 55346, Madison, WI 53705.

NORTHEAST

KOHLER-ANDRAE STATE PARK

Kohler Beach is a 3/4 mile-long stretch of beach and dunes bordering Lake Michigan on the north end of Kohler-Andrae State Park. Behind the beach are trails into Kohler Wildlife Refuge. Under jurisdiction of the DNR, the refuge has few clothed visitors on weekdays and after 3 p.m. weekends (every hour or two), moderate traffic on weekends before 3 p.m. (every half hour or so). Be discreet.

☞ Take I-43 to exit 120 three miles south of Sheboygan. Turn east on County V and drive 2.2 miles to where it makes a 90-degree left turn. Park on the shoulder of the road and walk east on Beach Park Lane 1/4 mile to lake. Turn left and hike 1/4 mile to refuge.

Or, from the park entrance (state park sticker required), drive 50 yards past the entrance, turn left and continue 1 mile. Park in the North Beach lot. Walk to beach, turn left and hike 1/4 mile to refuge.

Wisconsin River. Park in the lot and take the short path to the beach. At the beach, go left (downstream) and proceed to the southern-most part of the beach which is clothing-optional. Remain dressed during your walks to and from the naturist area.

From northwest. Off I-94 at the Baraboo exit. Highway 12 south 20 miles to Sauk City. Cross river and right on County Y, to Laws Road and right.

From Madison. Highway 14 west to Mazomanie. Turn right (north) on County Y. Go 4 miles and turn left on Laws Road, and as above.

TOFT POINT

Well north on the Door County peninsula is little-visited Toft Point. This wildlife sanctuary was acquired by the Nature Conservancy and turned over to the University of Wisconsin-Green Bay. Old growth makes you think of Canadian forests. Dilapidated wood buildings have a ghost town appeal. UW groups sometimes visit as do New Age folks from The Clearing. The most relaxed, lovely nude sunbathing spot in northeast Wisconsin, with a rocky shoreline on chilly Lake Michigan, a reedy bay with sandy shading to muck, and grassy sunning lawns.

☞ Route 57 to Bailey's Harbor. At Sandpiper restaurant, east on Ridge Road for 1 1/4 miles. Where the road forks right for Bailey's Harbor Yacht Club, go left. Another mile brings you to a small parking lot area but skinny-dippers continue either 0.5 or 1 mile. At either of these two points, there are trails to the beach, and if there are not a lot of cars, one may park on the side of the road or pull off into the drive-in spots that lead into the trails. If going with a group, it's best to park cars at the main lot and shuttle people to either one of the two trails.

This Page Bottom: Michael Cooney, At "Mazo" Beach On the Wisconsin River. Top: Michael Cooney, Claudette Richards Hosts the Mazo Beach Visitor Center. Facing Page: Kathleen A. Galley, Yosemite National Park: Immersed In Nature.

CANADA

A thinly populated expanse of forests and the countless moraine lakes offer many tempting chances to skinny-dip while hiking or canuding. "Skinny dipping in a moderate sense is something that has been a bit of a way of life in Canada," said British Columbia Attorney General Gardom in 1977.

FCN President David Basford explains (1995): "Canadian law is generally reasonable in its application to nudists. While it states that 'Where the accused is completely naked in a public place…the offense…is committed,' it goes on, 'This offense is not aimed at conduct such as swimming nude at an isolated beach.' Thus, Canadian naturists regularly enjoy nude relaxation in many secluded and partially secluded areas. Even where they are observed, tolerance for well-behaved naturists is generally very high."

For a more detailed listing of Canadian sites, the FCN and FQN each publish a guide book and periodical that list the naturist resorts, clubs, groups and free beaches of Canada. Write: Federation of Canadian Naturists: P.O. Box 186-WG, Islington, Ontario M9A 4X2. Fédération Québécoise de Naturisme: 4545 Avenue Pierre-de-Coubertin, C.P. 1000, Succursale M, Montréal, Québec H1V 3R2.

Many Canadian naturist clubs are vividly photographed by Richard West, *Canada Naturally*, 1993. From *Events Unlimited*, P.O. Box 317, Newfoundland, NJ 07435, which also supplies two excellent companion videos from Heritage.

This Page: Merv Krull. Houseboating On Lake Shuswap Near Salmon Arm, British Columbia.

Facing Page: Wreck Beach CANADA helicopter photo by Uwe Meyer© on May 22, 1994, using a 4" x 5" camera & 50 Fujichrome Velvia film. Available as 25" x 39" high quality poster. US $16 + $7 mailing tube & shipping. Adam's Creations, 2617 W. 7 Ave., Vancouver, BC V6K 1Z2, Canada. (604) 732-7111, Fax (604) 736-3686.

Wreck Beach
✦ CANADA ✦

ALBERTA

SUNNY CHINOOKS ASSOCIATION

In the foothills of the Rocky Mountains at the James River, Sunny Chinooks' new campground is surrounded by 18 acres of forest. Clubhouse, hot tub, children's pool, horseshoes, volleyball court, fish-ing. Two hours north of Calgary. Couples/families only. Box 33030, 3919 Richmond Rd. S.W., Calgary, Alberta T3E 7E2. (403) 274-8166.

☆ HELIOS EDMONTON

Helios, with 22 acres, is 35 miles east of Edmonton. Tent, RV sites with water. Pool, spa, sauna, volleyball. May–Sept. Box 8 R.R. 2, Tofield, Alberta T0B 4J0. Phone (403) 662-2886.

BRITISH COLUMBIA

VANCOUVER AREA

WRECK BEACH PRESERVATION SOCIETY

An extremely hardworking conservation-ist and naturist group that integrates a clothing-optional life-style with natural preservation. WBPS has fought and won some amazing battles in the preservation of Wreck Beach.

The sparkplug from Day One has been Judy Williams, now also on the Naturist Action Committee. See reports in *Nude & Natural* magazine, *N* 10.3 pp. 67–70; *N* 11.1 pp. 66–80; *N* 11.2 pp. 88–90, 100–101.

WBPS, P.O. Box 602, Delta, BC V4K 4J7. Phone (604) 946-7545.

WRECK BEACH

Wreck Beach is a Naturist success story and home to 8,000 laid-back nude bathers on a hot weekend. See the page photo!

From the United States take Route 99 north, past the airport, and immediately get off at the river's far side onto Marine Drive. You'll exit going east and double back, passing under Route 99 and thread-ing through some small streets until you're on Southwest Marine Drive going west. Continue for several miles and enter the UBC campus.

Extending from the Musqueam Indian reserve to West Spanish Banks is a 6.5-km clothes-optional beach at the mouth of the north arm of the Fraser River. Since 1970, no nude bather on Wreck sands has been hassled for it by the law.

The Greater Vancouver Park Board has extended legal status but allocated no support to Wreck. So entrepreneurs have packed in food and drink. Police and res-cue, when required, have come by Hovercraft over the waves. When drug vendors began showing up, the Wreck Beach Preservation Society was ready to call for police work. WBPS urges visitors to strictly avoid lighting fires on the beach and not to camp, cause erosion or leave litter.

☞ The main beach is at Trail/Gate 6 (near the intersection of Northwest Marine Drive and University Boulevard, directly opposite Place Vanier Residence). You can pick up one of UBC's glossy, col-

Jerry Derbyshire. The North Channel, Ontario.

orful visitor maps; trails to Wreck Beach are indicated. Park in the visitor (pay) lot. On weekends, some staff parking lots are available (free) to the public, read the signs. Go down the steps, a little steep but no big deal, past signs informing visitors that clothing is optional.

Heading west from Spanish Banks Beach to a point below the cliffs takes you to the limit of the Wreck Beach nude area. This is, by far, the most accessible part of Wreck Beach, as the road in this area is almost at sea level. Just where NW Marine Drive starts uphill to the UBC campus, there is a small parking lot at the roadside. From this lot follow the trail west along the beach. A short walk takes you across a tiny bridge to the nude section. It is possible to walk to Trail 6 from here, but it is a long distance. Note: if the parking lot is full, there is usually ample parking at the textile beach.

A more secluded, smaller and very rocky area at Trail/Gate 4 is known as Tower Beach. Used mostly by couples; no food or drink available. Trail 4 begins behind the Museum of Anthropology. Like Trail 6, it is steep and tiring to climb up. The Towers area is immediately at the foot of the trail and extends to the left. Not a great place to swim but for those who go for sunbathing it's quiet.

VANCOUVER SUNBATHING ASSOCIATION

A new club just southeast of metro Vancouver. A city retreat with tent sites and extensive plantings, ringed by old-growth Tynehead Park. Sunning lawn, greenhouse, showers, huge deck, hot tub, barbecue, picnic area, weekend events.

Gordon Skillen, VSA, 10185-164th St., Surrey, BC V4N 2K4. Phone (604) 589-6848 or 1-800-667-2732; fax 589-1398.

☆ VAN TAN CLUB

Canada's oldest nudist club, established 1939, the rustic Van Tan Club is splendidly alpine, located on Mount Fromme southeast of Grouse Mountain. Pool, sauna, showers, playground. Tent and RV sites. P.O. Box 423 Station A, Vancouver, BC V6C 2N2. Phone (604) 980-2400.

☆ SUNNY TRAILS CLUB

On 18 acres of parkland with mountain views in the Fraser Valley, one hour east of Vancouver on Route 7, the new Sunny Trails Club has 50 campsites, 35 fully-serviced; rental units, pool, spa, clubhouse, sauna, picnic area, trails, children's playground. Reasonable day rates. Open all year. 43955 Highway 7, Box 18, Lake Errock, BC V0M 1N0. Phone (604) 826-3419.

LILLOOET RIVER HOT SPRINGS

British Columbia has a wealth of hot springs. Most easily accessible sources have been commercially developed but a number of natural springs in the back-country are worth the trek. Of note in the Vancouver area are the Meager Creek and Skookumchuck hot springs along the Lillooet River.

☞ From Vancouver take Route 99 north to Pemberton; for Meager Creek follow the logging road northwest along the Lillooet to where it meets Meager Creek; the springs are a 10-km hike up the creek bed. For Skookumchuck continue on Route 99 to Mount Currie, then south along the forest road for 54 km until you see the BC Hydro tower #682. The spring is located between markers 22 and 21.

BRUNSWICK BEACH

"Little Wreck Beach," as Whistler Mountain ski buffs dub Brunswick Beach, causes problems for its namesake. Problem is, the Canadian Criminal Code still treats nudity as illegal although provincial policy autonomy in the matter has been tolerated since the 1960s. Wealthy Brunswick Point neighbors want the code enforced.

Brunswick Beach Bares, 308-1150 Burnaby, Vancouver, BC V6E 1P2. Phone (604) 687-5686.

☞ From North Vancouver, northwest on Route 99 (the road to Squamish) to 1 mile north of Lions Bay. Take trails towards Brunswick Point, go to clothed public beach (500-foot long) on south (Howe Sound) side of point, then walk east, cross 5-feet-high rock groin to 1000-foot nude beach, a mellow place.

WHISTLER

The Dock on Lost Lake, a 20-minute walk west on the valley trail from Whistler Village, is well-known locally for nudity; very cold water. If the lot for the public (clothed) beach is open, simply park there and walk 5 minutes until you reach a wooden dock, the marker for naturists that they are in the right place.

☞ Past the C.P. Chateau Whistler, take Lost Lake Road beyond the golf course to the car park/warming hut on the Lost Lake Trail. Follow trail to the right about 600 metres. The dock is down a short but steep path.

VANCOUVER ISLAND

THETIS LAKE PARK

Victoria, the capital of British Columbia, is a charming city on the southern tip of Vancouver Island. Victorians (at least those who do not live up to their name) established a free beachhead at Prior Lake, within Thetis Lake Park. In July 1978, city officials conceded it would be pointless to enforce laws against nude bathing.

Prior Lake doesn't have a beach—rather, a pier on which to sunbathe. The pier gets hot and there are no nearby amenities.

On Thetis Lake itself, nude use sometimes occurs on Upper Thetis Lake, at the western side. Mounties have been known to direct naturists to Prior Lake if the nude bathers are not discreet enough.

☞ From Victoria take Route 1 North for about 12 km to Highland Road. Drive up Highland Road (paved) about 3 km to 300 yd. beyond the walking track, and a sign: "Thetis Lake Park – Prior Lake." Park here. Walk 100 yd. to clothing-optional area. Prior Lake is not very large and the only access appears to be via a jetty at the end of the walking track.

SOL SANTE

Forest, trails and pond on 175 acres. Showers, sauna, clubhouse, children's area. Volleyball, badminton, shuffleboard, swimming and fishing. Tent and RV camping with hookups. Open all year; reservations required. 3120 Cameron Taggart Road, Cobble Hill, BC V0R 1L0. Phone (250) 743-2400.

DESWIN HOUSE BED & BREAKFAST

Open July through October. Deswin House Bed & Breakfast offers a relaxed, clean and quiet atmosphere. Facilities include private sunning deck, outdoor smoking area, hot tub and RV parking. Excellent rates for singles, couples, families. Within walking distance of Saxe Point Park and Olde England Inn. P.O. Box 38022, 794 Fort St., Victoria, BC, Canada V8W 3N2. Phone (250) 383-5814; fax (250) 381-2877.

SOOKE POTHOLES

The Sooke River Potholes are well-known to clothed visitors, especially for the waterfalls. The hike along the river involves scaling rocks and wading waist-deep in chilly water. Skinny-dippers just go a bit farther along before stripping down.

☞ About 30 km from Victoria. Drive west on Route 14 almost to the town of Sooke; turn right on Sooke River Road and then into the parking area. Hike 1 km beyond the clothed beach to the nude zone.

PACIFIC RIM NATIONAL PARK: LONG BEACH

From Victoria, Route 1 to Parksville then Route 4 past Port Alberni to Pacific Rim National Park. North end of Long Beach is used nude—past the camping towards Schooner Cove. Couples, gays, a beach backed by tall trees.

HORNBY ISLAND

From Victoria, Route 19 north. From Denman Island, take ferry to Hornby Island. Drive to Little Tribute Bay, where nude use has been established. Clean and sandy.

QUALICUM BEACH

The Esquimalt and Nanaimo Dayliners (the E&Q) run from Victoria terminal at 450 Pandora Avenue. The train makes a daily round trip, leaving at 8:15 a.m., traversing Vancouver Island's eastern seaboard. Reservation required: 383-4324. Marvelous wild scenes, terrifying trestles. Cost to Qualicum round trip is Canadian $20. You'll have two hours there, time for a midday nude swim, sunning and a picnic or restaurant lunch.

HOT SPRINGS COVE

Jamie's Whaling Station, Tofino, offers charter cruises on its 26-ft. cabin yacht, Golly Gee, upcoast to Hot Springs Cove. The springs accept up to 12 soakers and nudity is commonplace. Camp next to the springs if you like, or lodge nearby with natives; or do it as a day trip. Much wildlife including whales, sharks and eagles. Daily March through October.

To reach Tofino, take the ferry from Vancouver to Nanaimo, on Vancouver Island. Drive 23 miles north on Hwy 19 to Parksville. Turn west on Highway 4 and drive 110 miles. Hot Springs Cove is on Sharp Point in Maquinna Provincial Park. P.O. Box 590, Tofino, BC V0R 2Z0. Phone (250) 725-3919 or 1-800-667-9913.

CENTRAL

OKANAGAN SHUSWAP NUDIST SOCIETY

Okanagan Shuswap Nudist Society bought 22 wooded acres on water for a new nudist park near Vernon. Write for directions/fees. Okanagan Shuswap Nudist Society, c/o Secretary, Box 5149 Station A, Kelowna, BC V1Y 7V8, Canada. Phone (250) 832-7326.

MANITOBA

☆ CROCUS GROVE SUN CLUB

This 60-acre club 50 miles northeast of Winnipeg has a community kitchen, pool, sauna, spa, volleyball, tent and RV sites, two rental units. R.R. 3, Beausejour, Manitoba R0E 0C0. Phone (204) 265-3469.

PATRICIA BEACH

This provincial park at the south end of Lake Winnipeg is an hour's drive north of Winnipeg on Route 59. Pay fee and park in northernmost lot behind beach. Walk 1/2 mile north, ford the wide creek, to enjoy 3/4 mile of fine sand that is nude by custom.

☆ HIDDEN LAKES RESORT

Hidden Lakes Resort, a clothes-optional retreat, is a 3-hour drive from Winnipeg. Main facilities include hotel-style rooms with private bath, lounge area, sun deck, sauna and hot tub; lakefront tent/trailer sites available. Very secluded, beautiful scenery. Reservations required. 23-845 Dakota St., Suite 302, Winnipeg, Manitoba, R2M 5M3, Canada. Phone (204) 475-0777; fax (204) 477-4006.

NOVA SCOTIA

HALIFAX AREA

CRYSTAL CRESCENT BEACH

The capital of this eastern maritime province, Halifax has its own tolerated nude ocean beach—recommended to visitors who ask the Tourist Bureau. Great scenery, up to 300 friendly people on a weekend.

Bluenose Naturist Club formed after arrests were made at Crystal Crescent Beach on a weekend of August 1990. It organizes swims and house parties in the winter. Contact Dave Paquet (902) 469-0998.

☞ From Armdale Rotary at the head of the Northwest Arm in Halifax, drive south on Route 349 for 2.6 km and turn right, following the Old Sambro Road for 18.1 km via Harrietsfield. In Sambro at the stop sign and Harts Store, turn right and drive 2.4 km, following the signs to park at Crystal Crescent Beach. From its lot, to the right you'll see the first two beaches which are clothes-required. Walk 20 minutes south, past the second beach to the third, whether by shore or overland path. Starting with the third beach and south along the rocks, the entire coast and peninsula are openly clothes-optional.

☆ SUNNYVALE NATURE PARK

SunnyVale Nature Park opened in 1991. Located on 100 partially-wooded acres, the park is north of Halifax. Tent, RV sites, swimming pool, snack bar, rec hall and outdoor sports. Reservations required. SunnyVale Nature Park, R.R. 1 Stewiacke, Nova Scotia B0N 2J0. Phone (902) 639-9036; next dial local 215 to bypass automated attendant.

BAY OF FUNDY

ANNAPOLIS RIVER ISLAND

On the Bay of Fundy find the historic town of Annapolis Royal, then take the road toward Bridgetown. About 5 to 6 kilometers on your way, an inconspicuous dirt road leads from Route 201 down to the beach at the island. If in doubt, ask for directions. The beach is lovely, on the shore of a dammed causeway of the Annapolis River. Long used for skinny-dipping. Heavy river traffic on weekends, so be discreet.

CAPE BRETON ISLAND

INVERNESS BEACH

On northernmost Cape Breton Island, Inverness features a waterfall that crashes down into the ocean. A virtual paradise that resembles Big Sur, it's a favorite spot with the locals.

☞ Take Trans-Canada Route 2 from Moncton, New Brunswick, to Amherst, Nova Scotia, then Route 104 to the Canso Causeway. From here take Route 19 along the western shore for 85 km. Just before crossing the railroad tracks into Inverness, take a left onto Sight Point Road. Follow this road for 10 km and park along the side near the farm buildings. Walk an additional 1.5 km until you see the path that leads to the beach.

ONTARIO

his is the heartland of membership and influence for the Federation of Canadian Naturists, P.O. Box 186-WG, Islington, Ontario M9A 4X2; phone/fax (416) 410-NUDE.

FCN's members may try varied nudist places and activities through The Roaming Bares, 25 Esterbrooke Avenue, Suite 117, North York, Ontario M2J 2C5.

EAST ONTARIO

☆ CLUB NATURISTE RICHARD BRUNET

Francophone club of 60 wooded acres, just across the border into Ontario at 50 minutes from Montréal via Trans-Canada 417. Pool, sauna, playground, restaurant, clubhouse, sports games. Bonfires, youth olympiads, dances, films, golf. 400 Concession #2, St.-Eugène, Ontario K0B 1P0. Phone (613) 674-5277.

EAST HAVEN SUN CLUB

Seventy acres bordered by the South Nation River, providing excellent fishing and canoeing. Volleyball, pool, tent and trailer sites. Fifty km from Ottawa; 130 km from Montréal. P.O. Box 440, Casselman, Ontario K0A 1M0. Phone (613) 764-3595.

OTTAWA NATURISTS

Ottawa Naturists offer many activities. P.O. Box 64201, 1620 Scott St., Ottawa, Ontario K1Y 4V1. Phone (613) 860-2600.

GATINEAU PARK: OLD MILL (QUÉBEC)

Gatineau Park lies within Québec, but serves Ottawa, the nation's capital. The Old Mill is a popular site and the oldest established nude beach in Eastern Canada. The name conjures up images of a 17th century grinding mill, but don't be fooled. This is an abandoned hydroelectric power station and "old" is circa 1914. Legal and other history in *Going Natural,* Spring 1990, from the FCN. The pond is nice, and the surrounding mountains are authentic. Camping is at the north end.

☞ From Ottawa drive Route 105 north to Gatineau Park, which has four public beaches on various lakes. Locate Meech Lake, pay to park in the O'Brien Beach lot, and walk up the winding foot trail, actually a cross-country ski trail. The number "36" should appear on some trees and after 1 km, you will see a signpost for Herridge Lodge. Turn right at the first trail past this sign—up, into woods, and eventually down a steep incline, going right after crossing a wood bridge, to the Old Mill site. The total distance from the parking lot to the site is about 1.5 km.

Another site in Gatineau Park is Lake Lapêche. Take Route 105 from Ottawa

general stores, restaurants and entertainment are available in nearby Calabogie. 309-1568 Merivale Road, Nepean, ON K2G 5Y7. Phone (613) 752-2575.

☆ LAKESUN NATURIST RESORT

Unspoiled large lake with wilderness nude hiking. To protect the loons, no motorboats allowed. Sailing, fishing, camping. Families and singles welcome at this family-operated resort with European tradition (the first in North America to call itself "naturist"). Easter to Labor Day. It's 25 miles north of Kingston; near Watertown, NY; reached by US 81 North. R.R. #1, Perth Road Village, Ontario K0H 2L0. Phone (613) 353-2463.

☆ BUFFALO'S GETAWAY: LILLY VALLEY PARK

Just across the international bridge, Lilly Valley spells relief for Buffaloans. Indoor heated pool, sauna, spa, tent and RV sites, and the only steam bath in North America. 1863 Pettit Road, P.O. Box 261, Fort Erie, Ontario L2A 5M9. Phone (905) 871-4208.

TORONTO AREA

☆ FOUR SEASONS NATURE RESORT

Ten miles from Hamilton, an hour southwest of Toronto, luxurious Four Seasons Nature Resort has 50 acres, three lighted tennis courts, volleyball, indoor and outdoor pools, whirlpool, sauna, fitness center, lake boating and fishing, restaurant, convenience store and nightclub. Tent and trailer sites, rooms. Handicapped accessible. P.O. Box 9, Freelton, Ontario L0R 1K0. Phone (905) 659-7784.

☆ PONDEROSA PARK

Open all year, 100 acres, southwest of Toronto. Indoor/outdoor pool and whirlpool, sauna, TV lounge, restaurant and snack bar, tennis, par 3 69-yd. golf pitching green, pétanque courts, volleyball and basketball courts, hiking trails, dances, playground. Tent/RV sites and trailer/room rentals. Box 501, R.R. #3, Puslinch, Ontario N0B 2J0. Phone (905) 659-3410.

SCARBOROUGH: BEECHGROVE BEACH

Located in Toronto's east end, Scarborough offers secluded Beechgrove Beach,

with washed-up logs, natural dune vegetation on Lake Ontario, no facilities and no hassles. The lake can be nice for swimming, depending on the wind. Old picnic table and BBQ. Frequented by a small group of regulars, mostly families with children, the area is often posted with "Beyond This Point" signs to avoid complaints.

☞ Take 401 to the eastern edge of Toronto/Scarborough, exit at Morningside and go south to Lawrence Ave. (just past Kingston Road). Turn east and drive several blocks to Beechgrove Drive. Go south on the residential road; at the end it will zigzag over a railroad line and pass a water treatment plant. Park in lot where road ends and follow footpath at the northeast corner for a 10-minute walk to the beach.

☆ GLEN ECHO PARK

Toronto Gymnosophical Society's comfortable and lovely quarters north of Toronto. Indoor pool, whirlpool, sauna, snack bar, tent and trailer sites. 15400 Con. 7, R.R. 2, Kettleby, Ontario L0G 1J0. Phone (905) 939-7736.

UNICAMP

The Unitarian Universalist Unicamp and Conference Center northwest from Toronto at Honeywood Springs includes a clothing-optional beach. Only U/U members and participants in special events at the Camp are welcome to use the private beach. Information: Summer, (519) 925-6432. Off-season (416) 250-8549.

McREA LAKE

Some 110 miles north of Toronto with lots of bays and rocky points to camp. Some campsites even have sandy beaches. Accessible from Route 69 on the east and Georgian Bay on the west, and can only be reached by water which tends to keep out undesirables. Not an organized camping area patrolled by rangers, but rather reasonably remote and unspoiled by cottages. One must portage a canoe over the hill adjacent to the rapids and proceed west along the river to the lake. Don't let the 50 or so cars in the parking lot discourage you; these people use canoes and the lake remains uncrowded.

LAKE SIMCOE

Bare boaters are reported along Georgiana Island's south shore, making Lake Simcoe one of the more popular nude recreation spots for Torontoans. Take Route 404 north to the launch points.

through Hull, Chelsea, and several small towns to St. Cecil. In St. Cecil look for a dirt road turnoff to the left for Lake Lapêche. Park at the lake, and walk past the restaurant and picnic tables and around the peninsula by way of the lake to the nude bathing zone, where you may find up to a hundred fellow naturists.

☆ SUNWARD CLUB

Almost 500 acres of dense woods, a 70-foot-deep lake, rustic campsites, on rented farm. Located one hour west from Ottawa, Sunward offers fishing, swimming, volleyball. Golfing, craft shops,

WINDSOR-CHATHAM AREA

Ontario has a long shoreline on Lake Erie and several informants report most of it hassle-free—partly because it isn't the warmest or most desirable water—all the way from Detroit to Buffalo on the Canadian shore. Hillman Marsh Conservation Area, where County Road 20 meets Lake Erie east of Wheatley, was lately in favor.

☆ SUNNY GLADES

Located near junction of highways 79 and 2 between Chatham and London, 80 miles from Detroit/Windsor. The 94-acre grounds include pool, whirlpool, hiking trails, a lovely restored barn as rec hall. Tent and trailer sites, rental rooms and cottage. May 1–Sept. 30. P.O. Box 309, Bothwell, Ontario N0P 1C0. Phone (519) 695-3619.

NORTHWESTERN

LAKE NIPIGON

Popular Point is the free beach, a naturally-sheltered cove with many sandbars. Turn off Route 11 at Beardmore, and drive to the sandy beach 3 km south of the provincial park.

☆ TYLARA HILLS NATURIST RETREAT

Located on 100 acres, 25 miles southwest of Thunder Bay, just north of Minnesota, Tylara Hills Naturist Retreat provides hiking trails, fishing, swimming, volleyball. The house has 5 bedrooms, 3 bathrooms, jacuzzi, rec room, community kitchen, piano, sunporch and a great view. Finnish sauna, camping/RV sites, English/ French speaking. Open May–October. Tylara Hills, R.R. 1, Nolalu, ON P0T 2K0. Phone (807) 473-0630.

☆ JEWEL LAKE

Naturist camping resort with 100-acre lake amid 640 acres of forest. Canoes, paddleboat, beaches, hiking trails. Tent, trailer and RV sites available. Box 21077, 1950 Algonquin Ave., North Bay, Ontario, P1B 9N8; phone (705) 495-3134.

NOTE: captions to photos run along the inside edge of pages.

QUÉBEC

Québec's attorney general does not consent to prosecution of nude recreation. The policy of his office has consistently been more enlightened than that in neighboring Ontario, and the more remarkable when it is remembered that, until the 1960s, Québec was virtually without individual liberty, bowing to a quasi-ecclesiastical provincial government.

Fédération Québécoise de Naturisme, 4545 Avenue Pierre-de-Coubertin, C.P. 1000, Succursale M, Montréal, Québec H1V 3R2. Phone (514) 252-3014; fax 254-1363. The FQN enjoys the support of the Regroupement Loisir Québec in maintaining an office and is consulted by the Ministry of Tourism on relevant matters. The FQN journal *Au Naturel* includes updates; send $5 for the latest issue.

GASPÉ PENINSULA

PLAGE DE BOOM DÉFENSE

Beautiful sand beaches on either side of this long, gently-curved narrow spit of sand. With long grasses, driftwood and the Forillon National Park across water in the distance, this is an ideal place for swimming and sunbathing.

☞ From downtown Gaspé, take Route 132 east for 6 km and turn left on rue Alexander, which becomes a dirt road. Go 1/2 mile to the beach and park. Walk left past the textile section and wade across the shallow river to find other naturists.

QUÉBEC CITY

BAIE ST.-PAUL: RIVIÈRE BRAS DU NORD-OUEST

From Québec City, take Route 138 northeast to a traffic light at the Irving Garage by the small "Village" shopping center of Baie St.-Paul. Here take the Chemin de R'Équerre, and stay on it to the first road after Chemin du Golf. Turn left and after street address #40 on your right, take the small sand road on the right. Drive to the beach, turn left, go to the end and park. A trail leads down to a pond where you'll be able to hear and find the rapids. A mix of clad, topfree and naturists sun on the rocks and dip.

CAP-AUX-OIES

From Baie St.-Paul take Route 362 east past Les Eboulements. Find small sign on right for Cap-aux-Oies, take road toward the river. At official blue sign, go left to end and park, cross tracks to beach, walk left (east) along the bay. Nudity begins beyond the boulders. A beautiful setting and white sand beach.

NATURE-DÉTENTE

East 30 km from Québec City on Route 40, take Route 365 north 24 km to St.-Raymond. Tent and RV sites, restaurant, snack bar, whirlpool and sauna. Tennis and volleyball courts, children's play area and lounge, spring-fed lake fishing. Camping Nature-Détente, 615 rang Bourglouis, C.P. 2007, St.-Raymond, Québec G0A 4G0. Phone (418) 337-4491.

VALCARTIER: JACQUES CARTIER RIVER

Drive to Loretteville, where Routes 371 and 369 join west of Charlesbourg. Take Route 371 (Boul. Valcartier) north to the village of St.-Gabriel-de-Valcartier and continue to the bridge over the Jacques Cartier River. Park by the road, on the west side (the south bank), and take a path down to the river. The water is warm and deep. The sandspit island is 700 m upstream and is perfect for nuding and camping.

POINTE-TAILLON BEACH

Pointe-Taillon Beach on great Lac Sainte-

Jean is clean, sandy and tranquil. For a time it was an offical nude beach extending a mile along the shore. A mile northwest of the free beach area is a public campground.

☞ From Québec City take Route 175, then Route 169 north to Alma and beyond, to the village of Saint-Henri-Taillon. Here is a large car park and textile beach. Walk west to and beyond Pointe-Taillon's main beach to the nude beach. Wilderness camping is possible.

STE.-AGATHE FALLS

A magnificent site, well worth the trip yet off the tourist map. Several spots suitable to dive and swim in the gorge. Wilderness and commercial camping available.

☞ Take Route 20 from Québec City, to exit 278 (Laurier Station). Take Route 271 South to Ste.-Agathe. Turn right to take Route 218 west, to the first fork to the left. Follow it along the river to the covered bridge. Park, and walk downstream, passing the clothed areas, until you reach the rocks which are the naturist area.

MONTRÉAL EAST

CLUB NATURISTE LOISIRS AIR-SOLEIL

Club Naturiste Loisirs Air-Soleil is a co-op, youth-oriented resort on a river. Perfectly kept, 235 sites with full hookups. Heated pool, restaurant, rec hall, open-air cinema, campfires, dances, volleyball, pétanque, archery, Ping-Pong, shuffleboard, playground. Handicap accessible, no singles. Route 20 east of Montréal. 238 Chemin Allard, Boite Municipale 2, L'Avenis, Québec, J0R 1C0. Phone (819) 394-2556.

SOLEIL DE AMITIÉ

Restaurant and snack bar, clubhouse, tennis and volleyball courts, children's playground. Handicapped accessible. Tent and RV sites, rental trailers. 3000 Rang 3, St. Cyrille, Drummondville, Québec J0C 1H0. Phone (819) 478-3661.

MONTRÉAL SOUTH

CLUB LA POMMERIE

La Pommerie—"Apple Orchard" is 35 miles south of Montréal and 30 miles north of Plattsburgh (NY). It has 400 acres of cedars and working trees, a get-away with *esprit* and *savoir faire* that is favored by many. A trout-stocked quarry pond, pool with sunning lawn, volleyball, massage, shiatsu, yoga, pétanque, Ping-Pong, aerobics, t'ai chi, ceramics and macramé, archery, campfires, dances. Camping, newly-built cabins, mobile homesites, chalets to rent, gourmet restaurant, convenience store, fashion boutique, a 1,000-vine vineyard. May–August. 209 St-Antoine Abbé, Québec J0S 1N0. Phone (514) 826-4723.

☞ From Montréal, Pont Mercier and Route 138 southwest towards Huntington. At Ormstown turn left on Route 201, and left again at St-Antoine Abbé on Route 209. Go less than a mile and enter on right.

☆ VALLÉE RUSTIQUE

Club Naturiste la Vallée Rustique is a quaint, well-equipped club with friendly atmosphere. Pool, tennis, archery, volleyball, shuffleboard, restaurant, bar, motel. Just across border from Enosburg Falls. 40 Chemin des Bouleaux, Frelighsburg, Québec J0J 1C0. Phone 1-888-Nudiste.

MONTRÉAL NORTH

DOMAINE DE L'ÉDEN

On the near north of Montréal; restaurant and nightclub, artificial lake with beach, spa, large pool, tennis, youth club, playground, picnic tables, camping. Rooms to rent. 63 St-Stanislas, C.P. 1197, Laurentides, Québec J0R 1C0. Phone (514) 439-6012; fax 439-3916.

SHAWINIGAN: LE CYPRÈS

This 560-acre club is intersected by the unpolluted Batiscan River 2 1/2 hours northeast of Montréal; canuding is part of club experience along with the volleyball, baseball, archery, hiking, community dinners, bonfires, dances. Hundreds of tent/RV sites; chalet rentals, boat rentals, restaurant. Recent improvements include renovated beach, enlarged restaurant and new tennis courts. Cté Portneuf, Québec G0X 1W0. Phone (418) 336-2573.

MONTRÉAL WEST

OKA BEACH

Located within Paul-Sauvé Park with its cycle trails, forest and water sports. Oka Beach attracts a mixture of textiles and nudes, singles and families and unfortunately, some voyeurs.

☞ Route 640, Montréal's beltline on the north, will take you 35 km southwest, through St-Eustache, becoming Route 344, ending at Oka on the Ottawa River. Many nudists arrive by boat. The sandy beach is on the north shore of Lac des deux Montagnes—it's even on a Montréal bus route. Nude bathers go to the east end of the 3.5 km strand, past the end of the lifeguarded beach, marked by a flagpole.

RIVIÉRE ROUGE

Just north of the Ottawa River, a 3-mile granite gorge on the Rivière Rouge with white water rapids and lovely waterfalls. Above the last falls (30-minute walk), white sand beaches. In season, rafters come through, don't mind them. You might do the rafting too—New World River Expeditions, phone (819) 242-7238; fax 242-0207.

Plenty of large smooth rocks for sunning with deep pools upriver for cooling off. Fish for your dinner? Take in a trash bag; carry out some of the garbage.

SASKATCHEWAN

SASKATOON: BARE-ASS BEACH

The Saskatchewan River flows through the capital city of Saskatoon, offering many fine spots for skinny-dippers. Most popular of the "bare-ass" beaches is south of the city on the west river bank. Take the old Pike Lake Road and go about 5 km past "The Berry Barn."

A second beach is located on the east riverbank. Go south out of the city on Lorne Avenue, then follow the signs to **Cranberry Flats.** Clothing-optional area is south of the main beach.

A native advises that, in the prairie provinces, "every town has a summer skinny-dipping hole—the nearest water,

Informal camping.

☞ Seventy-five minutes from Montréal, near Hawkesbury (Ontario) and Petite Nation Provincial Park, midway to Ottawa. The park straddles Route 148 west of Calumet and before Pointe-au-Chêne Park where the highway crosses the river. Park and take one of two paths that descend on the east side to the river. Walk upstream beyond the first rock outcropping to a second rocky zone where the clothes-optional use begins. The walk is moderate to difficult as you continue upstream for the seven waterfalls.

OUTAOUAIS: LAC SIMON

Halfway between Montréal and Hull on Route 148, take Route 321 north to Duhamel, which has a deli and a hotel. Park at the S.E.P.A.Q.-operated public beach and walk east along Lac Simon. Reaching the shallow Nation Nord River, ford it and you're there!

be it the town reservoir or river, lake or slough." That goes for much of Canada—but do remember to check police practice before creating your Eden.

REGINA AREA

GREEN HAVEN SUN CLUB

Camping and trailer facilities, and 25 acres of gentle rolling land with large open grass areas and shade trees. Sauna, clubhouse. P.O. Box 3374, Regina, Saskatchewan S4P 3H1. Phone (306) 699-2515.

YUKON

WHITEHORSE: EAR LAKE

Ear Lake is close to Whitehorse. The shallow water is relatively warm for the Yukon, another attraction. Sunbathers disperse among the many coves, mostly on weekdays, for they have to allay gossip; Whitehorse has 15,000 curious citizens.

Alternative is **Long Lake,** also near town. Access at one end. By walking halfway around you find more privacy.

For the Liard River Hot Springs, see Alaska, U.S. listings.

☆ – *The star symbol before a resort name is your guarantee that The Naturist Society card is accepted and earns a discount at the resort. To obtain Naturist Society membership, see the inside front cover.*

CENTRAL & SOUTH AMERICA

ARGENTINA

BUENOS AIRES

NATURIST ARGENTINA

Co-founder Ramón Rodríguez was the one publicly-named officer of the nation's sole naturist club, *Primera Asociación Naturo-Desnudista Argentina*. Started in 1934, PANDA was by far Latin America's oldest naturist association. The Rodríguez family also owned the land on a Tigre River Delta island 40 km from Buenos Aires where members met for gymnastics and vegetarian repasts. PANDA's membership as well as rigor declined as the founders aged. In 1985 the family simply took back the land, closing the club.

Naturist Argentina regrouped, including former PANDA members, as NAT in 1991. The NAT goal is to win legal nude beaches.

NAT gathers on Sundays, Nov. 1–March 30, on land owned by Jorge Biagosch at Benavídez, 40 km north of Buenos Aires and just blocks from the Pan American Highway. Pool, restaurant, sauna, volleyball, Ping-Pong. Families and singles welcome. Phone Cristian Vogt, (541) 824-7398, or Biagosch, 0327-81566.

Recently, Argentinians have sunbathed by hiding among the dunes near popular public beaches. Or they drive or fly to more liberal beaches in Uruguay and Brazil.

BRAZIL

F ederação Brasileira de Naturismo, led by Celso Rossi, founder of Brazil's first legal nude beach (Praia do Pinho), is making great progress in the 1990s. Contact: Edo H. Moennich, FBdN, C.P. 328, Gramado, RS 95670-000, Brazil. Phone (5554) 282-1907. Also see *N* 16.3, pp. 36–40.

SANTA CATARINA

PRAIA DO PINHO

Brazil's southerly state of Santa Catarina is pretty and popular for snowy mountains, natural hot springs, sweeping beaches, chic discos and high rises. German settlers left their influence.

Tourist information in English comes from Florianópolis. Officials accept topfree and some nudity on resort beaches of **Camboriú** county. But the naturist mecca is 4 km south of Camboriú at Pine Beach, **Praia do Pinho.** The crescent sand beach lies between rocky points with good snorkeling, lobsters and shellfish, volleyball, surfing, pool, bonfires. Snackbars, camping, bungalows and motel with bar/restaurant. Main season is Christmas to March 30.

Associação amigos da Praia do Pinho, C.P. 272, 88330-000 Balneário Camboriú SC, Brazil. Phone 047 983 7536.

☞ By air, to Florianópolis. Bus or rental car for 70 km north almost to Camboriú. Turn off coastal route 101 at km marker 140. Eight km to the beach on a dirt road.

PRAIA DA GALHETA

On Ilha de Santa Catarina 30 km east of Florianópolis, Praia Galheta is south of Barra da Lagoa (itself near Lagoa da Conceição). Reached by a trail through the rocks which starts at the bridge at the north end of Praia Mole. Galheta Beach earlier was a refuge for transvestites and it remains clothing-optional.

PRAIA DAS PEDRAS ALTAS

Official small nude beach on BR-101, 30 km south of Florianópolis in Palhoça county. Calm clear water, with rustic motel, bar and restaurant. Clube Naturista Pedras Altas (CNPA), Av. Atlantica 860, Florianópolis, SC 88095-070.

SÃO PAULO

SITIO IBATIPORÃ

Five-acre luxurious naturist ranch with garden swimming pool, tennis court, soccer field, private lake with boat, and large house with accommodations for six families. Excellent cuisine.

Only 100 km from São Paulo. Turn right at kilometer 122 on Highway SP 300, going from Itu to Porto Feliz, and follow for 2 miles on the sand road to the site. Full nudity all year, mostly families. Inquiries to Eduardo S. Prado Jr., C.P. 83, Porto Feliz, SP 18540-000, Brazil. Phone (0152) 62-3252.

SITIO RINCÃO

One hundred fifty miles from São Paulo near the city of Guarantinguetá, Rincão ranch is a legal nude site of 330 acres with small lakes and waterfalls. Hiking, camping, lodging, restaurant. Alexandre & Ana, C.P. 651267, São Paulo, SP 01390-970. Phone +55 125 27 1142; fax +55 11 289 7184.

PRAIA BRAVA

A small remote "wild" beach usually without hassle, thanks to difficult access. Close to São Paulo between Bertioga and São Sebastiao on the Rio-Santos Highway; look for and hike along the oil pipe going down to the bay east of Ponta Grossa between the towns of Boiçucanga and Maresias.

RIO DE JANEIRO

BÚZIOS: PRAIA OLHO DE BOI

East-northeast 125 miles from Rio de Janeiro, Búzios—the fishing village that became an international symbol of chic— once had local nude beaches. Now, like St.-Tropez or Provincetown, Búzios' nude beaches have shifted to more acknowledged and durable locations, where no

one need be offended.

In Búzios, find the clothed local Praia Brava beach. Park, walk past Praia Brava and over the hill to the secluded **Ponta Olho de Boi.**

PRAIA BRAVA

Praia Brava, "wild beach," is closer to Rio than is Búzios and is reached by the same highway. The mayor of Cabo Frio, Ivo Saldanha, had it officially designated in 1991. Saldanha would have dedicated it himself, clothes-free, but the church, which opposes nudity, made a stink. With that mayor out of office, it is again unofficial.

Praia Brava is supervised by the Rio de Janeiro Naturist Association—Sérgio de Oliveira, RIO NAT, C.P. 136, Rio de Janeiro RJ 20001-970—who offers help to visitors. Phone (5521) 537-2767. In Rio itself, you can visit the RIO NAT solarium, Guaratiba, phone (5521) 395-2786.

☞ From Rio, Praia Brava is 191 km or 2 1/2 hours drive to Cabo Frio. Leave Rio by the Niteroi Bridge and follow the Amaral Peixote to Cabo Frio. In its center, cross the bridge and follow Bikinis Street. Your next landmark will be the Canal das Ostras on your right as you drive on Av. do Espadarte to Porto Veliero. Encountering the inlet you must angle left along it, until opposite Japanese Island. You'll have passed the windmills of a saline (salt evaporation yard) on your left. Park at Nacil Bar, walking the final 300 yards. The fine beach is free of pollution and open to the sea.

LAGOA GRANDE

An emerging Brazilian clothing-optional site west of Itacuruca. Take Rio-Santos Highway (BR-101) south from Rio. At 92 km mark (7 km past Itacuruca) find turnoff toward beach. Park before railroad tracks and continue on foot to the lagoon.

ESPIRITO SANTO

PRAIA DA BARRA SECA

A pristine official naturist beach near Linhares on the coastal road halfway between São Paulo–Bahia. Sea turtles lay eggs here. To visit, contact Gilson and Maria Luzia at NATES, C.P. 010697, Vitória, ES 29001-970. Phone (5527) 325-4430.

MATO GROSSO

CHAPADA DOS GUIMARÃES

A beautiful canyon park 68 km from Cuiabá, the capital of Mato Grosso state in west central Brazil. Chapada dos Guimarães has waterfalls and rivers where skinny-dipping has become a tradition. According to the 2-89 edition of *Pinho é*, nude use is well-established and growing due to influence of the nearby "hippie community" since the early 1970s. Campsites available. Cuiabá is the gateway to an immense ecological preserve, the Pantanal, well worth a visit.

BAHÍA

TRANCOSO: PRAIA DA PEDRA GRANDE

In the south of Bahía this town on a hill overlooking the Big Rock Beach remains a tranquil place. Hippies dominate without a heavy drug scene. *Pousadas* offer rooms or you can stay with local people. The 28 km of fine secluded beach extend south from Trancoso to Caraíva.

☞ Bus to Porto Seguro. Across from its bus terminal, catch the ferry across the river, and then another bus to Trancoso. If you arrive at Porto Seguro at night, stay over and go to Trancoso the next morning. If you know how long you're going to stay, book your return bus from Porto Seguro when you arrive, especially between December and March, and on holidays.

DA LAGOA AZUL

This Blue Lagoon has a lovely beach as well as medicinal mudbaths. Not far south of Arraial d'Ajuda, across the river from Porto Seguro, at the mouth of Rio Taipe on the road to Trancoso.

AREMBEPE

Fifty km northeast of Salvador, capital of Bahía, Arembepe was the original hangout for hippies in the late '60s. Now it is quiet and peaceful. The beach is long and lined with palms. You can find lodgings but most people make a day trip from Salvador. The nude portion is 2 km north.

☞ On BR-099. Buses run daily from Salvador at Terminal Franges in Cidaele Baixa (lower city). Best to check with your bus to find out when the last bus returns from Arembepe.

PARAÍBA

PRAIA TAMBABA

Conde, a city off BR-101 at 98 km north of Recife or 118 km south of Natal in the northeast of Brazil, had a naturist prefect, Aluisio Régis. Régis designated Tambaba —one of the 10 most beautiful Atlantic beaches of Brazil, according to Quatro Rodas—as the first Paraíba state legal nude beach. The beach extends for 24 km south from Jacumã. Hotel Vale das Cascatas, 48 km from the beach in João Pessoa, is a good base; phone (5583) 221-4514.

Information on Praia Tambaba from: Prefeitura, Rua general Perousse 121, Conde, PB 58322. Phone (5521) 241-1042; fax 221-2376.

CEARÁ

JERICOACOARA

Young hip Brazilians put the fishing town of Jericoacoara on their maps. Ringed by sand dunes and lakes in the northern state of Ceará, it lacks electricity or tap water, with only a town pump. Some families convert parlors to restaurants serving catch of the day. No hotels but locals rent rooms. Nude bathing is a 3-km walk west of town.

☞ A bus leaves daily at 8 a.m. from Fortaleza to a town called Jijoca. It is very important that you book in advance and, if you know when you'll be returning, buy your tickets when you arrive in Jijoca. From Jijoca jeeps meet the bus to take you for an hour ride around the dunes to Jericoacoara.

CANOA QUEBRADA

Canoa is growing in popularity and can be crowded in January and February. A few bars and restaurants and a dance hall for *Furro*, a traditional dance. The beach is long and clean, and you can buy cold drinks and fresh fish plates there.

Northeast of Mossoró on BR-304. Buses leave daily from Fortaleza to Aracati, a small historic fishing village with a lively carnival and not on most maps, where the young Brazilian vacationers rent rooms or sleep out of doors in hammocks. Several hundred will be on the nearby nude beach, with its big sand dunes, even in midweek. Find the area to the left of the main beach.

COSTA RICA

MANUEL ANTONIO NATIONAL PARK

On the Pacific Coast south from San Jose, on the southeastern outskirts of Quepos, is the 1,686-acre Manuel Antonio National Park and its clothes-optional beach, **Playita** (Little Beach). It's an amazing jungle coast with army ants, sloths and monkeys, wonderful flora and fauna. Closed Mondays. Arrive early as the park seals the gate when the daily attendance limit is reached. In 1995 a national $15 park entry fee was set for noncitizens.

Playita is 500 yards of calm warm water in a half-moon cove, with great white sand shaded by palm trees. Drive into the park at the first entrance past the Hotel Karahé. Proceed to Playa Espadilla, the main beach, where you will walk northwest, wade a small estuary, cross a small cove then clamber over a rock barrier at its north end to Playita. Plan your time: no access in or out of Playita at high tide!

On the southern end of Playa Espadilla there's a Bar del Mar with drinks, snacks, snorkel and flippers, lounge chair, umbrella and frisbee rental. You can also arrange a kayak tour of the park, its nearby islands and rivers: Iguana Tours/Rios Tropicales, phone (506) 770574.

You might lodge at the convenient, family-oriented Hotel Karahé, phone (506) 770170; fax 770152. Or the delightful, moderately-priced Villas Nicolás in Quepos, phone (506) 770481. Luxury inns are Makanda by the Sea, phone (506) 770442, and La Mariposa, phone (506) 770355; fax 770050.

If you're looking for more privacy, drive to Puntarenas—the Fiesta resort makes a good base—and hire a boat to visit your pick of over 20 islets in the **Golfo de Nicoya.** Then drive out onto the sparsely-settled Nicoya Penninsula near the Nicaraguan border, and visit the marvelous waterfall north of Montezuma that plunges into the Atlantic—there is skinny-dipping among the boulders.

MEXICO

he 16th-century Spanish takeover of Central America was enabled in part by a body-rejecting Catholic doctrine that confirms Mexicans in their misery. A new gentry now looks upon nakedness as the evidence and punishment of poverty and unworthiness. Thus does nudity default to the unchurched, desperate status of the *indio*. No wonder Mexicans feel troubled by nude beaches! Before going nude anywhere in Mexico, the visitor must ask at the hotel about current custom, law and enforcement.

NOTE: captions to photos run along the inside edge of pages.

YUCATAN

CANCÚN

Magnificent Mayan ruins—some of them overlooking the white sand beach and turquoise sea—the superb yet competitively-priced hotels, and low-cost air access have coaxed the Yucatan Peninsula into a world-class destination.

The upgrading clientele often request topfree or nude sunning, for which the Mexican tradition is ill-prepared. The public beaches of Cancún Island see the topfree option more and more asserted, particularly by European women. And full body freedom occurs at the Cancún Club Med nude sunning zone. Displaced by the Conrad Hotel to its north, Club Med nudity shifted onto the lagoon side just past the windsurfing pavilion.

Beyond this incremental acceptance by Cancún proper, the Playa del Carmen, Cozumel Island, Playa Paraiso at Tulum and Isla Mujeres beckon. Special report in *Nude & Natural* magazine *N* 11.2, pp. 41–47.

ISLA MUJERES

About 6 miles off the coast from Cancún, Isla Mujeres is a mellow fishing village with tourist restaurants, shops and several hotels. On the edge of town, *playa cocos* (Coco Beach/North Beach) is best for topfree sunbathing—confirmed by the island monthly *Isla Mujeres Today*. The southern end has good snorkeling and sailing. Prices are cheaper here than in Cancún and many prefer it. Ferry service from Punta Sam and Puerto Juárez and daily boat excursions from Cancún hotels.

PUERTO MORELOS

Puerto Morelos is just south of Cancún. From the Posada Amor bathers are driven to a deserted nude beach. A room at the inn, including 2 meals, is about $30 per day. Sr. Rogoello Fernandez, Posada Amor, Apartado Postal 806, Cancún, Puerto Morelos, Q. Roo, Mexico.

PLAYA DEL CARMEN

South of Cancún—north of Tulum along the coastal highway is the town of Playa del Carmen. Europeans welcome its quiet accepting way. Broad white sand beach, giant palms, many small restaurants and posadas, plus bus terminal, airstrip and the Cozumel Island ferry. From the pier north for 1/2 mile it's topfree.

☞ The stretch of beach along the Touresta Corredor (Highway 307), south from Cancún International Airport to Playa del Carmen, often invites clothes-optional use. About 0.5 km from **Shangri-La Caribe** is a sand road to Coco Beach which branches off to the left just short of the resort entrance. The road goes north for 200 m, turns right and eventually passes through a vehicle gate before heading towards Coco. Go north, up the beach, past the cafes for a few hundred meters. The nude area is about 1 km. The water is clear and clean, with sandy bottom and patch reefs and fine snorkeling. Do not leave anything unattended on beach.

COZUMEL ISLAND

Directly across from Playa del Carmen is Cozumel Island. If you're lodging at a Cancún hotel you can make a day visit by a cheap 20-minute commuter flight. The 2-hour boat connection leaves Cancún at 9:30 a.m., returns at 5:30 p.m., except Tuesdays. Cozumel dock or airport local authorities will direct you to the nude beaches; just ask.

Nudity is accepted at Punta Celarain on the miles-long **El Mirador Beach,** which runs northward from the lighthouse at Punta Celarain. Rent a car, or a bicycle or motorbike at Rueben's 2 blocks behind the San Miguel central square. Go south, past El Presidente Hotel, and you'll see the lighthouse from the Coastal road. Access is by a gravel hard right turnoff that doubles back south where the Coastal road angles northward. Halfway between the cutoff and the lighthouse is a small Mayan ruin the size of a backyard storage shed. A path behind the ruin leads to the beach. Nearing the lighthouse, park on its left.

Other secluded beaches on the eastern coast are north of where the paved Coastal road ends upon joining the Cross Island road. Take the dirt spur north, stopping at Mescalito's. The owner can suggest good nude sunning spots.

AKUMAL

Akumal, south of Playa Del Carmen, has superior diving and is less developed than Cancún. Some topfree sunning. Good accommodations. Club Akumal Caribe phone 1-800-351-1622.

X-Cacel Beach, 5 miles south, has tent camping, good surf, restaurant. The far north end has parts suited for nude use; topfree is accepted on either end of the beach. $2 entrance fee.

TULUM

Starting from the ancient Maya coastal city of Tulum, 75 miles south of Cancún, topfree and some nude use is made of the beach, at **El Mirador Campground** and farther south. A couple of native restaurants, a bakery and other supplies can be found at the ruins; another restaurant, El Crucero, is at the crossroads where the bus stops. Small hotels here, very reasonable, with communal hot showers and other amenities, are Cabañas Don Armandos and Cabañas Chac Mool. Along the highway heading south from the parking lot entrance, you'll see signs on roads leading to various *cabañas* (small cabins with thatched roofs to rent).

☞ To **El Paraiso Beach:** Best bet is by bus; it's fast and cheap; only 12 pesos from Carmen. Get off the bus at the Highway 307 entrance to Tulum, walk to the cab stand at the southwest corner and tell the driver you want to go to El Paraiso playa. It is three miles east on an arrow-straight road which ends in a "T." Turning left, toward El Paraiso, you will pass a small beach resort under

reconstruction (two hurricanes), named Gatos. This is 400 m beyond the south end of the nude beach. Continuing north about 1 km, you will arrive at El Paraiso. It looks closed (storm damage). Walk through main building to the beach. It is clothing-optional from the south walls of Tulum ruins to the rocks near Gatos. Take water.

OAXACA COAST

PUERTO ANGEL

Puerto Angel is often described as a left-over hippie town from the Sixties which developers ignored due to its rugged setting—be grateful!

First, get updated in Puerto Angel (and we recommend you rent a room) from a California woman, Susanne Lopez, who runs La Posada Cañon de Vata, A.P. 74, Pochutla, Oaxaca, Mexico; no phone. The Posada evening meal is family style and cosmopolitan. Or try deluxe hotel Angel del Mar. Both overlook the west harbor Playa del Panteón.

The best nude beach is 4 km west of Puerto Angel; you'll need a taxi to Playa Zipolite. Go to the far end, beyond the clothed people and the dangerous surf. The headland marks the end of the beach, and you'll find, up the cliff, a vegetarian food place with camping, run by yet another American woman who is helpful. Suggested lodging is Hotel Gloria at Playa Zipolite.

Another nude beach is at **Esatca-huites,** a 20-minute walk from the bus/taxi stop near the Navy (marina) base. Walk up the highway towards Pochutla for 1/2 km. The dirt road to

Esatcahuites is on the right and an 8-minute walk will bring you to several sandy coves. Do not leave your gear unattended. Swimming is dangerous. The beach has a refreshment stand.

PUERTO ESCONDIDO

An international airport now makes the access easy. It's still a small town, on a small and now crowded cove. Municipal Playa Marinero separates most town hotels from lightly used **Playa Zikatela,** which stretches 2 miles eastward inviting nude bathers. Recommended: Hotel Santa Fe, 25 rooms, fine restaurant, freshwater pool, right at start of Playa Zikatela, phone (52958) 20170.

You may hire a boat to go north around the point to *playa sin ropa* (naked beach) or to the best surfing beach.

You may also take the interurban bus 50 miles south to Puerto Angel for a few day's visit. See report in *Nude & Natural* magazine *N* 11.2, pp. 47–50.

ACAPULCO

You won't choose to go to Acapulco if a great nude beach is your priority. Once there, enjoy the best of what there is.

BOCA CHICA

Boca Chica is a fine hotel of 40 rooms with excellent food, lush grounds, a good pool, and a private swimming/snorkeling cove. The resident boatman will take you to the deserted beach of a nearby island. Reasonable rates include breakfast and dinner. Hotel Boca Chica, Playa Caletilla, Acapulco. Phone (52748) 36741.

HACIENDA INN

Hacienda Inn, at Los Magotes, 25 km north of Acapulco, is hosted by a fun-loving French Canadian and his Mexican wife. Price in 1995 season: Canadian $300 per week, includes room, meals, airport transfers, bicycles and beach equipment. Quiet 17-km clothes-optional beach with palapas; hike to waterfall. Season is December to April. Information: Michel Lauzon, 6000–29e Ave. No. 21, Montréal, Québec, Canada H1T 3G9. Phone (514) 721-4678.

MANZANILLO

TENACATITA BAY

Surrounded by lush jungle, Manzanillo is a Pacific fishing port with white sand beaches and a sunny climate, becoming a world-class destination. Located an hour from the airport is the Los Angeles Loco, a deluxe resort overlooking Tenacatita Bay, popular with Canadians and Americans. Phone (52333) 70220.

The beach in front of the hotel is textile; topfree sunning occurs at both ends. South of the villas are large rock formations, and beyond the rocks is a large beach used for nude sunbathing. But not swimming! There is a strong undertow, and the beach can only be reached at low tide.

PLAYA BLANCA

On Chamela Bay in Colima province, Club Med Playa Blanca is a huge complex designed for 660 guests. Scuba, sailing, snorkeling, tennis and more. Many French guests. Nudity occurs on the large, high, terrace above the scuba shack next to the beach, with a great view. Side trips to Guadalajara and Puerto Vallarta. Guests fly into Manzanillo for a 1 1/4-hour bus ride to the club.

PUERTO VALLARTA

CLUB MAEVA

Club Maeva, an all-inclusive resort opened in 1991, is 4.5 km south of Puerto Vallarta. At the north end of the waterfront is a small, man-made beach; if you follow the path past the shower, down the stairs to the real beach and go around the rocks, you will find the small, secluded nude beach. The hotel staff will carry beach furniture to the nude area for guests. It is the only section of beach with enough room for sunbathing, so clothed bathers occasionally share it.

P.O. Box 385, Puerto Vallarta, Jalisco 48300; phone (52322) 22787; fax (52322) 22105.

YELAPA & QUIMIXTO: UPPER FALLS

Located near a charming seaside town of the same name, reached only by sea, Yelapa Waterfall is well-known in town. Intrepid naturists learned of a lovely pool at the top of the falls, deep enough to allow you to relax in without worrying about being carried over the top. Surrounded by lush vegetation, skinnysoakers enjoy an unobstructed view of the bay below.

Your access is through Puerto Vallarta, Mexico's most popular resort with Californians. Take the 9 a.m. tourist ferry to Yelapa, walk through town and ask for the waterfall. Climb the poorly-defined path up the right side of the falls, and you'll find access to the pool.

Better, take the midday supplies boat, chat with the boatman, and plan to stay overnight at the Lagunita Hotel or in a local palapa or a U.S. expatriate's house.

A similar waterfall, with little-visited pools above the falls for skinny-dipping, is at **Quimixto.** Rental horses can be used to go 20 minutes from beach to falls.

You may find that Yelapa or Quimixto is what Puerto Vallarta is all about! Leave your hairblower home, there's no electricity in the coastal villages.

SAYULITA BEACH

About 46 km north of Puerto Vallarta. Non-naturist camper park and restaurants in Sayulita. Very remote beach in a cove below rocky cliffs. Try to avoid high tide.

☞ The beach is a mile or so north of the turnoff for the village of Sayulita. Instead of turning off Highway 200 onto the paved road leading to the village, stay on the highway (traveling north) and look for a seldom-used dirt road to the left. This road branches several times; each time keep to the right until you come to the beautiful isolated beach.

MAZATLÁN

ISLA DE LA PIEDRA

Mazatlán people encourage the *gringo* to go *desnudo* offshore at Stone Island on weekdays, since weekends they want to have well-dressed picnics on those beaches!

☞ On a weekday, find the Mazatlán Navy Yard; just to the north is "la barca a Isla de la Piedra," a 20-foot rowboat with motor and awning. A 5-minute ride deposits you opposite the cruise boats on Stone Island; walk inland along the harbor edge and then follow the main (dirt) road around the hill, bringing you to the beach by a restaurant with great smoked fish. Here, you walk left, out of sight of the restaurant, and strip down. Sometimes a horse cart is available to *la playa desnuda.*

BAJA CALIFORNIA

BAJA PENINSULA

Ah, Baja! The word evokes its rough and exotic terrain, true southwest—unspoiled, untamed, warmer and more liberal than mainland Mexico. May, June, October and November are best. It's 1000 well-paved miles, Tijuana—Cabo San Lucas by MEX-1. Or fly cheaply from Tijuana to the Cabo. Ferry service is Mazatlán—La Paz or Puerto Vallarta—Cabo. Naturists have explored Baja's desert, Pacific Coast islands and beaches, hot springs and the Sea of Cortez, and recommend:

The Camping Bares, a San Diego-based naturist "disorganization," organizes outings to **Cañon de Guadelupe** hot springs, near La Rumorosa, and to **Todos Santos Island** off Ensenada. Phone for dates and membership: (714) 646-8851 evenings.

The hot springs 50 miles south of San Felipe on the Sea of Cortez, where the sea rushes in to mingle with the hot water (ask a local boy, when you're near, to direct you there, as no map includes them).

Five hours south from San Diego on a fine paved highway, find **Bahia de los Angeles** on the shore of the Sea of Cortez. Hot days of nude snorkeling in warm clear waters; nights are wonderful. Spectacular scenery, sparsely populated, with no hassles from the local people. Bring your own water!

In the **Loreta** area contact Bob Peffley c/o Tripui Trailer Park, Puerto Escondido, Baja California Sur, Mexico. He has charters available for fishing, diving, sailing, and excursions to hot springs and beautiful beaches.

For a clothing-optional naturist boat excursion on the **Sea of Cortez,** write either Moorings Yacht Charters, or Capt. Johnny Ramos of the Yacht Hay Chihuahua, c/o Port Captain, La Paz, Baja California Sur. Ask to be phoned collect.

The vast rocky beach near **Hotel Solmar** in Cabo San Lucas at the tip of Baja. Go left from the hotel and squeeze through the rocks to a beautiful cave and nude beach, 200 yards from the Baja point. Great sports fishing. Hotel Cabo San Lucas illustrates topfree beach use in recent ads and it touts its "miles of private swimming beaches." Younger, less posh set stays at Hotel Mar de Cortez off the beach.

BAJA TOURING

Enjoy a Baja vacation more, by booking on the live-aboard bus operated by the Green Tortoise. They attract mellow, clothes-optional vacationers to sail, windsurf, explore, just hang out—or whale watch from November to March.

It is not your average bus trip. Green Tortoise shows that public transportation can be fun, with travel from major stop to stop at night, so passengers can make the most of daylight hours. Sleeping is on the bus itself, which has been converted into comfortable, living-room style space. Passengers are encouraged to bring musical instruments and additional sporting equipment. Average age of passengers is 20–30 but all ages have participated; singles, couples, families alike.

☞ Green Tortoise picks up in Seattle, Portland, Eugene, San Francisco, or Los Angeles. Write: Box 24459, San Francisco, CA 94124. Phone 1-800-TOR-TOIS or (415) 956-7500.

LORETO EDEN

In Loreto, halfway down Baja on the Gulf side, is Loreto Eden. The hotel sports a clothing-optional 200-foot sand beach, nearby bar and large hot tub. The beach is protected by a series of small breakwaters which allows the bottom to grow a carpet of seaweed. The hotel itself has nice rooms, restaurant with floor shows, a disco, clothed beach and swimming pool. Activities include golf, tennis, scuba, snorkeling and sports fishing at extra cost. Inclusive packages start at $400/per person from Aero California, phone 1-800-524-9191; or book from Go Classy Tours, Inc., 1-800-329-8145.

PANAMA

CONTADORA ISLAND RESORT

Contadora Island Resort shares the 11th largest of the Pearl Islands, 35 miles off the Panama Pacific Coast, with about 80 other co-owners. It is accessible by a 16-minute plane ride from Panama City and offers an all-inclusive package, international cuisine, pool with swim-up bar, golf and tennis courts and a small casino.

From the right end of the main beach, a path leads through a wooded area up a small hill for about 5 minutes, to a lovely white sand beach used topfree. Just past this area and over some rocks (impassible at high tide) is a designated nude beach, perhaps 400 yards long, pleasant and clean, called **Playa Suecas,** used by a dozen or so couples and singles. Best time to visit is Dec. 15–April 15. Popular with Canadians and Germans.

Contadora Island International Resort, P.O. Box 1880, Panama City 1, Panama. Phone (507) 27-2904.

URUGUAY

PUNTA DEL ESTE

Playa Chihuahua—Chihuahua Beach. A broad white sand playground on the South Atlantic ocean in Portezuelo that is backed by woods and accepted for full nudity. Only 40 minutes by air from Argentina, 90% of the users are nonetheless Uruguayan or Brazilian. Punta del Este is an international resort and even the hotel guests are often topfree.

☞ At kilometer 124 on the Montevideo—Punta del Este highway, turn on a dirt road towards the ocean. Park, wade the lagoon. Is waist-deep wading unacceptable? Get off instead at marker 125. Park at the hotel named Cabaña del Tío Tom. Walk back along the beach to reach the clothes-optional zone without hassles.

Michael Cooney, Bare Necessities Tour & Travel Co.'s 1995 Nude Caribbean 10-Day Cruise Aboard the Regent Rainbow. Facing Page: Michael Cooney, INF Vice-President Petra Scheller in Jamaica.

THE CARIBBEAN

For the pale-skinned, inhibited denizens of eastern North America, the Caribbean beckons like a paradise. The constant sweet warmth, the palms, the white sand beaches, the exotic names and lilting rhythms spell relief from rules and schedules. The anonymity of a distant resort is often as important as its beauty; it permits experiments with one's life-style.

Have you ever wondered what skinny-dipping for adults would be like: lounging without clothes, a soft trade wind stroking flesh that has never been exposed, with families and couples mixing unashamedly beneath a forgiving, embracing sun? Numerous resorts—many of them on Jamaica and St. Martin—now cater to this wish.

If you, a spouse or child are not confident about choosing a clothes-optional adventure, remember that the accented word is *optional*. Remain clothed at the destinations described here without embarrassment...just as you may remove most or all of your clothing.

Another way to be clothes-optional in the Caribbean is to make up your own small party on a motorized sailboat with a capacity of four to 15. A host couple or crew will skipper you to the skinny-dip beaches of the Bahamas or Virgin Islands.

Moreover, the clothes-optional, week-long chartering of major cruise ships is now popular; whether the quaint windjammers, or the "loveboat" cruise ships that offer water sports.

These travel agencies specialize in packaged tropical nude vacations ashore and afloat:

• Bare Necessities Tour & Travel Company—1802 W. 6th St., Suite B, Austin, TX 78703. Phone 1-800-743-0405 or (512) 499-0405; fax (512) 469-0179.

• Skinny-Dip Tours & Caribbean Hideaways—R.D. 1, Box 294, Bloomingburg, NY 12721. Phone 1-800-828-9356 or (914) 733-4596; fax (914) 733-5298.

• Travel Au Naturel—35246 U.S. 19 N., #112, Palm Harbor, FL 34684. Phone 1-800-728-0185 or (813) 948-2007; fax (813) 948-2832.

• Go Classy Tours—2676 West Lake Drive, Palm Harbor, FL 34684. Phone 1-800-329-8145 or (813) 786-8145.

ANTIGUA

HAWKSBILL BEACH

Antigua's chief clothes-optional beach is the farthest south (left) of the four maintained by the deluxe, sedate Hawksbill Beach Hotel, 3 miles southwest of St. John. It has several large sandy areas, and a hotel "beach officer" from 8 a.m. to 4 p.m. to provide security. There are fine coconut palms and the hotel supplies umbrellas and chaises. Bring any food or drink you need, and definitely use footwear. Great snorkeling off the nude beach; bring your own gear. Air travel from Miami to Antigua is quite reasonable. You needn't stay at the hotel to use the beach.

Hawksbill Hotel, phone: 1-800-223-6510 or (268) 462-0301. Fax (268) 462-1515.

Prices comparable to Club Orient but here only the beach is nude. Coolers with ice are provided in each of the 85 rooms and refilled daily.

Jerre Blank, Hawksbill Hotel Nude Beach.

ARUBA

THE BEACHES

With lots of fine beaches, a hot desert-like climate tempered by constant breezes, and European-oriented (topfree) resort hotels, Aruba has convenient flights from the U.S.

The recently opened **Sonesta Hotel** in downtown Oranjestad owns a private island, 1 mi off the coast and opposite the airport, with bar, restaurant, showers, rest rooms, a gym, tennis, and topfree beach. Continuous ferry service to the island for the hotel guests. There's also an excellent, very "nudism-friendly" beach at the western tip of the island, a ten-minute stroll from the facilities.

On the southwestern coast north of Oranjestad, a 4-mile palm beach of low-rise hotels is topfree-friendly. The **Manchebo Beach** and **Bucuti** hotels (adjacent and both operated by Best Western, 1-800-334-7234), and the **Divi-Divi** and **Tamarijn** hotels are recommended.

Nudity is also accepted on the shore behind the **Tierra del Sol** complex. It incorporates the California Lighthouse referred to in earlier editions. Due to golfing it has lost some of its seclusion.

A still-undeveloped area is **Dos Playa** on the northeast coast. Named for two lovely sand beaches divided by a great rock in the sea, the rear beach is traditionally nude and can be accessed only on foot or by 4WD. Nudity is also okay on Dos Playa's front beach, except when families picnic there which is mostly on Sundays.

In the **Seroe Colorado** residential area at the southeastern tip, topfree sunbathing is popular.

BAHAMAS

North from the Caribbean Basin and due east from Florida. The large islands are heavily developed. The Out Islands—some only 50 miles from Florida—have gorgeous, deserted beaches. Many small yachts are available for charter to reach these sites.

CAT ISLAND

CUTLASS BAY: CLUB & CAMPGROUND

Fifty miles in length, with many small Bahamian villages, this narrow, hilly, perhaps most beautiful island in the Bahamas was a pirate haven.

Cutlass Bay Club has a clothing-optional freshwater pool and a warm, shallow 10-mile beach for guests. Veranda dining, beach barbecues, tennis, snorkeling, bicycling, dancing. Hosts Robby and Sandy also organize island tours. See report in *Nude & Natural* magazine *N* 11.2 pp. 33–36.

Port Howe, Cat Island, Bahamas. Phone 1-800-723-5688 or (813) 269-0153.

FERNANDEZ BAY VILLAGE

Fernandez Bay Village near New Bight rents housekeeping villas. Each with maid service, windsurfer, small sailboat, and secluded by vegetation for deck sunning. Beach permits nude swimming at either end. Airfield, anchorage, sunfish, windsurfers, minimart, restaurant, bonfires with local musicians, air transfers. Phone 1-800-940-1905.

GRAND BAHAMA

FREEPORT

Drive, taxi or motorbike to 3 miles east of the Holiday Inn. Turn right on a small dirt road that leads to El Club Carib, a honky-tonk bar and restaurant on **Fortuna Beach** adjacent to the Fortuna Complex. Enjoy the huge Fortuna Beach in your choice of dress code but be wary of beach thieves. The stretch from Holiday Inn to Club Carib, Churchill Beach, can be used with caution too.

The beach at the Xanadu Hotel can be reached conveniently by a shuttle bus from the Bahama Princess or Bahama Towers hotels. At **Xanadu,** walk east (right, as you face the water), past three stone breakwaters, to a quiet spot of your choice or as far as the water cut, a half mile.

The East side of Grand Bahama is undeveloped and largely open to nude use.

NEW PROVIDENCE

PARADISE ISLAND

Since 1994 under the control of Sun International and its nudity-friendly impresario from South Africa, Sol Kerzner, this enclave, until 1960 known as Hog Island, has become a world-class but clothed water theme park. A ferry runs from Nassau to the Holiday Inn on Paradise Island ($2 fee charged). Or taxi across a bridge from Nassau, four miles long and a mile wide, where there are nine resorts on a perfected beach, plus golf, casino, many restaurants and nightclubs.

For nude use, however, walk left on the beach past **Club Med,** and the Yoga Center where g-strings and topfree are okay, over and around some major coral rocks and boulders, to the open sandy beach close to the lighthouse on the northwestern tip, before the rock jetty. It gets very hot so bring sunblock and drinking water. Be wary of sea currents and thieves.

You may more conveniently reach Lighthouse Beach if you hire a small boat at almost any hotel or at the cruise boat pier, which is *adjacent* to the lighthouse. So you may skip the whole tedious taxi trip into Nassau and across the bridge and then the long beach hike. Surprise!

ANDROS ISLAND

SMALL HOPE BAY LODGE

Andros is a low-slung coral island on which little grows large but casuarina trees. Comfortable cottages are lined up by the shore facing the main attraction, the fabulous sea. A small rock islet with a hot tub that you may use "starkers" also looks out. A solarium hedged with palm fronds provide nude privacy. Scuba, snorkel, bicycles, minimart, air transfer from Nassau. Small Hope Bay Lodge, Fresh Creek, Andros, phone 1-800-223-6961 or (242) 368-2014.

Bahamas: Lee Baxandall, Nude Beach At the Paradise Island Lighthouse, Nassau. Dolphin Island. Scuba Diving Off Grand Bahama Island.

Cuba, Cayo Largo: Vittorio Buono, Quebec Naturists Vacation At Villa Capricho & Its Beach. Insets: Terry Roscoe.

GREAT EXUMA

PEACE & PLENTY BEACH

George Town is a laid-back, friendly spot to forget time. Direct flights from Miami and Ft. Lauderdale. Gentleness on its unspoiled beaches, which admittedly don't have the bright lights and concrete of Nassau and Freeport.

On Elizabeth Harbor are several inns—try Peace and Plenty Hotel. Pool, lounge, restaurant, pier, scuba, windsurf, 32 air-conditioned rooms. Phone (242) 336-2551.

Peace & Plenty operates a Beach Club on Stocking Island a mile across the harbor. It provides transportation; you do not have to be a hotel guest. A clothes-optional beach is to the left of the club as you go ashore, past the rocky breakwater.

LONG ISLAND

STELLA MARIS INN

At the north end of 90-mile Long Island, between Exuma and Cat Islands. Scheduled Bahamasair service from Nassau and George Town.

The German managers support free body culture, if integrated with vacation activities—not as "cult" behavior in itself or on the grounds. Shark feeding is a specialty (integrate that, scuba-dippers!). Three-mile beach extending east is in au naturel use. Scuba, snorkel, jet ski, windsurf, bone fishing, tennis, six beaches, three pools, 120-guest capacity. Bungalows, hotel rooms; superb cuisine. Phone 1-800-426-0466 or (242) 336-2106.

ELEUTHERA

CLUB MED ET AL.

An island, 120 miles long, named with the Greek word for freedom. Rightfully, if *eleuthera* thrives on the solitude to go nude, select from hundreds of beaches with powdery white sand and clear warm water under sunny skies.

Choose a boat or small hotel as your base. Put together your own clothes-free group of 7 to 10 and enjoy the all-inclusive price, routing and convenience of a week at the lodge of **Outpost Eleuthera.** Phone Pat Meidl, (715) 435-3823.

Or try **Club Med Eleuthera.** It's set on traditionally clothes-optional French Leave Beach. Club personnel now deny—at government request—knowledge that nude sunbathing occurs starting 100 yards to the left outside the club's (topfree) enclave. Some vacationers sun here while lodging at Governor's Harbour a short walk away.

BONAIRE

SOROBON RESORT

On the south end of the Caribbean Sea, close to Venezuela, is the small Dutch island of Bonaire. It is quiet, dry and temperate. Flamingos wade in salt ponds and offshore coral reefs are protected.

Sorobon is an upscale clothes-optional resort with 20 double-bedroom kitchen-equipped units, built in 1984. Full-service restaurant. Fine sand private beach, windsurfing and snorkeling, with scuba options. Superb reef life that you can wade to across Sorobon Bay.

Not for partiers, Sorobon Resort is praised and promoted by Bonaire officials. P.O. Box 14, Bonaire, Netherlands Antilles. Phone 1-800-432-3471 or (5997) 8080; fax (5997) 6080.

CUBA

Το he Caribbean's finest white sand beaches, at the lowest air-plus-resort prices, and an official policy that supports nude beaches—this attracts many sunlovers to Cuba from Europe and Canada. United States passport holders, discouraged from travel to Cuba by U.S. government political posturing, will find they may readily visit Cuba and Cayo Largo.

CAYO LARGO

Cuba's satellite Big Key (Cayo Largo del Sur), 35 miles south of the western part of the main island, is reached by nonstop flights within the Caribbean. From the north, direct flights pass through Havana or Varadero. Many private planes and yachts also stop at Cayo Largo.

"Naturists from all the world are welcome here," says Omar Rigñack Asencio, spokesman for Gran Caribe Grupo Hotelero in Cayo Largo. "You may be nude anywhere on our 25 km of fine white sand beaches, only not in front of hotels. At the **Villa Capricho,** you may also be nude on the grounds and the water sports beach."

Playa Sirena, a short boat ride from the airstrip, is what most day-trippers from Havana see. Its central beach offers water sports, beach bar, restaurant, trips to Iguana Island or for scuba, and is topfree. Walk just off the central beach to be fully nude.

Multiday naturist visitors choose a plan at the nearby *complejo hotelero.* The clothes-optional, 72-unit **Villa Capricho** is the obvious choice. A lovely pine woods extends eastward sheltering many raptors and other birds. Cayo Largo is nearly flat and 15 square miles in area.

International phone and fax are available. English is widely spoken. Cuba is a member of the Caribbean Hotel Association.

The *complexo* has a choice of restaurants, pools, boutiques, squash and tennis courts, room TVs with CNN and HBO, water craft, horses, bicycles, ATVs and fine reefs for snorkeling and scuba. Dive master is Pipin Ferrera who holds the world record (67 m) for diving without equipment.

All expenses at Cayo Largo plus the Canada–Cuba round-trip airfare come to less than the ground costs alone at anywhere else a naturist might go in the Caribbean.

Toronto's Four Seasons nudist club visited Cayo Largo; the Quebec Naturist Federation (FQN) makes an annual event of it (see *Nude & Natural* magazine N 14.2 for a detailed report).

Flight access to Cuba for U.S. citizens is generally from Jamaica, the Dominican Republic, the Caymans, the Bahamas, Cancún or Mexico City, Toronto or Montreal. Ask Magna Holidays of Toronto, phone 416-665-7330; Champagne Tours of Montreal, phone 514-866-3695; or the FQN's Royal du Perron, phone 514-252-3014.

While U.S. credit cards and traveler's checks are not accepted, U.S. currency is; and Cuban authorities issue visas on the spot rather than stamp passports. Visits by U.S. citizens are climbing.

CURAÇAO

CORAL CLIFF HOTEL

On Santa Marta Bay, toward the little-developed, picturesque western end of the Dutch island near Venezuela in the south Caribbean, quiet Coral Cliff Resort reserves a third of its beach for nudity and its charter boats welcome nude scuba charters. There are 35 villa units with sea view, air conditioning, kitchenette; patio restaurant, tennis, and now a pool. Phone (5999) 642 666; fax 641 781.

An islet, Little Curaçao, is host to nude beach picnics that originate at Coral Cliff's sister hotel, The Curaçao Carib-bean. Ask the clerk how to connect.

Divide a visit in the south Caribbean between a Coral Cliff base for Curaçao's activities and nightlife, and laid-back, naturist Sorobon Beach Resort on Bonaire.

GRENADA & GRENADINES

GRENADA

La Sagesse Nature Center is said by some to be the place to check in if you hope to find a secluded beach during a stay on this former British possession—"liberated" from local nationalists by Pres. Reagan and U.S. troops. The island's current politicians can't seem to get anything right. So look north, up the chain of smaller islands known to small craft charters as The Grenadines, reaching to St. Vincent.

CARRIACOU

The largest of The Grenadines, most-easily reached by flying into Grenada, this undeveloped and uncrowded island has several small hotels, guest houses, rooms and houses for rent. Nude hiking is possible on the windward side of the island and discreet nudity is possible on almost all of the beautiful beaches. Offshore islets are easily accessible by kayak or boat for a picnic lunch, snorkeling, fishing and exploring. The nicest of these may be White Island off the south coast.

Anse La Roche beach on the Atlantic shore is recommended, as is the nearby Caribee Inn, hosted by an English couple. Phone (809) 443-7380. Annual visitor Bill Heyne can answer your questions—phone him at (908) 496-4347. More information in *N* magazine 12.1.

PETIT ST. VINCENT RESORT

"Some of our guests never put on any clothes until dinner time," or so the advertising goes at Petit St. Vincent Resort, a bungalow complex on this 113-acre private island in The Grenadines.

Each bungalow has its own sundeck where many guests prefer to spend their time—when they're not in one of the secluded coves. An exquisite spot, arranged with care and taste to satisfy the hedonist in all of us and with a price tag to match. Petit St. Vincent, St. Vincent-Grenadines, W.I. (U.S. office: P.O. Box 12506, Cincinnati, OH 45212.)

UNION ISLAND

Chatham Bay on the east coast is said to be used nude. Sailing cruises from Union Island can be arranged to the nearby Tabago Cays, where the majority of boaters may be nude. The beautiful palm-fringed beaches on these nearby islets have an abundance of marine life.

PALM ISLAND

Palm Island owner John Caldwell speaks plainly about nude sunbathers: "We don't mind." Welcoming its nudity-positive attitude and "string of comfy, breeze-conditioned cottages designed for privacy," author Peter Passell in his 1987 book *The Best* nominates Palm Island Beach Club as "the world's best nude beach."

Your party may fly to Barbados or Grenada, arrange a charter flight to Union Island's Funny International Airport, then a launch for the 1-mile crossing to Palm Island. Or just sail your charter boat to anchorage. Lovely stone beachfront cottages and 5 private villas; water sports, tennis, boutique and grocery store. Palm Island Beach Club, Grenadines, St. Vincent, W.I. Phone (809) 458-4804 or 800-999-7256; fax (212) 242-4768.

NOTE: captions to photos run along the inside edge of pages.

152

GUADELOUPE

uadeloupe, in 1964, designated Pointe Tarare as the first official nude beach of the Western Hemisphere, thanks above all to the initiative of Jean Rocquemont, a French naturist and engineer.

Contact for information: Marc Mottet, President, Association Naturiste de la Guadeloupe (ANG), B.P. 1152, F-97182 Pointe-a-Pitre, Guadeloupe, F.W.I. Phone (590) 88 72 45; fax 90 73 79. The ANG is not affiliated to the French Naturist Federation, but it is the larger local organization.

The FFN affiliate is ANGECEPERT, c/o Natasha Kvasnikoff, Les Jardins de Vetiver, Les Esses 3, 97139 Reizet, Abymes, Guadeloupe, F.W.I. Fax (590) 83 19 79.

GRANDE-TERRE

STE.-ANNE: JEAN ROCQUEMONT BEACH (CLUB MED CARAVELLE)

Backed by groomed palms and lawns, with a gorgeous view across a protected bay to the cloud-capped Soufriére volcano, Plage Jean Rocquemont Beach adjoins and is somewhat maintained by **Club Med Caravelle.** Architecture of the Club Med is spectacular, you will agree, and you may wish to attend as a week-long paying guest.

Access to the beach is open to the public under French law, but a fee is charged if you use Club Med facilities. The entire white sand **Anse Bourdel** is topfree and the nude portion normally extends to the berm.

☞ From Pointe-á-Pitre take south coastal Route d'Argent (RN 4) 18 km east. Just 1 km west from the limits of Ste.-Anne, find the Shell station on your left. The access road to Jean Rocquemont Beach is just opposite. Drive in and, if you are not a guest, curve left along the outside of the Club Med fence to the east end of the beach. Or park farther out and walk in. You may also ride the bus that runs often to St.-François and ask to be dropped at the Caravelle entrance. Walk right onto the Jean Rocquemont Beach from the east end fence, where a snack bar serves nonguests. While you may mingle with the Club Med guests, remember that the Anse Bourdel beach, not the resort grounds, is public domain. Your coopera-

tion with the club is recommended.

Make Club Med Caravelle reservations through the usual travel agencies, or phone 1-800-CLUB-MED.

Comfortable bungalows 2 minutes east along the beach may be rented from Mme. Giroux, **Le Barrière de Corail,** Durivage, F-97180 Sainte-Anne, Guadeloupe, F.W.I. Phone (590) 88 20 03.

The **Motel de Ste.-Anne** (F-97180, Guadeloupe, F.W.I.) is comfortable, with a good restaurant. Turn left beyond the Esso station, which is the next left after the Shell station. Mme. Giroux's is 200 m farther on the right, the first of two gates in a low stone wall, just before a bridge and cemetery beyond on the left. Other low-cost accommodations also available nearby.

Le Rotabas is located between the cabins rented by Mme. Giroux and the nude beach. Featuring 20 small but air-conditioned, double-bedded rooms, each with a shower and phone, the hotel has its own restaurant, au Matete, with native Creole as well as continental French cuisine and bar. Clothing required everywhere except the beach. Le Rotabas, B.P. 30, F-97180 Ste.-Anne, Guadeloupe, F.W.I. Phone (590) 88 25 60. Telex ROTABA 919 445 GL.

Hotel Toubana accepts full nudity on tiny beaches at the foot of the cliff. Price includes use of tennis courts, canoe, sailboard, catamaran or pedalboat. Horseback, fishing and scuba are extra. B.P. 63, 97180 Sainte-Anne, Guadeloupe, F.W.I. Phone (590) 88 25 78 or (590) 88 25 57. Telex GL 919434. U.S. representative: French Caribbean International, 1-800-322-2223; fax (805) 967-7798.

Be aware that the pressures on Jean Rocquemont Beach increase, due both to the small beach businesses and unsupervised behavior; no local individual or association of naturists has really taken responsibility since the beach's namesake retired.

POINTE TARARE

Eight kilometers east of Saint-François on the north shore of Pointe-des-Châteaux, at the eastern tip of Grande-Terre, is Pointe Tarare, the first legally-designated nude beach of the Western Hemisphere.

Pointe Tarare often has wild surf breaking on its protective reef and is very picturesque, with firm sand for wading. Palms provide nice shade from the sun. On weekdays there are few people on the beach, and some may be clothed. Weekends the beach is entirely nude with 50 or 60 users. You also may climb the bluff of Pointe Tarare in the buff to enjoy a great view down to the Pointe-des-Châteaux, itself a mandatory visit.

☞ Continue beyond St.-François on the coastal highway, past the airport and Hotel Méridien on your right,

over the narrow single-lane stone bridge. At this point check your odometer; the turnoff to the Point Tarare Beach is a one-lane gravel road on the left 3 km from the bridge. A vine-covered steel cyclone fence is on the left, but is now virtually obscured by growth. The best way to find the correct turnoff is to look for a Creole restaurant sign (painted with a large shrimp) on the left side of the road. The top of the sign reads "Plage Tarare" and the other side of the sign reads "Plage Naturiste Ici Tarare." A white turnoff stripe marks the rockstrewn lane that leads to the small parking lot. Park at the lot and walk the 100 m to the beach.

Or try the beach near the Pointe-des-Châteaux parking lot. Cross to the far (north) side of the entry road, walk west and wade through ankle-deep water to the beach which extends for 2 miles west. Do not use the small crescent beach directly at Pointe-des-Châteaux; it is dangerous as well as too public.

ILET DU GOSIER

For cruise passengers who come ashore at the capital city of Pointe-á-Pitre and are given just a few hours to "see" Guadeloupe, a taxi ride east of Pointe-á-Pitre to Gosier, the "Riviera," may help.

Ilet du Gosier is 1,000 m offshore, away from the cluster of Gosier hotels. The hotels have traditionally taken guests to the ilet to go nude weekdays. Local families claim the ilet on weekends; clothes are required on Sundays. In addition, avoid the manchineel trees, which are uniquely corrosive to the skin and lungs; stay on the sands. The sandy side is the part you see as you go over.

☞ A 15-minute taxi ride will take you from Pointe-á-Pitre to Gosier. Sun Beach Restaurant is straight down to the beach from the Gosier Church and has a lovely topfree beach with a near view of the ilet. To swim nude, you might walk east (left) 200 m on the beach, where you'll find seclusion beneath a cliff.

To reach the islet go east of Gosier town to the boat rental house of the Callingo Hotel, located at the base of

the jetty separating the Arawak and Callingo hotel beaches. The fee is reasonable, and you will be picked up as part of the arrangement.

LES SAINTES

TERRE-DE-HAUT: ANSE CRAWEN (HOTEL BOIS JOLI)

Terre-de-Haut is one of 8 islets in the offshore Les Saintes group. Its charming harbor has a fine view of Mt. Soufrière, and is remarkable for fishermen who preserve ways learned long ago in Brittany. **Crawen Beach** is on the southwest tip of Terre-de-Haut and is visited by the guests of Bois Joli, the casual but pricey hillside hotel with fine creole seafood and watersports.

Direct phone to Bois Joli, (590) 99 50 38; U.S. reservations through French Caribbean International, 1-800-322-2223; fax (805) 967-9850. Cheaper is Jeanne d'Arc near the pier; direct phone (590) 99 50 41.

☞ Drive to Trois Riviéres on the south of Guadeloupe's Basse-Terre. Take the 40-minute ferry which leaves in the morning and afternoon. A ferry also departs from Pointe-á-Pitre harbor. Air to Terre-de-Haut connects with international flights several times daily. Current schedules, phone (590) 82 09 30.

MARIE-GALANTE

CAYE Á POIRIER

Best reached by a 35-minute Jet Kat II ferry from Pointe-á-Pitre harbor, this nearby little-visited island of sugarcane, rum and zouk bands, affords a glimpse into the old colonial days. There is clothing-optional use of the very pleasant Caye á Poirier beach, northeast of Capesterre, and the white sands of Anse du Vieux Fort and Anse Canot north of St. Louis. Contact Philippe Bavarday, phone (590) 97 83 94.

JAMAICA

Jamaica could be your perfect getaway —with family or friends—for a first exposure to social nudity. A week in Negril has led many into a life of body acceptance.

An English-speaking Eden by the sea, Jamaica causes the feeling of nakedness to seem almost like a destiny. "No problem, mon, do what you like!"

Nudity is tried by about half of the vacationers to Jamaica, where it is permitted on a growing number of hotel beaches.

It's not really expensive. Air Jamaica competes with U.S. airlines, which improves your choice of departure cities, times and fares. Pick an upscale or a bargain package, an all-inclusive resort or improvise as you travel. Stick to a beach or venture to the mountains, rivers and islets. For assistance with your Naturist travel plans, contact Pauline (Polly) Stewart at **Destinations; phone** 1-800-532-2271.

NEGRIL BEACH

Six miles of superb white sand beaches subside into the wadeable turquoise sea. Great sunsets are applauded at Rick's Cafe. World-class resorts offer energetic sports and partying while bungalow colonies feature relaxation. All benefit from Negril's lively Afro-Baptist-Rastafarai community.

The tourists who forget their swimsuits? They descend from the hippies of a generation ago—college and corporate dropouts who wandered to Negril. There they found the sight, sound, and spliffs of Rastafarai's different drummers and DJs.

The hippies contributed a white-race body confidence to the mix. And Negril became an influence on its time.

Beyond the listed resorts, some bungalow colonies in the west end permit nude sunbathing. Spartan guest rooms can be rented in some Negril homes. Be sure to patronize the Paradise Yard Restaurant, 600 yards down the road to Savanna from the Negril Roundabout. Loraine, its busy owner, who takes vacations to Florida and Kansas as a naturist, can advise you on naturist opportunites at Negril.

GRAND LIDO

On Negril's Bloody Bay this upscale, inclusive-price resort has Jamaica's best-developed nude beach. The 200 rooms have TV, stereo, separate sitting area, porch or deck. Exercise room, tennis, scuba, sailing. Clothing isn't required in walking between the "nude beach zone" rooms and their shore, pool, jacuzzi, bar and sundeck complex. Lido guests also have access to Hedonism II next door. Phone 1-800-858-8009; in Canada, 1-800-553-4320. All travel agents can book Grand Lido.

HEDONISM II

The original "Nude or Prude Beach" getaway is SuperClub's Hedonism II. A single fee covers air, transfers, lodging, sumptuous meals, sports, gymnastics, entertainment and drinks.

Not "covering" you in unwanted garments is the SuperClub's philosophy of personal freedom. There is no mandated nude beach, and you may, in principle (although it is rare in practice), initiate nudity anywhere you and others are comfortable with it.

There is a nude beach area by consensus. It has its own bar and hot spa, nice lounge chairs and shade trees too. Its fans return repeatedly. Phone 1-800-858-8009 or (809) 957-4201, or through your agent.

POINT VILLAGE

On the peninsula between Hedonism II and Grand Lido, the new 14-acre Point Village offers a mix of studios and 1-, 2- and 3-bedroom suites, 255 units in all, with restaurants in several price brackets or self-catering (all units have kitchens, air conditioning and TV).

"Nudie Bay" has its own lifeguard. Tennis, water sports, gym, clothed pool and jacuzzi, gym, nightly entertainment. Phone (809) 957-9170; fax 957-4351.

FIREFLY COTTAGES

Nudity on its part of Negril Beach, also windsurfing rental, bar. Studios, housekeeping cottages. Food staples sold nearby; many restaurants. A budget base to explore the area. Phone (809) 957-4358; fax (809) 925-5728.

NEGRIL CABINS

Negril Cabins are comfortable budget lodging only 100 yards from nude-use Bloody Bay on the east end of Negril Beach. Phone (809) 957-4350; fax 957-4381.

CATCHA FALLING STAR

Six clothing-optional vacation resort cottages available with fridges, maid service and complimentary breakfast. Private cove for snorkeling, several restaurants within 10-minute walking distance. P.O. Box 22, Negril, Westmoreland, Jamaica; phone (809) 957-4446.

NEGRIL CLIFFSIDE LODGINGS

Home Sweet Home has nude use on the cliffs. Pool, six sunning decks, jacuzzi and gift shop.

Rock Cliff allows nudity on the cliffs with three semi-private decks. Pool, bar, massage, hair-braiding, scuba instructors.

Mirage has two bungalows and three cottages. Restaurant, bar, French-inspired food, activities/yoga hut. Employees indicate they're not interested in what the guests wear or don't wear.

Nudity is the norm at **Hog Heaven** and **Secret Paradise.** Both are secluded with cottages, restaurant and pool.

The cliffside **Heartbeat Cottages,** the sixth resort from the center of town, permits full nude use of the property. Twelve rooms, four sunning decks at water's edge.

MONTEGO BAY

SEAWIND BEACH

Radisson Sunset Island Resort has a nude beach area. Brochure/reservations at the new resort (one part of Seawinds) can be had by calling (809) 979-8070.

Secured on a peninsula jutting into Montego Bay, with bus service to local

MoBay shopping and night spots. The nude beach is on the point. Preferred lodging is in the east bloc of villas. Nudes may relax and watch MoBay air traffic.

GRAND LIDO BRACO

Emphasizing Jamaican culture, music and foods, the new 180-unit SuperClubs Grand Lido Braco Resort is on a 2,000-foot white sand beach—part of it nude. Golf course, tennis, health club, water sports, Olympic pool, soccer field. At Rio Bueno, 38 miles east of Montego Bay. Phone 1-800-329-8145 or (809) 975-7330.

Y.S. FALLS

Arguably the most breathtaking falls on the island, seldom visited or even known about, are about 35 miles from Montego Bay on the Y.S. Ranch, owned by cattle breeder Tony Browning. You almost certainly can skinny-dip in the pools to your heart's content.

RUNAWAY BAY

BREEZES RUNAWAY BAY

Breezes Runaway Bay (formerly Jamaica Jamica) is a SuperClub and its west beach and jacuzzi are in nude use. Nor are they screened from the "prude" beach.

Breezes Runaway Bay is a class act: a gourmet restaurant offers native cuisine, exotic birds, a Nautilus and spa in the main lobby, clean convenient rooms, snorkeling, catamaran, windsurfing, sailing, soccer, tennis, golf, cricket all with instruction available. Any travel agency can book or phone 1-800-858-8009.

CLUB CARIBBEAN

Attractive north coast cottage resort between Montego Bay and Ocho Rios. A 30-m clothes-optional beach fronts two bungalows, from cabin 17 to the end: be sure to request these, nudity is prohibited elsewhere. Restaurant, disco, pool, tennis, scuba, volleyball. Children welcomed and provided for—unusual in the Caribbean. Reasonably priced. Phone 1-800-221-4558 or (212) 355-6605.

OCHO RIOS

COUPLES

SuperClub Couples Resort is spotless, dining superb, drinks free-flowing. Nudity is restricted to an offshore islet with open bar, hammocks, mats, on-call boat shuttle. Rocks discourage swimming. A pleasant spot to get basted while dozing or chatting. Adult couples only; no singles. Do not confuse SuperClub resorts with their arch-competitor, the prudish Sandals resorts. Any travel agency can book, or phone (809) 974-4271.

EASTERN

PORT ANTONIO: NAVY ISLAND

A cove for nude use is provided on 64-acre Navy Island, described by the Admiralty Club brochure, confirms a reputation for sophistication set by former owner and film swashbuckler Errol Flynn. The lodge has a 30-person capacity, pool, restaurant and bar. A quarter mile offshore from bustling Port Antonio and its reggae disco, The Roof. Ferry is about $4.

Admiralty Club Resort & Marina, P.O. Box 188, Port Antonio, Jamaica. Phone (809) 993-2667.

REACH FALLS

Reach River is a refreshing stream that flows from the mountains, cutting into limestone. Delight in nakedly entering the cave under Reach Falls, and riding the sluiceways downstream. Hike upstream a half mile to where Reach River emerges from a "blue hole." Or 2 1/2 miles downstream to the coast road where you may be picked up. Visit on a weekday morning to minimize user conflict possibility.

☞ Six miles south from Port Antonio on the coastal road then 2 miles inland. A highway sign announces it. Check your way with locals as you probe the roads. Tell caretaker Frank Clark we sent you: he's naturist-friendly.

Jamaica: Glen Martin, The Apple Valley Great House Near Magotty (SENSE Adventures).

Jamaica: Michael Cooney, First Timers Ask To Be Photographed At Hedonism II. Bottom: Claude Richards, Naturist Officials & Police Officers At Reach Falls, Port Antonio.

MARTINIQUE

Sister island to Guadeloupe, you may be able to visit both on a single ticket. Martinique is rich in history and natural geography. Its aristocracy—unlike that of Guadeloupe—survived the French Revolution and, 200 years later, still exercises an authority and emphasizes a conservativism that is based on large landholdings. A consequence evidently is that social nude beaches are not allowed to emerge.

STE.-ANNE

The dry, hot southern tip of Martinique has a string of beautiful, deserted beaches a 10-minute drive south from Ste.-Anne. **Grande Anse des Salines** offers no facilities of any kind, so bring your lunch. Some Martiniquans permanently pitch tents on this wild, desolate beach and come out for weekends. A large salt pond gives it its name. You also will find a strange "petrified savannah forest," as it's called, if you can make it over the ruts. Cacti grow among bleak rocks that, on inspection, turn out to be wood turned to stone. The golden sands attract nude and clad bathers alike.

Anse Trabaud, on the Baie des Anglais, is 3/4 mile of fine sand and crashing surf backed by shade trees and located on the Atlantic.

☞ From Ste.-Anne take the paved road north. Pass the Club Med on the outskirts. After another 1/2 mile, where the road bends left, continue straight on a gravel road. Follow it 3 miles to the Baie des Anglais. The road winds through grazing goats and cows. The farmer charges a small parking fee. Be sure to leave by late afternoon or they may lock the cattle gate on you.

PUERTO RICO

Do drive around the splendid mountains of Puerto Rico; the beaches are not worth the hassle. Even topfree for the ladies is generally not tolerated. The islands listed below are the exception.

CONQUISTADOR RESORT: PALOMINO ISLAND

Spectacularly set on the northeast tip of Puerto Rico (with direct transfer from San Juan airport), at Las Croabas, is El Conquistador, a $200 million, 918-room casino hotel with 9 restaurants, huge pool, luxury spa, golf, tennis, water sports—and a nude beach on the backside of its own island, 3 miles offshore. Just go over the steep ridge, behind the main (clothed) beach, to a clean, 100-m, clothes-optional beach with lounge chairs and a pleasant breeze. Continuous ferry service. Box 270001, Fajardo, PR 00738. Phone 1-800-468-8365; fax (787) 860-3280.

VIEQUES ISLAND

Off the eastern shore, Isla de Vieques is reached by a 90-minute ferry ride from the Port of Fajardo (for ferry schedule, phone (787) 863-0705; autos require a week's advance reservation), or a 30-minute flight from the Isla Grande charter air terminal at San Juan.

Lodging: Try Sea Gate Guest House, phone (787) 741-4661, or Casa del Frances, phone (787) 741-3751. Camping is permitted at Sun Bay Beach with a free permit; phone (787) 722-1551. Car rental at most hotels. The U.S. Navy controls much of Vieques; it allows private boats to anchor off the west coast.

Drive south from the town of Isabel Secunda to the entrance of Camp Garcia, show the gate guard your driver's license, and from the gate drive due east on a bumpy dirt road 1-1/2 miles to a sign for Red Beach. You might turn right here, go south 1/2 mile and again take a right, and follow (going left at the fork) to topfree **Garcia Beach,** seldom used, with many shade trees. Walk right on Garcia Beach to be nude. Red Beach, the other beach in this area, is mostly family with some topfree at its far right.

For **Secret Beach:** drive east 1 mile past the above-mentioned Red Beach sign, to the next right dirt road turnoff; take it 1/4 mile to a low hilltop. Secret Beach with topfree and nude use is to your right.

East of the main road's Red Beach sign by almost 1-1/2 miles is a small bridge; anywhere on your right past it (prior to reaching the Blue Beach turnoff sign) is okay for topfree and nude. Or continue to Blue Beach sign, turn right, go 1/4 mile to the first left, take this another 1/2 mile to **Silver Beach** (nudity at left). Do NOT drive straight past Blue Beach sign, it's a gunnery range!

Or instead head west along the north shore for **Green Beach** on western Vieques. Show your ID to the base guard and drive an unveering, bumpy 8 miles from the gate to Green Beach. Here turn left at the fork and continue to the end. Park and walk around the point for 10 minutes or more, to enjoy the great afternoon sun au naturel and a fine view of eastern Puerto Rico.

Port Fajardo, too, has a beach in nude use—**Convento Beach.** In Fajardo, follow the signs to Seven Seas Public Beach ($1 parking). Walk to the ocean then along the beach to the right, to the end of the sand beach. Cross the coral reef (50 feet) to more sand and look for the path on your right. Follow it to a 3-mile beach of beautiful sand, crystal water and you alone! Total walking, 30 minutes.

CULEBRA ISLAND

Isla de Culebra is midway between Puerto Rico and St. Thomas, reached by air from San Juan's Isla Grande charter airport or by ferry from Fajardo in eastern Puerto Rico. Its 3,000 residents are friendly. About 1,500 acres are included in the Roosevelt National Wildlife Refuge; you may share a beach with a sea turtle.

On the north shore the sugary sand of Flamenco Beach is pretty but the hotel has posted it against nudity and you had best avoid it now. Not to despair; Culebra is the entry to an archipelago of 23 deserted islets. The best option is to visit the many coves and islets by kayak or boat. Kayaks and tips from Ocean Safari, phone (787) 742-3177.

Lodgings, all reasonable, are Posada la Hamaca (787) 742-3516 or Mamacitas (787) 742-0090, both in Dewey; Coral Island Guest House (203) 268-4964 overlooking the town pier; and Seafarer's Inn (787) 742-3171 with 15 basic rooms. Culebra Tourism, P.O. Box 189, Culebra PR 00775; phone (787) 742-3291.

ST. BARTHÉLEMY

Saint Barths is a universally accepted contraction for St. Barthélemy, smallest of the French island departments. You can drive around in an hour. It is the only island with a predominantly white population descended from early French and Swedish settlers. A New Jersey reader calls St. Barths "the low-key alternative to the boorish throng of New Yorkers who overrun Sint Maarten."

ARRIVING & LODGING

St. Barths may be reached from Guadeloupe or St. Martin by a heart-stopping STOL aircraft flight, or with one of many boat charters at St. Martin. A sign at the airport warns, "Nudisme est interdit à St. Barthélemy," yet the beaches get extensive nude use.

From St. Martin, try White Octopus, a 75-foot motor catamaran, $70 includes round-trip boat, lunch, rental car. Picks you up at any resort. Phone 2-4096. Or Quicksilver, arrives at Gustavia at 10 a.m., same package $65. Phone 2-2167. Boats generally depart from the Phillipsburg port. Flights are from the small Grand-Cage airport near Club Oriënt.

For a good price on a housekeeping bungalow on lovely Anse des Flamands, plus a car, contact Constant Gumbs at the airport. Phone (590) 276193; fax 277899.

The island is notable for expensive secluded inns such as the Emeraude Plage Hotel on an excellent beach of St. Jean Bay. The hotels and bungalow and villa rentals are surveyed in *Vendôme Guide: Saint Barthélemey* ($11 from West Indies Management Co., P.O. Box 1461, Newport, RI 02840. Phone 1-800-932-3222).

ANSE DE GRANDE SALINE

Anse de Grande Saline is a delightful and safe beach on the south coast, only a 10-minute drive from Gustavia and the airport. The turnoff is near the far (east) end of St. Jean Bay. Every cab driver knows the way.

Long accepted as a nude haven, its long crescent is never crowded. The bodysurfing can be great. There is now a pleasant cafe and snack bar on the trail to the beach.

COLUMBIER BEACH

Anse de Columbier is at the northwest tip, below the hilly Rockefeller estate. A taxi may take you as far as La Petite Anse just past Anse des Flamands; or alternatively to descend a trail from the hill village of Colombier. Trekking from either trailhead (wear boots and long pants) is 30 minutes. Stunning views make it worthwhile. Or have a small boat rented in Gustavia take you to this sandy, boulder-studded bay where yachts anchor.

ANSE DU GOUVERNEUR

Anse du Gouverneur gets nude bathers. Secluded and beautiful, this south coast beach has a sharp drop-off near the shore. It can be very wind-blown. It is reached by 10 minutes of driving a very steep, winding road beginning in the back street of Gustavia via Lurin. A regular vacationer to St. Barths says the biggest change regarding nudity is that the local residents now outnumber the tourists.

ST. JEAN BAY

St. Jean Bay on the north shore, which you pass in driving to Saline Beach, has been called a Caribbean St.-Tropez. The topfree beach has attracted wonderful inns and restaurants. Golden youth of French and international origin sip aperitifs and glance at the STOL arrivals to the nearby airstrip.

A recommended hotel on sandy St. Jean Bay is Hotel Filao Beach. Fresh water pool complex with decking and lounges, huge palms, deep baths in each of 30 bungalows. B.P. 167, St. Barthélemy FWI-97133. Phone (590) 276484; fax 276224. See *Vendôme Guide* for full selection.

Villa and studio rentals here and island-wide: Sibarth, B.P. 55, St. Barthélemy FWI-97133. Phone (590) 276238; fax 276052.

St. Barths: Doug Wahl, Anse de Grande Saline.

Top: St. Martin: Edin Velez, Horseback On Oriënt Bay. Bottom: Lee Baxandall, First Buildings On Oriënt Bay, 1979; Reint Brink, Owner, With Curious Couple.

161

ST. MARTIN

int Maarten— Saint Martin. The Dutch and French share this smallish, sunnily dry and temperate island. This sparks a concurrence, beneficial to *Naturisme*, because Dutchside *hoteliers* and investors are acceptive of the French tolerance.

You fly into Philipsburg on the Dutch side. Casino hotels generally have abundant rooms. Electronics and other buys are touted by duty-free shops. Rent a car, and on the French side find all but one of the nude beaches plus green hills and tiny restaurants, in Marigot and Grand-Case, with cuisines *très chic et cher*. Theft is a problem—don't walk away from valuables on a beach or in a car. Visas aren't required. English is *lingua franca*. US $ OK *partout*.

ORIËNT BAY

THE NEW ST.-TROPEZ

Plage baie oriëntale—Oriënt Bay Beach, on the northeastern coast—is generally considered one of the best beaches of the entire Caribbean. Gentle transparent water, white sand bottom, protective reef and offshore islands delight all.

Cruise ships that often stop in Philipsburg send their guests here for a first glimpse of naturism as **Oriënt Beach** is open and free to the public. Rental sailing/snorkeling/windsurfing gear, and snorkel/sail day-cruises are available.

Go first class: reserve at the all-clothing-optional **Hotel Club Oriënt** and enjoy its perks.

Or stay at a non-naturist resort and try Oriënt Beach nudity for a day. Dine at Club Oriënt's moderate-price restaurant; or perhaps at low-cost Pedro's Barbecue on the beach.

Constables have sought with indifferent results to contain the full nudity at the Club Oriënt end of the beach only. A number of bar-restaurants and water sport concessions have appeared on the middle beach, impairing its once pristine quality.

A major luxury resort on Oriënt Beach allows topfree at pool and beach but not full nudity. The 227-unit **Hotel Mont Vernon** would do well to revoke its ban, for its niche and destiny as "the other anchor" of Oriënt Beach is to add synergy for a Caribbean version of St.-Tropez in France.

In mid-Oriënt Beach, **Esmerelda Resort** has built 53 villa-style suites; pools, restaurant, lighted tennis courts.

Other non-naturist lodging options near Oriënt Bay include upscale Alizea (a long walk from the nude beach), and budget-kind Sunrise Hotel (across Oriënt Bay, but you'll want a car). For a good selection phone Caribbean Islands Travel Service at (301) 854-2027.

☞ Take the island's circle road westerly from Philipsburg's airport, passing Marigot and Grand-Case. Beyond the Grand-Case airfield find a sign for Club Oriënt, turn left on a paved road and then another left, following signs and a dirt road. From Philipsburg's port area, take the circle road north to Orleans; Club Oriënt turnoff lies beyond.

HOTEL CLUB ORIËNT

Hotel Club Oriënt, opened in 1978, was the Caribbean's first fully clothes-optional resort—dreamt, designed, constructed, managed, promoted and up to a point financed, by self-made Dutch millionaire

Reint "Ray" Brink, who still holds forth.

Club Oriënt consistently has the highest occupancy rates on St. Martin. The idyllic *Baie orientale*, the water sports, tennis and volleyball, bar-restaurant and Finnish-log bungalows make this a destination that naturist patrons return to. Auto rentals on premises. Clothing is optional everywhere on the grounds. L'Orientíque, Club Oriënt's clothes-optional store, carries food items and fresh French baking. The story of Oriënt Bay and its development is fascinating, and is told in *Nude & Natural* magazine *N* 10.2, 12.1, 13.1, 15.2, and 16.3, available from N Editions.

F-97150 St. Martin. Phone (590) 873-385; fax 873-376. Skinny-Dip Tours reservation (914) 733-4596 or 1-800-828-9356.

WEST PENINSULA

CUPECOY BEACH

Backed by low sandstone cliffs, secluded Cupecoy Beach is always nude. Cupecoy Bay is on the Dutch western coast of the far-flung west peninsula of St. Martin known by locals as the lowlands or *terres basses*. Cupecoy is a mile west of Sheraton's huge Mullet Bay Hotel. Peaceful, beautiful and no hassles.

☞ Drive west from Juliana Airport, through the Mullet Bay Resort, then the Cupecoy Hotel, and watch for the Atlantis Casino on the right. The dirt road on left is at the main road's right turn just past the Sapphire Club on the sea side. Park in the lot after the Sapphire Beach hotel and walk west. You can scamper down to smaller beaches or go to the main nude beach about 300 yards away. Rent lounge chairs, buy a Heineken or soft drink from the store-under-an-umbrella.

BAIE ROUGE

At Pointe du Bluff ("the Bluff"), Red Bay is a great beach for those staying in Marigot—they drive 5 minutes west instead of 25 minutes to Oriënt Bay. Breathtaking rock formations, lively beach scene. Ample parking. Bar and snacks.

☞ Starting westward from Philipsburg on the circle road, at 4 km beyond the French border—between la Samanna and the PLM St.-Tropez Beach hotels—find the sign for Baie Rouge. Turn left and follow dirt road to parking. The beach area to the right (east) is topfree; a *plage naturiste* is 100 yards to the left (west).

St. Martin: Lee Baxandall, Annie, Owner Of Adam & Eve Beach Boutique On Oriënt Bay.

THE VIRGIN ISLANDS

Tourist experience in the English and American Caribbean seems to turn out more prudish and packaged than the ambience that tourists can find in the independent Caribbean nations and the French islands.

Travelers to the Virgins find it enhances their safety and convenience to be cocooned on a boat or in a bungalow or tent colony or a rental villa. This generalization is only partly true; it is truer of St. Thomas than of St. John. Still, the contemporary Anglo-American tourism packaging and marketing do respond effectively to the restive racial and economic underclass in the Virgin Islands. Anger, theft, riot and murder encourage keeping a distance. For a classy, clothes-optional sailing yacht without the need to charter the boat: Sail Vacations Ltd., P.O. Box 823, Road Town, Tortola, BVI. Phone 1-800-368-9905 or (809) 494-3656; fax (809) 494-4731.

Start with villa rentals in the British and U.S. Virgins. *The Vendôme Guide* costs $11 from West Indies Management Co., P.O. Box 1461, Newport, RI 02840. Phone 1-800-932-3222.

BRITISH VIRGINS

Cottage colonies flourish in the British Virgin Islands. Proprietors focus their services on a handful of guests. Now just think of the fleet of charter boats in these islands only 60 miles east of Puerto Rico. They're a floating "cottage" industry. The skippers outdo themselves to please their guests. Check updated boat listings in *Nude & Natural* **magazine.**

VIRGIN GORDA

Virgin Gorda makes a memorable day-trip by air from San Juan. South end nude sunning centers on one-mile **Savana Bay** and neighboring **Pond Bay,** both about 3 miles north of The Baths. Walk to Savana Bay around Blowing Point from Little Dix Bay Hotel. Or from the airport proceed straight to a T-intersection, go right, continue past Olde Yard Inn another 2 km. **Valley Trunk,** about 0.5 km north of The Baths, is an alternative.

Devil's Bay is your best south end bet, and it's next to a boat landing for The Baths. Drive to Baths roadhead; an established trail connects the very popular Baths to Devil's Bay. Topfree is best in the mornings, before the main load of boats moor up and come ashore. Bring snorkel gear.

Turtle Bay is another strand where the nude frolic. From the airport take the main road north, through the valley toward North Sound. Look for the sign on your left for Turtle Bay Vacation Villas; turn here. At the triple fork take the leftmost road, park at the end, walk through the gate marked "No Trespassing" and down to the beach. Sea urchins live here, so use caution when swimming.

Recommended accommodations are at Fischer's Cove or Gauva Berry Spring Bay, and you may fly in on Crown Airways or Air BVI from San Juan, PR.

TORTOLA

Many natives on this most populated BVI take a dim view of naturism. Avoid any busy beaches or anchorages. So too Josiah's Bay, going by 4WD.

Long Beach, the next bay east of Josias Bay on Tortola, southeast of Guana Island, is recommended. Walk to right on Long Beach to the end of the bay. Fine swimming and snorkeling. The guests of Marine Cay Hotel cross over to Great Camanoe island offshore for private sunbathing.

Or go to east point, cross the bridge onto **Beef Island,** pass the first road on

the left, then a pond, to find doubtful-looking tire tracks. They take you across sand (it's firm) until you must park. Go another 100 yards on foot.

ANEGADA

Anegada Island, alone among the BVI, has a coral, not a volcanic origin. Its 23-mile, low-slung, little-visited shore allows you to doze au naturel on sand, instead of on sharp rocks. Anegada Reefs Hotel is reasonable and recommended.

NORMAN ISLAND

The Bight, the main bay of Norman Island, is largely clothing optional. Only anchored boats are there and onboard rules are determined by the passengers. A short sail away are **The Indians** and **Pelican Island** where topless prevails.

JOST VAN DYKE AREA

Green Cay is a little island just east of Jost Van Dyke. Nudity is hopeful.

South of Green Cay and due east of Little Harbor on Jost Van Dyke is **Sandy Cay,** a national park that is completely undeveloped. This is the most reliably clothing-optional shoreline in the BVIs. The south side of the island is a quarter mile sandy beach, 40 to 50 feet cliffs on the north side, and a nature trail following the perimeter of the island links the two. This is an archetypical desert island with cactus on the cliffs but a tropical forest and thousands of lizards just behind the ridge, extending to the beach. Wear plenty of insect repellent.

White Bay, at the west end of Jost Van Dyke, has fantastic snorkeling and is clothing-optional at its west end. The west end is sometimes briefly inundated with cruise ships, making it less than ideal, but we have been told that many of the women enjoy the beach topfree, particularly those from the Club Med boats.

U.S. VIRGINS

Over time they have been held by Spain, France, England, Holland, even the Knights of Malta. Eventually, Denmark sold them to the U.S. for $25 million; our military sought a presence in the eastern Caribbean.

ST. JOHN

Virgin Islands National Park holds 9,500 acres, two-thirds of St. John. Packaged activities include an underwater reef "trail," tours of a Danish plantation and tours through lush tropical forest. Check with a shuttle driver on arrival for the best available skinny-dipping; many visitors to St. John quietly skinny-dip.

"No nudity–NPS" signs serve to prevent aggressive nudity. Rangers just wave to discreet and deferential sunbathers—who strip again when the ranger goes.

Jumbaie Bay, the first cove west of Trunk Bay on the north coast, offers shade, snorkeling and a great view of Trunk Bay. This 100-yard beach at the 3-mile marker on the north shore road is the local naturists' favorite and St. John's best. Limited parking (3–4 vehicles) prevents crowding. Arrive by 9:30 a.m. for your pick of parking and dress code.

Solomon's Beach is another option. Go east on North Shore Road from Cruz Bay; at top of first hill, turn left on paved road that goes to NPS housing. Opposite the second house from the end, take the trail to the right. Proceeding across two intersecting trails, the trail then bears right along the shore and emerges at Solomon Bay, which is cautiously clothes-optional. The beach is a 20-minute walk from the center of Cruz Bay. Or park in the Caneel Bay Plantation lot and walk west from Honeymoon Beach.

Jumbaie Beach is in easy reach of Cinnamon Bay Campground, a clothed, reasonably-priced tent and cottage establishment. Each unit comes complete with cots, linen, picnic table, charcoal grill, ice chest and cooking utensils. Cinnamon Bay Campground, P.O. Box 720, Cruz Bay, St. John, VI 00831. Phone 1-800-539-9998; fax (809) 693-8280.

Maho Bay Camp, an inexpensive clothed resort has grown to 102 units. The permanent tents are comfortable and place little barrier between you and a felicitous nature. You'll also observe minimalist technology in use: compost toilets, energy-generating windmill and an elaborate system that utilizes the water from sinks and showers for irrigation and fresh-water pools. No hot water available. Bring repellent against the sand flies that you may encounter. Maho Bay Camps Inc., 17A E. 73rd St., New York, NY 10021. Phone (212) 472-9453; fax (212) 861-6210.

Francis Bay Beach, east of Maho Bay Camp, serves as an anchorage for private yachts attracted by the snorkeling, lovely sunsets and nude swimming and sunning common in the area away from the parking lot. The sun gets hot here and there are few shade areas; bring water and food as there are no facilities other than port-a-potties. Parking lot holds 10 cars max, arrive early.

Reef Bay Beach is increasingly popular, a safe 90-minute hike down Reef Bay Trail on the central south coast, lagoon, scenic cliffs, small beach.

ST. CROIX

Isaacks Cove, on the eastern tip, is the most private beach on the island—you can share a mile of sand with one or two other couples. The beach is protected by a reef 1/2 mile from the shore, filled with 20- to 30-foot red coral trees that pierce the water.

☞ Take the gravel road to the eastern tip of the island. About 50 yards before you reach the turnaround are two parallel 4WD roads that wind their way steeply down from the south side of the road. Once at the bottom, park and head west over hill for 1/2 mile. Isaacks Cove is the long white sand beach over the crest of the hill.

ST. THOMAS

Morningstar Beach is now topfree at the far end and very popular. Stay at or visit the Frenchman's Reef Hotel (Holiday Inn owns it); proceed past the tennis courts to the far east end of the beach. Great snorkeling here, and close to town.

Also, **Brewer's Bay Beach,** by the airport and university, has nude and topless bathing.

Other St. Thomas beaches cannot be confirmed at this time for your safety in nude use.

Instead, look into a small-craft day charter. Most skippers are comfortable with your nudity. The skipper may be able to make up the rest of the party if your group can't afford it alone. Before paying make sure the skipper is willing and your companions are congenial—just one prude aboard can ruin a great day of sunning and snorkeling. The local Yellow Pages are your source of charter craft.

165

FREUDE AM KÖRPER

1,50 M

BLÄTTER
FREIER MENSCHEN
KÖRPERBILDUNG – NACKTKULTUR
SONDERHEFT 12

WERNICKE

Adolf Koch, FREUDE AM KÖRPER "Joy in the Body," pamphlet for Physical Education/Naked Culture, 1920s. Koch was perhaps the most talented and daring of early leaders of FKK – free body culture. See

EUROPE

urope's naturist beaches, campgrounds, resorts and spas are burgeoning. Our world-girdling illustrated guide cannot contain all the worthwhile sites. Our aim, for Europe, is to survey the most popular and best.

OTHER INTERNATIONAL GUIDES. Experienced travelers will want the *INF Nude Travel Guide,* available from the Naturist Society; phone (920) 426-5009. Eurocentric, the International Naturist Federation abstracts encyclopædic data for 850 clubs and resorts. Omitted from the listings are a number of unaffiliated clothes-optional resorts. The beach information is spotty and slight.

A wide-ranging *Naturist Guide to Europe* in two notebook-style volumes is issued by David Martin. Coast & Country Naturist Publications, 3 Mayfield Ave., Scarborough, N. Yorkshire YO12 GDF, England. Phone (0723) 503 456; fax 500 576.

Continuing updates for Europe appear in *Nude & Natural* magazine published by The Naturist Society, P.O. Box 132, Oshkosh, WI 54902, USA. Phone (920) 426-5009 or fax (920) 426-5184 for catalog.

NATURIST TRAVEL AGENCIES. Clothes-optional resorts and campgrounds are often a complete mystery to a general travel agency. You'll benefit by going to the specialists. At this time one North American agency stands out for experience, range of European and world naturist destinations offered, and full-service competence: Skinny-Dip Tours, R.D. 1, Box 294, Bloomingburg, NY 12721. Phone 1-800-828-9356.

Other agencies specialized in naturist destinations advertise their varied and changing offerings in *Nude & Natural* magazine (see above).

Wolfgang Hiob, FKK Beach Bestensee Near Berlin, GDR, 1980s.

167

AUSTRIA

The mountain lakes and streams are frequently used au naturel by campers and local people. "Topfree (*oben ohne*) is practiced nearly everywhere," reports the ÖNV journal *Nahtlos Braun* (*Seamless Tan*). Austrians did not lead in the early FKK movement, but tourism to Yugoslavia's Istrian Coast after 1960 exposed many Austrians.

Austrian campgrounds listed in the *INF Handbook* have no rental lodgings, only empty sites. Information: Österreichischer Naturistenverband (ÖNV), Postfach 53, A-1024 Wien. Phone: (0222) 218 08 31.

VIENNA (WIEN)

DANUBE ISLAND

Danube Island is more or less in the center of Vienna. A flood control project mandated this 22-km "fill" in the famous river creating a separate Drainage Canal (sometimes called the New Danube). Tens of thousands enjoy the setting on warm summer days.

In clothes-optional use are both sides of the north and the south ends of the Canal—about 15 km of pebbly river beaches in all, with barbecue pits, meadows, woods and trails. Fine restaurants are at hand. A mobile Konditorei with petit fours and ices, coffees and liquors, might drive right up to your cove! Bask or swim, play cards or picnic, it's your free choice. (See *N* 12.4, pp. 32–35.)

Topfree (*oben ohne*) is accepted almost anywhere that bathing costumes are worn in Vienna. It was officially adopted in 1981 at the popular Gänsehäufl bathing island, on an arm of the "old" Danube. In 1982 FKK areas were extended to Gänsehäufl and the Danube Island.

☞ Autos are allowed on the Island but parking is very limited. The

bus system requires more study than you may have patience. The subway carries you in minutes from the western or southern peripheral districts to the Island. The tram and inter-city Schnellbahn have stations on or near the Island. A ferry across the Danube is a pleasant access.

DANUBE FLOAT

The Viennese love to take outings by auto up the gorgeous Danube River to enjoy a fine day. Some will make this 80-km excursion by train so as to float home to the metropolis on an air mattress, sunbathing on the way (watch out for the steamers). Check the shores as you go for the nude beaches—there's one on the sandspit in the Danube between Melk (with its famous monastery) and Aggsbach, on the right bank as you float.

☞ From Vienna take the Melk train, or drive A-1 to Melk. Exit at Wachaustrasse, follow the signs for Krem for 7 km and then take the left-hand fork, which will bring you to the beach. No facilities, and no camping.

KÄRNTEN

CARINTHIA PROVINCE

Kärnten–Carinthia, the southern province of Austria, bordering on former Yugoslavia, is a sunny region of small lakes and large mountains. Major naturist resorts nestle among the Alpine mead-

ows and forests. Day trips will include castles, cathedrals and chateaux. The provincial capital, Klagenfurt, is of interest as are many towns that retain medieval qualities. If possible, attend the Carinthian Summer Festival July–August in Ossiach and Villach. Mention your naturist interests if you contact the Austrian National Tourist Office, 500 Fifth Avenue, New York, NY 10110. Phone (212) 944-6880.

KEUTSCHACHER SEE

The free beach adjoins a huge naturist campground with showers, sauna, sports field, restaurant. RV rentals. **Camping Sabotnik,** Dobein 9, A-9074 Keutschach. Phone (04273) 2509.

Next door is **FKK-Camping Müllerhof,** Dobein 10. Phone (04273) 2517. With 350 campsites Müllerhof is less crowded than its older and popular neighbor.

Take E-94 south from Klagenfurt. Turn west to Wörther See and continue on to the southwest shore of Keutschach Lake.

TIGRINGER SEE

West of Klagenfurt, north of Moosburg, is Tigring Lake. Again a popular nude bathing site adjoins a large and impressive naturist campground. F. Kogler, Tigring 19-a, 9062 Moosburg. Phone (04272) 83542.

RUTAR LIDO

On 25 acres with 365 campsites, 50 rental RVs and a magnificent view of the mountains. Tennis, hiking, fishing, water gymnastics, indoor wave pool, outdoor heated pool, massage, sauna, volleyball, chapel, facilities for children and the disabled; restaurant and minimart; a large artificial lake. No single males—otherwise it is a small luxurious smoothly-regulated city. Located 22 km east of Klagenfurt. English-language brochure from Rutar Lido, A-9141 Eberndorf. Phone (0043) 4236 2262/0; fax (0043) 4236 2220; telex 42 29 43.

FORST SEE

An Edenic site near Wörther See. Forst See (lake in the woods) can be reached by well-marked hiking trails. Flat sunning rocks and sandy beaches at this large former quarry cause picnickers to get naked. No facilities on site.

☞ From Velden on the west end of Wörther See, go 3.5 km east along the north shore to the aluminum works. Turn left, drive 1.5 km, hang a left and after 500 m park on the shoulder. Or hike

Otto Wiesner, On Vienna's Danube Island.

from Unterwinklern (eastern Velden) for 90 minutes uphill on trail number 5, 15, following signs to Forst See.

HELIO-CARINTHIA

Helio-Carinthia Naturist Park has tent and RV camping, bungalows, playground, grocery store in an awesome natural setting on a mountain. Hike nude for hours or visit the nearby town of Gmünd for the Porsche car museum. Familie de Graaf, Pressingberg 31-32, A-9861 Eisentratten. Phone (04735) 268.

PESENTHEIN

This health facility on the Milstätter See has a public beach with a section reserved for naturist use. Strandbad Pesenthein, 9872 Millstadt. Phone (04766) 2021/44 – 2021/31.

STEIERMARK

THERME LOIPERSDORF

In the verdant, hilly Styrian countryside east of Graz, a hot spring site has been wedded with modern architecture to provide vast indoor and outdoor pools, "brooks," "waterfall," water slides, spas, saunas, and sunning areas for the clad and semiclad. Plus restaurant, children's rooms, steam bath, massage, solarium, and sports and exercise programs.

The Schaffelbad, a smaller area with indoor and outdoor decks, spa and sauna, offers FKK use on Fridays 5–9 p.m. Schaffelbad continually provides a huge lawn for nude sunbathing.

Contact: Therme Loipersdorf bei Fürstenfeld, A-8282 Loipersdorf 152. Phone 33 82-8204.

RABNITZBACHGELÄNDE

About 10 km northeast of Graz, Rabnitzbach is set in a rich agricultural valley of rolling hills. Its 17 acres include two sunbathing meadows, sports fields, tennis and volleyball, a pond surrounded by woods, playgrounds, swimming pool, a canteen with a sun terrace. Visitors are always welcome. Rabnitzbachgelände, Volkersdorf, bei Eggersdorf, 8063 Eggersdorf; phone (03132) 32 82.

TIROL

VÖLS CAMPGROUND

Völs' convenience to Innsbruck makes it popular despite being crowded. You need your own tent or RV. Pavilion with snack bar, fine swimming pool, playground, very friendly. Reservations: LffL Innsbruck, Postfach 17, A-6022 Innsbruck 3. Phone (0512) 30 31 45.

SALZBURG

HALLSTÄTTER SEE

Local initiative succeeded in gaining a section of Hallstätter See at Untersee for naturist use. Open to all; facilities nearby. The best access is Route 145 from Bad Goisern toward Pötschenpass. After St. Agatha, bear right toward lake and FKK area. Kurverwaltung, 4822 Bad Goisern; phone (06135) 8329; fax (06135) 832974.

LESSER RHINE

BREGENZ

In western Austria the Lesser Rhine flows into the Bodensee (a.k.a. Lake Constance) north of Lustenau. Its delta forms a wetland with sandy "islets." Here the town of Hard has a nude recreation area with lockers, showers, a marsh walk and a buffet-biergarten!

☞ Take B-202 (Rheinstrasse) for 7 km west from Bregenz. Go all the way through Hard and at the city limit of Fussach, after the bridge over the so-called "New Rhine," turn right and follow signs for FKK beach. After the gravel plant look for the reception area. Adjoining guest houses.

THE BALTIC STATES

Latvian "Saule" Naturists On Inchupe Beach.

North from Poland, and south from Finland along the Baltic Sea, lie three tiny nations, now again independent after being long controlled by Russia to their East. Naturism has a long proud history on this coast.

LITHUANIA

THE COURIAN ISTHMUS

The Courian Isthmus extends from Zelenogradsk in Kaliningrad, an exclave of Russia, northeast nearly to Klaipeda (Memel) in Lithuania—which is where the users from Vilnius, 180 miles to the east, enter. The Russians for a time called it simply "Neringa," or isthmus. The northern half is Lithuanian.

Several nude enclaves—described as "health beaches"—are found along this sandspit. One of these, **Palanga Beach,** reserved for women only, became notorious in 1985 when authorities denounced it as a black market in clothing, food and medicine. However, undercover policemen could not enter the area and undercover policewomen refused to strip so as to seek evidence. This popular nude beach market survived its notoriety.

LATVIA

INCHUPE BEACH

Saule (Sun), the club of the Latvian Nudist Society, *Latvuas Nüdistu Biedriba*, founded 1990, in 1991 issued an explanatory booklet, *Brivais Cilveks* ("Free Man"), the first USSR post-Stalinist nudist publication.

Named after an earlier LNB magazine (1932), "Free Man" outlined in clear concepts a defense and history of Latvian naturism.

The Inchupe (peatbog) River is 40 km northwest of Riga on Riga Bay, 6 km from the nearest town. By wading across the river you reach the nude beach that extends for 3 km. This nude Inchupe Beach has crude permanent bunkers for shelter, a rough-hewn sauna, and a natural spring. Since 1991, it has been legal.

There is no current winter activity or newsletter.

Nikolai Manyuck, LNB, P.O. Box 30, LR-1011 Riga, Latvia. Phone (0132) 280 019.

ESTONIA

KLOOGA BEACH

Klooga-Rand is located on the Gulf of Finland about 40 km east of the Estonian capital, Tallinn. Up to 3,000 locals used the 200-m organized nude beach in the early 1980s.

The coast is backed by dense pine woods and seems always to have been clothes-optional. Actor Peter Ustinov

recalled in 1977 that as a boy, in 1928, "most people bathed and sculpted (the beach clay) naked, only dressing again to meet the hazards of the forest."

Some Estonians, thumbing their noses at Russia, copied the Poles' 1980s nudist parading of sexy women on Baltic beaches. A Miss Nude Estonia pageant telecast by the Tallinn station in 1983 led the authorities to crack down. Pageant organizers built clay walls around their beach area with a bulldozer, blocking sight lines. Ordered to knock down the walls, the pageant entrepreneurs appealed to the Estonian Supreme Court and won! To mollify civil authorities the pageant organizers then raised the clay wall up to ten feet.

On March 30, 1989 an Estonian Nudist Union with 200 petitioning members was officially registered as the first nudist group recognized by government in the USSR.

Local opponents then got officials in 1990 to forbid nude groups on Klooga Beach. With the grim economy the beach activity has collapsed. Sauna evenings continue to be held twice a month, nine months a year in Tallinn.

Eesti Nudistide Selts, c/o Olev Meremaa, pres., pk 941, EW-0034-Tallinn, Estonia. Or c/o Kaljo Piiskop, pk 907, 200034-Tallinn, Estonia.

BELGIUM

Commencing 1981, Belgium allowed the topfree option but not full nudity on its 65 km of *haute coûture* but cheek-by-jowl North Sea beaches.

The development of landed nudist clubs goes forward; they were long banned. Belgium is up to 20 clubs and 20,000 FBN members. Many of these naturists still go nude only on holidays to the French and Spanish beaches, which were long their only option. Nudity is now an option at some inland hotels and municipal pools, however; and Belgium like Germany has huge spa complexes with nude options.

Contact: Fédération Belge de Naturisme, St. Hubertusstraat 5, B-2600 Antwerp, Belgium. A Belgium–Luxemburg guide, *Beneluxgids Naturisme*, is available from SNU, Antwoordnummer 4058, NL-3500 VB Utrecht, Netherlands.

LANDED CLUBS: ATHENA

Clubs came first. Land later, when possible and if allowed. Many clubs developed ties with South European FKK campgrounds; others with Dutch ones. Contracts for winter use of Belgium's municipal pools are a later and now widespread practice.

Sustained naturist club activity appeared in Belgium only with Robert Lambrechts who started the Athena Club (1955). Lambrechts was to become a dynamic INF general secretary. For safety, early Athena Club members had to cross an international border to their club grounds at Ossendrecht, Netherlands.

Lambrechts later established native Athena terrains for Brussels, Liege, Ghent and Hasselt. The Antwerp terrain, 16 km distant at Ossendrecht, has 350 member sites, 70 rental units and a proud tradition.

For a landed club experience in Belgium begin with the prime mover: **Athena Club,** office at St. Thomasstraat 24, B-2018 Antwerpen. Phone/fax: 164 672 489.

BULGARIA

Organized social nudity emerged at the Black Sea in the mid-1960s as Balkan Tours earned hard currency promoting FKK to West Germans. Sites at Nessebâr and the Ropotomo River were controlled to serve only these tourists. Conservative Bulgarian elements soon forced even tourists to cover up.

Today, beach freedom rules. The modern hotels and 120 mostly modern campgrounds remain inexpensive. Private rooms are often rented by local fishermen.

Bulgarian Naturist Association c/o Dr. Rumen Bostandjiev, Bl. Tolbuhin no. 36, BG-1142 Sofia. Varna Naturist Society c/o Veselin Dimitrov, Bl. "8 Polk" no. 75, BG-9002 Varna. Phone (35952) 224987. Bulgarian reservations (including good AYH facilities): Pirin Travel, 30 Al. Stamboliiski Blvd., Sofia.

BLACK SEA

VARNA NORTH

The Naturist Society of Varna has a favorite nude beach 15 km north on the road to Golden Sands (Zlatni Pyassatsi) Hotel, located on the north shore below the well-known restaurant Trifon Zerezan. Bus No. 9 stops at the restaurant.

Further north, in the attractive resort Albena, is a nude beach beyond the most southward hotel, the Gergana. Wade across a small stream to find a nude area just beyond that runs about 100 m. Users (mostly German) tend to use the dunes but the area has little wind and much sun. Don't mind the food vendors.

SUNNY BEACH

The clear, warm Black Sea has a tourist section 80 km from Varna, 30 km from Burgas. The FKK area is 4–6 km north of this sunny shore, called Sunny Beach (Slanchev Bryag), near Nessebâr, designated by UNESCO as a World Heritage city and now an artists/writers hideaway. The beach is just past the Morski sanatorium; the Dolphin Restaurant abutts it. Another FKK beach is 1 km north of the Vlas textile campground.

SOZOPOL–KITEN

Tourists who come for FKK beaches from Eastern Europe often choose the South Coast—many exquisite coves receive individuals and couples.

Here, south from Burgas, the Sozopol peninsula is "a natural" for nudity and the town is an artist colony. Near Arkutino, the oak forests march down to the sea. Kiten Beach is in an exotic nature park at the delta of the famous Ropotomo River. Hospitable fisher families take in guests as far south as Ahtopol, and there are fine campgrounds—all FKK-friendly.

CROATIA

Before the political break-up of Yugoslavia, its Adriatic seacoast, including 1,185 islands, totalled 6,116 kilometers—of which fully 5,790 kilometers lay within Croatia. By possessing this immense shoreline within its 21.9% share of the total area of Yugoslavia, Croatia had earned over 80% of the foreign tourist income, much of it from the uniquely developed FKK centers, 27 of Yugoslavia's 30 being in Croatia. As the war-weary region now rebuilds, its Naturist assets benefit Croatia.

Croatian families rent comfortable rooms to tourists and make them welcome. Naturist camping/RV sites with hookups and minimarts are widespread, supplementing the revived resorts and hotels. European Naturists enjoy low prices as well as the camaraderie of helping out.

Croatia will open tourist offices abroad. A current tourism contact is Croatian Air Tours, 3408 Broadway, Astoria, NY 11106. Phone (718) 777-0555. A Naturist contact is Bruno Cernelic, Drusto Naturista Hrvatske, TRG Küküljevica 9, HR-41090 Zagreb.

ISTRIA COAST

Bulging into the Adriatic Sea at the northwest point of Croatia, Istria is the magnet and gateway for descending German and Austrian tourists with RVs and tents, the bread-and-butter of the naturist tour trade. A lovely jagged/rocky coast, wooded bays, picturesque seaside towns, a green hilly inland and mild climate.

THE RESORTS

Lanterna Peninsula—Solaris. The popular resorts Solaris and Lanterna share Lanterna Peninsula, 10 km from Porec. Rocky beaches and woods along 5 km of shore allow guests to spread out. These self-contained resorts provide everything from supermarkets to hammock rental. The Lanterna beach is clothes-required. Only Solaris is a true naturist resort with clothing-optional everything. Naturist Solaris, V. Nazora 9, HR-51440 Porec. Phone (0385) 52 44 34 00; fax (0385) 52 44 30 64.

Koversada, the dowager summer-city of Croatian naturism, is at Vrsar. Begun as a camping area on the small offshore island of Koversada, over the years the resort has spread onto the mainland and along the shore of the fjord. Covering 280 acres, it can accommodate 1,600 people in its pavilions alone. Add to that the camping and caravan sites for 8,000, and it's easy to see why this is former Yugoslavia's renowned naturist resort. The beach is of sharp limestone that doesn't seem to deter the many users. Sea swimming, sailing, tennis, minigolf, windsurfing, disco. Boat/bus excursions to Lim Fjord with its own beautiful beaches, coves, and archipelago of 18 small islands. Koversada ANITA, HR-51450 Vrsar. Phone (0385) 52 441 111; fax (0385) 52 441 122.

Valalta. On the shore of the Lim Fjord opposite Koversada, Valalta is popular with the camping set. A single-story bungalow area is well away from the campgrounds. The pebble beach is backed by a large lawn. Naturist Camping Valalta, HR-52210 Rovinj. Phone (0385) 552 811 033; fax 811 463.

Monsena resort has a splendid view of the Rovinj church of St. Euphemia. Located amid olive, pine, and laurel trees, its bungalows have small flower gardens. Contact Jadran Turist, Nazora 6, HR-52210 Rovinj. Phone (0385) 552 813 111; fax 813 497.

Pula—Medulin Beach & Kazela Camping. A Roman settlement in southern Istria, Pula is rewarding with an ancient temple, medieval churches, a famous Roman amphitheatre. Ten km from Pula, Medulin has a nude beach worth a visit. To the southwest is the Kastel Peninsula with 2 km of beach and a pine forest. Naturist camp Kazela is on Medulin Bay. Arenaturist Splitska 1, HR-53000 Pula. Phone (0385) 552 23811.

Croatia's Solaris Resort At Porec On Istria.

KVARNER COAST

KVARNER BAY

The islands southeast of Pula in Kvarner Bay offer some of the Mediterranean's most natural and historical settings for nude recreation. Ferry service (autos accepted) goes to the larger islands.

THE ISLANDS

Cres Island & Beaches. On a long narrow island, Cres is an ancient village center with gate and defensive towers, town hall, several churches, amphora museum. The naturist resort **Nedemisju** is on the northeast of the bay of Cres. South is a free beach at **Martinscica**. Farther south are resorts featuring nude recreation—**Baldarin** and **Bokinic**—in easier reach of Osor, now a town on the isthmus connecting Cres and Losinj; once an important harbor city. UTP Jadranka, HR-51550 Mali Losinj. Phone (0385) 512 31518.

Krk. The largest island, reached by ferries from Kraljevica and Crikvenica. Bastion of the Dukes of Krk who played a decisive role in Croatian history; the island was renowned in Roman times. Krk town has a sandy FKK beach at a scenic site which is recommended. North of Krk the villages of **Omisalj**, **Njivice**, and **Malinska** have FKK beaches. South are free beaches at **Baska** and the famous resort **Akapulka**, HR-51521 Punat. Phone (0385) 532 227036.

Losinj. This island "continues" Cres. Verdant, with mild climate, the Romans had their summer villas on Losinj and it is a tourist favorite. The towns of **Mali Losinj** and **Veli Losinj** on the southeastern coast have clothing-optional beaches, and the naturist beach of the **Suncana Uvala** resort is near Mali Losinj.

Rab. Among the best-known yet ancient resorts of the Adriatic; well-preserved palaces and churches and a 1,500-m rocky FKK beach on three coves, the largest windshielded with a lovely view of open sea. The resorts **Kandoralo** and **Suha Punta** share this beach in thick pine forest.

Pag. Offshore from Rab, Pag Island has a bridge to the mainland. The town has many Roman and Christian remains. Nearby **Strasko** is the largest island naturist settlement on the Adriatic coast, accommodating 4,000 campers. Pag has little fresh ground water so showers are rationed. The snack bar is cheap and terrific. The beach is of sharp limestone but otherwise excellent. Autocamp Strasko, HR-51291 Novalja, Pag. Phone (0385) 518 96226.

Silba. Medium-sized with secluded coves. In one of these is a designated FKK beach. Formerly a sailors' refuge/playground, Silba is known for wine and cheese. No hotels here; private homes accept up to 330 visitors.

DALMATIAN COAST

RESORTS

Alan Hotel. As the first hotel in Europe built exclusively for naturists, Hotel Alan at Punta Skala, east of Zadar at the south end of Kvarner Bay, once set a direction for international tourism. Its 1,345 beds in a 400-acre park signaled a major commitment. In 1989 Punta Skala dropped its "naturist hotel" status, reflecting an acceptance by average Dalmatians of nudism outside the hotel grounds. A rocky FKK coast extends 5 km north of the hotel, satisfying many old clients who like to go nude out-of-doors with some privacy.

Hotel Adriatic and **Hotel Niko Solaris** in nearby Sibenik have taken their lead from the Alan Hotel and encourage nude sunbathing.

Region of Split. Halfway down the Dalmatian Coast and southeast of Split, **Omis** has a free beach. But if you fly into Split and have only a day in the region **Ruskamen Resort** is convenient with a clothes-optional area. Hotel Omis, HR-58310 Omis. Phone (0385) 58 68144.

Makarska is downcoast. Its harbor, between small peninsulas, has a main nude beach over a mile long. The Makarska Riviera owes its vitality to such offshore islands as **Brac** and **Hvar**, discussed below. A few miles south, the village of **Tucepi** has a free beach. Hotel Nimfa, HR-58331, Zivogosce. Phone (0385) 58 627086.

Orebic. Our most southerly focus on the Dalmatian coast, on the south shore of the Peljesac Peninsula, Orebic is developing fine modern hotels, a pleasant ambiance and clothes-optional beaches.

ISLANDS

Dugi Otok. Offshore from Zadar is Dugi Otok—a long, narrow island with villages, **Bozava** and **Sali**, that encourage naturist tourists.

On nearby **Ugljan Island**, Kukljica has the tourist complex **Zlatna Punta**, with a major free beach.

Brac. The north coast offers the calm coves and beaches of a naturist zone at **Povlja**. **Bol** is a noted ancient town on the south coast, and few visitors are not excited by the Gothic art and monuments, the Renaissance palace and Dominican monastery. Bol even has a lengthy but grotty nude beach.

Hvar. The ancient island of vineyards and olive groves takes its name from the Greek for lighthouse, *pharos*. The oldest known European image of a ship is in the Grapceva Cave on Hvar.

Hvar city, on the western end, has a reputation for excellent, sunny climate.

Offshore islet **Palmizan** has a delightful sandy nude beach and **Jerolim** also has numerous nude recreation facilities.

Rivaling Hvar city is **Stari Grad**, built on the old Greek settlement at Pharos. Stari Grad has a naturist campground and beach at **Helos**. Just west of Stari Grad lies **Vrboska**, another small town with Renaissance master paintings and, of course, a skinny-dipping beach. **Jelsa**, the most eastern naturist destination on Hvar, has Illyrian and Greek relics, a nearby prehistoric cave and a beautiful sandy beach with woods that descend to the sea.

Zecovo, offshore Hvar, is part of the Yugoslav naturist paradise and offers unspoiled landscape, a fine yacht harbor and restaurant.

Korcula. South of Hvar, this island's mild climate, verdancy and history make it a favorite. Korcula town, on the east shore, is a museum city with a cathedral built in the 13th–16th centuries, paintings by Tintoretto and others, ancient towers, the Doge's palace and others of the patrician families. **Adria Club** provides a naturist hotel convenient to Dubrovnik yet with FKK sports facilities.

To the east of Korcula in the **Peljesae Channel** is an archipelago of some 20 islets. Of these, **Vela** and **Mala Stupa** offer a chance to get back to nature. The village of Luka on Vela's western shore offers bathing in many coves. For swimming, you may want to go to the island of **Osjak** in the middle of the bay.

SOUTHERN ADRIATIC

DUBROVNIK REGION

Dubrovnik is the most beautiful and interesting of Croatian destinations, and, a smart gateway to begin a visit. Settled in the 7th Century, Dubrovnik is today as it was at the end of the 15th Century. Stone walls encircle the town. Each house and public building has its unique page of history.

Two villages to the north—**Slano** and **Trsteno**—feature naturist beaches. Slano has naturist **Hotel Osmine** with a modern restaurant and bar, sauna, and disco. HR-50232 Slano; phone (0385) 50 87244.

South of Dubrovnik are other lodgings to attract naturists. **Mlini**—a village set deep within Zupa Bay—has two hotels, the Astarea and the Mlini, with beaches set aside for nude use. **Cavtat**, in the southern part of Zupa Bay, has a cove. **Lokrum Island** is a 15-minute launch-ride from Dubrovnik. Its rocky shore is used for nude sunning.

Access is convenient by air, rail, or ferry—including direct flights from the U.S. and auto ferries from Trieste and Bari in Italy.

THE CZECH REPUBLIC

Czechoslovakia split on 1 January 1993 into the Czech Republic and Slovakia. By Summer 1990, naturist organizations had already emerged in both states.

Slovaks organized UNS (*Unia Naturistov Slovenska*, P.O. 14, 94603-Kolárovo, Slovakia). UNS' one campground and its magazine failed in 1993, and this *Guide* omits Slovakia. However, from Hotel Danube in Bratislava you may take Bus 116 south on E-65 to a popular naturist quarry with entry just before Rosovce village.

The Czechs established UNA—*Unie naturistú Cech a Moravy* (P.O. Box 96, Olsanská 9, CZ-13000 Prague 3). The phone/fax for UNA as well as Natur Travel is (422) 541-659. (A second Naturist-friendly agency is Globtour, Jáchymova 4, CZ-11630 Prague 1; phone (422) 232-4160, fax 5420.) UNA claims 17 local clubs, most with nude beaches, some renting a sauna and pool.

PRAGUE AREA

BEACHES

Seberák, slang for the pond *Seberovsky rybník* in the southeastern suburb of Kunratice, has an FKK sector which in the Eighties became the first legal nude beach in Czech history. It is fully enclosed to control gawkers and keep nudity mandatory, collecting an entrance fee. Volleyball, toilets, buffet. 9 a.m.–7 p.m. daily.

☞ Take the Metro (subway), line C, to Kacerov. Transfer to bus 114 which runs at 13-minute intervals, 8 a.m.–6 p.m. Kunratice–Seberák is its last stop. The bus halts at the textile beach entry; walk another 200 yards to naturist access.

A lawn and top decks for nude sunning are available at **Podolí,** in the south district of Prague, where the public pool is textile.

East of Prague, naturist Oáza beach at Hostivár has over 1000 users on a good day.

At **Lhota u Brandyse nad Labem,** 20 km northeast of Prague, is a clear-water quarry where the public skinny-dip in numbers up to 6,000 on hot days!

Northwest of Prague, in Central Bohemia at Vokovice, **Lake Dzbán** has an official nude facility back of Pavilion A. Naturists often camp at the textiled TJ Aritma Dzbán, Nad Lávkou 3, CZ-16000 Prague 6. Phone (42) 02-368551. Rental tents; buffet, sports equipment. June–August.

One can find up to 100 nude users at the official nude beach on **Stvanice Island,** in the middle of Prague.

A sauna, open to the public, is located in the **Hotel Oshanka** at the Central European University, Táboritská 23, 130 87 Prague 3.

BOHEMIA

WESTERN

In Western Bohemia, official naturist sites are at the **Borská prehrada** dam, next to the naturist tent camping in Plzen; at the **Bolevecky rybník** pond, north of Plzen-Bolevec; and at the outdoor swimming pool in **Klatovy,** where nudes and textiles mix peacefully.

NORTHERN

In Northern Bohemia, **Benedikt** lake in Most; and the **Barbora** lake, northwest of Teplice-Oldrichov, are both officially nude. There are two naturist beaches north of Máchovo jezero lake. One is next to the textile camp, **Na Klúcku** on Doksy, and the second is the opposite bank, **Pod Bornym.**

In Chomutov, **Kamencové jezero** lake, next to the non-naturist camp Kamencové jezero, has legal nudity.

EASTERN

Nudity is tolerated at two sites in East Bohemia, **Opatovice n. Labem,** south of Hradec Králové, and at **Hrádek,** northwest of Pardubice. Both sites see over 600 users on a good day.

MORAVIA

NORTHERN

Five official naturist beaches are located in the North Moravian Region. The **Olse/Olza** river, near Karviná, and **Podédbrady Lake,** north of Olomouc-Repcín, both get up to 150 users each day. The terrace at the outdoor swimming pool at **U Hanyskü,** 10 km north of Prerov, is an official naturist location.

Olesna Lake is 3 km southwest of Frydek-Místek. **Koblov-Antosovice,** north of Ostrava, gets over 1,000 nude users on a good day.

SOUTHERN

Brnénská Prehrada, the Brno dam site below Osada (Pod Osadou) on the left side of the lake, is long in FKK use. From Brno center take tram #10 or 18 northwest to Bystrc, walk to the main harbor (Bystrc) and board a lake steamer to its third stop, Osada. Steamers leave every half hour. Contact in German: Dr. Dusan Rysánek, Vránova 55, CZ-62100 Brno.

Nudity is tolerated at the **Plumlov** lake, next to the textile campground Zralok in Plumlov, west of Prostéjov.

Otrokovice-by-Zlín was established with official permission in 1992. Grassy beach, shade trees; toilets, showers, pool, volleyball, tennis, minigolf, boats, disco, swings, buffet, tent sites. Hotels, supermarket, and Otrokovice city bus stop (no. 55) are in walking distance. (See *N* 13.1, p. 48.)

☞ From Prague, to Brno, to Hodejice on Rt. 50 toward Uherské

Hradiste; before reaching it, turn left at Staré Mesto onto Rt. 55 toward Zlín, through Napajedla and Otrokovice, then across two bridges. From the last bridge you can see the lake on the left. Take an offramp turning sharply to the right, and go under the bridge (underpass). Train #270, Prague–Prerov–Hodonin, makes a stop at Otrokovice.

NOTE: captions to photos run along the inside edge of pages.

This Page: Leif Heilberg, The Beach At Antosovice In Northern Moravia, 1994.

Leif Heilberg, The ACN Beach At Otrokovice, 1994.

DENMARK

ere is a true complete list of the public beaches where nudity is ILLEGAL in Denmark: Aabenraa and Holmsland–Klit. The remaining 4,700 kilometers of Danish coast are authorized for public nudity.

This acceptance needed major lobbying and educational efforts by Danish naturists. These culminated with a public, then-illegal, "wade-in" by some 300 nude beachers—finally jumpstarting a transformation of public policy in 1969.

A number of beaches were then posted as officially nude. The Danish Tourist Board emphasizes: "Public nude beaches are open to everybody whether they want to bathe with or without clothes, but only a few of these beaches are specially marked by signs."

At all other beaches too —with the two exceptions noted—*nudity which does not lead to complaints* is permitted. A sensitivity to others' comfort level is the key.

If you choose a beach that is not specially posted for nudity, watch others' behavior. Perhaps ask Danes for advice. At some mixed-custom beaches it's okay to lie down without covering oneself but it's not acceptable to get up and stroll to the water nude. Considerate behavior is a small price to pay for extensive freedom.

For a map of the coastal accesses, contact any Danish Tourist Office. For Naturist clubs and campgrounds contact the Danish Naturist Union, c/o Ella Pihl, Fuglebakkevej 103, I. th., DK-2000 Frederiksberg. Heritage video's "Freedom Denmark" is excellent.

JUTLAND

RØMØ ISLAND

Rømø is the most southerly vacation island on Jutland's west coast—popular with naturists from all of northwestern Europe. Those who tire of Sylt may move to Rømø by a 45-minute ferry ride. A causeway connects to Denmark's autoroute A-11. Rømø's wide open spaces, quaint Frisian villages, shepherds and modern hotels are easily reached. Contact: Tourist Office, Rømø, DK-6791 Kongsmark.

☞ The most popular nude beach is Sonder Strand, 1,500-m long, located near the hotels and campgrounds of Havneby, the port for the ferry from Sylt,

Politikens Presse: 14 km South Of Copenhagen, Ishoj Strand In 1979: Koge Bay Becomes A Designated Nude Beach; Erik Arcgemes, Right, Leads the First Plunge

on the southeastern shore. Drive A-11 to Skærbæk and take the Rømø Island exit.

FANØ ISLAND

North of Rømø, Fanø Island has 18 km of fine sandy beaches and dunes that stretch from Vesterhavsbad in the north to Sønderho in the south.

Most beach nudity is at **Søren Jessens Strand,** at the island's north tip. Take A-12 into Esbjerg, where a ferry connects to Nordby. Contact: Tourist Office, Torvet 21, DK-6700 Esbjerg.

WEST COAST

The Jutland Peninsula is Denmark's leading choice for vacation campers, being inexpensive and convenient to the Dutch and Germans. The surf of the North Sea crashes onto wide sandy beaches. Grass-covered dunes and vast moors also make it a romantic sight. But not only can strong currents drag the swimmer out to sea—bathers are sometimes kept on shore by frothy fish-killing yellow sea algae.

☞ Take A-11 north past the Rømø and Fanø Island accesses, to the 40 km of North Sea beaches which stretch from **Kærgard** beach north to Skalingen, with Kærgard the most popular. Beyond Esbjerg take the Varde exit and drive west to Oksbøl. Past Oksbøl, where the road angles south, continue west to Grærup, where you take the coastal road north, past Børsmose, to Kærgard.

North of Kærgard beach is the town of Henne with its **Houstrup** nude beach (*see below*) touted by the tourist office (Turist-Kontoret, Bredgade 44, DK-6830 Nr., Nebel; phone 75 28 86 70). Its dunes are wildly romantic. The Blåbjerg Plantation is here, and Lyngbo naturist campground is in walking distance of the beach. Curiously, Holmsland–Klit beach to the north is one of two in Denmark that forbid nudity.

On Jutland's northwest coast, find the **Jammerbugten.** Coastal A-11 diverges from the main A-11 at Østerild, rejoining it beyond Fjerritslev. Shortly before Fjerritslev take another road leading northeast to Hjortdal. Then follow the signs to Svinklov and Slettestrand—Jammerbugt Beach lies between the two.

From Løkken on A-11, drive north 7 km to just before Gølstrup, and turn west to the coast between Rubjerg Knude and Nørre-Lyngby-Molle. The road to a nude beach begins from the restaurant at Molle.

LYNGBO PARK

Lyngbo Park, West Jutland, offers naturist camping. Nudity is not required and activities such as volleyball are clothing-optional. Restaurant, laundromat, mini-mart. Young people are made welcome by lower rates and a special camping area

where radios and late partying is okay. May 1–Sept. 15. Strandfogedvej 15, DK-6854 Henne. Phone (75) 25 50 92.

BALTIC COAST

Skagen, at Jutland's northern tip, faces Sweden to the east. Its 65 km of windswept dunes and sands are clothing-optional. Reach by A-10 along the Baltic Coast.

North of the Fyn Island causeway, the tourist board recommends a site on the southern hook of Vejle Fjord. Take A-18 south from Vejle to the Vinding exit; then east to Trelde Næs. Or from Fyn Island, take A-1 northwest across the causeway; at the Erritse exit, go north, through the city of Fredericia, to Trelde.

BALTIC ISLANDS

Most of us visualize the Jutland Peninsula when we think of Denmark. In reality, industrial activity and population are centered on Denmark's Baltic Islands.

ANHOLT ISLAND

Anholt is small and remote with a fine, unspoiled shoreline. Reached by a 3-hour ferry from Grena or by air. A free beach on the eastern shore is popular.

BORNHOLM ISLAND

Bornholm is a 7-hour ferry ride southeast from Copenhagen or 2 1/2 hours by ferry from Ystad, Sweden. Air travel is available. Nudity at the Dueodde, Jom-fru-gaard and Vester Somark beaches.

FALSTER ISLAND

Falster Island is en route to Copenhagen, if you take the auto ferry from northeastern Germany. Boto Strand is 18 km south on A-2 from Nykøbing, the principal city. Between Boto and Marielyst, look for the large graphic sign.

FYN ISLAND

Fyn Island is linked by causeway to Jutland and to Langeland Island and by ferry to Sjælland.

Thurø By beach is on a cove just east of the A-9 causeway from Fyn to Langeland Island. It's pebble-free and safe for bathing.

Hverringe Skov beach, near Kerteminde to the northeast of Odense, is 800 m long with parking at the Forest of Hverringe.

In Odense is naturist **Fyn Bøjden Næs,** Horne, DK-5600 Faaborg 62; phone 62 60 17 02. Tent and RV sites, shower, playground, sports courts.

Near Middelfart is **Lillebaelt,**

Strandvaenget 34, DK-6000 Kolding; phone/fax 64 40 33 59. Tent and RV sites, clubhouse, bike rental.

LOLLAND ISLAND

From Nakskov, drive southwest to Lange and make your way to Albuen at Lolland Island's western tip. Albuen is a hamlet on a sandspit in Nakskov Fjord.

SJÆLLAND ISLAND

Sjælland is largest and most populous of the Baltic Islands.

☞ A designated nude beach is on **Køge Bay** 15 km south of Copenhagen between Ishoj and Brondby Strand. The suburban train goes to Ishoj (with bus connection to Ishoj Strand) as well as to "youth" beaches some 10 km north at Helsigor and Klampenborg.

A more southerly nude beach is at **Feddet** on Fakse Bugt. From Copenhagen take E-4 south to Tappernøje. Turn off in the direction of Orup. The Feddet Peninsula is accessible to the east about halfway to Orup.

The most popular nude beach—recommended by the tourist board—is near **Tisvilde,** bordering Troldeskoven (the troll forest). Tisvilde is special in Sjælland for its beauty and the quality of the sand and water. Drive northwest on A-16 to Frederiksværk, then A-205 N to A-237, then to coastal Tisvildeleje and the nude beach 3/4 mile to the west. Closest parking is Stangehus P-Plads. Camping facilities in Tisvildeleje.

The westernmost free beach, **Vesterlyng,** is reached by A-4. Follow signs for Kalundborg and take the exit after Viskinge to Eskebjerg. From Eskebjerg take the road west toward Alleshave; Vesterlyng will be on your right.

Another beach, **Ordrup Naes,** offers a solitary naturist idyll within a state park 60 miles from Copenhagen. Lush meadows back a part-sand, part-gravel beach. Take A-4 west to Holbæk. Five miles outside of Holbæk—while following signs to Kalundborg—turn right toward Gislinge and Fårevejle. In Fårevejle drive past the train station and turn left for 100 yards at the main intersection in town, then right again in the direction of Ordrup Næs. After 2 miles, look for the village store and the Blaa Ged Restaurant. Turn off the road at Næsvej about 600 yards beyond the park and walk to the beach.

WHERE TO STAY

The hotels of *Københaven* (Copenhagen) are expensive and often full. The Sleep-In is an adventurous, unadvertised alternative. Those who arrive in the summer without a bed can ask for it. About $4 a night buys a private bunk, toilet and shower use, and breakfast. Some 250 travelers comfortably share this converted ice rink nightly. Children under 12 free.

Denmark

Coastal areas feature Vacation Villages, liked by European visitors. Rental about $25 per night. Write Vacation Centers Inc., Box 186, Spring Lake, NJ 07762.

Country inns and farms are another cost-saving option. Write for a list to Danish Tourist Board, 75 Rockefeller Plaza, New York, NY 10019.

Solvennerne offers a relaxing naturist base in a piney woods as you visit Copenhagen. It's 10 km due west on A-1 and off onto E-4 N at Glostrup. It's even near Copenhagen's suburban tram. Community kitchen, large pool, volleyball. May 1–Sept. 15. Tysmosen, Nybøllevej 21, DK-2765 Smørum. Phone (44) 97 34 02.

Farther west on A-1, 22 km beyond Roskilde, *Naturistforeningen Sjælland*—or **Solbakken**—welcomes foreign visitors. Rental chalets, community kitchen and clubhouse, fjord waterfront. April–Sept. Solbakkenvei 4, Kyndeløse Sydmark, DK-4070 Kirke Hyllinge.

Phone (46) 40 51 07. The largest Naturist club in Denmark, Solbakken organizes winter swims in Copenhagen.

North of Kirke Hyllinge at Skibby is a popular winter solarium-pool-sauna for naturists, *Hellas.* Camp at **Nordisk Solsport,** Leif Hierwagen, Solen 3B, Torup, 3390 Hundested; phone (47) 98 88 80.

Roskilde Fjord harbors *Hyldeholm*—from 1936 the "naturism on one island" project of Søren Sørensen and Eila Pfeiffer.

FINLAND

With thousands of small lakes, Finland offers many sites for enjoying the great outdoors in the altogether. Yet there are only four official naturist beaches: Helsinki (location: Pihlajasaari), Punkaharju (location: Kultakivi), Pori (location: Yyteri) and Turku (location: Ruissalo Camping).

The Finns are sometimes misunderstood. The sauna is their invention and gift to the world, yet traditionally they do not practice mixed-sex nudity except among family and close friends. Every household has its sauna. The result is a dearth of public naturism with the exception of municipal and hotel saunas.

One solution is to cross the Russian border and visit the beach also used by St. Petersburg naturists, described in N 16.3 pp. 100–101. It is at Terijoki, scene of WWII battles between Finnish and Russian troops.

The small but energetic Finnish naturist group is reached through Erkki Husu, Luonnonmukaiset, Killintie 3, FIN-4520 Kouvola 20; phone + 35 80 29 88 344.

ÅLAND ISLAND

MÖCKELÖ BEACH

The thousands of southwestern Finnish islands in the Åland archipelago—formerly Swedish—have become a sunbathing haven. Even Swedish nationals boat and ferry over to Åland to enjoy camping/sunning. A social nude beach has emerged and is advertised in tourist brochures at Möckelö—on the first peninsula west of the principal Åland town of Mariehamn. Official camping is adjacent.

Finnish Sauna Borrowed By Norwegian Naturists.

181

FRANCE

France followed Germany's lead in establishing organized Naturism and was the second nation to do so with significant numbers. Today the Fédération Française de Naturisme is the world's largest and leads the way in forming the European Naturist Union.

Kienné de Mongeot was primarily responsible for early development. A tall, aristocratic free spirit, he edited *Vivre* (later *Vivre d'Abord*), the focal nudist magazine of the 1930s and 1940s. De Mongeot also founded the Sparta Club, near Paris, where a classic Greek norm of social nudism was developed, acceptive of the male and female singles and not family-oriented. Like other European clubs of the time, Sparta Club set rigorous codes of nudity.

Albert Lecocq, de Mongeot's disciple and successor in French naturism, was not, at heart, more Christian or family-oriented, but he made more concessions to the popular prejudices in the interests of popularizing Naturism. The era of Lecocq is still with us: the terrain he founded, Club du Soleil; the ocean resort, Montalivet and the journal, *La Vie au Soleil* continue, even if they have changed hands.

Today's FFN president

Philippe Cardin and his ideas are profiled in *Nude & Natural* magazine 13.4, pp. 60-63.

Some FFN club naturists resisted the rise of nude beaches and resorts in the 1970s while other FFN members helped create public clothes-free zones. In 1994, French penal code article 330—"*outrage public á la pudeur*," now rarely invoked against mere nudity on public lands—was abolished. The private clubs presently seek to extend education and benefits to reattract members. Brochures in major languages; 65 rue de Tocqueville, F-75017 Paris. Phone (331) 4764 3282; fax (331) 4764 3263. Its magazine and vacation guide is *NAT-Info*, 160 F/year from S.E.D.N., 11 rue Galin, F-33100 Bordeaux. Phone (33) 5677 3248; fax (33) 5677 3232.

NORTHWEST

DUNKERQUE TO NORMANDY BEACHES

Nord—Ghyvelde. Municipal nude beach, east of Zuydcoote Marine Hospital. The deprived next-door Belgians benefit. Access by coastal N-1 or D-60 then north on D-947 to park at Bray Dunes.

Pas-de-Calais—Berck-sur-Mer. At 42 km south of Boulogne, turn off N-40 west onto Blvd. de Boulogne, then right on Chemin des Anglais to sea. Park at Dr. Calot St. lot. Cross to Terminus Beach, walk north 15–20 minutes for nude beach. Stay out of the handsome dunes.

Somme—Quend Plage Rue. Enjoy the Channel dunes north of Abbeville. From Rue drive by D-940 to Quend then

D-102 to Quend Plage; walk south towards Le Crotoy.

Manche—Hatainville. Drive south from Cherbourg on D-904 to just north of Le Moitiers d'Allone, then D-242 west through Hatainville to the beach. Walk 1 km south halfway to Cap de Carteret.

Manche—Agon-Coutainville. From Granville take D-72 north. Turn left on D-44 to Agon. There go south onto the hook. Just before the lighthouse, take a sand road on the right (just before the Lechanteur monument), park, walk north to the huge sand beach. Note that low tides go far out.

Manche—Bréville-sur-Mer. Exit D-971 (Graville-Constances Road) at Grand Chemin heading for the Bréville airport (D-236). Take this road over the dunes to the beach, then continue left. The beach is north of Vanlée Camping and opposite the rifle range.

BRITTANY BEACHES

Cote d'Emeraude—Crique de Fréhel. From N-786, east of Pluvien, take D-34a northeast via Pléhérel-Plage. Follow signs for Cap Fréhel and park atop Trou du Poulifer. A goat path leads down to Port-du-Sud-Est beach, on the east shore of Cap Fréhel, halfway between the point and La Guette beaches.

Cap d'Erquy—Le Lourtuais. Leave N-786 at Erquy, direction Cap d'Erquy. Take the right-hand road at the ruins. Park when the road becomes too steep; walk to the gathering spot, east of Cap d'Erquy, a large beach of black rocks backed by hilly pinewoods.

St.-Brieuc—Plage des Rosaires. Easy access. From St-Brieuc drive northwest on D-786, turn right (north) at Piérin to Grève des Rosaires. Walk right.

Lannion—Beg-Léguer. At the mouth of Le Léguer River, 10 km west of B-786, is Beg-Léguer and Mez an Aod beach. Take D-21 north from Lannion and exit left at Le Raudour, direction Pointe Servel. Confusing intersections abound— follow your nose, due west. Past Beg-Léguer Church and before the lighthouse, turn left at the road with a stone marker. Park your car here on the side of the road. Walk 10 minutes west to a small cove surrounded by granite boulders. Walk north over the rocks to Mez an Aod. Try Camping Beg-Léguer, F-22300 Servel-Lannion. Phone 9648 7520.

Quimper—Cap Sizun to Tregunc. North of Audierne, Pors-Péron beach at Beuzec-Cap-Sizun has a nude cove beyond the rocks on its west end. On the Bay of Audierne, naturists use the ends of Prat-ar-Hastel beach, southeast of Treguennec; D-156 east from Plonéour-

Lanvern goes there. For Treffiagat beach: take D-102 coastal route south from Pont-L'Abbé, and 1 km beyond Lesconil (going west now) turn left onto a dirt road. Camping des Dunes, Phone 9887 8178. Tregunc's Plage de Kerouini is south on D-1 to Pointe de Trévignon.

Fouesnant—Kerler Beach. A portion of Kerler Plage is now officially naturist. Sunbathers also use the beach and dunes between Mousterlin and Bénodet.

Lorient—Ploémeur. From Lorient drive south then west on the D-152 loop to Plage des Kaolins near St.-Jude Church.

Morbihan-Erdéven—Kerminihy Beach. Easily reached and popular. Via Auray or Ploemel to Erdéven (where D-781 and D-105 meet). At Erdéven Church go due west to Kerminihy, drive through, turn left at last house and go to the second right. Beach is between the rivière d'Etel and Roche-Sèche World War II gun block-house. Lodging: Association Naturiste Morbihannaise, B.P. 8, F-56106 Lorient.

KOAD AR ROC'H

Koad Ar Roc'h is a chateau in the Brocéliande Forest 50 km west of Rennes, now a magnificent naturist park. Rolling woods and fields, lakes, restaurant, bar, crêperie, disco, handicrafts, yoga, volleyball, soccer, canoeing, riding.

Rental RVs, stone-built bungalows; a fine base for visiting Brittany. June 15–Sept. 15. Chateau de Bois de la Roche, F-56820 Néant-sur-Yvel. Phone (97) 74 4211; fax (97) 74 4499.

PARIS AREA

HÉLIOMONDE

An innovator and paragon among the federated clubs. Huge outdoor heated pool, volleyball, tennis, restaurant, bar, clubhouse and library, on wooded 45 ha. Rent a bungalow or caravan (RV). South 50 km from Paris, close to N-20, with metro bus and rail only a mile away at St.-Chéron. Thirty km from Orly; open all year. La Petite Beauce, F-95130 St. Chéron. Phone (331) 6456 6137. Inquires to SOC-NAT, 16 rue Drouet, F-75009 Paris. Phone (331) 4246 4387.

CLUB DU SOLEIL

The FFN's sophisticated Parisian suburb haven, located between La Défense and Chaton metros at 14 rue Victor-Hugo, F-78420 Carrières-sur-Seine. Phone (331) 3914 6265. Outdoor pool, sun terrace, sauna, cafe, game room. Open all year. Some camping and lodging.

CHEATEAU DE BARNEAU

Sun meadows, woods for tent/RV camping in a 14-ha cheateau park just 20 km from Euro-Disneyland. Some rooms. Restaurant, bar, pool, tennis, volleyball. L'Elan Gymnique, 104 rue de Champeaux, F-77111 Soignolles-en-Brie. Phone (331) 6406 7024.

ATLANTIC COAST

TURBALLE TO VENDÉE BEACHES

La Turballe—Pen-Bron Beach. Brittany's most popular nude beach: sunny, fine sand, good swimming, boating and fishing. La Turballe is west-northwest on D-99 from Nantes, near the mouth of the Loire River. From La Turballe take Route D-92 south. Drive 1 km past signs for Village Vacances Famille to the T-intersection, and park on left. Walk in entrance and through forest for 10 minutes, past the lifeguard station, then right over dunes to beach. No lodging within 30 km.

St.-Nazaire—Les Jaunais. Pointe de Chémoulin. West on D-92 from St.-Nazaire, south on D-292 through St.-

France

Edin Velez, Giant Chess At Montalivet.

Marc. Ask, and perhaps stay just beyond the nude beach, at Camping des Jaunais–St. Marc, F-44600 St.-Nazaire. Phone 4045 9260.

Île de Noirmoutier—Luzéronde Beach. Nudity is long-established on the island's west coast between L'Herbaudiére and L'Épine among free spirits who mostly stay at Camping de la Bosse (phone 39 01 07) or Camping de L'Oasis (39 09 77) in L'Épine, or Camping de la Pointe (39 16 70) in L'Herbaudiére. Île de Noirmoutier can be reached by D-38 via Fromentine.

Fromentine—La Barre-de-Monts. Just south of Île de Noirmoutier, another well-known free beach. La Barre-de-Monts is at the center of a pine-shaded, undeveloped 7-km beach from La Barre-de-Monts to Notre-Dame-de-Monts. At hamlet of Les Lays on D-38, park and follow trail across dunes. Or drive 2 km south of St.-Jean-de-Monts to the new official naturist beach, le Grand-Bec.

St.-Gilles—Brétignolles-sur-Mer. On D-38 south of coastal St.-Gilles, west of La Roche-S-Yon. Access to a splendid 2-km beach is at L'auberge du Petit-Pont (La Rhumerie) just north of Brétignolles. Drive around the inn, park and walk 1 km west to the beach. Camping Les Cyprès, phone 5255 3898.

Olonne-sur-Mer—Sauveterre Beach. International set enjoys sun and seclusion. North on D-32 from Sables-d'Olonne, then west on D-80 to Sauveterre and continue west through the Olonne Forest to parking on the sea. Walk 1 km north.

La-Faute-sur-Mer—Pointe d'Arçay. A bird sanctuary runs the length of this wild and calming sandy beach. Approach by N-746 west through L'Alguillon. Park at sanctuary entrance, walk 2.5 km south to naturist portion. Or drive full length south, park and cut west across woods to the beach. Phone 5156 4519.

CHARENTE—MARITIME BEACHES

La Rochelle—Île de Ré. Popular beaches are Lisay and Petit-Bec on the island's north shore, and between La Couarde and Bois-Plage-en-Ré at the gun blockhouse on the central southwest coast. Causeway is from La Pallice near La Rochelle. Information: 4629 4609. **Île d'Oléron,** an overlooked beauty spot, has official nude beaches south of the bridge access (St.-Trojan-Les-Bains and Vert-Bois) and just north of Bayardville (Les Soumonards). **Club Naturiste Atlantique,** in Royan, is beautifully laid out about one km from the sea. Naturism is allowed where indicated.

Pointe d'Arvert—Tremblade Beaches. On the west coast of the peninsula, which juts above the Gironde River mouth, a large free beach extends along coastal D-25 from Pointe Espagnole south. Northern access is via the parking lot at Pointe Espagnole (Pointe d'Arvert). From the south look for the ranger station Bouverie at the junction of D-268 and D-25. It's a long hike in. Nudity resumes farther south at Pointe de la Coubre and at La Palmyre/Plage de la Grande Côte. Close to it all is naturist camping at **Atlantique Soleil,** F-17570 Les Mathes. Phone 4622 4035. Two pools, restaurant, volleyball, playground, activities, rental bikes and RVs. April–Oct.

GIRONDE PENINSULA

The Gironde Peninsula was "liberated" by naturists after World War II. With a pleasant climate, and rather convenient to Paris and much urban FFN membership in a time of more difficult travel, the Gironde was attracting campers to its sandy pine woods and Atlantic beach surf. A bid to buy land seemed right.

Today the resorts of Montalivet and Euronat mark the success of organized naturism. But many families still drive to the area for no-frills clothes-free camping—at **Naujac-sur-Mer** (northern part, from Pin Sec); **Hourtin** (south); **Carcans** (south and right of the ranger station Alexander); and **Lacanau.** A part of **St. Nicolas Beach,** as **Verdon-sur-Mer,** is officially naturist.

Also of interest are the northernmost and southernmost points of Gironde. Just 10 km from Soulac-sur-Mer, the former is **Le Gurp,** named for the street which leads to it. The high dunes provide a beautiful backdrop and ensure that naturism is widely practiced. At the southernmost tip is **Cap Ferret** and the campground Truc Vert (F-33979 Cap Ferret). Though not a naturist campground it does boast a naturist beach.

EURONAT

South of Royan and the Gironde River lies Soulac. South from Soulac via D-101, amid coast pines and dunes, is Euronat with double the area of its model, Montalivet, on a 1.5-km, broad sand beach. English-speaking assistance at check-in. Bicycle a necessity, may be rented. Rents 50 RVs and 300 bungalows fully supplied, and 790 tent/RV sites. Camping rated ****. Baker, butcher, deli, wine and fish shops, minimart, restaurant, boutiques, newsstand, bank, post office. Huge all-year heated indoor pool, with children's section, and special camping area for ages 16–25. Riding stable, all sports. Thalassotherapy spa and fitness program. From the Bordeaux airport, 90 km. Centre Naturiste Euronat, F-33590 Grayan-l'Hôpital. Phone (33) 05 5673 2451; fax (33) 05 5609 3973. In USA, 1-800-828-9356.

MONTALIVET

Montalivet—the premiere campground of the Fédération Française de Naturisme—dates from 1949. Albert Lecocq and his FFN colleagues intensively negotiated with a Vendays mayor and councilmen, who were sceptical of admitting nudists to their community, yet fearful—after a forest fire charred the sandy coast—that no sensible person would bring money into a devastated region.

The FFN accepted strict conditions: nudity was confined at first to areas screened by scrub pine. They began reforestation and built primitive bungalows and common buildings. The numbers increased until, by 1970, Vendays was overshadowed by its stepchild. Now, over 20,000 vacationers come to Montalivet each year, many repeaters, spending two to four weeks.

Montalivet now offers its own 2-km nude beach with much spillover at the ends, tall pines, 1,250 chalets (200 for rent), 1,200 tent/RV sites (camping rated **). Children's pool and club, 16 volleyball courts, 8 tennis courts, heated pool, sauna, massage, spa, Ping-Pong tables, amphitheater, films, crafts, library, TV,

disco, bakery, wine and fish stores. All year. It's 80 km from Bordeaux airport. Avenue de l'Europe, F-33930 Vendays-Montalivet. Phone 5673 2670; fax 5609 3215. Paris phone (331) 4246 4387.

☞ From the north, take ferry at Royan to Pointe de Grave. Continue via Verdon to Soulac, and take D-102 south through Vendays to the coast and Montalivet. Rail to Bordeaux and then Queyrac, 14 km distant. Couples and families only. INF membership required, may be purchased at gate.

LABORDE

On 20 ha of beautifully landscaped wooded area, Laborde has a sauna, bar, restaurant, laundry facilities, clubhouse, heated indoor pool, children's area, sports games, two lakes. Paulhiac, F-47150 Monflanquin. Phone 5362 1488; fax 5361 6023.

LE COUDERC

Due east from Bordeaux, Le Couderc is situated on 44 acres in the heart of Périgord, close to the town of Beaumont. Camping areas are surrounded by woods. RV sites and fully-equipped

chalets are also available. Facilities are handicap accessible and include showers, European-style toilets, solar-heated pool, children's pool, restaurant, bar and grocery store. Owners speak English and French. Fam. Postel, Naussannes 24440 Beaumont du Périgord, Dordogne, France. Phone 5322 4040; fax 5323 9098.

LE CRO MAGNON

Just east of Le Couderc, Le Cro Magnon is located in the center of the Dordogne, with an excellent view of the valley and the Beynac castle. Bar/restaurant, grocery store, archery, canoeing down the Dordogne River. Information from English-speaking Ed and Liduin Beitsma, Le Cro Magnon, Allas-Les-Mines, 24220 Beynac, France or phone 5329 1370; fax 5329 1579.

GIRONDE BEACHES

Lacanau—Bunker Beach. During its Occupation, the German army laid a road from Lacanau south to the defensive bunkers. Ask for "l'Route Allemagne." The 15-km beach—59 km due west of Bordeaux via D-2—has a naturist B&B, **La Forestière**, phone 5603 2050. Otherwise lacks facilities. Good surfing.

Arcachon—La Test-de-Buch Beach on the Dune du Pilat Lagoon. A very popular, superb naturist zone of dunes and pines. Reached by D-63, southwest from Bordeaux to Arcachon, then D-112 south, towards Biscarrosse-Plage; a km past Petit Nice Camping, turn in to Parking La Lagune—safe, with hotels/restaurants; try Le Sablonney, phone 5622 7101.

LA JENNY

An elaborate and popular naturist complex between the Médoc and the Arcachon Basin 50 km west of Bordeaux, La Jenny has 300 acres of pine forest on the coast. Opened 1983, 300 fully-equipped (including mopeds), self-catering rental chalets for 2 to 7 persons—and no tents or RVs. With 4 pools, 10 tennis courts, trails, surfing, archery, yoga, sauna, cultural evenings, newsstand, terrace restaurant and bar, food shops, fitness center. Almost endless nude beach, many children's activities. Book your departure inspection early. June–Sept. La Jenny, Route de Lauros, F-33680 Le Porge. Phone 5626 5690; fax 5626 5651.

South of La Jenny on the Arcachon Basin is an official nude beach, **La Teste-de-Buch,** frequented by military personnel.

ARNAOUTCHOT

Family camping, rated ****, in a pine forest between the Landes and Basque country. Atlantic sandy beach of 1.5 km. Heated indoor pool, playground, golf, 4 tennis courts, riding stables, water sports, films, disco. Canuding in Hutchet River reserve nearby; excursions to Pyrenees and Basque country. Rental chalets, RVs, tent sites. Minimart, bakery. Biarritz airport 65 km. May–Oct. Domaine d'Arnaoutchot, F-40560 Vielle St.-Girons. Phone 5848 1111; fax 5848 5712.

WESTERN MEDITERRANEAN

PYRENEES ORIENTALES BEACHES

Argelés-sur-Mer—Bocal del Tech. Near the Spanish border is a magnificent expanse of beach at the mouth of the Tech River. The cleanest water on the French Mediterranean coast; swimming is encouraged. Catalan and Sardice folklore shows two nights a week in town and the Festival de Prades at the end of July–start of August.

☞ Drive north from Argelés-sur-Mer and turn off D-81 on its west side between le pont de la Ribérette (Ribérette Bridge) and le pont du Tech (Tech Bridge). The turnoff soon loops back under D-81, and east a mile to the coast. Drive carefully across the sand. When it gets treacherous do park, walk 5 to 10 minutes. Naturists often stay at the nearby (clothed) Le Soleil campground, rated ****, phone 6881 1448.

Torreilles—Bourdigou Plage. Exit D-81 between the Bourdigou and Agly rivers, drive to Torreilles' Village des Sables on the coast and then south, staying north of the Bourdigou River.

PERPIGNAN

La Clapère. Located between the mountains and sea, on 50 ha of unspoilt wooded countryside. Children and adult pools, clubhouse, playground. Tent/RV sites. 35 Route de Las Illas, F-66480 Maureillas; phone 6883 3604.

Domaine Le Clols has 63 ha of natural wooded areas and exceptional views. Pool, sports games, massage, library, guided mountain walks, golf, close to Spanish border. Tent/RV camping. F-66260 St. Laurent de Cerdans; phone 6839 5168.

PORT-LEUCATE

Quartier Naturiste Port-Leucate was built (1976) as a nude-use zone anchored by the resort-villages Aphrodite and Ulysse. Since 1989, the quartier has been expanded. A 2-km, clean, windy, unvegetated beach framed by jetties that stop beach walkers. With an INF card you may ask for a free day pass. Pools, tennis and volleyball courts, water-ski, windsurfing, balneotherapy, children's activities, mini-marts, restaurant and bar with beach terrace, newsstand, discos.

Aphrodite Village has 546 garden villas and apartments around a marina. **Oasis Village**—of classy design, and on the beach, with a pool–palm oasis—now extends Aphrodite. F-11370 Port Leucate. Phone 6840 9042.

Club Nature Ulysse has 130 studios and apartments, and features 150 tent/caravan sites rated **. New **Eden** apartments extend the Ulysse holdings. F-11370 Port Leucate. Phone 6840 9921; fax 6840 6395.

☞ Thirty km north of Perpignan and 50 km south of Narbonne. Turn off A-9 at Leucate, and then by RN-9 on the left after 200 m take D-627.

LANGUEDOC— ROUSSILON BEACHES

Port-la-Nouvelle—Les Montilles. A posted, public nude beach south of Port-la-Nouvelle, most often used by visitors to the naturist campground Le Clapotis, 7 km away. Directly on the lagoon (Étang) of Lapalme, Clapotis has 220 campsites rated ****, a restaurant, bar, supermarket, sauna, boat rentals, lagoon beach, volleyball and basketball courts. Le Clapotis, F-11480 Lapalme. Phone 6848 1540.

To Les Montilles Beach from Port-la-Nouvelle: South on B-9 from Narbonne, off at Sigean, then N-9D east. Drive south to the nude beach on a dirt road that is 500 m behind the shore. Park and continue walking.

For Le Clapotis: from Port-la-Nouvelle drive south on D-709 to Lapalme and beyond, hugging the Étang de Lapalme on your left. Its campers have walking access to Les Montilles beach via Camping Côte Vermeille, off D-709.

Gruissan—Fleury d'Aude. Between the beach villages of Gruissan-Plage and Les Cabanes de Fleury is a breezy, lovely strand of campgrounds and naturist beaches. The tarmac road to St-Pierre-le-Mer offers convenient entry. So too from Gruissan via Blvd. de Pech-Maynaud toward Narbonne-Plage, taking the first exit to the right at the traffic circle, continuing on to sand tracks, angling north. Write: Camping municipal de l'Etang, F-11560 Fleury-d'Aude. Phone only: Gruisson Promag, 6849 0900. Campgrounds: Les Ayguades, 6833 8159 (rated ***, on the nude beach). Naturist camping **Grand-Cosse,** 480 RV/tent sites, where migrating shorebirds are an off-season attraction. F-11560 Fleury-d'Aude. Phone 6833 6187; fax 6833 3223.

Domaine de Lambeyran. Private and semiprivate camping areas on 340 ha; large pool, recreational facilities. 34700 Lodéve. Phone 6744 1399; fax 6744 0991.

Le Village du Bosc. 50 km from Montpellier. Pool, volleyball, restaurant, river swimming. Tent/RV sites. Ricazouls – 34800 Octon. Phone 6796 0737; fax 6796 3575.

Grau-du-Roi—Espiguette Lighthouse. Directly east of Montpellier; a.k.a. plage des Barronets. The local FFN club was instrumental in gaining this lovely beach as an official naturist site. The club now maintains it as a first-class beach with ample parking (fee required) and signs. Take D-62b out of Grau-du-Roi, circle around the Arena, exit with the Port Camargue on your right onto Route du Phare de l'Espiguette. Go straight past the lighthouse to the natural parking lot. Beach vendors bring refreshments.

SÉRIGNAN

West of Agde, this official naturist beach was restricted to guests of the Clos-du-Ferrand and Gymno-Club Méditerranéen campgrounds when decreed in 1972. The general public now uses it, entering by public Sérignan-Plage. Better, park on the right 100 m before Gymno-Club gate, for direct access onto the nude beach. Refreshments on beach.

Gymno-Club Méditeranéen, F-34410 Sérignan. Phone 6732 0361; fax 6732 2636. Rated *** with 300 tent/RV sites, restaurant, all water sports, volleyball, clubhouse, disco. Right on the beach, 10 ha, open all year.

Le Clos Ferrand, F-34410 Sérignan-Plage. Phone 6732 1559. Rated ***, a small and satisfying naturist campground on the beach.

CAP D'AGDE

Begun as a small naturist campground in 1956 by the Oltra family on their coastal farm, Cap d'Agde now covers 90 ha—truly a naturist city and a model for developers internationally. Government investment was vital to make Cap d'Agde what it is today. The four distinct complexes each accommodate thousands as well as a wealth of enterprises. The unique aspect of Agde is the integration of naturism with everyday town life. Only here can you do all your shopping, banking,

garage visits, and other daily business in the nude. This lends a tremendous sense of freedom, and causes one to wonder what a clothes-optional world might be like.

Centre Helio-Marin is the campgrounds—with 3,000 sites. March 15–Oct. 15. Agence Oltra, BP 884, F-34307 Cap d'Agde. Phone 6726 3378. If your notion of camping is to get away from it all and commune with nature, this isn't for you. The French like to bring their suburbia with them when they camp, including social events such as Tupperware parties and niceties such as garden fences. It's a good thing that the visitors aren't all that interested in nature—the beach that serves the Naturist complex is only 3 km, hardly adequate for all those bodies.

Hotel Eve, near the entrance, built 1983, rated ***, offers convenience, a heated private pool and terrace, solarium and full services. BP 654, F-34308 Cap d'Agde. Phone 6726 7170.

Cap d'Agde can accommodate up to 40,000 persons, and indeed does in the peak season July 15–Aug. 20. The international clientele creates a cosmopolitan atmosphere. The last few years have seen an increase of Japanese and American naturists. Readers may obtain a brochure in English about the rental agencies, RV/campsites, hotels, area attractions. Office Municipal du Tourisme et des Loisirs, BP 544, F-34305 Agde Cedex. Phone 6726 3858; fax 6726 2299.

Travel consultants for visiting Agde include: Skinny-Dip Tours (1-800-828-9356) in association with Peng Travel and Pru & Larry Beck, an American couple at Agde who can make your on-site and travel reservations: 34 Helio Village, F-34308 Cap d'Agde, phone 6726 0341; fax 6726 0341.

☞ Driving: Take motorway A-9, exit Agde/Pezenas southwest of Montpellier. Road signs to the Quartier Naturiste. Rail: Agde Station has direct day/night connection with Paris, Nice, Bordeaux, Strasbourg, Spain, Switzerland, Germany and Italy. Air: Air France, Air Inter and other airlines have daily flights from Paris and London to Montpellier, 50 miles from Agde. Transfer service is available, airport and rail, with Agde.

AVIGNON AREA

DOMAINE DE BELEZY

Drawn to France and the beach-city of nudists, Agde? Do also visit Belezy, an energetically bucolic retreat for family naturist camping; you'll enjoy making the comparison. Olympic pool, smaller heated pool, tennis, volleyball, soccer. Over

35 workshops in high season: archery, aquatics, French, astronomy, photography, computer use, sculpture, et al. Child care, youth programs. Choral and instrumental performance. Restaurant/bar on terrace. Minimarket, massage, yoga. 25 ha. Campsites, dormitory, bungalows, RVs. East of Avignon and Carpentras, below Mont Ventoux; great area for excursions. May–Oct. Domaine de Belezy, BP 3, F-84410 Bédoin. Phone 9065 6018; fax 9065 9445.

You may also wish to visit **Le Romegas,** an exceptional naturist RV park to the northeast that perches high on a hillside and has a terrific view of the Mediterranean coast, huge pool, restaurant and hotel, grocery store. Rated ***. Nearby towns such as Vaison-la-Romaine, Orange, and Nyons offer plenty to the tourist. F-26170 Buis les Baronnies. Phone 7528 1078.

CÈZE RIVER CAMPING

Europeans since prehistoric times have enjoyed clothes-free campgrounds along the cliff-lined, sandy banks of the Cèze River in the foothills of the Cévennes.

Northwest of Avignon, 120 km from Cap d'Agde and 30 km south of the Ardèche river gorges—the naturist camps have a "lock" on their part of the Cèze, freeing a 530-acre, 3-km zone for canuding, rafting, fishing, hiking, rock climbing, caving and swimming. Pleasant into October.

La Genése is on the south bank—drivers note, as the others are by north bank access! It's a most sophisticated Cèze naturist center, 30 ha, 400 sites. Pool, volleyball, tennis, Ardèche excursions, craft workshops, archery, playground, minimart, restaurant, crêperie, fine new bungalows. Rated ****. May–Sept. F-30430 Méjannes-le-Clap. Reservations: SOCNAT, 16 rue Drouot, F-75009 Paris. Phone 6624 5173; fax 6624 5038.

Domaine de la Sablière offers 300 campsites on 60 ha, rated ****. Ecology emphasis. Canuding beneath a towering rock face. Beautiful pool, sauna, fitness gym, tennis, disco, restaurant, bar. Rental RVs, bungalows. April–Oct. 15. St.-Privat-de-Champclos, F-30430 Barjac, France. Phone 6624 5116; fax 6624 5869.

Le Martinet de L'Elze, on 15 ha, borders the Cèze atop the Cévennes plateau for 1,300 m. Rated ***, 132 sites. Pool, children's playground, clubhouse. Aujac, F-30450 Genolhac. Phone/fax 6661 1237.

The best nearby non-naturist accommodation—if you make a day visit or don't camp—would be Le Dolmen, a small hotel at Mejannes le Clap near Barjac, only 4 km from the Cèze nude zone.

Top: J. Riera Rovira, The Cap d'Agde Beach. Left: Lee Baxandall, Jan Smith Shops Agde. Right Top: John Sathre, Robin Skinner Orders Take-Out. Right Bottom: Richard Pasco, Baskin-Robbins At Agde.

188

France

CENTRAL EAST

HAUTE PROVENCE

Tamier. Restaurant, bar, clubhouse, children's play area, pool, windsurfing. Tent/RV sites. Route de col de Pomerol, 05150 Rosans. Phone/fax 9266 6155.

Club Origan. Wooded and cleared 35 acres with restaurant, clubhouse, volleyball, pool. Tent/RV sites. Alpes d'Alzur – 06260 Puget-Theniers. Phone 9305 0600; fax 9305 0934.

Le Haut Chandelalar. Adult and wading pools, general store, recreation center, children's playground. 06850 Briançon. Phone 9360 4009; fax 9360 4964.

La Chamarade, in the Haute Provence, has wooded campsites, restaurant, large pool, volleyball and children's playground. Tent/RV sites with hookups. F-26230 Chamaret, France. Phone 7546 5767.

Les Faucons. Pool, restaurant, clubhouse, children's playground, water sports. Tent/RV sites, rental apartments. Route de Ries, F-04210 Valensole; phone

France

9274 8270.

Les Clapiéres. Beautiful mountain scenery surrounds 3 ha of wooded and cleared tent/RV sites. Rental studios available. 05100 Briançon. Phone/fax 9221 1583.

EASTERN MEDITERRANEAN

BOUCHES-DU-RHÔNE BEACHES

The Camargue—Saintes-Maries-de-la-Mer. From Arles south via Albaron on N-570. Drive east from Stes.-Maries to this vast delta beach of the Rhône River; passing 5 km of parking to the last lot. The eastern 9 km are a clothes-free utopia—look for the lighthouse, "phare du Rousty," and the FKK signs are located to its right. The farther you stroll the more naked and clean you and the beach get. Beach camping is now banned. There's a big campground at the beach entrance. Provisions in town. In August, the gypsies gather. Office de Tourisme, Ave. van Gogh, BP 34, F-13460 Saintes-Maries-de-la-Mer. Phone 9047 8255.

Salin-de-Giraud—Arles Beach. A vast flat like Stes.-Maries to its west; with a 5-km designated-nude zone. Follow the south bank of the Rhône southeast from Arles for 35 km to Salin-de-Giraud (get your water here; last chance); there's also a ferry here for cars to cross from D-35 (direction Marseille, Aix). Continue southeast on CR-38 past salt flats and bird marshes for 11 km, and turn right at signs to Le Grau du Piémançon. Just short of the sea turn left, drive on hard sand to signs for naturist zone. Camping okay. Office de Tourisme, esplanade des Lices, F-13200 Arles. Phone 9096 2935.

Fos-sur-Mer-Cavaou Beach. At its far end is a 700 m officially nude sandy beach. From the harbor, find the lighthouse and follow the signs.

Marseille—Martigues. A small cove of sand and large, flat rocks, at the Plaine de Bonnieux, south of Martigues, which isn't far west of Marseille. The local FFN club provides for amenities and vets INF cards. Bring snorkel, sneakers and mask—good waters to catch your next bouillabaisse. Naturistes de Martigues, BP 123, F-13695 Martigues Cedex. Camping l'Arquet, phone 4242 8100.

Marseille—Southeastern Calanques. The lovely secluded coves east of Marseille draw au naturel picnics. Hire a fisherman at Morgiou to take you to the calanque of Pierres Tombées, Sugiton, or Port-Pin, picking you up hours later. You can also hike from Morgiou but it's rugged. From Marseille by N-559 and les Baumettes—but driving to Morgiou is chancy—controlled access. Drive on a weekday mid-morning, or better, try public transportation.

TOULON BEACHES

La-Seyne-sur-Mer—Le Jonquet. West of Toulon, approached by paths through the sloping Cap Sicié woodlands, then over rocks between the seven small coves. Each interesting and unique, some have natural springs. Signs limit naturism to the east side of the cape on the beaches of Malpasset and St.-Selon. Jonquet is much loved. Parking lot above beach, off the Route de la Corniche opposite a fire lane leading inland. Office de Tourisme, 6 rue Léon Blum, F-83500 Seyne-sur-Mer. Phone 9494 7309.

The FFN maintains a nude beach at **Les Sablettes.**

Carqueiranne—Bau-Rouge. Unblessed with a sand coast, Toulon makes do with Le Bau-Rouge's pebbles—bring portable comfort. From Carqueiranne take N-559 toward Le Pradet, exit at D-86 south, follow signs for Le Bau Rouge. At the hilltop settlement take the somewhat treacherous path to the beach. The FKK section is clearly marked.

Plage du Pellegrin east of Toulon near Lalonde/Miramar gets nude use, as well as rocky outcrops east of Plage du Pellegrin, between three beaches on peninsula. Or try some of the coves/creeks on **Cap de Leoube.** Stay at Le Grand Hotel in Bormes les Mimosas.

Iles des Porquerolles, a beautiful offshore island near Hyeres and Ile du Levant, has nude use. Try the northern tip of the island, near Pointe du Grand Langoustier. The area is rocky. Take caution; no official status.

Les Salins d'Hyeres. Nudism is officially recognized on a portion of Plage des Vieux Salins, located east of town.

ÎLE DU LEVANT

This earliest naturist seaside colony owes its establishment to a decision of two doctors, the brothers Durville, to purchase a large section of the rock island of Levant when it was discontinued as a penal colony in 1930. They installed carefully selected naturists on subleased plots, creating a community dedicated to harmony with the elements and simple living. The French military stepped in and built a naval base in World War II, disrupting the hegemony of health and limiting the recreation and lodging to only 220 acres.

You must wear *le minimum*, a kind of g-string, or another cache-sex, everywhere when off the beach. The "Levantines" even dress formally for dinner. Even the rockiness of the shoreline (excepting a sandy cove) doesn't daunt devotees, who return year after year to this sun-baked island. Lodgings are booked far in advance. Naturists interested in a living "museum" of the movement's past might take the ferry over for a day, lodging on the mainland.

Lodge at **Lavandou.** It's a ferry port to Île du Levant. East of Lavandou on D-559 around the Pointe du Layet, there's a good nude beach—Plage du Layet—down a stairway painted green. Look for the iron walkway, park there. The path to the beach is 100 m in the direction of Lavandou. Two stone markers are at the entrance. This nude beach has a restaurant! It rents umbrellas and chairs too.

Hotels, restaurants, bars, shops, campgrounds, windsurfing, discos, are described by information from Union des Commercants, F-83146 Île du Levant.

CAVALAIRE

Cavalaire—Pointe de La Nasque. Cavalaire (not to be confused with nearby Cavaliére) has a nude beach accessed across from the Bon Porteau Campground (rated ****, 9464 0324). Take N 559 south from Cavalaire-sur-Mer, park at Bon Porteau and walk toward the beach, as you pass the concessions, take a right along a very stony ascending path so rugged that many choose to enter the water at the family beach, to swim around the rocks. The nudes gather toward La Nasque Point to the south.

ST.-TROPEZ BEACHES

St.-Tropez—Ramatuelle—Plage de Pampelonne. The ancient fishing village St.-Tropez set an example to the youth of the Côte d'Azur in the mid-1950s thanks to Brigitte Bardot, rock musicians and other creative rebels. Nudity was a big part of the "St.-Tropez scene," started by topfree women at Plage de Pampelonne in 1964. Bardot fled the tourist throngs in 1990. The new St.-Tropez mayor caters to conservatives and has "banned nudity." Is naturism finished? No.

Clothes-free fashion was rare enough, in this style-setting town, even at its media zenith. Topfree cannot be stopped in St.-Tropez. And full nudity occurs just east, on the Ramatuelle peninsula where it has flourished since the mid-1960s at several places including Plage de

Pampelonne, located southeast of St.-Tropez town on the Ramatuelle peninsula. It's a 3-mile stretch of granular sand; much of it is broken into small private sub-beaches and only a small portion in the center of the Pampelonne public beach gets nude use. To find it, get on the eastern shore road that parallels the Baie de Pampelonne and look among the many beach signs for **Liberty** beach/restaurant. Turn off toward beach and park (pay small fee).

Just south of Liberty are **Neptune, Le Blouch** and **Kon-Tiki,** all restaurant-and-lounge concessions encouraging nudity and all owned by Norbert Luftman, who recently built similar beach bar-restaurants at Orient Bay on St.-Martin, see *N* 13.1, p. 41. Kon-Tiki has an off-beach, clothed RV-and-camping area (rental units too) that is ideal for your stay. The entire Plage de Pampelonne may be strolled nude but in practice, you'll want to rent a lounge chair at one of these establishments.

Or try the "wild" nuding at **Cap Cartaya, Cap Taillat** and **Plage de l'Escalet.** Cap Camarat is reached by going south on the road backing the Plage de Pampelonne, then turning left (east) where the road west leads into Ramatuelle. At Cap Camarat find the free parking for Plage de l'Escalet. Walk west through a parking lot that requires a fee. Walk down steps on to the small, gorgeous cove beaches of Plage de l'Escalet, then walk east to find nude, rocky coves before reaching the Cap Camarat lighthouse.

Plage de Briande is a clothing-optional beach with a bay-like cove and shallow, crystal waters. Get there by taking D-61 to Ramatuelle and continue to look for Plage de l'Escalet signs. Park west at Plage de l'Escalet and walk a half hour to the beach, past Cap Cartaya. The beach is within the Domaine du Conservatoise.

Fréjus—St. Aygulf Plage. From the road from Fréjus to Fréjus-Plage turn south on D-98, cross two bridges to town line with St.-Aygulf. At Snack Bar Sammoa instantly turn around, park in lot on right, walk 300 m north to official Fréjus naturist beach—of fine sand and lifeguarded, posted for nude recreation, and nice rollers come in. Shallow enough for children to enjoy, sandy all the way out to where you can swim. Neat backdrop of a high-rise coastline eastward toward Cannes.

CANNES

Cannes enforces a nudity ban. This limits seamless tanning to la Pointe du Dragon on l'Île Sainte-Marguerite, reached by boat from le Suquet. There's also Pointe Fourcade between Cannes–Golfe Juan. Most of the rocky 2 km between Pointe Fourcade and Pointe-de-l'Aube also gets nude use. The

small areas of sand are usually crowded during summer months. Most annoying here are the loud trains passing through next to the beach. To get there, take National 7 (N7) road that hugs the coastline. There are no train stops near the Pointe.

Pointe du Cap Roux—Le Trayas, on the D-98 Corniche de L'Esterel road between St. Raphael and Cannes lies the massive Esterel outcrop plunging into the sea. The coves, creeks and rocks off the road get nude use. The coves at **Théoule** between Pointe St. Marc and Pointe Aiguille also get nude use but access is difficult.

CAP DE NICE

On the old Riviera, Cap de Nice gets the most nude exposure, partly because Nice is a port from which many sail to that nude haven, Corsica. Recommended is the Eze-sur-Mer beach. Follow the road to Monaco. The clothes-optional beach, **Plage Pissarelle,** is reached beyond the Eze-sur-Mer exit on the way to Cap d'Ail, 1 km from Cap Estel. Bus 100, which goes along the Lower Corniche from Nice to Menton, will drop you about 100 m beyond the old Fina station. The sign across the street, "Domaine des Pissarelle" is visible if driving from the east. Walk directly opposite the station to a road (signed Pissarelle), leading down to above the beach. There is parking for only a few cars; park and walk 40–50 m to beach where mostly gays, some singles/families can be found relaxing in the nude. It is a must to visit nearby Eze Village which perches alone on a mountaintop.

Some of the peninsulas in the Cap de Nice-Monaco area get nude use. Try the western portion of the southern tip of **St. Jean Cap Ferrat** peninsula. From the tip (southern part of Cap Ferrat lighthouse) of the peninsula, continue walking west on the pathway that circumnavigates it. Look for isolated trails leading down to the sea. It is all rocky—there are no real beaches.

Youth hostel in Cap d'Ail, the convenient rail station and 35 minutes walk from the beach. Naturist camping, 45 minutes from Nice International Airport at **Club Origin,** Côte d'Azur, c/o Nat'Azur, 23 Ave. Jean Médecin, F-06000 Nice. Phone 9305 0600. Want to rub bare elbows with the yacht set? Neptune III, 20 Quai Lunel, F-06300 Nice.

CORSICA

After World War II, naturists were still searching for subtropical strands where officials would accept their social nudity. Corsican developers were trying to think of a tourist market that could be attracted to this

somewhat remote destination, off the Côte d'Azur but closer to Italy, where rugged terrain makes farming and manufacture difficult.

Voilá! Vacationing Naturists! The east coast around San Nicolao (central) and Porto Vecchio (south) was given over to clothes-free campgrounds. Northern Europeans flocked in, enchanted by snowcapped peaks, meadows of wild flowers, ancient ruins, yet lovely beaches.

Rarely do Americans visit Corsica; we miss some of Europe's finest long sand beaches, great weather lacking mistral gusts, and low prices. Skinny-Dip Tours books Corsica: phone 1-800-828-9356.

Fly into Bastia or Figary—not Ajaccio, it's on the wrong side of a 10,000-foot mountain range. Perhaps hire an airport car or book a car ferry; you'll want to see the island. Be sure to go nude only where prescribed; Corsican nationalists fiercely dislike foreign tourists, especially the naked ones.

BAIE DE GIUNCHETU

Along the north coast from Cap Côrse west to Calvi are many secluded lovely coves, including a favorite, Baie de Giunchetu, west from L'Île-Rousse.

☞ The train from L'Île-Rousse to Palaga takes you to Baie de Giunchetu beach; or by auto, follow N 199 from L'Île-Rousse to Algajola, then signs for Le Bodri campground. Park at Le Bodri and walk to Botre Beach, then by goat trail over the rocks southwesterly; the naturist cove is at the tip of Punta di Ginebre.

Another recommendation: **Anse de Peraiola,** near Santo-Pietro-di-Trenda, east of L'Île-Rousse. Follow D 81 to where it bends with an overlook of the water; park well off the road and descend to the beach, then walk out of sight of this road. Or continue on D 81 and exit at Casta, following directions to Saleccia, and then find the turnoff for Faggiola Cove, reached by a 12-km trail.

At the main beach of **Calvi** is a restaurant, Le Plein Soleil, with a nude sunbathing roof terrace; get your cold beer here!

CLUB CORSICANA

Club Corsicana is the largest Corsican naturist facility with 530 chalets, largely filled by German tour organizers. Guests share a 4-mile beach with Tropica and other naturist resorts—there's enough beach, and beach restaurants, for everyone! (Cf. *N,* 9.3) Club Corsicana: Linguizzeta, F-20230 San Nicolao, Côrse, France. Phone (95) 38 80 25. Or Tropica, 20230-San Nicolao, Côrse, France. Phone (95) 38 80 71.

SAN NICOLAO

North of Aleria, the town of San Nicolao focalizes a number of naturist campgrounds. Access is by ferry or airport via Bastia. Drive 60 km south on Route 193 to 198, and look for signs to the campgrounds on your left.

Continuing south beyond San Nicolao find the friendly **Club Bagheera** and **Riva Bella,** with lodgings, restaurants and minimarts that U.S. travelers usually require. Club Bagherra, F-20230 San Nicolao, Côrse, France. Phone (95) 38 83 20; fax (95) 38 83 47. Riva Bella, F-20270 Aleria, Côrse, France. Phone (95) 38 81 10 or (95) 38 85 97; fax (95) 38 91 29.

PORTO VECCHIO

High-priced, well-appreciated for its efficiency and development by largely German clientele, **Club La Chiappa** resort has panoramic restaurant, sauna, barber, laundromat, minimart, water sports, lawn games, nightly dances. F-20137 Porto Vecchio, Côrse, France. Phone (95) 70 00 31.

Aptly-named, Porto Vecchio harbored **Villata,** the earliest naturist camp on Corsica. Primarily a campground for the young on a beautiful beach, with some bungalows. Villata is tranquil, self-contained. Villata, F-20144 Ste. Lucie de Porto Vecchio, Côrse, France. Phone (95) 71 62 90.

Ten kilometers inland is **U'Furo,** formerly Au Moulen; the only naturist complex that is not on the coast. The "wild" landscape of water and rocks rewards a drive even if you do not stay at the Mill. U'Furo, Route de Nota, F-20137 Porto Vecchio, Côrse, France. Phone (95) 70 58 05.

At the southern tip is the wildly awesome Capo di Feno with its Camping-Club **Les Amis de Neptune.** F-20169 Bonifacio. Phone (95) 73 00 80. Scuba, restaurant, lodgings. Only one ferry a week.

Karl H. Reddies, The Beach At Club Corsicana.

192

GERMANY

Bone-chilled Germans began heading for the Mediterranean some 1,800 years ago, but were stopped by Roman legions. Since 1950 an estimated 12 million Germans, seeking nude beaches for their holidays, have resumed heading south. Innkeepers of Yugoslavia, Corsica, Turkey, the Baléaric and Canary Islands, Crete, southern France and Italy are pleased.

Germans also look to the Caribbean, even to repressive Florida, for *Freikörperkultur*—FKK, or free body culture—vacations. They visit their own lakes and north coast for sun. Not to overlook the luxurious indoor/outdoor, sauna/swim/ fitness leisure centers that now serve many German cities.

Less and less do they join the clubs of the German FKK Association (DFK), which is floundering.

Acceptance grew during a century. In 1904, Richard Ungewitter wrote the manifesto, *Die Nacktheit* (Nakedness). It grew out of 19th Century health ideas and focused an organized movement worldwide. Ungewitter put morals and history, art and health in a new light.

Deutscher Verband für Freikörperkultur E.V, Uhlemeyerstrasse 14, D-30175

Hannover 1. Phone (0511) 34 22 33; fax (0511) 318 08 38. Its magazine is *Freikörperkultur*. For more information, obtain the *INF Guide* for club data in symbols and English.

NORDSEE

EAST FRISIAN ISLANDS

Borkum Island. Westernmost of the East Frisian Islands. Easily reached from Holland, Borkum has a 1,200-m FKK beach of 100-m depth in walking distance of the ferry port at Emden, with toilets/showers, shops, playground, lifeguards, and even a beach for those nude people who prefer the company of nude dogs. May 15–October 1. Kurverwaltung, PF 1680, D-26742 Borkum. Phone (04922) 30301.

Norderney Island. A bus runs to the lighthouse FKK beach on the north

shore, 7 km from Norderney town—lifeguards, toilets, restaurant at the Oase. 20,000 tourist beds on the island 1 hour by boat from Norden–Norddeich. DFK Norderney, PF 1148, D-26533 Norderney. Phone (04932) 8910.

Helgoland. The northernmost and most distant East Frisian island, served from Hamburg by Elbe River packet and by air. It has a remarkable history—from Viking outpost to Nazi submarine base—indeed, the British bombed it to smithereens *after* World War II. Nothing old stands, but the beaches deserve an excellent reputation, including the free beach in the north shore dunes. Bungalows, camping nearby. Rent a bike; no vehicles on Helgoland except minibuses and electric cars. Ferry service connects with offshore nude bathing islets and Cuxhaven. Kurverwaltung, Postfach Rathaus, D-27498 Helgoland. Phone (04725) 701.

ELBE RIVER MOUTH

The "hooks" of the Elbe River delta are convenient for northwest Germany. Caution: If you want to swim, choose a high tide. The mudflats exposed at low tide are amazing.

Cuxhaven. Spa town on south shore of the Elbe. North from Bremen. FKK was earlier confined to the remote "nude dunes" between the Duhnen and Döse campgrounds. This area has expanded; moreover, Neu-Nackeduhnien are on the tidal Wattenmeer, at the south end of Duhn beach. Visit on Tuesday, and from 5:30 you can enjoy FKK night at a grand local sauna/pool complex. Kurverwaltung, Cuxhavener Str., D-27476 Cuxhaven. Phone (04721) 404.

Cappel-Neufeld/Nordholz—Familien Ferienplatz. Opened in 1984 by the DFK, on the Wattenmeer between Bremerhaven and Cuxhaven. Tent/RV sites, playground, volleyball, North Sea access. Bahnhofstr. 50, D-27637 Nordholz. Phone (0421) 874385; fax (04206) 6214.

Büsum—Westerdeichstrich. North of the Elbe near Büsum. The town's grassy 700-m FKK beach with camping is reached from Hamburg by Routes 5 and 23. Parking, showers. Kurverwaltung, D-25761 Westerdeichstrich. Phone (04834) 2336.

NORTH FRISIANS

From the Elbe River mouth north to Denmark, the North Frisian Islands offer:

Pellworm. The northwest shore on Hök-Hallig near Nordermühle is FKK. Showers/toilets. Ferry from Nordstrand. Kurverwaltung, D-25849 Pellworm. Phone (04844) 544.

Amrum. Windswept dunes and broad beaches enjoy the FKK overflow from neighboring Sylt on the **Nebel** town beach at the north. Phone (04682) 544: the southern section of **Norddorf** town beach. Phone 811: south of the Frisian village **Süddorf**; and **Wittdün DFK campsite,** D-25946 Wittdün, phone 2406. Ferry from Dagebüll.

Föhr Island—Goting Beach. With 13,000 beds for tourists, Föhr's Old Frisian character competes vigorously with Sylt's night life. On the main Sandkasten beach, 1 km is reserved for FKK at Nieblum-Goting-am-Wikinger, with lifeguard, showers, beach chairs—amenities not everywhere supplied to naked people. Dagebüll ferry departures to Amrum Island also serve Föhr. Car ferry, phone (04681) 701. Kurverwaltung, D-25938 Wyk. Phone 3040.

SYLT ISLAND

At the Danish border, the most northerly of the Frisians, Sylt is a historic outpost of Naturism and High Society. From the 1850s Westerland's Dr. Jenner urged nude bathing upon his patients. Over 70% of today's tourists do choose FKK. If southern climes now attract many younger beachgoers Sylt more than survives, retaining FKK sophisticates with *la dolce vita:* lifeguards, cabanas, windbreaks/chairs, beach

showers, refreshments, convenient lodgings, and night life.

Access is over a causeway on a train which can take cars. The first town you reach is **Westerland** with a beautiful beach and an FKK section a 50-minute stroll south. Concerts, mudbaths, tennis, shopping, discos. Kurbetrieb, D-25980 Westerland. Phone (04651) 81224. No camping. Lodging: phone 24001, fax 24060.

Driving south, **Rantum** has two FKK beaches, Samoa, phone (04651) 26504; and Zanzibar, phone 6128 (do the names make you warmer?).

Hörnum, farther south, has an FKK beach a 15-minute walk from the village. Kurverwaltung, D-25997 Hörnum. Phone (04653) 1065.

Driving north: north of **Wenningstedt** is a 1,000-m nude beach beneath cliffs. Camping available. Kurverwaltung, D-25996 Wenningstedt. Phone (04651) 41081. Lodging: phone 41892.

The next north, elegant **Kampen** has 3 km of nude beach beneath red cliffs reaching north and south of a clothed central beach. Riding stables. Kurverwaltung and lodging, D-25999 Kampen. Phone (04651) 41091.

Northernmost, **List** has an excellent FKK beach to its west, served by town trails and buses. Kurverwaltung, D-25992 List. Phone (04652) 1015.

BALTIC COAST (OSTSEE)

Beaches are the great holiday attraction of Germany's northeastern (Baltic) coast and islands. This Ostsee region extends between the Danish and Polish borders.

For 40 years, much of it, from Travemünde to the Polish border, lay in East Germany (GDR). Almost every town has an FKK beach, some 90 sites serving 200,000 campers/lodgers annually; more FKK than textile beaches. A GDR poll found 57% of the population approving of nude recreation, 30% had no opinion, and only 13% opposed.

Until 1990, GDR-led factory and sports federations organized affordable family vacations at campgrounds, often with mixed-use beaches attached. The "last word" on these GDR beaches was *FKK Zwischen Ostsee und Vogtland* by Friedrich Hagen (VEB Tourist Verlag, Leipzig, 1987).

Reservations like Prerow should be placed early with Campingzentrum Ostsee, Barther Str. 64b, D-18437 Stralsund. Phone 5015.

GLÜCKSBURG AREA

Holnis Peninsula—Glücksburg Beach. North of Glücksburg at Holnis town on the Flensburger Fjord, Germany's northern border with Denmark, is an FKK beach and camping. Kurverwaltung, Sandwigstr. 1-A, D-24960 Glücksburg. Phone (04631) 921.

Gelting—Gammeldamm Beach. From Glücksburg east on Route #199 to the hook of Flensburg Fjord. At Gelting continue east to Falshöft village. The famous nude beach now has campsites, toilets. Phone (04643) 777.

Schönhagen—Camping Seestern. South from Gelting and north from Eckernförde, a very pleasant FKK camping/beach. Bungalow/RV rentals. Camping Seestern, D-24398 Karby. Phone (04644) 305.

KIEL BAY

Straight north from Hamburg to Ostsee.

Eckernförde Bay southside has a 1-km FKK beach below the Hohenhain cliffs, between Dänisch-Nienhof and Surendorf. From Kiel take B-503 north to Dänisch-Nienhof via Sprenge. Spot the towns of Eckerholm and Hopenheim and look for clustered parked cars; the beach is nearby. Kurverwaltung, P.F. 1440, D-2330 Eckernförde. Phone (04351) 90520.

Another west Kiel Bay spot is **Schilksee,** below the bluff at the coastal radio station.

Wendtorf Beach on the east bay draws up to 4,000 naturists on a good weekend. From Kiel, B-502 toward Schönberg to the Marina Wendtorf turnoff, and park in the day lot (no charge). Walk along the dike toward Bottsand 1,200 m. A nature preserve. Verkehrsverein, Strandstr., D-2304 Wendtorf. Phone (04343) 631.

LÜBECK AREA

North of Lübeck, **Behrensdorf Beach** has broad sands and a romantic setting. Drive 10 km from Lütjenburg to Behrensdorf Strand, park, walk just 150 m from the textile section and you're clothes-free—all the way, if you choose, for 10 km to Lippe. Verkehrsamt, Alte Dorfstr. 17, D-24321 Behrensdorf. Phone (04381) 286.

Weissenhäuser Strand is a class resort on Hohwachter Bay reached by E-4 via Wangels…with an all-comfort FKK beach just down the strand. Lifeguards, the ubiquitous wicker chairs (*Körbe*), restaurant, sports, accommodations. Kurverwaltung, D-2440 Weissenhäuser. Phone (04361) 490 731.

Fehmarn Island. E-4 takes you all the way. Three campgrounds have FKK beaches: **Wallnau Camping** with 1,100 sites and a mile-long beach. Mehnert Camping, D-23769 Wallnau. Phone (04372) 456. **Camping Wulfener Hals**

with 515 tent/RV sites plus rental bungalows, near Burg in the west, rated ****. D-2449 Wulfen. Phone 4250.

Textilcamping Fehmarnbelt near Altenteil in the northwest. D-23769 Dänschendorf. Phone 445. Kurverwaltung, D-23769 Burg auf Fehmar. Phone (04371) 4011.

Neustadt Bay—Pelzerhaken Beach. Between Neustadt (north of Lübeck by E-207) and Rettin, the sandy Pelzerhakenstrand has 40,000 sq m of officially FKK beach on its south. Beach showers. Fitness center next to beach. Convenient parking. Nearby camping. Kurverwaltung, D-23730 Pelzerhaken. Phone (04561) 7011.

Neustadt—Scharbeutz Beach. South of Neustadt on the bay, Scharbeutz lies between the harbor and the Timmendorf city limits. About 200 m long.

Grömitz Beach north of Neustadt was quietly pioneered by local FKK people. As nudity became accepted, municipal authority began to supply services. Kurverwaltung, D-23743 Grömitz. Phone (04562) 520.

DFK-Familiengelände "Erhard Wächtler." North of Grömitz, a German Naturist Federation FKK family shore camp. A 1,200-m beach. Rental cabins. Tent/RV sites. Minimart, snack bar. Must obtain INF card. D-23749 Grube (Rosenfelde). Phone (04365) 222; fax (04365) 7574.

Travemünde. East across the Lübeck Bay from Neustadt, Travemünde gained notoriety as "the nude beach under barbed wire, machine guns and searchlights" because located at the border with the GDR. Guards' binoculars were believed to sweep the FKK beach intently. Perhaps for this reason, Travemünde's nude section has been highly popular. Kurverwaltung, Auenallee 10-A, D-23570 Travemünde. Phone (04502) 84362.

WISMAR BAY

Wismar, the first major city east of the old GDR border.

Hohen Wieschendorf Beach. Northwest of Wismar. Very popular beach despite a knee-high depth for 400 m out and little shade. Why? The water warms rapidly; children are safe; the 1.5-km beach is sandy; wild camping is allowed. Facilities, water, restaurant in the village. Preferred campground 6 km away at Wohlenberg Wiek, Gramkow, has 2,100 capacity.

Kühlungsborn—Rerik Beach. Southwest of Warnemünde–Rostock, north of Wismar, reached by a road off Route 105 from Heiligendamm to Kühlungsborn, is Rerik FKK beach. Ostseebad Camping has 1500 capacity.

ROSTOCK BEACHES

The most-frequented FKK beach on the "GDR Baltic" is at southwest Fischland, between Graal Müritz and Markgrafenheide campsites—northeast of Rostock and Warnemünde. Parking provided; camping at Rosenort, 1 km away. Strong undertow.

DARSS PENINSULA

Darss—Prerow. North of Rostock. Access from Ribnitz-Damgarten. Fine nude beaches at Arenshoop, Fischland West, and Prerow. Don't miss the Darsser Heimatmuseum.

Only Prerow Beach has a legal FKK campground, with its 4,300 capacity usually full—and that directly on the 5-km beach, with good sand, no pebbles, and sheltered from cool westerly winds by the Darss town highland, while currents warm the coastal waters. Blueberry picking in the Darss Woods from mid-July. Post office, minimart.

Day visitors to FKK beach must park a mile before reaching it, on Bernsteinweg.

RÜGEN ISLAND

Rügen, largest of the Baltic islands, has a number of FKK beaches along its 570-km sand coast. Relatively "undiscovered," Rügen is still an uncommercialized haven. Drive northeast of Rostock by way of Stralsund and across the Rügendamm causeway.

Rappin Beach. An FKK beach at Gr. Banzelwitz on an inlet of the Ostsee, Rappin has a swampy coast and a bog inland. However, it abuts camping Zeltplatz Rappin (phone 0131) and is popular with water sports fans.

Schaabe Beach is a thin 6-km-long crescent of wooded dunes on the Tromper Wiek, a relatively sheltered and sunny landbridge between the towns of Breege and Glowe. The Schaabe is of fine sand with no stones, a delightful 6-minute stroll from the parking through a woods. It draws FKK bathers from afar. Some field toilets provided. Camping at Glowe (phone 0128). Recommended parking is on the second lot when driving northwest from Glowe. Public bus A-404 and A-419 to Glowe.

Vitt, northeast from Breege, is a fine ancient village, well worth a visit, although the stoney beach is difficult to reach.

Dranske-Nonnevitz Beach on the northern coast west from Breege, is a lovely and popular strand with high cliffs and a view that draws regulars (phone 0126). A 15-minute walk through the woods and campgrounds from the parking. Try to reserve in campsite areas I to III.

Thiessow Camping at the southeast point has a fine 2-km white sand FKK beach. Thousands, primarily families, throng to the beach to claim windbreaks as the sun appears or wind drops and vendors appear. Camping behind beach at Zeltplatz Thiessow (phone 0136) or 1 km away at Zeltplatz Middelhagen-Lobbe (phone 0136). It's a 2-minute hike through woods from the parking. Frequent breezes and waves here, and a view of ship traffic.

HIDDENSEE ISLAND

In the 1920s Hiddensee had a colony of artists-nudists. FKK is now on 1.5 km of the west shore, south of Neuendorf village. Windy; keep out of dunes. No autos allowed. Park in the crowded lot at Schaprode on Rügen to take ferry over. Or take "the white fleet" from Stralsund harbor.

USEDOM ISLAND

Usedom Island is at the Polish border, directly north from Berlin on E-6 and Route 197; or drive east from Rostock. Most-loved, 3-km FKK beach lies between Zempin and Koserow campgrounds.

An 1,100-camper "village," largest on the east Baltic, lies between Bansin and Ückeritz. FKK beach of 2 km has permanent volleyball courts, even private permanent windbreak screens.

FRANKFURT AM MAIN

THE FIRST OF GERMANY

For many who fly to Germany, Frankfurt will be the gateway to first impressions:

Langener Waldsee with its grassy lawn sloping to the 500-m lake, is large enough to host windsurfer and sailing regattas. On a fine day, hundreds enjoy the clean FKK beach (there's also a small separate textile beach). Toilets, showers, snack bar, large parking lot. June–Sept. Take B-44 south from Frankfurt to E-451 junction and Walldorf exit. Take overpass east. Find the sandpits behind the Langener Sand Company.

Badesee Walldorf. If you don't cross B-44 after exiting it, you're in Walldorf. Park on street southeast of B-44 intersection with Aschaffenburgerstr. Badesee north shore is FKK.

Grueneburg Park. At lunchtime on

Leif Heilberg, Rügen Island, Baltic Coast, 1985.

hot days as downtown office workers pour into this park, the dress code goes south.

Morfelden Kiesgruben—about 10 km south of Frankfurt near the city of Morfelden has many quarries outside of town with wonderful freshwater springs. Cool water but feels great. Many city pools in Frankfurt have at least one day a week for clothing-optional swimming.

Bad Homburg—Taunus Therme. Plan a layover at this temple of body indulgence. It's northwest of Frankfurt, public transportation goes. The upper level is all FKK: a "Finnish sauna world" with 6 cabins of varying temperature; 2 sauna pools, a sauna-bar; "Irish-Roman" steambath; indoor and outdoor pools linked by canal; "Japanese" solarium; 150 face-tanners, massage, travel agency, restaurant and bar. Elsewhere: cinemas, gym, waterfalls, spas, fountains, barbecue terrace, and more. Moderately-priced hotels nearby. Phone (06172) 43076.

Hattstein Schloss. Hattstein Castle in the Taunus Hills has a small, popular FKK pond in a forest clearing. Ask at the castle park, the access eludes summary.

BERLIN AREA

In 1987, on the advice of its lawyers, the City of West Berlin ceased to fine for "bathing in public without a bathing suit." No longer would the police pronounce on what is "decent" and what is **"contrary to community standards of dress."** (*FKK, 1/1988*).

BERLIN PARKS

For 40 years the Berlin Wall severed West Berlin naturist clubs from their grounds, famous in the 1920s, dormant in the Hitler years. However, clothes-optional was accepted by the West Berlin Senate at a number of sites. Nudity also continued on the communist side. West Berlin parks had well-known free-sun areas years before the City acted:

Halensee, Rathenauplatz, offers a small FKK beach between the radio tower and the highway access road; to its north, a huge sunning meadow with up to 2,000 nudes on a sunny day.

Nearly a third of the total beach at **Tegeler See** is now in nude use.

Grunewaldsee has sandy terraces for nude sunbathing as you walk the lakeshore. The Grunewald Castle art museum is on the walk, and a "hunting-lodge" restaurant with terrace awaits at the parking.

Teufelsee is a small nude lake on a tidy trail deep in the woods, with a snack van.

At a parking lane for walking into Teufelsee is FKK sports club **Helios**—mostly for members—telephoning could open the gate to use of its competition-level heated pool, tennis, table tennis, and volleyball. Im Jagen 57/58, D-14193 Berlin. Phone (030) 301 75 76. A 10-minute walk from S-Bahnhof Grunewald.

Berlin tourist information will supply indoor FKK swims and emerging lake sites.

WANNSEE BEACH

The beach of choice for Berlin's clothed bathers over the years, Wannsee is increasingly nude although the original area remains textile. Truly a cross-section of Berlin. Chairs rented, beach showers, pier, swans, wading paddle-ball, snacks and beer. In the southwest and readily reached by urban transit.

VEREIN DER SAUNAFREUNDE

This Band of Sauna Friends offers much more than a sauna at its relaxing, happy family club on a lush and large lake, Heiligensee, in Berlin's northwest suburbs. Diving board, beach shower, fishing, windsurfing, boules, tennis, volleyball, snacks, children's playground. Camping. Day guests welcomed. Süderholmer Steig 3, D-13503 Berlin. Phone (030) 431 10 79.

MÜGGELSEE BEACH

Strandbad Grosser Müggelsee in "East Berlin" is a large suburban lake with birch, oak and pine trees and sloping sun meadows on a sandy shore. It's reachable by urban transit or by private boat via Berlin's waterways—and this is well, since parking is very limited, and up to 15,000 may be on the FKK west end plus

Germany

textile use at original facility. Many boats anchor offshore to join in. FKK biergarten, snacks, volleyball, Ping-Pong, children's gym, bowling, giant chess/checkers, lifeguards. A "must do!"

Want your Müggelsee wilder? Get off trolley at stop before the "pay" FKK beach. Or wade around a fence west of the pay beach. The wild beach predates 1965, its core bathers establishing the broader nude acceptance.

☞ From Friedrichstrasse Bahnhof, take the S-Bahn in direction of Erkner, get off at Friedrichshagen station. Cross under viaduct and street to take #25 tram. It follows the S-Bahn track farther. At fifth stop, get off and cross tracks to FKK Beach gatehouse. Or get off at fourth stop and go through woods to shore without paying. You can also drive from Friedrichshagen station east on Fürstenwalder Damm to the sign and parking.

EUROPA CENTER THERMEN

This fine, large penthouse spa in downtown Berlin is clothing-optional. Outdoor heated canal pool with sundeck and city view (office workers may also observe the sundeck), 4 Finnish saunas, cold plunge, 2 Russo-Roman steam baths, table tennis, billiards, backgammon, chess, exercise room, TV lounge, massage, sunlamps, bar, restaurant, large indoor pool. Parking discount at Europa Center Parkhaus (the spa is on the roof). From 10 a.m. daily. Nürnbergerstr. 7, D-10787 Berlin. Phone 261 60 31.

BLUB PARADISE

BLUB, Berliner Luft-und Badparadies, in the southeast Neukölln district, offers an extravagant family water park. FKK garden, hot whirlpool, pool, 4 saunas with a bar, fireplace, quiet rooms, tanning center, massage. Water slide, wild water canal, rock caverns and waterfall, huge central pool, wave pool, geyser, exercise center, hydrobics and aerobics—some clothing-optional. Take #7 U-bahn to Grenzallee, walk 10 minutes to BLUB. Buses 41 and 73 stop at entrance. Free parking. Buschkrugallee 64, D-12359 Berlin. Phone 606 60 60.

POTSDAM: CECILIENHOF

Thousands now sun in the grass and swim nude in the Heiligensee, a willow-and-birch-surrounded lake at Cecilienhof, a country mansion where Churchill, Stalin and Roosevelt signed their

Germany

Potsdam Agreement in 1945.

Next to Sans Souci, the wonderful pleasure park of Frederick the Great, Cecilienhof is the leading attraction of Potsdam. Both are worth your visit; a full day is hardly enough time. You may get to Potsdam and Cecilienhof by taking the southwest expressway, or an intercity bus or excursion boat from Berlin.

DRESDEN

VOLKERSDORF

Volkersdorf may be the oldest FKK site in continuous use in the world, tracing its origin to around 1900. Beaches, swans, sauna, beer garden, snack bar, minimart, sports. Tent/RV sites available; day visitors welcome. Familiensport-und FKK-Bund, D-01468 Volkersdorf. Phone (035207) 285.

☞ From Berlin, by A-13 to Bärnsdorf exit, north of Dresden; continue through Volkersdorf to Niederen Waldteich.

BAVARIA

This is the fun-loving province. How are you gonna keep Bavarians in Lederhosen after they've been clothes-free? Munich Mayor Dr. Scarnagel was confronted by an opponent with a photo of himself naked, taking part in a "chicken fight" in the pool of a local FKK club. Scarnagel endorsed it as his campaign photo.

Voters re-elected him.

Public opinion polls cue Bavarian officials that nudity is here to stay. An Isar River cruise passenger complained about nude bathers along the bank. It became a tourism issue. Instead of banning nudity from such public areas, the Ministry of the Interior instructed boatsmen to issue "nude alerts"—asking passengers who might be offended to look the other way.

MUNICH

Today, Germans from all walks of life may relax, topfree or fully nude, in more or less discreet areas of the city parks throughout the nation.

Munich led the way by its decision (1981) to accommodate naked people within urban public settings. The officially accepted areas for sunbathing without a stitch were published in the June 4, 1985 *Münchner Stadtanzeiger* as follows:

Feldmochinger See—In north Munich; at the southwest end of the lake. Parking at the Karlsfelder-Str. access. Toilets, refreshments.

Englischer Garten—It's twice the size of New York's Central Park. Nude sunbathing is at the north end, at a meadow—the "Schwabing Bucht"—on the west side of a loop of the chilly brook that runs through the English Garden. East of U-bahn station Studentenstadt. Southwest of Aumeister Biergarten.

Oberföhring Island—On the east shore of the Isar River, facing the northern part of English Garden. FKK from the English Garden footbridge at Mittlere-Isar-Str. north.

Schönfeldwiese—An oval field within a riding track, north of the Haus der Kunst at the south end of the Englischer Garten. (In practice, this nude area has often expanded.) The art museum is on Prince Regent Street, a main concourse. U-bahn station Universität, walk east. Next to the Japanese Teahouse.

South Isar River— (1) Along the dike ("Wehrsteg") in the river south from the **Marienklause Bridge** in city center at Lukas Kirche. (And in practice, often north of it on the south end of Praterinsel, and along Zellstr. on the facing east bank of the Isar, north of the Volksbad.) S-bahn Isartor and walk east. (2) Along the dike on the east bank of Isar, from Braunau Railway bridge south to **Brudermühle Bridge** (the Flaucher Island crossing of the Mittlerer Ring). Blue line bus #45, or U-bahn to Implerstr. and walk east. (3) Farther south along the Isar, sunbathing informally continues at Hellabrunn Zoo (bus #52).

Munich Police Chief Manfred Schreiber said that citations for provocative nudity would be issued only in "the gravest cases."

Curiously, many expected the Bavarian Naturist Federation to lead the expansion of nude rights—in fact, it disassociated itself, saying: "It is not our goal to turn everyone into a naturist…it would be a shame should the undisciplined, "wild nudity" in public places create a mistaken impression of naturism for authorities." Fortunately, others led, and led well.

MUNICH AREA
Munich south—

Hollman: Man With Medicine Ball, Berlin 1940.

Composer Kurt Weill & Boys, Berlin FKK Grounds, 1920s.

northeastern Unterföhring—an S-bahn stop—on fine weekends to enjoy nude windsurfing on Lake Fertinga. From Nördliches Moos, near the S-3 intersection, cross south on Gleissach under the Ostumgehung Autobahn to parking at the peninsula. Near ZDF Television. Toilets, refreshments.

Munich—Amperland. Friendly DFK naturist club welcomes travelers. On the Amper River by Fürsten-Feldbruck, off A-8; minutes by train northwest from Olympic City. Dormitory, RV rentals, 350 tent/RV sites, open kitchen, restaurant, pool, sports. April–Sept. Postfach 1161, D-82275 Emmering. Phone (08141) 43600.

DIVERSE INLAND BEACHES & BATHS

HAMBURG AREA

Hamburg—gateway to the **Schleswig-Holstein** peninsula, which is, next after Bavaria, Germany's top vacation region. FKK beaches ring its Nordsee and Ostsee coasts, Kiel Bay and Lübeck Bay.

Hamburg—Volksdorf. Visit the DFK's lake in the woods. Clubhouse, sauna, volleyball, tennis, badminton, bowling, gymnastics, folk dances, disco, youth club. RV park but no tent sites. June–Sept. Metro Buchenkamp then bus 174, exit Farenkoppel. HFK Hamburg Bund für FKK und Familiensport EV, Moorbekweg 100, 22359 Hamburg 67. Phone (040) 603 47 30. Also try FUN-Familiensport-und Naturistik Verein Hamburg, Dortstr., D-21514 Fitzen. Phone (04155) 5129.

Hamburg—Hallenbad Holtenhusen. The popular sauna-spa goes FKK on Sat.–Sun. after 7:30 p.m. Subway U-I to Kellinghusenstr.; exit the station left.

Staffelsee—Murnau Freibad. On the west-shore peninsula of Lake Staffel is a nude beach. Park on the eastern shore at the Murnau Freibad and walk around.

Wolfratshausen—Pupplinger Au. Naturist bonfire picnics are a custom; make up a party. On a summer evening friends and families gather black bread, cheese, radishes, and beer and drive 33 km south of Munich on the autobahn to Garmisch-Partenkirchen. Turn off, drive to Wolfratshausen, then follow the signs to Puppling (Iking). Park where the bridge crosses the Isar or at the nearby inn. Ask where the trail begins to the Pupplinger Au river flats, in the forest preserve on the banks of the Isar.

Seeshaupt—Ostersee. From Seeshaupt, drive in direction of Penzberg; after 1 km park at entrance to Lauterbachmühle. Walk around Lake Oster 10 minutes to the site.

Munich north—

Fertingasee. Nude bathers flock to

Germany

St. Peter—Ording. Sand-yachters skitter about this 10-km offshore sandbar. Naturists find their place in the littoral order at the north point (100 ha). Cars may drive over. Camping. Kurverwaltung, PF 100, D-25823 St. Peter–Ording. Phone (04863) 830.

Bremen—Stadtwaldsee. The southeast shore of Bremen's city lake is a legal FKK beach—often with volleyball.

HANNOVER

The Ricklinger Lakes—where Hannoverians go to play—include an official FKK beach on Sieben-Meter-Teich. Playing fields too. Via Südschnellweg.

Hereford—Bad Salzuflen. Four pools (two outside), solarium, FKK meadow, sauna, bowling, fitness room, gardens, restaurant. FKK Sunday 5–8 p.m. Near Hereford, south of Hannover on A-2, Salzuflen exit, follow Badkur signs.

DÜSSELDORF

Unterbacher See is southeast of Düsseldorf. Follow map towards Eller, find Unterbacher See–Südstrand exit. Bus 891 also goes, get off at Vennhauser Allee. Half of the south beach is FKK. Snack van, toilet.

Baggersee entrance is along the Ratingen-to-Kalkum Road; marked "Baggersee;" 1 km west of A-52 intersection. From a grassy parking lot, walk down a paved single-lane road, across a field and through a woods to popular lake.

DARMSTADT

Darmstädter have skinny-dipped for years at Erlensee-bei-Bickenbach. From Darmstadt, B-3 south 10 km to Bickenbach. Follow signs to Bahnhof (rail station), cross tracks, turn left, take overpass above Autobahn, then first right to parking. From Autobahn, exit Seeheim/Jugendheim. Most FKK is on north shore. Toilets, snack bar.

Freizeitgelände Prinz von Hessen (Hessian Sand Pit, a.k.a. Prince Emil's Sand Pit). From Darmstadt City Ring, leave the ruin of the old city theater in direction Dieburg. Pass the Steinbrücker-Teiche park, to the Prinz von Hessen preserve. Parking along the old Dieburgerstrasse. In the middle of the woods, a quiet beach with a nice core group of users.

Darmstadt—Schwimhalle. Downtown on Landgraf Georg Str. FKK swim Sat. p.m.

Pfungstadt—Wellenbad (wave pool), south and west of Darmstadt. FKK Wed. eves.

Orplid. A proud DFK family sports club since 1923, with courts, woods and meadows in northwest Darmstadt. Pool, sauna, restaurant. INF cardholders may visit and lodge. Weiterstädterstr., 150, D-64291Darmstadt-Arheilgen. Phone (06151) 372600.

MANNHEIM

As soon as Weinheim authorities planned to build Germany's first indoor wave pool, area naturists asked for FKK hours. A single nude night was set. The demand raised it to three nights: Saturday, Sunday and Tuesday after 7 p.m. Several saunas, a variety of pools, two restaurants, indoor–outdoor sunbathing, and the famous, mini-lake wave pool.

☞ Heidelberg–Frankfurt Autobahn north from Mannheim and take the first turn into Weinheim, cross the railroad tracks and follow the priority road. In Weinheim, follow signs for Miramar, located on the east end of a lake. The multicolored fabric arches that provide a roof can be seen from the Autobahn. To 10 p.m. daily.

BODENSEE

Bodensee, a.k.a. Lake Constance, is an immense lake at the Swiss border, long

Popular Wannsee Beach in Berlin.

200

favored for vacations. The free beach is between Überlingen and Sipplingen 1 km from where the lake drains; cross the rail tracks from B-30 by a small tunnel.

Konstanz—Freibad Horn. Since 1982 a designated nude beach is accessed by bus #5 from downtown.

BADEN-BADEN

Baden-Baden—Black Forest Spa. Younger Europeans are less likely than their parents to "take the waters" at a spa. Many traditional spa resorts are in trouble, although state of the art therapies and exotic and flamboyant additions do bring customers.

A spa making the transition is venerable Baden-Baden, renaming itself The Black Forest Spa. **Caracall Therme,** a great winter retreat, has indoor/outdoor warm water public baths with an FKK sauna on top deck. Brochure from German National Tourism Office, phone (212) 308-3300. Direct: Augustaplatz 8, D-76530 Baden-Baden.

FREIBURG

Freiburg—Opfingersee. Lake Opfinger is 9 km west of Freiburg, beside the north-south Rhine River Valley autobahn. There's no exit from the Autobahn at this point. So turn off on Opfingerstrasse west

(at first it's called Carl-Kistner-Str.). Just after crossing the Autobahn watch for the turnoff to the right into a parking area at the south end of the lake. Take the path along the east side for about 800 feet to a grassy terrace with shrubbery top shielding the Autobahn. No facilities.

Freiburg—Zähringen Bath. North Freiburg at Lameystr. 4. Phone 216-3771. Nude Sundays, 10–3.

BOCHUM

Aquadome am Ruhrpark. Extravagant water slides and tropical pools, and for naturists, a sauna paradise: five "grotto" choices of dry steam temperatures plus Turkish bath, massage, sun meadow and restaurant. Exit Bochum–Werne from A-2, east of Essen, turn right and follow Aquadome signs.

KASSEL—GÖTTINGEN

Sport-und Freizeitpark Bördel. Brochure in English. Family FKK club welcomes visitors. May–Sept. Nikolaistr. 30, 37127 Dransfelf – Ortsteil Bördel. Phone (05502) 1255.

BONN—COLOGNE

Bonn—Panorama. Every German metro area now has at least one clothes-

free, sauna-spa-pool health wonderland. Blind masseur Josef Schmidt had the vision to create Panorama—6 saunas, 4 hot tubs, galvanic foot bath, Roman-Irish steam bath, sun garden and ponds, heated outdoor pool, buffet, biergarten, massage, beautician, the works! and more; 100,000 happily naked customers annually. From Cologne south by A-1 then A-61 (30 min.), or from Bonn southwest by A-565 (20 min.), exiting at Meckenheim. Via Gelsdorf and Vettelhoven to Grafschaft. D-53501 Grafschaft-Holzweiler. Phone (02641) 34736.

Aachen—Cologne. Heavily-promoted Hotel Zum Walde is 10 miles from Aachen. FKK pool–bar–terrace with meals available, fitness gym, sauna. Klosterstr. 4, D-52224 Stolberg-Zweifall. Phone (02402) 7690; fax (02402) 76910.

ESSEN

From Essen in North Rhineland go north to Münster. From Münster, drive or take a bus north on Schiffahrter Damm towards Greven, turning off in Gelmar, into the village of Gittrup. The Kü is a disused mile-long section of concrete canal crossing the Ems River overhead. Both sides are in nude use and there's a lifeguard but no toilets or other facilities.

GREECE

Greece, in its precocious cultural adolescence some 2,500 years ago, learned how to benefit its citizens by combining nakedness with civilization.

The early Greek influentials saw no shame in displaying a fit body or a fine mind. They preferred their athletics nude and on this basis they invented the Olympic Games. *Gymno* as in *gymnastics* means *naked*.

The glory that was humanistic Greece sets a challenge to modern prophets of fear. Our ecclesiastical and civic authorities may confine the naked body, but they will not eradicate the Greek ideal which lives today in the Naturist idea.

Orthodox Church clerics blocked licensing of naturism in modern Greece until 1981, when elections favored a progressive government. Now a few clothes-free enterprises complement the many nude beaches in the islands.

Naturist contact: Angelos Mimikopoulos, P.O. Box 52 894, GR-14610, Nea Erithrea, Greece. Phone/fax (301) 813 4182.

Further reading, maps: John Dunn, *Sunseekers' Greek Islands*, from Sunseeker Publications, The Barn, Brighton Road, Lower Beeding, West Sussex, RH13 6PT, England.

ATHENS AREA

RAMNOUS BEACH

"Cradle of modern Athenian nude beachgoing" (ca. 1974), according to Angelos Mimikopoulos, it's popular with Athenians who lack money or time for a boat or air transfer to the islands.

Ramnous is named for a thorny bush encountered on the way in. Permanence as a nude beach was enhanced when the National Archeological Service made access harder by fencing the area directly above the beach. In ancient times the 150-foot statue of Nemesis, goddess of vengeance, stood over this beach and remnants remain. Regulars now clean the shoreline. Clear sea with snorkeling, scuba and fishing. Octopi up to 5 kilos are taken and cooked on the spot as delicacies. March–November. August can be windswept.

☞ Bus from Athens—1 1/2 hours, about US $2.50. National Archeological Museum is 5 minutes walk from Mavromateon St. bus station at Areos Park. Catch bus for "Athens-Kato-Souli-Aghia Marina" ferry terminal—it's northeast, past Marathon. Departures have been 6:00, 8:15, 10:15, 12:30, 3:30, subject to change and added busses. Phone Mimikopoulos for update (813-4182).

Leave bus at Ramnous Tavern stop, the last before Aghia Marina. Walk up the asphalt road at the right side for 1 1/2 miles, past vineyards to a clearing by the gate of the ancient shrine of Ramnous. Here walk either right or left on a footpath around the fenced area for about 10–15 minutes to a cove of four small pebbly beaches. Bring beach footwear, snacks and drinks.

If you drive, proceed as above to the entrance of the shrine, where a bad non-asphalt road opposite the entrance leads 3.5 miles to a clearing by the sea with a church of Aghia Marina. Park, take path to coast, you'll soon find the cove.

Limited tent sites available at the Naturist Ramblers and Friends of the Sun, 6 Filomilas St., GR-145 65 Ekali. Phone (301) 813 1738; fax (301) 813 4182.

IONIAN ISLANDS

CORFU

The seven Ionian Islands along the west coast of central Greece provide a gateway with ferry service from Italy and a direct London–Corfu airlink that keeps the beaches crowded. Indeed, just beyond Pelekas, **Myrtiotissa Beach** is a rare unharmed and unhassled nude getaway, praised by L. Durrell and other writers. It's sandy with fine swimming, even a small waterfall, but lacks shade—come with your own. Corfu has other beaches

202

that are used nude—but as elsewhere in this book, we highlight the best.

☞ Rent a car or moped at San Rocco Square or take a bus from the New Fortress (Spilia) bus station in Corfu. Take the main road west across the island to Pelekas.

There turn right and go halfway to Glyfadas. Find a broad track through trees on your left, probably marked on the right by a sign "Myrtiotissa" (bus drivers will let you off here). Drive it a half mile to the parking. Hiking down the 800 ft. cliff takes 15 minutes; coming up depends on your stamina.

Easier than climbing, rent a pedal-boat at the north end of Glyfadas Beach. Pedal north around the headland for 10 minutes and you're there!

ZAKYNTHOS

Southerly Zakynthos (Zante), the most-visited Ionian Island after Corfu, is accessible by air from London with direct busses daily from Athens. Many beaches are afflicted by tiny black oil pellets that may get on your feet. Nude beaches located off the metalled road south from Argassi have included Dafni Beach, Agios Nikolaos, and Garakas Beach. Arrive early, set the dress code in high season.

KEFALONIA

Topfree is common at **Paliostifado Beach**, left of the Hotel Mediterranee outside of the capital of Argostoli. From Argostoli, boat to Lixouri where one may find many isolated beach stretches for nude use. Beaches outside the communities of **Blaxata** and **Myrto** also have nude use.

Kefalonia is not a major tourist attraction; the beaches are uncrowded. The 1953 earthquake destroyed many towns which have since been rebuilt. Although the island lacks historic points of interest, the Melissani Cave near Vlahana features an underground lake.

LEFKADA

Lefkada Island features Levka's **Kathisma Beach,** a long, clean beach where nude use is common from the middle to south end. Park at the south end; walk about 50 m to the beach area. Large open-air beach restaurant at north end sells seafood, pizza and beverages.

PELOPONNESE

IDRA—SPETSES

Off the Peloponnese eastern shore, in sight of the Lena-Mary Beach Hotel (and easily visited from it), these islands delight many tourists.

Many a modern Croesus has sailed to Idra to sun nude with his entourage. A kind of St.-Tropez, this small port rich in naval history draws yachts from everywhere, with numerous fine mansions from the days of sailing fortunes. If you lack your own keel, ferry service runs from Piræus near Athens, and from Ermioni on the Peloponnese.

Idra (Hydra) sadly lacks a public nude beach—Spetses provides one. By rental moped, bicycle, horse-drawn buggy (no motor taxis), or caique, you can follow a track through the pine woods to Agios Anargheri, and next to it is the clothes-optional **Paraskevi Bay**. Or find your own small cove—**Vrellore, Ligoneri, Ksilokeriza**—by boat or scrambling down from the road circling Spetses.

MACEDONIA

SITHONIA

Long ignored by the Greek government, Macedonia has emerged as a popular travel destination. It has monasteries, harbors and campsites, and nude recreation happens in the countless small coves along the coast of Sithonia, the central spur of Chalcidice, a three-pronged peninsula that juts into the Aegean.

Notable beaches are at the **Platamitsi** and **Armenistis** coves on the east coast, and at the small beaches **Azapiko** and **Triptistas** between Nikitas and Koufos on the western shore. Camping is unrestricted, provisions are available in the towns of Sartis, Nikolaos and Koufos. Sailing, spear fishing and swimming are a delight in the bright, clear waters.

THASSOS

The most northerly of the eastern Ægean islands, not far from Sithonia. Thassos is Macedonian, with ferry transfer from Kavalos and Keramoti. Many campgrounds, and also much "wild" camping at beaches. **Pefkari Beach**, 2 miles east of Limenaria, is nude, and **Paradise Beach** on the east coast south of Skala Potomia is officially so. Busses run hourly.

DODECANESE ISLANDS

RHODES

Hic Rhodus, hic saltus. Tourists who come this far should try a nude beach even if it's a crowded tourist island. Be prepared to go miles away from Rhodes town, by bus or (more pleasurably) boat, to the currently best nude beach. The "best" shifts often at this mass travel destination—so, go, then ask. We recommend southern **Falirahi Beach.**

Tsambika Beach, a gorgeous mile-long sandy stretch between two mountaintops on the eastern side of Rhodes has nude use on the southern (right) side.

KOS

The Dodecanese Islands lie off Turkey's southwest coast, with ferry service via Piræus or flights Athens–Kos.

Kos has many fine beaches but the best, to our mind, is **Tropical Beach**, a 30-minute walk west from Kardamena. Accessible also from Kardamena (by boat) is **Bubble Beach** with a separate nude section.

Hotel Caravia has a naturist beach that stretches most of the way to Tigaki, 8 miles west of Kos town. **Marmari**, 4 km farther west along the main road from Tigaki, has a nude beach as do **Mastichorio** and **Kamario**.

PATMOS

Quiet lovely Patmos is a museum "must" with its St. John monastery. Naturists love **Psiliamos Beach** for its beauty, shade trees, and a taverna owner who keeps it all tidy and rents umbrellas and beach chairs. Too remote for most to walk, access to Psiliamos Beach is by bus, moped or daily boat. Caiques also run to nearby islands and the Turkish coast, an alternative to fast antiseptic ferries.

CYCLADES ISLANDS

CYCLADES ISLANDS

The Cyclades Islands—southeast of Athens and Central Greece—cluster around Delos Island, said to be the place of birth of Apollo the sun god.

They're rocky outcrops from the blue Ægean Sea. Small white chapels with blue domes and windmills too hover over towns made up of square planes—a pleasing asymmetricity. A number of smaller Cyclades have lovely deserted beaches that welcome the sun worshiper. Only the more established are mentioned here.

An extensive network of ferries connects the islands with the mainland—at Piræus and Rafina—and with each other, making island hopping convenient and one of the best buys in European travel. Airfields are located on the free beach islands of Mykonos, Santorini and Paros.

KÉA

Near to the Attica mainland, Kéa's sheltered rocky coves have long been enjoyed by naturists. **Kéa Beach Hotel** even has a designated nude beach only

Top: Scandinavian Campers Attracted Greek Men In the 1970s. Bottom Left, Leif Heilberg, A Bather At Paradise; Right, Fisherman, Ancient Fresco, Santorini.

204

205

15 minutes to the north of the hotel. **Otzias Beach**, near Korissía, has discreet nude users.

SYROS

Galyssas on Syros quadrupled in 10 years owing mainly to its discovery by low-budget campers. Unofficial ("wild") often-nude camping centers on coves near the white church on the hill, but rooms-to-let are everywhere and hotels are going up. Take a ferry to Ermoupolis then the bus to Galyssas.

PAROS

A beach accepted for nude use is 1 km southwest of bustling Paros town.

Agia Irini, west of Parasporos, is nude at the north end with access via a dirt track from the main road. It has a stone wall, shade trees but no other amenities.

Platis Ammos and **Kolimbithres** are reached from the port town of Naoussa; and try the beaches of **Lageri** and **Santa Maria**. **Chrissi Akti** (Golden Beach) near Drios has nudity at one end. Don't miss the Venetian fortress in Paroikia. Paros is served daily by flights from Athens and fast Piræus–Paros hydrofoil ferries.

Antiparos Island—a half hour transfer by small caique from Poros town—has a friendly town with rooms to rent, rocky coves and secluded sandy beaches with "wild" camping. The First World Naturist Society's Congress on Nude Beaches (1986) met at Camping Antiparos which has a buffet, minimart, tent and sleeping bag rental, shower block, and large sand beach. GR-84007 Antiparos. Phone (30) 284 61221.

MYKONOS

The sun god's place of birth, Delos, is across a strait so it's apt that Mykonos' sunbathing beaches attract young travelers from afar. Cosmopolitan ambience, high-fashion shops and artisan boutiques heighten the charm. With international flights and the Golden Olympic Supercat 2-hour ferry from Piræus, Mykonos has "arrived."

East from Plati Gialos (Yialos), the south coast terminus of a 15-minute bus ride from central Mykonos, fishing boats will ferry jet-setters along a dry and rocky coastline which lacks a road, straight to **Paradise**, or **Super Paradise** (gays to the left), or **Agrari**, or the last stop, **Hell** (Elias to the Greeks), as you may wish.

Those desiring a more secluded sunning spot may choose the west side of **Panormos Bay**. You must walk for an hour or so, or take a taxi from central Mykonos. The prevailing north winds deter the fainthearted but there is a taverna nearby for refuge if needed. Nudity is the norm.

A clothes-optional beach is found at **Hotel Aphroditi** in Kalafti, served by bus.

☞ You'll be met in Mykonos by many landladies offering rooms. Instead, go to Plati Gialos Bay. Try the Patasos Beach Hotel with a panoramic dining veranda—phone (30289) 23437.

Or continue by boat to **Paradise Beach & Camping**—justly popular because owner Fredy Dactylidis indulges guests with very affordable tent sites and rooms, modern toilets with hot showers, fine buffet restaurant with bar, newsstand and minimart, music and dancing nightly, moped, dive and sailing rental. Staff speaks English. The other clothes-optional beaches have no amenities approaching this! You can look for Paradise shuttle bus in the town or phone for it. GR-84600 Mykonos. Phone (30289) 22852 or 22937; fax (30289) 24350.

NAXOS

Largest and most fertile of the island group, Naxos has a rich history. Of particular interest are the temple of Apollo, the Mycenæan tombs and giant archaic sculptures, "Kouri." Free beach lovers relax and pay their respects to Apollo on the southwest beach Agia Anna, reached by bus from Naxos town, then walking left around the point. Day boat visits from Mykonos appeal to many.

IOS

Daily ferries serve Mykonos–Ios. Fleeing mass tour packaging of Mykonos, sophisticated world travelers flock to Ios' dreamy beaches and lively discos.

Mylopotas is legendary. A half hour walk or a frequent bus will take you from the port, Gialos, or Ios town to **Mylopotas Beach.** There, tavernas let your sunning coincide with gastronomic sinning. Water sport rentals. You may lodge almost on the sand at the Hotel Delfini, phone (30286) 991341, or perhaps at Soulis Campground.

Less thronged, **Coumbara** nude beach is reached by walking a path around a rocky point northwest of Ios town. **Manganari Bay** on the south coast is served by day-trip caiques from the port.

SANTORINI

A volcano island drawing many visitors with spectacular views, cobbled streets, and remains of Phoenician, Dorian, Roman, Byzantine and Minoan cultures. Beaches are secondary. In nude use, the most popular is the rather fine black sand beach, running for miles south from developed **Perissa Beach** on the southeastern shore. Tavernas and shade are amenities.

Red Beach road is opposite the gate of the Akrotiri archeological site. Follow road uphill for 20 minutes to taverna, chapel, then path down and round the point.

Monolithos is the best of beaches on the east coast. Walk left pass the textiles to enjoy au naturel.

CRETE

The first European civilization— Minoan—emerged on Crete 4,500 years ago. This historic, ruggedly beautiful and largely unspoiled island can exhilarate you. A "must" visit is the palace of Knossos, 6 km south of Iraklion, evoking the time of King Minos and the Minotaur, Theseus and the Labyrinth. If the coast doesn't quite measure up, enjoy the good climate and many other features. Accommodations from campgrounds to three modern resorts for naturists. Cretians are tolerant of tactful beach nudity.

KALYPSO CRETIAN VILLAGE

A Class-A resort hotel built in 1982, Kalypso Cretian Village has Greek National Tourist Office naturist status, granted in 1989.

Located in a garden setting on a dramatic fjord in south-central Crete—offering easy access (and bus or boat tours) to the historical sites, the mountains and Samara Gorge, Matala nude beach, the island of Santorini and more—Kalypso is eager to please a naturist visitor. English spoken.

Looking out over the warm Libyan sea—swimmable even in January—are 102 air-conditioned bungalows with showers and telephones, restaurant and minimart, disco, main and pool bar, TV lounge, folklore evenings, Olympic pool, children's pool, playground, veranda with cafe, private beach with dock, deck chess, 2 lighted tennis courts, volleyball, Ping-Pong, water sports, sauna and massage.

Clothes are required only in public indoor areas. Prices are ridiculously low. International airports at Heraklion and Hania. P.O. Box 16, GR-Rethymno, Crete. Phone (30832) 31210 or 31296; fax (30831) 23392. Air-land packages from

VRITOMARTIS

Vritomartis Hotel and Bungalows, built in 1989 next to the Samaria Gorge, became naturist in 1994. April–Oct. Approved by NTOG as a Class-B hotel. Many German guests. Large pool with bar, grassy lawns, restaurant, shuttle to beach, tennis, volleyball, excursions. GR-73011 Chora Sfakion. Phone (30825) 91112; fax 91222.

THE BEACHES

Over the years many small coves and out-of-the-way beaches of Crete have seen nude use, but none as much as **Vai** at the far northeastern tip. Beginning in March and into November you could find California surfers living out of tents, French youths with nothing but hammocks, bedrolls and motorcycles, as well as whole German families with elaborate camping equipment and no clothing, all mixing easily. The northern coastal road takes you east to Sitia ending at Palekastron. Here turn north for Itanos and Vai Beach. Ample tavernas, rooms to rent and visiting Greeks.

Sougia is now what Vai Beach was before discovered. On the southwest coast, this village has a wide, clean pebble beach a mile long; the eastern half is nude. A taverna on the beach, Cafebar Maria, marks the division. It has a cool shower that all use nude. Accommodations can be found cheaply in the village.

☞ Sougia can be reached from the Hania air gateway by auto or bus in less than 2 1/2 hours. Already on Crete? Ride an early-morning bus from Hania to Omalos, where the Samaria Gorge, Europe's largest, begins. Hike the Gorge (5–6 hours) to its shore terminus at Chora Sfakion. Refresh yourself until a ferry takes you that afternoon to Sougia, an hour west, where you may live like a beach bum until deciding to bus back to Hania…or get on a boat going east to Kalypso hotel, or beyond to Matala.

Matala—Red Beach is accessed by following the track which begins opposite the Zafarina Pension in Matala. The 25-minute trek to the beach is of steep climbs and dangerous descents—not recommended for everybody. The 75-m beach has red sand and a nearby taverna.

Near Matala find sign for **Kalamaki Beach**. The road turns to dirt for a short time and then back to pavement. Pull into the small town of Kalamaki. Follow the road straight to the sand beach and

park. Walk 150 yards west and you're clothes-free. Mostly German couples and families enjoy the rocky cliffs and warm water of the Libyan Sea.

A nude beach, **Agia Fotia**, can also be found east of Ierapetra. Access is down a steep, driveable road from highway at clearly marked sign. Nude use is beyond rocks to the left as you face the water.

Dammoni Beach, east of the main beach in the town of Dammoni, becomes crowded quickly; get there early if you want a good spot. Camping and nudity at either end of the beach. Two tavernas in town can provide a simple meal and friendly conversation. Dammoni is about 35 minutes by car from Plakias on Road E.

Hersonissos. About 15 miles from Iraklion is a shadeless beach where nudity is the norm. From the Creta Maris complex, take the cliff-top road northwest for about 1 km until you reach a ravine. Descend the crude steps of the ravine and continue along the seaweed-covered beach to the next headland until you reach the 200-m beach of sand and rocks. No facilities.

From the port of Iraklion drive west on the main auto route. Park at the **Geropotamos Bridge**, several kilometers east of Rethimno. There's a fine black sand, clothed beach here where the river meets the sea. Better, there's a "hidden" sand beach beneath the towering cliffs, with even a fine natural rock bridge—inaccessible to climbers—just 1 km west of the river. The water is pellucid and shallow at shore. Swim down to the secluded cove, get naked and enjoy!

On the northwest end of Crete, **Falasarna Beach**, 40 miles west of Xania is a 2-mile beach nestled beneath a cliff. Popular with backpackers, who camp on the sand and enjoy the shallow waters. A nearby inn provides local food. No problems with the natives here, especially if you can make yourself understood in either Greek or German.

☞ Take Highway 41 from Xania, through Platanias and Malene to Kalidonia, past Koleni and Drapanias to Kastelli. Go past Kastelli 6 km and when the road splits, take the Agnos Georgios, then go through Lardas to Platanos. At Platanos, the road splits. Take the right to Falasarna. After 5 km of turns, the road splits again. Make sure you bear to the right to Falasarna, not straight to Limani. At Falasarna, park along the bluffs above the beach and climb down the hill. Make sure to bring everything you need and wear sneakers to climb up and down the hill.

THE SPORADES

SKOPELOS

The Sporades are in the northern Ægean Sea east of Central Greece. Airlink from Athens to nearby Skiathos then by fast boat to Skopelos, which is verdant with pines and orchards and wonderful, little-visited beaches. **Velanio Beach** offers serendipity itself—at one end, a cooling natural spring, perfect respite after your hot sun bath or salty sea dip. A native, instead of plowing under the spring, added an unofficial campground!

Velanio Beach is 5 km southeast of Skopelos town, reached from the bus stop for Stafylos beach, which has a taverna. Hike around the Stafylos headland. Walk along the beach; a rocky outcrop serves as a dividing line for nudes and textiles.

SKIATHOS

Reached in 25 minutes by air from Athens, modern Skiathos is famed for its clothed Koukounaries (Golden Sand) Beach, Lalaria Beach (reached by caique, nude at one end), and best of all, Ammoudia Krassa (Banana) Beach. There's only one city, Skiathos; nearly all stay there who aren't camping.

Banana Beach surprises visitors with its superb tavernas, shady pines and wildflowers. It's a 15-minute walk from the Agia Eleni or the Koukounaries ("Koukou") bus stops. Or go by caique. Beach vendors will mix your lettuce, feta cheese and olive oil to taste, and charge by salad size. If the beach becomes crowded, walk south past the rocks to secluded coves. Banana is mostly clothed in high season, when you can shift to the next bay north, **Banana Two** (Spartacus), with a taverna but fewer visitors.

On the north coast, **Megalos Asselinos Beach** has nudity. So too does **Elias** and **Mandraki Beach**, reached by a lovely 45-minute walk north (taking a left fork) through pines from the Mandraki Hotel, two bus stops before Koukounaries.

There are also some deserted beaches on **Tsougria Island,** just north of where the boats arrive, that see little use, clothed or nude.

HUNGARY

Hungary's first naturist park, on Lake Balaton, was announced in December 1981. At once the Roman Catholic prelate lept to denounce the "immoral Communist" plan. The government backed out but Hungarians come to body acceptance as they cleave to horses' backs, which is to say, superbly, so the prelate's dictum was not the end.

Roving skinny-dippers focused on quarry-made lakes near Délegyháza, less than an hour south of Budapest, and in 1983 their camp was officially recognized. A number of other locations have since appeared.

Hungary is among the most scenic, historic, economical and enjoyable of European nations. Its Naturist facilities offer friendly bases to tourists moving in unusual regions.

Magyar Naturisták Egyesülete (MNE), Csaba Molnár, Ady útca 21, H-1221 Budapest. Fax (361) 226 3585. Napóra, P. O. Box 25, H-1553, Budapest. Phone (361) 206 791 or 406 097.

BUDAPEST

THERMAL WATERS

Budapest is literally built upon hot springs: 31 mineral wells, fed by 123 thermal springs, surface within the city limits, with a yield over 14 million gallons a day. At least half of these springs emerge hotter than 86°F, some surfacing at a scalding 169°F. To bask in spas is cultivated, and nudity no big thing here. Local leaders and workers, and you, will indulge in thermal baths, massages, radioactive mudpack, solariums, pedicure and electrotherapy—naturally.

Choose the modern **Thermal Hotel,** situated in a vast park on Margitsziget (Margaret) Island in the Danube River which divides Budapest. Phone (361) 111 1000; fax 533 029. Or just visit the park, which includes jacuzzis, saunas and a big wave-making pool.

For tradition, stay at or visit the landmark **Hotel Gellért**. Its panoramic rooftop (with bathing), and the top terrace above the outdoor wave pool, offer nude sunning. Enter by the cafe at the side, pay cashier and get directions to all facilities. Insist on going to the thermal bath *(furdo)*. Phone (361) 185 2200; fax 166 6631.

Other spas beckon. Near the Gellért, the famed Turkish **Rudas Baths,** Döbrentei tér. 9, phone (361) 156 1322. **Császár Baths**, Frankel Leó útca 17; phone (361) 115 4680. **Rác Baths** (Turkish; 16th Century) put the Oriental touch into soaking, steam and massage; fitness room too; try the whole package. Hadnagy útca 8, phone (361) 156 1322. If you enjoy these, keep trying others; there's nothing like it.

For spa and hotel packages: Hungarian Hotels Sales office, phone 1 800 448 4321 (in California, 1 800 231 8704).

NAPÓRA KLUB

Napóra Klub offers winter fitness and social activities: sauna, massage, Ping-Pong, badminton, gymnastics, yoga, occasional parties, as well as information. Begun in 1988 by the energetic Judit Halász, with Miklos Bende, Gustäv Hellebronth, and Dr. Béla Tomor, it counts over 400 members nationwide. Napóra Club meets Autumn through Spring, on the 1st and 3rd Saturdays at 4 p.m., Hotel Lido, III. Nánási útca 67, Budapest. Phone (361) 180 5549.

Summer Napóra activities include use of sun meadows north of Budapest on the Danube at Szentendre Island, **Horány**

Gyöngye—an elite bathing resort fallen on hard times. Suburban rail north to Szentendre/Horány. RV hookups, room rentals; FKK camping, boating, fishing, river swimming. June–Aug. Organized by Passzió, Ltd., H-2015 Szigetmonostor, Horány, Duna sor 1. Phone (36) 23544. Horány Gyöngye, Dunátours, Bp. Baycsy-Zsilinszky útca 17, H-1065 Budapest; phone (361) 31 45 33.

The informative *Napóra* magazine of East European Naturism—published by Angelos Mimikopoulos—is the journal of the East European Documentation Centre on Naturism & Related Subjects. The Naturist Society may be able to provide issues or contact EEDC, P.O. Box 52 894, GR-14610 Nea Erithrea, Greece.

BUDAKALÁSZ

Three popular sand-pit lakes in Omska Park are in view of a towering memorial depicting Soviet soldiers who died while driving the Germans from Budapest. They draw up to 1,500 nude sunbathers on hot weekends. Mobile buffet, toilets, no fees, grassy lawns.

☞ Take the suburban rail line north toward Szentendre (St. Andre).

You can board the train on the Buda side of the Danube at the Arpad Bridge, among other stops. Get off at Budakalasz. Walk right up the street, keeping the monument on your left, then take the next right, then left to the lake. Or in driving out Route 11 to St. Andre, you can watch for the monument and find the lake.

DÉLEGYHÁZA

The premiere naturist campground of Hungary, opened in 1983 after years of "wild" use. Up to 5,000 recreate on 425 hilly acres, MNE supervised. Site of 1987 International Meeting organized by The Naturist Society, (*Clothed with the Sun* 7.4).

Windsurfing, fishing, swimming in large landscaped gravel-pit lakes. Children everywhere. Restaurants, creperies and snack bars with beer/wine, greengrocers, bakery, toilets/showers, volleyball, disco, 900 permanent and 600 rental sites. May 1–Sept. 15. Volántourist agency can make reservations at the 10-room motel. Phone (3626) 72072.

☞ Délegyháza village is south of Budapest, direction Baja; reached

by a left turn between Taksony and Kiskunlachaza, after the 31 km marker on Route 51.

From Budapest's Józsefváros Station, take a "slow" train, on line 150, direction Kelebia; get off in 40 minutes at Délegyháza and ask for the local bus to the "osztalyzo" (quarry-lake). It's 2 km, you might walk. Bus 38 from Budapest, direction Szigethalom-Volan.

SZEGED

SZIKSÓSFÜRDÖ

Sziksósfürdö Naturist Camping, west of Szeged, occupies 3 acres on a natural lake in the south of Hungary. Still a tranquil retreat with 75 sites, 24 with RV hookups. Limited room rental. Holds a Sports Meeting in July. Volleyball, snack bar, fishing, playground, rafting, toilets/showers, phone. Nearby town has everything else needed. May–Sept. Natours, Ltd., P.O. Box 26, 6791 Szeged-Kiskundorozsma, Hungary. Phone/fax László Kiss or Gabriella Dérénnyi, in winter (3662) 478 336; summer (3662) 361 488.

Hungary

☞ By bus or car, 11 km from Szeged to Sziksóstó.

LAKE BALATON

BALATONBERÉNY

After state initiative failed in 1981, businessman Lajos Szabó brought naturism to Lake Balaton in 1987. Restaurant, changing rooms, 7-acre sun meadow under huge trees, boat rentals and beach, on southwestern shore of the vast but very shallow lake. Popular with Germans. RV/tent sites. About 500 visitors daily. May 15–Sept. 15, 9 a.m.–7 p.m. H-8649 **Balatonberény.** Phone 85 377 715; fax 85 377 857.

While this near, run over to **Lake Héviz** at Keszthely—a natural thermal lake, its source water 37°C, 86 million litres of it a day! Two Danubius hotels provide spa services and amenities.

No camping here. At the north end of Lake Balaton, 50 miles closer to Budapest, however, is **FKK Camping Piroska**, with 130 RV/tent sites, sunning lawn and trees, jetty on lake, shops. Aligai útca 15, H-8172 Balatonakarattya.

Phone/fax 88 381 084. Or rent in a private home in Balatonberény through local IBUSZ agency.

☞ From Budapest via Sopron on Route 84. At Balaton take Route 71 via Keszthely (7 km) and watch for big FKK sign. Line 30 bus from Budapest via Nagy and Kanizsa.

PÉCS

MOHÁCS

Mohács nude beach—on an island of the Danube River at the Yugoslav border, 100 miles south of Budapest, abuts a 500-site campground that is in part FKK. A serenely beautiful site with sports, playground, toilets/showers. No hookups. The Danube is too polluted for swimming or drinking; owner Aréna Camping dug a well. May 15–Sept. 30. Transfer service from Hotel Csele at Mohács. Zoltá and Emöke Bistei, 39-ES Dandár útca 9, H-7633 Pécs. Phone (3672) 21 032.

DEBRECEN

LÁTÓKÉP

Látókép, near Max, is in eastern Hungary off Route 33 between Füzesabony and Debrecen. It is convenient on a visit to the *puszta* country. The naturist area is clearly marked by signs near 96 km post leading the 2.5 km through a fishcamp from Route 33. Two piers, shelter, toilet, beach. Winter saunas also offered. Peter Papp, Piac útca 36, H-4024 Debrecen. Phone (3622) 22 286.

IRELAND

DUBLIN AREA

A self-confident beach-and-sauna naturist core has formed in Dublin with nearly 500 adherents. The government, local and national, have yet to recognize an official nude beach, but the group uses a primitive camping site with safe swimming for the children near Brittas Bay, on the east coast 40 miles from Dublin. Year-round there is a swimming/sauna session in Dublin every second Saturday. Irish Naturist Association, P.O. Box 1077, Churchtown, Dublin 14, Ireland.

ITALY

Giuseppe Feroldi, The International Naturist Federation Awards
Winners Of Youth Swim Meet; INF President Karl Dressen At Left.

In 1978 Italian courts and the police first c o n d o n e d nude beaches. *Panorama* newsweekly explained: "The reason was at bottom economic. Foreign tourists would no longer put up with the whims of this or that magistrate. Even Italian tourists, 75 percent from the north, were looking for quiet beaches and places where they might experience nature directly. They weren't going to be deprived of this elementary naturist contact by being forced into bathing suits."

A Milanese prosecutor ordered a survey to determine community standards of decency. Seventy-one percent responded that they were not offended by the sight of a naked body. Nonetheless, a Rome superior appeals court in January 1979 found beach nudity *contrarie al buon costume*, contrary to morality or custom.

In Spring 1981 the national legislature made topfree a legal option for all beaches, and in 1985, Rome appeals judge Mario Giarruso performed a similar service for "discreet and natural" genital nudity. "The sight of the naked body is not indecent to the majority of citizens"—he wrote—"as long as it is not done in a

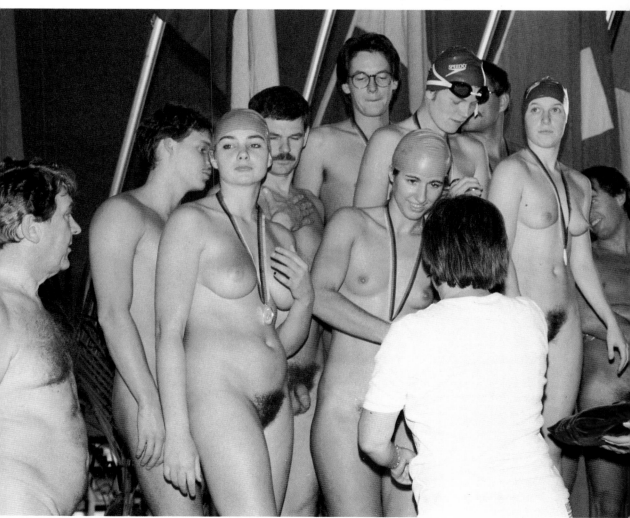

213

show-off or provocative way."

Despite the multipronged progress, recreational nudity remains a red-hot issue. Some magistrates still seek ways to punish it. Dress codes were passed by some tourist city destinations in 1987-88. Beatings of nude bathers on remote beaches have occurred.

In 1993, Northern League rightist mayors of Alassio and Pietra Ligure, leading resorts on the Italian Riviera, banned the bikini from their towns. Retorted the Franciscan Father Nicola Giandomenico: "Wearing a bikini is not a sin. You can be fully dressed and offend the people around you, just as you can be naked and not offend anyone." Check the local custom and practices before disrobing.

The Italian Naturist Federation (FE.NA.IT.) is splintered and only 4,000 strong. Yet its leading personalities have made a difference, especially at Elba, Sardinia, Turin and Bologna. Federazione Naturista Italiana, c/o Andrea Garuglieri, Via Eritrea 7, I-22050 Colle Brianza Como; phone +39 92 60.

SARDINIA

THE FIRST CLUB

Sardinia is an island with a history of "many rulers but no masters." Perhaps this explains why, years ago, a naturist settlement, the first in Italy, was able to take hold here, when the ecclesiastical mainland would have none of it.

The mild climate and numerous beach-

es have made Sardinia a perfect destination for a naturist holiday. The delights of Sardinia are becoming better known as tourists pack into the better beaches. Avoid July and August if you want some peace and come in June or September.

The northeast coast from Santa Teresa Gallura to Capo Comino has seen considerable resort growth. Convenient to the ferry port of Olbia, nude bathing occurs on islands of the **Madgalena** archipelago. (Proximity to Corsica, long a favorite naturist destination, has helped to free the spirits here.)

Near the village of Posada on the northeast coast is beautiful **Su Tiriarzu Beach. Ermosa Beach,** near the defunct campground, has nude use about 200 yards from the beach trailhead. **Bèrchida Beach,** a few miles south, is even finer.

Beaches at **Muravera** and **Villasimius,** near the southern city of Carbonia, see frequent nude use. Also consider Isola Serpentara, an islet off southeasterly Capo Carbonara, to which day-trippers travel from hotels on the Capo such as the Stone Age Club.

Lovely s'Archittu village is on Sardinia's delightfully undeveloped west coast between Bosa and Oristano. About 1.5 miles south of the village, on the right side, is a common entrance to several campgrounds. One of these, **Nurapolis,** offers direct access to a 3-mile long sandy beach, of which the 2.5-mile stretch south of the campground is often used nude. A small hotel in s'Archittu is the alternative to camping.

These locations are most conveniently reached by air (Cagliari has the only airport) or ferry from either Sicily or mainland Italy. Beaches have no facilities.

ISOLA D'ELBA

THE FIRST BEACHES

Established nude beaches date from the late '70s on the Italian mainland. They were tolerated long before on Tuscany's vacation island of Elba, in the Tyrrhenian Sea. Don't expect a highly developed resort; the many sections of coastline accepted for naturist use are in isolated areas, and possess no amenities. You'll want a car to get around in; transport it on the Piombino–Portoferraio ferry, it takes an hour.

Campsites include Camping Acquaviva at the ferry port and Camping Stella Mare at Lacona on the south-central coast. South of Marina di Campo on the south coast is *Spiaggia Seccheto* with rooms to be rented in fishermen's homes.

On the whole, Elba's coastline is rocky or pebbly, but occasional sandy bays can be found. Six km of the coast of **Punta dei Ripalta,** Elba's large southeastern peninsula, are set aside for naturist use.

From Capoliveri take Strada Panoramica (Fattoria Ripalte) to the south. After 7 km look for a path leading down to Punta della Calamita's sandy bays.

All along the northeast coast from Cavo to Rio Marina are lovely sandbars long enjoyed by naturists. Take any of the paths leading to the shore and find your private bay. The waters are shallow here, and access is easy, making this an ideal area for children. Of special interest are Capo Pero's many sandy bays.

On the Costa di Barbarossa at **Porto Azzuro,** try a 500-m long rocky section between the fine "Spiaggia Barbarossa" and "Spiaggia Reale" (*spiaggia* means beach), set aside for discreet naturist use. It's hard not to feel like a second-class citizen here, yet one can only hope that this small, liberated area will expand due to increasing popularity.

Local tourist offices will supply directions to naturist beaches and ANITA, the Italian naturist organization, publishes map and tourist information. Write to Gruppo Naturisti Isola d'Elba, Via Andrea Vitaliani 20, 57036 Porto Azzurro, LI, Italy. A donation is appreciated.

Ferries make the 1-hour crossing from Piombino in Tuscany to the ports of Portoferraio and Porto Azurro several times daily. Reservations for ferry and accommodations in high season are recommended.

TUSCANY

ITALIAN RIVIERA

Named for the Etruscans, original settlers of the region, Tuscany has produced Michelangelo, Dante, Leonardo da Vinci, Boccaccio, Petrarch, the cities of Florence and Pisa—and now some attractive nude beaches. With the exception of Elba Island, nudity is not officially allowed in the Tuscany area and magistrates may fine. However, by avoiding crowded places and keeping watch for patrols, nudity is possible on many Tuscany beach strands. Not recommended at the Marina de Albereto.

The beaches north of Castiglione della Pescala strictly forbid nude use and should be avoided. The coastline from Castiglione della Pescala south to the Argentaria Peninsula is open for discreet clothes-free use. Southernmost is most popular. Orbetello's Etruscan ruins, 5 km from town, are well worth the visit, and the nearby fishing villages of Porto Santo Stefano and Port 'Ercole have long been popular with the jet set. The beaches are excellent from June to September, and Florence is most beautiful in May or June.

For a naturist experience on the Tuscan coast try Chiarone. A whistle-stop on the coastal rail line with a campgrounds and a hunter hotel and bar, Chiarone is the preferred beach of jet-

Italy

setters vacationing at ancient Capalbio, the nearest village. By road: Drive Via Aurelia (SS I) to a sign for Chiarone Camp just north of the Latium–Tuscany border.

Indeed, the old Tuscan Duchy's toll office from A.D. 800 is here along with milestones in the high dunes inscribed "E.F. XVIII," i.e., 18th year of Fascist Era. But back to the beach: just outwalk the clothed ones to find your sandy spot.

LE BETULLE

Le Betulle, "The Birches" was the first Italian family naturist park. Perennial president Tom Operti lived here. Founded in 1969 to much media hullaballoo, and still the model. Tent, RV sites. Splendid pool, archery, bocce ball, volleyball, Ping-Pong, rec hall. Restaurant, minimart within 10 minutes walk. Temperate; just over the Alps from France, two hours from the coast, and a good base for visiting NE Italy. Requires proof of INF membership and advance reservation by letter. Open all year. Just 15 minutes from the airport. B.P. 1, I-10040 La Cassa, Turin. Phone (011) 98 42 819; fax (011) 54 80 77.

ROME AREA

TOR VAIANICA BEACH

One of the most heavily used and interesting nude beaches is Tor Vaianica, an hour outside Rome and well maintained with litter bags, refreshment stands and a makeshift camping area. This beautiful, broad, white sand beach extends for miles with the nude section 1 km long. Awnings provide shade over picnic tables where many a family sits au naturel to a bowl of pasta, good sandwiches and wine.

☞ From Rome take the Statale (state road) 148 south through the EUR complex and continue 20 km. Look for a right-hand turn to Tor Vaianica, then right again at Tor Vaianica and drive north along the beach for 6 km. Park on your left at the nude section.

Or take the Roma-Ostia train (station at the Porta S. Paolo) to Lido Cristoforo Columbo, the last stop. Directly in front of the station get on the 07X bus which goes south along the coast (not 07 which leads north to Lido di Ostia) to the end of the line (15 min.). Walk farther south along the beach for another 15 minutes. Total transportation cost is about $2.

CAPOCOTTA BEACH

It's the favorite today. Like many beaches serving greater Rome, Capocotta Beach had teetered between anarchy and regulation, filth and freedom. Many thought it Rome's best nude beach—relatively tidy, still natural, naturist-friendly yet inhospitable to voyeurs. Small merchants had gone from selling to sunbathers out of baskets to creating capanni, "arbors"—l Battello Ubriaco (The Drunken Boat, after Rimbaud's poem, the best if too-loud disco), Zagaja (The Stutterer), L'Aragosta (The Lobster), Le Vagoo, The Dunes, Tropical, Andrea, Disco Surf. These unregulated stalls served ices, drinks, hot meals, whatever people wanted. They also cleaned up, imposed etiquette, and supported nude use.

☞ Take Via Christopher Colombo to Ostia. The intersection with the beach road (Hwy 601) is a large traffic circle; just under 9 km south of this circle is Capocotta Beach. There is an entrance about a kilometer closer to Ostia, but the best facilities are at 8.8 km.

Or by Metro, take line B to the Magliana station then change to the Rome-Lido line for Lido Ostia Centro. From Ostia, take an ATAC line bus #7, leaving Lido Centro every 12 minutes. There are bus stops in both directions at the Capocotta Beach entrance.

LAKE MARTIGNANO

"Feel like getting an all-over tan?" inquired the newspaper *Il Messaggero*. "You needn't go to an elite watering hole in Sardinia. You can do it right here in the Commune of Rome"—at Lake Martignano.

☞ Drive out from Rome on Via Boccea and take either Via Santa Maria di Galeria or Via Anguillarese to get on the Via di Ponte Valle Trave and follow the signs. At the lake, park in the county lot (fee charged) and hike on the trail through woods and brush to the main beach. Hidden coves along the volcanic shore to right or left of the main beach provide possibilities for nude bathing.

SABAUDIA: SPERLONGA

About halfway down the coast toward Naples, Sperlonga's nude beach has long been popular with natives and tourists alike. Carabinieri sometimes patrol the sands, but their attitude toward nudity has relaxed considerably and they oftentimes stop to give you time to dress. Nonnaturist camping nearby.

☞ Route 7 from Rome south to the turnoff before Terracina, then 213 in town to Sperlonga Park. Park and walk as though for the Grotto. It's 100 yards from the Grotto.

NAPLES

THE LAST BEACH

Very nice and popular. Saturday mornings are best because most Italians work or go to school until noon. Sundays are crowded and forget about August as the whole country takes the month off. Best to arrive before 9 a.m.

☞ From Naples, take the Via Domiziana north through the villages of Mondragone, Minutino, Scuari and Formia into Gaeta. At Gaeta, take S.S. 213 (the first busy intersection in Gaeta, bear to the right) towards Terracina. Go about 5 miles north along the cliff road. To your left look for a small white sign saying La Ultimo Spiaggio. Park alongside the road. Someone may ask for lire to watch your car. Pay it and they'll keep your car safe from thieves. Walk down the stairs (181 of them) to the beach. At the snack bar, the owner will want 3000 lire per person. Turn to the left—to the right is the textile beach. The farther along you walk, the less clothing is encountered. If you wade out into the sea and around a rocky point, there is a small cove that is very nice.

TYRRHENIAN SEA

Ponza is the largest of the Isole Ponziane in the Tyrrhenian Sea. Although it is well out to sea, the heavily polluted Gulf of Gaeta flows toward Ponza—so forget swimming and work on your total tan.

While there see legendary Isola di Capri, the "sin" island of the Romans where Tiberius is said to have orgied and where pirates lorded it in the sun for many centuries. Today Capri is tame by comparision, but topfree and beginnings of full nudity can be seen.

SICILY

The offshore isles of this vast, historic island have seen more nude use with the years—but with the exception of the beaches near sophisticated Taormina, it was deemed advisable to stay dressed on Sicily proper.

No longer is this so; every major city now has beaches with some nude use. Palermo has Terrasini, along Route 113 towards Cefalù. Trapani has Calanpisu, near Capo San Vito. Siracusa has Brucoli. Messina has Patti Beach. Catania has the rocky right end of the Fontane Bianche beach. A beach near Agrigento is nude at either end.

ISOLE EOLIE

The rugged coastlines of these volcanic islands off Sicily's northern coast offer numerous possibilities for secluded nude swimming and sunning. Of special note is the famous "Le Punte" beach on Isola Filicudi. Visitors to Villaggio Turistico "Phenicusa" (Phone (3990) 914114) pioneered the nude beach between two promontories. On Isola Vulcano stay at Camping Sicilia Vulcano: phone (3990) 9852164. A number of clothes-free coves and beaches are nearby.

ISOLE EGADI

The Egadi Islands are offshore from Trapani and the ancient city of Erice on westernmost Sicily. Lots to explore here, off-beach too: medieval castles, mysterious grottos, fishing villages.

PELAGIAN ISLANDS

ISOLA DI LAMPEDUSA

You'll strain your eyes trying to find this vacation retreat off Italy's coast: it is east of Souse, Tunisia, and the Arab influence is strongly felt. Happily, this does not extend to mores. Lampedusa's main beach is topfree and nearby beaches are totally nude. Access is from Sicily; flights leave from Palermo airport and ferries from Agrigento's Porto Empedocle. Stay at Villaggio Turistico Cala Creta. Phone (39922) 970 545. Or at Camping La Roccia, Via Madonna, I-92010 Lampedusa. Phone (39922) 970 055.

CALABRIA

PIZZO GRECO

A naturist campground at what was a "wild" nude beach near Capo Rizzuto. Pizzo Greco has official nude status. Its 7 acres, on a secured bluff above a fine sandy beach, offer some bungalows, RVs and tents to rent, as well as tent and RV sites, with shade trees, clean and ample toilets, showering and shared kitchen facilities, restaurant with bar and disco, and minimart. Recreation includes bocce ball, volleyball, Ping-Pong, horse riding, evening entertainment, and windsurfing or sunning on a fine red sand beach lapped by clean Ionian sea. Families and couples only.

Air and sea ports serve Pizzo Greco at Crotone, 8 km distant. Or fly to Lamezio and a car will bring you 50 miles over the mountains to the campgrounds. You can locate Pizzo Greco by thinking of Italy as a boot descending south: Pizzo Greco and Isola Capo Rizzuto are on the ball of the foot.

Contact Rosso Sergio (who speaks English) off-season at (39) 142 70338, evenings. May to October at Pizzo Greco: (39962) 79 22 49 or 79 17 71. Pizzo Greco Naturist Club, P.O. Box 57, Loc. Fratte, I-88076 Isola Capo Rizzuto CZ.

ADRIATIC COAST

GARGONA PENINSULA AND TREMITI

Forty miles of sandy beach lie on the northern Gargona Peninsula, better known as the "spur" sticking out of the back of Italy's boot. Vieste, commercial center of the area is where accommodations are most likely to be found. Crowded with tourists in the hot months. The beaches south of the city see the most nude use. The Isle of Tremiti, to the north of Gargona, also permits nude sunning and swimming.

ANCONA

Ancona, coincidentally a major ferryport access to Yugoslavia's nude resort coast, is blossoming with a nude zone in its own right. Keep to the south of town; there's a fining magistrate with jurisdiction to the north.

SAN MARINO

CLUB CAMPEGGIATORI

Club Campeggiatori designated a portion of its grounds naturist in 1989. The site is

on the Adriatic coast near Ravenna, 150 km south of Venice. Modern camping facilities. Day visitors welcome.

RAVENNA

LIDO DI DANTE: CAMPING CLASSE

Camping Classe offers three-star naturist campsites with hookups, pool, restaurant and tennis courts, in a shady pine woods a short walk from an Adriatic clothing-optional beach. Byzantine, Roman antiquities. I-48100 Ravenna, phone (0544) 49 20 05 or 49 20 58; fax (0544) 49 20 58.

BOLOGNA

ASSOCIAZIONE NATURISTA BOLOGNESE (ANB)

In downtown Bologna the 2,500-member ANB maintains its Centro Naturista—a health club and vegetarian restaurant in a 300-year-old building. It has 2 gyms, sauna, Turkish bath, massage, yoga, aikido, shiatzu, shops. Mon.–Fri. Via degli Albari 6, I-40126 Bologna. Phone (3951) 235 643.

Forty km away in a vast mountain forest preserve and only 80 km from Florence, is ANB's campgrounds, Ca'le Scope, with the home of ANB's guiding spirit and founder Luigi Bolelli. Tent, RV sites, gym, vegetarian restaurant. Bocce ball, Ping-Pong, hiking. Localita Cimitero di San Martino, La Quercia, I-40043 Marzabotto. Phone (051) 932 328.

NETHERLANDS

T he Netherlands Naturist Federation has now grown to be the second largest in the world, larger even than Germany's. According to a 1986 government-sponsored inquiry, nine percent of the Dutch population "regularly sunbathe, swim or hike in the nude" and another 70 percent did not disapprove of this practice.

Surprisingly, Dutch acceptance of public nudity is of recent development. At the start of the 1950s naturists still often had to travel to Germany or France to find a private park; nudity was prohibited at the Noordzee.

But this dour sky opened by the early 1970s. Emboldened by emerging national consensus for individual freedom, naturists acted to be nude on public lands. When progressive television stations brought full-frontal nudity into living rooms, and it was accepted, new community standards were affirmed. A last spur was the hot summer of 1975. Naturism took a firm footing on the Dutch beaches.

Concurrently the Minister of Justice, addressing Parliament, asked that nudity be accepted on locally approved beaches that are "out of the way, of limited size, marked and labelled as such." By the early 1980s the NFN could point to official FKK beaches. The adoption of Article 430a in 1986 established the right of public nudity wherever it is appropriate.

A woman was found guilty of nudity by the town of Ouddorp on Goeree Island in Zeeland. She appealed and the Sommelsdijk Justice of the Peace dismissed the charges in 1987, establishing in case law that Article 430a, toleration of *geschikte* (appropriate) public nudity, takes priority over a local law that condemns mere nudity.

In our listing are only the best social and comfortable beaches for naturists. Information from Netherlands Tourism offices or from Nederlandse Federatie van Naturistenverenigingen (NFN), Drift 3 Postbus 783, NL-3500 AT Utrecht. Phone (3130) 232 88 10, 10 a.m.–3 p.m. daily; fax (3130) 233 29 57.

Naturists from abroad might contact the singles coordinator SOLONAT, J. Boschstraat 35, NL-5171 AH Kaatscheuvel. Camping and sauna activities are coordinated by NKZ, Postbus 1633, NL-2000 BR Haarlem. INTERNATUUR makes vacation arrangements: phone (3126) 6317134.

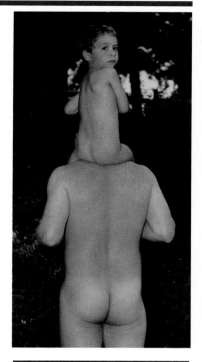

ZEELAND

SERVING BELGIUM

The conservative Zeeland tourist authorities insisted into the 1980s that no beaches could be enjoyed au naturel in the southernmost province. Yet naturists did find secluded beaches at Brouwersdam, on the south bank; between Renesse and Haamstede by the Verklikkers dunes; between Vrouwenpolder and Oost-Kappelle, turning right near the Oranjezon camping; at Domburg behind the golf links; and in Vlissingen at Nollestrand, walking toward Dishoek.

Belgians, repressed in their own country, went to Zeeland on weekends. As legal Dutch nude beaches appeared in the north a demand in the Flemish Catholic south grew. At last Oostburg authorities designated a nude beach in 1985 at Breskens between poles 21–22, 13 km north of Cadzand. Sampling landed clubs:

Vlissingen—Seelandia. On the water where the ferry from Sheerness docks. RV rentals. PB 343, NL-4330 AH Middelburg. Phone (01184) 67290.

Bergen Op Zoom—Camping Athena. The main Belgian retreat in Zeeland; 70 RV rentals. Zandvlietseweg 15, NL-4641 SR Ossendrecht. Phone/fax (01646) 72489.

217

SOUTH HOLLAND

HOEK VAN HOLLAND

The Hook of Holland, where ferries dock from England, is south of The Hague at the Harbor of Rotterdam entrance. A small official FKK beach with two pavilions is northeast on the sea towards 's-Gravenzande. Beach pavilion serves drink and light meals and may be used nude. Toilets and showers. Off Rechtsestraat to the right, then left. Between km poles 116.360–116.110.

ROTTERDAM

Kralingen—Kralingseplas. In the northeastern suburb of Kralingen is the Kralingseplas, a large lake surrounded by wooded public land where you can enjoy space to walk, cycle or ride horses. The lake offers swimming, sailing and windsurfing as well as a haven for wildlife.

☞ From the car park at the south west corner of the lake walk north along the shore past the official swimming beaches (topfree like all Dutch beaches) to the first clump of trees. A path leads beyond this to a sheltered grassy clearing, where on any fine day you will find a dozen or so fellow naturists. Take a plastic groundsheet as the ground is often damp here. Locals bring their bicycles in with them.

Rotterdam Harbor—Maasvlakte. A desolate flat in the bend of the Europa Way by the Mississippi Harbor, Maasvlakte is a popular spot with Rotterdammers. Naturists delight in wandering the strand naked for miles, with perhaps no other companions but the sand, the sea, and if in luck, the sun.

☞ From Rotterdam follow signs to Europoort, then signs to Maasvlakte when they appear, until a road turns off to the left marked for Strand Slufter. Take this road and follow it right along to the end. There is a series of steps down to the beach on the left of the road. The nude section is to the right of the last set of steps. During the summer a small mobile café is at the top of the steps. Plenty of parking; no access by public transport.

KIJKDUIN

With a shopping center and hotels it's a favorite seaside resort for Germans; the Dutch and "Deutsch" strip off between poles 107–108.5, to either side of the clothed beach for Ockenburg Camping.

SCHEVENINGEN

The Hague (Den Haag)—Scheveningen. Ceding no freedom edge to Amsterdam, *Hagenaars* too have an FKK beach at their world-famous sea resort.

Toilets and showers for small fee; light meals and drinks, two beach buffets. Buses and trams run often to Scheveningen Pier. There, walk north for 20 minutes to just south of the Wassenaar town line between km markers 98 and 96. Also at Westduinpark between poles 103–105.5. VVV, PF 85973, NL-2508 Den Haag. Phone (070) 354 62 00.

MAARSEVEENSE LAKE

Freshwater nude bathing can be found on the Maarseveense Lake in Westbroek, a suburb of Utrecht. Access is via the Westbroekse Binnenweg—look for the beach on the northeast shore. The NFN crown-jewel Zon en Leven Camp, Gravingen, is located nearby; no RVs. Zon en Leven, Kanaalstraat 200, 3531 CR Utrecht; phone (3130) 939 222.

NORTH HOLLAND

AMSTERDAM

The train to Zandvoort is supplemented by Amsterdam's suburban options:

Het Twiske—10 km north of Amsterdam between the towns of Oostzaan and Landsmeer. A wooded parkland of meadows, lakes and trails. Good swimming, windsurfing, picnicking. Seldom crowded; clothing-optional except for a small area signed for no nudity. Easily reached by bus (to Oostzaan or Den Iip), auto or bicycle. Naturists gather in the north end at "De Wezenlanden." Brochures at Central Station in Amsterdam. Phone 075 6844338.

Sloterplas Lake—In the western suburbs, the lake has two small islands for naturists. From downtown Amsterdam take trolley #1 or 13 or bus #23. Driving, follow signs for Amsterdam West and watch for Slotervaart near Osdorp.

Amstelveen—Amsterdamse Bos. To the south; a secluded sunning meadow.

ZANDVOORT BEACH

Amsterdam—Zandvoort. Where the city lies down by the sea in summer. A world-class, lifeguarded, clothes-optional beach; with the beach buffets Adam & Eva, Amerika, Trocadero and Sans Tout, which also provide showers/toilets and rent chairs.

☞ Frequent and comfortable trains make the trip in 30 minutes. The rail terminal is only steps from the sands. At the southern pavilion walk south to poles 68–74. Camping het Helmgat is 2 km north at Bloemendaal aan Zee, phone (02326) 0820.

FLEVO-NATUUR

Flevoland—Flevo-Natuur. Built by NFN, a recreation center open to all. Opened 1978; 30 ha with indoor/outdoor

heated pool, sports courts, sauna, restaurant. Tent/RV sites, bungalows, minimart. Wheelchair accessible. East of Amsterdam 55 km by Amersfoort–Zwolle highway; on the south of the Flevopolder (Zuider Zee after drainage) across from Nijkerk. Open all year. Managed by Creatief Vakantieparken, PB 352, NL-9700 AJ Groningen. Phone (050) 314 3434. Grounds: Flevo-Natuur, Wielseweg 3, NL-3896 LA Zeewolde. Phone (036) 522 8880; fax (036) 522 8783.

Elburg—Veluwe Lake. A free beach on the Flevoland, opposite the mainland town of Elburg. Look for a restaurant "De Klink" and the Riviere Campgrounds. The beach lies between the two. From Flevo-Natuur, 40 km.

BERGEN AAN ZEE

A lively beach resort located near Alkmaar, famous for its cheese market; within an hour of Amsterdam. Take bus 168 to Bergen aan Zee, walk south along the beach to marker 36 and strip down. Or walk north in the direction of Schoorl, between markers 29.5 and 32.4. Near Castricum between poles 46–49 is another option.

CALLANTSOOG

The first sanctioned nude beach was voted in at this small North Sea resort straight north of Amsterdam, with a wide strand and dunes. Off the beaten track of tourists who think that Amsterdam is the Netherlands, it's a popular holiday spot. The nude sector has its own refreshment pavilion, named "Natural." A splendid reserve for waterfowl is just south, Het Zwanenwater.

For FKK, from the main beach entrance walk 30 minutes south. Or enter beach at St. Maartenszee to walk 15 minutes north. FKK zone is km markers 14.5–16.8 and 8.4–9.4. VVV, Jewelweg 8, NL-1759 HA Callantsoog. Phone (02248) 1541.

NOORDZEE

North Sea beaches are not for all of us! Often austerely beautiful, with romantic moors and good sand, the weather may be bracing—well, chilly! A brisk wind often blows with a hint of shower. Not bothersome enough to stop people from claiming their place (or their windbreak) in the hazy sun, year after year.

Enjoy. And be careful swimming. Riptides take lives of even hardy swimmers.

The Dutch Frisian Islands, off the North Sea coast, offer much for lovers of fish, wildfowl and dunes. Ferries travel to the Frisians from a number of mainland ports. The Dutch love

them as a place to get away from it all. When you're not sunning, try a guided tour through the Waddenzee tidal flats—at low tide the shallows teem with life.

DEN HELDER

Den Helder, departure point for liberated Texel, has nude beaches south of the city: between poles 2–3, between markers 4–6 and at Julianadorp between poles 8.4–9.4.

TEXEL ISLAND

Southernmost of the Dutch Frisian Islands, Texel has night life and all water sports as well as two official FKK beaches. One is at the north point near the village of De Cocksdorp, between km markers 26.4 and 27.4, best reached from the parking lot at De Krim. A second is at Den Hoorn where FKK is south of pole 9, complete with beach buffet, next to the Hoornderslag parking on the Witteweg. Note that wind from the east will ruin your beach day. Ferry from Den Helder. VVV Texel, PF 3, NL-1790 AA Den Hoorn.

VLIELAND

Northeast of Texel, Vlieland Island's beach and dunes are completely free for nude sunbathers. Ferry from Harlingen.

AMELAND ISLAND

It is entirely clothes-optional except along roads. Ferry from Holwerd, reached through Dokkum.

SCHIERMONNIKOOG ISLAND

Northernmost of the Frisians, friendly and traditional; very popular with cyclists and walkers in an undeveloped nature. The Schiermonnikoog town council decided in 1981 that given the many nude beachgoers, it made more sense to define a part of the beach where clothing *must be worn*. This is between the two main beach entrances (km markers 2–7). The rest of the island shore is clothing-optional. Ferry from Lamwersoog. VVV, PF 13, NL-9166 PW Schiermonnikoog. Phone (051953) 1233.

NOTE: captions to photos run along the inside edge of pages.

NORWAY

With thousands of miles of a granite fjord shoreline, the Norwegians easily find secluded ledges for sunbathing. Most rely on these rocky "free beaches" rather than purchase land for naturist clubs.

Increasingly, municipalities make legal provision for the nude sunbathers. The Norwegian Naturist Union did buy a seaside center and campground, Sjøhaug, in 1980. Municipal pools are used for nude swims in winter. See full report in N magazine, 13.3 pp. 57-62.

Contact: Norsk Naturist-förbund, Postboks 189 Sentrum, N-0102 Oslo. Phone or fax: 22 33 70 53. Its travel agency is Vidy Reiser, Boks 427, N-4001 Stavanger, phone (51) 527140; fax (51) 532430.

Nude beaches and naturist campgrounds of Denmark, Norway and Sweden are listed in the *Scandinavian Naturist Guide* (all listings repeated in English) from Sveriges Naturistförbund, Box 160, 20121 Malmö; phone (040) 931016.

SOUTHERN

CAMP ISEFJAER

Located 21 km north of Kristiansand, along coastal road RV-401, the campground borders a large national park, famous for wildlife and fishing.

Purchased by Sorlandets Naturistforening (SNF), the site is fully equipped with houses and cottages, restaurant, dance floor and bar, and large sauna. The beach is about 80 m long on Isefjaer Bay with warm seawater for swimming. RV/tent camping also available. For information contact Bjørg and Magné Nodeland, phone +47 38 15 70 03; telefax +47 38 15 70 35.

OSLO AREA

Increased naturist activity in southern Norway prompted the Oslo City Council to designate official FKK sites.

If it's not sunbathing weather, go to view the pulpit in St. Mary's Cathedral—"the most naturist pulpit in the world," says Per Lonning, the State Church bishop and outspoken naturist. Visit Vigeland Sculpture Park for its vast portrayal of naked humanity. And view the giant nude Oslo Fjord mural in the banquet room of Oslo City Hall.

OSLO AREA BEACHES

Topfree is generally accepted on Norwegian beaches. Nude beaches on Oslo Fjord:

Langøyene Island, the rocky southeastern shore. Idyllic view, no vehicles on island, camping permitted. Ferry service from Aker Brygge, Oslo.

Indre Huk Beach. At Strømborgveien 49 on Bygdøy at Oslo's western city limits—near Kontiki raft museum on the Frognerkillen. Sandy beach, shower facility, nearby restaurant.

Kalvøya Beach. Take E-18 west about 10 kilometers to Sandvika town hall. Park on the facing Kadettangen peninsula. Walk across bridge onto forested Kalvøya Island. Official nude beach is on its east side.

Strandskog Beach, at Ingierstrandvei 100–108, Oppegaard. Two km beyond Ingierstrand Baths; a small blue sign on shore side should identify site. Tiny sandy area among rocks beneath trees.

A small lake north of Oslo, **Svartkulp** has a popular nude beach; many users stay at Panorama Sommerhotel. Also of note is **Lille Aklungen,** a lake northwest of Svartkulp, with an established naturist area and good fishing.

SJØHAUG NATURIST CENTER

Sjøhaug, owned by Norwegian Naturist Union, has 12 1/2 acres of fields and woods. Its quarter mile beach winds around two bays on a fjord. Fishing, swimming, windsurfing, boating. Volleyball, hiking, playground. Rustic farm lodgings, camping, community kitchen.

Inexpensive, congenial base for visiting Oslo. Ferry, train, and bus make Oslo–Moss connections. Sjøhaug Naturistsenter, Renneflottveien, Stopp nr. 18-N-Jeløy, 1514 Moss. Phone (09) 69 27 00 50.

☞ From Oslo, take E-6 south. After 55 km take E-120 into Moss city, cross Mossesundet bridge onto Jeløya Island. Drive north on Nesveien to Sjøhaug on the eastern shore.

NORTH SEA COAST

ORRESANDEN

On the North Sea lies Norway's bustling port of Stavanger, with the only well-established nude beach on the western coast.

Take Route 510 south to Bora, then Route 507 for 8 km until you see signs for the Orresanden beach zone. Park in the lot and walk north to the nude section. Ferries connect Stavanger with ports in Germany (Hamburg), Holland (Amsterdam) and England (New Castle).

POLAND

Poles avid for the freedom of social nudity at lakes, saunas and the Baltic Coast were very numerous as the country freed itself from USSR control. The media came to them. The Polish Naturist Association, formed in February 1988 by Józef Kubicki of Lódz, enrolled 2,000 and its magazine claimed 200,000 newsstand circulation.

But a vast misconception shaped this interest. Exploitative Miss Natura pageants were staged on FKK beaches. Much of what passed as naturism, purported in magazines like the popular weekly *Veto* and Kubicki's *Natura Naturyzm*, derived from *Playboy* or *Penthouse*. Kubicki himself promoted sexual massage parlors, videos and night-clubs.

Many local naturists were outraged and the Association disbanded in June 1991, as did the magazine. The INF did not even acknowledge Polish naturism in its 1994 *Guide*. It does continue locally, especially in Wroclaw and Warsaw, despite the economic desperation, which has cancelled government subsidy of saunas, pools and solaria; and despite the hostility of freshly powerful Roman Catholicism, which now teaches its dogmas in all public schools.

WARSAW AREA

VISTULA BEACHES

Swidry Beach. The first-tolerated Warsaw area nude beach is 10 miles southeast of Warsaw, just north of where the Swider River enters the Vistula. Express bus C from the intersection of Warsaw's main avenues, Marszalkowska and Jerozolimski. At Falenica transfer to bus 702, 717 or 719, direction Otwock or Józefów. Get off at the *gola plaza* (nude beach) stop at the restaurant Pod Debami between Swidry Male and Swidry Wielke. Or take bus 146 from Warszawa Wschodnia train station (Praga district) in direction of Falenica; at Byslawska St., transfer to bus 702, 717 or 719. Walk west from Pod Debami towards the Vistula. At dead end cross the small stream, Swidry Male, or turn left (southwest) on a well-trod path to the sandbar island beach.

Aleya Romantyczna—Miedzeszyn Beach. Also on the Vistula River, and an alternative to Swidry Beach. Many families and couples, a clubby and cultured group. A lovely sand beach 400 feet wide, within Warsaw city limits; 2 miles north of Swidry Beach and on the same side. Parking; no facilities. Contact: Stanislaw Dziadowicz, úlca Kardynale Wyszynskiego 4 m. 25, PL-01015 Warsaw; or Stanislaw Wydzka, Klarysewska 32, PL-02923, Warsaw. Phone (4822) 420275.

☞ Take bus 113 and then 146 in direction of Falenica and get off at the crossroads of Trakt Lubelski and Wat Miedzeszynski and walk back 200 m along the latter. Or get off at Miedzeszynski and Romantyczna streets and walk 1 km on the latter, past the country club. Then 700 m to the river, with a military area on the left, along the Rychnowska alley; the weekend nudity on the shore and islets is evident. Or drive from downtown Warsaw, across the Vistula River on General Berlinga Bridge, then upriver (southwest) for 10 km on the left bank. At Al. Romantyczna turn right to the river.

Grand Hotel Warsaw. Naturists socialize at its sauna/pool. Daily 10–8. Al. Krucza 28. Phone (4822) 294051.

Gerhard Skagestein, On A Norwegian Fjord.

220

LÓDZ AREA

LÓDZ SOLARIUM

Lódz, in the geographic center of Poland, was also at the heart of the controversy over true and false naturism. Józef Kubicki, the porn-promoter-publisher-SNP president, and the true naturism leader Adam Chrzuszcz both live there. Garden-variety naturists meet daily in good weather at the solarium of a city pool. Zespót Basenów "Fala," Park Kultury i Wypoczynku na Zdrowiu, al. Unii 4. Phone 28664.

Local contact: Jola and Adam Chrzuszcz, al. Sowinskiego 24, PL-91485 Lódz, phone 575254 or 551595.

KRAKOW AREA

KRYSPYNÓW LAKE

Kryspynów Village is 10 km west of Krakow. Express bus K goes directly to Kryspynów Lake from the Krakow west Old Town "Salvator" bus stop, below Kosciuszko Mound. Parking, boat rentals, windsurfers, kayaks, sailboats, and facilities at the *tekstylni* village beach. Walk 10 minutes to opposite (north) side, past rye fields, for nudity, clean water, and a nice view of a Baroque monastery.

BALTIC COAST

BEACHES

Coastal Route 52 sweeps across the Polish Baltic coast and its beaches from western Szczecin (access to Uznam–Wolin) to Gdansk in the east (the access to Hel Peninsula). Train and bus offer parallel service, but a rental car is best.

Swinoujscie—Uznam Beach at Poland's German border is cheek-by-jowl with an FKK beach on Usedom. Ferries operate from the bank of the river Odra in Szczecin to Mielenska Island.

Wolin Island—Miedzyzdroje Beach. In walking distance of rail station, with a second beach east of Wiselka. Fine white sand, wading depth, not cold, good for families. "Camping Pomerania" is at the beach and popular with naturists.

Dziwnówek Beach. A mile east of clothed Dziwnów beach, northeast of Wolin.

Koszalin—Uniescie. East of Mielno, west of Lazy, on the barrier beach between Lake Jamno and the Baltic. Take Koszalin city bus 2 to Uniescie, walk 2.5 km east along coast road to Lake Jamno canal and follow it to beach. Parking by the road is suppressed; walk in.

Slupsk—Rowy Beach. Drive from Slupsk north to coast, then east to park at Rowy, and walk a mile east, then cross the wooded dunes onto the white sand beach, with its *plaza naturystowa*. Camping reservations, phone Rowy 11980.

Lebork—Leba provides another access to miles of nude beach on a sandspit between Lake Lefskoand Sea, 3 km to the left of the last campsite on the road in.

Debek–Bialogóra Beach. Reach Debek village by crowded interurban bus from Wladyslawowo (also gateway to Hel), or drive. West along the beach, fording the Piasnica River, toward Bialogóra hamlet. A beautiful beach, very popular.

Chalupy Beach, Poland's best-known FKK beach for over 50 years, drew thousands of beachgoers to the **Hel Peninsula.** Closed by Chalupy town council after controversial "Miss Natura" contests were staged in early 1980s. A more quiet naturism survives today at **Jastarnia Campground.** Turn east from Wladyslawowo, 40 minutes north from Gdynia and served by an express train from Warsaw. Park in lot 5, cross the tracks to the beach, walk left.

Gdansk—Stogi. This beach to the east on the Bay of Gdansk is too "urban" and polluted but convenient. Take tram 8 to the end of line and walk south 20 minutes along the beach. Strong winds, no refreshments.

Winter swims Sundays Sept.–June in Sopot. Area contact is Zbigniew Marchewicz, al.Kolberga 4b/27, PL-81881 Sopot. Phone (4858) 519232.

221

PORTUGAL

Lusitanian hospitality survived 40 years of dictatorship and now combines with liberalism. Many Portuguese welcome the naturists. You may safely mix *praias gymnicas* with your affordable vacation. Do be cautious in disrobing, however; for nudity remains controversial.

Make Lisbon your gateway—and make your first visit to Aldeia de Meco, a beautiful Lisbon beach beneath sandstone bluffs!

Or take a bus, car or train (5 hours), or directly fly to Faro—the gateway of the southern Algarve Coast, with many small coves and barrier sandbars. Direct flights from London or Montréal. You can still camp at most beaches—unlike in many countries of Europe.

Parliament approved legislation that legalized naturism on April 19, 1988; this legislation was developed by the Federaçao Portuguesa de Naturismo, founded 1977. Contact the FPN at Apto. 3232, P-1306 Lisbon Codex, Portugal. Phone +351 1 44 33 29 2; fax +351 1 44 37 60 8. It was pushed through Parliament by the tiny Green Party, winning by 92/31 (with 130 abstentions).

ALGARVE COAST

Segregated at the extreme south of Portugal by sea, river and mountains, the Algarve Coast took the imprint of successive settlers: Phoenicians, Greeks, Carthaginians, Romans and Moors. The strong Arab flavor in customs and architecture remains, including in the name—originally Al-Gharb. "The Land Beyond."

Developers are rapidly building on the attractions. Modernization has also meant acceptance of the monokini—and no-bikini—on a number of beaches including Praia da Salema, Praia das Furnas and Praia de Fiqueira—all near Quinta dos Carriços, a beautiful camping area with a naturist section.

Faro is the capital of the Algarve, its international airport, and most civilized place to stay: an old port with narrow streets, a walled inner city and impressive church surrounded by low, tile-roof houses and patterned dark stone streets. A bit north is Estoi with an amazing palace. For leather and tile shopping don't miss Quinta do Logo.

From Faro you may go east or west on the 120 km coastal Route 125. Good bus and electric train service.

FARO EAST

East from Faro the nude beaches:

Faro–Olhão Ilhas. Faro area islands are reached from the port of Olhão. Camping and nudity are prevalent, well down the beaches. Ilha da Armona is nearest, but more busy. Ilha do Farol/Culatra is a better choice

Tavira—Ilha de Tavira. Drive to a housing estate, Pedras del Rei, 4 km east of Tavira. There's a sometime nude beach here. Better, a ferry goes every half hour to the 13 km sandy barrier island of Tavira. On the Ilha find a pool, minimart, buffet and disco. Walk down the beach to be nude.

FARO WEST

The beaches from Faro west:

Vale do Lobo. Before Qaurteira. Drive to Almansil; turn towards the coast and Vale do Lobo; at the sandy road parallel to the coast turn left, direction of Quinta do Largo, and watch for a cluster of signs including Mad Max's. Park by the restaurants and walk east to the nude area, past Julia's Beach Cafe.

Albufeira—Praia de Gale–Armacao da Pera. Numerous coves accessible at low tide. Discreet nudity at the beach steps in Falesia and by Hotel Alta-Mar, also east of Praia da Oura.

Portimão—Carvoeiro and Ferragudo. Southeast of Portimão, Carvoeiro is between river estuary and Lagos.

Lagos—Ponta da Piedade. A cove amid scenic cliffs at the lighthouse of Ponta da Piedade, 1 mi south of Lagos. Preferred by youth from chillier climes who camp in the cliffside caves and clean the beach, suggesting a need to the Portuguese authorities. Much of the glorious Lagos coast is too rocky for land access; on calm days, fishermen can be hired to drop your party at a sublime cove.

Salema—Quinta dos Carriços. Portugal's first naturist (in part) campground. Open all year, 50 sites; also studios, apartments for naturists. Restaurant, bar, laundromat, money-exchanging facilities. Entire region is a gorgeous nature park. Accessible by public transportation. Quinta dos Carriços, Praia da Salema, 8650 Vila do Bispo, Algarve. Phone (082) 65 400, fax (082) 65 122.

Sagres—Praia Ingrini. At 7 km east of Sagres take a road signposted for Praia Ingrini; park at the beach buffet, and walk left.

Zavial Beach. Route 125 west past Logos towards Vila do Bispo to Rasposeira village. Turn south toward beach and take a left fork, marked Zavial, which winds to the beach, 12 km from Sagres at the old Barrançao fort. East from the snackbar is nude. Many live at a hippie squatter campground.

LISBON AREA

LISBON AREA

Nudity occurs, often discreetly, south of Lisbon from Costa de Caparica to Sesimbra and Setúbal.

Costa da Caparica. Clean water, nice breeze; too active now for fully comfortable nude use; but if you're there, take the little beach tram, direction Fonte da Telha, to the next to last stop (#19) and check out the dunes. Early pro-nudity actions were here. Or drive over the Tagus (Tejo) Bridge, following signs for Ponte da Telha, then drive north behind the dunes as far as the road goes, and park (you're near #19 beach). You can get from Lisbon to the Costa by direct bus from the Praça de Espanha (Metro Palhavã) or with the ferry across to Cacilhas.

Setúbal—Troia Beach. A beautiful, narrow peninsula at the mouth of the Rio Sado offers tranquility on the Baia de Setúbal. Access by N-253-1 via Alcacer do Sal: Troia Beach is 1 km beyond the enclosed campground, so park beside the road and hike in. Or better, by ferry or hovercraft from Lisbon to Setúbal, and cross the river mouth to Praia do Troia.

Sesimbra—L'Aldeia do Meco. Your first choice near Lisbon. Thirty km directly south, on point of a peninsula near the fishing village of Sesimbra (with lodging, minimart, restaurants and camping). Farmers with donkeys sell mulberries, figs and grapes to sunbathers. A natural spring provides showers and mudbaths. Good windsurfing. Camping in nearby pine woods.

☞ There are two ways. Drive from Lisbon via Fogueteiro, Marco de Grillo and Alfarim; then as below. Or exit Lisbon by the April 25 Bridge over the Rio Tejo (Tagus River) on E-4, and turn off south on N-378 at the Sesimbra exit. Go toward Sisimbra until Marco do Grilo. Here, turn right to Lagoa de Albufeira and on to Alfarim. Entering Alfarim, turn right at the primary school. This road leads to Aldeia de Meco, which you pass through, bearing right on a potholed road. In 2 km you arrive at the parking lot. It's a 300 m walk to the bay; the beautiful 4 km naturist sand beach, backed with cliffs and pine trees, is on the south. (Fonte da Telha is at the north end of the textiled "north" beach.)

CENTRAL

SÃO PEDRO DE MUEL

Limited beach access, a rough coast and unsafe swimming make these 50 kilometers of fine sand an unexpected haven. Patrols will wave you out of the water but generally do accept nudity.

☞ Arriving in São Pedro from Marinho Grande, turn right at the second roundabout. Follow signs to Figuera La Foz. Pass the lighthouse, take the winding road to the second left turn, at a small roundabout. Take this dirt road to parking at the vast beach.

Or drive south from São Pedro towards Praia da Victoire. At Pentieira, you want the beach between Agua de Madeiros and Polvoeira.

NORTHERN

PORTO: AFIFA BEACH

North of Porto (airport) on the Costa Verde, conservatives rule and a nude beach struggles on. The FPN believes success of naturism depends on growing acceptance in the north. Focus is the dunes and beach at Afifa, north of Viana do Castelo and south of Valencia (Spain).

In Porto, check with Hotel Boa Vista, Esplanada do Castelo 58, Foz do Doura, P-4100 Porto. Phone 683 176.

RUMANIA

Rumania largely treats modern naturist values as extensions of agrarian ways. Yes, of course you take off your clothes and bathe when the need is there. Of course you do it with your own sex gender. All the reasons for a free body culture with gender integration, evolved over a century, elude the public policy in Rumania. A modern approach seems yet to come, and there is no organization to bring it about.

After the coup against the longtime communist regime, however, citizens began taking such decisions into their own hands. The Bucharest daily *Evenimentul* for July 14, 1993, reported "hundreds of men and women sunbathing, playing volleyball and enjoying themselves without a stitch on" along the 124-mile Black Sea coast.

CONSTANTA

CONSTANTA SOUTH

Eforie, 14 km south of Constanta, an historic Black Sea resort that includes heliotherapy with other cures. Sections for women only, men, and families. Eforie led Rumanian attitudes on the body and its maintenance.

Lake Techirghiol. Its mudbaths are the finest, most unique naturist activity at the Black Sea. Just west of Eforie North. A modest fee admits you to the shower and locker area where you leave your garments. Then walk to a huge vat of mud and smear it over yourself. Stand under the sun to let it bake you dry (10–12 minutes). Finally walk into the lake to rinse off, and sunbathe till dry. Repeat as often as desired. The mud's medicinal effect is every visitor's rationale for attending—and in truth, it's great fun. Buses and taxis go to Techirghiol from all Black Sea hotels. Gender-segregated.

Continesti has a 1 km nude beach—in our sense—on its north coast. Lively, youth-oriented. Here the forest reaches to a Black Sea which is clear.

Mangalia near the Bulgarian border has a "therapy" hotel on its north shore, Neptune, which includes beach solarium.

Camping 2nd May is 3 km south of Mangalia, has a clothes-optional beach.

223

RUSSIA

Social nudity in Russia as in other Slavic states has a dual tradition: folk and avant-garde. The peasant tradition includes family nude bathing, usually gender-segregated. Thus the last czar was photographed with his retinue in full frontal nudity on a pier of a lake. The early years after the 1917 revolution saw a good deal of intellectually-founded nudity in art or as social protest—but with the consolidation of the Stalinist regime, all of that ended.

In the 1970s nudity became a theme of Soviet art and fiction. Young writers brought skinny-dipping and sexual freedom to small literary magazines. *Literaturnaya Gazeta*, then the cultural arbiter, denounced the themes as "immoral." But by 1990, the Stalinist straitjacket was ripped off.

Today old customs survive without fanfare. Baltic States Estonia, Latvia and Lithuania (see listings) harbor nude bathing at chill, austerely beautiful sites. The Black Sea resorts allow some, too, for "therapeutic" reasons. Russian steam baths are a refuge for the clothes-optional soul. A dozen or so Naturist groups have sprung up, from St. Petersburg to Omsk, from Yaraslavl to Astrakhan, with total membership in 1994 of perhaps 1,000.

Surely much of it is tutored by *Playboy*, little by Naturism. Yet the beaches can provide an experience of body acceptance that is without exploitation. Here are the best sites to date, and the key organizations to contact. See also major reports in *Nude & Natural* magazine N 12.2 pp. 86–93, N 14.2 pp. 71–80, and N 16.3 pp. 97–102.

MOSCOW AREA

SEREBRJANYJ BOR

Since 1988, Moscovites gather on a site near the Moscow Ring road, one of several sandy beaches along a side loop on the left bank of the Moscow River. On the left part of "Serebrjanyj bor 3" beach they swim or sunbathe, play volleyball, cards or chess, as an occasional drunk gawps. Up to 500 men, women and families may be present. As of mid-1994 this beach has been officially designated for nudity.

The leading local group (there are several) is Moscow Naturist Society, 107553 Moscow, P.O.B. 36; phone 095 462 51 48. The MNS sponsors a national organization, Free Association of Naturists (FAN), Igor Nezovibatko, president.

☞ **Serebrjanyj bor**—Silver Pine park—lies between the Borossilovski and Kuncjevskij districts. From central Moscow you can get to the park, at the northwest quadrant of the city, by excursion boat to "Serebrjanyj bor."

Driving, the nearest prominent name on a map is Tatanskaja Street, which leads directly into the park from the Ring road.

By metro, get off at "Polezhaevskaja" station, transfer to electric tram 20 or 65, and go to the last stop. There go left, past a beer bar and a 50-m fence, and turn right, pass a children's playground, go over two footbridges, veer right and the nude beach is about 200 m through pine trees, on the river just before the lifesaving station.

ASTRAKHAN

Located in an island park almost in the center of Astrakhan, the nude beach is on the delta of the Volga River 100 km from the Caspian Sea. No alcohol permitted. Regular users formed the Astrakhan Naturist Association, P.O. Box 84, 414040 Astrakhan, Russia. Phone: 7 (8512) 252-198.

The president of this local group, Valery V. Karpov, was elected president of the Russian Naturist Federation in August 1992. A co-vice president, Nesovibatko (Moscow), led a splinter group out in 1993.

SPAIN

Summarized *Cambio 16*, Spain's leading magazine in 1990: "The idea of Naturism has had a profound transformation in recent years. From being a hotly-debated attitude of the 1960s, it has become customary for entire families."

A clothes-free campground was first licensed only in 1978, in Alméria. Since then, developers have created naturist residence communities; and a 500-room, all-naturist grand resort hotel went up in Andalucia in 1989. Caterers to the British holiday trade employ naturism as a marketing tool. Exciting times, after almost 40 years of paralyzing dictatorship!

Todo Naturismo magazine, started 1997. Subs to the U.S. (4xyr), US $45, payable with U.S. credit card info by e-mail to: focus100@ctv.es

Also see "Naturist Travel to Spain," *N* 17.1 (1997), for an overview.

COSTA BRAVA

MAS PERICOT

Only 40 km south of the French Mediterranean border on 154 ha of forest and prairie, with a river and commanding view of Roses Bay and Lake Boadella. Pool, *boules*, volleyball, Ping-Pong, community barbecue, tent/RV sites. Dirt road is difficult. Mas Pericot, E-17720 Maçanet de Cabrenys.

RELAX-NAT CAMPING

Since 1983. Primarily chosen by visitors to the Costa Brava nude beaches. On an 8 ha farmstead at Mont-Ras, 4 km from coast. Ample tent/RV sites all hookups. Rental RVs. Minimart, snack bar, tennis, volleyball, basketball, 2 pools (one heated), spa, playground, video room. April–Sept. No singles. Relax-Nat, Aptdo. de Correos 19, 17230 Palamós, Girona. Phone (72) 30 08 18; fax (72) 60 11 00.

THE BEACHES

The Mediterranean Coast from the French border to Blanes has sandy coves protected by rocky headlands, and nude bathing is entirely natural. July–August are crowded but May and September have fine weather and Easter is a festive time; come off-season!

Cap de Creus—Cadaqués. Wonderfully clean waters and small sea caves to explore. Best coves accessible only by boat. From Perpignan, take coastal Route 114 across Spanish border to Llansá, keep east along shore to Port de la Selva, cut south to Cadaqués, then by boat or foot northeast towards Cap de Creus. Just south is:

Ampurias—Golf de Roses. Ampurias is famous for Greco-Roman ruins. Figueres has a Dali museum and bullfights. From the Figueres–Roses road, turn right to Playa Ampuria-Brava. Find the most southerly parking and wade across Riu Muga to a 4-mi nude beach, Platja al Golf de Roses. Alternatively, drive south from Castelló d'Empúries in direction Armentera; turn northeast to the Gulf after crossing Riu Fluvià, just south of St. Pere Pescador; park at Camping Nàutic Almata and walk north. Another nude beach is reached by driving south from Nàutic Almata.

Bagur—Platja de Pals. Massos de Pals is an ancient commune. Its spectacular cove, El Salt d'en Ribes, is often visited by Barcelonians and guests of Relax-Camping. Drive east from Palafrugell to Pals, and continue, turning right at sign for Platja de Pals. Park at Mar Blau restaurant near Voice of America transmitting towers. Climb the stairway over the boulders to the south, and you're in the free zone at a giant offshore butte, Illa Roja. Fine campgrounds to south (not nude, but with nude coves).

Palamós—Cala Estreta. Between Punta del Castell and Cap Roig. Take C-255 north from Palamós for 2.5 km, follow signs to the Benelux Campground. Continue past Benelux, with the shore on your right, for 1.5 km. Park under the pines and follow the path down to the beach. The last of four coves is Cala Estreta. More recently in nude use are Cala Bona and Cala Gamarús.

Sant Felíu de Guixols—Tossa de Mar Coast. A variety of naturist beaches along the road: **Cala del Senyor Ramón**—the name is on a roadside rock, next to Cala Salions—a beautiful private sandy beach with refreshment stand, umbrellas, etc. **Santa Cristina**, just south of Sr. Ramón; take the path before the bridge.**Vall Presona** and **Givarola**, facing Cap Péntine.

BARCELONA

The Gaudí church, '92 Olympics, distinctive Catalan customs, language and anarchist tradition, the Picasso museum, great restaurants and night life, rocky coves and beaches, San Felíu and Montserrat monastery; cheaper than the French Riviera and more developed than the Italian—Catalonia is a popular vacation choice for the French, for the French naturists too, and Barcelona is the capital and port. The shirt of freedom on Spanish beaches was first pulled off in Catalonia and homage is due.

The association, founded 1978, has a lively bulletin in Catalan, *Naturisme*. Club Català de Naturisme, Hotel d'Entitats, C/Pere Vergés, 1, 08020 Barcelona. Phone (93) 278 0294; fax (93) 278 0174.

BALÉARIC ISLANDS

The beautiful Baléaric Islands were the first venue officially to allow nudity on the Spanish coast. Ibiza's first nude beach, *Aqua Blanca,* became a popular destination with the young international set in the early 1970s.

IBIZA

Always-sunny Ibiza (*Eivissa*, in Catalan)—a small island with a major airport, and boat connections to Marseilles and Alicante—was a natural to be "the pioneer of nudism in Spain" as *Cambio 16* noted. Two of 40 beaches are officially naturist. Unofficially, add dozens of coves. Topfree is accepted everywhere.

From San Carlos in the north you can reach official and popular **Es Figueral** (a.k.a. Playa Agua Blanca) to its east, a "morning sun" beach.

On Cabo Falcon—10 miles from Ibiza

city at the southern point—is **Es Cavallet**, a second officially naturist beach. Restaurant/bar, snack bar, restrooms, umbrella rentals, big Sunday parties. Connected with Es Cavallet by a headland and string of small coves is **Ses Salines** with shallow water, water sport rentals, refreshment stands. To either, there's bus service from Ibiza town, or drive out airport road and turn left on "La Canal" at the salt mound, to parking at either beach.

Also check **d'En Bossa** beach. The Guardia Civil raided it in June 1977 and cited a dozen nude bathers, only to be hooted by clothed bathers who resented the interference of the Guard with innocent practices. Its far end still has some FKK use despite development.

Both **Cala Conta** (go left of main beach) and **Cala Bassa** (FKK at the ends) can be reached by bus or ferry from San Antonio, and have secluded coves to enjoy au naturel. **Portinax**, where "South Pacific" was filmed, has an end bay in nude use.

FORMENTERA

If anywhere in the Mediterranean is still a vacation haven—it is Formentera, south of Ibiza. The official beach, Las Illetas, is only part of the good news. Most other island beaches are also nude with no hassle or gawkers.

Accommodations: Es Pujols is most convenient to Las Illetas. Bicycles are *de riguer* and can be rented in every village. Regular ferry service from Ibiza Port (about 5 km from the Ibiza airport) several times daily. Day trips are organized from Ibiza and San Antonio (both on Ibiza) directly to Las Illetas.

An isthmus extending several miles northward, with surf on one side and quiet sea on the other.

On the south coast the **Bay of Mitjorn** offers 4 miles of golden sands with at least 75 percent of the bathers openly nude. The western shore secluded bays are also primarily nude; the most popular have beach bars.

MALLORCA

This largest of the Baléarics is easily visited by sea from Marseilles, Barcelona, Alicante and Valencia. Mallorca has well-tolerated nude beaches, among them Cala Pi, Ses Covettes and d'Es Trenc. The civil governor, Marin Arias, noted that "naturism is a sociological reality, and for this reason it is necessary to regulate it with the most open attitude that is possible." Beginning in 1979, naturist camping on Ibiza and Formentera was authorized by the government. The situation continually develops. Check current patterns before you get naked.

Es Trenc is an "ideal" nude beach with white sand, a gentle surf and safe swimming, snack and beverage vendors and umbrella rentals. From Palma drive east

30 mi to Campos. Turn right at center of Campos to La Rapita, and go 7 miles toward the coast. A mile before La Rapita turn left at sign for **"Ses Covetes."** Proceed along narrow road to T-intersection. Turn right, go a mile, turn on a short sandy road to the left towards beach. Nude use between two snack bars.

El Mago, center of three coves, is small, officially nude and very beautiful. Clean sand, gentle slope, refreshments, superb swimming, and flat rocks on east side for sunning. Take freeway from Palma towards Andraix 15 mi to turnoff to Cala Figueroa. Continue to second intersection where sign points past east side of a golf course to El Mago. Go that way and after 2 mi observe sign pointing way down hillside toward coves on the left.

MENORCA

Menorca has, on its northeast coast, naturist beaches at **Capifort, Es Grau,** and **Illa d'En Colum.** On its south coast it has **Macarelleta** and **Binigaus.** A fast ferry runs from Puerto Alcudia, Mallorca to Ciudadela, Menorca.

Even the major hotel beach Son Bou is used clothes-free. The tourist level is low enough, and beaches extensive enough, that most things are possible, for nudity is now expected on Menorca.

To reach Playa Son Bou from the parking lot of Hotel Sol Milanos, walk to the main beach. Continue walking down the beach, away from the main area, to the rocky headland and shallow bay where naturists gather.

COSTA DORADA

SOUTH OF BARCELONA

Since Barcelona lacks suburban *playas desnudas* that are popular, many Catalonians will drive south on Route 246 to the beaches from the Hospitalet del Infante to Peñiscola.

Sitges—l'Home Mort. Located 35 km southwest of Barcelona, Sitges is "the Provincetown of Europe." From the Carreta Pau, a *tren* will take you west along the promenade to Hotel Terramar. Continue west on foot, parallel to the tracks, past the golf course and car park of Platja les Coves, then behind the filtering station and over the hill. The first, W-shaped bay is naturist. If you go on, there's another bay mostly in gay nude use. Both beaches are pebbly. Refreshments are brought in by a donkey during high season. No facilities. *Naturist Hotel Antemar*, Av. Virgen de Montserrat 48, Sitges.

Tarragona—El Torn (L'Hospitalet de L'Enfant Beach). Officially nude.

On highway N-340, at km 1130, turn for

the Hospitalet de L'Enfant. The entrance to the official parking lot is just past the railway crossing. It is regularly patrolled. A small fee is charged.

Or use an alternative turnoff just before the rail crossing, drive 1 km and park anywhere you can; this is unofficial, unprotected, free parking. Cross the rail tracks and follow one of the many paths down to the midpoint of the beach.

El Torn Beach, a mile long, offers a generally quiet sea with refreshing breezes, lifeguards, and a beach bar at the northern end which serves meals and rents chairs and umbrellas.

Camping El Templo Del Sol, E-43980 L'Hospitalet de L'Enfant, Tarragona, Spain. Phone 011 (34-977) 823-434; fax 011 (34-977) 811-306, serves El Torn naturists.

COSTA BLANCA

WHITE COAST BEACHES

The Costa Blanca, accessed via Alicante, caters to naturist seekers of calm and quiet with night life and tourism convenient if desired.

La Rosina. Rents apartments with fine view and total privacy. Two nude beaches nearby, pool on grounds, supermarket at 1.5 km. Inland are grottos, castles, old villages. Owners promise personalized service including baby-sitting. Auto necessary. Phone (65) 73 08 98.

Altea—Punta del Mascarat. Rows of concrete housing monoliths testify to the greed of coastal developers pushing one more condo for one more tourist dollar. Nude beaches help the tourist to recoup and prepare for the next night's adventures.

From Alicante take Route 332 north to Altea. Just before the tunnels under the mountain, look for the house named El Aramo Mascarat on the right. Turn here and continue down the road (which turns into a dirt track) for 2 km. Park at the end; scramble down the steep path to the broad, pebbly beach.

Bénidorm—Playa Cala. A bleak memorial to Spain's juggernaut to build a tourist industry, Bénidorm's 100,000 annual tourists move through 50 discos and countless restaurants and bars. For them, Playa Cala, south of Bénidorm, is an FKK zone. A fence may be constructed to screen out the merely curious, and refreshments are available.

Santa Pola del Este—El Carabasi. This huge beach sees frequent if spotty nude use. The police cite only on complaints as natives are tolerant. Rumor has it that a naturist resort is planned to dominate the view over the pebbly beach. From Alicante take N-352 south. Follow signs to Santa Pola del Este and look for the north beach.

Spain

J. Riera Rovira, Cala de Pals, Costa Brava, Spain.

approval for naturist values, portend the end of a tradition of poverty that is Alméria's image. There is a new kind of "strip" where previously no one wanted to come.

VERA–MOJÁCAR AREA

Vera village and Mojácar are in Eastern Andalucia, 220 km south of Alicante or 100 km from Alméria airport:

Vera Playa Club, a grand hotel for Naturists, is sited on 1.5 km white sand Vera Beach with a panorama of mountains, across a clean, warm, somewhat choppy sea. Huge pool, windsurfing, volleyball, restaurant/bar, beach bar, minimart, disco, tennis, bike rentals, even Spanish lessons, trilingual bingo. Coach trips or rental car to nearby caves and villages. Beachside bungalows and, since 1989, 500 hotel rooms (ask for South wing). Rated ***; reasonable rates.

North of the port city Garruchia. Vera-Playa, Hoteles Playa, E-04740 Roquetas de Mar (Alméria). Phone 950 46 70 27; fax 950 46 70 28. Packaged air/land from USA: 1-800-828-9356.

Camping Almanzora. Managed by Asociación Naturista de Andalucia y Murcia. Formerly Las Palmeras. Its 220 tent/RV sites next to Vera Playa Club are a fertile oasis, with a vast outdoor pool, indoor heated pool, restaurant/bar, minimart. Free access to Playa Vera Club. Open all year. Centera de Garrucha a Villaricos, Aptdo. 60, Vera, Alméria. Phone 34 50 46 74 74; fax 34 50 46 64 76.

Las Rozas. Five km north of Vera Playa, a restored mine manager's mansion on a wooded hillside at base of 3,000-foot mountains. Cottages, camping and bike rentals. Pool, restaurant, bar, minimart, playground, volleyball, miniten. Owner-sculptor Kevin Heffernan and his wife Denise, Yorkshire expatriates, extend a hearty welcome. El Cortijo Las Rozas, E-04610 Las Herrerias, Cuevas del Amanzora, Alméria.

Mojácar–Torre del Peñon. A gorgeous Moorish village, Mojácar clings to a hillside; 2 km south of it naturists gather at lovely "wild" Macenas Beach beyond Torre del Peñon.

El Cabo de Gata. Thinly-settled Sierra de Gata peninsula is suited to "wild camping" and *desnudismo salvaje*. Get a local map and check out the national park for the Carboneras zone, San Pedro de las Negras, Las Sirenas and the Payazo Rodalquilar. Due east from Alméria.

SUN COAST BEACHES

The Sun Coast boasts an extension into southeast Spain of Saharan Africa dry and

COSTA CALIDA

EL PORTÚS

Some bungalow and RV rentals, and 480 tent/RV sites, with sea and mountain view, an hour from Alicante airport. Pool, kids' pool, tennis, terrace restaurant/bar, shops, disco. Fish, snorkel, sail, surf (at times).

Drive 12 km southwest of Cartagena, direction Mazarron, to the sign Centre Naturista (the town of Portús is tiny). Open all year. Camping Naturista, El Portús, E-30393 Cartagena, Murcia. Phone (3468) 55 30 52; fax (3468) 55 30 53.

ANDALUCIA

COSTA DE ALMÉRIA

South from the highly commercial Valencia-to-Cartagena beach strip, the 195-km Alméria Coast was neglected; but that's changing. Its quiet coves and beaches, and dry, hot climate, supported by improved transportation and official sunny climate: hot in summer, mild in winter.

Malaga—Torremolinos. Topfree is common on the hotel beaches. And find nude Benalnatura Beach just two bays before the Casino Torrequebrada, going toward Torremolinas. Access is from the turn lane of N-340 for Viborilla, 100 m following the roundabout for the casino. Umbrellas, refreshments.

COSTA DEL SOL

COSTA NATURA

Between the Rock of Gibralter (27 miles west) and Malaga (airport—60 miles east), don't miss this successful outcome of a gleam in a developer's eye. Two hundred Andalusian-style garden villas nestle into a lushly planted coastal hillside on 7 ha with a view of the Straits. Condos, resident community; holiday weekly rentals; solar-heated pool, tennis, volleyball, jacuzzi, sauna, activities, restaurant. Open all year.

Playa Natura, km 151, Carretera de Cadiz, Estepona 29680 Malaga. Phone (52) 80 15 00; fax (52) 80 28 00. Packaged, air/land from USA: 1-800-828-9356.

Las Dunas. Every success has camp followers and this inexpensive, German-operated naturist campground operates on the beach next to Costa Natura.

ATLANTIC COAST

GULF OF CÁDIZ

Little-visited Gulfo de Cádiz offers a stark landscape for *desnudismo salvaje*. Preferred area is **Matalascañas,** north of Cádiz in the Parque de Donana, and Cala de los Castillejos and Los Canos de Meca near Jerez de la Frontera. Seville or Gibraltar are the accesses. Beware auto break-ins.

Los Caños de Meca is 10 km south of Cádiz on the road to Punto de Tarifa. It has a large adjacent campground, natural caves, clean fine sand and a freshwater run-off into the ocean suitable for natural showers.

MADRID AREA

PARK SOLARIA

Elipa Solarium. The capital of Spain has an official nude sunbathing area posted in a park—a thatched solarium on a hill at a popular sports complex, Elipa. From the pool you can mount earthen steps to the entrance. A sign calls for "complete nudity" inside. This enclosure was created after desnudismo salvaje began to take over the extensive lawns at Elipa—and you'll still find the unruly on the grass. There is both official and unofficial nude sunbathing at other Madrid pools.

☞ From the center of Madrid, drive east on Calle de Alcalá along the north edge of the park. In 300 meters Alcalá forks, take the right (Calle de O'Donnell). Two km further, after the road crosses M30, go right for 300 m and take the first left. Drive 200 m to the entrance of Complejo Polideportivo. Buy an entrance ticket and pick up a map.

For background: Association for the Naturist Development of the Madrid Community. Aptdo. de Correos 47147, E-28080 Madrid. Phone (93) 734 9598 or 617 9563 or 522 9152.

> NOTE: captions to photos run along the inside edge of pages.

SWEDEN

Sweden can be reached by car ferry through its southern ports Ystad, Trelleborg and Malmö. Starting there, your opportunities follow.

Naked recreation fits well into a Swedish life: "You have to be clothed up to your ears for nine months, then summer comes," a Swede told us—"Wow, just take it all off!" The long coasts and many lakes offer the chance at every turn.

The Danes are said to be more plain and direct than the Swedes about being publicly nude. In both countries, however, it is acceptable anywhere that due thought and consideration is shown.

We list leading nude beaches. Most are established near favorite (often textile) campgrounds with telephones. Naturist clubs typically gravitate to these and do not own their own grounds, although a few do. Brochure available from Sveriges Naturistförbund, Box 160, 20121 Malmö; phone/fax (040) 931016.

SOUTHERN

Malmö now has its own official nude beach, **Ribersborg.** The 5 km-long beach located in the center of the city has a clothing-optional portion.

Skanör Peninsula—Svanrevet (Swan's Reef) is 29 km south of Malmö by E-6, turning on Route 100. Skanör was famous in Hanseatic herring trade; visit early chapel. A bird refuge with broad white sand nude beach reached via SNF.

☆**Solhejdan Campground.** Volleyball, miniten, badminton, playground, tent/caravan sites with hookups, pool, showers, sauna, community kitchen, room or caravan rental. June 15–Aug. 15. Welcoming naturists in any season. Box 60, S-23921 Skanör. Phone (046) 40 47 50 88.

Ystad—Backåkra. Direct road from Malmö. The 2 km *fribadstrand* links Löderup Strandbad and Sandhammaren Lighthouse. Turn right at Backåkra and go through Hagestad Naturreservat (wildlife reserve) to the beach. Phone (0411) 77288.

Yngsjö—Gropahalet Beach. Seventeen km south of Kristianstad. Route 63 from Filipstad for 8 km toward Hallefors to Lake Yngen. A government clothes-optional beach is at the south end of Yngsjö town beach. Toilets, play equipment, campsites.

Olofström—Partisanens Naturistcamping. S-29060 Kyrkhult. Phone (0454) 71210; fax 71080. Drive east from Kristianstad on Route 116 at Bromolla, turn left and go to Olofström, continue on Route 121 to Vilshult. Turn right to Kyrkhult and Galaxy Hotel and find Partisanens Naturistcamping in the back. Lake, tentsites, toilets/showers, playground.

Snapphanens Camping is near Skälmershult and Partisanens. Phone (035) 115237 or (0454) 71384.

Aplanabben is 20 km east of Karlskrona, 10 km from Jämjö and 6 km

230

south of Kristianopel. Seventy campsites, half with hookups; sauna, lake, playground. Contact Irene Knutsen, phone (0455) 68000.

WESTERN

Helsingborg—Knähaken Beach. North of Malmö next to Raa Vallar Campground (clothed). Phone (042) 26 06 85.

Laholm—Mällby Beach. Half of 600 m sandy beach is naturist. Adjunct campground is clothed. Marias Camping, S-31200 Laholm. Phone (0430) 25294.

South Göteborg—Smithska Udden Beach. Famous recreation area on Näset Peninsula, south of Vastra Frölunda, has very popular nude sector on north end. Drive out, or trolleys 2 and 3 go from Frölunda Square to Näset and change to bus 92.

Göteborg—Stora Amundön Beach. Take the Linnéplatsen-Brottkar bus line in the direction of Amundön. Or drive from Järntorget on Route 158 toward Särö. The Amundön exit is well marked. At the beach cross the bridge and the island to end of the path, turn south, cross two hills, and you're at the leeward, clothes-free area.

Hamburgsund—Kiddön Island. From Oslo go south—or from Göteborg go north on E-6, past Uddevalla, towards Fjällbacka. The last 35 km take Route 163 toward Fjällbacka and turn left for Hamburgsund. **Kiddön Camping.** S-45070 Hamburgsund. Phone (0525) 33147.

Stora Ekenäset is an island in Lake Frisjön reached by boat from Arnäsholm, on the road between Roasjö and Aplared, east of Göteborg. Phone (0321) 72161.

Strömstad—Kattholmen. An official nude beach, 30 km south of Halden (Norway).

BALTIC COAST

Karlskrona—Salto Beach. The *fribadstrand* is at Karlskrona's core recreation complex. From city center take Järnvägstorget–Borgmästarekajen–Fisktorget–Björkholmskajen–Björkholm en to Saltö Beach and signs for *fribadstrand*. Campground is clothed, with van to beach; May–Aug: Dragsö Camping, S-37103 Karlskrona. Phone (0455) 153 54.

Kalmar—Värsnäs Beach. The town at the causeway to Öland Island has a vast nude beach, Värsnäs, at Vassnäseudd 5 km north.

Öland Island—is lovely with windmills and wildflowers. Driving onto it from Kalmar, turn north for **Borgholm Beach,** midway to tip. Close to Ekerum

Campground (textile). Phone (0485) 555 90. **Böda-Bukten Beach** is on the north point. No campground. For a third beach, Näckstrand, in **Mörbylånga,** south from the causeway and 9 km south of Farjestaden: drive Route 136 south to Vickleby, turn right to the inland shore. The beach is near Haga Park Camping (textile), phone (0485) 406 70.

Gotland Island—reached by ferry from Oskarshalm, north of Kalmar—is a pagan wonderland for the Swedes! June 19th (Midsummer's Eve) kicks off festivities that include July's Stangaspelen (Viking Olympics) and August's Kraftorfest (Crayfish festival that rivals Munich's Oktoberfest for partying). The allure of Visby—a medieval town with city walls that attest to its prominence in the Hanseatic League—is captivating. Be sure to visit **Sjaustre-viken** nude beach between Ljugarn and Gammelgarn on the east coast, and **Norsta Aura** by Faarö in the north.

Vikbolandets Naturistförening, formerly Camp Tyrol. Drive Route 209 east 30 km toward Arkösund, turn right for Rönö. After 3 km find sign for Tobo, and 2 km later signs to the camp. May–Aug. 60307 Norrköping. Phone (0125) 30 139.

STOCKHOLM AREA

Nyköping/Buskhyttan—Västra Kovik Beach. Take Route 53 from Nyköping south toward Oxelösund. After 3 km turn right to Navekvarn and continue for 9 km to the turnoff for Tunaberg. After 3 km find a road going off left opposite a lake. Take that road another 3 km to the parking of Västra Kovik which has cliffs and a sandy beach. No camping.

Djursnäs Naturistcamping. South from Stockholm on Route 73 toward Nynäshamn to Östmo where you turn right on Route 225. Soon turn left to St. Vika and find road to Djursnäs. Campground belongs to Naturistföreningen Stockholms Nynäs. Situated on inlet of the Baltic. Åbovägon 6, 14539 Huddinge. Phone (08) 520 370 26.

Ågestasjön Beach. From Stockholm drive south to Farsta Strand, continue south Agesta Bridge-Lansvagen-Vidjevagen, turning left on Bonasvagen. Help phone (08) 746 6886.

Stockholm—City. On hot days visit the Långholm Park in western Stockholm on the south side of Västerbron Bridge. Take subway to Hornstull stop, then bus 54 or 66 or walk to Högalidsgatan or Bergsund street beaches. Contact: Naturistentusiasterna, Box 15127, S-10465 Stockholm; phone (0480) 41 69 00.

Stockholm Archipelago—Stora Idskär. Tentsites, rental cabins, kitchen, grocery, clubhouse. Island of Naturistföreningen Stockholms Naturvänner. Game courts, water sports. Visitors welcome. June–Aug. Box 444, S-10128 Stockholm. Phone (08) 5413 9306.

Mullhyttan—Trumöbadet. Drive west from Stockholm to Örebro, continuing on E-18 towards Karlskoga. Turn left on Route 204 to Mullhyttan, where signs appear for Trumöbadet, in the Örebro Nature Reserve, near Öna. No camping or sand beach and few facilities but has charm. Phone (0585) 107 20.

Plan to stay at **Gustavsberg Camping,** 32 km northwest of Örebro in Bergslagen, a vast forest with abandoned mines and lakes. From Nora, drive north toward Siggebohyttan. After a few km find Gustavsberg Camping on right: 140 tent/caravan sites, 60 hookups, 10 rental rooms. June–Aug. Box 86, 71322 Nora. Phone (0587) 105 45.

Sandviken Camping lies 15 km east of Filipstad on Lake Yngen. Sites for 70 RVs, most with hookups. Box 122, 66423 Grums; phone (0590) 21100.

Sandvikarna nude beach on Vålön Island, offshore from a famed Picasso sculpture, is 7 km south of Kristinehamn, east of Karlstad on Route 64. Skymningens Camping, not nude, is 4 km.

Skutberget. Follow Route E18 toward Grums 7 km from Karlstad. From there follow signs to Skutberget Camping. Phone (054) 535130.

GULF OF BOTHNIA

Öregrund—Tallparksbadet. From Uppsala North, Öregrund is where ferries leave for Gräsö Island. The town beach includes a nude sector in the Tallparksbadet on the ferry harbor. Go via Uppsala by Route 288 northeast, or from Stockholm by E-3 to Norrtälje and then Route 76.

Rullsand Beach. Straight north from Uppsala to coastal Skutskär is an official *fribadstrand*. Said to be one of the finest beaches in the Uplands, 1-km Rullsand Beach has both shallow and deep shelf for swimming, and surfing at the mouth of the Dalalvens River.

Rullsands Camping with 350 tent/caravan sites (122 with hookups) rents 10 cabins. Cafe, restaurant. Canuding, fishing; boat and bike rentals. 81400 Skutskär. Phone (026) 860 46. Local SNF contact phone (018) 367569.

Killingsands Camping is on the Gulf 70 km north of Umeå, with a nude beach. Phone (0934) 14000; fax (0934) 14014.

SWITZERLAND

owhere outside Switzerland is an equal contrast found between "traditional" Naturists, who generally abstain from the use of tobacco, alcohol, and meat as part of a philosophical ethic of a free body culture; and youth who pull on underwear as outerwear, or become casual nudists at the drop of their trousers, without having to articulate a coherent freedom reason or context.

In the latter spirit of liberty, topfree and nude sunbathing are tolerated in many Swiss parks, somewhat in the way drugs are condoned. A Zurich ordinance of 1989 has offically accepted nudity, called *blütteln,* in municipal pools after a public opinion poll found only 18% opposition. Whatever a quest for freedom may be, Swiss officials rarely interfere.

In contrast, the 17 Swiss Naturist clubs (5 are in Italian- and 1 in French-speaking cantons) mostly demand an INF membership card for entrance. They articulate a philosophy, and they're happy to be exclusive. To visitors, they open a fascinating world of standards that are almost unconsidered in other nations. To visit these clubs, obtain information from the *INF Handbook* and the *Organisation naturiste suisse,* PF 12, CH-2075 Thielle (NE), phone (032) 83 23 95.

Switzerland is also becoming exclusive due to prices—few outsiders can afford the cost of living. An exception is the simple, wholesome, cost-conscious way of life at the Swiss Naturist club grounds. To base a visit at a club such as Die Neue Zeit (Thielle) is at once an eye-opener into a valuable tradition and the way to beat the high cost of visiting Switzerland.

DIE NEUE ZEIT

"Thielle" is the fond common name for Switzerland's most honored Naturist terrain—now in the midst of decisions and changes. The keepers of the flame of traditional Swiss Naturism are mostly aging. They perform rituals of vegetarian meal preparation in the great house of legendary founders Edi and Elsi Fankhauser. A modern hotel is proposed, which would displace many tents and caravans; bringing more money, allowing more memberships, but essentially paving over the natural character of Neue Zeit.

The grounds fill on weekends with young families. Whether they keep the dietary standard is uncertain; they rarely join the workshops in FKK practices conducted by the old-timers. However, they certainly are fit and happy, a credit to body acceptance.

Some bungalow, dormitory, tent/RV site rentals at this club on Lake Neuchâtel. Rather than a public restaurant a community kitchen and common vegetarian dining. Playground, trampoline, aquacise, volleyball, boules, dance, crafts, singing. Open all year. CH-2075 Thielle. Phone (032) 83 22 34.

GENEVA: THONON PLAGE

Beyond Thonon on the south (French) side of Lake Geneva is Thonon Plage and next to it, an attractive free beach with round pebbles, shade trees and agreeable atmosphere. Information: Georges Gervais, Bonnatrait CH-74140 Sciez. Phone (50) 72 77 37.

☞ On the west side, walk between the beautifully landscaped (but not nude) Thonon Beach and the picturesque old Chateau de Ripaille. Find the path between the Domaine vineyard and the lake and follow it to the clothed bathers; the nude section is on the east end.

LAUSANNE: CAMPING CLUB LÉMAN

A verdant, landscaped site, on the Venoge River just off Lake Léman. Welcomes visitors, a splendid base for visiting French Switzerland. Dorm, tent/RV sites, some rentals. Pool, playground, boules, badminton, community kitchen, minimart. June–Sept. Off N-1 at Morges. Chemin de la Venoge 31, CH-1028 Préverenges. Phone (021) 801-83-98.

Die Neue Zeit, Thielle. Dance exercise on lake lawn.

UNITED KINGDOM

VICTORIA SUN BEACH CLUB, Lincolnshire, made this show of the Union Jack. Seen, in 1980, are Pamela Holesworth and her sister.

Slow, low-profile development of naturism in the UK since the 1930s leaves members of the national organization, British Naturism, essentially club-based. Most clubs operate a family- and couples-only admission policy. The 20,000 signed-up Naturists are joined by some 200,000 unofficial naturists who enjoy regular nude holidays in Europe—particularly France—and on numerous coves and bays around the 3,000 miles of Britain's interesting and underrated coastline.

With only six or so official beaches to choose from, many naturists park on a cliff-top road away from the arcades and piers typical of British seaside towns, hike down to the beach and strip off. Explorative natives and visitors find such discreet and enjoyable nude bathing and sunning spots by trial and error. Although guides and magazines list locations, they cannot be complete, and as a general rule, the farther one walks away from beach facilities, the more opportunities for nude recreation increase, particularly on the south and east coasts.

Increasing use of inland locations suits naturists who tire easily of sand and sea. Nude rambling groups wander freely over remoter parts of the huge national parks and common lakes that make up the patchwork of town and country, which is the green, wooded and farmed British landscape. Lakes, reservoirs and numerous rivers host private spots for nude use. Half an hour out of any town or city provides a field or park for naturism, and there are few complaints against the discreet.

British summers—May to September—are short, and weather patterns are peculiar. Although August is often the hottest month

it can also be the wettest. September has cool nights but days can be hot and evenings humid. Early summer can be surprisingly warm and holiday spots are less crowded.

Short unpredictable summers have inspired rapid growth in indoor naturism. Sports complexes and health suites are regularly booked for naturist use only in winter and summer—particularly around larger towns and cities. We describe some of the more welcoming facilities and accessible beaches. Key resources:

Central Council for British Naturism, 30-32 Wycliffe Rd., Northampton NN1 5JF, England. Phone (01604) 20361; fax (01604) 230176. CCBN's magazine *British Naturism* is US $5 for a sample copy or $18/year by surface; $25/year by air. Autumn issue updates the winter swim and

sauna locales and phones.

Naturist Guide Book to Britain, by David Martin. US $20 from Coast & Country Publications, 3 Mayfield Ave., Scarborough, N. Yorkshire, Y012 6DF; phone (01723) 503456; fax (01723) 370691.

Singles Outdoor Club, BM/SOC, London WC1N 3XX. Facilitates admission to England's many reclusive local sun clubs if you're a newcomer.

Suntrekkers, c/o M. Banner, 17 Shearwater Road, Woodlands, Lincoln LN6 0UZ. Contains listings of swims/saunas in each issue; organizes RV/tenting rallies and weekends.

Starkers, "the magazine that uncovers it all." BCM Box 4681, London WC1N 3XX England; phone (01202) 429 189, fax 44-1-202-427-081.

England

LONDON AREA

LANDED CLUBS

Brocken Hurst is impressive; owned and operated on 50 acres of parkland by the Naturist Foundation. Tent/RV sites and extensive recreation facilities include a pool lined with Venetian tiles. Historically a major force in British Naturism. Naturist Foundation, Orpington, Kent BR5 4ET. Phone (01689) 87 12 00.

Silverleigh Health & Fitness Center. Spas, sauna, steam baths, massage, tanning areas, aromatherapy, naturopathy. Clothes-optional, with nudity required weekends and Tuesday and Friday evenings. Driving, leave M-2 at Junction 3 and follow signs for Brands Hatch and West Kingsdown. From Brands Hatch continue to a Texaco garage. Silverleigh is the fourth building on the left after Texaco. Phone (01474) 85 34 38.

Rio's, London's premier indoor clothing–optional venue, features saunas, steam rooms and whirlpools. Secluded gardens, TV lounge, sun beds. Open 24 hours. 239-241 Kentish Town Road, NW5 2JT. Phone (01714) 85 06 07.

There are several gay swim clubs in London—one uses the Oasis Swimming Baths at High Holborn. A favorite club is **Gymnos,** phone (01816) 51 64 99. They swim on Tuesdays, Fridays, and Sundays from 9 to 10 p.m. at Haggerston Baths, a newly-remodeled recreation center. Though this is an all-male swim, don't be surprised that women are continuously coming out of the building preceding 9 p.m. To get there from Liverpool Street Station (Bishopgate exit) take either Bus 22A, 22B or #149 north on Shoreditch High St. (it soon becomes Kingsland Road). You will pass Geffrye Museum on the right. At Whiston Road, walk east about 1/4 mile to Haggerston Baths on the left.

EAST ANGLIA

ESSEX

St. Osyth Beach is the most convenient nude beach for day use leaving London without a car. Or drive the 50 miles and park right behind this sandy, friendly naturist beach. Hutleys Caravan Park owns it and collects parking fees, offering toilets, showers and restaurant in the large clothes-required trailer section. Phone for weather (0255) 82 07 12.

☞ By car, into East Anglia and from Colchester in direction of Clacton by B1027 to St. Osyth Village Crossroads thence to Hutleys Coine Point. By train: from Liverpool Station on the hourly train to Clacton, an 80-minute ride. At Clacton-on-Sea walk to other end of Station Rd., find bus stops on left. Take #2 bus (runs each half hour) to end of line (Jaywick Tower Camp); walk 10 min. in same direction along seawall to Hutleys.

NORFOLK

Holkham Hall Bay Beach. Privately-owned Holkham Bay beach—between Wells and Burnham—is on the Holkham Hall estate. The Viscount Coke controls the property and makes 700 m of shore available to naturist use. Phone (01263) 82 43 29. One can swim safely here but the North Sea is not noted for warmth.

☞ Drive A-149 from Wells towards Hunstanton. Opposite the gates of Holkham Hall, turn right on Lady Anne Road to parking. You will see a posted map showing where the naturist area is located. Walk along the beach or the wooded paths to the west past the small lake and chalet. The clothes-free zone begins here and extends west. Nudity to the east of the chalet is discouraged.

SUFFOLK

Corton Sands. Accorded official nude status by a margin of more than 2-to-1 in the vote of the Waveney District Council. The CCBN termed Corton Sands (a.k.a. Gunton Sands) "possibly the best stretch of official nude beach to date." Nice sand backed by a concrete retaining wall, easy access, draws many Londoners on hot days. Included in tourist brochure. Phone (01502) 56 59 89.

☞ Route A-12 takes you northeast from London to Lowestoft. From there continue on A-12 (now Yarmouth Road) north toward Corton, then B-1385 (Corton Road) north, a total of 2 miles. Park on the road at Pleasurewood Hills American Theme Park. Locate the Tramps Alley cliff driveway (local bus 603 also runs to the top of Tramps Alley). Descend it to the beach, turn north (left) and walk 200 m. Toilets are a 10-minute walk toward Lowestoft; a pub is just 10 minutes in the other direction.

LANDED CLUBS

Broadlands is a good base if you visit Lowestoft's Corton Beach and other East Anglia attractions northeast of London. Heated indoor and outdoor pools, tent/RV sites, restaurant, sports. Brickle Road, Stoke Holy Cross, Norwich NR14 8NG. Phone (015086) 49 29 07.

Tything Barn. Twenty acres of ancient quarries, little meadows and a salt marsh. Two fully-equipped rental cottages, tent sites. Carew, Kilgetty, Pembrokeshire SA68 0TN; phone (01646) 65 14 52.

THAMES & CHILTERNS

LANDED CLUBS

St.-Albans—Spielplatz Club. Founded in 1930, the oldest and largest naturist club of England, venerable yet lively Spielplatz is 25 miles from London. Displaying linkage with the German origins of naturism, it's the only fully-residential grounds with 120 permanent residents and 650 visiting members. Marble-lined pool, sauna, miniten, badminton, 12 acres of woodland, rental cabins, restaurant. Write before visiting to Spielplatz, Lye Lane, Bricket Wood, St. Albans, Herts. AL2 3TD. Phone (01973) 67 21 26.

Sunfolk Society, c/o The Spinney, Hazel Road, Park St., St. Albans, Herts, AL2 2AJ. Phone (0181) 346 4094. Tent/RV sites, showers, playground. Others include **Gardenia** (01923) 67 27 55; and **Fiveacres** (01923) 67 30 73, both singles-friendly.

EAST MIDLANDS

LINCOLNSHIRE

Saltfleetby—Theddlethorpe Dunes Nature Reserve—North. Just to the north of the preserve is a spot favored by the Victoria Sun Beach Club. Along Coast Road 1031, look for the Sea Lane exactly halfway between Saltfleet and Meers Bridge. Take the right-hand fork of the Sea Lane toward the nature reserve parking area. Access to the beach is by the derelict gun site; walk along the beach for 400 yards to the favored area. A bylaw excludes use of the fine beach and dunes that extend south to Mablethorpe's North End.

SOUTH EAST

BRIGHTON BEACH

Brighton—an hour's lark by train from London—is notorious for its catchpenny arcades and fun fairs. It added an official nude beach to its brochures just 50 m east of the main town promenade. It's a pebble beach slipped between the marina and Peter Pan's Playground. Take the Volks Railway to the end of the line and walk back along the beach to the naturist signs.

BEACHES

Hastings—Fairlight Glen. An official nude beach has been likewise termed "a very grotty cove." It's scenic and warmed by the sun under 600-foot cliffs. Fairlight has limited the parking so it's best to park at Hastings County Park on Fairlight Road and ask for the path. Or park at Fishmarket Car Park on the Hastings seafront and climb or take the lift up the cliff at the end of Rock A Nore Road, and walk by the footpath in the direction of Fire Hills, past Ecclesbourne Glen. At Fairlight Glen, rough steps descend to the rocky shore. Care should be taken after rainy weather as the path gets very slippery. Nearest facilities at Hastings. Or enjoy the convenience of camping on nearby Barley Lane at Shearbarn Caravan Site, phone (0424) 42 35 83.

SOUTHERN

LANDED CLUBS

Bournemouth & District Outdoor Club & Holiday Centre. With a view of the Avon Valley, this large site, 11 km from Bournemouth and convenient to Studland Beach, offers numerous activities, outdoor and indoor. New in 1996 is a year-round complex with a large, heated "swirlpool," 14-person jacuzzi. Finnish sauna, bar lounge with sun beds. Matchams Drive, Matchams, Ringwood, Hants. BH24 2BU. Phone (01425) 47 21 21.

St. Anne's Cottage, near Three Legged Cross. Six wooded acres with hookups, tent sites. Reservations required; contact Roy Rogers, St. Anne's Cottage, Horton Road, Three Legged Cross, Nr Wimborne, Dorset, BH21 6SD or phone (01202) 822 377.

South Hants Sun Club welcomes visitors to the Portsmouth area, the ferry port to Isle of Wight, Channel Islands, France. Hotel rooms, tent/RV rentals and sites. Heated pool, hot tub, sauna, volleyball, restaurant and darts. Open year round. Color brochure from Blackhouse Lane, North Boarhunt, Fareham, Hants. PO17 6JS. Phone (01329) 83 29 19.

Aztecs Recreational & Sun Club, a prime home base for touring East and West Sussex and Surrey. Clubhouse, sauna, heated pool, children's area. Crawley, Sussex, RH10 3PE; phone (01293) 88 21 71.

Brighton Sun Club with its undulating woodland, sunning lawn, snack bar, large sauna, swim pool, welcomes visitors from other clubs. Scaynes Hill, West Sussex, RH17 7NP; phone (01444) 83 16 75.

BOURNEMOUTH

Studland Bay. Fine sands with good dunes and swimming. Studland is popular with naturists and accepted locally due to many years of sensible behavior. A good spot for families. Top of the pick. Featured in *N* 16.3, pp. 88–91.

Local tourism information, including nude beach, phone (0929) 42 28 85.

Beach User Group Studland (BUGS) phone Barry, (0202) 69 99 08.

Recommended naturist camping is contacted in advance c/o Studland Summer Camp, 183 Brighton Road, Lancing, Sussex BN15 8JB. July only, cold showers, chemical toilets, no singles, no hookups; a noncommerical act of generosity, congenial times organized by Roger, because he's glad to do it.

☞ Access to Studland Bay can be by chain ferry across the harbor, leaving car in Poole. Or drive around Poole Harbor via Wareham and Corfe Castle and drive north on the ferryport road. Turn right into Knoll National Trust Carpark just past Knoll Hotel, park and walk north on the beach 25 minutes. Or drive north closer to the ferry dock, watch for clustered cars by the road, a sure sign of a nude beach over the dunes.

Weymouth—Durdle Door. This beach area is larger than first appears and is both sandy and rocky. A large rock juts out of the clear water and can be used for sunning or diving. A tunnel in the rock can be swum through, leading to a smaller, deserted beach. The beach and adjoining Durdle Door Caravan Park are privately owned. Phone (01929) 41200.

☞ Find Durdle Door on the map next to Lulworth Cove (Weymouth side); it is well-marked by road signs. At the campground pay to park on the cliff, descend it taking a trail fork to right. On the beach walk right (westward) away from Durdle Door, to the secluded naturist area.

WEST COUNTRY

DEVON

Slapton Sands—Pilchards Cove. This site is England's oldest nude beach. Holding a secured place in the hearts of naturist Britons, Pilchards attracts a new, under-40 crowd despite only a grotty beach, occasional falling rocks, and dangerous undertow. A windbreak is helpful too, yet a loyal cadre comes, you'll see why. Route 379 south from Dartmouth to the north end of Slapton Sands. Park at Strete Gate, where the road intersects the coast; walk ten minutes north to the rock fall at the beach end.

Exmouth—Littleham Cove. A good walk west from the Steamer Steps at the middle of the Budleigh-Salterton Beach. Some shelter from wind and privacy is afforded by large rocks and a 500-foot

cliff. Use the right end of the beach, away from suited swimmers, to avoid trouble from the authorities.

CORNWALL

Perranporth Beach. This nude beach was a vote shy of official designation, but has won the town's acceptance. Dunes, sandy beach. Swim with caution. Take 3285 from Perranporth toward Goonhaven. At the top of a hill find the Perran Sands Holiday Village on the left. The next left is the one you want (marked Menter). Take this road past the Army range and park. Follow a path to Lost Church (1 mile), then over the dunes to the beach. The nude zone is 200 yards north.

Gorran Haven—Vault or Bow Beach. Drive south from St. Austell on B-3273 to Gorran Haven. There drive west up narrow, steep, "no through" Lamledra Road toward the youth hostel. Park in the National Trust carpark. A 3/4-mile footpath leads in front of a hotel west to Bow beach (the map name); keep going through the textile end to the free beach.

Pednevounder Beach. There's a free zone between Logan Rock and Porthcumo, on a clean sandy beach called Pednevounder. Spectacular coast. With its good swimming, Pednevounder gets growing use from both Brits and tourists. A somewhat difficult cliff access means caution by the elderly and young children, who may well handle it.

☞ Off Route 3315, almost to Land's End, find the hamlet of Treen down a "No Through" road. Naturists lunch at Treen's Logan Rock Inn, and may camp here too. Path to beach is southwest from the Treen post office down a farm road, crossing the Cornwall North Coast Footpath.

St.-Austell—Polgaver Bay: Carlyon Bay Camping and Caravan Park. Benefitting from a miniature train that can chug you down to the beach, family use increases. Formerly Cornish Leisure World. This private naturist beach opens daily 10 a.m.–6 p.m., May–Sept. The 15 acres of white sandy beach are backed with brushy dunes. From St. Austell, take A-390 toward Plymouth. At Holmbush turn right and follow signs to Carlyon Bay. St. Austell, Cornwall PL25 3RE; phone (01726) 81 42 61.

Starting in 1991 *naturist* tent/RV sites are offered by top-rated textile **Bethesda Farm Camping,** a 5-minute walk from the nude beach. Phone (0726) 81 27 35.

LANDED CLUBS

Tara Club. Lovely wooded grounds east of Bristol is open to visitors. Tent/RV rentals. Heated pool, sports courts. Tara, Mapleridge Road, Chipping Sodbury, Bristol, Avon BS17 6PB. Phone (01454) 29 42 56.

England

Southleigh Manor. Conveniently and centrally located in Cornwall, with caravans and possibly B & B to rent. Heated pool, sauna, spa, social activities, near the beaches. Southleigh Manor, St. Columb Major, Cornwall TR9 6HY. Phone (01637) 88 09 38.

NORTH WEST

AINSDALE: FORMBY BEACH

Serving Liverpudlians with the tranquility of a nature preservation area, dune sunning at Formby is sheltered and can even get very warm. It's a pleasant walk to the water's edge for a dip. Main area is a mile south of Ainsdale rail station. Beach access is at Pontings. A small road leads off toward the sea. Park as far south as you can, walk south (left) and strip down, staying out of cordoned areas!

YORKSHIRE

BEACHES

Bridlington—Fraisthorpe Sands. Two miles south of Bridlington, now official with a 30-year tradition of nude use.

☞ From Hull take A-165 north toward Bridlington. At Fraisthorpe town make a turn for Auburn Farm and follow its unpaved track to a parking lot, pay, walk 1.5 miles to the shore. On the beach

walk south until you reach Earls Dyke Stream; the nude beach is there. Toilets at Auburn Farm. Phone (01262) 67 34 74.

Scarborough Region. Several unofficial naturist areas. Recommended:

Johnny Flintons Harbour at the north end of Cayton Bay (a.k.a. Osgodby Beach). Owned by the National Trust, and once an official beach, naturists have been on this spot for over 40 years. Park at Killerby Cliff and walk north one mile. Or park in Osgodby and take the path down Knipe Point Drive through the woods and to the cove.

Other Scarborough options: **Red Cliffs** (park at Killerby Cliff and descend a path to Cayton Bay), and **Cornelian Bay** where discretion is needed when fishermen are about. To reach Cornelian Bay, go to Johnny Flintons Harbour and scramble northwards over the huge boulders at the foot of the cliffs. If the tide is in, follow a similar route over the grassy cliff which forms the back of Camels Hump. Or park on Cornelian Avenue, being mindful of the residents, and walk along farm track that runs next to golf course and ends in car park. Go left and down 50 feet to the stream or ditch. Follow the cliff footpath and veer along a grass path that leads to the bay.

HUMBERSIDE

BEACHES

Hull—Easington Beach. North of Spurn Head and east of Hull is an

unspoiled sand beach frequented by birds alone. North Sea air can be chilling yet on a bright warm day this spot can't be beat. Park just north of Easington and walk to the north. The area used extends to Holmpton.

NORTHUMBRIA

BEACHES

Ross Back Sands consists of 2 miles of deserted golden sand, clean if cold water, and dunes for wind shelter and privacy. The hamlet of Ross is north of Bedford off A-1. In Ross, look for the green lane that leads to the sea; park here—do not block the access—and follow the pathway through the fields to the dunes. The beach can be enjoyed for a mile north or south.

Berwick—Holy Island (Lindesfarne). A mile-long causeway leads to this pagan attraction and possible naturist use, away from locals and tourists, on the east and north shores. Please note: the causeway vanishes twice daily during high tide. Do plan!

Northumbria naturists also visit unofficial beaches in Redcar, Skinningrove, Hummersea, Druridge Bay and Cheswick.

237

Scotland

BEACHES

The reader may wish to visit these unofficial clothes-optional beaches.

Near **Dunbar**, in the John Muir Country Park towards Peffer Burn, is an expansive sandy beach.

Tentsmuir Forest on the far north side, away from the parking area, has naturist use. A nearby Bed and Breakfast welcomes naturists: phone (025) 08 42 18.

Old Barn Beach, 2 miles north of Nairn, is used au naturel by locals.

Isle of Arran—Lagg Inn Beach. Not far offshore the Scottish mainland in the Irish Sea is this fascinating island. Ferries traverse the Firth of Clyde from Ardossan to the town of Broderick on Arran about five times a day and from there a short ride will bring you to the lovely, remote beach called Cleats Shore that has been set aside for nude use. Buses meet each ferry and arrive at the hospitable Lagg Inn, at the southern tip, within 45 minutes. The track from the bus stop to the beach is 1/2 mile long. Cars can be parked at the beach. Tourist info 0770-2140.

Solway Firth coast with its many coves and bays is the discreet choice of some. Other possibilities:

Southerness Beach, Powillimount Beach, The Isle Of Mull.

An excellent source for Scottish naturist sites is the *Naturist Guide Book,* by David Martin. A Coast & Country Publication, 3 Mayfield Ave., Scarborough, North Yorkshire, Y012 6DF; phone (0723) 503456.

CLUBS

Scottish Outdoor Club. Private 12-acre, 3-mile-long Inchmurrin Island on fabled Loch Lomond lake. A popular site over 50 years old—a milestone of British naturism, and a resource where you may tent (or rent a room) and cook, play volleyball, socialize and disco with the veterans, and of course lake swim. Inchmurrin Hotel/restaurant shares the island. You'll be met at arranged time and ferried over. It is required that you make contact in advance with an SAE to Scottish Outdoor Club, 2 Birk Hill Ave., Glasgow C64 2 LE. Phone (041) 772 6023.

Sunnybroom Sun Club. Alford, 20 miles west of Aberdeen. Tent/RV sites, playground, clubhouse, sports. Write c/o Les Walker, 43 Prince St., Peterhead, AB42 6QQ; phone (0778) 74803.

Winter Swims—Western Baths, Glasgow, has Winter swims on Sunday mornings. Such nude swims are organized at other Scottish pools. For current times/places call Archie, phone (0324) 48 54 85. You may also ask Archie about the Scottish Outdoor Club camping on Inchmurrin Island.

Wales

GOWER PENINSULA

West from London by M-4 is Swansea. A few miles west of Swansea is The Gower, a large peninsula on the Bristol Channel whose southern exposure has a dune expanse delightful to all naturists—the best of Britain au naturel!

The coast has many coves, spectacular cliffs, great sandy beaches. The National Trust keeps up a cliff path most of the way around The Gower. It will lead you to the hidden coves, and a tide table from the Tourist Office in Swansea will help you to avoid surprises.

Naturism on The Gower is popular albeit unofficial. Naturist lodgings on The Gower, phone (0792) 85 02 86.

☞ These areas are regularly visited by naturists. You may obtain tourist information to other, wide-ranging possibilities. Also check the U.K. Naturist guides for maps and details.

Drive A-4118 out of Swansea. Turn right at Little Reynoldston, left at Burry Green, and follow the road south to Llangennith.

Go through the village, turning left at the roundabout, to the parking at the end of the road. Follow the path onto the beach, and walk west 10 minutes.

Another frequented area is near the point of Whitford Burrows. Reached by SS-4493. Park at Llanmadoc, walk to Cwm Ivy Farm, then north up the Burrows nearly to its end.

HARLECH: MORFA DYFFRYN

An excellent beach south of Harlech, between the towns of Llanbedr and Dyffryn Ardudwy. Although unofficially naturist, some say its camaraderie makes Morfa Dyffryn (pron. *Duffrin*) the "British Montalivet." Backed by the Morfa Nature Reserve the undeveloped beach stretches for miles and yet, an ice cream vendor visits!

Many beachgoers rent a tent/RV site at clothing-mandatory Benar Beach Campsite on the shore a mile south, phone (0317) 571.

☞ Access is by the Harlech to Barmouth road. Turn off A-496 just south of Llanenddwyn. Take Fford Benar Lane, over a rail crossing, to parking at Benar Beach Campsite. Then it's a 20-minute walk north (stay off the dunes!).

LLEYN PENINSULA: PORTH NEIGWL

The middle two miles of the popular beach at Porth Neigwl, known as Hell's Mouth, see frequent nude use. A beguiling strand backed by clay-grass, gently sloping cliffs. An ideal spot to bring children.

The best access is from the east—Llanengan—where a minor road leads to within 300 yards of the beach and even has space for parking. Take Route 497 turnoff from 487 and follow it toward Abersoch. At Llanbedrog take Route 4413 to Llanengan.

YUGOSLAVIA

onde Nast's *Traveler* magazine for May 1988 offered this factoid: "Number of designated nude public beaches in the United States: two. Number of beaches in Yugoslavia for naturists: 1,100."

The 1988 Yugotour Travel Catalog amplified this startling information: "The naturist idea is on the increase throughout Europe. Yugoslavia was the first country on the continent to provide ample restriction-free facilities for naturists and sun lovers. Yugoslavia has just about everything a naturist requires: blue and clear waters of the Adriatic Sea and long hot summers, not to mention miles of beautiful coastline with lush vegetation and shade-giving pinewoods. You will find professional couples with their children, young people and the elderly; a whole variety of sun lovers from a score of countries, of all ages and from all walks of life."

But by 1991, Slovenia and Croatia were in deadly conflict with Serbia. Tourists fled. A Yugoslav success story knitted together 45 years earlier was unravelling.

The Yugoslav ruling party was the world's first investor to provide major capital to emerging Naturist Tourism.

Then, it took courage to recognize and finance the naked people market.

However, even before the Balkan Compromise came apart the Naturist sector was in trouble due to competition and aging facilities. In May 1990 the INF met with longtime Yugoslav advocate of naturism Jerko Sladoljev. The news was that Yugoslav occupancy rates at naturist holiday centers dropped about 30% since 1980. Duration of stay dropped from 12 to 10 days. Punta Skala, renowned for nudity, already shut its doors to naturists. More centers might follow. On the positive side, central and south Adriatic nude facilities continued to show a 2% annual occupancy growth. These were late to develop. They also have more contemporary appeal with sophisticated attractions.

Other poor countries—Greece, Portugal, Turkey, Spain—now have naturist appeal. Also most beaches of Yugoslavia now have some naturist use. "There are two kinds of naturist centers in Yugoslavia. You can stay in a hotel which caters for all holiday makers and spend the day on a nearby naturist beach. Or stay at a naturist center."

This speculation ended with the political break-up

of Yugoslavia. Croatia took nearly all of the Naturist centers—see listings in this *Guide*. Yugoslavia, as the union of Serbia and Montenegro, retains a short coast north of Albania.

MONTENEGRO COAST

GULF OF KOTOR TO ALBANIA

Herceg–Novi Igalo is a tourist center at the mouth of the Gulf, which has a mile-long sandy naturist beach ideal for children. Another local beach, this one with curative muds, is supervised by the Institute of Physical and Medical Rehabilitation. Nearby **Njivice** has a nude beach that is well-sheltered from the wind.

Ulcinj, the southernmost city, boasts a 7-mile sandy FKK beach. The ancient city Budva is nearby, and en route is a fishing village, **Sveti Stefan–Milocer,** now kept as a museum-hotel. To its south is a campground with a clean pebbly beach and a younger crowd. Only "FKK" appears on the sign by the road.

Ada Bojana. An exclusively naturist resort island of sand near Ulcinj, offers mostly bungalow living, some RV and camping, minimart, good restaurants, all water sports, tennis, volleyball, night life. A uniquely free-spirited FKK holiday grounds across the Bojana river from Albania. Montenegroturist, OOUR ADA, YU-85360 Ulcinj. Phone (085) 81834.

Ironically, Yugoslavia ended up with very little Adriatic shoreline but it got the sandy part! Access may remain difficult for some time due to the economic blockade of Serbia.

In the past, how has one reached Ulcinj? Titograd has the international airport. Buses make the connection. Or fly to Belgrade and take the 9 a.m. express train; it's very scenic, passing through 253 mountain tunnels over the 300-mile route to Bar, a local bus ride from Ulcinj. Bus runs to Ada. A ferry connects Bari in Italy with Montenegro's Stari Bar port. And Albania is open to some tourism.

AFRICA &
THE MIDDLE EAST

A reporter writing from Libreville, capital of Gabon, notes a "reversal of attitudes." If the *National Geographic* were to depict truly the fashions in body acceptance, "now it is the white man, or more shockingly significant, the *female* of the species, who goes topless in the tropical sun, while the demure natives, taught by the missionaries to cover their breasts as in socially more advanced countries, look on in amusement.

"All Africa seems to have gone suddenly topless as wave after wave of European tourists hit the beaches...'It is very disconcerting to my parishioners,' shuddered an Irish missionary...'Here we have been telling these people for years to clothe the upper body as a matter of decency and as a sure step toward social modernization, and now these European tourists arrive in hordes like the Gaderene swine and upset the whole cultural applecart, with their immodest dress on the beaches.'"

However, the missionaries who invest shame in the tribal patterns of dress do violence to an integral culture with its natural imperatives. This taking command of another culture's clothing customs can be literally deadly.

Central Intelligence Organization chief Ken Flower of the white-minority [now Zimbabwe] Rhodesian government revealed in his memoir *Serving Secretly* that he had poisoned clothing given to hundreds of black Rhodesians who were volunteering for guerrilla training. The turncoat black Christian minister who did the dirty deed handed out vests, underwear, and shirts sprayed with a powerful but slow-acting poison. Before they reached training camps they died lingeringly in the bush. "Many hundreds of recruits became victims of this operation," confessed Flower. "It became so diabolically successful that the principal perpetrators had to be eliminated," meaning the black-robed black minister.

This may be the most shocking instance in colonial history of missionaries distributing harmful clothing. But the shame in one's own custom, the trust in one's oppressor, are commonplace.

SUB-SAHARAN SURVEY

These are incomplete reports from Africa south of the Sahara desert.

Djibouti. The French invested heavily in tourist infrastructure for this Red Sea port city before leaving. With temperatures often around 100°F, many head for the beaches and seek to get naked. Some natives, Islamic in culture, are offended. The Tourist Office sends the bathers to hotel beaches outside Djibouti City.

Ethiopia. The **Omo River Raft Trip** has been a peak experience for naturists. Jungle and savannah, hippos, baboons, gators, exotic birds, a 1,300 m gorge and a 120 m waterfall, tribesmen who go without clothes and are pleased you do too. Only way to go is SOBEK Expeditions, 6420 Fairmont Ave., El Cerrito, CA 94530. Phone 1-800-227-2384.

At **Lake Langano,** Hotel Bekele Molla is on the left side, 220 km out of Addis Ababa en route to Moyale at the Kenya border. Leftside of the hotel beach is topfree. A 20-minute walk along lake to the left is an established fitfully used nude beach, drawing nudists from Addis on weekends.

On the same road **Shalla Lake** is 230 km from Addis. Turn off and drive 6 km to the shore, then left for 4 km, cross the bridge, and go 2 km farther to a well-known nude beach where you can park.

Gambia—Wadner Beach Hotel. Banjul, the capital city. The beach is mostly topfree and 1 km west is a deserted, free zone. There is also a small hassle-free offshore island. Avoid during rainy April–Oct.

Ivory Coast—Club du Soleil. Atlantic Coast expatriate French resort, 20 km from the capital of Abidjan, 13 km from airport (flights can be met). Sophisticated, landscaped grounds. Pool, restaurant, Ping-Pong, petanque, volleyball. Some bungalow, tent/RV site rentals. Visitors stay at Abidjan or nearby Gonzaqueville (4.5 km), drive a rental car to the club. Open all year. FFN affiliated. Fédération Ivoirienne de Naturisme, B.P. 1653, Abidjan CI, Ivory Coast. Phone 36 75 30 Ques.

Other Ivory Coast possibilities are **Club Med** Vacation Village at Assanie and the nearby **Les Paletuviers** resort that it helps to administer.

Kenya. The four-star **New Nyali Beach Hotel** has three pools and a km of beach on the Io, with a tramp-steamer wreck for amusement on the sandbar. Women of three races appear topfree at the wet bars, even at the ice cream bar.

Lamu Island is regarded as the best refuge from Muslim custom in Kenya. Ask at Petley's Hotel & Restaurant for current suggestions. Many visitors hire a dhow to drop them at a remote beach. Or book at Peponi's Inn or the expensive Kiwayuu Island Lodge, both near a nude beach.

Nigeria. Expatriate whites carry on with nude river bathing at the Butum River near Obudu and on the Cross River near Ugep. In the Lagos area around Badagny and Tarkwa Bay, and at Eket, there is Atlantic Coast nude sea bathing. Usually a group is on picnic or rents a block of villas ensuring some privacy.

As whites looked for ways to get naked, Adwali Kazir, the governor of Kwara state, launched "Operation Get Them Dressed Up"—them, being Kambari tribal women slow to adopt the now-discredited "European" custom of prudery.

Senegal. Like the Ivory Coast, this former colony keeps its French connection. The Senegal newspaper *Le Soleil* attacked French tourists who, "ignoring all sense of decency, practice nude sunbathing on Senegal beaches." The "official" line is now anti-public nudity but topfree women are a common sight at hotel pools.

A free beach at **Aldiana,** 120 km from Dakar, was established by German tourists. La Somone Hotel is near the clothes-optional beach, N'Gaparou. **Savana Saly** and the **Baobab Club** at Nianing on the Atlantic Coast have naturist beaches.

CANARY ISLANDS

Governed by Spain, the Canary Islands are 100% Saharan in origin. The natives wear djellabas, ride camels and herd goats like their Moroccan neighbors. The wealth of the Canaries lies primarily in sand, ocean vistas, and balmy breezes. The Spanish were swift to note that this touristic value was central; moreover the island administrators long have condoned nude sunning areas. Although Moorish in local mores, the Canaries have harbored an international lifestyle for decades.

They're free of the dominant Muslim code of conduct found at that warm latitude. This has made a winter trip to the Canaries very attractive to Germans and British sick of the cold damp streets. The Canaries are, in a sense, Europe's Florida.

But times change. When European Mediterranean beaches were almost as prudish as those in Algeria or Libya, it was understandable that many a European flew to the Canaries. Now many more options exist.

Yet the Canaries remain attractive. They enjoy a permanent "exhaust wind" from the sub-Saharan climate in Morocco and are guaranteed sunny and hot.

LANZAROTE

Lanzarote is the most eastern of the Canaries, about 40 by 15 miles, of volcanic composition with nearly 300 volcanoes. It has little vegetation but does enjoy over 300 days of sunshine a year in a temperature range of 65°–80°F. Must-sees include the fire mountain El Janubio and a water cavern complete with nightclub, called Jameos del Aqua.

The naturist apartment complex of **Las Piteras,** at Mala-Haria, about 20 miles north of Arrecife, offers modern facilities and reasonable prices. Three apartment buildings on a rocky coast, each unit furnished with kitchenette; a minimart and two restaurants; seawater tidal pool, volleyball, boules. Skinny-Dip Tours can book it, phone 1-800-828-9356.

Charco del Palo, formerly known as Castillo de Papagayo, consists of bungalows and apartments with terraces and swimming pool, restaurant, cafeteria, bar and supermarket. Charco del Palo has many German guests, and serves German, as well as Spanish, cuisine. Its lagoon is sheltered by rocks, and provides a lovely place to lunch and swim. You can rent a car to explore the rest of the island. About 2 km away is the former naturist village of Los Cocoteros, now in partial ruin. Charco del Palo, also at Mala-Haria, is booked by Oböna Reisen in Germany, phone 49-6032-8984.

Playa Blanca is a small fishing village at the southwestern tip. Lodging and food, water and wine are available. **Playa Papagayo** is used by many visitors, primarily English and German, nearly all nude. Drive out Playa Blanca's main street east, always taking the best-defined of many tracks that fork as you proceed. After 5 km you should come to a sign pointing right marked "Playa Papagayo." Avoiding potholes and goats for 1 km, you'll come to ample parking and a gorgeous 3/4 mile golden sand beach, with crystal-clear water and mild surf. An easy climb around the rocky point at the east end leads to several beautiful coves with tiny beaches.

GRAN CANARIA

This island has been called a "mini-continent" with mountains to 6,000 feet and tropical rainfall at one side, and desert dunes with fine white sand and camels at the other.

Playa Maspalomas. Immense dunes extend from Playa de Inglés 6 miles west to Maspalomas. The clothing-optional zone, 3 to 4 miles long, is in between. Hordes walk back and forth or play volleyball all day. As there are 150,000 tourist beds in the area it is easy to understand why there are thousands of nude users. The ****-rated **Palm Beach Hotel** in Maspalomas, near the nude beach, is recommended.

TENERIFE

Visit the barren Costa del Silencio and enjoy the warmth and sun on the dark sand beach **Playa del Confital,** west of the Punta Roja rock formation that dominates the coast. It is frequently used by locals, and nudity is accepted. The sand is a dark grey, the beach could be cleaner, but that holds true for all of the Canaries. The water is warm, making the swimming delightful. Coming from El Medano, turn left just after the 4 km post, or coming from Los Abrigos, turn right before you reach the 3 km post.

The beach is about 25 km from the resorts of Playa de las Americas and Los Christianos.

Playa Pavaiso. On a cove near Playa de Las Americas in South Tenerife between two mountains, this beach has black sand and a refreshment stand. Walk 2 km east from Pavaiso del Sur on a trail with cliffs and gullies. You'll see a marker, "Playa," for a trail to the beach.

Playa La Caleta. West of Playa de Las Americas is La Caleta village with another free beach. Park to the right of the village and walk across a soccer field over a well-used ridge to an idyllic bay, then around a headland to La Caleta Beach. Recommended hotel: Paraiso del Sur, Adeje, Tenerife. Phone: 349 78 0450.

El Medano—Playa Tejita West. A big public beach, with nude bathing accepted at the west end.

For a small bay in naturist use, go to El Medano Playa Tejita East from the autopista, turn right towards Los Abrigos, drive past the hotel and windsurfing beach and, 100 m short of the brick building on right, turn left across rough ground to a beach cafe. Park, cross a small sandstone promontory on left to the bay. Both East and West beaches are windy.

Playa Colmenares east of Chaparral on Costa Silencio has a rocky area used by naturists.

Las Gaviotas is a popular, weekdays-mostly, nude beach. Take the road from Santa Cruz to Igueste and continue uphill past the traffic lights at Teresitas Beach. In exactly 3.1 km, one of the hairpin bends has a cutoff right down to three beach cafes.

Playa de Los Patos. From Playa Bullullo at El Rincon, a path leads to naturist Playa de Los Patos with a difficult access over broken concrete steps and around a promontory that is cut off at high tide.

Playa de las Puntillas. From Playa de las Americas take route to San Juan. After 5 km make a left turn at road sign for Armenime. Opposite green-roofed houses on right, turn left carefully onto a sand track and go 3.5 km to beach. Initially follow telegraph poles; left at the first junction, and along a grey finca wall. At reservoir and house on left, turn right following track down to next junction. Turn left and park alongside a large disused finca. Walk across a wooden bridge, over a ridge to two sandy bays. Bring plenty of water.

A resident contact on Tenerife: Eric Tunnington, c/o Owen Booker, La Rambla del Mar 3, E-38412 Los Realejos Bajo, Tenerife.

FUERTEVENTURA ISLAND

Hotels pepper the coast of Fuerteventura (pronounced *Few-ert-e-ven-tura*) and at least three feature naturist beaches. They are Hotel Tres Islas at Corralejo on Fuerteventura's northern tip, and the hotels Casa Atlantica and Robinson Club at Jandia to the south. The island has not yet been commercialized, the beaches are unspoilt and the locals are very friendly.

GOMERA

Gomera, among the smaller, less developed islands of the Canary group, is beautiful—and an easy day trip from Tenerife. The free beach is at the south end of Gomera. Go to Santiago, and then to the second of three small beaches just east of town. This is the free beach; it has potato-sized black lava rocks, rolled smooth by the surf and delightfully warm to lie or sit upon. Geraldo and Mercedes are the resident "hosts" of the beach and genial welcomers.

Lodging: try El Cabrito, a colony of the free-spirited Otto Mühle's AAO, phone 3422-87 1233.

IRAN

Ayatollah Khomeini incited the meanest reign of dress-code terror in decades. The indecent exposure of a woman could mean the sight of a single lock of hair or of less-than-opaque stockings. Women omitting a headscarf were the target of an acid attack. The chador, a one-piece, head-to-toe veil, exposing but a small portion of a woman's face, became the preferred garment to be worn even when "swimming" on Iran's once-fashionable Caspian Riviera. Males continue to bathe in western swim trunks. The speaker of the Iranian Parliament explained the double standard and patronizing treatment: "Women have smaller brains than men."

How could this dismaying terror occur? The Koran, Islam's holy book, makes only this one, passing reference to the veil: "Say to the believing women, that they cast down their eyes…and reveal not their adornment…and let them cast their veils over their bosoms…." Koran, Sura XXIV:31.

In custom the veil goes back to ancient India and Persia. Nomadic Arab and Bedouin tribes instituted strict female modesty to ensure the safety and behavior of women under the suzerainty of absent warriors.

Wahhabism, a fundamentalist sect of Islam, put the full force of religious ideology behind ancient custom in the 18th Century. Under Khomeini, the muttawwiun moral police patrol, at times using cattle prods, shamed those who seem to fail the test of orthodoxy.

The paradox in Koranic tradition is that women enjoy in principle a fully independent legal personality. An Islamic woman may inherit and own property, divorce in certain circumstances, exercise the same religious functions as a male.

Custom it is which overrode the Koran's far more modest expectations. Coercion replaced the role of choice. The cultural fundamentalism, enforced by terror, has now spread to Egypt, Algeria, and other semi-modernized Islamic nations.

Sea area just north of the resort of En Gedi has possibilities for nude recreation, as well as the beaches of Ashdod, going southwest to the Gaza perimeter.

GA'ASH

Ga'ash, located half an hour's drive from Tel Aviv and less than 15 minutes from the tourist resort of Netanya, is an area where skinny-dippers are usually left alone. The beach is not well-maintained, but the weather, water and white sand make up for it.

Drive north from Tel Aviv on the Tel Aviv-Haifa highway. Six or seven kilometers past Herzeillya you'll see a little sign marking the entrance to the Kibbutz of Ga'ash. Turn left and after 100 m, turn right onto a dirt road which is parallel to the main highway. Follow the main dirt road until it turns left, then keep going westerly and you'll reach a large, free parking which hangs from the cliff over the beach. Park here; access to the beach is a short and easy climb through a narrow passageway in the cliffs at the south end of the lot. Bring drinking water.

EIN BOKEK PSORIASIS CENTER

On this shore of the Dead Sea, not far from the ancient site of Sodom and Gomorrah, luxury hotels have sprung up that cater to nude sunbathers from throughout the world. There is no need to fear the wrath of God, however, since the hotels are in the respectable business of providing sun cures for psoriasis patients. Situated 1,292 feet below sea level—the lowest spot on earth—the Dead Sea provides a unique environment. The dense atmosphere filters the

ISRAEL

The socialist rural communities of Israel, the *kibbutzim*, are scrambling for income. Some cater weddings, operate music festivals, launch fish farms or country clubs, do day care for city mothers or open a disco.

Kibbutz Kfar Szold is said by Carl Alpert, in his column "Israel Today" for *The Sentinel*, to "be toying with a proposal to operate a nudist colony on its premises, on the basis that this would be back to nature in the true sense."

Public nudity is unlawful but there are several places where this isn't enforced. In addition to the sites listed below, Nahariya on the coast north of Haifa has a beach where topfree and nudity is practiced and no one is bothered. The Dead

sun's rays allowing many people to spend up to eight hours a day on the beach after the first days. Nothing heals the scaly psoriasis sores better than sunshine. The nude sunbathing area is screened by a high fence and segregated by sex. And despite repeated complaints from the patients, the Israeli government doesn't intend to sanction mixed nude sunbathing even for the sake of psoriasis sufferers.

ELAT

As the world hung on CNN News reports, Scud rockets from Iraq pounded Haifa. Incongruously, the image of a holiday bus appeared on the screen. Israelis were seen boarding. They told a reporter they were off to Elat rather than sit under an equivalent of the V-2 blitzkrieg on London.

Elat is in Israel's far south at the head of the Gulf of Aqaba, 10 miles from Egypt's Taba Beach. With transfer of Sinai to Egypt, Taba Beach and Sharm el Sheikh with its *apres-plonge* sunbathers—and so too the nude haven at Neviot (now Nuweiba)—passed from Israeli control. Elat now serves as the bus gateway for pack-toting European sunbathers heading for the Gulf of Aqaba, as well as being Israel's sole equivalent of St. Tropez.

SEYCHELLES

SEYCHELLES

A cluster of 92 atolls 1,000 miles off the coast of Kenya in the Indian Ocean, the Seychelles offer white sand beaches, luxuriant rolling mountains and beautiful surf—the ideal backdrop for a romantic idyll. So perfect, in fact, that a former president actively courted the porn-movie trade, convinced that his islands were ideal to film flesh epics. He was replaced with a socialist regime.

Nature did not neglect the Seychelles. Centuries-old trees, giant ageless turtles and hundreds of species of birds set these islands apart. Latter-day Darwins delight in these wonders, and marvel at how unspoiled the islands remain.

Mahé, the largest, offers the most lodgings and restaurants. The best way to explore is by rented car and boat. Best avoided from December to March; monsoon season.

With so many perfect islets, your romantic scene is set; you supply the casting.

SOUTH AFRICA

S tarting off on a shaky basis in the late 1950s, Naturism carved a place for itself within the South African social set-up in the 1980s. Yet even in the 1990s Naturists keep very much to themselves avoiding interaction with broader society. This has led to only a small number of unofficial Naturist beaches and land-based clubs, with interrelationship between the different groupings, as well as a common purpose, for all practical purposes nonexistent. See our full report in N magazine, 14.3 and 14.4.

CAPE TOWN

SANDY BAY

The nation's most popular venue of Naturism, Sandy Bay lies on the Western coast of the Cape Peninsula, adjacent to the suburb of Llandudno 12 km from cen-

Model Poses at Beau Valley, Transvaal, South Africa.

tral Cape Town. Its beach nudity, technically "illegal" if today officially tolerated, is traced to the early 1940s. Complaints and arrests occurred through the 1980s until the case for nude beaches was made by brave activists. Some of South Africa's most powerful and progressive financial interests now protect Sandy Bay's ecological and lifestyle integrity.

☞ Directions: Leave Cape Town city limits at Bakoven and drive 5 kilometers along scenic seashore Victoria Drive. Turn off onto Llandudno Road; its name soon changes to Fisherman's Bend. At the cul-de-sac turn right into Sandy Bay Road which takes you to sea level and the start of the footpath. Park in the street.

For 900 yards the path runs above a rocky area then veers sharply to the right and an open area where a path leads to Shelly Beach, a profusion of shells with a nice stretch of sand between the massive boulders. When southeast winds blow the rocks afford some protection.

Beyond Shelly Beach lies the gay area, and then—1.3 km from the start of the path, where it drops to sea level, next to a refreshing sweetwater spring—35-meter-long, friendly, sandy Family Beach. Protected by boulders against the breakers, it is ideal for children who can play in shallow water and among the rocks.

Outjutting rocks on the south side of Family Beach are the Hammersteen. After passing this on the landward side or walking over it and around the ensuing highrising cliff on the seaward side, one reaches the northern end of Main Beach, stretching at least 600 meters to the south.

Main Beach is the actual Sandy Bay below the majestic Karbonkelberg. On a windless, sunny summer day, Main Beach has up to 2,000 nude beachgoers. On such a day luxury yachts and cabin cruisers lie out on the azure water of the bay. A flat section on the northern side is regularly used for volleyball. Closer to the water's edge beach tennis and frisbee are played, and Naturists stroll the water's edge from Main Beach to Shelly Beach and back.

The Albatross Bed & Breakfast, opened 1992 and a Naturist "first" for Cape Town, is located in the southern suburbs. Owner-hosts James and Birgitt Tindall welcome couples and singles. Four guest rooms, indoor jacuzzi, sundeck and pool for "tannuding," lounges and shuttle service to and from the airport or Sandy Bay. P.O. Box 347, Sea Point 8060. Phone (021) 697-3869.

PORT ELIZABETH

SECRET COVE

Naturism has a firm if quiet foothold in the Eastern Cape on the promontory south of the city of Port Elizabeth, within the Cape Recife Nature Reserve. Secret Cove lies west of Cape Recife whose beaches Naturists also use with no complaints from the anglers.

☞ Directions: travel south from the center of Port Elizabeth, over Baakens River to the seaside suburb of Humewood. Continue south along Marine Drive, leaving the city limits at Happy Valley recreational park. Go further south along the extension of Marine Drive; on the right is the University of Port Elizabeth. Where the road turns due west, find the parking area next to the rifle range, the jumping-off point for Secret Cove, a walk of 1 km.

Naturist activities at Secret Cove date from the late 1970s and apparently the Cape Recife Naturists have never been cited by Nature Conservation officials or the South African Police, unlike at Sandy Bay. Its regular patrons are mostly young couples from the city and students from nearby University hostels.

Information: Steve McVeigh, Naturist Promotions, P.O. Box 2025, Durbanville 7550; or Hilton Payne, Secret Cove Beach Group, 2 Langenhof, Middle Street, North End, Port Elizabeth 6001. Phone: 27-41-547863.

THE TRANSVAAL

Transvaal is the economic heartland of South Africa and much of the population lives here. While the eastern part of the province—the Lowveld—is subtropical, eminently suitable for Naturist activities, no known landed clubs are located within the region. Nude use is made of isolated rivers, streams and mountain ponds.

NATURE TRUST

Nature Trust (formerly Beau Valley Country Club), is 200 km north of Johannesburg in the Waterberg mountain range of The Transvaal. Previously a farm, it lies within a *kloof* or ravine, and is the largest and most popular of two dedicated naturist resorts in South Africa, the other being Kiepersol Kloof (see below). The scenery is breathtakingly beautiful; the vegetation particularly lush. Baboons, monkeys, other species of small game and birds abound. Pool, restaurant, steam bath, playground. Rental cabins available; day visitors welcome. P.O. Box 2382, Za-Nylstroom 0510. Phone 27-14-7364012.

SUN EDEN

Come and enjoy the real bushveld together with naturist friends at Sun Eden in Cullinan, 50 km from Pretoria. RV and tent sites available. Phone (12213) 51569.

KIEPERSOL KLOOF

In 1991 a group of ex-Beau Valley supporters established their own private nudist club near the town of Rustenburg 80 km west of Pretoria. Sun City, the nation's Las Vegas, is only 30 minutes distant. Kiepersol Kloof lies within a scenic valley with river and natural pools. Cooperating members have completed a swimming pool, 2 small, private pools, a sanitary block and kitchen, volleyball court and playground. Accommodations include luxury chalets, rustic bungalows, RV and tent sites. On the 210 ha property is a herd of kudu, smaller antelope, warthogs, a few baboons and smaller game. Contact The Secretary, Kiepersol Kloof, P.O. Box 9831, Hennopsmeer 0046; phone (int) 27-12-6632222.

JUNGLE KLOOF

In 1993 The Jungle Kloof opened to the west of Pretoria in the Silkaatsnek Nature Reserve on the north slope of the Magaliesberg mountain range. The Reserve has giraffe, kudu, waterbuck, impala, warthogs, duiker, teenbuck, African buffalo and an abundance of bird life. Like Kuipersol, Jungle Kloof is still rustic but provides camping/RV sites, kitchen, sanitary block, pool, volleyball and cabins for rent. Contact The Jungle Kloof, 92 12th Avenue, Edenvale 1610. Phone: 27-1211-502608.

TUNISIA

DJERBA ISLAND

Long proprietors at their crossroads of civilizations, the gentle-eyed Tunisians are now accommodating nude recreation as well. The mildest of Muslim countries, Tunisia has in Djerba Island a prime vacation spot, where topfree is yielding to full nudity. On Djerba, the 2,450-bed Dar Jerba Hotel is the largest in Africa and among the most handsome.

TURKEY

ISTANBUL

Recommended is the **Cagaloglu Hamami** in the old quarter of Istanbul. Here attendants practice what can only be characterized as a Turko-Esalen massage, sensitive to the body's tension and needs. The massage follows a 20-to-30 minute period of relaxation in the steaming chamber. One lies on the center marble podium, about 20 feet across, under the main Roman-style vault of the bath, with a pad for the head or even from head to the knees. The client is nude except for a small loincloth which one is expected to keep, however tokenly, in the region of the genitals. Following the massage, the attendant bathes and shampoos the client, rubbing the limbs with a camel's hair glove.

Mostly young Germans, Australians and New Zealanders, many on the long super-bus trip from Munich to Nepal, attend the Cagaloglu. There is a second Cagaloglu bath around the corner for women clientele.

Open days and evenings, except Sunday, to 10 p.m. Find it at Yerebatan Caddesi 34, 770 feet from the St. Sophia museum.

SOUTHWEST

TURQUOISE COAST

Emerging as a superb, low-cost, unspoiled area for yachting and basic camping with clothes-optional possibilities is the Turquoise Coast with long, lightly-used beaches and incredibly clear waters. Behind the coast are the Taurus Mountains which hold ruins of pre-Attic settlements of the Lycians. Due to earthquakes some of the ancient monuments have sunk under water, and only those with yachts can snorkel to inspect them, as at Kekova Island.

You can arrange a clothes-optional "Seaborne Safari" with worldwide traveler Roy Edwards, Megamar Yachting, Barbaros cad 87, Marmaris, Turkey. Inquiries are taken by phone/fax +90 252 487 10 71; or U.K. central agents, phone 01962 877 327, fax 01962 877 347.

One of Edwards' boats is featured in the video "Cast Off With Cockatoo," which highlights a fun, 10-day naturist cruise illustrating the magnificent coastline and country; available from Charlie Simonds, Parafotos Film Productions, 136 Bulford Road, Durrington, Salisbury, Wiltshire SP4 8HE; phone/fax 01980 652 034.

Prefer to rent a car or use public transportation? We'd nominate **Finike,** still a small town, as a base to explore the coast if arriving by bus or other vehicle. Finike has lots of local produce, is in a stunning setting on a lagoon, and low-cost beach shanties and campsites are abundant. However, many stay at **Kas** at least to get oriented.

Nudity is a matter of tact and opportunity—with a boat greatly enhancing your opportunities. Be aware this is a Muslim culture, not fundamentalist, but by no means fully modern either!

NOTE: captions to photos run along the inside edge of pages.

THE FAR EAST
& SOUTH PACIFIC

ANTARCTICA

SCOTT & McMURDO STATIONS

Recreational nudity is ritually encouraged at Antarctic sites. Where to go:

The **Lake Vanda Scientific Station,** in the ice-free valleys near McMurdo Sound, as reported by the *Wall Street Journal* for Dec. 10, 1985: "Several U.S. generals and a Congressman have achieved membership in the Royal Vanda Swimming Club, which is restricted to the lake's skinny-dippers.

"At the **South Pole Station,** membership in the 300 Club is earn d by leaping from a 200-degree sauna into 100 below air, again, naked.

" 'Hug a Husky Day' at New Zealand's

Scott Base on the Ross Sea was quickly abandoned when a diplomat from New Zealand was bitten in the worst imaginable place, after shedding his clothes and embracing one of the base's dogs."

The Scott Base claims the all-time coldest skinny-dip record. On April 21, 1986, the official start of Antarctic winter, 35 Americans and 9 New Zealanders "used a chainsaw to cut through meter-thick ice" to skinny-dip, reported Reuters.

Within crowded facilities of the polar stations women have lived the minimum 11-month tour of duty alongside men since 1974. The women say that "within 2 to 3 weeks in the saunas, showers, and restrooms, there are no secrets."

The Morning Edition of National

Public Radio on June 21, 1990 phoned the South Pole. On the equinox, NPR wanted to know, what was happening way down under?

South Pole Station communications officer Laura Folger reported that the Fahrenheit was minus 63, the wind chill minus 136.

"The 300 Club will happen if the wind chill gets up to minus 100," Folger reported.

The 300 Club? "Yes, that's when the temperature is minus 100 and we're all in the sauna which is plus 200. We run outside with just our boots on and run around the south pole and back into the sauna."

NOTE: captions to photos run along the inside edge of pages.

AUSTRALIA

Oz natives have a succinct phrase for skipping out of the 20th Century and on to the beach. "Slip slop slap," they nudge. Translation: slip out of anything you may be wearing, slop on sunscreen in place of clothes, and finally slap the broad-brim Aussie hat on the head, a small substitute for a proper ozone layer.

Australian Bare Facts is the essential print guide ($11.95). *Bare Facts of Oz* is the video guide ($49.95). Both from Elysium Book Nook-NN, 814 Robinson Rd., Topanga, CA 90290 USA.

Australian Sun & Health magazine, slickly informative bimonthly, $5.50 U.S./issue from Elysium.

N 14.1, the special issue on Australia, 1994 ($10) from TNS.

Australian Nudist Federation, Secretary, P.O. Box 741, Browns Plains 4118 QLD; phone/fax (07) 3806 8833.

NEW SOUTH WALES

Sydney is "the nude beach capital" of Australia. Cobblers, Lady Jane, Obelisk, Werrong and Tomaree beaches are officially designated and Aussies will create spontaneous nude beaches when the hot spirit of Summer (our Winter) grips them.

Topfree prevails for both genders on Sydney's municipal beaches—Avalon, Balmoral, Bilgola, Bundeena, Bungan, Cronullawanda, Curl Curl, Dee Why, Thompson's, Turimetta and Whale Beach.

SYDNEY BEACHES

Lady Jane Beach. The sandy beach is only 75 m long and legal nude use continues on rocks eastward to South Point. Some catch fish and abalone from the rocks, to barbecue; a boat comes by with drinks.

Weekdays preferred. The high weekend attendance is plagued by cliff and waterborne gawkers. The core users are unfazed by the "looky-Lous."

Get on direct bus #325 from King's Cross or Circular Quay/Opera House. Exit at Watsons Bay. A water taxi ($7 round-trip) also runs every half hour from Circular Quay. At Watsons Bay, walk east over a hill to the east end of Camp Cove and a large wooden sign pointing out the path to Lady Jane.

Werrong Beach. From Sydney 40 km south in the Royal National Park is a legal nude beach with outstanding scenery and wildlife; even camping by permit on the beach.

From Sydney south on Princess Highway (Route 1)—or north from Wollongong—to F-6 freeway north. Turn off towards Stanwell Park. At park entrance go straight, past lookout/gliderport for 2 km, to parking on right past the sign for Otford Railway Station. Park, follow path for Burning Palms and Werrong Beach. After 200 m the path forks—look for a "W" and arrow on a rock, and follow path down cliffside, a rugged 30-minute walk.

Obelisk Beach. This small, sheltered beach attracts a friendly crowd on George's Head in Sydney Harbour National Park. Crossing the Sydney Harbour Bridge, turn east onto Military Road, Route 14. Go 1.5 km and turn right onto Belmont Road, then left onto Middlehead Road, which becomes Chowder Bay Road. Take the first turn off it to the right, park, descend path to beach.

Or take the bus that departs every hour from the Cremone ferry wharf. It is a private bus that says "Middlehead." Otherwise, it is about 1.5 km walk from the public bus terminal at Mosman Junction.

SYDNEY NORTH

Newcastle—Birdie Beach. Off Sydney expressway at Newcastle exit. Route 1 to Elizabeth Bay, turn right, through town and turn left onto Birdie Beach Drive. Park at end, walk to the legal nude beach.

Lodging may be found at the naturist **Rosco Club**, founded by users of Birdie Beach. Tennis and volleyball courts, dart boards, clubhouse and cooking facilities, sauna, hot showers and social functions. Near beautiful Wattagan Mountain State Forest. Postal address is The Rosco Club International, P.O. Box 45, Toronto 2283.

Ghosties Beach, farther north, is reached by getting off Route 1 at Catherine Hill Bay. Drive south through town to Moonie Beach Caravan Park, behind a coal mine; park, walk south around headland.

Dudley Beach. South on Route 1 toward Belmont, off at Charlestown, find signs to Dudley Beach.

Samurai Point. About 25 km (about 10 km before Nelson) look for signs to right for Anna Bay and One Mile Beach. Park at south side of Sandfort Caravan Park at One Mile Beach lot, walk through to beach and north 1 km to beyond a rocky outcrop. From Newcastle, the right bus going to Port Stephens can drop you at the Sandfort Caravan Park. The legal nude area is Samurai Point on north One Mile Beach—accessible via a track between Middle Rock Caravan Park and Bardots Nude Village Resort.

Shelly Beach. A beautiful, long sandy nude beach with legal status. Bring snorkel, fishing gear.

From Sydney, take Pacific Highway for 270 km north to Bulahdelah. A km north of town, turn right on Lakes Way route to Forster. After 40 km of mountainous lake scenery you reach Pacific Palms. Go right to Elizabeth Beach, park at far end of lot, hike uphill for 10 minutes.

COFFS HARBOUR

Part way to Brisbane from Sydney, and a fine stop-off, are several unofficial nude beaches.

Little Diggers—Moonee Beaches. Little Diggers Beach is reached by a road opposite the Big Banana tourist complex at the northern outskirt of Coffs Harbour. Nude use is at north end. Moonee Beach turnoff from Route 1 is 10 km farther north; nudity at south end of beach.

Bundageree Beach is on the south shore of Coffs Harbour, a short distance beyond Sawtell. Farther south, Wenonah Head Beach can be reached by turning off Route 1 south of Uranga. Nude area is north end of beach.

Broken Head Nature Reserve—Kings Beach. Six miles south of Byron Bay, you may reach beautiful Kings Beach from the Broken Head parking lot. Keep to the established path on the cliff through rain forest to the beach; do not create your own path, erosion must be curtailed.

SYDNEY SOUTH

Scarborough—Wombarra Beach. A family-oriented beach with large rocks and pools. Topfree is common; full nudity at times, at ends of beach. Between Scarborough and Wombarra along the south coastal road. Parking near Surf Club, walk north to the beach.

From **Stanwell Park**, north on the coastal road, are 25 or more beaches where discreet nude sunning and swimming occur. The cliff drive offers a won-

drous view of the ocean and mountains as well as access.

East Corrimal Beach is smaller than Scarborough Wombarra Beach and used less. Go left from the parking lot; use discretion.

Batemans Bay—Richmond and Myrtle Beaches. In Murramarang National Park. Beautiful coast, colorful steep hills, semitropical rain forest. Affordable camping at Durras.

South on Route 1 past Ulladulla to Durras exit. From Durras, turn right on coast road for 1.5 km to Myrtle Beach. Richmond Beach is 1.3 km farther up coast.

Merimbula—Tura Head Beach. A white sand strand, beautiful setting near Yellow Pinch Wildlife Park. From Merimbula, go up hill toward Bega and turn right on to the Tathra Road, then turn right again onto Tura Beach Road. Continue on this road and turn right on first road past the turnoff for Tura Beach Estate. Follow road to North Tura beach, park at the southern end, walk south along the track (which heads inland at times) until you reach Tura Head Beach.

About 175 km south of Sydney, the **Jervis Bay** area has several beaches used with care weekdays by area nudists. Shallow clear water, no surf, clean white sand.

Greenfields Beach, near Jincentia, has modern facilities in the clothed area but nudity should only be attempted weekdays. Both the north and south ends of Long Beach are used au naturel. Murrays Beach, off Jervis Bay Road near the Naval College, has nude use east of the boat ramp. West of the ramp is Hole In The Wall Beach; also used nude.

LANDED CLUBS

Mittagong—River Island Nature Retreat. A family-oriented, clothing-optional resort 2 hours southwest of Sydney in a private valley along the Wollondilly River. Over 350 wooded acres where you may bushwalk and encounter such unique Australian wildlife as the platypus at dusk. Pool, sandy beaches, canuding, trout fishing, sauna, spa, tennis, 4WD club, volleyball. Tent/RV sites, health foods, store, barbecues, cafe, laundry. P.O. Box 456-WG, Mittagong 2575 NSW. Phone (048) 88 9236.

☞ Take the F-5 freeway south and at 5 km beyond Mittagong, turn right onto Wombeyan Caves Road. Follow it 34 km (half on dirt), turn into orange gate on left and follow the white posts 3 km to clubhouse.

Port Stevens—Bardots Nude Village Resort. Ambitious villa resort close to Newcastle white sand nude beaches 2 hours north of Sydney at Port Stevens. Studio, 1- and 2-bedroom suites, some with own spa. Heated pool, volleyball, bushwalking. Cafe, special events, already a "must" of Australian naturism. 288 Gan Road, Anna Bay, Port Stevens 2316 NSW. Phone (049) 82 2000.

AUSTRALIAN CAPITAL (A.C.T.)

KAMBAH POOL BEACH

On the Murrumbidgee River in "The ACT" is a lovely legal nude beach. Toilet facility, barbecues permitted.

ACT Nudist Club is the group of friends who battled for the legal Kambah Pool Beach. They now legally own 40 acres. Rental campsites, spa, tennis, pool, just 20 minutes from Canberra—a good base "if caught in the ACT." P.O. Box 242, Woden 2606 ACT. Phone (062) 38 1512.

From Canberra follow signs to Tuggeranong on Route 23. Turn right into Sulwood Drive; left into Kambah Pool Road. Go straight through the roundabout at Berritt Street to the lower car park. Walk downstream 200 m to the beach.

VICTORIA

What's in a name that Victorian attitudes were transmuted around the globe, down under and also a hundred years forward in time? The Victorian double standard lingers on in Victoria.

Finally The Nudist (Prescribed Areas) Act of 1983 made two beaches legal. Other beaches have since joined them. But it took many arrests before they were granted such status.

BEACHES

Melbourne—Point Impossible. A legal free beach with large sandy area for sunning or beach sports.

Route 1 from Melbourne west through Geelong towards Colac. Just outside of Geelong, look for the road to Breamlea (before Torquay), take a left and follow this road almost to the end. Then look for Black Gate Road, take another left, drive to the end and park. Nearby Corio Valley Nudist Club has camping; phone (052) 81 9200.

Port Phillip Bay—Sunnyside North Beach. Melbourne nudists worked determinedly for the legal status of this convenient beach on the Mornington Peninsula at Mount Eliza. Spotless, clean, friendly, popular with gays.

☞ From Melbourne take the Nepean Highway (Route 3) south 40 km to Frankston. Continue 8 km, looking for the sign to Sunnyside Beach. Turn right at the sign to the beach. Do not park in private driveways. From the beach, go north around the rocky point to the clothing-optional area.

Gippsland Lakes. About 320 km east of Melbourne off the Princess Highway with a variety of water sports and overnight facilities, these lakes, rivers and waterways offer numerous isolated beaches apt for nude use. Camping is possible. Avoid private property; heed "No Camping" signs. No campfires during dry months.

Second Beach. A wide sandy westerly beach with legal status; camping permitted. From the Newell Highway, turn west immediately before the bridge on the Victorian side of the river. Where the track runs beside the river do not bear right into the Time Out resort but go straight ahead, through a gate. Keep bearing right until you pass through a second gate. The beach is then just to the left.

LANDED CLUBS

Kerang—Border River. Tent/RV sites, Ping-Pong, trampoline, pool, boating, swim beach on the Murray River, children's petting pasture. Five acres farmland and woods. Oct.–April. Private Bag 75, Kerang 3579 VIC. Phone (054) 54 2311.

Echuca—Wyanda Park Naturist Holiday Farm. Clothing-optional 60-acre farm/bushland; formerly "Noah's Park." Sheep, goats, horses; milking, shearing and spinning demonstrated. Cabins, 60 tent/RV hookups, RV rentals, shower blocks, rec room, pool, creek, sandy beach, tennis, laundry, playground. No membership required, reasonable rates, open all year. P.O. Box 206, Tongala 3621 VIC. Phone (058) 67 3236.

Echuca—River Valley Nudist Holiday Resort. "A must." RV rentals, 100 tent/RV hookups, chalets, dorm. Playground, tennis, badminton, trampolines, miniten, volleyball, canuding. Open all year. Box 227, Echuca 3564 VIC. Phone (054) 82 6650.

Yandoit—Jajarawong. "Escape from civilization." Two-bedroom cottages rented day/week. Wood heater, gas light; no telephone or electricity. Playground, sauna, water sports, picnic area. RMB 2543 Yandoit Creek Road, Yandoit 3460 VIC. Phone (054) 76 4362.

Horsham—Emu Holiday Park. With 40 wooded acres of owned bushland and pools adjacent to Grampians National Park. Tent/RV sites, hookups, barbecues, water activities, volleyball. RMB 7371, Wartook 3401 VIC. Phone (053) 83 6304.

Glenrowan—Wairane Sun & Health School. Amateur farm on 98 acres with kitchen garden, farm animals, aviaries. Nearby attractions include wineries, Ned Kelly Museum, Drake's Airworld, water-skiing, and gliding. Forty tent/RV sites, 10 RV rentals. Open all year. RMB 4430, Glenrowan 3675 VIC. Phone (057) 65 2315.

Confest. Massage, yoga and other

Australia

activities are held at this camping event held near the NSW/Victoria border each January. Inexpensive vegetarian food. Contact: Down to Earth (Vic), Co-op Soc Ltd., 247 Flinders Lane, Melbourne VIC 3000.

TASMANIA

BEACHES

Asbestos Range National Park—Bakers Beach. The northeast section is okay for tactful nudity. Open to vehicles only 8 a.m. to 8 p.m., December–April; some folks do walk in at other times.

Seven Mile Beach, near Hobart, also has nude possibilities.

SOUTH AUSTRALIA

BEACHES

Adelaide—Maslin Beach. Australia's first legal public nude zone, "Maslin" offers 3 km of white sandy beach on a calm coast with gently sloping seabed. Sandstone cliffs protect on windy days. Beach users keep beach litter-free. Refreshments available. Nudity is on south end. Concrete stairs to the beach. Restrooms on the stairway.

☞ From Adelaide south for 45 km on Main South Road, going through Morphet Vale; do not turn left onto Victor Harbour Road at Noarlunga. Turn right onto Sandpits Road, turn left at the next intersection, go south for several km, turn right onto Tuit Road, go past Maslin Beach Caravan Park to the clifftop parking.

Lake Bonney—Pelican Point. A sandy, legal nude beach with shady areas, sailing, canuding, waterskiing. Bush camping is permitted. Barmera, at the south end of the lake, has shops, lodging, restaurants and water sport rentals. Turn off Sturt Highway, 2 km west of Barmera onto Morgan Road, then east onto Ireland Road, taking you to the beach.

LANDED CLUBS

Adelaide—Maslin Beach Caravan Park. Modern 10 ha wooded resort in walking distance of popular, officially nude Maslin Beach. Pool, tennis, rec room, playground, laundry. Tent/RV sites, RV rentals, cabins. See Beaches for directions. 2 Burnell Drive, Belair 5052 SA. Phone (085) 56 6113.

Adelaide—Whyalla Nudist Social &

Recreational Club. The members often use nearby and legally-nude Murrippi Beach. P.O. Box 2412, Whyalla Norrie 5608 SA. Phone (086) 42 3700.

St. Agnes—Sunland Holiday Village. An RV park—50 sites, some with hookups—at a legal, 500-m nude beach, between Beachport and Robe. Sunland has 100 ha of sand dunes and bushland with kangaroos, wombats, wallabies, a variety of wildflowers and bird species. Pool, miniten, table tennis, jogging trails. Nearby, the caves of Naracoorte and Tantanoola, wineries at Coonawarra. Newcomers welcome. P.O. Box 412, Robe 5276 SA. Phone (087) 35 7280.

Lake Bonney—Pelican Point Resort. Two hours from Adelaide in the Riverland district, the legal nude beach, boating, shaded campsites, kitchen, sports and playground draw many. P.O. Box 799, Barmera 5345 SA. Phone int + 88 73 66.

WESTERN AUSTRALIA

BEACHES

Esperance—Nine Mile Beach. From this lovely seaside town with a moderate climate and beautiful sandy beaches, take the short drive to legally-nude Nine Mile Beach. Follow the coastal road the 9 miles, look for the sign, park and go down steps to the beach.

Perth—North Swanbourne Beach. Site of first Nude Beach Olympics. Traditionally nude as a Commonwealth property when the military used it, the WA government now has jurisdiction; the beach remains nude despite some objecting home owners. Highly popular. North Swanbourne Beach Users Association gets a lot of the credit. They maintain a clean safe beach, organize activities and discourage improper behavior. P.O. Box 35, Clairmont 6010 WA.

☞ From Perth, take Stirling Highway southwest. Turn right onto Eric Street and continue toward the coast. Turn right onto Marine Parade and follow the road to the car park. Walk 300 m north to the dress-optional area. By bus, take #207 from St. Georges Terrace, or train from Perth to Swanbourne station.

Perth—Rottnest Island. Take a scheduled ferry to this lovely island, then head for Parakeet Bay and Little Parakeet Bay on the northern end. Bicycles rented; you can find your own edenic cove.

Rockingham—Warnbro Beach. Clean sand, clear water, gentle waves; legally-nude, no facilities. Best visited in morning to avoid strong winds. Take

Rockingham Road south, turn left onto Mandurah Road, turn right onto Safety Bay Road, and left onto Fendham Street. Near the end of the road, Pollard Way leads off to the right into No. 3 car park. It's a 1-km walk to the designated nude area on the south end of the beach.

Perth-To-Darwin Coastal Drive. The North West Coastal Highway linking to the Great Northern Highway provides a scenic and delightful drive with many secluded beaches where nude use is possible. Do schedule a major stopover for Broome and nearby Cable Beach.

LANDED CLUBS

Perth—Sunseekers. A half hour from Perth near Parkerville; chalets and rental RVs in a peaceful hill setting. Pool, badminton, tennis, miniten, volleyball, darts, sunning lawns, an hour drive from Perth. Open all year. P.O. Box 220, Midland 6936 WA. Phone (09) 295 4346.

NORTHERN TERRITORY

BEACHES

Darwin—Casuarina Beach. A large, officially nude beach with toilets, showers, refreshments. May–October only, due to toxic jellyfish. Nearby Pandanus Holiday Center has camping facilities. From Darwin, follow signs on Stuart Highway to airport, but soon after the racetrack turn left onto Bagot Road (which becomes Talbot Rd.). Go past McMillans Road and turn right onto Trower Road. Turn right onto Casuarina Drive to the beach. The legal area is between Dripstone Caves and Sandy Creek.

QUEENSLAND

BEACHES

Noosa National Park. Queensland's Sunshine Coast, 100 miles north of Brisbane, is crowned by Noosa National Park with its lush tropical plantations, fine surfing, plenty of opportunities for nude recreation.

Noosa Main Beach is often topfree and the sandy inlet to its west, fronted by Noosa Parade, is topfree with some full nudity; these are the best beach and dune lands in the area.

Or drive northeast along Laguna Bay to parking in the national park area, and proceed on foot past Tea Tree Bay Beach to **Granite Beach.** When high tide swal-

Australia

lows the sandy beach, move on to the firm white sands of superb **Alexandria Bay.** Because of the long hike (about 3 km) take everything you'll need for the day. Naturists may rent a bungalow by the week, a walk down the beach from the Noosa nude beaches: Sunshine Beachfront Village, 26 Stevens St., Sunshine Beach 4567 QLD. Phone (074) 47 4739.

Maryborough—Toogoom Beach. Sheltered, clean white sand; part of Jefferson's Beach between Toogoom Caravan Park and O'Regans Creek. North from Maryborough by Route 1 toward Childers, turn off to coast at Torbanlea.

Prosperpine—Whitsundays Islands. Almost 75 islands off the coast of North Queensland. Water taxis or tourist boats can drop you off and pick you up at a predetermined place and time, allowing you to live out the fantasy of a deserted tropical island. Or you can rent a boat and chart your own course. Fishing is excellent, as is coral viewing at low tide. Usually the first to arrive on an island sets the dress code. Recommended: the west side of Blue Pearl Bay, Sunlovers Bay on the north end of Daydream Island (a.k.a. West Molle), Cataran Bay on Border Island, Whitehaven Beach on the southeastern tip of Whitsunday Island, Chalkies Beach on the northwest shore of Haslewood

Island. Many resorts allow topless bathing off of the main beaches and Grun Island has a small nude beach northwest of the main beach. All but 5 islands are national parks and many permit camping for as little as $2 per night. Permits from Ranger, Conway Range National Park, Shute Harbour, QLD 4802, phone (079) 46 9430. Outfitter: Airlie Camping and Gas Center, 2/398 Shute Harbour Rd., Airlie Beach, phone (079) 46 6145.

Townsville—Magnetic Island. Warm gentle surf, beautiful sandy beaches. Rocky Bay, a half mile northeast of Picnic Bay ferry terminal, has nude bathers as does the western end of Horseshoe Bay. Reached by car ferry; for schedule, phone (077) 71 6927. On-island bicycle/auto rentals and buses.

Cairns, north of Townsville, has nudity at Buchan Point. Head north along Cook Highway. The area is about 500 m from Palm Cove Resort. The nude area is south of a large rock and extends for 200 m. No facilities.

Or try Trinity Beach. Take the Beach Bus from Cairns City. Nudity is official on the last 150 m of the northern end. Cafe, swim shop, restaurants nearby.

Also along on Cook Highway are Yorkey's Knob and Ellis Beach; both are unofficial nude beaches.

For full information and personal atten-

tion, Brisbane travelers may contact **Peter Bentley,** 29 Lakeside Drive, Mountain View Village, Murwillumbah 2484 NSW Australia. Phone 6166 726041.

LANDED CLUBS

Brisbane—Sun Leisure. Overseas visitors welcome on 20 ha of bushland. Ample tent/RV hookups, pool, sauna, clubhouse, archery, canuding. Open all year. Reservations needed. P.O. Box 101, Woodridge 4114 QLD. Phone (075) 46 3215.

Pacific Sun Friends. Within an hour of Brisbane, with 100 acres of woodlands and green lawns. Camp, swim, canoe, fish in a nearby creek or join a game of cricket or volleyball. Open all year. P.O. Box 678, Caboolture 4510 QLD. Phone (071) 98 8333.

Marian—Hidden Valley. Abundant wildlife, picnic area, horseback riding, archery, rain forest, swimming in natural pools. On-site vans and guest house available. Reservations required. P.O. Box 104, Marian 4753 QLD. Phone (079) 59 1389.

Aquarius Nature Retreat welcomes weekend visitors. Close to Brisbane. In-ground pool, volleyball, tennis, clubhouse. Tent and RV camping. P.O. Box 49, Browns Plains 4118 QLD. Phone (07) 3800 7482.

Alexandria Beach at Noosa Heads, Queensland.

CHINA

In ancient times Chinese empires constructed a second, skintight, ideological reality, to foreshadow and control the intended behavior in social life. Thus with mannered fiction and fine arts the Confucian culture justified the binding and deforming of upper-class female feet, to secure their status as precious property.

Mao Zedong's cultural revolutionaries relied on the arts to expose such barbarisms, in the process substituting straitlaced revolutionary social models.

Emerging reform politicians from 1978 cautiously condoned a shift to natural body acceptance. That was the year of one individual's wall poster in Beijing, the first known published demand: "Unless we eliminate puritanism, our literature and our art cannot take a step forward. Our country will remain forever in a state of feudalism."

The economic changes of 1979 aided ideological shifts. By 1980 nudity in art was accepted. A Beijing airport restaurant mural ventured to portray Spring Water Festival nude bathing and splashing by women of the Dai ethnic minority.

257

In 1983, discovery of pornographic videotapes at Beijing Academy of Sciences led to a backlash. Nonetheless, arts academies were soon recruiting nude models, and a 1985 decree made the classic, nude-may-not-be-lewd distinction: "Literary works with artistic value, and paintings that show the beauty of the human body," are not pornographic.

The Chinese-language *Ming Pao Daily News* printed a photo on Jan. 1, 1987 of a young Chinese woman seen from the rear walking nude on a beach—the first China-mainland nude beach photo published to our knowledge.

An all-nudes exhibition of the Beijing Art Academy (Dec. 1988) drew a daily capacity of 10,000 visitors. It promoted painters like Xie Dongming, noted for his Western-influenced nude figures. In the 1990s, art and ideology are not as skin-tight. And pornography and repression continue to contend, as elsewhere.

HEILONGJIANG PROVINCE

HELIUNG: WU DA LIAN CHI

Chinese are prudish in comparison with Japanese at their baths—yet one traditional health spa with a custom of nude use draws hundreds of men and women daily to bathe together. Wu Da Lian Chi is a nonheated natural spring in Heliung

250 miles north of Harbin, near the Soviet border in the northeast corner of mainland China.

BEIJING REGION

TENTH RIVER CROSSING

In the mountains above Beijing, Tenth River Crossing resort town won a quiet fame among the intelligentsia in the early 1980s for a secluded river site which was modern China's first nude beach.

HONG KONG

HARBOR BASKING

Long a royal colony of Great Britain, now joining China. Nude swims that avoid hassles and crowds may be possible by going with friends, on a weekday, to Tai Long Wan Beach or Discovery Bay on Lantau Island where many Europeans reside; by boat or foot to Long Ke Wan's East (second) Beach in Sai King; or by boating from Cheung Chau. Topfree sunning happens on rocks bordering the beach at Lamma power station.

TIBET

SPRING FESTIVALS

According to *China Tourism* for Summer 1986: "During the Bathing Festival, Tibetan men are to be seen stark naked on the banks of the Lhasa River, taking a dip in the water. They look quite natural and unrestrained. Also, some young women are bold enough to sport about freely in the water."

Another Bathing Festival site is the Yarlung Zanbo river where the Tibetan woman bather seen on the previous page was photographed.

Hot springs on the Kosi River—a two-hour walk from Kyirong—are a traditional site of Tibetan Spring Bathing. H. Harrer wrote 55 years ago (Ch. 4, *Seven Years in Tibet*): "Swarms of Tibetans came along and bamboo huts sprang up…Men and women tumbled naked into the pool and any signs of prudishness provoked roars of laughter…The whole holiday season lasts only a short time as the river, swollen with melting snow, overflows the springs."

(The Dai minority Water-Splashing Festival, held April 15 in much of the

Xishuangbanna region of Yunnan Province, inspired Yuan Yunsheng's Beijing Airport mural.)

HAINAN REGION

SOUTH CHINA SEA

Gorgeous white sand islands sprawl in a turquoise South China Sea, 300 km or more from the gateway port of Sanya on Hainan Island. The archipelagos of most interest are Xisha (Paracel Islands), Nansha (Spratly Islands), and Zhongsha. Already the principal Xisha town of Yongxing has restaurants and lodging. Nearby Dongdao or East Island has abundant vegetation and a huge colony of red-footed boobies. Hawksbill turtles, giant lobsters and sea cucumbers throng the South China Sea coral reefs.

China's 23rd province was organized only in 1988. Access is now restricted by the military. The Naturist Society's Lee Baxandall visited the Chinese Ministry of Tourism at Beijing in October 1993 to deliver a copy of this *World Guide* and to urge attention to the Naturist resort niche in planning for South China Sea Tourism. The Hainan archipelagos could become a natural holiday Eden.

HAINAN ISLAND

Along with the Xishuangbanna region in Yunnan Province, Hainan Island is the favorite Winter holiday destination for both Han Chinese and foreigners.

As the second-largest island with 34,000 sq km, Hainan has good hotels and easily merits a one- to two-week visit—make it your R&R wind-up of a visit to mainland China, as do young Scandinavians.

CAAC has flights from Beijing, Shanghai and Hong Kong. The Hong Kong ship Malan makes a weekly run to Hainan Island.

See the capital of Haikou, then go several days to the tropical south coast and its port Sanya. On Xiiangshui Bay's fine sand beach with huge rocks, good surf, and few bathers, you can surely skinny-dip. Near Sanya, wide sandy Yalong Bay is scheduled for resort development; today it's unspoiled. East of Sanya at Tianya Haijiao, the beach vendors include moslem Hui women who drape their heads in bright yellow towels. China's variety is astonishing, no less on Hainan Island.

A good account of Hainan is in *China* (Lonely Planet: Berkeley, CA).

INDIA

Indians raised in the cosmopolitan states Goa and Kerala are often at ease with the secular nudity of Westerners. Nonetheless, body tolerance is in jeopardy not least in the attitudes of public officials in those states. The middle-class Indian who goes socially nude is ridiculed by his peers.

But at the last, nature does not tolerate a veil of respectability. "Primitive" tribes of India still go to their fields unclothed. During the Great Drought of 1979, unclad Uttar Pradesh women tilled the fields at night, believing nakedness might please the deities and bring rain and crops. A holy Jain tradition of "sky-clad" nudity lives still, which predates Greek gymnosophy. The temple sculptures of India can make Westerners blush.

TRADITION

SHALMALA'S RIVER OF 1,000 LINGAMS

The lingam is a carving from stone that literally represents the mystery of joined male and female sexual organs. It materializes the unmanifested energy of godhead.

Remarkable evidence of this body-affirming Hindu tradition, at the order of King Swadi these thousands of Siva lingams were carved from the rocks and boulders of the Shalmala River 350 years ago. Devotees flock to the river, especially during Mahasivaratri, to bathe and sit among the rocks. These may be the only truly divine genitalia at a nude bathing site.

Another remarkable lingam, a natural ice formation, is worshipped in Kashmir's Amarnath Cave.

CHANDRAGUTTI

President Rajiv Gandhi, the inheritor of the mantle of good politics in India and modernizer of the vast nation, glared at his Prime Minister, V. Pratap Singh.

"You now stand *exposed*, naked in front of the nation!" Gandhi roared. As a modernizer, Gandhi didn't appreciate the role of nakedness in the Hindu tradition.

Three years earlier, his social workers and police at the Chandragutti festival didn't get it either. On March 8–9, 1987, they kept the clothing upon the backs of some 100,000 celebrants, who wished to converge on this village of 3,000, some 200 miles northwest of Banglalore, as the believing lower castes had done since the 8th Century.

The purpose of the mass nudity is purification ending with new clothes. Entire families—10,000 persons in 1986—strip naked, bathe in the River Varada then walk, still nude, 4 km to the cave-shrine of the goddess Renukamba —whose willingness to flee her attackers while nude preserved her innocence.

When police and social workers interfered in 1986 and tried to clothe the faithful, dozens of government workers were compelled to strip, the better to purify them. Greatly outnumbered, police were compelled to walk naked to the shrine.

In 1987 the Chandragutti festival was blockaded; 2,000 police patrolled with rifles and clubs. The town's inhabitants were forced to remain inside. Roadblocks kept the faithful from Chandragutti and the river.

The festival was not held in 1988. In 1989 it returned, fully clothed. So is the true festival of naked purity finished? Doubtful. The roots of innocence are deeper than temporal power....

KERALA

KOVALAM BEACH

Kerala State in the south of India has on its west coast, at 15 km from Trivandrum, the five-star, clifftop Ashoka Resort at Kovalam Beach. To one side is a palm-bordered "Hawaii Beach" that may be used topfree, or clothes-free if discreet, by beachgoers who, we're told, must implicitly be non-Indian, or at least accompanied by a Westerner!

Some travelers to India rent rooms at nearby huts and small hotels to be near Hawaii Beach—known locally as "valley of the nudes."

As for Keralans, males shuck their shirts at home. Kerala Hindu tradition is that they must *not* wear shirts inside the temple. This hearkens back to a southern Indian standard of bare-breasted for both genders, which endured nearly 4,000 years until moslem incursions of the 12th–17th Centuries.

GOA

THE MALABAR COAST

Named *"Grove of Paradise"* by ancient Indian writings; located on a fertile coastal plain between the Ghats Mountains and the Arabian Sea, 485 km south of Bombay; with 100 km of sandy coastline, 78°F average temperature, and wonderful cuisine: Goa is the favorite clothes-optional destination of India.

"Destination" is the word for it. The clothing-compulsive of all India came to gawk, drawn initially by Goa Travel Board group tours to "hippie" hangouts. The rest of India was tutored in morals and sensibility for over a century by the British. The average Indian now has a horror of the body. He is attracted and repulsed to see the Western children enjoying a clothes-optional freedom on the Goa shore, which the Portuguese had ruled with an un-Victorian insouciance.

In 1988, the "impropriety" of public nudity was enunciated by tourism officials prodded by Roman Catholic hierarchy. Antinudity billboards went up. The harassment got little support from local innkeepers, restaurants or merchants, who often spoke quietly with the police who thereupon often turned, as they say, Nelson's Eye on the foreign naked people (fabled British Lord Nelson was blind in his right eye).

So is the party over? We seriously doubt it. Nonetheless, prudence remains wise. Goa is worth a trip, even if you discover that Nelson's left eye functions and you may have to curb your sunbathing.

British Airways flies nonstop London–Bombay and from Bombay you can steam to Goa overnight on a Mogul Lines boat. A helpful Bombay contact, pioneering modern naturism for India, is

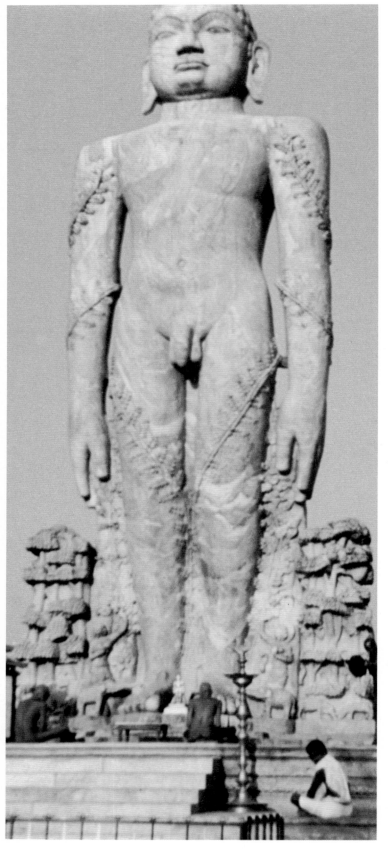

Shrine at Dharmasthala near Mangalore: Nude Jain Monks Meditate At A Modern Gommateshvara Statue.

Mr. Sudhir Surti, P.O. Box 11090, Bombay 400-020.

Only Lufthansa's Condor flies direct Frankfurt–Goa on a weeklong, bargain air/land package. Taxi, bus or bicycle get you around Goa. Sept.–March is the season; after which the weather turns hot, then rainy. Try for pre-Lenten Carnival as local Catholics spark the festivities.

BEACHES

At the north end of the Goa Coast, Vagator Beach South—**"Small Vagator," near Chapora**—is popular with Westerners in a g-string or less who enjoy people-watching, yoga, work on a craft, trade, a nap, massage, Frisbee, fishing.

Suggested lodging or simple access: **Vagator Beach Resort,** Bardez-Goa. Phone Bombay 377 089. Goa phone Siolim 41. Specify a cottage on the beach. A protected clothes-optional area is a walk south of the clothed resort beach, over or around a headland, and to a second cove. At its southern end the coconut groves end in jungle, a small stream and massive headland marked by a small cross.

Temple Cove is nice for a private idyll. Walk north and west from Chapora town on the main road, past the boats, to the end. Continue west along the river, past a small stone fort and tiny cove, a second cove with small Hindu temple, to a third cove where the river flows into the surf. You want to be nearly out of sight of the temple spire, and indeed, avoid nudity if the temple is in use.

Across the river by ferry is **Sweetwater Lake** which may still have a nude beach.

Check the attractive beach at **South Anjuna,** for long the clothes-optional site of a wonderful flea market on Wednesdays. Joe Banana's Restaurant is the information post. Aurobindo Ashram, Pondicherry, was a model for California's Esalen Institute. Also visit **Bagha Beach** across the estuary.

Calangute Beach, at the south end of traditional nudity and early part of it, is on a two-mile sandy coast of dunes, palm groves, and convenient lodgings and restaurants which appeal to Western tastes. Suggested first lodging: **Taj Holiday Village,** phone 1-800-458-8825; or in India, Goa 403 515. Once on site, consider renting a "beach lodge" cabin for $25/mo. or room with a hospitable Goan family near a tolerant beach.

A budget-package beach has developed at **Colva,** several km south; some nude use is developing.

NOTE: captions to photos run along the inside edge of pages.

repressive. Balinese continue their seminude social customs up in the hills—and do become upset if photographers or gawkers invade that etiquette. A similar freedom/privacy is accorded to visitors in their enclave to the south.

If you wish to visit traditional Bali, rent mountain bikes, take a *bemo* (minibus) to the top of the island, then leisurely, tactfully, peddle 200 km to the sea. See *Indonesia,* Lonely Planet Press.

With a rented vehicle one can easily find remote beaches where one can take everything off, especially in the southwest beyond the Kuta/Legian tourist strip. Local people bathe nude or near-nude in rivers and lakes at dusk every day, usually men and women in separate areas.

Kuta Beach, south of Denpasar, north of Tuban Airport, was a fishing village; it now has fruit and cake and sarong shops, bungalow-type hotels, beach peddlers and masseurs, but all low-key; you wish the wild Australians on rented motorcycles were as civilized. Beach admission fee; some of the best surfing in the world but strong undertow. Kuta Beach is usually topfree and full nudity is possible on portions.

North Legian Beach, 6 km from Kuta Beach, is reached by bemo or you may walk north on the beach to Legian Beach and Blue Ocean motels. Older Balinese women offer inexpensive massage. Topfree apart from morals police visits.

Oberoi Beach is north from Legian Beach, past the Oberoi Hotel; isolated with topfree possible.

Nusa Dua Beach, south then east from the airport, is seldom visited; opportunity for nudity.

Ubud Village is a lovely place to hang out. Go east along the main street and continue east along a small road at the T-junction to a bridge over a river in a deep valley. Go down to the river and then upstream along the bank around a couple of bends. The path is rough but you will find some rocks that form a large pool in the jungle where the water is deep enough to swim and dive au naturel.

INDONESIA

BALI

The 13,000 Malay Archipelago islands of Indonesia support the world's fifth largest population. In 1982, Tourism Director Joop Ave warned, "public exposure of the human body is alien to Indonesia's cul-ture." He ignored the fabled island of Bali and its 2 1/2 million people where a unique, ancient culture, with Hindu values ascendent over Koranic doctrine, explains how Bali can be so vibrant with sensuous customs and body acceptance while Moslem Indonesia as a whole is so

JAPAN

Dana Levi, Cable Car Hot Tubbing, Arita, Wakayama Peninsula.

Nude recreation in Japan isn't expressed with ocean or lake sunning and bathing. To offset urban alienation and sexual sublimation, Japanese males appear to lack antidotes other than a flourishing prostitution and pornographic drawing books.

Tradition does offer them communal baths—20,000 public bathhouses, nearly 3,000 in Tokyo alone. Often, they are oddly modernized and grotesquely mass-marketed. For instance, the Hot Tub in a Cable Car, jazzing up a business conference retreat on Wakayama Peninsula at Arita. Rows of one-man hot tubs line the sides of gondolas. As each glides out over a spectacular rocky coast, the soakers gaze at the surf and idly chat or scrub (see photo above).

Writes B. Barber in *Sensual Water: A Celebration of Bathing:* "The Japanese communal bath is not unlike those of ancient Greece and Rome. But whereas they have disappeared, the Japanese bath remains an integral part of today's culture. There is no other country today where public bathing is enjoyed by young, old, rich and poor alike."

HOT SPRINGS & PUBLIC BATHS

Japan is flush with *onsen,* natural hot springs. Skiiers in the northern islands take breaks by jumping into the nearest one. Resort towns are built around them.

Almost everywhere, they have been "improved"—constructed, often both homogenized and sensationalized, with access available only for a fee. Gender segregation is a result of this catering to the lowest common market denominator; unchanging backcountry inns are the exceptions.

"Turkish" baths, *toruko,* have proliferated in the cities, equivalent to Western sexual massage parlors, putting the sexes back together in a bath for the woman's exploitation. The growth of *toruko* occurred after prostitution became "illegal."

But sample both the urban public baths and the 1,600 vacation hotels that capitalize on volcanic hot waters. And look for the occasional still-traditional bath.

The Japan Tourist Office in major cities can provide a *Japan Ryokan Guide.* They also have booklets listing 422 no-frills hotels in 155 cities. Somewhat different ground is covered by *A Guide to Japanese Hot Springs* by Anne Hota with Yoko Ishiguro. It is 284 pages with color illustrations, maps, glossary, accommodations directory. *Pleasures of the Japanese Bath* by Peter Grilli and Dana Levi is valuable (Weatherhill: New York, 1992).

HONSHU

SAGAMI BAY

On Japan's main island above the seaside resort of Atami on Sagami Bay, is the Sekitei Ryokan, secluded within an old fortress. Guests are housed in 20 tiled cottages sharing a multilevel garden of rocks, hot waters and gardens with a beautifully-restored *onsen* and bathhouse. Traditional gender-mixing of nude bathers is restored. Fine restaurant. Bullet train goes from Tokyo to Atami Station in an hour for $25. Not cheap; reservations: Sekitei Ryokan, 6–17 Wadacho, Atami, Shizuoka 413. Phone (0557) 83 2841. Tokyo office, phone (03) 463 2841.

For a complete change of pace, Atami also hosts Japan's Museum of Pornography, a truly bizarre collection revealing more of the Japanese male psyche than you may care to know.

ODARU SPAS

Not far from Atami is Amagiso *ryokan* with more than 20 baths: an outdoor bath in the froth of a waterfall, several baths downstream from the waterfall next to a river in a steep gorge, a cave bath, a women-only outdoor bath, several baths on the side of the gorge, several indoor baths, and seven small iron tubs, named after the seven waterfalls nearby. Most outdoor baths and the cave bath are mixed bathing. To get here from Ito on the Izu peninsula, take the Izu Kyuko Line to Kawaza Station and then the bus to Odaru. The ryokan van will pick you up if you tell them what time you're arriving at the station; or, if you see it waiting for passengers, you are free to ride it. Amagiso Ryoken, Kawazu-cho, Kamo-gun, Shizuoka. Phone (0558) 35-7711. Just down the road is the more economical Urushiya Ryoken, phone (0558) 35-7289.

Other attractions on the Izu peninsula include an orchid farm, wildlife park, scenic rocky coastlines, a wild monkey habitat, an aquarium, a cactus park and numerous museums.

ARIMA SPA

One of Japan's three oldest spas and a national landmark, Arima presides over the Inland Sea west of Tokyo on Mount Rokko. Thirty *ryokan* (inns) and hotels range in price from $20 to $90 per night per person, including two meals. Gaze at the view, lounge on a tatami mat to eat, take tea and talk (with great room service), or go down the hall to the indoor natural hot spring. Or clog about the traditional town.

KYUSHU

IBUSUKI SPA

Ibusuki City, a seaside resort on the southern tip of the southernmost main island, Kyushu, is courting Western visitors. Fly to Kagoshima then take a 50-minute bus or train connection. A subtropical setting enhances the hot spring experience. Book at the 640-room Ibusuki Kanko Hotel with Jungle Bath, an indoor "beach" and 60 hot spring pools, 6 restaurants, dinner theater, mall, etc. Reasonable. 3755 Junicho, Ibusuki City 891-04. Phone (09932) 22131.

Ibusuki Beach is geothermally warmed. Attendants bury lightly-clad clients to the necks in rows along the beach for a unique *sunamushi* or hot sand bath.

BEPPU

Beppu, on Kyushu, is called the Miami Beach of hot spring resorts with over 4,000 hot springs, plus large ponds, or "hells," of water so hot that eggs are boiled in baskets held over them.

Some hot springs are free for public use. There are eight different major zones, each type different, in Beppu. In the Kamegawa area, bathers are buried up to their necks in sand. In the Myoban area, bathers lounge in acid-oxide-hydrogen waters topped with bits of orange peel.

Kannawa is the original *onsen* area: here, children crouch over steaming cracks in the crooked streets, cooking over the vapors, and the "hells" (*jigokus*) are truly formidable. *Chinoike jigoku* (Blood Red hell) gets its color from the iron oxide. *Tatsumaki jigoku* (Whirlwind hell) has a geyser erupting every 25 minutes. At *Oniyama jigoku* (Devil's Mountain hell) more than 100 crocodiles make their home in the steaming waters. And *Bozu jigoku* (Monk's hell) is bubbling hot mud, like the gate of Hell itself. While *Kamado jigoku* (Oven hell) supplies steam heat to hatch thousands of chicken eggs daily, and *Umi jigoku* (Ocean hell) heats the local zoo.

Many lodgings available, the biggest: Suginoi Hotel, 2272 Oaza minami-Tateishi, Beppu City 874. Phone (0977) 24 1141.

264

NEW ZEALAND

Kiwis sparsely populate their nation, a verdant pair of islands. Naturists are attracted by sand beaches that exist beyond any current human need, few of them near to private homes.

Impromptu nudity is thus easy to claim. The chief reason for leaving a nude beach is often merely that high tide may prevent escape from a cliffy cove. No statute in New Zealand law categorically forbids nudity in a public place. Legal recognition seems gratuitous. And yet, it's happening too: serendipity.

Indeed, some nude beaches are in residential areas, and one has a viewing platform built by spectators! The law basically is, if you are far enough away from other people so as not to cause offense, nudity is acceptable. Nor may people approach a nude-use area or nude person with the intention of being offended.

This was established by a 1973 court case and there has been no prosecution since for simple nudity—only for "offensive behavior" where the accused was causing trouble. It's live and let live…an uncrowded haven from urban madness.

Many visitors find it makes sense to rent a motor home to tour the islands and stay at nudist parks. Resources:

Free Beaches: maps, addresses, everything you need to find club and beach. US $7 and allow 2 months. Free Beach Group, P.O. Box 41-171, St. Lukes, Auckland 1030. Phone (04) 589 5461. Or Free Beach Group Wellington, 9858 Wellington. Phone (04) 387 9858.

New Zealand Nudist Federation, P.O. Box 74-257, Market Rd. PO, Auckland 1005. Phone/fax 09 520 0796. *New Zealand Naturist* quarterly magazine, P.O. Box 2925, Auckland. *New Zealand,* Lonely Planet Press. *Naked Down Under,* Heritage Video, is highly recommended.

NORTH ISLAND

METRO AUCKLAND

Auckland, the largest city, has the international airport and shipping. Situated on a land bridge—with Manukau Harbor on the west, Hauraki Gulf on the east—greater Auckland has many nude recreation possibilities.

A good way to "settle in" is by reserving at **Auckland Outdoor Health Club,** C.P.O. Box 2702, Auckland. Phone (09) 833 9209. RV hookups, rentals; 30 km from airport, 1 km from Ranui rail station. Volleyball, badminton, tenniquoit and miniten courts, pool, trampolines, playground, sunning lawn, and good advice.

Katikati Naturist Park is a new resort in 1996. Riverside location, pool, spa, sauna, sports. RV rentals, tent sites. 149 Wharawhara Road, RD 2, Katikati; phone 07 549 2158.

Takapuna—St. Leonard's Beach, is popular after 3 p.m. weekdays, anytime on weekends. Take Bay Bridge to Lake Road in Takapuna. Turn right, go south to Hauraki Corner. Turn left onto Hauraki Road, to the end and park. Walk south around the rocky head at the south end of Takapuna Beach and find sandy, secluded coves. Alternately, continue down Lake Road to St. Leonard's Street, turn left and proceed to the end. Park and take stairs to the beach; walk north to the free zone.

Caution: Takapuna legislated in 1992 to permit prosecution of "offensive" (i.e. overtly sexual) beach nudity, as a precaution. However, no prosecution has resulted. Simple nudity is even more popular on Auckland's North Shore.

Waiheke Island—Little Palm Beach. In Hauraki Gulf; boat from Auckland. Official nude section, west of the rocks. Ferry leaves from Queen Street; on island, take bus to Palm Beach. Also on the island is **Onetangi Beach,** near the hotel of the same name. Water is cold, no facilities. Take the Onetangi bus from ferry terminal for a 10-minute ride. At the beach, go to the west end and cross rocks (be sure to get out before high tide).

Manukau Harbor—Huia Beach. Drive through New Lynn, turn left onto Titirangi Road, follow signs to Huia. After

Cornwallis, turn left at the sign for Huia Point Lookout. Park off road, take path to left.

Manukau Heads—Kariotaki. Take Southern Motorway to Drury, turn west and drive to Waiuku. Turn right, then immediately left onto Constable Road. Look for Kariotaki Road, take that to Gap Road and park at the beach. Walk south for 15 minutes from Surf Club car park.

Hamilton—Waikato Outdoor Society. Miniten, pool, sundeck, clubhouse, playground, tent/RV sites, community kitchen. Pick blackberries, fish a mountain stream, hike Mount Pirongia, tour Waitomo Caves, take a shovel to Kawhai beach to dig your own hot pool and soak. P.O. Box 619, Hamilton. Phone Hamilton 435 779.

Long Bay. An ARA Reserve on the northernmost of Auckland's east coast bays; often used nude. From Harbour Bridge, turn right onto Rosedale Road. Turn left on East Coast Bays, go 3 km and turn right onto Carlisle Road. Follow to reserve and drive through grounds, parking at the far end. Walk north on cliff path around rocks to second beach, next to cow pasture. Access up to 1 1/2 hours each side of high tide, or walk over the clifftop.

Hauraki Gulf—Tawhitokino Beach. With 1.5 km of white sand, the finest beach in southeast Auckland. Drive east through Clevedon to Kawakawa Bay, and continue on coastal road (signed No Exit) for 4 km to the car park at the end. A large map board here shows the trail. The nude beach is an hour's strenuous hike south of the lot, and worth it. Be sure to arrive and depart during low tide!

You may alternately park at Kawakawa Bay where the road comes down to the beach. Walk back along the beach, around the point to the nude zone. Again, avoid high tide.

NEAR NORTH

Warkworth—Omaha Beach. From Auckland take Route 1 north to Warkworth. Turn right and go 8 km to a turnoff with multiple signs. Follow signs for the beaches, a right-hand turn. Walk south from the beach entrance at Matakana.

Wellsford—Pakiri Beach. North on Route 1 to just beyond Wellsford, find Pakiri sign. Park in lot, walk north to miles of uncrowded sand dunes.

Uretiti Beach. A popular beach in a recreational Reserve south of Whangarei. Camping, water, flush toilets, showers. Take Route 1 to a mile north of Waipu, turn right on Uretiti Road, park at beach, walk south. Ruakaka Motor Camp, a few miles north of Waipu, has tent/RV hookups. Box 14, Ruakaka.

NORTHLAND

Bland Bay—Whangaruru Harbour, 35 minutes north of Whangarei City, sparse-ly-visited coves. Recommended is Waione Bay, an easy walk from Whangaruru North (except at high tide), and beaches at Southern Bland Bay.

Bay of Islands—Long Beach. Access from Russell east over the peninsula to Long Beach. Park at the west end of lot, walk around a rock outcrop (wear shoes!) at the south end to reach a small, secluded cove—Donkey Beach. Be sure to attempt this only at low tide; the trail down is not recommended.

Oke Bay. Take the Rawhite Road through to outside Rawhite, watch for sign on right: "Walking Track to Oke Bay." Not a large beach; unsuitable for suitless use if crowded.

Whatuwhiwhi—Puheke Beach. Drive past the lake, watch for the left turn signed Puheke Beach. Park at road's end, walk around hillock to your right to the nude zone.

Kaeo—Wainui Bay. From Route 10 south of Kaeo, take Matauri Bay Road. At the top of the hill, above the bay, turn left and continue past Te Ngaire for 2 km. Watch for the bridge, and turn off into the paddock preceding it. Wade across the stream and walk north around the rocks to the beach. Camping nearby.

COROMANDEL PENINSULA

Matarangi Beach. Southeast of Auckland, take Highway 25 past Kuaotuna and look for the Matarangi Beach turnoff. Park at the lot and walk for 15 minutes to the 3-mile nude beach.

Whangapoua—New Chums Beach. Take Highway 25 to find Whangapoua Beach on the east coast, total distance 24 km. Park and walk from north end along the rocks and over the track for 15 minutes. The nude zone is near the point.

Opoutere Beach. Discreet nude use in center section. Youth hostel within walking distance.

Whitianga—Hot Water Beach. Lodging at Hot Water Beach Motor Camp.

BAY OF PLENTY

Mount Maunganui—Papamoa Beach. Just east of Tauranga on the Bay of Plenty. Drive north from the rail crossing to Mt. Maunganui, turn right on Girven Road opposite Mt. Hire, and go past the D.B. Hotel. Go right on Papamoa Beach Road. Continue past Bay Park Raceway and Ocean Pines Motor Camp, and park near a "Welcome to Papamoa" sign. Walk to the left, keeping out of the dunes. Legally designated (but not marked) "Nude Bathing Area" is located a few kilometers northwest from the main entance. Tauranga has shops, campgrounds, motels.

Rotota Sun Club, inland from Bay of Plenty on the central volcanic plateau, is convenient to Orakei Korako Thermal Wonderland with its geysers and boiling mud. Tent/RV rentals. No food service or electricity. P.O. Box 164, Reporoa. Phone (073) 38 371.

GISBORNE AREA

Mahia Peninsula—Mahanga Beach. From Gisborne, on North Island's south eastern exposure, take Route 2 south to Morere and follow signs to Mahanga on the Mahia Peninsula. At the 8 km dune beach, walk south; there are houses at the north end.

Waimarama Beach. From Havelock North, drive south and turn left onto Ocean Road, then right on Waimarama Road. Find the inconspicuous Dump Road entrance on your left before the main beach entrance, and turn in; at the tenting site, turn left, proceed cautiously in sandy ruts to the beach. Across the creek to the left is the nude area.

Gisborne Country Club features pool, hot tub, sauna, courts, a few rental units; on Makaraka Highway. P.O. Box 391, Gisborne. Phone 867-8157 or 867-3607.

WELLINGTON AREA

Peka Peka Beach. The first accessible beach north of Wellington that's not developed. Take Highway 1 north 40 miles, through Waikanae to Peka Peka Road on the left, 3 miles north of the town. At the beach park and walk north 1 km past the Sandcastle Motel and a creek to the free beach area. Nearest facilities at Te Horo Beach, 3 miles north.

Breaker Bay. Designated for nudity. From Wellington centre, go east "around the bay" following signs for airport, to Evans Bay. At the last roundabout, head south toward the airport then east for Strathmore Park and Seatoun. After the road tunnel take the first right (Ludlam Street) to Inglis Street. Turn right and south and through the Pass of Brands to the coast. Park on the left. Walk back and down to the beach after Breaker Bay, where nudity is normal after the rock arch right along to Point Dorset. Public bus to Strathmore Park and Seatoun.

Tararua Forest Park river has nudity. **Clouston Park** and **Otaki Forks** have nude possibilities and camping areas. Nude enthusiasts might try the northern ends of **Tasman, Foxton** and **Hokio** beaches on the west coast. The east coast offers little in way of nude recreation, with the exception **Baring Head** at the eastern end of Fitzroy which has an isolated beach area. If you travel the Wellington area beaches and see a yellow flag (with Fred Bare) marking the location, stop and visit the flag owners.

Wellington Sun Club has 14 acres and many tent/RV rental units available for naturists at Te Marua. P.O. Box 2854, Wellington. Phone (04) 267 853.

Manakau—Waikawa Beach.
Midway between Levin and Otaki, west of Manakau. Cross the footbridge, walk past the pines and hills to the beach.

Please note attractions immediately south of Wellington on South Island…

SOUTH ISLAND

Nelson—Mapua Leisure Park. New Zealand's only clothing-optional resort offers pool, sauna, spa, volleyball, golf course, tennis, unique children's playground, rafting, private beach. Tent/RV sites, rental. Open all year. Local attractions include caves, Nelson National Parks, golf. 33 Toru St., Mapua, Nelson. Phone (03) 540 2666.

Nelson Sun Club. Tent/RV/room rentals. Miniten, golf course, table tennis, playground, barbecue, community kitchen, clubhouse with TV lounge. Open all year. P.O. Box 467, Nelson. Phone Nelson (054) 44 616.

Christchurch—Spencerville Beach. From Christchurch, follow Marshlands Road. Turn on Lower Styx Road toward Spencerville. At beach, stay left and park at end of road.

Otago Peninsula Beaches—Sandfly Bay. Just 15 km from Dunedin. Take Seal Point Road, walk north on trail to the bay and beach beyond the sand hill. **Allans Beach,** a 20-minute walk from entrance. **Victory Beach,** on north shore of Papanui Inlet. **Ryans Beach,** south 20 minutes from entrance to Pipikaretu Beach. With a much cooler climate, South Island beaches get use only in "Down Under" summer months.

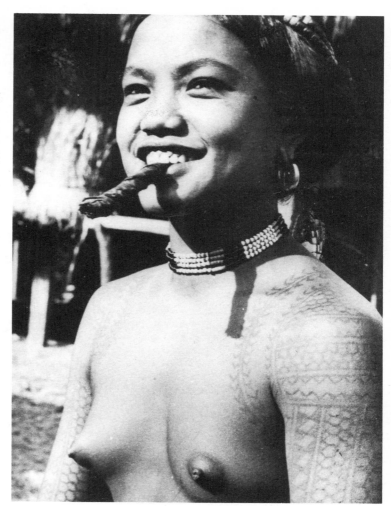

PHILIPPINES

BEACH CLUBS

The whole country is a mass of islands—if you can't find a nude beach resort, hire a boat (it's not expensive) and find your own deserted beach. Specify a time for the boatman to come back and pick you up; be sure to take precautions against the fierce tropical sun if there's no shade. Remember, though, Philippine law strictly forbids nudity. Be sure what's currently tolerated before you strip.

Mactan Island—Tambuli Beach Resort and Seafood Restaurant on Buyong Beach, and **Argao Beach Club,** both located 70 km south of Cebu City, offer the possibility of topfree in a country where this is far from common on public beaches. In the mid-1980s, Argao Resort (not the previously mentioned beach club) 35 km from Cebu City was owned by Imelda Marcos. The beach is usually topfree and full nudity will be allowed depending on the guests present. The resort has comfortable air-conditioned cabins, flush facilities, hot water, shower; restaurant has international menu and is excellent.

Aklan Province—Boracay Island. Bo-RAY-cay, as it is pronounced, offers clear, emerald water and a white, sugar-like sand beach at the northern tip of Aklan province. Reached through Aklan's capital city, Kalibo, Boracay Island has developed a European reputation as a little Eden. Flights to Kalibo should be reserved weeks ahead—two months, if you time your visit to January's great Atihan festival week.

A 2 1/2 hour jeepney ride to Caticlan at the northern tip connects with a pumpboat for the 15-minute ride over. The nude beach is to the left from the landing site, around some large boulders extending down to the water, on the side of the island facing the main island, Panay. Mostly German visitors enjoy disco, exotic bungalows, some potent mushrooms, water sports.

Palawan Island—Coco-Loco Beach Resort. Beautiful white sand beach, tennis, squash, sailing, snorkeling, paddle boat, fishing, cottages. Jean Pierre Riccio is your host. To get there, travel from Puerto City to Roxas (144 km) and then go from Roxas to Palawan Island by the Coco-Loco Pumpboat service which runs daily.

Nagarao Island, South Philippine Sea. Nude beach only. Oböna Reisen 1991 package tour, phone: Germany (06032) 8901.

Puerto Galera on Mindoro Island tolerates topfree and nude swimmers.

Swagman Playa Blanca Beach Resort, Currimao, Victoria, Laoag, Ilocos Norte, Luzon.

Mindanao-Dakak also has a nude beach. Tours are available from Hong Kong.

POLYNESIA

Tahiti, the island with the international airport, gets 100,000 visitors annually compared with Hawaii's 4 million, and the outlying islands receive far fewer. So you're able to get down to nature rather quickly. Topfree is accepted nearly everywhere. The fabled South Seas paradise, French Polynesia is halfway across the Pacific from California to Australia.

Best prices are November 15 to April 3, which is also hot and moist time. Package tours are the cheapest way to go; check Club Med (1-800-583-3100) or Islands in the Sun (1-800-854-3413 U.S., 1-800-432-7080 CA). Airlines: Air France, Air New Zealand, and Quantas, from Los Angeles and San Francisco.

A great way to view these fabulous islands is from the sea. Charter a small boat or crew on a friend's craft if you are lucky. For Tahiti's naturist charter, Danæ IV, contact Claudine Goché, P.O. Box 251, Uturoa-Raiatea, French Polynesia, fax (689) 66 39 37.

TAHITI

Few fully nude beaches will be found. The **Beachcomber Hotel** provides three rafts specifically for nude sunning. You can swim to them, or take the hotel's boat for a fee.

Next to the **Tahiti Museum** is an ex-hotel, now condominium, where nudity goes unnoticed at either side of the main beach area.

"Le Truck" circles the island and costs little. You could hop off at—or bicycle to—other small secluded beaches and rivers on the island for private nude sunning. Nobody's been hassled for tactful nudity despite the prevalence of clothing.

BORA BORA

About 165 miles from Tahiti, Bora Bora may be the most beautiful island on earth, a craggy emerald set in a luminous blue lagoon encircled by a reef. It also has splendid beaches on offshore *motus*.

The **Bora Bora Hotel** beach is topfree, with some nudity at the ends. The **Marara Hotel** beach also is topfree, a 64-bungalow village with two nude-use motus and lots of activities.

The **Club Med** is small and some find it dull; but the offshore nude motu is lovely and the main beach is, of course, topfree. A short walk up the beach from the Club Med is the **Hotel Oa Oa,** very pleasant and inexpensive.

MOOREA

Clustered are the **Club Med Moorea;** a low-cost **private campground** with showers, toilets, grocery store to its south; and **Hotel Moorea Village.**

Offshore a quarter mile are two small islands or motus, utilized by bolder spirits for nude sunning. The larger, which lacks transportation to it, has a wealthy Italian's

Durand Stiener. Americans Sailing Polynesian Waters.

house but the beaches, as all French beaches, are public and available. The smaller motu is served by a Club Med boat shuttle which clients of the neighboring lodgings also use. The small motu is often littered and overpopulated by people with no idea of nude sunbathing.

Elsewhere on Moorea the **Bali Hai Hotel** beach is topfree, with some nudity at the ends. This hotel also features a "Leaky Tiki" day cruise picnic with snorkeling, which is topfree and fun. The beach between the Moorea Airport and Kia Ora Resort gets some nude use. Best prices for a room on Moorea may be Chez Albert, which rents one- and two-bedroom bungalows with kitchen and bath for as little as $30/day for up to three guests. Phone Albert (Moorea 6-12-76) to reserve, then send deposit.

TETIAROA

Marlon Brando's atoll, Tetiaroa, is of great interest to naturists. Purchased by

Brando in 1965 when he was in Tahiti to film *Mutiny on the Bounty,* Tetiaroa is open to the public. Since Brando owns it, he can make his own rules; and Brando is all for nudity. This is the beach which Brando was quoted as saying he frequently strolled unclad: one of his peak experiences.

Care was taken in developing this island 30 miles north of Tahiti. Each bungalow is a few feet from the beach, and a dining room, lounge, and bar pamper guests. Moreover, the resident manager encourages private groups to "hire" Tetiaroa from Monday to Friday at a discount and then use it nude if they please. Twenty or more required in the party; less than $400 per person would cover air fare from Papeete, food, lodging, boats and so on. Or you could fly over for a day, $100 per person, airfare and lunch included. Sign up at the kiosk in the Papeete airport or write to H. Monad, B.P. 2417, Papeete, Tahiti, French Polynesia.

RANGIROA

A friendly little resort village, Sans Souci is on the virtually uninhabited side of the island of Rangiroa—one of the largest Pacific atolls, 200 nautical miles northeast of Tahiti, in the Tuamotus. Located 9 miles from the airport; interisland flights daily. Tall coconut palms, 12 thatched bungalows, restaurant/bar, store, kitchen. Bungalows are on stilts; showers and toilets are centrally-located. All water is supplied by rain-catchment and electricity is 12-volt and supplied through solar panels. There are miles and miles of uninhabited beach for nude enjoyment and the owner indicates the entire complex is clothing-optional anytime the registered guests agree. If six or more naturist couples book together, the policy is to hold non-naturist bookings so the entire complex can be clothes-free. Contact Bill Fox, 16823 Scofield Ave., Wasco, CA 93280 or (805) 758-3809; state your naturist preference.

THAILAND

INTERIOR

Chieng Mai—Wat Phrathat Waterfalls. Thailand can be beastly hot. Chieng Mai, 500 miles north of Bangkok in the mountains, is a cooler "summer capital" with lower humidity. Take the #3 city bus from the railroad station to the base of a series of waterfalls descending a mountain to the City Zoo. Hike up among the swimming holes, natural rock slides and sunning rocks, you'll love it. Weekdays are best.

GULF OF THAILAND

KO PHANGAN ISLAND

Pauper's Paradise must be somewhere in the Gulf of Thailand.

On precipitous islands off the Thai coast, sleepy fishing villages of food stalls, Chinese hotels and economy shops have seen first, hippies, then rapid commercial development. The glorious silver-white beaches, thatched huts ($6/night), and fresh seafood for even less drew a young and knowing crowd, many staying for months.

Earliest was Phuket Island's Kata Beach, in the Andaman Sea. Hippie interest soon drew the Club Med and other luxury hotel chains. The thrill was gone, the prices high, and refugees switched to Samui Island and its Chaweng and Lamai beaches in the Gulf of Thailand. But an airport opening in 1989 made Samui too convenient and trendy.

So, cheaper, less developed, "hot now," is neighboring Phangan Island, its **Haad Rin Beach** and **Sunrise Beach,** just north of Samui.

Lighthouse Beach, near the main beach, is clothing-optional. Some shady areas. The water is not always deep enough to swim but there is always enough water for splashing around. Good coral for snorkeling. In Haad Rin East, there is one road that runs south to north. Go south along this, over the low hill behind some bungalows. At the first fork, turn right and continue 1/2 km to the beach.

From Bangkok, reserve a 16-hour train ride to Surat Thani, then by taxi to Ban Don port, where you board a ferry to Phangan—or to wherever next may be hot.

Or, oh hell, fly! Indeed you can wing it on Northwest nonstop to Bangkok then by frequently-flying Bangkok Airways to Samui.

Facing Page: Peter Simon, A Child Will Lead.

VANUATU

TANNA ISLAND: WHITE GRASS BUNGALOWS

The sole public place at Tanna Island where women may sunbathe topfree is Tom Numake's White Grass Bungalows. A feature is its restaurant/bar, built upon a rock overlooking the sea. Or order a picnic lunch and walk three minutes to the private white sand nude beach at the edge of a savannah with wild horses.

Vanuatu is near Fiji and New Caledonia. A short flight transfers you from Vila, the capital, to Tanna Island, a worthwhile Pacific stopover: the active Yasar volcano, coves, lush jungle, traditional villages, excellent seafood, great coral reefs for snorkeling and scuba, coffee and fruit plantations, hot springs and waterfalls. Best avoided January–March, hurricane season.

For a brochure, write or phone Mr. Tom Numake, White Grass Bungalows, P.O. Box 5, Lenakel, Tanna Island, Vanuatu. Phone (678) 68660 or (678) 68661; fax (678) 68688.

Vanuatu: White Grass Resort Hotel host Tom Numake.